AIRFRAME & POWERPLANT MECHANICS HANDBOOK

AIRFRAME
VOLUME 1 OF 2

FAA-H-8083-31-ATB

U.S. Department of Transportation
Federal Aviation Administration
Flight Standards Service

Revisions by Aircraft Technical Book Company

2nd Edition

Printed and Published by
Aircraft Technical Book Company
72413 US Hwy 40
Tabernash, CO 80478-0270 USA
1 970.726.5111 FAX 1 970.726.5115
www.actechbooks.com

PREFACE

Airframe & Powerplant Mechanics Handbook—Airframe (FAA-H-8083-31 & FAA-H-8083-31-ATB) is one of a set of 3 handbooks for persons preparing for certification as an Airframe or Powerplant mechanic. It is intended that this handbook provide the basic information on principles and technical procedures relating to the airframe rating. It is designed to aid students enrolled in a formal course of instruction, as well as individuals studying on his or her own.

Because there are so many types of aircraft in use today, it is reasonable to expect that differences exist in airframe components and systems. To avoid repetition, the practice of using representative systems and units is carried out throughout the handbook. Subject matter is from a generalized point of view and should be supplemented by manufacturer's manuals and other textbooks if more detail is desired. This handbook is not intended to replace, or supersede official regulations or the manufacturer's instructions. Occasionally the word "must" or similar language is used where the desired action is deemed critical. The use of such language is not intended to add to, interpret, or relieve a duty imposed by Title 14 of the Code of Federal Regulations (14 CFR).

This book has been developed by the U.S. Department of Transportation, Federal Aviation Administration, Airman Testing Standards Branch, AFS-630, Oklahoma City, OK 73125 and published and distributed by Aircraft Technical Book Company, Tabernash, CO 80478. Comments regarding this publication may be sent to FAA at *AFS630comments@faa.gov* and to Aircraft Technical Book Company at *techsupport@actechbooks.com* or by phone to 970.726.5111

Revisions and updates to this book:
Each book in this series (the H-8083-ATB editions) are subject to constant updates, corrections, and clarifications by Aircraft Technical Book Company. Typically revision suggestions are identified by A&P instructors. Those suggestions are then sent for peer review by other working instructors and if agreed, the change is made; immediately to the eBook and with the next printing to the printed book. Nothing is removed from the original FAA text. All revisions are corrections, or clarifications. If you are a working A&P instructor and would like to participate on the ATB peer review team, please call 970.726.5111.

Related publications for your A&P training:
Available in eBook or Printed format - *www.actechbooks.com*

General Handbook
8083-30-ATB
ISBN 978-194114409-1

Airframe Handbook Vol 2
8083-31-ATB
ISBN 978-194114411-4

Powerplant Handbook
8083-32-ATB
ISBN 978-194114412-1

AC 43.13 1B/2B
ISBN 978-097748969-5

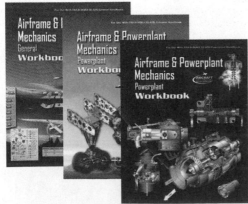

Matching Workbooks for 8083-ATB Series
General ISBN 978-097748968-8
Airframe ISBN 978-098386584-1
Powerplant ISBN 978-098386585-8

Matching Test Guides for 8083-ATB Series
General - ISBN 978-097748966-5
Airframe - ISBN 978-098386587-2
Powerplant - ISBN 978-098386588-9

From original FAA-H-8083-31 through this printing.

Airframe Volume 1

1-38 Corrected to current identification of AC43.13 1B/2B.

2-12 Figure 2-12; removed the trim tab locations shown on the flaps. Added trim tab to aileron. Removed trim tab shown on second elevator.

2-29 Corrected sequence of images and labeling on Figure 2-45 so that lowering the collective lowers pitch angle, and raising the collective increases pitch.

2-30 Figure 2-46; Replaced figure to show a collective lever with an actual twist grip throttle.

2-46 Figure 2-75; replaced line drawing with picture of an actual aircraft type cable tensiometer.

3-5 Figure 3-4; noted that specifications for on cotton is for reference only as it is no longer produced.

4-5/47 Replace 32 images of various tools for clarity and modernization.

4-6 Figure 4-10; replaced drawing of heavy duty punch with photo of an aircraft appropriate light weight automatic center punch.

4-14 Added and clarified procedural text on filing technique for clarity.

4-33 E (KE) rivets are alloy 7050 aluminum, not 2017. 2117-T rivets are heat treated by the manufacturer.

4-34/35 Section rewrite: rivet pitch is same as rivet spacing; clarified rivet spacing minimums for protruding and flush rivets; clarified "must" vs. "may"; corrected additional typos.

4-59 In Figure 4-121, setback is measured R+T; (not R+1)

4-62/63 Adjusted incorrect equations and results.

4-65 In Figure 4-127, multiplier is 44.5% of T

4-68 In Figure 4-132, sight line is located one radius outboard.

4-87 Clarified contradictory statement regarding acceptability of repairing or splicing a damaged metal component based on AC43.13 1B/2B

4-83 Replaced Figure 4-165 depicting an actual joggle

7-14 Deleted false statement that "damage to composite structures is sometimes allowed to go unchecked."

7-15 Figure 7-21 replaced with clearer representation of topic

9-6 Figure 9-8 corrected to show proper north/south polarity.

9-16 Figure 9-25, replaced incorrect formula L=0.021

9-17 Fixed incorrect equation (right column, top line)

9-18 Adjusted incorrect formula as 1/equation shown

9-20 Replaced incorrect formula S + E × I

9-33 Figure 9-51, labels for parallel and series windings were reversed.

Airframe Volume 2

10-10 Figure 10-15 safety wiring on transducer shown loosening the fitting. Image corrected.

10-10 Figure 10-16 needle in MP gauge shown out of acceptable range. Redrawn in the green arc.

10-13 Figure 10-23 drain hole in pitot tube shown in the wrong location. Redrawn, placing it in an acceptable place.

10-37 Clarified confusing caption on Figure 10-69.

10-47/48 Corrected mixed placement of Figure 10-84 and 10-86 and Figure 10-84 caption.

10-53 Figure 10-93, bracket attach points on sample D were 90 degrees off. Redrawn with top/bottom alignment.

11-7 Corrected text errors regarding number of electrons in each shell of an atom.

11-22 Circuits have "virtually" no gain, not vertically.

11-69 GPS satellites at 12,625 miles, not 12,625 feet.

11-71 Finished incomplete figure 11-154.

11-76 Added that sealant on an antenna mount interface also acts as a moisture barrier.

12-3 Removed comment of "complete interchangeability of mineral based fluids

12-4 Corrected typo; "elastomers", not elastoiners.

12-9 Eliminated reference to obscure 1960s military application

12-38 Corrected figure numbering references.

13-15/17 Numerous references to "tow-in/tow-out" corrected to "toe-in/toe-out".

16-18 Figure. 16-32 vertical column is measured in hundreds, not thousands.

16-39 Left column; rewrote portions of paragraph for improved clarity.

16-48 Replaced worthless Figure 16-79 with photo of aircraft evaporator from AirComm Corp.

16-50 Two references to "compressors" in 2nd paragraph corrected to "condensers".

16-55 Replaced poor drawing of condenser with photo of damaged condenser fins and enhanced caption.

16-56 Added improved photo of iced condenser fins.

iii

Volume Contents

Volume 1

Preface ii

Revision Log iii

Volume Contents v

Table of Contents vii

Acknowledgments xvii

Chapter 1
Aircraft Structures 1-1

Chapter 2
Aerodynamics Aircraft Assembly and Rigging 2-1

Chapter 3
Aircraft Fabric Covering 3-1

Chapter 4
Aircraft Metal Structural Repair 4-1

Chapter 5
Aircraft Welding 5-1

Chapter 6
Aircraft Wood 6-1

Chapter 7
Advanced Composite Materials 7-1

Chapter 8
Aircraft Painting and Finishing.................... 8-1

Chapter 9
Aircraft Electrical System 9-1

Glossary...G-1

Index I-1

Volume 2

Revision Log..iii

Volume Contents...v

Table of Contents vii

Chapter 10
Aircraft Instrument 10-1

Chapter 11
Communication and Navigation.................11-1

Chapter 12
Hydraulic and Pneumatic 12-1

Chapter 13
Aircraft Landing 13-1

Chapter 14
Aircraft Fuel System 14-1

Chapter 15
Ice and Rain Protection 15-1

Chapter 16
Cabin Environmental 16-1

Chapter 17
Fire Protection Systems.............................17-1

Glossary...G-1

Index I-1

Table of Contents

Preface ii

Volume Contents...v

Table of Contents...vii

Acknowledgments xvii

Chapter 1
Aircraft Structures 1-1
A Brief History of Aircraft Structures 1-1
General...1-5
Major Structural Stresses 1-6
Fixed-Wing Aircraft...1-8
  Fuselage...1-8
    Truss Type 1-8
    Monocoque Type 1-9
    Semimonocoque Type 1-9
  Pressurization 1-10
Wings 1-10
  Wing Configurations 1-10
  Wing Structure 1-11
  Wing Spars 1-13
  Wing Ribs 1-15
  Wing Skin 1-17
  Nacelles 1-19
Empennage...1-22
Flight Control Surfaces 1-24
  Primary Flight Control Surfaces..............1-24
    Ailerons......................................1-26
    Elevator......................................1-27
    Rudder..1-27
  Dual Purpose Flight Control Surfaces.......1-27
  Secondary or Auxiliary Control Surfaces ..1-28
    Flaps...1-28
    Slats..1-30
    Spoilers and Speed Brakes..............1-30
    Tabs...1-31
  Other Wing Features 1-34
Landing Gear 1-35
  Tail Wheel Gear Configuration 1-37
  Tricycle Gear.......................................1-38
Maintaining the Aircraft 1-38
  Location Numbering Systems 1-39
  Access and Inspection Panels.................1-40
Helicopter Structures 1-40

Airframe 1-40
Fuselage..1-42
Landing Gear or Skids..1-42
Powerplant and Transmission 1-42
  Turbine Engines..................................1-42
  Transmission......................................1-43
Main Rotor System...1-43
  Rigid Rotor System..............................1-44
  Semirigid Rotor System.........................1-44
Fully Articulated Rotor System..............................1-44
Antitorque System..1-45
Controls 1-46

Chapter 2
**Aerodynamics, Aircraft Assembly,
and Rigging**.. 2-1
Introduction..2-1
Basic Aerodynamics 2-2
The Atmosphere...2-2
  Pressure 2-2
  Density 2-3
  Humidity..2-3
Aerodynamics and the Laws of Physics 2-3
  Velocity and Acceleration......................2-3
  Newton's Laws of Motion.......................2-4
  Bernoulli's Principle and Subsonic Flow....2-4
Airfoil..2-5
  Shape of the Airfoil 2-5
  Angle of Incidence 2-6
  Angle of Attack (AOA)...........................2-6
  Boundary Layer....................................2-7
Thrust and Drag 2-7
Center of Gravity (CG) 2-9
The Axes of an Aircraft 2-9
Stability and Control...2-9
  Static Stability 2-9
  Dynamic Stability.................................2-11
  Longitudinal Stability............................2-11
  Directional Stability 2-11
  Lateral Stability 2-11
  Dutch Roll 2-11
Primary Flight Controls 2-12
Trim Controls...2-12
Auxiliary Lift Devices 2-13
  Winglets...2-14
  Canard Wings......................................2-14

Wing Fences 2-14
Control Systems for Large Aircraft 2-14
  Mechanical Control 2-14
  Hydromechanical Control 2-15
  Fly-By-Wire Control 2-15
High-Speed Aerodynamics 2-15
Rotary-Wing Aircraft Assembly and Rigging 2-16
Configurations of Rotary-Wing Aircraft 2-18
  Autogyro 2-18
  Single Rotor Helicopter 2-18
  Dual Rotor Helicopter 2-18
Types of Rotor Systems 2-18
  Fully Articulated Rotor 2-18
  Semirigid Rotor 2-19
  Rigid Rotor 2-19
Forces Acting on the Helicopter 2-19
  Torque Compensation 2-19
  Gyroscopic Forces 2-20
Helicopter Flight Conditions 2-22
  Hovering Flight 2-22
    Translating Tendency or Drift 2-22
    Ground Effect 2-23
    Coriolis Effect (Law of Conservation of
    Angular Momentum) 2-23
  Vertical Flight 2-24
  Forward Flight 2-24
    Translational Lift 2-24
    Effective Translational Lift (ETL) 2-25
    Dissymmetry of Lift 2-26
  Autorotation 2-28
Rotorcraft Controls 2-29
  Swash Plate Assembly 2-29
  Collective Pitch Control 2-29
  Throttle Control 2-30
  Governor/Correlator 2-30
  Cyclic Pitch Control 2-30
  Antitorque Pedals 2-31
Stabilizer Systems 2-31
  Bell Stabilizer Bar System 2-31
  Offset Flapping Hinge 2-32
  Stability Augmentation Systems (SAS) 2-32
  Helicopter Vibration 2-32
    Extreme Low Frequency Vibration 2-32
    Low Frequency Vibration 2-32
    Medium Frequency Vibration 2-32
    High Frequency Vibration 2-32
  Rotor Blade Tracking 2-32
    Flag and Pole 2-32
    Electronic Blade Tracker 2-33
  Tail Rotor Tracking 2-34
    Marking Method 2-34
    Electronic Method 2-34
  Rotor Blade Preservation and Storage 2-35
Helicopter Power Systems 2-35
  Powerplant 2-35

Reciprocating Engine 2-35
Turbine Engine 2-36
Transmission System 2-36
  Main Rotor Transmission 2-36
  Clutch 2-37
    Centrifugal Clutch 2-37
    Belt Drive Clutch 2-37
  Freewheeling Unit 2-38
  Airplane Assembly and Rigging 2-38
  Rebalancing of Control Surfaces 2-38
    Static Balance 2-38
    Dynamic Balance 2-38
  Rebalancing Procedures 2-39
  Rebalancing Methods 2-40
Aircraft Rigging 2-41
  Rigging Specification 2-41
    Type Certificate Data Sheet 2-41
    Maintenance Manual 2-41
    Structural Repair Manual (SRM) 2-41
    Manufacturer's Service Information 2-41
  Airplane Assembly 2-41
    Aileron Installation 2-41
    Flap Installation 2-41
    Empennage Installation 2-41
  Control Operating Systems 2-41
    Cable Systems 2-41
    Cable Inspection 2-44
    Cable System Installation 2-44
    Push Rods (Control Rods) 2-47
    Torque Tubes 2-48
    Cable Drums 2-48
  Rigging Checks 2-48
    Structural Alignment 2-48
    Cable Tension 2-52
    Control Surface Travel 2-53
    Checking and Safetying the System 2-55
  Biplane Assembly and Rigging 2-58
Aircraft Inspection 2-60
  Purpose of Inspection Programs 2-60
  Perform an Airframe Conformity and
  Airworthiness Inspection 2-61
  Required Inspections 2-61
    Preflight 2-61
    Periodic Maintenance Inspections 2-61
    Altimeter and Static System Inspections 2-63
    Air Traffic Control (ATC) Transponder Inspections 2-63
    Emergency Locator Transmitter (ELT) Operational
    and Maintenance Practices in Accordance With
    Advisory Circular (AC) 91-44 2-64
  Annual and 100-Hour Inspections 2-64
    Preparation 2-64
Other Aircraft Inspection and Maintenance Programs .. 2-66
  Continuous Airworthiness Maintenance
  Program (CAMP) 2-68

Title 14 CFR part 125, section 125247, Inspection
Programs and Maintenance 2-68
Helicopter Inspections, Piston-Engine and
Turbine-Powered 2-69
Light-Sport Aircraft, Powered Parachute, and
Weight-Shift Control Aircraft 2-69

Chapter 3
Aircraft Fabric Covering 3-1
General History 3-1
Fabric Terms 3-3
Legal Aspects of Fabric Covering 3-3
Approved Materials 3-4
Fabric 3-4
Other Fabric Covering Materials 3-5
Anti-Chafe Tape 3-5
Reinforcing Tape 3-5
Rib Bracing 3-5
Surface Tape 3-5
Rib Lacing Cord 3-5
Sewing Thread 3-6
Special Fabric Fasteners 3-6
Grommets 3-6
Inspection Rings 3-6
Primer 3-7
Fabric Cement 3-7
Fabric Sealer 3-8
Fillers 3-8
Topcoats 3-8
Available Covering Processes 3-8
Determining Fabric Condition—Repair or Recover? 3-9
Fabric Strength 3-9
How Fabric Breaking Strength is Determined 3-10
Fabric Testing Devices 3-11
General Fabric Covering Process 3-11
Blanket Method vs Envelope Method 3-12
Preparation for Fabric Covering Work 3-12
Removal of Old Fabric Coverings 3-13
Preparation of the Airframe Before Covering 3-14
Attaching Polyester Fabric to the Airframe 3-15
Seams 3-16
Fabric Cement 3-16
Fabric Heat Shrinking 3-17
Attaching Fabric to the Wing Ribs 3-18
Rib Lacing 3-18
Rings, Grommets, and Gussets 3-21
Finishing Tapes 3-21
Coating the Fabric 3-22
Polyester Fabric Repairs 3-23
Applicable Instructions 3-23
Repair Considerations 3-23
Cotton-Covered Aircraft 3-23
Fiberglass Coverings 3-24

Chapter 4
Aircraft Metal Structural Repair 4-1
Aircraft Metal Structural Repair 4-1
Stresses in Structural Members 4-2
Tension 4-2
Compression 4-3
Shear 4-3
Bearing 4-3
Torsion 4-3
Bending 4-4
Tools for Sheet Metal Construction and Repair 4-4
Layout Tools 4-4
Scales 4-4
Combination Square 4-4
Dividers 4-4
Rivet Spacers 4-4
Marking Tools 4-4
Pens 4-4
Scribes 4-5
Punches 4-5
Prick Punch 4-6
Center Punch 4-6
Automatic Center Punch 4-6
Transfer Punch 4-6
Drive Punch 4-6
Pin Punch 4-7
Chassis Punch 4-7
Awl 4-7
Hole Duplicator 4-8
Cutting Tools 4-8
Circular-Cutting Saws 4-8
Kett Saw 4-8
Pneumatic Circular Cutting Saw 4-8
Reciprocating Saw 4-9
Cut-off Wheel 4-9
Nibblers 4-9
Shop Tools 4-9
Squaring Shear 4-9
Throatless Shear 4-10
Scroll Shears 4-10
Rotary Punch Press 4-10
Band Saw 4-11
Disk Sander 4-11
Belt Sander 4-11
Notcher 4-12
Grinding Wheels 4-13
Hand Cutting Tools 4-13
Straight Snips 4-13
Aviation Snips 4-13
Files 4-13
Die Grinder 4-14
Burring Tool 4-14
Hole Drilling 4-14
Portable Power Drills 4-15
Pneumatic Drill Motors 4-15

Right Angle and 45° Drill Motors 4-15
Two Hole 4-15
Drill Press..4-15
Drill Extensions and Adapters 4-16
Extension Drill Bits 4-16
Straight Extension..4-16
Angle Adapters 4-16
Snake Attachment 4-16
Types of Drill Bits...4-17
Step Drill Bits 4-17
Cobalt Alloy Drill Bits.......................................4-17
Twist Drill Bits 4-17
Drill Bit Sizes 4-18
Drill Lubrication 4-18
Reamers 4-19
Drill Stops 4-19
Drill Bushings and Guides.................................4-19
Drill Bushing Holder Types...............................4-19
Hole Drilling Techniques 4-20
Drilling Large Holes 4-20
Chip Chasers 4-20
Forming Tools...4-21
Bar Folding Machine...4-21
Cornice Brake..4-22
Box and Pan Brake (Finger Brake) 4-22
Press Brake 4-22
Slip Roll Former 4-23
Rotary Machine 4-24
Stretch Forming 4-24
Drop Hammer..4-24
Hydropress Forming..4-24
Spin Forming 4-25
Forming With an English Wheel..........................4-26
Piccolo Former 4-26
Shrinking and Stretching Tools...........................4-26
Shrinking Tools 4-26
Stretching Tools 4-27
Manual Foot-Operated Sheet Metal Shrinker........4-27
Hand-Operated Shrinker and Stretcher..................4-27
Hardwood Form Blocks......................................4-27
V-Blocks 4-27
Shrinking Blocks 4-28
Sandbags 4-28
Sheet Metal Hammers and Mallets.....................4-28
Sheet Metal Holding Devices 4-28
Clamps and Vises 4-28
C-Clamps 4-28
Vises 4-29
Reusable Sheet Metal Fasteners 4-29
Cleco Fasteners..4-29
Hex Nut and Wing Nut Temporary
Sheet Fasteners 4-30
Aluminum Alloys...4-30
Structural Fasteners...4-31
Solid Shank Rivet 4-31

Description..4-31
Installation of Rivets...4-32
Rivet Installation Tools...4-36
Riveting Procedure 4-40
Countersunk Rivets...4-41
Evaluating the Rivet 4-44
Removal of Rivets 4-45
Replacing Rivets...4-46
National Advisory Committee for Aeronautics
(NACA) Method of Double Flush Riveting 4-46
Special Purpose Fasteners 4-47
Blind Rivets 4-47
Pin Fastening Systems (High-Shear Fasteners)......4-50
Lockbolt Fastening Systems 4-52
Blind Bolts 4-54
Rivet Nut...4-56
Blind Fasteners (Nonstructural).........................4-57
Forming Process..4-57
Forming Operations and Terms 4-58
Stretching 4-58
Shrinking 4-58
Bumping 4-59
Crimping..4-59
Folding Sheet Metal 4-59
Layout and Forming..4-59
Terminology...4-59
Layout or Flat Pattern Development 4-60
Making Straight Line Bends.................................4-61
Bending a U-Channel 4-62
Using a J-Chart To Calculate Total
Developed Width 4-67
How To Find the Total Developed Width Using
A J-Chart..4-67
Using a Sheet Metal Brake to Fold Metal 4-68
Step 1: Adjustment of Bend Radius......................4-68
Step 2: Adjusting Clamping Pressure 4-70
Step 3: Adjusting the Nose Gap............................4-71
Folding a Box 4-71
Relief Hole Location...4-73
Layout Method..4-73
Open and Closed Bends 4-74
Open End Bend (Less Than 90°)...........................4-74
Closed End Bend (More Than 90°).......................4-74
Hand Forming 4-74
Straight Line Bends 4-75
Formed or Extruded Angles..................................4-75
Flanged Angles..4-76
Shrinking...4-76
Stretching..4-77
Curved Flanged Parts...4-77
Forming by Bumping...4-80
Joggling...4-81
Lightening Holes 4-82
Working Stainless Steel...4-83
Working Inconel® Alloys 625 and 718..................4-83

Working Magnesium..4-84
Working Titanium 4-85
   Description of Titanium.......................................4-85
Basic Principles of Sheet Metal Repair 4-86
Maintaining Original Strength....................................4-87
Shear Strength and Bearing Strength 4-88
Maintaining Original Contour 4-89
Keeping Weight to a Minimum..................................4-89
Flutter and Vibration Precautions..............................4-89
Inspection of Damage...4-90
Types of Damage and Defects.....................................4-90
Classification of Damage...4-91
   Negligible Damage..4-91
   Damage Repairable by Patching.........................4-91
   Damage Repairable by Insertion 4-92
   Damage Necessitating Replacement of Parts 4-92
Repairability of Sheet Metal Structure 4-92
Structural Support During Repair..............................4-92
Assessment of Damage 4-92
Inspection of Riveted Joints 4-92
Inspection for Corrosion...4-93
Damage Removal 4-93
   Repair Material Selection 4-93
   Repair Parts Layout 4-93
   Rivet Selection..4-94
   Rivet Spacing and Edge Distance.......................4-94
   Corrosion Treatment..4-94
Approval of Repair 4-94
Repair of Stressed Skin Structure................................4-95
   Patches 4-95
Typical Repairs for Aircraft Structures 4-97
   Floats..4-97
   Corrugated Skin Repair 4-97
   Replacement of a Panel 4-97
   Outside the Member 4-97
   Inside the Member 4-97
   Edges of the Panel 4-97
   Repair of Lightening Holes 4-100
   Repairs to a Pressurized Area 4-100
   Stringer Repair...4-100
   Former or Bulkhead Repair 4-102
   Longeron Repair 4-103
   Spar Repair 4-103
   Rib and Web Repair..4-104
   Leading Edge Repair 4-105
   Trailing Edge Repair...4-105
   Specialized Repairs...4-108
   Inspection Openings 4-108

Chapter 5
Aircraft Welding **5-1**
Introduction..5-1
Types of Welding...5-2
   Gas Welding...5-2
   Electric Arc Welding..5-2

   Shielded Metal Arc Welding (SMAW)...................5-2
   Gas Metal Arc Welding (GMAW) 5-3
   Gas Tungsten Arc Welding (GTAW).....................5-3
Electric Resistance Welding...5-5
   Spot Welding 5-6
   Seam Welding..5-6
Plasma Arc Welding (PAW) 5-6
Plasma Arc Cutting...5-7
Gas Welding and Cutting Equipment 5-7
Welding Gases...5-7
   Acetylene 5-7
   Argon 5-7
   Helium 5-7
   Hydrogen 5-7
   Oxygen...5-7
Pressure Regulators 5-7
Welding Hose 5-8
Check Valves and Flashback Arrestors.........................5-8
Torches 5-9
   Equal Pressure Torch 5-9
   Injector Torch 5-9
   Cutting Torch 5-9
Torch Tips 5-9
Welding Eyewear 5-9
   Filler Rod 5-10
Equipment Setup 5-10
   Gas Cylinders..5-10
   Regulators 5-11
   Hoses...5-11
   Connecting Torch 5-11
   Select the Tip Size 5-11
   Adjusting the Regulator Working Pressure 5-13
Lighting and Adjusting the Torch 5-13
Different Flames...5-13
   Neutral Flame 5-13
   Carburizing Flame 5-13
   Oxidizing Flame 5-13
   Soft or Harsh Flames 5-13
   Handling of the Torch..5-14
Oxy-acetylene Cutting 5-14
   Shutting Down the Gas Welding Equipment 5-15
Gas Welding Procedures and Techniques....................5-15
   Correct Forming of a Weld 5-16
   Characteristics of a Good Weld..........................5-16
Oxy-Acetylene Welding of Ferrous Metals..................5-16
   Steel (Including SAE 4130) 5-16
   Chrome Molybdenum 5-17
   Stainless Steel..5-17
Oxy-Acetylene Welding of Nonferrous Metals............5-18
   Aluminum Welding..5-18
   Magnesium Welding 5-19
Brazing and Soldering..5-20
   Torch Brazing of Steel 5-20
   Torch Brazing of Aluminum 5-21
   Soldering 5-21

Aluminum Soldering 5-21
Silver Soldering 5-22
Gas Metal Arc Welding (TIG Welding) 5-22
TIG Welding 4130 Steel Tubing 5-23
TIG Welding Stainless Steel 5-23
TIG Welding Aluminum 5-24
TIG Welding Magnesium......................................5-24
TIG Welding Titanium...5-24
Arc Welding Procedures, Techniques, and Welding
Safety Equipment..5-25
Multiple Pass Welding 5-27
Techniques of Position Welding 5-28
Flat Position Welding...5-28
Bead Weld 5-28
Groove Weld 5-28
Fillet Weld 5-28
Lap Joint Weld 5-29
Vertical Position Welding 5-29
Overhead Position Welding.................................5-29
Expansion and Contraction of Metals.....................5-30
Welded Joints Using Oxy-Acetylene Torch 5-31
Butt Joints...5-31
Tee Joints..5-31
Edge Joints 5-31
Corner Joints 5-32
Lap Joints 5-32
Repair of Steel Tubing Aircraft Structure by Welding..5-32
Dents at a Cluster Weld......................................5-32
Dents Between Clusters.......................................5-32
Tube Splicing with Inside Sleeve Reinforcement 5-33
Tube Splicing with Outer Split Sleeve Reinforcement 5-34
Landing Gear Repairs...5-35
Engine Mount Repairs..5-36
Rosette Welding 5-37

Chapter 6
Aircraft Wood and Structural Repair 6-1
Aircraft Wood and Structural Repair........................6-1
Wood Aircraft Construction and Repairs 6-2
Inspection of Wood Structures..............................6-3
External and Internal Inspection 6-3
Glued Joint Inspection 6-4
Wood Condition...6-5
Repair of Wood Aircraft Structures..........................6-7
Materials 6-7
Suitable Wood 6-7
Defects Permitted...6-9
Defects Not Permitted...6-9
Glues (Adhesives)...6-10
Definition of Terms Used in the Glue Process 6-10
Preparation of Wood for Gluing............................6-11
Preparing Glues for Use......................................6-12
Applying the Glue/Adhesive 6-12
Pressure on the Joint 6-12
Testing Glued Joints 6-13

Repair of Wood Aircraft Components 6-13
Wing Rib Repairs 6-13
Wing Spar Repairs...6-15
Bolt and Bushing Holes 6-20
Plywood Skin Repairs...6-20
Fabric patch 6-20
Splayed Patch..6-20
Surface Patch 6-20
Plug Patch 6-21
Scarf Patch 6-24
The Back of the Skin is Accessible for Repair 6-25
The Back of the Skin Is Not Accessible for Repair 6-25

Chapter 7
Advanced Composite Materials 7-1
Description of Composite Structures 7-1
Introduction 7-1
Laminated Structures..7-2
Major Components of a Laminate 7-2
Strength Characteristics 7-2
Fiber Orientation...7-2
Warp Clock 7-3
Fiber Forms 7-3
Roving...7-3
Unidirectional (Tape)......................................7-3
Bidirectional (Fabric)......................................7-3
Nonwoven (Knitted or Stitched)........................7-4
Types of Fiber 7-4
Fiberglass..7-4
Kevlar®...7-4
Carbon/Graphite 7-6
Boron 7-6
Ceramic Fibers 7-6
Lightning Protection Fibers 7-6
Matrix Materials...7-7
Thermosetting Resins 7-7
Curing Stages of Resins 7-8
Pre-Impregnated Products (Prepregs) 7-8
Dry Fiber Material..7-9
Thixotropic Agents...7-9
Adhesives 7-9
Film Adhesives 7-9
Paste Adhesives 7-9
Foaming Adhesives 7-10
Description of Sandwich Structures.........................7-10
Properties..7-11
Facing Materials...7-11
Core Materials...7-11
Honeycomb...7-11
Foam 7-12
Balsa Wood...7-13
Manufacturing and In-Service Damage 7-13
Manufacturing Defects..7-13
Fiber Breakage...7-13
Matrix Imperfections.......................................7-13

Delamination and Debonds..............................7-14
Combinations of Damages............................7-14
Flawed Fastener Holes.................................7-14
In-Service Defects 7-14
Corrosion 7-15
Nondestructive Inspection (NDI) of Composites 7-15
Visual Inspection 7-15
Audible Sonic Testing (Coin Tapping) 7-16
Automated Tap Test 7-16
Ultrasonic Inspection.......................................7-17
Through Transmission Ultrasonic Inspection.........7-17
Pulse Echo Ultrasonic Inspection 7-18
Ultrasonic Bondtester Inspection.....................7-18
Phased Array Inspection 7-18
Radiography 7-19
Thermography 7-19
Neutron Radiography 7-19
Moisture Detector 7-19
Composite Repairs 7-19
Layup Materials..7-19
Hand Tools..7-19
Air Tools 7-20
Caul Plate 7-20
Support Tooling and Molds 7-20
Vacuum Bag Materials 7-21
Release Agents...7-21
Bleeder Ply...7-21
Peel Ply 7-21
Layup Tapes...7-21
Perforated Release Film....................................7-21
Solid Release Film 7-21
Breather Material 7-21
Vacuum Bag 7-21
Vacuum Equipment..7-22
Vacuum Compaction Table 7-22
Heat Sources 7-22
Oven...7-22
Autoclave 7-23
Heat Bonder and Heat Lamps.............................7-23
Thermocouples 7-25
Types of Layups 7-26
Wet Layups 7-26
Prepreg...7-27
Co-curing 7-28
Secondary Bonding......................................7-28
Co-bonding 7-28
Layup Process (Typical Laminated Wet Layup).........7-28
Layup Techniques.......................................7-28
Bleedout Technique 7-29
No Bleedout 7-29
Ply Orientation Warp Clock 7-29
Mixing Resins 7-30
Saturation Techniques 7-30
Fabric Impregnation With a Brush or Squeegee.....7-30
Fabric Impregnation Using a Vacuum Bag 7-30

Vacuum Bagging Techniques 7-31
Single Side Vacuum Bagging...........................7-31
Envelope Bagging.......................................7-31
Alternate Pressure Application...............................7-32
Shrink Tape..7-32
C-Clamps 7-32
Shotbags and Weights..................................7-32
Curing of Composite Materials 7-32
Room Temperature Curing 7-32
Elevated Temperature Curing 7-32
Composite Honeycomb Sandwich Repairs....................7-33
Damage Classification..7-34
Sandwich Structures 7-34
Minor Core Damage (Filler and Potting Repairs) ..7-34
Damage Requiring Core Replacement and
Repair to One or Both Faceplates 7-34
Solid Laminates..7-37
Bonded Flush Patch Repairs............................7-37
Trailing Edge and Transition Area Patch
Repairs 7-40
Resin Injection Repairs.................................7-40
Composite Patch Bonded to Aluminum
Structure..7-40
Fiberglass Molded Mat Repairs.........................7-41
Radome Repairs 7-41
External Bonded Patch Repairs 7-41
Bolted Repairs 7-44
Fasteners Used with Composite Laminates.................7-46
Corrosion Precautions...................................7-46
Fastener Materials......................................7-46
Fastener System for Sandwich Honeycomb
Structures (SPS Technologies Comp Tite).............7-46
Hi-Lok® and Huck-Spin® Lockbolt Fasteners 7-46
Eddie-Bolt® Fasteners 7-46
Cherry's E-Z Buck® (CSR90433) Hollow Rivet....7-47
Blind Fasteners 7-47
Blind Bolts..7-48
Fiberlite..7-48
Screws and Nutplates in Composite Structures......7-48
Machining Processes and Equipment........................7-49
Drilling...7-49
Countersinking..7-52
Cutting Processes and Precautions 7-52
Cutting Equipment......................................7-52
Repair Safety 7-53
Eye Protection...7-53
Respiratory Protection 7-53
Skin Protection..7-53
Fire Protection..7-53
Transparent Plastics 7-54
Optical Considerations 7-54
Identification..7-54
Storage and Handling 7-54
Forming Procedures and Techniques 7-54
Heating..7-54

Forms 7-55
Forming Methods 7-55
Sawing and Drilling 7-55
Sawing 7-55
Drilling 7-55
Cementing 7-56
Application of Cement 7-56
Repairs 7-56
Cleaning 7-57
Polishing 7-57
Windshield Installation 7-57
Installation Procedures 7-57

Chapter 8
Aircraft Painting and Finishing 8-1
Introduction 8-1
Finishing Materials 8-2
Acetone 8-2
Alcohol 8-2
Benzene 8-2
Methyl Ethyl Ketone (MEK) 8-2
Methylene Chloride 8-2
Toluene 8-2
Turpentine 8-3
Mineral Spirits 8-3
Naphtha 8-3
Linseed Oil 8-3
Thinners 8-3
Varnish 8-3
Primers 8-3
Wash Primers 8-3
Red Iron Oxide 8-3
Gray Enamel Undercoat 8-4
Urethane 8-4
Epoxy 8-4
Zinc Chromate 8-4
Identification of Paint 8-4
Dope 8-4
Synthetic Enamel 8-4
Lacquers 8-4
Polyurethane 8-5
Urethane Coating 8-5
Acrylic Urethanes 8-5
Methods of Applying Finish 8-5
Dipping 8-5
Brushing 8-5
Spraying 8-5
Finishing Equipment 8-6
Paint Booth 8-6
Air Supply 8-6
Spray Equipment 8-6
Air Compressors 8-6
Large Coating Containers 8-7
System Air Filters 8-7
Miscellaneous Painting Tools and Equipment ... 8-7

Spray Guns 8-7
Fresh Air Breathing Systems 8-8
Viscosity Measuring Cup 8-9
Mixing Equipment 8-9
Preparation 8-10
Surfaces 8-10
Primer and Paint 8-10
Spray Gun Operation 8-11
Adjusting the Spray Pattern 8-11
Applying the Finish 8-11
Common Spray Gun Problems 8-12
Sequence for Painting a Single-Engine or Light
Twin Airplane 8-13
Common Paint Troubles 8-13
Poor Adhesion 8-13
Blushing 8-13
Pinholes 8-14
Sags and Runs 8-14
Orange Peel 8-14
Fisheyes 8-15
Sanding Scratches 8-15
Wrinkling 8-15
Spray Dust 8-16
Painting Trim and Identification Mark 8-16
Masking and Applying the Trim 8-16
Masking Materials 8-16
Masking for the Trim 8-16
Display of Nationality and Registration Marks ... 8-17
Display of Marks 8-17
Location and Placement of Marks 8-17
Size Requirements for Different Aircraft ... 8-18
Decals 8-18
Paper Decals 8-18
Metal Decals with Cellophane Backing ... 8-18
Metal Decals With Paper Backing 8-18
Metal Decals with No Adhesive 8-18
Vinyl Film Decals 8-18
Removal of Decals 8-19
Paint System Compatibility 8-19
Paint Touchup 8-19
Identification of Paint Finished 8-19
Surface Preparation for Touchup 8-20
Stripping the Finish 8-20
Chemical Stripping 8-21
Plastic Media Blasting (PMB) 8-21
New Stripping Methods 8-21
Safety in the Paint Shop 8-21
Storage of Finishing Materials 8-21
Protective Equipment for Personnel 8-22

Chapter 9
Aircraft Electrical System 9-1
Introduction 9-1
Ohm's Law 9-2
Current 9-2

Conventional Current Theory and Electron Theory .9-3
Electromotive Force (Voltage)...................................9-4
Resistance...9-4
Factors Affecting Resistance 9-4
Electromagnetic Generation of Power 9-5
Alternating Current (AC) Introduction....................9-9
Definition 9-9
Opposition to Current Flow of AC.........................9-12
Resistance 9-12
Inductive Reactance..9-12
Capacitive Reactance..9-14
Impedance..9-15
Parallel AC Circuits..9-18
Power in AC Circuits..9-20
True Power..9-20
Apparent Power..9-20
Power Factor...9-20
Aircraft Batteries..9-21
Type of Batteries 9-21
Lead-Acid Batteries...9-21
NiCd Batteries..9-22
Capacity 9-22
Aircraft Battery Ratings by Specification..............9-23
Storing and Servicing Facilities............................9-23
Battery Freezing...9-23
Temperature Correction......................................9-23
Battery Charging..9-24
Battery Maintenance 9-24
Battery and Charger Characteristics 9-25
Aircraft Battery Inspection 9-26
Ventilation Systems...9-26
Installation Practices...9-26
Troubleshooting...9-27
DC Generators and Controls 9-27
Generators..9-27
Construction Features of DC Generators.............9-29
Types of DC Generators 9-32
Generator Ratings 9-33
DC Generator Maintenance 9-33
Generator Controls 9-34
Theory of Generator Control 9-34
Functions of Generator Control Systems 9-35
Generator Controls for High Output Generators 9-35
Generator Controls for Low-Output Generators....9-36
DC Alternators and Controls....................................9-38
DC Alternators...9-39
Alternator Voltage Regulators.............................9-40
Solid-State Regulators 9-40
Power Systems 9-41
AC Alternators 9-41
Alternator Drive 9-42
AC Alternators Control Systems..............................9-45
Aircraft Electrical Systems 9-47
Small Single-Engine Aircraft....................................9-47
Battery Circuit 9-47

Generator Circuit 9-48
Alternator Circuit...9-48
External Power Circuit 9-50
Starter Circuit...9-50
Avionics Power Circuit...9-51
Landing Gear Circuit 9-52
AC Supply 9-55
Light Multiengine Aircraft 9-57
Paralleling Alternators or Generators 9-57
Power Distribution on Multiengine Aircraft..........9-58
Large Multiengine Aircraft 9-60
AC Power Systems 9-60
Wiring Installation 9-65
Wiring Diagrams 9-65
Block Diagrams 9-65
Pictorial Diagrams 9-65
Schematic Diagrams 9-65
Wire Types 9-65
Conductor 9-67
Plating 9-68
Insulation 9-68
Wire Shielding 9-68
Wire Substitutions 9-69
Areas Designated as Severe Wind and
Moisture Problem (SWAMP)...............................9-69
Wire Size Selection 9-69
Current Carrying Capacity...................................9-71
Allowable Voltage Drop.......................................9-75
Wire Identification...9-77
Placement of Identification Marking 9-77
Types of Wire Markings..9-77
Wire Installation and Routing 9-78
Open Wiring 9-78
Wire Groups and Bundles and Routing..................9-78
Conduit 9-83
Wire Shielding 9-85
Lacing and Tying Wire Bundles 9-88
Tying..9-89
Wire Termination 9-90
Stripping Wire 9-90
Terminal Strips 9-91
Terminal Lugs...9-91
Emergency Splicing Repairs.................................9-92
Junction Boxes..9-92
AN/MS Connectors 9-93
Coaxial Cable...9-96
Wire Inspection 9-96
Electrical System Components 9-96
Switches 9-96
Type of Switches 9-98
Toggle and Rocker Switches 9-98
Rotary Switches 9-99
Precision (Micro) Switches..................................9-99
Relays and Solenoids (Electromagnetic Switches) 9-99
Solenoids...9-99

    Relays 9-99
  Current Limiting Devices 9-100
    Fuses 9-100
    Circuit Breakers 9-100
Aircraft Lighting Systems 9-101
  Exterior Lights 9-101
    Position Lights 9-101
    Anticollision Lights 9-102
    Landing and Taxi Lights 9-103
    Wing Inspection Lights 9-104
  Interior Lights 9-104
  Maintenance and Inspection of Lighting Systems ... 9-105

Glossary **G-1**

Index **I-1**

Acknowledgments

The Aviation Maintenance Technician Handbook—Airframe (FAA-H-8083-31) was produced by the Federal Aviation Administration (FAA) with the assistance of Safety Research Corporation of America (SRCA). The FAA wishes to acknowledge the following contributors:

Mr. Chris Brady (*www.b737.org.uk*) for images used throughout this handbook

Captain Karl Eiríksson for image used in Chapter 1

Cessna Aircraft Company for image used in Chapter 1

Mr. Andy Dawson (*www.mossie.org*) for images used throughout Chapter 1

Mr. Bill Shemley for image used in Chapter 1

Mr. Bruce R. Swanson for image used in Chapter 1

Mr. Burkhard Domke (*www.b-domke.de*) for images used throughout Chapter 1 and 2

Mr. Chris Wonnacott (*www.fromtheflightdeck.com*) for image used n Chapter 1

Mr. Christian Tremblay (*www.zodiac640.com*) for image used in Chapter 1

Mr. John Bailey (*www.knots2u.com*) for image used in Chapter 1

Mr. Rich Guerra (*www.rguerra.com*) for image used in Chapter 1

Mr. Ronald Lane for image used in Chapter 1

Mr. Tom Allensworth (*www.avsim.com*) for image used in Chapter 1

Navion Pilots Association's Tech Note 001 (*www.navionpilots.org*) for image used in Chapter 1

U.S. Coast Guard for image used in Chapter 1

Mr. Tony Bingelis and the Experimental Aircraft Association (EAA) for images used throughout Chapter 2

Mr. Benoit Viellefon (*www.johnjohn.co.uk/compare-tigermothflights/html/tigermoth_b o_aozh.html*) for image used in Chapter 3

Mr. Paul Harding of Safari Seaplanes–Bahamas (*www.safariseaplanes.com*) for image used in Chapter 3

Polyfiber/Consolidated Aircraft Coatings for images used throughout Chapter 3

Stewart Systems for images used throughout Chapter 3

Superflite for images used throughout Chapter 3

Cherry Aerospace (*www.cherryaerospace.com*) for images used in Chapters 4 and 7

Raytheon Aircraft (Structural Inspection and Repair Manual) for information used in Chapter 4

Mr. Scott Allen of Kalamazoo Industries, Inc. (*www.kalamazooind.com*) for image used in Chapter 4

Miller Electric Mfg. Co. (*www.millerwelds.com*) for images used in Chapter 5

Mr. Aaron Novak, contributing engineer, for charts used in Chapter 5

Mr. Bob Hall (*www.pro-fusiononline.com*) for image used in Chapter 5

Mr. Kent White of TM Technologies, Inc. for image used in Chapter 5

Safety Supplies Canada (*www.safetysuppliescanada.com*) for image used in Chapter 5

Smith Equipment (*www.smithequipment.com*) for images used in Chapter 5

Alcoa (*www.alcoa.com*) for images used in Chapter 7

Mr. Chuck Scott (*www.itwif.com*) for images used throughout Chapter 8

Mr. John Lagerlof of Paasche Airbrush Co. (*www.paascheairbrush.com*) for image used in Chapter 8

Mr. Philip Love of Turbine Products, LLC (*www.turbineproducts.com*) for image used in Chapter 8

Consolidated Aircraft Coatings for image used in Chapter 8

Tianjin Yonglida Material Testing Machine Co., Ltd for image used in Chapter 8

Mr. Jim Irwin of Aircraft Spruce & Specialty Co. (*www.aircraftspruce.com*) for images used in Chapters 9, 10, 11, 13, 14, 15

Mr. Kevan Hashemi for image used in Chapter 9

Mr. Michael Leasure, Aviation Multimedia Library (*www2.tech.purdue.edu/at/courses/aeml*) for images used in Chapters 9, 13, 14

Cobra Systems Inc. (*www.cobrasys.com*) for image used in Chapter 10 *www.free-online-private-pilot-ground-school.com* for image used in Chapters 10, 16

DAC International (*www.dacint.com*) for image used in Chapter 10

Dawson Aircraft Inc. (*www.aircraftpartsandsalvage.com*) for images used throughout Chapter 10

Mr. Kent Clingaman for image used in Chapter 10

TGH Aviation-FAA Instrument Repair Station (*www.tghaviation.com*) for image used in Chapter 10

The Vintage Aviator Ltd. (*www.thevintageaviator.co.nz*) for image used in Chapter 10

ACK Technologies Inc. (*www.ackavionics.com*) for image used in Chapter 11

ADS-B Technologies, LLC (*www.ads-b.com*) for images used in Chapter 11

Aviation Glossary (*www.aviationglossary.com*) for image used in Chapter 11

AT&T Archives and History Center for image used in Chapter 11

Electronics International Inc. (*www.buy-ei.com*) for image used in Chapter 11

Excelitas Technologies (*www.excelitas.com*) for image used in Chapter 11

Freestate Electronics, Inc. (*www.fse-inc.com*) for image used in Chapter 11

AirTrafficAtlanta.com for image used in Chapter 1

Western Historic Radio Museum, Virginia City, Nevada (*www.radioblvd.com*) for image used in Chapter 11

Avidyne Corporation (*www.avidyne.com*) for image used in Chapter 11

Kintronic Laboratories (*www.kintronic.com*) for image used in Chapter 11

Mr. Dan Wolfe (*www.flyboysalvage.com*) for image used in Chapter 1

Mr. Ken Shuck (*www.cessna150.net*) for image used in Chapter 11

Mr. Paul Tocknell (*www.askacfi.com*) for image used in Chapter 1

Mr. Stephen McGreevy (*www.auroralchorus.com*) for image used in Chapter 11

Mr. Todd Bennett (*www.bennettavionics.com*) for image used in Chapter 11

National Oceanic and Atmospheric Administration, U.S. Department of Commerce for image used in Chapter 11

RAMI (*www.rami.com*) for image used in Chapter 11

Rockwell Collins (*www.rockwellcollins.com*) for image used in Chapter 11

Sarasota Avionics International (*www.sarasotaavionics.com*) for images used in Chapter 11

Southeast Aerospace, Inc. (*www.seaerospace.com*) for image used in Chapter 11

Sporty's Pilot Shop (*www.sportys.com*) for image used in Chapter 11

Watts Antenna Company (*www.wattsantenna.com*) for image used in Chapter 11

Wings and Wheels (*www.wingsandwheels.com*) for image used in Chapter 11

Aeropin, Inc. (*www.aeropin.com*) for image used in Chapter 13

Airplane Mart Publishing (*www.airplanemart.com*) for image used in Chapter 13

Alberth Aviation (*www.alberthaviation.com*) for image used in Chapter 13

AVweb (*www.avweb.com*) for image used in Chapter 13

Belle Aire Aviation, Inc. (*www.belleaireaviation.com*) for image used in Chapter 13

Cold War Air Museum (*www.coldwarairmuseum.org*) for image used in Chapter 13

Comanche Gear (*www.comanchegear.com*) for image used in Chapter 13

CSOBeech (*www.csobeech.com*) for image used in Chapter 13

Desser Tire & Rubber Co., Inc. (*www.desser.com*) for image used in Chapter 13

DG Flugzeugbau GmbH (*www.dg-flugzeugbau.de*) for image used in Chapter 13

Expedition Exchange Inc. (*www.expeditionexchange.com*) for image used in Chapter 13

Fiddlers Green (*www.fiddlersgreen.net*) for image used in Chapter 1

Hitchcock Aviation (*www.hitchcockaviation.com*) for image used in Chapter 13

KUNZ GmbH aircraft equipment (*www.kunz-aircraft.com*) for images used in Chapter 13

Little Flyers (*www.littleflyers.com*) for images used in Chapter 1

Maple Leaf Aviation Ltd. (*www.aircraftspeedmods.ca*) for image used in Chapter 13

Mr. Budd Davisson (*Airbum.com*) for image used in Chapter 13

Mr. C. Jeff Dyrek (*www.yellowairplane.com*) for images used in Chapter 13

Mr. Jason Schappert (*www.m0a.com*) for image used in Chapter 13

Mr. John Baker (*www.hangar9aeroworks.com*) for image used in Chapter 13

Mr. Mike Schantz (*www.trailer411.com*) for image used in Chapter 13

Mr. Robert Hughes (*www.escapadebuild.co.uk*) for image used in Chapter 13

Mr. Ron Blachut for image used in Chapter 13

Owls Head Transportation Museum (*www.owlshead.org*) for image used in Chapter 13

PPI Aerospace (*www.ppiaerospace.com*) for image used in Chapter 13

Protective Packaging Corp. (*www.protectivepackaging.net*), 1-800-945-2247 for image used in Chapter 13

Ravenware Industries, LLC (*www.ravenware.com*) for image used in Chapter 13

Renold (*www.renold.com*) for image used in Chapter 13

Rotor F/X, LLC (*www.rotorfx.com*) for image used in Chapter 13

SkyGeek (*www.skygeek.com*) for image used in Chapter 13

Taigh Ramey (*www.twinbeech.com*) for image used in Chapter 13

Texas Air Salvage (*www.texasairsalvage.com*) for image used in Chapter 13

The Bogert Group (*www.bogert-av.com*) for image used in Chapter 13

W. B. Graham, Welded Tube Pros LLC (*www.thefabricator.com*) for image used in Chapter 13

Zinko Hydraulic Jack (*www.zinkojack.com*) for image used in Chapter 13

Aviation Institute of Maintenance (*www.aimschool.com*) for image used in Chapter 14

Aviation Laboratories (*www.avlab.com*) for image used in Chapter 14

AVSIM (*www.avsim.com*) for image used in Chapter 14

Eggenfellner (*www.eggenfellneraircraft.com*) for image used in Chapter 14

FlightSim.Com, Inc. (*www.flightsim.com*) for image used in Chapter 1

Fluid Components International LLC (*www.fluidcomponents.com*) for image used in Chapter 1

Fuel Quality Services, Inc. (*www.fqsinc.com*) for image used in Chapter 14

Hammonds Fuel Additives, Inc. (*www.biobor.com*) for image used in Chapter 14

Jeppesen (*www.jeppesen.com*) for image used in Chapter 14

MGL Avionics (*www.mglavionics.com*) for image used in Chapter 14

Mid-Atlantic Air Museum (*www.maam.org*) for image used in Chapter 14

MISCO Refractometer (*www.misco.com*) for image used in Chapter 14

Mr. Gary Brossett via the Aircraft Engine Historical Society (*www.enginehistory.org*) for image used in Chapter 14

Mr. Jeff McCombs (*www.heyeng.com*) for image used in Chapter 14

NASA for image used in Chapter 14

On-Track Aviation Limited (*www.ontrackaviation.com*) for image used in Chapter 14

Stewart Systems for image used in Chapter 14

Prist Aerospace Products (*www.pristaerospace.com*) for image used in Chapter 14

The Sundowners, Inc. (*www.sdpleecounty.org*) for image used in Chapter 14

Velcon Filters, LLC (*www.velcon.com*) for image used in Chapter 14

Aerox Aviation Oxygen Systems, Inc. (*www.aerox.com*) for image used in Chapter 16

Biggles Software (*www.biggles-software.com*) for image used in Chapter 16

C&D Associates, Inc. (*www.aircraftheater.com*) for image used in Chapter 16

Cobham (Carleton Technologies Inc.) (*www.cobham.com*) for image used in Chapter 16

Cool Africa (*www.coolafrica.co.za*) for image used in Chapter 16

Cumulus Soaring, Inc. (*www.cumulus-soaring.com*) for image used in Chapter 16

Essex Cryogenics of Missouri, Inc. (*www.essexind.com*) for image used in Chapter 16

Flightline AC, Inc. (*www.flightlineac.com*) for image used in Chapter 1

IDQ Holdings (*www.idqusa.com*) for image used in Chapter 16

Manchester Tank & Equipment (*www.mantank.com*) for image used in Chapter 16

Mountain High E&S Co. (*www.MHoxygen.com*) for images used throughout Chapter 16

Mr. Bill Sherwood (*www.billzilla.org*) for image used in Chapter 16

Mr. Boris Comazzi (*www.flightgear.ch*) for image used in Chapter 1

Mr. Chris Rudge (*www.warbirdsite.com*) for image used in Chapter 16

Mr. Richard Pfiffner (*www.craggyaero.com*) for image used in Chapter 1

Mr. Stephen Sweet (*www.stephensweet.com*) for image used in Chapter 16

Precise Flight, Inc. (*www.preciseflight.com*) for image used in Chapter 1

SPX Service Solutions (*www.spx.com*) for image used in Chapter 16

SuperFlash Compressed Gas Equipment (*www.oxyfuelsafety.com*)

Mr. Tim Mara (*www.wingsandwheels.com*) for images used in Chapter 16

Mr. Bill Abbott for image used in Chapter 17

Additional appreciation is extended to Dr. Ronald Sterkenburg, Purdue University; Mr. Bryan Rahm, Dr. Thomas K. Eismain, Purdue University; Mr. George McNeill, Mr. Thomas Forenz, Mr. Peng Wang, and the National Oceanic and Atmospheric Administration (NOAA) for their technical support and input.

Chapter 1
Aircraft Structures

A Brief History of Aircraft Structures

The history of aircraft structures underlies the history of aviation in general. Advances in materials and processes used to construct aircraft have led to their evolution from simple wood truss structures to the sleek aerodynamic flying machines of today. Combined with continuous powerplant development, the structures of "flying machines" have changed significantly.

The key discovery that "lift" could be created by passing air over the top of a curved surface set the development of fixed and rotary-wing aircraft in motion. George Cayley developed an efficient cambered airfoil in the early 1800s, as well as successful manned gliders later in that century. He established the principles of flight, including the existence of lift, weight, thrust, and drag. It was Cayley who first stacked wings and created a tri-wing glider that flew a man in 1853.

Earlier, Cayley studied the center of gravity of flying machines, as well as the effects of wing dihedral. Furthermore, he pioneered directional control of aircraft by including the earliest form of a rudder on his gliders. *[Figure 1-1]*

In the late 1800s, Otto Lilienthal built upon Cayley's discoveries. He manufactured and flew his own gliders on over 2,000 flights. His willow and cloth aircraft had wings designed from extensive study of the wings of birds. Lilienthal also made standard use of vertical and horizontal fins behind the wings and pilot station. Above all, Lilienthal proved that man could fly. *[Figure 1-2]*

Octave Chanute, a retired railroad and bridge engineer, was active in aviation during the 1890s. *[Figure 1-3]* His interest was so great that, among other things, he published a definitive work called "Progress in Flying Machines." This was the culmination of his effort to gather and study all the

Figure 1-2. *Master of gliding and wing study, Otto Lilienthal (top) and one of his more than 2,000 glider flights (bottom).*

Figure 1-1. *George Cayley, the father of aeronautics (top) and a flying replica of his 1853 glider (bottom).*

information available on aviation. With the assistance of others, he built gliders similar to Lilienthal's and then his own. In addition to his publication, Chanute advanced aircraft structure development by building a glider with stacked wings incorporating the use of wires as wing supports.

The work of all of these men was known to the Wright Brothers when they built their successful, powered airplane in 1903. The first of its kind to carry a man aloft, the Wright Flyer had thin, cloth-covered wings attached to what was primarily truss structures made of wood. The wings contained forward and rear spars and were supported with both struts and wires. Stacked wings (two sets) were also part of the Wright Flyer. *[Figure 1-4]*

Figure 1-3. *Octave Chanute gathered and published all of the aeronautical knowledge known to date in the late 1890s. Many early aviators benefited from this knowledge.*

Powered heavier-than-air aviation grew from the Wright design. Inventors and fledgling aviators began building their own aircraft. Early on, many were similar to that constructed by the Wrights using wood and fabric with wires and struts to support the wing structure. In 1909, Frenchman Louis Bleriot produced an aircraft with notable design differences. He built a successful mono-wing aircraft. The wings were still supported by wires, but a mast extending above the fuselage enabled the wings to be supported from above, as well as underneath. This made possible the extended wing length needed to lift an aircraft with a single set of wings. Bleriot used a Pratt truss-type fuselage frame. *[Figure 1-5]*

Figure 1-5. *The world's first mono-wing by Louis Bleriot.*

More powerful engines were developed and airframe structures changed to take advantage of the benefits. As early as 1910, German Hugo Junkers was able to build an aircraft with metal truss construction and metal skin due to the availability of stronger powerplants to thrust the plane forward and into the sky. The use of metal instead of wood for the primary structure eliminated the need for external wing braces and wires. His J-1 also had a single set of wings (a monoplane) instead of a stacked set. *[Figure 1-6]*

Figure 1-4. *The Wright Flyer was the first successful powered aircraft. It was made primarily of wood and fabric.*

Figure 1-6. *The Junker J-1 all metal construction in 1910.*

Leading up to World War I (WWI), stronger engines also allowed designers to develop thicker wings with stronger spars. Wire wing bracing was no longer needed. Flatter, lower wing surfaces on high-camber wings created more lift. WWI expanded the need for large quantities of reliable aircraft. Used mostly for reconnaissance, stacked-wing tail draggers with wood and metal truss frames with mostly fabric skin dominated the wartime sky. *[Figure 1-7]* The Red Baron's Fokker DR-1 was typical.

Figure 1-7. *World War I aircraft were typically stacked-wing fabric-covered aircraft like this Breguet 14 (circa 1917).*

In the 1920s, the use of metal in aircraft construction increased. Fuselages able to carry cargo and passengers were developed. The early flying boats with their hull-type construction from the shipbuilding industry provided the blueprints for semimonocoque construction of fuselages. *[Figure 1-8]* Truss-type designs faded. A tendency toward cleaner monowing designs prevailed.

Into the 1930s, all-metal aircraft accompanied new lighter and more powerful engines. Larger semimonocoque fuselages were complimented with stress-skin wing designs. Fewer truss and fabric aircraft were built. World War II (WWII) brought about a myriad of aircraft designs using all metal technology. Deep fuel-carrying wings were the norm, but the desire for higher flight speeds prompted the development of thin-winged aircraft in which fuel was carried in the fuselage. The first composite structure aircraft, the De Havilland Mosquito, used a balsa wood sandwich material in the

Figure 1-8. *The flying boat hull was an early semimonocoque design like this Curtiss HS-2L.*

construction of the fuselage. *[Figure 1-9]* The fiberglass radome was also developed during this period.

After WWII, the development of turbine engines led to higher altitude flight. The need for pressurized aircraft pervaded aviation. Semimonocoque construction needed to be made even stronger as a result. Refinements to the all-metal semimonocoque fuselage structure were made to increase strength and combat metal fatigue caused by the pressurization-depressurization cycle. Rounded windows and door openings were developed to avoid weak areas where cracks could form. Integrally machined copper alloy aluminum skin resisted cracking and allowed thicker skin and controlled tapering. Chemical milling of wing skin structures provided great strength and smooth high performance surfaces. Variable contour wings became easier

Figure 1-9. *The DeHavilland Mosquito, the first aircraft with foam core honeycomb in the fuselage.*

Figure 1-10. *The nearly all composite Cessna Citation Mustang very light jet (VLJ).*

to construct. Increases in flight speed accompanying jet travel brought about the need for thinner wings. Wing loading also increased greatly. Multispar and box beam wing designs were developed in response.

In the 1960s, ever larger aircraft were developed to carry passengers. As engine technology improved, the jumbo jet was engineered and built. Still primarily aluminum with a semimonocoque fuselage, the sheer size of the airliners of the day initiated a search for lighter and stronger materials from which to build them. The use of honeycomb constructed panels in Boeing's airline series saved weight while not compromising strength. Initially, aluminum core with aluminum or fiberglass skin sandwich panels were used on wing panels, flight control surfaces, cabin floor boards, and other applications.

A steady increase in the use of honeycomb and foam core sandwich components and a wide variety of composite materials characterizes the state of aviation structures from the 1970s to the present. Advanced techniques and material combinations have resulted in a gradual shift from aluminum to carbon fiber and other strong, lightweight materials. These new materials are engineered to meet specific performance requirements for various components on the aircraft. Many airframe structures are made of more than 50 percent advanced composites, with some airframes approaching 100 percent. The term "very light jet" (VLJ) has come to describe a new generation of jet aircraft made almost entirely of advanced composite materials. *[Figure 1-10]* It is possible that noncomposite aluminum aircraft structures will become obsolete as did the methods and materials of construction used by Cayley, Lilienthal, and the Wright Brothers.

General

An aircraft is a device that is used for, or is intended to be used for, flight in the air. Major categories of aircraft are airplane, rotorcraft, glider, and lighter-than-air vehicles. *[Figure 1-11]* Each of these may be divided further by major distinguishing features of the aircraft, such as airships and balloons. Both are lighter-than-air aircraft but have differentiating features and are operated differently.

The concentration of this handbook is on the airframe of aircraft; specifically, the fuselage, booms, nacelles, cowlings, fairings, airfoil surfaces, and landing gear. Also included are the various accessories and controls that accompany these structures. Note that the rotors of a helicopter are considered part of the airframe since they are actually rotating wings. By contrast, propellers and rotating airfoils of an engine on an airplane are not considered part of the airframe.

The most common aircraft is the fixed-wing aircraft. As the name implies, the wings on this type of flying machine are attached to the fuselage and are not intended to move independently in a fashion that results in the creation of lift. One, two, or three sets of wings have all been successfully utilized. *[Figure 1-12]* Rotary-wing aircraft such as helicopters are also widespread. This handbook discusses features and maintenance aspects common to both fixed-wing and rotary-wing categories of aircraft. Also, in certain cases, explanations focus on information specific to only one or the other. Glider airframes are very similar to fixed-wing aircraft. Unless otherwise noted, maintenance practices described for fixed-wing aircraft also apply to gliders. The same is true for lighter-than-air aircraft, although thorough

Figure 1-11. *Examples of different categories of aircraft, clockwise from top left: lighter-than-air, glider, rotorcraft, and airplane.*

Figure 1-12. *A monoplane (top), biplane (middle), and tri-wing aircraft (bottom).*

coverage of the unique airframe structures and maintenance practices for lighter-than-air flying machines is not included in this handbook.

The airframe of a fixed-wing aircraft consists of five principal units: the fuselage, wings, stabilizers, flight control surfaces, and landing gear. *[Figure 1-13]* Helicopter airframes consist of the fuselage, main rotor and related gearbox, tail rotor (on helicopters with a single main rotor), and the landing gear.

Airframe structural components are constructed from a wide variety of materials. The earliest aircraft were constructed primarily of wood. Steel tubing and the most common material, aluminum, followed. Many newly certified aircraft are built from molded composite materials, such as carbon fiber. Structural members of an aircraft's fuselage include stringers, longerons, ribs, bulkheads, and more. The main structural member in a wing is called the wing spar.

The skin of aircraft can also be made from a variety of materials, ranging from impregnated fabric to plywood, aluminum, or composites. Under the skin and attached to the structural fuselage are the many components that support airframe function. The entire airframe and its components are joined by rivets, bolts, screws, and other fasteners. Welding, adhesives, and special bonding techniques are also used.

Major Structural Stresses

Aircraft structural members are designed to carry a load or to resist stress. In designing an aircraft, every square inch of wing and fuselage, every rib, spar, and even each metal fitting must be considered in relation to the physical characteristics of the material of which it is made. Every part of the aircraft must be planned to carry the load to be imposed upon it.

Figure 1-13. *Principal airframe units.*

The determination of such loads is called stress analysis. Although planning the design is not the function of the aircraft technician, it is, nevertheless, important that the technician understand and appreciate the stresses involved in order to avoid changes in the original design through improper repairs.

The term "stress" is often used interchangeably with the word "strain." While related, they are not the same thing. External loads or forces cause stress. Stress is a material's internal resistance, or counterforce, that opposes deformation. The degree of deformation of a material is strain. When a material is subjected to a load or force, that material is deformed, regardless of how strong the material is or how light the load is.

There are five major stresses *[Figure 1-14]* to which all aircraft are subjected:

- Tension
- Compression
- Torsion
- Shear
- Bending

Tension is the stress that resists a force that tends to pull something apart. *[Figure 1-14A]* The engine pulls the aircraft forward, but air resistance tries to hold it back. The result is tension, which stretches the aircraft. The tensile strength of a material is measured in pounds per square inch (psi) and is calculated by dividing the load (in pounds) required to pull the material apart by its cross-sectional area (in square inches).

Compression is the stress that resists a crushing force. *[Figure 1-14B]* The compressive strength of a material is also measured in psi. Compression is the stress that tends to shorten or squeeze aircraft parts.

Torsion is the stress that produces twisting. *[Figure 1-14C]* While moving the aircraft forward, the engine also tends to twist it to one side, but other aircraft components hold it on course. Thus, torsion is created. The torsion strength of a material is its resistance to twisting or torque.

Shear is the stress that resists the force tending to cause one layer of a material to slide over an adjacent layer. *[Figure 1-14D]* Two riveted plates in tension subject the rivets to a shearing force. Usually, the shearing strength of a material is either equal to or less than its tensile or compressive strength. Aircraft parts, especially screws, bolts, and rivets, are often subject to a shearing force.

Bending stress is a combination of compression and tension. The rod in *Figure 1-14E* has been shortened (compressed) on the inside of the bend and stretched on the outside of the bend.

Figure 1-14. *The five stresses that may act on an aircraft and its parts.*

A single member of the structure may be subjected to a combination of stresses. In most cases, the structural members are designed to carry end loads rather than side loads. They are designed to be subjected to tension or compression rather than bending.

Strength or resistance to the external loads imposed during operation may be the principal requirement in certain structures. However, there are numerous other characteristics in addition to designing to control the five major stresses that engineers must consider. For example, cowling, fairings, and similar parts may not be subject to significant loads requiring a high degree of strength. However, these parts must have streamlined shapes to meet aerodynamic requirements, such as reducing drag or directing airflow.

Fixed-Wing Aircraft

Fuselage

The fuselage is the main structure or body of the fixed-wing aircraft. It provides space for cargo, controls, accessories, passengers, and other equipment. In single-engine aircraft, the fuselage houses the powerplant. In multiengine aircraft, the engines may be either in the fuselage, attached to the fuselage, or suspended from the wing structure. There are two general types of fuselage construction: truss and monocoque.

Truss Type

A truss is a rigid framework made up of members, such as beams, struts, and bars to resist deformation by applied loads. The truss-framed fuselage is generally covered with fabric.

The truss-type fuselage frame is usually constructed of steel tubing welded together in such a manner that all members of the truss can carry both tension and compression loads. *[Figure 1-15]* In some aircraft, principally the light, single-engine models, truss fuselage frames may be constructed of aluminum alloy and may be riveted or bolted into one piece, with cross-bracing achieved by using solid rods or tubes.

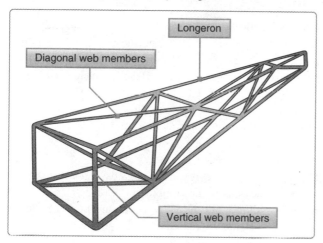

Figure 1-15. *A truss-type fuselage. A Warren truss uses mostly diagonal bracing.*

Monocoque Type

The monocoque (single shell) fuselage relies largely on the strength of the skin or covering to carry the primary loads. The design may be divided into two classes:

1. Monocoque
2. Semimonocoque

Different portions of the same fuselage may belong to either of the two classes, but most modern aircraft are considered to be of semimonocoque type construction.

The true monocoque construction uses formers, frame assemblies, and bulkheads to give shape to the fuselage. *[Figure 1-16]* The heaviest of these structural members are located at intervals to carry concentrated loads and at points where fittings are used to attach other units such as wings, powerplants, and stabilizers. Since no other bracing members are present, the skin must carry the primary stresses and keep the fuselage rigid. Thus, the biggest problem involved in monocoque construction is maintaining enough strength while keeping the weight within allowable limits.

Semimonocoque Type

To overcome the strength/weight problem of monocoque construction, a modification called semimonocoque construction was developed. It also consists of frame assemblies, bulkheads, and formers as used in the monocoque

Figure 1-16. *An airframe using monocoque construction.*

design but, additionally, the skin is reinforced by longitudinal members called longerons. Longerons usually extend across several frame members and help the skin support primary bending loads. They are typically made of aluminum alloy either of a single piece or a built-up construction.

Stringers are also used in the semimonocoque fuselage. These longitudinal members are typically more numerous and lighter in weight than the longerons. They come in a variety of shapes and are usually made from single piece aluminum alloy extrusions or formed aluminum. Stringers have some rigidity but are chiefly used for giving shape and for attachment of the skin. Stringers and longerons together prevent tension and compression from bending the fuselage. *[Figure 1-17]*

Figure 1-17. *The most common airframe construction is semimonocoque.*

Other bracing between the longerons and stringers can also be used. Often referred to as web members, these additional support pieces may be installed vertically or diagonally. It must be noted that manufacturers use different nomenclature to describe structural members. For example, there is often little difference between some rings, frames, and formers. One manufacturer may call the same type of brace a ring or a frame. Manufacturer instructions and specifications for a specific aircraft are the best guides.

The semimonocoque fuselage is constructed primarily of alloys of aluminum and magnesium, although steel and titanium are sometimes found in areas of high temperatures. Individually, no one of the aforementioned components is strong enough to carry the loads imposed during flight and landing. But, when combined, those components form a strong, rigid framework. This is accomplished with gussets, rivets, nuts and bolts, screws, and even friction stir welding. A gusset is a type of connection bracket that adds strength. *[Figure 1-18]*

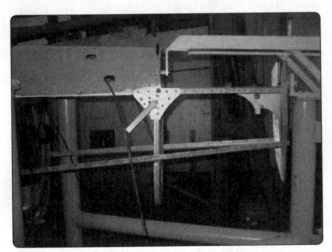

Figure 1-18. *Gussets are used to increase strength.*

To summarize, in semimonocoque fuselages, the strong, heavy longerons hold the bulkheads and formers, and these, in turn, hold the stringers, braces, web members, etc. All are designed to be attached together and to the skin to achieve the full strength benefits of semimonocoque design. It is important to recognize that the metal skin or covering carries part of the load. The fuselage skin thickness can vary with the load carried and the stresses sustained at a particular location.

The advantages of the semimonocoque fuselage are many. The bulkheads, frames, stringers, and longerons facilitate the design and construction of a streamlined fuselage that is both rigid and strong. Spreading loads among these structures and the skin means no single piece is failure critical. This means that a semimonocoque fuselage, because of its stressed-skin construction, may withstand considerable damage and still be strong enough to hold together.

Fuselages are generally constructed in two or more sections. On small aircraft, they are generally made in two or three sections, while larger aircraft may be made up of as many as six sections or more before being assembled.

Pressurization

Many aircraft are pressurized. This means that air is pumped into the cabin after takeoff and a difference in pressure between the air inside the cabin and the air outside the cabin is established. This differential is regulated and maintained. In this manner, enough oxygen is made available for passengers to breathe normally and move around the cabin without special equipment at high altitudes.

Pressurization causes significant stress on the fuselage structure and adds to the complexity of design. In addition to withstanding the difference in pressure between the air inside and outside the cabin, cycling from unpressurized to pressurized and back again each flight causes metal fatigue. To deal with these impacts and the other stresses of flight, nearly all pressurized aircraft are semimonocoque in design. Pressurized fuselage structures undergo extensive periodic inspections to ensure that any damage is discovered and repaired. Repeated weakness or failure in an area of structure may require that section of the fuselage be modified or redesigned.

Wings

Wing Configurations

Wings are airfoils that, when moved rapidly through the air, create lift. They are built in many shapes and sizes. Wing design can vary to provide certain desirable flight characteristics. Control at various operating speeds, the amount of lift generated, balance, and stability all change as the shape of the wing is altered. Both the leading edge and the trailing edge of the wing may be straight or curved, or one edge may be straight and the other curved. One or both edges may be tapered so that the wing is narrower at the tip than at the root where it joins the fuselage. The wing tip may be square, rounded, or even pointed. *Figure 1-19* shows a number of typical wing leading and trailing edge shapes.

The wings of an aircraft can be attached to the fuselage at the top, mid-fuselage, or at the bottom. They may extend perpendicular to the horizontal plain of the fuselage or can angle up or down slightly. This angle is known as the wing dihedral. The dihedral angle affects the lateral stability of the aircraft. *Figure 1-20* shows some common wing attach points and dihedral angle.

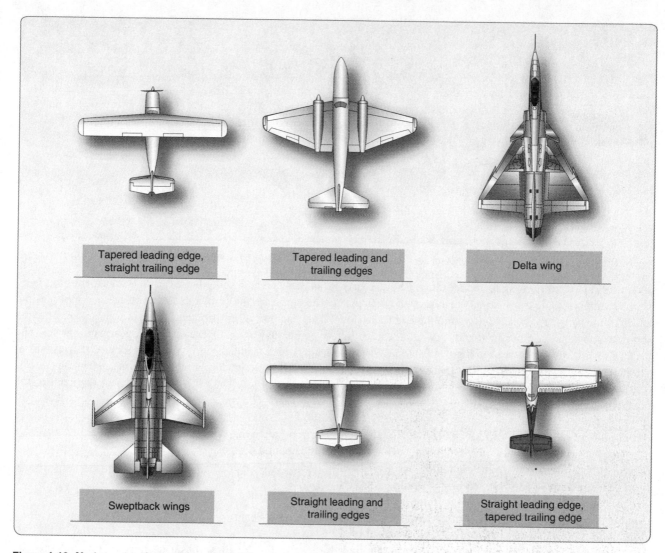

Figure 1-19. *Various wing design shapes yield different performance.*

Tapered leading edge, straight trailing edge

Tapered leading and trailing edges

Delta wing

Sweptback wings

Straight leading and trailing edges

Straight leading edge, tapered trailing edge

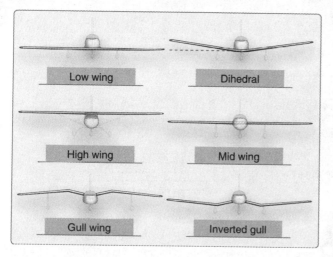

Low wing

Dihedral

High wing

Mid wing

Gull wing

Inverted gull

Figure 1-20. *Wing attach points and wing dihedrals.*

Wing Structure

The wings of an aircraft are designed to lift it into the air. Their particular design for any given aircraft depends on a number of factors, such as size, weight, use of the aircraft, desired speed in flight and at landing, and desired rate of climb. The wings of aircraft are designated left and right, corresponding to the left and right sides of the operator when seated in the cockpit. *[Figure 1-21]*

Often wings are of full cantilever design. This means they are built so that no external bracing is needed. They are supported internally by structural members assisted by the skin of the aircraft. Other aircraft wings use external struts or wires to assist in supporting the wing and carrying the aerodynamic and landing loads. Wing support cables and struts are generally made from steel. Many struts and their

Figure 1-21. *"Left" and "right" on an aircraft are oriented to the perspective of a pilot sitting in the cockpit.*

attach fittings have fairings to reduce drag. Short, nearly vertical supports called jury struts are found on struts that attach to the wings a great distance from the fuselage. This serves to subdue strut movement and oscillation caused by the air flowing around the strut in flight. *Figure 1-22* shows samples of wings using external bracing, also known as semicantilever wings. Cantilever wings built with no external bracing are also shown.

Aluminum is the most common material from which to construct wings, but they can be wood covered with fabric, and occasionally a magnesium alloy has been used. Moreover, modern aircraft are tending toward lighter and stronger materials throughout the airframe and in wing construction. Wings made entirely of carbon fiber or other composite materials exist, as well as wings made of a combination of materials for maximum strength to weight performance.

The internal structures of most wings are made up of spars and stringers running spanwise and ribs and formers or bulkheads running chordwise (leading edge to trailing edge). The spars are the principle structural members of a wing. They support all distributed loads, as well as concentrated weights such as the fuselage, landing gear, and engines. The skin, which is attached to the wing structure, carries part of the loads imposed during flight. It also transfers the stresses to the wing ribs. The ribs, in turn, transfer the loads to the wing spars. *[Figure 1-23]*

In general, wing construction is based on one of three fundamental designs:

1. Monospar

2. Multispar

3. Box beam

Modification of these basic designs may be adopted by various manufacturers.

The monospar wing incorporates only one main spanwise or longitudinal member in its construction. Ribs or bulkheads

Figure 1-22. *Externally braced wings, also called semicantilever wings, have wires or struts to support the wing. Full cantilever wings have no external bracing and are supported internally.*

Figure 1-23. *Wing structure nomenclature.*

supply the necessary contour or shape to the airfoil. Although the strict monospar wing is not common, this type of design modified by the addition of false spars or light shear webs along the trailing edge for support of control surfaces is sometimes used.

The multispar wing incorporates more than one main longitudinal member in its construction. To give the wing contour, ribs or bulkheads are often included.

The box beam type of wing construction uses two main longitudinal members with connecting bulkheads to furnish additional strength and to give contour to the wing. *[Figure 1-24]* A corrugated sheet may be placed between the bulkheads and the smooth outer skin so that the wing can better carry tension and compression loads. In some cases, heavy longitudinal stiffeners are substituted for the corrugated sheets. A combination of corrugated sheets on

the upper surface of the wing and stiffeners on the lower surface is sometimes used. Air transport category aircraft often utilize box beam wing construction.

Wing Spars

Spars are the principal structural members of the wing. They correspond to the longerons of the fuselage. They run parallel to the lateral axis of the aircraft, from the fuselage toward the tip of the wing, and are usually attached to the fuselage by wing fittings, plain beams, or a truss.

Spars may be made of metal, wood, or composite materials depending on the design criteria of a specific aircraft. Wooden spars are usually made from spruce. They can be generally classified into four different types by their cross-sectional configuration. As shown in *Figure 1-25,* they may be (A) solid, (B) box shaped, (C) partly hollow, or (D) in the form of an I-beam. Lamination of solid wood spars is

Figure 1-24. *Box beam construction.*

Figure 1-25. *Typical wooden wing spar cross-sections.*

often used to increase strength. Laminated wood can also be found in box shaped spars. The spar in *Figure 1-25E* has had material removed to reduce weight but retains the strength of a rectangular spar. As can be seen, most wing spars are basically rectangular in shape with the long dimension of the cross-section oriented up and down in the wing.

Currently, most manufactured aircraft have wing spars made of solid extruded aluminum or aluminum extrusions riveted together to form the spar. The increased use of composites and the combining of materials should make airmen vigilant for wings spars made from a variety of materials. *Figure 1-26* shows examples of metal wing spar cross-sections.

In an I–beam spar, the top and bottom of the I–beam are called the caps and the vertical section is called the web. The entire spar can be extruded from one piece of metal but often it is built up from multiple extrusions or formed angles. The web forms the principal depth portion of the spar and the cap strips (extrusions, formed angles, or milled sections) are attached to it. Together, these members carry the loads caused by wing bending, with the caps providing a

foundation for attaching the skin. Although the spar shapes in *Figure 1-26* are typical, actual wing spar configurations assume many forms. For example, the web of a spar may be a plate or a truss as shown in *Figure 1-27*. It could be built up from light weight materials with vertical stiffeners employed for strength. *[Figure 1-28]*

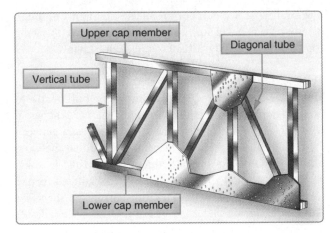

Figure 1-27. *A truss wing spar.*

Figure 1-26. *Examples of metal wing spar shapes.*

Figure 1-28. *A plate web wing spar with vertical stiffeners.*

It could also have no stiffeners but might contain flanged holes for reducing weight but maintaining strength. Some metal and composite wing spars retain the I-beam concept but use a sine wave web. *[Figure 1-29]*

Figure 1-29. *A sine wave wing spar can be made from aluminum or composite materials.*

Additionally, fail-safe spar web design exists. Fail-safe means that should one member of a complex structure fail, some other part of the structure assumes the load of the failed member and permits continued operation. A spar with fail-safe construction is shown in *Figure 1-30.* This spar is made in two sections. The top section consists of a cap riveted to the upper web plate. The lower section is a single extrusion consisting of the lower cap and web plate. These two sections are spliced together to form the spar. If either section of this type of spar breaks, the other section can still carry the load. This is the fail-safe feature.

As a rule, a wing has two spars. One spar is usually located near the front of the wing, and the other about two-thirds of the distance toward the wing's trailing edge. Regardless of type, the spar is the most important part of the wing. When other structural members of the wing are placed under load, most of the resulting stress is passed on to the wing spar.

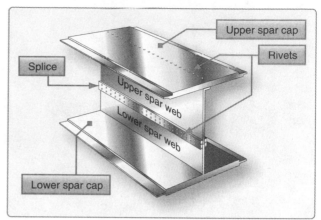

Figure 1-30. *A fail-safe spar with a riveted spar web.*

False spars are commonly used in wing design. They are longitudinal members like spars but do not extend the entire spanwise length of the wing. Often, they are used as hinge attach points for control surfaces, such as an aileron spar.

Wing Ribs

Ribs are the structural crosspieces that combine with spars and stringers to make up the framework of the wing. They usually extend from the wing leading edge to the rear spar or to the trailing edge of the wing. The ribs give the wing its cambered shape and transmit the load from the skin and stringers to the spars. Similar ribs are also used in ailerons, elevators, rudders, and stabilizers.

Wing ribs are usually manufactured from either wood or metal. Aircraft with wood wing spars may have wood or metal ribs while most aircraft with metal spars have metal ribs. Wood ribs are usually manufactured from spruce. The three most common types of wooden ribs are the plywood web, the lightened plywood web, and the truss types. Of these three, the truss type is the most efficient because it is strong and lightweight, but it is also the most complex to construct.

Figure 1-31 shows wood truss web ribs and a lightened plywood web rib. Wood ribs have a rib cap or cap strip fastened around the entire perimeter of the rib. It is usually made of the same material as the rib itself. The rib cap stiffens and strengthens the rib and provides an attaching surface for the wing covering. In *Figure 1-31A,* the cross-section of a wing rib with a truss-type web is illustrated. The dark rectangular sections are the front and rear wing spars. Note that to reinforce the truss, gussets are used. In *Figure 1-31B,* a truss web rib is shown with a continuous gusset. It provides greater support throughout the entire rib with very little additional weight. A continuous gusset stiffens the cap strip in the plane of the rib. This aids in preventing buckling and helps to obtain better rib/skin joints where nail-gluing is used. Such a rib can resist the driving force of nails better than the other types.

Figure 1-31. *Examples of wing ribs constructed of wood.*

Continuous gussets are also more easily handled than the many small separate gussets otherwise required. *Figure 1-31C* shows a rib with a lighten plywood web. It also contains gussets to support the web/cap strip interface. The cap strip is usually laminated to the web, especially at the leading edge.

A wing rib may also be referred to as a plain rib or a main rib. Wing ribs with specialized locations or functions are given names that reflect their uniqueness. For example, ribs that are located entirely forward of the front spar that are used to shape and strengthen the wing leading edge are called nose ribs or false ribs. False ribs are ribs that do not span the entire wing chord, which is the distance from the leading edge to the trailing edge of the wing. Wing butt ribs may be found at the inboard edge of the wing where the wing attaches to the fuselage. Depending on its location and method of attachment, a butt rib may also be called a bulkhead rib or a compression rib if it is designed to receive compression loads that tend to force the wing spars together.

Since the ribs are laterally weak, they are strengthened in some wings by tapes that are woven above and below rib sections to prevent sidewise bending of the ribs. Drag and anti-drag wires may also be found in a wing. In *Figure 1-32*, they are shown crisscrossed between the spars to form a truss to resist forces acting on the wing in the direction of the wing chord. These tension wires are also referred to as tie rods. The wire designed to resist the backward forces is called a drag wire; the anti-drag wire resists the forward forces in the chord direction. *Figure 1-32* illustrates the structural components of a basic wood wing.

At the inboard end of the wing spars is some form of wing attach fitting as illustrated in *Figure 1-32*. These provide a strong and secure method for attaching the wing to the fuselage. The interface between the wing and fuselage is often covered with a fairing to achieve smooth airflow in this area. The fairing(s) can be removed for access to the wing attach fittings. *[Figure 1-33]*

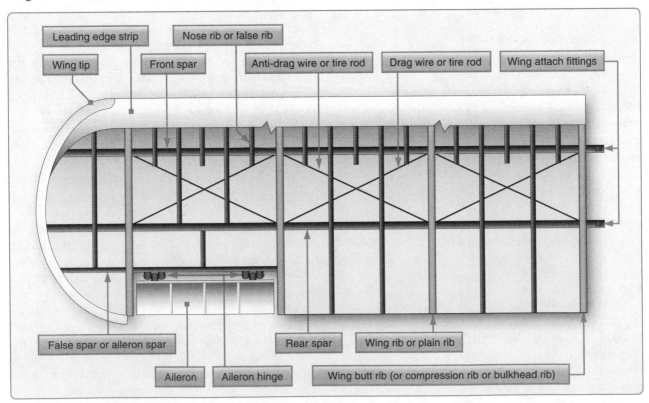

Figure 1-32. *Basic wood wing structure and components.*

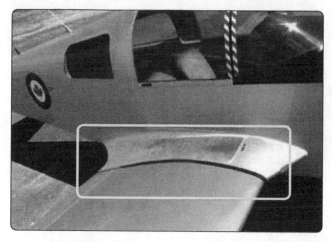

Figure 1-33. *Wing root fairings smooth airflow and hide wing attach fittings.*

The wing tip is often a removable unit, bolted to the outboard end of the wing panel. One reason for this is the vulnerability of the wing tips to damage, especially during ground handling and taxiing. *Figure 1-34* shows a removable wing tip for a large aircraft wing. Others are different. The wing tip assembly is of aluminum alloy construction. The wing tip cap is secured to the tip with countersunk screws and is secured to the interspar structure at four points with ¼-inch diameter bolts. To prevent ice from forming on the leading edge of the wings of large aircraft, hot air from an engine is often channeled through the leading edge from wing root to wing tip. A louver on the top surface of the wingtip allows this warm air to be exhausted overboard. Wing position lights are located at the center of the tip and are not directly visible from the cockpit. As an indication that the wing tip light is operating, some wing tips are equipped with a Lucite rod to transmit the light to the leading edge.

Wing Skin

Often, the skin on a wing is designed to carry part of the flight and ground loads in combination with the spars and ribs. This is known as a stressed-skin design. The all-metal, full cantilever wing section illustrated in *Figure 1-35* shows the structure of one such design. The lack of extra internal or external bracing requires that the skin share some of the load. Notice the skin is stiffened to aid with this function.

Figure 1-34. *A removable metal wing tip.*

Fuel is often carried inside the wings of a stressed-skin aircraft. The joints in the wing can be sealed with a special fuel resistant sealant enabling fuel to be stored directly inside the structure. This is known as wet wing design. Alternately, a fuel-carrying bladder or tank can be fitted inside a wing. *Figure 1-36* shows a wing section with a box beam structural design such as one that might be found in a transport category aircraft. This structure increases strength while reducing weight. Proper sealing of the structure allows fuel to be stored in the box sections of the wing.

The wing skin on an aircraft may be made from a wide variety of materials such as fabric, wood, or aluminum. But a single thin sheet of material is not always employed. Chemically milled aluminum skin can provide skin of varied thicknesses.

On aircraft with stressed-skin wing design, honeycomb structured wing panels are often used as skin. A honeycomb structure is built up from a core material resembling a bee hive's honeycomb which is laminated or sandwiched between thin outer skin sheets. *Figure 1-37* illustrates honeycomb panes and their components. Panels formed like this are lightweight and very strong. They have a variety of uses on the aircraft, such as floor panels, bulkheads, and control surfaces, as well as wing skin panels. *Figure 1-38* shows the locations of honeycomb construction wing panels on a jet transport aircraft.

A honeycomb panel can be made from a wide variety of materials. Aluminum core honeycomb with an outer skin of aluminum is common. But honeycomb in which the core is

Figure 1-35. *The skin is an integral load carrying part of a stressed skin design.*

Figure 1-36. *Fuel is often carried in the wings.*

an Arimid® fiber and the outer sheets are coated Phenolic® is common as well. In fact, a myriad of other material combinations such as those using fiberglass, plastic, Nomex®, Kevlar®, and carbon fiber all exist. Each honeycomb structure possesses unique characteristics depending upon the materials, dimensions, and manufacturing techniques employed. *Figure 1-39* shows an entire wing leading edge formed from honeycomb structure.

Nacelles

Nacelles (sometimes called "pods") are streamlined enclosures used primarily to house the engine and its components. They usually present a round or elliptical profile to the wind thus reducing aerodynamic drag. On most single-engine aircraft, the engine and nacelle are at the forward end of the fuselage. On multiengine aircraft, engine nacelles are built into the wings or attached to the fuselage at the empennage (tail section). Occasionally, a multiengine aircraft is designed with a nacelle in line with the fuselage aft of the passenger compartment. Regardless of its location, a nacelle contains the engine and accessories, engine mounts, structural members, a firewall, and skin and cowling on the exterior to fare the nacelle to the wind.

Some aircraft have nacelles that are designed to house the landing gear when retracted. Retracting the gear to reduce wind resistance is standard procedure on high-performance/ high-speed aircraft. The wheel well is the area where the landing gear is attached and stowed when retracted. Wheel wells can be located in the wings and/or fuselage when not part of the nacelle. *Figure 1-40* shows an engine nacelle incorporating the landing gear with the wheel well extending into the wing root.

Figure 1-37. *The honeycomb panel is a staple in aircraft construction. Cores can be either constant thickness (A) or tapered (B). Tapered core honeycomb panels are frequently used as flight control surfaces and wing trailing edges.*

Figure 1-38. *Honeycomb wing construction on a large jet transport aircraft.*

The framework of a nacelle usually consists of structural members similar to those of the fuselage. Lengthwise members, such as longerons and stringers, combine with horizontal/vertical members, such as rings, formers, and bulkheads, to give the nacelle its shape and structural integrity. A firewall is incorporated to isolate the engine compartment from the rest of the aircraft. This is basically a stainless steel or titanium bulkhead that contains a fire in the confines of the nacelle rather than letting it spread throughout the airframe. *[Figure 1-41]*

Engine mounts are also found in the nacelle. These are the structural assemblies to which the engine is fastened. They are usually constructed from chrome/molybdenum steel tubing in light aircraft and forged chrome/nickel/molybdenum assemblies in larger aircraft. *[Figure 1-42]*

The exterior of a nacelle is covered with a skin or fitted with a cowling which can be opened to access the engine and

components inside. Both are usually made of sheet aluminum or magnesium alloy with stainless steel or titanium alloys being used in high-temperature areas, such as around the exhaust exit. Regardless of the material used, the skin is typically attached to the framework with rivets.

Cowling refers to the detachable panels covering those areas into which access must be gained regularly, such as the engine and its accessories. It is designed to provide a smooth airflow over the nacelle and to protect the engine from damage. Cowl panels are generally made of aluminum alloy construction. However, stainless steel is often used as the inner skin aft of the power section and for cowl flaps and near cowl flap openings. It is also used for oil cooler ducts. Cowl flaps are moveable parts of the nacelle cowling that open and close to regulate engine temperature.

There are many engine cowl designs. *Figure 1-43* shows an exploded view of the pieces of cowling for a horizontally

Figure 1-39. *A wing leading edge formed from honeycomb material bonded to the aluminum spar structure.*

Figure 1-40. *Wheel wells in a wing engine nacelle with gear coming down (inset).*

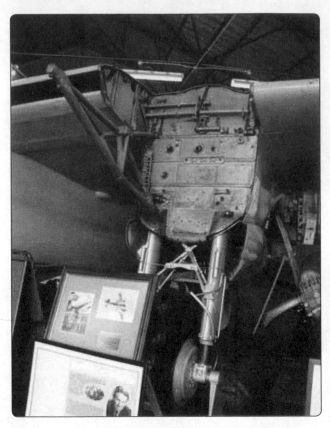

Figure 1-41. An e*ngine nacelle firewall.*

Figure 1-42. *Various aircraft engine mounts.*

opposed engine on a light aircraft. It is attached to the nacelle by means of screws and/or quick release fasteners. Some large reciprocating engines are enclosed by "orange peel" cowlings which provide excellent access to components inside the nacelle. *[Figure 1-44]* These cowl panels are attached to the forward firewall by mounts which also serve as hinges for opening the cowl. The lower cowl mounts are secured to the hinge brackets by quick release pins. The side and top panels are held open by rods and the lower panel is retained in the open position by a spring and a cable. All of the cowling panels are locked in the closed position by over-center steel latches which are secured in the closed position by spring-loaded safety catches.

An example of a turbojet engine nacelle can be seen in *Figure 1-45.* The cowl panels are a combination of fixed and easily removable panels which can be opened and closed during maintenance. A nose cowl is also a feature on a jet engine nacelle. It guides air into the engine.

Empennage

The empennage of an aircraft is also known as the tail section. Most empennage designs consist of a tail cone, fixed aerodynamic surfaces or stabilizers, and movable aerodynamic surfaces.

Figure 1-43. *Typical cowling for a horizontally opposed reciprocating engine.*

The tail cone serves to close and streamline the aft end of most fuselages. The cone is made up of structural members like those of the fuselage; however, cones are usually of lighter construction since they receive less stress than the fuselage. *[Figure 1-46]*

Figure 1-44. *Orange peel cowling for large radial reciprocating engine.*

Figure 1-45. *Cowling on a transport category turbine engine nacelle.*

Figure 1-46. *The fuselage terminates at the tail cone with similar but more lightweight construction.*

The other components of the typical empennage are of heavier construction than the tail cone. These members include fixed surfaces that help stabilize the aircraft and movable surfaces that help to direct an aircraft during flight. The fixed surfaces are the horizontal stabilizer and vertical stabilizer. The movable surfaces are usually a rudder located at the aft edge of the vertical stabilizer and an elevator located at the aft edge the horizontal stabilizer. *[Figure 1-47]*

Figure 1-47. *Components of a typical empennage.*

The structure of the stabilizers is very similar to that which is used in wing construction. *Figure 1-48* shows a typical vertical stabilizer. Notice the use of spars, ribs, stringers, and skin like those found in a wing. They perform the same functions shaping and supporting the stabilizer and transferring stresses. Bending, torsion, and shear created by air loads in flight pass from one structural member to another. Each member absorbs some of the stress and passes the remainder on to the others. Ultimately, the spar transmits

Figure 1-48. *Vertical stabilizer.*

any overloads to the fuselage. A horizontal stabilizer is built the same way.

The rudder and elevator are flight control surfaces that are also part of the empennage discussed in the next section of this chapter.

Flight Control Surfaces

The directional control of a fixed-wing aircraft takes place around the lateral, longitudinal, and vertical axes by means of flight control surfaces designed to create movement about these axes. These control devices are hinged or movable surfaces through which the attitude of an aircraft is controlled during takeoff, flight, and landing. They are usually divided into two major groups: 1) primary or main flight control surfaces and 2) secondary or auxiliary control surfaces.

Primary Flight Control Surfaces

The primary flight control surfaces on a fixed-wing aircraft include: ailerons, elevators, and the rudder. The ailerons are attached to the trailing edge of both wings and when moved, rotate the aircraft around the longitudinal axis. The elevator is attached to the trailing edge of the horizontal stabilizer. When it is moved, it alters aircraft pitch, which is the attitude about the horizontal or lateral axis. The rudder is hinged to the trailing edge of the vertical stabilizer. When the rudder changes position, the aircraft rotates about the vertical axis (yaw). *Figure 1-49* shows the primary flight controls of a light aircraft and the movement they create relative to the three axes of flight.

Primary control surfaces are usually similar in construction to one another and vary only in size, shape, and methods of

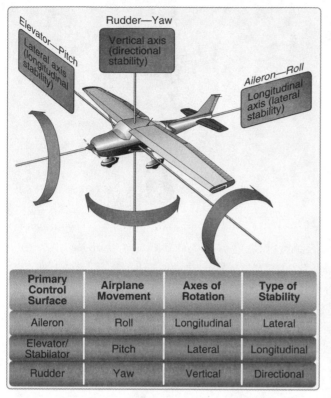

Primary Control Surface	Airplane Movement	Axes of Rotation	Type of Stability
Aileron	Roll	Longitudinal	Lateral
Elevator/Stabilator	Pitch	Lateral	Longitudinal
Rudder	Yaw	Vertical	Directional

Figure 1-49. *Flight control surfaces move the aircraft around the three axes of flight.*

attachment. On aluminum light aircraft, their structure is often similar to an all-metal wing. This is appropriate because the primary control surfaces are simply smaller aerodynamic devices. They are typically made from an aluminum alloy structure built around a single spar member or torque tube to which ribs are fitted and a skin is attached. The lightweight ribs are, in many cases, stamped out from flat aluminum sheet stock. Holes in the ribs lighten the assembly. An aluminum skin is attached with rivets. *Figure 1-50* illustrates this type of structure, which can be found on the primary control surfaces of light aircraft as well as on medium and heavy aircraft.

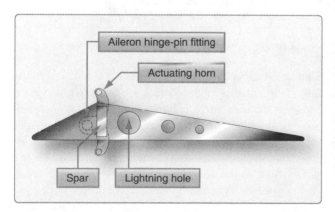

Figure 1-50. *Typical structure of an aluminum flight control surface.*

Primary control surfaces constructed from composite materials are also commonly used. These are found on many heavy and high-performance aircraft, as well as gliders, home-built, and light-sport aircraft. The weight and strength advantages over traditional construction can be significant. A wide variety of materials and construction techniques are employed. *Figure 1-51* shows examples of aircraft that use composite technology on primary flight control surfaces. Note that the control surfaces of fabric-covered aircraft often have fabric-covered surfaces just as aluminum-skinned (light) aircraft typically have all-aluminum control surfaces. There is a critical need for primary control surfaces to be balanced so they do not vibrate or flutter in the wind.

Figure 1-51. *Composite control surfaces and some of the many aircraft that utilize them.*

Performed to manufacturer's instructions, balancing usually consists of assuring that the center of gravity of a particular device is at or forward of the hinge point. Failure to properly balance a control surface could lead to catastrophic failure. *Figure 1-52* illustrates several aileron configurations with their hinge points well aft of the leading edge. This is a common design feature used to prevent flutter.

Figure 1-52. *Aileron hinge locations are very close to but aft of the center of gravity to prevent flutter.*

Ailerons

Ailerons are the primary flight control surfaces that move the aircraft about the longitudinal axis. In other words, movement of the ailerons in flight causes the aircraft to roll. Ailerons are usually located on the outboard trailing edge of each of the wings. They are built into the wing and are calculated as part of the wing's surface area. *Figure 1-53* shows aileron locations on various wing tip designs.

Figure 1-53. *Aileron location on various wings.*

Ailerons are controlled by a side-to-side motion of the control stick in the cockpit or a rotation of the control yoke. When the aileron on one wing deflects down, the aileron on the opposite wing deflects upward. This amplifies the movement of the aircraft around the longitudinal axis. On the wing on which the aileron trailing edge moves downward, camber is increased and lift is increased. Conversely, on the other wing, the raised aileron decreases lift. *[Figure 1-54]* The result is a sensitive response to the control input to roll the aircraft.

Figure 1-54. *Differential aileron control movement. When one aileron is moved down, the aileron on the opposite wing is deflected upward.*

The pilot's request for aileron movement and roll are transmitted from the cockpit to the actual control surface in a variety of ways depending on the aircraft. A system of control cables and pulleys, push-pull tubes, hydraulics, electric, or a combination of these can be employed. *[Figure 1-55]*

Figure 1-55. *Transferring control surface inputs from the cockpit.*

Simple, light aircraft usually do not have hydraulic or electric fly-by-wire aileron control. These are found on heavy and high-performance aircraft. Large aircraft and some high-performance aircraft may also have a second set of ailerons located inboard on the trailing edge of the wings. These are part of a complex system of primary and secondary control surfaces used to provide lateral control and stability in flight. At low speeds, the ailerons may be augmented by the use of flaps and spoilers. At high speeds, only inboard aileron deflection is required to roll the aircraft while the other control surfaces are locked out or remain stationary. *Figure 1-56* illustrates the location of the typical flight control surfaces found on a transport category aircraft.

Elevator

The elevator is the primary flight control surface that moves the aircraft around the horizontal or lateral axis. This causes the nose of the aircraft to pitch up or down. The elevator is hinged to the trailing edge of the horizontal stabilizer and typically spans most or all of its width. It is controlled in the cockpit by pushing or pulling the control yoke forward or aft.

Light aircraft use a system of control cables and pulleys or push pull tubes to transfer cockpit inputs to the movement of the elevator. High performance and large aircraft typically employ more complex systems. Hydraulic power is commonly used to move the elevator on these aircraft. On aircraft equipped with fly-by-wire controls, a combination of electrical and hydraulic power is used.

Rudder

The rudder is the primary control surface that causes an aircraft to yaw or move about the vertical axis. This provides directional control and thus points the nose of the aircraft in the direction desired. Most aircraft have a single rudder hinged to the trailing edge of the vertical stabilizer. It is controlled by a pair of foot-operated rudder pedals in the cockpit. When the right pedal is pushed forward, it deflects the rudder to the right which moves the nose of the aircraft

to the right. The left pedal is rigged to simultaneously move aft. When the left pedal is pushed forward, the nose of the aircraft moves to the left.

As with the other primary flight controls, the transfer of the movement of the cockpit controls to the rudder varies with the complexity of the aircraft. Many aircraft incorporate the directional movement of the nose or tail wheel into the rudder control system for ground operation. This allows the operator to steer the aircraft with the rudder pedals during taxi when the airspeed is not high enough for the control surfaces to be effective. Some large aircraft have a split rudder arrangement. This is actually two rudders, one above the other. At low speeds, both rudders deflect in the same direction when the pedals are pushed. At higher speeds, one of the rudders becomes inoperative as the deflection of a single rudder is aerodynamically sufficient to maneuver the aircraft.

Dual Purpose Flight Control Surfaces

The ailerons, elevators, and rudder are considered conventional primary control surfaces. However, some aircraft are designed with a control surface that may serve a dual purpose. For example, elevons perform the combined functions of the ailerons and the elevator. *[Figure 1-57]*

A movable horizontal tail section, called a stabilator, is a control surface that combines the action of both the horizontal stabilizer and the elevator. *[Figure 1-58]* Basically, a

Figure 1-56. *Typical flight control surfaces on a transport category aircraft.*

Figure 1-57. *Elevons.*

Figure 1-58. *A stabilizer and index marks on a transport category aircraft.*

stabilator is a horizontal stabilizer that can also be rotated about the horizontal axis to affect the pitch of the aircraft. A ruddervator combines the action of the rudder and elevator. *[Figure 1-59]* This is possible on aircraft with V–tail empennages where the traditional horizontal and vertical stabilizers do not exist. Instead, two stabilizers angle upward and outward from the aft fuselage in a "V" configuration. Each contains a movable ruddervator built into the trailing

Figure 1-59. *Ruddervator.*

edge. Movement of the ruddervators can alter the movement of the aircraft around the horizontal and/or vertical axis. Additionally, some aircraft are equipped with flaperons. *[Figure 1-60]* Flaperons are ailerons which can also act as flaps. Flaps are secondary control surfaces on most wings, discussed in the next section of this chapter.

Figure 1-60. *Flaperons.*

Secondary or Auxiliary Control Surfaces

There are several secondary or auxiliary flight control surfaces. Their names, locations, and functions of those for most large aircraft are listed in *Figure 1-61.*

Flaps

Flaps are found on most aircraft. They are usually inboard on the wings' trailing edges adjacent to the fuselage. Leading edge flaps are also common. They extend forward and down from the inboard wing leading edge. The flaps are lowered to increase the camber of the wings and provide greater lift and control at slow speeds. They enable landing at slower speeds and shorten the amount of runway required for takeoff and landing. The amount that the flaps extend and the angle they form with the wing can be selected from the cockpit. Typically, flaps can extend up to 45–50°. *Figure 1-62* shows various aircraft with flaps in the extended position.

Flaps are usually constructed of materials and with techniques used on the other airfoils and control surfaces of a particular aircraft. Aluminum skin and structure flaps are the norm on light aircraft. Heavy and high-performance aircraft flaps may also be aluminum, but the use of composite structures is also common.

There are various kinds of flaps. Plain flaps form the trailing edge of the wing when the flap is in the retracted position. *[Figure 1-63A]* The airflow over the wing continues over the upper and lower surfaces of the flap, making the trailing edge of the flap essentially the trailing edge of the wing. The plain

Secondary/Auxiliary Flight Control Surfaces		
Name	Location	Function
Flaps	Inboard trailing edge of wings	Extends the camber of the wing for greater lift and slower flight. Allows control at low speeds for short field takeoffs and landings.
Trim tabs	Trailing edge of primary flight control surfaces	Reduces the force needed to move a primary control surface.
Balance tabs	Trailing edge of primary flight control surfaces	Reduces the force needed to move a primary control surface.
Anti-balance tabs	Trailing edge of primary flight control surfaces	Increases feel and effectiveness of primary control surface.
Servo tabs	Trailing edge of primary flight control surfaces	Assists or provides the force for moving a primary flight control.
Spoilers	Upper and/or trailing edge of wing	Decreases (spoils) lift. Can augment aileron function.
Slats	Mid to outboard leading edge of wing	Extends the camber of the wing for greater lift and slower flight. Allows control at low speeds for short field takeoffs and landings.
Slots	Outer leading edge of wing forward of ailerons	Directs air over upper surface of wing during high angle of attack. Lowers stall speed and provides control during slow flight.
Leading edge flap	Inboard leading edge of wing	Extends the camber of the wing for greater lift and slower flight. Allows control at low speeds for short field takeoffs and landings.

NOTE: An aircraft may possess none, one, or a combination of the above control surfaces.

Figure 1-61. *Secondary or auxiliary control surfaces and respective locations for larger aircraft.*

Figure 1-62. *Various aircraft with flaps in the extended position.*

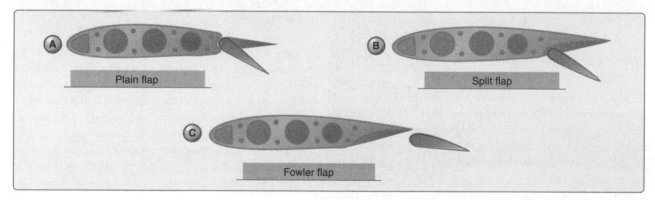

Figure 1-63. *Various types of flaps.*

flap is hinged so that the trailing edge can be lowered. This increases wing camber and provides greater lift.

A split flap is normally housed under the trailing edge of the wing. [Figure 1-63B] It is usually just a braced flat metal plate hinged at several places along its leading edge. The upper surface of the wing extends to the trailing edge of the flap. When deployed, the split flap trailing edge lowers away from the trailing edge of the wing. Airflow over the top of the wing remains the same. Airflow under the wing now follows the camber created by the lowered split flap, increasing lift.

Fowler flaps not only lower the trailing edge of the wing when deployed but also slide aft, effectively increasing the area of the wing. [Figure 1-63C] This creates more lift via the increased surface area, as well as the wing camber. When stowed, the fowler flap typically retracts up under the wing trailing edge similar to a split flap. The sliding motion of a fowler flap can be accomplished with a worm drive and flap tracks.

An enhanced version of the fowler flap is a set of flaps that actually contains more than one aerodynamic surface. Figure 1-64 shows a triple-slotted flap. In this configuration, the flap consists of a fore flap, a mid flap, and an aft flap. When deployed, each flap section slides aft on tracks as it lowers. The flap sections also separate leaving an open slot between the wing and the fore flap, as well as between each of the flap sections. Air from the underside of the wing flows through these slots. The result is that the laminar flow on the upper surfaces is enhanced. The greater camber and effective wing area increase overall lift.

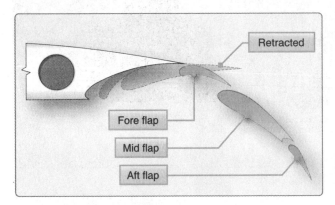

Figure 1-64. *Triple slotted flap.*

Heavy aircraft often have leading edge flaps that are used in conjunction with the trailing edge flaps. [Figure 1-65] They can be made of machined magnesium or can have an aluminum or composite structure. While they are not installed or operate independently, their use with trailing edge flaps can greatly increase wing camber and lift. When stowed, leading edge flaps retract into the leading edge of the wing.

Figure 1-65. *Leading edge flaps.*

The differing designs of leading edge flaps essentially provide the same effect. Activation of the trailing edge flaps automatically deploys the leading edge flaps, which are driven out of the leading edge and downward, extending the camber of the wing. *Figure 1-66* shows a Krueger flap, recognizable by its flat mid-section.

Slats

Another leading-edge device which extends wing camber is a slat. Slats can be operated independently of the flaps with their own switch in the cockpit. Slats not only extend out of the leading edge of the wing increasing camber and lift, but most often, when fully deployed leave a slot between their trailing edges and the leading edge of the wing. [Figure 1-67] This increases the angle of attack at which the wing will maintain its laminar airflow, resulting in the ability to fly the aircraft slower and still maintain control.

Spoilers and Speed Brakes

A spoiler is a device found on the upper surface of many heavy and high-performance aircraft. It is stowed flush to the wing's upper surface. When deployed, it raises up into the airstream and disrupts the laminar airflow of the wing, thus reducing lift.

Spoilers are made with similar construction materials and techniques as the other flight control surfaces on the aircraft. Often, they are honeycomb-core flat panels. At low speeds, spoilers are rigged to operate when the ailerons operate to assist with the lateral movement and stability of the aircraft. On the wing where the aileron is moved up, the spoilers also raise thus amplifying the reduction of lift on that wing. [Figure 1-68] On the wing with downward aileron deflection, the spoilers remain stowed. As the speed of the aircraft

Figure 1-66. *Side view (left) and front view (right) of a Krueger flap on a Boeing 737.*

Figure 1-67. *Air passing through the slot aft of the slat promotes boundary layer airflow on the upper surface at high angles of attack,*

increases, the ailerons become more effective and the spoiler interconnect disengages.

Spoilers are unique in that they may also be fully deployed on both wings to act as speed brakes. The reduced lift and increased drag can quickly reduce the speed of the aircraft in flight. Dedicated speed brake panels similar to flight spoilers in construction can also be found on the upper surface of the wings of heavy and high-performance aircraft. They are designed specifically to increase drag and reduce the speed of the aircraft when deployed. These speed brake panels do not operate differentially with the ailerons at low speed.

Figure 1-68. *Spoilers deployed upon landing on a transport category aircraft.*

The speed brake control in the cockpit can deploy all spoiler and speed brake surfaces fully when operated. Often, these surfaces are also rigged to deploy on the ground automatically when engine thrust reversers are activated.

Tabs

The force of the air against a control surface during the high speed of flight can make it difficult to move and hold that control surface in the deflected position. A control surface might also be too sensitive for similar reasons. Several different tabs are used to aid with these types of problems. The table in *Figure 1-69* summarizes the various tabs and their uses.

Flight Control Tabs			
Type	Direction of Motion (in relation to control surface)	Activation	Effect
Trim	Opposite	Set by pilot from cockpit. Uses independent linkage.	Statically balances the aircraft in flight. Allows "hands off" maintenance of flight condition.
Balance	Opposite	Moves when pilot moves control surface. Coupled to control surface linkage.	Aids pilot in overcoming the force needed to move the control surface.
Servo	Opposite	Directly linked to flight control input device. Can be primary or back-up means of control.	Aerodynamically positions control surfaces that require too much force to move manually.
Anti-balance or Anti-servo	Same	Directly linked to flight control input device.	Increases force needed by pilot to change flight control position. De-sensitizes flight controls.
Spring	Opposite	Located in line of direct linkage to servo tab. Spring assists when control forces become too high in high-speed flight.	Enables moving control surface when forces are high. Inactive during slow flight.

Figure 1-69. *Various tabs and their uses.*

While in flight, it is desirable for the pilot to be able to take his or her hands and feet off of the controls and have the aircraft maintain its flight condition. Trims tabs are designed to allow this. Most trim tabs are small movable surfaces located on the trailing edge of a primary flight control surface. A small movement of the tab in the direction opposite of the direction the flight control surface is deflected, causing air to strike the tab, in turn producing a force that aids in maintaining the flight control surface in the desired position. Through linkage set from the cockpit, the tab can be positioned so that it is actually holding the control surface in position rather than the pilot. Therefore, elevator tabs are used to maintain the speed of the aircraft since they assist in maintaining the selected pitch. Rudder tabs can be set to hold yaw in check and maintain heading. Aileron tabs can help keep the wings level.

Occasionally, a simple light aircraft may have a stationary metal plate attached to the trailing edge of a primary flight control, usually the rudder. This is also a trim tab as shown in *Figure 1-70.* It can be bent slightly on the ground to trim the aircraft in flight to a hands-off condition when flying straight and level. The correct amount of bend can be determined only by flying the aircraft after an adjustment. Note that a small amount of bending is usually sufficient.

The aerodynamic phenomenon of moving a trim tab in one direction to cause the control surface to experience a force moving in the opposite direction is exactly what occurs with the use of balance tabs. *[Figure 1-71]* Often, it is difficult to move a primary control surface due to its surface area and the speed of the air rushing over it. Deflecting a balance tab hinged at the trailing edge of the control surface in the opposite

Ground adjustable rudder trim

Figure 1-70. *Example of a trim tab.*

direction of the desired control surface movement causes a force to position the surface in the proper direction with reduced force to do so. Balance tabs are usually linked directly to the control surface linkage so that they move automatically when there is an input for control surface movement. They also can double as trim tabs, if adjustable in the flight deck.

A servo tab is similar to a balance tab in location and effect, but it is designed to operate the primary flight control surface, not just reduce the force needed to do so. It is usually used as a means to back up the primary control of the flight control surfaces. *[Figure 1-72]*

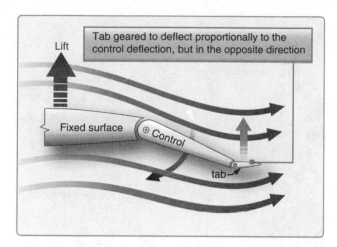

Figure 1-71. *Balance tabs assist with forces needed to position control surfaces.*

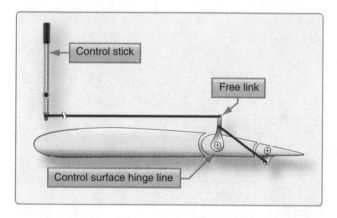

Figure 1-72. *Servo tabs can be used to position flight control surfaces in case of hydraulic failure.*

On heavy aircraft, large control surfaces require too much force to be moved manually and are usually deflected out of the neutral position by hydraulic actuators. These power control units are signaled via a system of hydraulic valves connected to the yoke and rudder pedals. On fly-by-wire aircraft, the hydraulic actuators that move the flight control surfaces are signaled by electric input. In the case of hydraulic system failure(s), manual linkage to a servo tab can be used to deflect it. This, in turn, provides an aerodynamic force that moves the primary control surface.

A control surface may require excessive force to move only in the final stages of travel. When this is the case, a spring tab can be used. This is essentially a servo tab that does not activate until an effort is made to move the control surface beyond a certain point. When reached, a spring in line of the control linkage aids in moving the control surface through the remainder of its travel. *[Figure 1-73]*

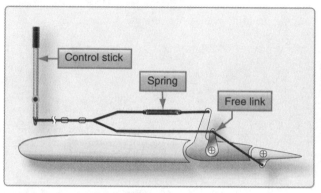

Figure 1-73. *Many tab linkages have a spring tab that kicks in as the forces needed to deflect a control increase with speed and the angle of desired deflection.*

Figure 1-74 shows another way of assisting the movement of an aileron on a large aircraft. It is called an aileron balance panel. Not visible when approaching the aircraft, it is positioned in the linkage that hinges the aileron to the wing.

Balance panels have been constructed typically of aluminum skin-covered frame assemblies or aluminum honeycomb structures. The trailing edge of the wing just forward of the leading edge of the aileron is sealed to allow controlled airflow in and out of the hinge area where the balance panel is located.

Figure 1-74. *An aileron balance panel and linkage uses varying air pressure to assist in control surface positioning.*

[Figure 1-75] When the aileron is moved from the neutral position, differential pressure builds up on one side of the balance panel. This differential pressure acts on the balance panel in a direction that assists the aileron movement. For slight movements, deflecting the control tab at the trailing edge of the aileron is easy enough to not require significant assistance from the balance tab. (Moving the control tab moves the ailerons as desired.) But, as greater deflection is requested, the force resisting control tab and aileron movement becomes greater and augmentation from the balance tab is needed. The seals and mounting geometry allow the differential pressure of airflow on the balance panel to increase as deflection of the ailerons is increased. This makes the resistance felt when moving the aileron controls relatively constant.

Figure 1-75. *The trailing edge of the wing just forward of the leading edge of the aileron is sealed to allow controlled airflow in and out of the hinge area where the balance panel is located.*

Antiservo tabs, as the name suggests, are like servo tabs but move in the same direction as the primary control surface. On some aircraft, especially those with a movable horizontal stabilizer, the input to the control surface can be too sensitive. An antiservo tab tied through the control linkage creates an aerodynamic force that increases the effort needed to move the control surface. This makes flying the aircraft more stable for the pilot. *Figure 1-76* shows an antiservo tab in the near neutral position. Deflected in the same direction as the desired stabilator movement, it increases the required control surface input.

Other Wing Features

There may be other structures visible on the wings of an aircraft that contribute to performance. Winglets, vortex generators, stall fences, and gap seals are all common wing features. Introductory descriptions of each are given in the following paragraphs.

A winglet is an obvious vertical upturn of the wing's tip resembling a vertical stabilizer. It is an aerodynamic device designed to reduce the drag created by wing tip vortices in flight. Usually made from aluminum or composite materials, winglets can be designed to optimize performance at a desired speed. *[Figure 1-77]*

Figure 1-76. *An antiservo tab moves in the same direction as the control tab. Shown here on a stabilator, it desensitizes the pitch control.*

Figure 1-77. *A winglet reduces aerodynamic drag caused by air spilling off of the wing tip.*

Vortex generators are small airfoil sections usually attached to the upper surface of a wing. *[Figure 1-78]* They are designed to promote positive laminar airflow over the wing and control surfaces. Usually made of aluminum and installed in a spanwise line or lines, the vortices created by these devices swirl downward assisting maintenance of the boundary layer of air flowing over the wing. They can also be found on the fuselage and empennage. *Figure 1-79* shows the unique vortex generators on a Symphony SA-160 wing.

A chordwise barrier on the upper surface of the wing, called a stall fence, is used to halt the spanwise flow of air. During low speed flight, this can maintain proper chordwise airflow reducing the tendency for the wing to stall. Usually made of aluminum, the fence is a fixed structure most common on swept wings, which have a natural spanwise tending boundary air flow. *[Figure 1-80]*

Figure 1-78. *Vortex generators.*

Figure 1-79. *The Symphony SA-160 has two unique vortex generators on its wing to ensure aileron effectiveness through the stall.*

Often, a gap can exist between the stationary trailing edge of a wing or stabilizer and the movable control surface(s). At high angles of attack, high pressure air from the lower wing surface can be disrupted at this gap. The result can be turbulent airflow, which increases drag. There is also a tendency for some lower wing boundary air to enter the gap

Figure 1-80. *A stall fence aids in maintaining chordwise airflow over the wing.*

and disrupt the upper wing surface airflow, which in turn reduces lift and control surface responsiveness. The use of gap seals is common to promote smooth airflow in these gap areas. Gap seals can be made of a wide variety of materials ranging from aluminum and impregnated fabric to foam and plastic. *Figure 1-81* shows some gap seals installed on various aircraft.

Landing Gear

The landing gear supports the aircraft during landing and while it is on the ground. Simple aircraft that fly at low speeds generally have fixed gear. This means the gear is stationary and does not retract for flight. Faster, more complex aircraft have retractable landing gear. After takeoff, the landing gear is retracted into the fuselage or wings and out of the airstream. This is important because extended gear create significant parasite drag which reduces performance. Parasite drag is caused by the friction of the air flowing over the gear. It increases with speed. On very light, slow aircraft, the

Figure 1-81. *Gap seals promote the smooth flow of air over gaps between fixed and movable surfaces.*

extra weight that accompanies a retractable landing gear is more of a detriment than the drag caused by the fixed gear. Lightweight fairings and wheel pants can be used to keep drag to a minimum. *Figure 1-82* shows examples of fixed and retractable gear.

Landing gear must be strong enough to withstand the forces of landing when the aircraft is fully loaded. In addition to strength, a major design goal is to have the gear assembly be as light as possible. To accomplish this, landing gear are made from a wide range of materials including steel, aluminum, and magnesium. Wheels and tires are designed specifically for aviation use and have unique operating characteristics. Main wheel assemblies usually have a braking system. To aid with the potentially high impact of landing, most landing gear have a means of either absorbing shock or accepting shock and distributing it so that the structure is not damaged.

Not all aircraft landing gear are configured with wheels. Helicopters, for example, have such high maneuverability and low landing speeds that a set of fixed skids is common and quite functional with lower maintenance. The same is true for free balloons which fly slowly and land on wood skids affixed to the floor of the gondola. Other aircraft landing gear are equipped with pontoons or floats for operation on water. A large amount of drag accompanies this type of gear, but an aircraft that can land and take off on water can be very useful in certain environments. Even skis can be found under some aircraft for operation on snow and ice. *Figure 1-83* shows some of these alternative landing gear, the majority of which are the fixed gear type.

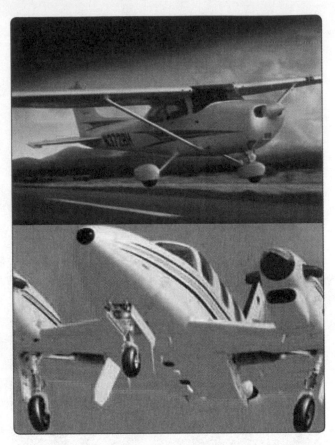

Figure 1-82. *Landing gear can be fixed (top) or retractable (bottom).*

Amphibious aircraft are aircraft than can land either on land or on water. On some aircraft designed for such dual usage, the bottom half of the fuselage acts as a hull. Usually, it is accompanied by outriggers on the underside of the wings near the tips to aid in water landing and taxi. Main gear that retract into the fuselage are only extended when landing on

Figure 1-83. *Aircraft landing gear without wheels.*

the ground or a runway. This type of amphibious aircraft is sometimes called a flying boat. [Figure 1-84]

Figure 1-84. *An amphibious aircraft is sometimes called a flying boat because the fuselage doubles as a hull.*

Many aircraft originally designed for land use can be fitted with floats with retractable wheels for amphibious use. [Figure 1-85] Typically, the gear retracts into the float when not needed. Sometimes a dorsal fin is added to the aft underside of the fuselage for longitudinal stability during water operations. It is even possible on some aircraft to direct this type of fin by tying its control into the aircraft's rudder pedals. Skis can also be fitted with wheels that retract to allow landing on solid ground or on snow and ice.

Figure 1-85. *Retractable wheels make this aircraft amphibious.*

Tail Wheel Gear Configuration

There are two basic configurations of airplane landing gear: conventional gear or tail wheel gear and the tricycle gear. Tail wheel gear dominated early aviation and therefore has become known as conventional gear. In addition to its two main wheels which are positioned under most of the weight of the aircraft, the conventional gear aircraft also has a smaller wheel located at the aft end of the fuselage. [Figure 1-86] Often this tail wheel is able to be steered

by rigging cables attached to the rudder pedals. Other conventional gear have no tail wheel at all using just a steel skid plate under the aft fuselage instead. The small tail wheel or skid plate allows the fuselage to incline, thus giving clearance for the long propellers that prevailed in aviation through WWII. It also gives greater clearance between the propeller and loose debris when operating on an unpaved runway. But the inclined fuselage blocks the straight ahead vision of the pilot during ground operations. Until up to speed where the elevator becomes effective to lift the tail wheel off the ground, the pilot must lean his head out the side of the cockpit to see directly ahead of the aircraft.

Figure 1-86. *An aircraft with tail wheel gear.*

The use of tail wheel gear can pose another difficulty. When landing, tail wheel aircraft can easily ground loop. A ground loop is when the tail of the aircraft swings around and comes forward of the nose of the aircraft. The reason this happens is due to the two main wheels being forward of the aircraft's center of gravity. The tail wheel is aft of the center of gravity. If the aircraft swerves upon landing, the tail wheel can swing out to the side of the intended path of travel. If far enough to the side, the tail can pull the center of gravity out from its desired location slightly aft of but between the main gear. Once the center of gravity is no longer trailing the mains, the tail of the aircraft freely pivots around the main wheels causing the ground loop.

Conventional gear is useful and is still found on certain models of aircraft manufactured today, particularly aerobatic aircraft, crop dusters, and aircraft designed for unpaved runway use. It is typically lighter than tricycle gear which requires a stout, fully shock absorbing nose wheel assembly. The tail wheel configuration excels when operating out of unpaved runways. With the two strong main gear forward providing stability and directional control during takeoff roll, the lightweight tail wheel does little more than keep the aft end of the fuselage from striking the ground. As mentioned, at a certain speed, the air flowing over the elevator is sufficient for it to raise the tail off the ground. As speed increases further, the two main wheels under the center of gravity are very stable.

Tricycle Gear

Tricycle gear is the most prevalent landing gear configuration in aviation. In addition to the main wheels, a shock absorbing nose wheel is at the forward end of the fuselage. Thus, the center of gravity is then forward of the main wheels. The tail of the aircraft is suspended off the ground and clear view straight ahead from the cockpit is given. Ground looping is nearly eliminated since the center of gravity follows the directional nose wheel and remains between the mains.

Light aircraft use tricycle gear, as well as heavy aircraft. Twin nose wheels on the single forward strut and massive multistrut/multiwheel main gear may be found supporting the world's largest aircraft, but the basic configuration is still tricycle. The nose wheel may be steered with the rudder pedals on small aircraft. Larger aircraft often have a nose wheel steering wheel located off to the side of the cockpit. *Figure 1-87* shows aircraft with tricycle gear. Chapter 13, Aircraft Landing Gear Systems, discusses landing gear in detail.

Maintaining the Aircraft

Maintenance of an aircraft is of the utmost importance for safe flight. Licensed technicians are committed to perform timely maintenance functions in accordance with the manufacturer's instructions and under the 14 CFR. At no time is an act of aircraft maintenance taken lightly or improvised. The consequences of such action could be fatal and the technician could lose his or her license and face criminal charges.

Airframe, engine, and aircraft component manufacturers are responsible for documenting the maintenance procedures that guide managers and technicians on when and how to perform maintenance on their products. A small aircraft may only require a few manuals, including the aircraft maintenance manual. This volume usually contains the most frequently used information required to maintain the aircraft properly. The Type Certificate Data Sheet (TCDS) for an aircraft also contains critical information. Complex and large aircraft require several manuals to convey correct maintenance procedures adequately. In addition to the maintenance manual, manufacturers may produce such volumes as structural repair manuals, overhaul manuals, wiring diagram manuals, component manuals, and more.

Note that the use of the word "manual" is meant to include electronic as well as printed information. Also, proper maintenance extends to the use of designated tools and fixtures called out in the manufacturer's maintenance documents. In the past, not using the proper tooling has caused damage to critical components, which subsequently failed and led to aircraft crashes and the loss of human life. The technician is responsible for sourcing the correct information, procedures, and tools needed to perform airworthy maintenance or repairs.

Standard aircraft maintenance procedures do exist and can be used by the technician when performing maintenance or a repair. These are found in the Federal Aviation Administration (FAA) approved advisory circulars AC 43.13-1B and -2B. If not addressed by the manufacturer's literature, the technician may use the procedures outlined in these manuals to complete the work in an acceptable manner. These procedures are not specific to any aircraft or component and typically cover methods used during maintenance of all aircraft. Note that the manufacturer's instructions supersede the general procedures found in AC 43.13-1B and -2B.

All maintenance related actions on an aircraft or component are required to be documented by the performing technician in the aircraft or component logbook. Light aircraft may have only one logbook for all work performed. Some aircraft may have a separate engine logbook for any work performed on the engine(s). Other aircraft have separate propeller logbooks.

Figure 1-87. *Tricycle landing gear is the most predominant landing gear configuration in aviation.*

Large aircraft require volumes of maintenance documentation comprised of thousands of procedures performed by hundreds of technicians. Electronic dispatch and recordkeeping of maintenance performed on large aircraft such as airliners is common. The importance of correct maintenance recordkeeping should not be overlooked.

Location Numbering Systems

Even on small, light aircraft, a method of precisely locating each structural component is required. Various numbering systems are used to facilitate the location of specific wing frames, fuselage bulkheads, or any other structural members on an aircraft. Most manufacturers use some system of station marking. For example, the nose of the aircraft may be designated "zero station," and all other stations are located at measured distances in inches behind the zero station. Thus, when a blueprint reads "fuselage frame station 137," that particular frame station can be located 137 inches behind the nose of the aircraft.

To locate structures to the right or left of the center line of an aircraft, a similar method is employed. Many manufacturers consider the center line of the aircraft to be a zero station from which measurements can be taken to the right or left to locate an airframe member. This is often used on the horizontal stabilizer and wings.

The applicable manufacturer's numbering system and abbreviated designations or symbols should always be reviewed before attempting to locate a structural member. They are not always the same. The following list includes location designations typical of those used by many manufacturers.

- Fuselage stations (Fus. Sta. or FS) are numbered in inches from a reference or zero point known as the reference datum. *[Figure 1-88]* The reference datum is an imaginary vertical plane at or near the nose of the aircraft from which all fore and aft distances are measured. The distance to a given point is measured in inches parallel to a center line extending through the aircraft from the nose through the center of the tail cone. Some manufacturers may call the fuselage station a body station, abbreviated BS.

- Buttock line or butt line (BL) is a vertical reference plane down the center of the aircraft from which measurements left or right can be made. *[Figure 1-89]*

- Water line (WL) is the measurement of height in inches perpendicular from a horizontal plane usually located at the ground, cabin floor, or some other easily referenced location. *[Figure 1-90]*

- Aileron station (AS) is measured outboard from, and parallel to, the inboard edge of the aileron, perpendicular to the rear beam of the wing.

- Flap station (KS) is measured perpendicular to the rear beam of the wing and parallel to, and outboard from, the inboard edge of the flap.

- Nacelle station (NC or Nac. Sta.) is measured either forward of or behind the front spar of the wing and perpendicular to a designated water line.

In addition to the location stations listed above, other measurements are used, especially on large aircraft. Thus, there may be horizontal stabilizer stations (HSS), vertical stabilizer stations (VSS) or powerplant stations (PPS). *[Figure 1-91]* In every case, the manufacturer's terminology and station location system should be consulted before locating a point on a particular aircraft.

Another method is used to facilitate the location of aircraft components on air transport aircraft. This involves dividing the aircraft into zones. These large areas or major zones are further divided into sequentially numbered zones and subzones. The digits of the zone number are reserved and

Figure 1-88. *The various body stations relative to a single point of origin illustrated in inches or some other measurement (if of foreign development).*

Figure 1-89. *Butt line diagram of a horizontal stabilizer.*

indexed to indicate the location and type of system of which the component is a part. *Figure 1-92* illustrates these zones and subzones on a transport category aircraft.

Access and Inspection Panels

Knowing where a particular structure or component is located on an aircraft needs to be combined with gaining access to that area to perform the required inspections or maintenance. To facilitate this, access and inspection panels are located on most surfaces of the aircraft. Small panels that are hinged or removable allow inspection and servicing. Large panels and doors allow components to be removed and installed, as well as human entry for maintenance purposes.

The underside of a wing, for example, sometimes contains dozens of small panels through which control cable components can be monitored and fittings greased. Various drains and jack points may also be on the underside of the wing. The upper surface of the wings typically have fewer access panels because a smooth surface promotes

better laminar airflow, which causes lift. On large aircraft, walkways are sometimes designated on the wing upper surface to permit safe navigation by mechanics and inspectors to critical structures and components located along the wing's leading and trailing edges. Wheel wells and special component bays are places where numerous components and accessories are grouped together for easy maintenance access.

Panels and doors on aircraft are numbered for positive identification. On large aircraft, panels are usually numbered sequentially containing zone and subzone information in the panel number. Designation for a left or right side location on the aircraft is often indicated in the panel number. This could be with an "L" or "R," or panels on one side of the aircraft could be odd numbered and the other side even numbered. The manufacturer's maintenance manual explains the panel numbering system and often has numerous diagrams and tables showing the location of various components and under which panel they may be found. Each manufacturer is entitled to develop its own panel numbering system.

Helicopter Structures

The structures of the helicopter are designed to give the helicopter its unique flight characteristics. A simplified explanation of how a helicopter flies is that the rotors are rotating airfoils that provide lift similar to the way wings provide lift on a fixed-wing aircraft. Air flows faster over the curved upper surface of the rotors, causing a negative pressure and thus, lifting the aircraft. Changing the angle of attack of the rotating blades increases or decreases lift, respectively raising or lowering the helicopter. Tilting the rotor plane of rotation causes the aircraft to move horizontally. *Figure 1-93* shows the major components of a typical helicopter.

Airframe

The airframe, or fundamental structure, of a helicopter can be made of either metal or wood composite materials, or some combination of the two. Typically, a composite component

Figure 1-90. *Water line diagram.*

Figure 1-91. *Wing stations are often referenced off the butt line, which bisects the center of the fuselage longitudinally. Horizontal stabilizer stations referenced to the butt line and engine nacelle stations are also shown.*

Figure 1-92. *Large aircraft are divided into zones and subzones for identifying the location of various components.*

consists of many layers of fiber-impregnated resins, bonded to form a smooth panel. Tubular and sheet metal substructures are usually made of aluminum, though stainless steel or titanium are sometimes used in areas subject to higher stress or heat. Airframe design encompasses engineering, aerodynamics, materials technology, and manufacturing methods to achieve favorable balances of performance, reliability, and cost.

Fuselage

As with fixed-wing aircraft, helicopter fuselages and tail booms are often truss-type or semimonocoque structures of stress-skin design. Steel and aluminum tubing, formed aluminum, and aluminum skin are commonly used. Modern helicopter fuselage design includes an increasing utilization of advanced composites as well. Firewalls and engine decks are usually stainless steel. Helicopter fuselages vary widely from those with a truss frame, two seats, no doors, and a monocoque shell flight compartment to those with fully enclosed airplane-style cabins as found on larger twin-engine helicopters. The multidirectional nature of helicopter flight makes wide-range visibility from the cockpit essential. Large, formed polycarbonate, glass, or plexiglass windscreens are common.

Landing Gear or Skids

As mentioned, a helicopter's landing gear can be simply a set of tubular metal skids. Many helicopters do have landing gear with wheels, some retractable.

Powerplant and Transmission

The two most common types of engine used in helicopters are the reciprocating engine and the turbine engine. Reciprocating engines, also called piston engines, are generally used in smaller helicopters. Most training helicopters use reciprocating engines because they are relatively simple and inexpensive to operate. Refer to the Pilot's Handbook of Aeronautical Knowledge for a detailed explanation and illustrations of the piston engine.

Turbine Engines

Turbine engines are more powerful and are used in a wide variety of helicopters. They produce a tremendous amount of power for their size but are generally more expensive to operate. The turbine engine used in helicopters operates differently than those used in airplane applications. In most applications, the exhaust outlets simply release expended gases and do not contribute to the forward motion of the helicopter. Because the airflow is not a straight line pass through as in jet engines and is not used for propulsion, the

Figure 1-93. *The major components of a helicopter are the airframe, fuselage, landing gear, powerplant/transmission, main rotor system, and antitorque system.*

1-42

cooling effect of the air is limited. Approximately 75 percent of the incoming airflow is used to cool the engine.

The gas turbine engine mounted on most helicopters is made up of a compressor, combustion chamber, turbine, and accessory gearbox assembly. The compressor draws filtered air into the plenum chamber and compresses it. Common type filters are centrifugal swirl tubes where debris is ejected outward and blown overboard prior to entering the compressor, or engine barrier filters (EBF), similar to the K&N filter element used in automotive applications. This design significantly reduces the ingestion of foreign object debris (FOD). The compressed air is directed to the combustion section through discharge tubes where atomized fuel is injected into it. The fuel/air mixture is ignited and allowed to expand. This combustion gas is then forced through a series of turbine wheels causing them to turn. These turbine wheels provide power to both the engine compressor and the accessory gearbox. Depending on model and manufacturer, the rpm range can vary from a range low of 20,000 to a range high of 51,600.

Power is provided to the main rotor and tail rotor systems through the freewheeling unit which is attached to the accessory gearbox power output gear shaft. The combustion gas is finally expelled through an exhaust outlet. The temperature of gas is measured at different locations and is referenced differently by each manufacturer. Some common terms are: inter-turbine temperature (ITT), exhaust gas temperature (EGT), or turbine outlet temperature (TOT). TOT is used throughout this discussion for simplicity purposes. [Figure 1-94]

Transmission

The transmission system transfers power from the engine to the main rotor, tail rotor, and other accessories during normal flight conditions. The main components of the transmission system are the main rotor transmission, tail rotor drive system, clutch, and freewheeling unit. The freewheeling unit, or autorotative clutch, allows the main rotor transmission to drive the tail rotor drive shaft during autorotation. Helicopter transmissions are normally lubricated and cooled with their own oil supply. A sight gauge is provided to check the oil level. Some transmissions have chip detectors located in the sump. These detectors are wired to warning lights located on the pilot's instrument panel that illuminate in the event of an internal problem. Some chip detectors on modern helicopters have a "burn off" capability and attempt to correct the situation without pilot action. If the problem cannot be corrected on its own, the pilot must refer to the emergency procedures for that particular helicopter.

Main Rotor System

The rotor system is the rotating part of a helicopter which generates lift. The rotor consists of a mast, hub, and rotor blades. The mast is a cylindrical metal shaft that extends upwards from and is driven, and sometimes supported, by the transmission. At the top of the mast is the attachment point for the rotor blades called the hub. The rotor blades are then attached to the hub by any number of different methods. Main rotor systems are classified according to how the main rotor blades are attached and move relative to the main rotor hub. There are three basic classifications: rigid, semirigid, or fully articulated.

Figure 1-94. *Many helicopters use a turboshaft engine to drive the main transmission and rotor systems. The main difference between a turboshaft and a turbojet engine is that most of the energy produced by the expanding gases is used to drive a turbine rather than producing thrust through the expulsion of exhaust gases.*

Rigid Rotor System

The simplest is the rigid rotor system. In this system, the rotor blades are rigidly attached to the main rotor hub and are not free to slide back and forth (drag) or move up and down (flap). The forces tending to make the rotor blades do so are absorbed by the flexible properties of the blade. The pitch of the blades, however, can be adjusted by rotation about the spanwise axis via the feathering hinges. [*Figure 1-95*]

Figure 1-95. *The teetering hinge allows the main rotor hub to tilt, and the feathering hinge enables the pitch angle of the blades to change.*

Semirigid Rotor System

The semirigid rotor system in *Figure 1-96* makes use of a teetering hinge at the blade attach point. While held in check from sliding back and forth, the teetering hinge does allow

Figure 1-96. *The semirigid rotor system of the Robinson R22.*

the blades to flap up and down. With this hinge, when one blade flaps up, the other flaps down.

Flapping is caused by a phenomenon known as dissymmetry of lift. As the plane of rotation of the rotor blades is tilted and the helicopter begins to move forward, an advancing blade and a retreating blade become established (on two-bladed systems). The relative windspeed is greater on an advancing blade than it is on a retreating blade. This causes greater lift to be developed on the advancing blade, causing it to rise up or flap. When blade rotation reaches the point where the blade becomes the retreating blade, the extra lift is lost and the blade flaps downward. [*Figure 1-97*]

Figure 1-97. *The blade tip speed of this helicopter is approximately 300 knots. If the helicopter is moving forward at 100 knots, the relative windspeed on the advancing side is 400 knots. On the retreating side, it is only 200 knots. This difference in speed causes a dissymetry of lift.*

Fully Articulated Rotor System

Fully articulated rotor blade systems provide hinges that allow the rotors to move fore and aft, as well as up and down. This lead-lag, drag, or hunting movement as it is called is in response to the Coriolis effect during rotational speed changes. When first starting to spin, the blades lag until centrifugal force is fully developed. Once rotating, a reduction in speed causes the blades to lead the main rotor hub until forces come into balance. Constant fluctuations in rotor blade speeds cause the blades to "hunt." They are free to do so in a fully articulating system due to being mounted on the vertical drag hinge.

One or more horizontal hinges provide for flapping on a fully articulated rotor system. Also, the feathering hinge allows blade pitch changes by permitting rotation about the spanwise axis. Various dampers and stops can be found on different designs to reduce shock and limit travel in certain directions. *Figure 1-98* shows a fully articulated main rotor system with the features discussed.

Figure 1-98. *Fully articulated rotor system.*

Numerous designs and variations on the three types of main rotor systems exist. Engineers continually search for ways to reduce vibration and noise caused by the rotating parts of the helicopter. Toward that end, the use of elastomeric bearings in main rotor systems is increasing. These polymer bearings have the ability to deform and return to their original shape. As such, they can absorb vibration that would normally be transferred by steel bearings. They also do not require regular lubrication, which reduces maintenance.

Some modern helicopter main rotors have been designed with flextures. These are hubs and hub components that are made out of advanced composite materials. They are designed to take up the forces of blade hunting and dissymmetry of lift by flexing. As such, many hinges and bearings can be eliminated from the tradition main rotor system. The result is a simpler rotor mast with lower maintenance due to fewer moving parts. Often designs using flextures incorporate elastomeric bearings. *[Figure 1-99]*

Antitorque System

Ordinarily, helicopters have between two and seven main rotor blades. These rotors are usually made of a composite structure. The large rotating mass of the main rotor blades of a helicopter produce torque. This torque increases with engine power and tries to spin the fuselage in the opposite direction. The tail boom and tail rotor, or antitorque rotor, counteract this torque effect. *[Figure 1-100]* Controlled with foot pedals, the countertorque of the tail rotor must be modulated as engine power levels are changed. This is done

Figure 1-99. *Five-blade articulated main rotor with elastomeric bearings.*

by changing the pitch of the tail rotor blades. This, in turn, changes the amount of countertorque, and the aircraft can be rotated about its vertical axis, allowing the pilot to control the direction the helicopter is facing.

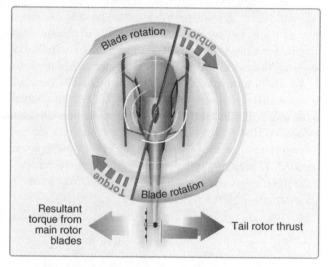

Figure 1-100. *A tail rotor is designed to produce thrust in a direction opposite to that of the torque produced by the rotation of the main rotor blades. It is sometimes called an antitorque rotor.*

Similar to a vertical stabilizer on the empennage of an airplane, a fin or pylon is also a common feature on rotorcraft. Normally, it supports the tail rotor assembly, although some tail rotors are mounted on the tail cone of the boom. Additionally, a horizontal member called a stabilizer is often constructed at the tail cone or on the pylon.

A Fenestron® is a unique tail rotor design which is actually a multiblade ducted fan mounted in the vertical pylon. It works the same way as an ordinary tail rotor, providing sideways thrust to counter the torque produced by the main rotors. *[Figure 1-101]*

Figure 1-101. *A Fenestron or "fan-in-tail" antitorque system. This design provides an improved margin of safety during ground operations.*

A NOTAR® antitorque system has no visible rotor mounted on the tail boom. Instead, an engine-driven adjustable fan is located inside the tail boom. NOTAR® is an acronym that stands for "no tail rotor." As the speed of the main rotor changes, the speed of the NOTAR® fan changes. Air is vented out of two long slots on the right side of the tail boom, entraining main rotor wash to hug the right side of the tail boom, in turn causing laminar flow and a low pressure (Coanda Effect). This low pressure causes a force counter to the torque produced by the main rotor. Additionally, the remainder of the air from the fan is sent through the tail boom to a vent on the aft left side of the boom where it is expelled. This action to the left causes an opposite reaction to the right, which is the direction needed to counter the main rotor torque. *[Figures 1-102]*

Figure 1-102. *While in a hover, Coanda Effect supplies approximately two-thirds of the lift necessary to maintain directional control. The rest is created by directing the thrust from the controllable rotating nozzle.*

Controls

The controls of a helicopter differ slightly from those found in an aircraft. The collective, operated by the pilot with the left hand, is pulled up or pushed down to increase or decrease the angle of attack on all of the rotor blades simultaneously. This increases or decreases lift and moves the aircraft up or down. The engine throttle control is located on the hand grip at the end of the collective. The cyclic is the control "stick" located between the pilot's legs. It can be moved in any direction to tilt the plane of rotation of the rotor blades. This causes the helicopter to move in the direction that the cyclic is moved. As stated, the foot pedals control the pitch of the tail rotor blades thereby balancing main rotor torque. *Figures 1-103* and *1-104* illustrate the controls found in a typical helicopter.

Figure 1-103. *The collective changes the pitch of all of the rotor blades simultaneously and by the same amount, thereby increasing or decreasing lift.*

Figure 1-104. *The cyclic changes the angle of the swash plate which changes the plane of rotation of the rotor blades. This moves the aircraft horizontally in any direction depending on the positioning of the cyclic.*

Chapter 2

Aerodynamics, Aircraft Assembly, and Rigging

Introduction

Three topics that are directly related to the manufacture, operation, and repair of aircraft are: aerodynamics, aircraft assembly, and rigging. Each of these subject areas, though studied separately, eventually connect to provide a scientific and physical understanding of how an aircraft is prepared for flight. A logical place to start with these three topics is the study of basic aerodynamics. By studying aerodynamics, a person becomes familiar with the fundamentals of aircraft flight.

Basic Aerodynamics

Aerodynamics is the study of the dynamics of gases, the interaction between a moving object and the atmosphere being of primary interest for this handbook. The movement of an object and its reaction to the air flow around it can be seen when watching water passing the bow of a ship. The major difference between water and air is that air is compressible and water is incompressible. The action of the airflow over a body is a large part of the study of aerodynamics. Some common aircraft terms, such as rudder, hull, water line, and keel beam, were borrowed from nautical terms.

Many textbooks have been written about the aerodynamics of aircraft flight. It is not necessary for an airframe and powerplant (A&P) mechanic to be as knowledgeable as an aeronautical engineer about aerodynamics. The mechanic must be able to understand the relationships between how an aircraft performs in flight and its reaction to the forces acting on its structural parts. Understanding why aircraft are designed with particular types of primary and secondary control systems and why the surfaces must be aerodynamically smooth becomes essential when maintaining today's complex aircraft.

The theory of flight should be described in terms of the laws of flight because what happens to an aircraft when it flies is not based upon assumptions, but upon a series of facts. Aerodynamics is a study of laws which have been proven to be the physical reasons why an airplane flies. The term aerodynamics is derived from the combination of two Greek words: "aero," meaning air, and "dyne," meaning force of power. Thus, when "aero" joins "dynamics" the result is "aerodynamics"—the study of objects in motion through the air and the forces that produce or change such motion.

Aerodynamically, an aircraft can be defined as an object traveling through space that is affected by the changes in atmospheric conditions. To state it another way, aerodynamics covers the relationships between the aircraft, relative wind, and atmosphere.

The Atmosphere

Before examining the fundamental laws of flight, several basic facts must be considered, namely that an aircraft operates in the air. Therefore, those properties of air that affect the control and performance of an aircraft must be understood.

The air in the earth's atmosphere is composed mostly of nitrogen and oxygen. Air is considered a fluid because it fits the definition of a substance that has the ability to flow or assume the shape of the container in which it is enclosed. If the container is heated, pressure increases; if cooled, the pressure decreases. The weight of air is heaviest at sea level where it has been compressed by all of the air above. This compression of air is called atmospheric pressure.

Pressure

Atmospheric pressure is usually defined as the force exerted against the earth's surface by the weight of the air above that surface. Weight is force applied to an area that results in pressure. Force (F) equals area (A) times pressure (P), or F = AP. Therefore, to find the amount of pressure, divide area into force (P = F/A). A column of air (one square inch) extending from sea level to the top of the atmosphere weighs approximately 14.7 pounds; therefore, atmospheric pressure is stated in pounds per square inch (psi). Thus, atmospheric pressure at sea level is 14.7 psi.

Atmospheric pressure is measured with an instrument called a barometer, composed of mercury in a tube that records atmospheric pressure in inches of mercury ("Hg). *[Figure 2-1]* The standard measurement in aviation altimeters and U.S. weather reports has been "Hg. However, world-wide weather maps and some non-U.S. manufactured aircraft instruments indicate pressure in millibars (mb), a metric unit.

Figure 2-1. *Barometer used to measure atmospheric pressure.*

At sea level, when the average atmospheric pressure is 14.7 psi, the barometric pressure is 29.92 "Hg, and the metric measurement is 1013.25 mb.

An important consideration is that atmospheric pressure varies with altitude. As an aircraft ascends, atmospheric pressure drops, oxygen content of the air decreases, and temperature drops. The changes in altitude affect an aircraft's performance in such areas as lift and engine horsepower. The effects of temperature, altitude, and density of air on aircraft performance are covered in the following paragraphs.

Density

Density is weight per unit of volume. Since air is a mixture of gases, it can be compressed. If the air in one container is under half as much pressure as an equal amount of air in an identical container, the air under the greater pressure weighs twice as much as that in the container under lower pressure. The air under greater pressure is twice as dense as that in the other container. For the equal weight of air, that which is under the greater pressure occupies only half the volume of that under half the pressure.

The density of gases is governed by the following rules:

1. Density varies in direct proportion with the pressure.

2. Density varies inversely with the temperature.

Thus, air at high altitudes is less dense than air at low altitudes, and a mass of hot air is less dense than a mass of cool air.

Changes in density affect the aerodynamic performance of aircraft with the same horsepower. An aircraft can fly faster at a high altitude where the density is low than at a low altitude where the density is greater. This is because air offers less resistance to the aircraft when it contains a smaller number of air particles per unit of volume.

Humidity

Humidity is the amount of water vapor in the air. The maximum amount of water vapor that air can hold varies with the temperature. The higher the temperature of the air, the more water vapor it can absorb.

1. Absolute humidity is the weight of water vapor in a unit volume of air.

2. Relative humidity is the ratio, in percent, of the moisture actually in the air to the moisture it would hold if it were saturated at the same temperature and pressure.

Assuming that the temperature and pressure remain the same, the density of the air varies inversely with the humidity. On damp days, the air density is less than on dry days. For this reason, an aircraft requires a longer runway for takeoff on damp days than it does on dry days.

By itself, water vapor weighs approximately five-eighths as much as an equal amount of perfectly dry air. Therefore, when air contains water vapor, it is not as heavy as dry air containing no moisture.

Aerodynamics and the Laws of Physics

The law of conservation of energy states that energy may neither be created nor destroyed.

Motion is the act or process of changing place or position. An object may be in motion with respect to one object and motionless with respect to another. For example, a person sitting quietly in an aircraft flying at 200 knots is at rest or motionless with respect to the aircraft; however, the person and the aircraft are in motion with respect to the air and to the earth.

Air has no force or power, except pressure, unless it is in motion. When it is moving, however, its force becomes apparent. A moving object in motionless air has a force exerted on it as a result of its own motion. It makes no difference in the effect then, whether an object is moving with respect to the air or the air is moving with respect to the object. The flow of air around an object caused by the movement of either the air or the object, or both, is called the relative wind.

Velocity and Acceleration

The terms "speed" and "velocity" are often used interchangeably, but they do not have the same meaning. Speed is the rate of motion in relation to time, and velocity is the rate of motion in a particular direction in relation to time.

An aircraft starts from New York City and flies 10 hours at an average speed of 260 miles per hour (mph). At the end of this time, the aircraft may be over the Atlantic Ocean, Pacific Ocean, Gulf of Mexico, or, if its flight were in a circular path, it may even be back over New York City. If this same aircraft flew at a velocity of 260 mph in a southwestward direction, it would arrive in Los Angeles in about 10 hours. Only the rate of motion is indicated in the first example and denotes the speed of the aircraft. In the last example, the particular direction is included with the rate of motion, thus, denoting the velocity of the aircraft.

Acceleration is defined as the rate of change of velocity. An aircraft increasing in velocity is an example of positive acceleration, while another aircraft reducing its velocity is an example of negative acceleration, or deceleration.

Newton's Laws of Motion

The fundamental laws governing the action of air about a wing are known as Newton's laws of motion.

Newton's first law is normally referred to as the law of inertia. It simply means that a body at rest does not move unless force is applied to it. If a body is moving at uniform speed in a straight line, force must be applied to increase or decrease the speed.

According to Newton's law, since air has mass, it is a body. When an aircraft is on the ground with its engines off, inertia keeps the aircraft at rest. An aircraft is moved from its state of rest by the thrust force created by a propeller, or by the expanding exhaust, or both. When an aircraft is flying at uniform speed in a straight line, inertia tends to keep the aircraft moving. Some external force is required to change the aircraft from its path of flight.

Newton's second law states that if a body moving with uniform speed is acted upon by an external force, the change of motion is proportional to the amount of the force, and motion takes place in the direction in which the force acts. This law may be stated mathematically as follows:

$$\text{Force} = \text{mass} \times \text{acceleration (F = ma)}$$

If an aircraft is flying against a headwind, it is slowed down. If the wind is coming from either side of the aircraft's heading, the aircraft is pushed off course unless the pilot takes corrective action against the wind direction.

Newton's third law is the law of action and reaction. This law states that for every action (force) there is an equal and opposite reaction (force). This law can be illustrated by the example of firing a gun. The action is the forward movement of the bullet while the reaction is the backward recoil of the gun.

The three laws of motion that have been discussed apply to the theory of flight. In many cases, all three laws may be operating on an aircraft at the same time.

Bernoulli's Principle and Subsonic Flow

Bernoulli's principle states that when a fluid (air) flowing through a tube reaches a constriction, or narrowing, of the tube, the speed of the fluid flowing through that constriction is increased and its pressure is decreased. The cambered (curved) surface of an airfoil (wing) affects the airflow exactly as a constriction in a tube affects airflow. *[Figure 2-2]* Diagram A of *Figure 2-2* illustrates the effect of air passing through a constriction in a tube. In B, air is flowing past a cambered surface, such as an airfoil, and the effect is similar to that of air passing through a restriction.

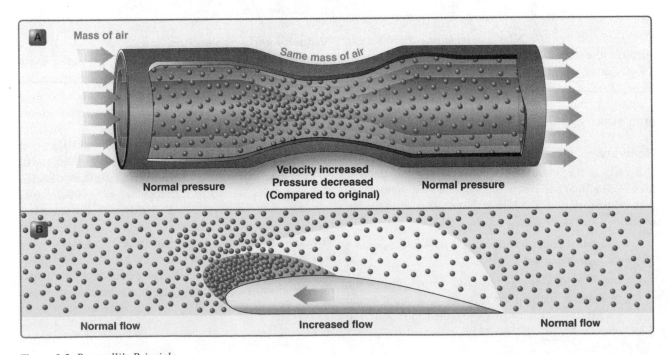

Figure 2-2. *Bernoulli's Principle.*

As the air flows over the upper surface of an airfoil, its velocity increases and its pressure decreases; an area of low pressure is formed. There is an area of greater pressure on the lower surface of the airfoil, and this greater pressure tends to move the wing upward. The difference in pressure between the upper and lower surfaces of the wing is called lift. Three-fourths of the total lift of an airfoil is the result of the decrease in pressure over the upper surface. The impact of air on the under surface of an airfoil produces the other one-fourth of the total lift.

Airfoil

An airfoil is a surface designed to obtain lift from the air through which it moves. Thus, it can be stated that any part of the aircraft that converts air resistance into lift is an airfoil. The profile of a conventional wing is an excellent example of an airfoil. *[Figure 2-3]* Notice that the top surface of the wing profile has greater curvature than the lower surface.

Figure 2-3. *Airflow over a wing section.*

The difference in curvature of the upper and lower surfaces of the wing builds up the lift force. Air flowing over the top surface of the wing must reach the trailing edge of the wing in the same amount of time as the air flowing under the wing. To do this, the air passing over the top surface moves at a greater velocity than the air passing below the wing because of the greater distance it must travel along the top surface. This increased velocity, according to Bernoulli's Principle, means a corresponding decrease in pressure on the surface. Thus, a pressure differential is created between the upper and lower surfaces of the wing, forcing the wing upward in the direction of the lower pressure.

Within limits, lift can be increased by increasing the angle of attack (AOA), wing area, velocity, density of the air, or by changing the shape of the airfoil. When the force of lift on an aircraft's wing equals the force of gravity, the aircraft maintains level flight.

Shape of the Airfoil

Individual airfoil section properties differ from those properties of the wing or aircraft as a whole because of the effect of the wing planform. A wing may have various airfoil sections from root to tip, with taper, twist, and sweepback. The resulting aerodynamic properties of the wing are determined by the action of each section along the span.

The shape of the airfoil determines the amount of turbulence or skin friction that it produces, consequently affecting the efficiency of the wing. Turbulence and skin friction are controlled mainly by the fineness ratio, which is defined as the ratio of the chord of the airfoil to the maximum thickness. If the wing has a high fineness ratio, it is a very thin wing. A thick wing has a low fineness ratio. A wing with a high fineness ratio produces a large amount of skin friction. A wing with a low fineness ratio produces a large amount of turbulence. The best wing is a compromise between these two extremes to hold both turbulence and skin friction to a minimum.

The efficiency of a wing is measured in terms of the lift to drag ratio (L/D). This ratio varies with the AOA but reaches a definite maximum value for a particular AOA. At this angle, the wing has reached its maximum efficiency. The shape of the airfoil is the factor that determines the AOA at which the wing is most efficient; it also determines the degree of efficiency. Research has shown that the most efficient airfoils for general use have the maximum thickness occurring about one-third of the way back from the leading edge of the wing.

High-lift wings and high-lift devices for wings have been developed by shaping the airfoils to produce the desired effect. The amount of lift produced by an airfoil increases with an increase in wing camber. Camber refers to the curvature of an airfoil above and below the chord line surface. Upper camber refers to the upper surface, lower camber to the lower surface, and mean camber to the mean line of the section. Camber is positive when departure from the chord line is outward and negative when it is inward. Thus, high-lift wings have a large positive camber on the upper surface and a slightly negative camber on the lower surface. Wing flaps cause an ordinary wing to approximate this same condition by increasing the upper camber and by creating a negative lower camber.

It is also known that the larger the wingspan, as compared to the chord, the greater the lift obtained. This comparison is called aspect ratio. The higher the aspect ratio, the greater the lift. In spite of the benefits from an increase in aspect ratio, it was found that definite limitations were defined by structural and drag considerations.

On the other hand, an airfoil that is perfectly streamlined and offers little wind resistance sometimes does not have enough lifting power to take the aircraft off the ground. Thus, modern aircraft have airfoils which strike a medium between extremes, the shape depending on the purposes of the aircraft for which it is designed.

Angle of Incidence

The acute angle the wing chord makes with the longitudinal axis of the aircraft is called the angle of incidence, or the angle of wing setting. *[Figure 2-4]* The angle of incidence in most cases is a fixed, built-in angle. When the leading edge of the wing is higher than the trailing edge, the angle of incidence is said to be positive. The angle of incidence is negative when the leading edge is lower than the trailing edge of the wing.

Figure 2-4. *Angle of incidence.*

Angle of Attack (AOA)

Before beginning the discussion on AOA and its effect on airfoils, first consider the terms chord and center of pressure (CP) as illustrated in *Figure 2-5*.

The chord of an airfoil or wing section is an imaginary straight line that passes through the section from the leading edge to the trailing edge, as shown in *Figure 2-5*. The chord line provides one side of an angle that ultimately forms the AOA. The other side of the angle is formed by a line indicating the direction of the relative airstream. Thus, AOA is defined as the angle between the chord line of the wing and the direction of the relative wind. This is not to be confused with the angle of incidence, illustrated in *Figure 2-4*, which is the angle between the chord line of the wing and the longitudinal axis of the aircraft.

Figure 2-5. *Airflow over a wing section.*

On each part of an airfoil or wing surface, a small force is present. This force is of a different magnitude and direction from any forces acting on other areas forward or rearward from this point. It is possible to add all of these small forces mathematically. That sum is called the "resultant force" (lift). This resultant force has magnitude, direction, and location, and can be represented as a vector, as shown in *Figure 2-5*. The point of intersection of the resultant force line with the chord line of the airfoil is called the center of pressure (CP). The CP moves along the airfoil chord as the AOA changes. Throughout most of the flight range, the CP moves forward with increasing AOA and rearward as the AOA decreases. The effect of increasing AOA on the CP is shown in *Figure 2-6*.

The AOA changes as the aircraft's attitude changes. Since the AOA has a great deal to do with determining lift, it is given primary consideration when designing airfoils. In a properly designed airfoil, the lift increases as the AOA is increased.

When the AOA is increased gradually toward a positive AOA, the lift component increases rapidly up to a certain point and then suddenly begins to drop off. During this action the drag component increases slowly at first, then rapidly as lift begins to drop off.

When the AOA increases to the angle of maximum lift, the burble point is reached. This is known as the critical angle. When the critical angle is reached, the air ceases to flow smoothly over the top surface of the airfoil and begins to burble or eddy. This means that air breaks away from the upper camber line of the wing. What was formerly the area of decreased pressure is now filled by this burbling air. When this occurs, the amount of lift drops and drag becomes excessive. The force of gravity exerts itself, and the nose of the aircraft drops. This is a stall. Thus, the burble point is the stalling angle.

A | Angle of attack = 0°

Resultant

Negative pressure pattern

Relative airstream

Positive pressure — Center of pressure

B | Angle of attack = 6°

Resultant

Negative pressure pattern moves forward

Relative airstream

Positive pressure —

C | Angle of attack = 12°

Resultant

Center of pressure moves forward

Relative airstream

Positive pressure —

D | Angle of attack = 18°

Wing completely stalled

Positive pressure —

Figure 2-6. *Effect on increasing angle of attack.*

As previously seen, the distribution of the pressure forces over the airfoil varies with the AOA. The application of the resultant force, or CP, varies correspondingly. As this angle increases, the CP moves forward; as the angle decreases, the CP moves back. The unstable travel of the CP is characteristic of almost all airfoils.

Boundary Layer

In the study of physics and fluid mechanics, a boundary layer is that layer of fluid in the immediate vicinity of a bounding surface. In relation to an aircraft, the boundary layer is the part of the airflow closest to the surface of the aircraft. In designing high-performance aircraft, considerable attention is paid to controlling the behavior of the boundary layer to minimize pressure drag and skin friction drag.

Thrust and Drag

An aircraft in flight is the center of a continuous battle of forces. Actually, this conflict is not as violent as it sounds, but it is the key to all maneuvers performed in the air. There is nothing mysterious about these forces; they are definite and known. The directions in which they act can be calculated, and the aircraft itself is designed to take advantage of each of them. In all types of flying, flight calculations are based on the magnitude and direction of four forces: weight, lift, drag, and thrust. *[Figure 2-7]*

Figure 2-7. *Forces in action during flight.*

An aircraft in flight is acted upon by four forces:

1. Gravity or weight—the force that pulls the aircraft toward the earth. Weight is the force of gravity acting downward upon everything that goes into the aircraft, such as the aircraft itself, crew, fuel, and cargo.

2. Lift—the force that pushes the aircraft upward. Lift acts vertically and counteracts the effects of weight.

3. Thrust—the force that moves the aircraft forward. Thrust is the forward force produced by the powerplant that overcomes the force of drag.

3. Drag—the force that exerts a braking action to hold the aircraft back. Drag is a backward deterrent force and is caused by the disruption of the airflow by the wings, fuselage, and protruding objects.

These four forces are in perfect balance only when the aircraft is in straight-and-level unaccelerated flight.

The forces of lift and drag are the direct result of the relationship between the relative wind and the aircraft. The force of lift always acts perpendicular to the relative wind, and the force of drag always acts parallel to and in the same direction as the relative wind. These forces are actually the components that produce a resultant lift force on the wing. *[Figure 2-8]*

Figure 2-8. *Resultant of lift and drag.*

Weight has a definite relationship with lift, and thrust with drag. These relationships are quite simple, but very important in understanding the aerodynamics of flying. As stated previously, lift is the upward force on the wing perpendicular to the relative wind. Lift is required to counteract the aircraft's weight, caused by the force of gravity acting on the mass of the aircraft. This weight force acts downward through a point called the center of gravity (CG). The CG is the point at which all the weight of the aircraft is considered to be concentrated. When the lift force is in equilibrium with the weight force, the aircraft neither gains nor loses altitude. If lift becomes less than weight, the aircraft loses altitude. When the lift is greater than the weight, the aircraft gains altitude.

Wing area is measured in square feet and includes the part blanked out by the fuselage. Wing area is adequately described as the area of the shadow cast by the wing at high noon. Tests show that lift and drag forces acting on a wing are roughly proportional to the wing area. This means that if the wing area is doubled, all other variables remaining the same, the lift and drag created by the wing is doubled. If the area is tripled, lift and drag are tripled.

Drag must be overcome for the aircraft to move, and movement is essential to obtain lift. To overcome drag and move the aircraft forward, another force is essential. This force is thrust. Thrust is derived from jet propulsion or from a propeller and engine combination. Jet propulsion theory is based on Newton's third law of motion *(page 2-4)*. The turbine engine causes a mass of air to be moved backward at high velocity causing a reaction that moves the aircraft forward.

In a propeller/engine combination, the propeller is actually two or more revolving airfoils mounted on a horizontal shaft. The motion of the blades through the air produces lift similar to the lift on the wing, but acts in a horizontal direction, pulling the aircraft forward.

Before the aircraft begins to move, thrust must be exerted. The aircraft continues to move and gain speed until thrust and drag are equal. In order to maintain a steady speed, thrust and drag must remain equal, just as lift and weight must be equal for steady, horizontal flight. Increasing the lift means that the aircraft moves upward, whereas decreasing the lift so that it is less than the weight causes the aircraft to lose altitude. A similar rule applies to the two forces of thrust and drag. If the revolutions per minute (rpm) of the engine is reduced, the thrust is lessened, and the aircraft slows down. As long as the thrust is less than the drag, the aircraft travels more and more slowly until its speed is insufficient to support it in the air.

Likewise, if the rpm of the engine is increased, thrust becomes greater than drag, and the speed of the aircraft increases. As long as the thrust continues to be greater than the drag, the aircraft continues to accelerate. When drag equals thrust, the aircraft flies at a steady speed.

The relative motion of the air over an object that produces lift also produces drag. Drag is the resistance of the air to objects moving through it. If an aircraft is flying on a level course, the lift force acts vertically to support it while the drag force acts horizontally to hold it back. The total amount of drag on an aircraft is made up of many drag forces, but this handbook considers three: parasite drag, profile drag, and induced drag.

Parasite drag is made up of a combination of many different drag forces. Any exposed object on an aircraft offers some resistance to the air, and the more objects in the airstream, the more parasite drag. While parasite drag can be reduced by reducing the number of exposed parts to as few as practical and streamlining their shape, skin friction is the type of parasite drag most difficult to reduce. No surface is perfectly smooth. Even machined surfaces have a ragged uneven appearance when inspected under magnification. These ragged surfaces deflect the air near the surface causing resistance to smooth airflow. Skin friction can be reduced by using glossy smooth finishes and eliminating protruding rivet heads, roughness, and other irregularities.

Profile drag may be considered the parasite drag of the airfoil. The various components of parasite drag are all of the same nature as profile drag.

The action of the airfoil that creates lift also causes induced drag. Remember, the pressure above the wing is less than atmospheric pressure, and the pressure below the wing is equal to or greater than atmospheric pressure. Since fluids always move from high pressure toward low pressure, there is a spanwise movement of air from the bottom of the wing outward from the fuselage and upward around the wing tip. This flow of air results in spillage over the wing tip, thereby setting up a whirlpool of air called a "vortex." *[Figure 2-9]*

Figure 2-9. *Wingtip vortices.*

The air on the upper surface has a tendency to move in toward the fuselage and off the trailing edge. This air current forms a similar vortex at the inner portion of the trailing edge of the wing. These vortices increase drag because of the turbulence produced, and constitute induced drag.

Just as lift increases with an increase in AOA, induced drag also increases as the AOA becomes greater. This occurs because, as the AOA is increased, the pressure difference between the top and bottom of the wing becomes greater. This causes more violent vortices to be set up, resulting in more turbulence and more induced drag.

Center of Gravity (CG)

Gravity is the pulling force that tends to draw all bodies within the earth's gravitational field to the center of the earth. The CG may be considered the point at which all the weight of the aircraft is concentrated. If the aircraft were supported at its exact CG, it would balance in any position. CG is of major importance in an aircraft, for its position has a great bearing upon stability.

The CG is determined by the general design of the aircraft. The designers estimate how far the CP travels. They then fix the CG in front of the CP for the corresponding flight speed in order to provide an adequate restoring moment for flight equilibrium.

The Axes of an Aircraft

Whenever an aircraft changes its attitude in flight, it must turn about one or more of three axis. *Figure 2-10* shows the three axes, which are imaginary lines passing through the center of the aircraft.

The axes of an aircraft can be considered as imaginary axles around which the aircraft turns like a wheel. At the center, where all three axes intersect, each is perpendicular to the other two. The axis that extends lengthwise through the fuselage from the nose to the tail is called the longitudinal axis. The axis that extends crosswise from wing tip to wing tip is the lateral, or pitch, axis. The axis that passes through the center, from top to bottom, is called the vertical, or yaw, axis. Roll, pitch, and yaw are controlled by three control surfaces. Roll is produced by the ailerons, which are located at the trailing edges of the wings. Pitch is affected by the elevators, the rear portion of the horizontal tail assembly. Yaw is controlled by the rudder, the rear portion of the vertical tail assembly.

Stability and Control

An aircraft must have sufficient stability to maintain a uniform flightpath and recover from the various upsetting forces. Also, to achieve the best performance, the aircraft must have the proper response to the movement of the controls. Control is the pilot action of moving the flight controls, providing the aerodynamic force that induces the aircraft to follow a desired flightpath. When an aircraft is said to be controllable, it means that the aircraft responds easily and promptly to movement of the controls. Different control surfaces are used to control the aircraft about each of the three axes. Moving the control surfaces on an aircraft changes the airflow over the aircraft's surface. This, in turn, creates changes in the balance of forces acting to keep the aircraft flying straight and level.

Three terms that appear in any discussion of stability and control are: stability, maneuverability, and controllability. Stability is the characteristic of an aircraft that tends to cause it to fly (hands off) in a straight-and-level flightpath. Maneuverability is the characteristic of an aircraft to be directed along a desired flightpath and to withstand the stresses imposed. Controllability is the quality of the response of an aircraft to the pilot's commands while maneuvering the aircraft.

Static Stability

An aircraft is in a state of equilibrium when the sum of all the forces acting on the aircraft and all the moments is equal to zero. An aircraft in equilibrium experiences no accelerations, and the aircraft continues in a steady condition of flight. A gust of wind or a deflection of the controls disturbs the equilibrium, and the aircraft experiences acceleration due to the unbalance of moment or force.

Figure 2-10. *Motion of an aircraft about its axes.*

The three types of static stability are defined by the character of movement following some disturbance from equilibrium. Positive static stability exists when the disturbed object tends to return to equilibrium. Negative static stability, or static instability, exists when the disturbed object tends to continue in the direction of disturbance. Neutral static stability exists when the disturbed object has neither tendency, but remains in equilibrium in the direction of disturbance. These three types of stability are illustrated in *Figure 2-11*.

Dynamic Stability

While static stability deals with the tendency of a displaced body to return to equilibrium, dynamic stability deals with the resulting motion with time. If an object is disturbed from equilibrium, the time history of the resulting motion defines the dynamic stability of the object. In general, an object demonstrates positive dynamic stability if the amplitude of motion decreases with time. If the amplitude of motion increases with time, the object is said to possess dynamic instability.

Any aircraft must demonstrate the required degrees of static and dynamic stability. If an aircraft were designed with static instability and a rapid rate of dynamic instability, the aircraft would be very difficult, if not impossible, to fly. Usually, positive dynamic stability is required in an aircraft design to prevent objectionable continued oscillations of the aircraft.

Longitudinal Stability

When an aircraft has a tendency to keep a constant AOA with reference to the relative wind (i.e., it does not tend to put its nose down and dive or lift its nose and stall); it is said to have longitudinal stability. Longitudinal stability refers to motion in pitch. The horizontal stabilizer is the primary surface which controls longitudinal stability. The action of the stabilizer depends upon the speed and AOA of the aircraft.

Directional Stability

Stability about the vertical axis is referred to as directional stability. The aircraft should be designed so that when it is in straight-and-level flight it remains on its course heading even though the pilot takes his or her hands and feet off the controls. If an aircraft recovers automatically from a skid, it has been well designed for directional balance. The vertical stabilizer is the primary surface that controls directional stability. Directional stability can be designed into an aircraft, where appropriate, by using a large dorsal fin, a long fuselage, and sweptback wings.

Lateral Stability

Motion about the aircraft's longitudinal (fore and aft) axis is a lateral, or rolling, motion. The tendency to return to the original attitude from such motion is called lateral stability.

Dutch Roll

A Dutch Roll is an aircraft motion consisting of an out-of-phase combination of yaw and roll. Dutch roll stability can be artificially increased by the installation of a yaw damper.

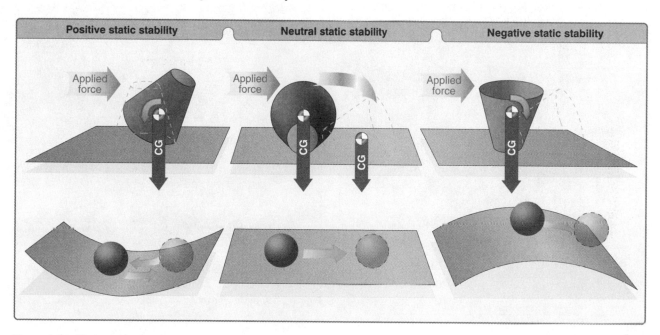

Figure 2-11. *Three types of stability.*

Primary Flight Controls

The primary controls are the ailerons, elevator, and the rudder, which provide the aerodynamic force to make the aircraft follow a desired flightpath. *[Figure 2-10]* The flight control surfaces are hinged or movable airfoils designed to change the attitude of the aircraft by changing the airflow over the aircraft's surface during flight. These surfaces are used for moving the aircraft about its three axes.

Typically, the ailerons and elevators are operated from the flight deck by means of a control stick, a wheel, and yoke assembly and on some of the newer design aircraft, a joystick. The rudder is normally operated by foot pedals on most aircraft. Lateral control is the banking movement or roll of an aircraft that is controlled by the ailerons. Longitudinal control is the climb and dive movement or pitch of an aircraft that is controlled by the elevator. Directional control is the left and right movement or yaw of an aircraft that is controlled by the rudder.

Trim Controls

Included in the trim controls are the trim tabs, servo tabs, balance tabs, and spring tabs. Trim tabs are small airfoils recessed into the trailing edges of the primary control surfaces. *[Figure 2-12]* Trim tabs can be used to correct any tendency of the aircraft to move toward an undesirable flight attitude. Their purpose is to enable the pilot to trim out any unbalanced condition which may exist during flight, without exerting any pressure on the primary controls.

Figure 2-12. *Trim tabs.*

Servo tabs, sometimes referred to as flight tabs, are used primarily on the large main control surfaces. They aid in moving the main control surface and holding it in the desired position. Only the servo tab moves in response to movement by the pilot of the primary flight controls.

Balance tabs are designed to move in the opposite direction of the primary flight control. Thus, aerodynamic forces acting on the tab assist in moving the primary control surface.

Spring tabs are similar in appearance to trim tabs, but serve an entirely different purpose. Spring tabs are used for the same purpose as hydraulic actuators—to aid the pilot in moving the primary control surface.

Figure 2-13 indicates how each trim tab is hinged to its parent primary control surface, but is operated by an independent control.

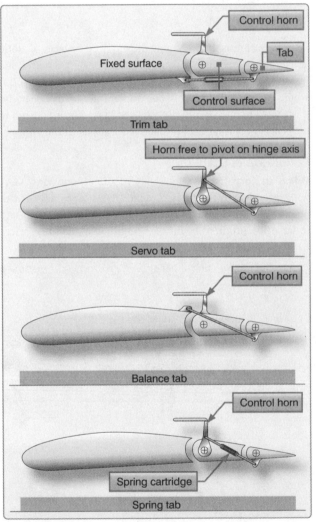

Figure 2-13. *Types of trim tabs.*

Auxiliary Lift Devices

Included in the auxiliary lift devices group of flight control surfaces are the wing flaps, spoilers, speed brakes, slats, leading edge flaps, and slots.

The auxiliary groups may be divided into two subgroups: those whose primary purpose is lift augmenting and those whose primary purpose is lift decreasing. In the first group are the flaps, both trailing edge and leading edge (slats), and slots. The lift decreasing devices are speed brakes and spoilers.

The trailing edge airfoils (flaps) increase the wing area, thereby increasing lift on takeoff, and decrease the speed during landing. These airfoils are retractable and fair into the wing contour. Others are simply a portion of the lower skin which extends into the airstream, thereby slowing the aircraft. Leading edge flaps are airfoils extended from and retracted into the leading edge of the wing. Some installations create a slot (an opening between the extended airfoil and the leading edge). The flap (termed slat by some manufacturers) and slot create additional lift at the lower speeds of takeoff and landing. *[Figure 2-14]*

Other installations have permanent slots built in the leading edge of the wing. At cruising speeds, the trailing edge and leading edge flaps (slats) are retracted into the wing proper. Slats are movable control surfaces attached to the leading edges of the wings. When the slat is closed, it forms the leading edge of the wing. When in the open position (extended forward), a slot is created between the slat and the wing leading edge. At low airspeeds, this increases lift and improves handling characteristics, allowing the aircraft to be controlled at airspeeds below the normal landing speed. *[Figure 2-15]*

Lift decreasing devices are the speed brakes (spoilers). In some installations, there are two types of spoilers. The ground spoiler is extended only after the aircraft is on the ground, thereby assisting in the braking action. The flight spoiler assists in lateral control by being extended whenever the aileron on that wing is rotated up. When actuated as speed brakes, the spoiler panels on both wings raise up. In-flight spoilers may also be located along the sides, underneath the fuselage, or back at the tail. *[Figure 2-16]* In some aircraft designs, the wing panel on the up aileron side rises more than the wing panel on the down aileron side. This provides speed brake operation and lateral control simultaneously.

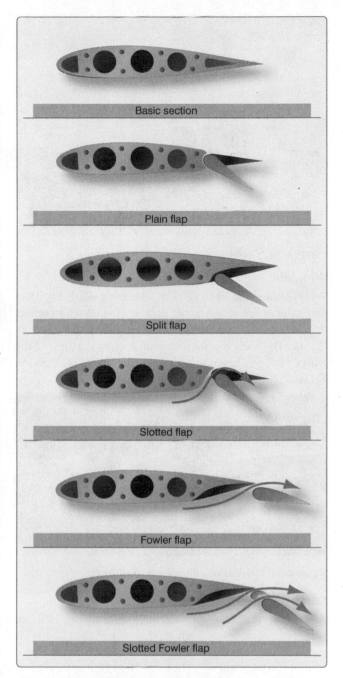

Figure 2-14. *Types of wing flaps.*

Figure 2-15. *Wing slots.*

Figure 2-16. *Speed brake.*

Winglets

Winglets are the near-vertical extension of the wingtip that reduces the aerodynamic drag associated with vortices that develop at the wingtips as the airplane moves through the air. By reducing the induced drag at the tips of the wings, fuel consumption goes down and range is extended. *Figure 2-17* Shows an example of a Boeing 737 with winglets.

Figure 2-17. *Winglets on a Bombardier Learjet 60.*

Canard Wings

A canard wing aircraft is an airframe configuration of a fixed-wing aircraft in which a small wing or horizontal airfoil is ahead of the main lifting surfaces, rather than behind them as in a conventional aircraft. The canard may be fixed, movable, or designed with elevators. Good examples of aircraft with canard wings are the Rutan VariEze and Beechcraft 2000 Starship. *[Figures 2-18* and *2-19]*

Figure 2-18. *Canard wings on a Rutan VariEze.*

Figure 2-19. *The Beechcraft 2000 Starship has canard wings.*

Wing Fences

Wing fences are flat metal vertical plates fixed to the upper surface of the wing. They obstruct spanwise airflow along the wing, and prevent the entire wing from stalling at once. They are often attached on swept-wing aircraft to prevent the spanwise movement of air at high angles of attack. Their purpose is to provide better slow speed handling and stall characteristics. *[Figure 2-20]*

Figure 2-20. *Aircraft stall fence.*

Control Systems for Large Aircraft

Mechanical Control

This is the basic type of system that was used to control early aircraft and is currently used in smaller aircraft where aerodynamic forces are not excessive. The controls are mechanical and manually operated.

The mechanical system of controlling an aircraft can include cables, push-pull tubes, and torque tubes. The cable system is the most widely used because deflections of the structure to which it is attached do not affect its operation. Some aircraft incorporate control systems that are a combination of all three. These systems incorporate cable assemblies, cable guides, linkage, adjustable stops, and control surface snubber or mechanical locking devices. These surface locking devices, usually referred to as a gust lock, limits the external wind forces from damaging the aircraft while it is parked or tied down.

Hydromechanical Control

As the size, complexity, and speed of aircraft increased, actuation of controls in flight became more difficult. It soon became apparent that the pilot needed assistance to overcome the aerodynamic forces to control aircraft movement. Spring tabs, which were operated by the conventional control system, were moved so that the airflow over them actually moved the primary control surface. This was sufficient for the aircraft operating in the lowest of the high speed ranges (250–300 mph). For higher speeds, a power-assisted (hydraulic) control system was designed.

Conventional cable or push-pull tube systems link the flight deck controls with the hydraulic system. With the system activated, the pilot's movement of a control causes the mechanical link to open servo valves, thereby directing hydraulic fluid to actuators, which convert hydraulic pressure into control surface movements.

Because of the efficiency of the hydromechanical flight control system, the aerodynamic forces on the control surfaces cannot be felt by the pilot, and there is a risk of overstressing the structure of the aircraft. To overcome this problem, aircraft designers incorporated artificial feel systems into the design that provided increased resistance to the controls at higher speeds. Additionally, some aircraft with hydraulically powered control systems are fitted with a device called a stick shaker, which provides an artificial stall warning to the pilot.

Fly-By-Wire Control

The fly-by-wire (FBW) control system employs electrical signals that transmit the pilot's actions from the flight deck through a computer to the various flight control actuators. The FBW system evolved as a way to reduce the system weight of the hydromechanical system, reduce maintenance costs, and improve reliability. Electronic FBW control systems can respond to changing aerodynamic conditions by adjusting flight control movements so that the aircraft response is consistent for all flight conditions. Additionally, the computers can be programmed to prevent undesirable and dangerous characteristics, such as stalling and spinning.

Many of the new military high-performance aircraft are not aerodynamically stable. This characteristic is designed into the aircraft for increased maneuverability and responsive performance. Without the computers reacting to the instability, the pilot would lose control of the aircraft.

The Airbus A-320 was the first commercial airliner to use FBW controls. Boeing used them in their 777 and newer design commercial aircraft. The Dassault Falcon 7X was the first business jet to use a FBW control system.

High-Speed Aerodynamics

High-speed aerodynamics, often called compressible aerodynamics, is a special branch of study of aeronautics. It is utilized by aircraft designers when designing aircraft capable of speeds approaching Mach 1 and above. Because it is beyond the scope and intent of this handbook, only a brief overview of the subject is provided.

In the study of high-speed aeronautics, the compressibility effects on air must be addressed. This flight regime is characterized by the Mach number, a special parameter named in honor of Ernst Mach, the late 19th century physicist who studied gas dynamics. Mach number is the ratio of the speed of the aircraft to the local speed of sound and determines the magnitude of many of the compressibility effects.

As an aircraft moves through the air, the air molecules near the aircraft are disturbed and move around the aircraft. The air molecules are pushed aside much like a boat creates a bow wave as it moves through the water. If the aircraft passes at a low speed, typically less than 250 mph, the density of the air remains constant. But at higher speeds, some of the energy of the aircraft goes into compressing the air and locally changing the density of the air. The bigger and heavier the aircraft, the more air it displaces and the greater effect compression has on the aircraft.

This effect becomes more important as speed increases. Near and beyond the speed of sound, about 760 mph (at sea level), sharp disturbances generate a shockwave that affects both the lift and drag of an aircraft and flow conditions downstream of the shockwave. The shockwave forms a cone of pressurized air molecules which move outward and rearward in all directions and extend to the ground. The sharp release of the pressure, after the buildup by the shockwave, is heard as the sonic boom. *[Figure 2-21]*

Figure 2-21. *Breaking the sound barrier.*

Listed below are a range of conditions that are encountered by aircraft as their designed speed increases.

- Subsonic conditions occur for Mach numbers less than one (100–350 mph). For the lowest subsonic conditions, compressibility can be ignored.

- As the speed of the object approaches the speed of sound, the flight Mach number is nearly equal to one, $M = 1$ (350–760 mph), and the flow is said to be transonic. At some locations on the object, the local speed of air exceeds the speed of sound. Compressibility effects are most important in transonic flows and lead to the early belief in a sound barrier. Flight faster than sound was thought to be impossible. In fact, the sound barrier was only an increase in the drag near sonic conditions because of compressibility effects. Because of the high drag associated with compressibility effects, aircraft are not operated in cruise conditions near Mach 1.

- Supersonic conditions occur for numbers greater than Mach 1, but less then Mach 3 (760–2,280 mph). Compressibility effects of gas are important in the design of supersonic aircraft because of the shockwaves that are generated by the surface of the object. For high supersonic speeds, between Mach 3 and Mach 5 (2,280–3,600 mph), aerodynamic heating becomes a very important factor in aircraft design.

- For speeds greater than Mach 5, the flow is said to be hypersonic. At these speeds, some of the energy of the object now goes into exciting the chemical bonds which hold together the nitrogen and oxygen molecules of the air. At hypersonic speeds, the chemistry of the air must be considered when determining forces on the object. When the Space Shuttle re-enters the atmosphere at high hypersonic speeds, close to Mach 25, the heated air becomes an ionized plasma of gas, and the spacecraft must be insulated from the extremely high temperatures.

Additional technical information pertaining to high-speed aerodynamics can be found at bookstores, libraries, and numerous sources on the Internet. As the design of aircraft evolves and the speeds of aircraft continue to increase into the hypersonic range, new materials and propulsion systems will need to be developed. This is the challenge for engineers, physicists, and designers of aircraft in the future.

Rotary-Wing Aircraft Assembly and Rigging

The flight control units located in the flight deck of all helicopters are very nearly the same. All helicopters have either one or two of each of the following: collective pitch control, throttle grip, cyclic pitch control, and directional control pedals. *[Figure 2-22]* Basically, these units do the same things, regardless of the type of helicopter on which they are installed; however, the operation of the control system varies greatly by helicopter model.

Rigging the helicopter coordinates the movements of the flight controls and establishes the relationship between the main rotor and its controls, and between the tail rotor and its controls. Rigging is not a difficult job, but it requires great precision and attention to detail. Strict adherence to rigging procedures described in the manufacturer's maintenance manuals and service instructions is a must. Adjustments, clearances, and tolerances must be exact.

Rigging of the various flight control systems can be broken down into the following three major steps:

1. Placing the control system in a specific position—holding it in position with pins, clamps, or jigs, then adjusting the various linkages to fit the immobilized control component.

2. Placing the control surfaces in a specific reference position—using a rigging jig, a precision bubble protractor, or a spirit level to check the angular difference between the control surface and some fixed surface on the aircraft. *[Figure 2-23]*

3. Setting the maximum range of travel of the various components—this adjustment limits the physical movement of the control system.

After completion of the static rigging, a functional check of the flight control system must be accomplished. The nature of the functional check varies with the type of helicopter and system concerned, but usually includes determining that:

1. The direction of movement of the main and tail rotor blades is correct in relation to movement of the pilot's controls.

Figure 2-22. *Controls of a helicopter and the principal function of each.*

Cyclic control stick
Controls attitude and direction of flight

Throttle
Controls rpm

Collective pitch stick
Controls altitude

Pedals
Maintain heading

Main rotor rigging protractor

CAUTION
Make sure blade
dampers are
positioned against
auto-rotation
inboard stops

Figure 2-23. *A typical rigging protractor.*

2. The operation of interconnected control systems (engine throttle and collective pitch) is properly coordinated.

3. The range of movement and neutral position of the pilot's controls are correct.

4. The maximum and minimum pitch angles of the main rotor blades are within specified limits. This includes checking the fore-and-aft and lateral cyclic pitch and collective pitch blade angles.

5. The tracking of the main rotor blades is correct.

6. In the case of multirotor aircraft, the rigging and movement of the rotor blades are synchronized.

7. When tabs are provided on main rotor blades, they are correctly set.

8. The neutral, maximum, and minimum pitch angles and coning angles of the tail rotor blades are correct.

9. When dual controls are provided, they function correctly and in synchronization.

Upon completion of rigging, a thorough check should be made of all attaching, securing, and pivot points. All bolts, nuts, and rod ends should be properly secured and safetied as specified in the manufacturers' maintenance and service instructions.

Configurations of Rotary-Wing Aircraft

Autogyro

An autogyro is an aircraft with a free-spinning horizontal rotor that turns due to passage of air upward through the rotor. This air motion is created from forward motion of the aircraft resulting from either a tractor or pusher configured engine/propeller design. *[Figure 2-24]*

Figure 2-24. *An autogyro.*

Single Rotor Helicopter

An aircraft with a single horizontal main rotor that provides both lift and direction of travel is a single rotor helicopter. A secondary rotor mounted vertically on the tail counteracts the rotational force (torque) of the main rotor to correct yaw of the fuselage. *[Figure 2-25]*

Figure 2-25. *Single rotor helicopter.*

Dual Rotor Helicopter

An aircraft with two horizontal rotors that provide both the lift and directional control is a dual rotor helicopter. The rotors are counterrotating to balance the aerodynamic torque and eliminate the need for a separate antitorque system. *[Figure 2-26]*

Figure 2-26. *Dual rotor helicopter.*

Types of Rotor Systems

Fully Articulated Rotor

A fully articulated rotor is found on aircraft with more than two blades and allows movement of each individual blade in three directions. In this design, each blade can rotate about the pitch axis to change lift; each blade can move back and forth in plane, lead and lag; and flap up and down through a hinge independent of the other blades. *[Figure 2-27]*

Pitch change axis

Flipping hinge

Drag hinge

Figure 2-27. *Articulated rotor head.*

Semirigid Rotor

The semirigid rotor design is found on aircraft with two rotor blades. The blades are connected in a manner such that as one blade flaps up, the opposite blade flaps down.

Rigid Rotor

The rigid rotor system is a rare design but potentially offers the best properties of both the fully articulated and semirigid rotors. In this design, the blade roots are rigidly attached to the rotor hub. The blades do not have hinges to allow lead-lag or flapping. Instead, the blades accommodate these motions by using elastomeric bearings. Elastomeric bearings are molded, rubber-like materials that are bonded to the appropriate parts. Instead of rotating like conventional bearings, they twist and flex to allow proper movement of the blades.

Forces Acting on the Helicopter

One of the differences between a helicopter and a fixed-wing aircraft is the main source of lift. The fixed-wing aircraft derives its lift from a fixed airfoil surface while the helicopter derives lift from a rotating airfoil called the rotor.

During hovering flight in a no-wind condition, the tip-path plane is horizontal, that is, parallel to the ground. Lift and thrust act straight up; weight and drag act straight down. The sum of the lift and thrust forces must equal the sum of the weight and drag forces in order for the helicopter to hover.

During vertical flight in a no-wind condition, the lift and thrust forces both act vertically upward. Weight and drag both act vertically downward. When lift and thrust equal weight and drag, the helicopter hovers; if lift and thrust are less than weight and drag, the helicopter descends vertically; if lift and thrust are greater than weight and drag, the helicopter rises vertically.

For forward flight, the tip-path plane is tilted forward, thus tilting the total lift-thrust force forward from the vertical. This resultant lift-thrust force can be resolved into two components: lift acting vertically upward and thrust acting horizontally in the direction of flight. In addition to lift and thrust, there is weight, the downward acting force, and drag, the rearward acting or retarding force of inertia and wind resistance.

In straight-and-level, unaccelerated forward flight, lift equals weight and thrust equals drag. (Straight-and-level flight is flight with a constant heading and at a constant altitude.) If lift exceeds weight, the helicopter climbs; if lift is less than weight, the helicopter descends. If thrust exceeds drag, the helicopter increases speed; if thrust is less than drag, it decreases speed.

In sideward flight, the tip-path plane is tilted sideward in the direction that flight is desired, thus tilting the total lift-thrust vector sideward. In this case, the vertical or lift component is still straight up, weight straight down, but the horizontal or thrust component now acts sideward with drag acting to the opposite side.

For rearward flight, the tip-path plane is tilted rearward and tilts the lift-thrust vector rearward. The thrust is then rearward and the drag component is forward, opposite that for forward flight. The lift component in rearward flight is straight up; weight, straight down.

Torque Compensation

Newton's third law of motion states "To every action there is an equal and opposite reaction." As the main rotor of a helicopter turns in one direction, the fuselage tends to rotate in the opposite direction. This tendency for the fuselage to rotate is called torque. Since torque effect on the fuselage is a direct result of engine power supplied to the main rotor, any change in engine power brings about a corresponding change in torque effect. The greater the engine power, the greater the torque effect. Since there is no engine power being supplied to the main rotor during autorotation, there is no torque reaction during autorotation.

The force that compensates for torque and provides for directional control can be produced by various means. The defining factor is dictated by the design of the helicopter, some of which do not have a torque issue. Single main rotor designs typically have an auxiliary rotor located on the end of the tail boom. This auxiliary rotor, generally referred to as a tail rotor, produces thrust in the direction opposite the torque reaction developed by the main rotor. [Figure 2-25] Foot pedals in the flight deck permit the pilot to increase or decrease tail rotor thrust, as needed, to neutralize torque effect.

Other methods of compensating for torque and providing directional control include the Fenestron® tail rotor system, an SUD Aviation design that employs a ducted fan enclosed by a shroud. Another design, called NOTAR®, a McDonald Douglas design with no tail rotor, employs air directed through a series of slots in the tail boom, with the balance exiting through a 90° duct located at the rear of the tail boom. [Figure 2-28]

Figure 2-28. *Aerospatiale Fenestron tail rotor system (left) and the McDonnell Douglas NOTAR® System (right).*

Gyroscopic Forces

The spinning main rotor of a helicopter acts like a gyroscope. As such, it has the properties of gyroscopic action, one of which is precession. Gyroscopic precession is the resultant action or deflection of a spinning object when a force is applied to this object. This action occurs approximately 90° in the direction of rotation from the point where the force is applied. *[Figure 2-29]* Through the use of this principle, the tip-path plane of the main rotor may be tilted from the horizontal.

Examine a two-bladed rotor system to see how gyroscopic precession affects the movement of the tip-path plane. Moving the cyclic pitch control increases the angle of attack (AOA) of one rotor blade with the result that a greater lifting force is applied at that point in the plane of rotation. This same control movement simultaneously decreases the AOA of the other blade the same amount, thus decreasing the lifting force applied at that point in the plane of rotation. The blade with the increased AOA tends to flap up; the blade with the

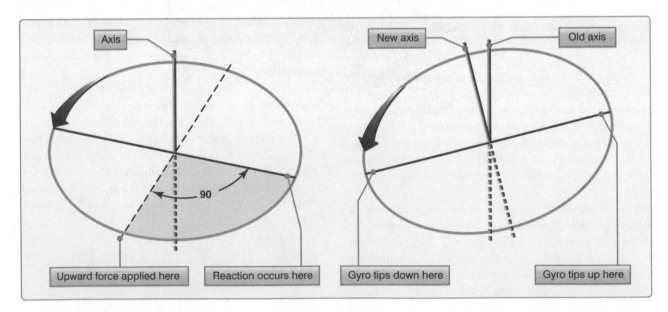

Figure 2-29. *Gyroscopic precession principle.*

decreased AOA tends to flap down. Because the rotor disk acts like a gyro, the blades reach maximum deflection at a point approximately 90° later in the plane of rotation. As shown in *Figure 2-30*, the retreating blade AOA is increased and the advancing blade AOA is decreased resulting in a tipping forward of the tip-path plane, since maximum deflection takes place 90° later when the blades are at the rear and front, respectively. In a rotor system using three or more blades, the movement of the cyclic pitch control changes the AOA of each blade an appropriate amount so that the end result is the same.

The movement of the cyclic pitch control in a two-bladed rotor system increases the AOA of one rotor blade with the result that a greater lifting force is applied at this point in the plane of rotation. This same control movement simultaneously decreases the AOA of the other blade a like amount, thus decreasing the lifting force applied at this point

in the plane of rotation. The blade with the increased AOA tends to rise; the blade with the decreased AOA tends to lower. However, gyroscopic precession prevents the blades from rising or lowering to maximum deflection until a point approximately 90° later in the plane of rotation.

In a three-bladed rotor, the movement of the cyclic pitch control changes the AOA of each blade an appropriate amount so that the end result is the same, a tipping forward of the tip-path plane when the maximum change in AOA is made as each blade passes the same points at which the maximum increase and decrease are made for the two-bladed rotor as shown in *Figure 2-30*. As each blade passes the 90° position on the left, the maximum increase in AOA occurs. As each blade passes the 90° position to the right, the maximum decrease in AOA occurs. Maximum deflection takes place 90° later, maximum upward deflection at the rear and maximum downward deflection at the front; the tip-path plane tips forward.

Figure 2-30. *Gyroscopic precession.*

Helicopter Flight Conditions

Hovering Flight

During hovering flight, a helicopter maintains a constant position over a selected point, usually a few feet above the ground. For a helicopter to hover, the lift and thrust produced by the rotor system act straight up and must equal the weight and drag, which act straight down. *[Figure 2-31]* While hovering, the amount of main rotor thrust can be changed to maintain the desired hovering altitude. This is done by changing the angle of incidence (by moving the collective) of the rotor blades and hence the AOA of the main rotor blades. Changing the AOA changes the drag on the rotor blades, and the power delivered by the engine must change as well to keep the rotor speed constant.

Figure 2-31. *To maintain a hover at a constant altitude, enough lift and thrust must be generated to equal the weight of the helicopter and the drag produced by the rotor blades.*

The weight that must be supported is the total weight of the helicopter and its occupants. If the amount of lift is greater than the actual weight, the helicopter accelerates upwards until the lift force equals the weight gain altitude; if thrust is less than weight, the helicopter accelerates downward. When operating near the ground, the effect of the closeness to the ground changes this response.

The drag of a hovering helicopter is mainly induced drag incurred while the blades are producing lift. There is, however, some profile drag on the blades as they rotate through the air. Throughout the rest of this discussion, the term drag includes both induced and profile drag.

An important consequence of producing thrust is torque. As discussed earlier, Newton's Third Law states that for every action there is an equal and opposite reaction. Therefore, as the engine turns the main rotor system in a counterclockwise direction, the helicopter fuselage tends to turn clockwise. The amount of torque is directly related to the amount of engine power being used to turn the main rotor system. Remember, as power changes, torque changes.

To counteract this torque-induced turning tendency, an antitorque rotor or tail rotor is incorporated into most helicopter designs. A pilot can vary the amount of thrust produced by the tail rotor in relation to the amount of torque produced by the engine. As the engine supplies more power to the main rotor, the tail rotor must produce more thrust to overcome the increased torque effect. This is done through the use of antitorque pedals.

Translating Tendency or Drift

During hovering flight, a single main rotor helicopter tends to drift or move in the direction of tail rotor thrust. This drifting tendency is called translating tendency. *[Figure 2-32]*

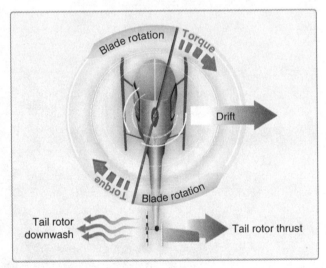

Figure 2-32. *A tail rotor is designed to produce thrust in a direction opposite torque. The thrust produced by the tail rotor is sufficient to move the helicopter laterally.*

To counteract this drift, one or more of the following features may be used. All examples are for a counterclockwise rotating main rotor system.

- The main transmission is mounted at a slight angle to the left (when viewed from behind) so that the rotor mast has a built-in tilt to oppose the tail rotor thrust.

- Flight controls can be rigged so that the rotor disk is tilted to the right slightly when the cyclic is centered. Whichever method is used, the tip-path plane is tilted slightly to the left in the hover.

- If the transmission is mounted so the rotor shaft is vertical with respect to the fuselage, the helicopter "hangs" left skid low in the hover. The opposite is true for rotor systems turning clockwise when viewed from above.

- In forward flight, the tail rotor continues to push to the right, and the helicopter makes a small angle with the wind when the rotors are level and the slip ball is in the middle. This is called inherent sideslip.

Ground Effect

When hovering near the ground, a phenomenon known as ground effect takes place. This effect usually occurs at heights between the surface and approximately one rotor diameter above the surface. The friction of the ground causes the downwash from the rotor to move outwards from the helicopter. This changes the relative direction of the downwash from a purely vertical motion to a combination of vertical and horizontal motion. As the induced airflow through the rotor disk is reduced by the surface friction, the lift vector increases. This allows a lower rotor blade angle for the same amount of lift, which reduces induced drag. Ground effect also restricts the generation of blade tip vortices due to the downward and outward airflow making a larger portion of the blade produce lift. When the helicopter gains altitude vertically, with no forward airspeed, induced airflow is no longer restricted, and the blade tip vortices increase with the decrease in outward airflow. As a result, drag increases which means a higher pitch angle, and more power is needed to move the air down through the rotor.

Ground effect is at its maximum in a no-wind condition over a firm, smooth surface. Tall grass, rough terrain, and water surfaces alter the airflow pattern, causing an increase in rotor tip vortices. *[Figure 2-33]*

Coriolis Effect (Law of Conservation of Angular Momentum)

The Coriolis effect is also referred to as the law of conservation of angular momentum. It states that the value of angular momentum of a rotating body does not change unless an external force is applied. In other words, a rotating body continues to rotate with the same rotational velocity until some external force is applied to change the speed of rotation. Angular momentum is moment of inertia (mass times distance from the center of rotation squared) multiplied by speed of rotation. Changes in angular velocity, known as angular acceleration and deceleration, take place as the mass of a rotating body is moved closer to or further away from the axis of rotation. The speed of the rotating mass increases or decreases in proportion to the square of the radius. An excellent example of this principle is a spinning ice skater. The skater begins rotation on one foot, with the other leg and both arms extended. The rotation of the skater's body is relatively slow. When a skater draws both arms and one leg inward, the moment of inertia (mass times radius squared) becomes much smaller and the body is rotating almost faster than the eye can follow. Because the angular momentum must remain constant (no external force applied), the angular velocity must increase. The rotor blade rotating about the rotor hub possesses angular momentum. As the rotor begins to cone due to G-loading maneuvers, the diameter or the disk shrinks. Due to conservation of angular momentum, the blades continue to travel the same speed even though the blade tips have a shorter distance to travel due to reduced disk diameter. The action results in an increase in rotor rpm. Most pilots arrest this increase with an increase in collective pitch. Conversely, as G-loading subsides and the rotor disk flattens out from the loss of G-load induced coning, the blade tips

Figure 2-33. *Air circulation patterns change when hovering out of ground effect (OGE) and when hovering in ground effect (IGE).*

now have a longer distance to travel at the same tip speed. This action results in a reduction of rotor rpm. However, if this drop in the rotor rpm continues to the point at which it attempts to decrease below normal operating rpm, the engine control system adds more fuel/power to maintain the specified engine rpm. If the pilot does not reduce collective pitch as the disk unloads, the combination of engine compensation for the rpm slow down and the additional pitch as G-loading increases may result in exceeding the torque limitations or power the engines can produce.

Vertical Flight

Hovering is actually an element of vertical flight. Increasing the AOA of the rotor blades (pitch) while keeping their rotation speed constant generates additional lift and the helicopter ascends. Decreasing the pitch causes the helicopter to descend. In a no wind condition, when lift and thrust are less than weight and drag, the helicopter descends vertically. If lift and thrust are greater than weight and drag, the helicopter ascends vertically. [Figure 2-34]

Figure 2-34. To ascend vertically, more lift and thrust must be generated to overcome the forces of weight and drag.

Forward Flight

In steady forward flight with no change in airspeed or vertical speed, the four forces of lift, thrust, drag, and weight must be in balance. Once the tip-path plane is tilted forward, the total lift-thrust force is also tilted forward. This resultant lift-thrust force can be resolved into two components—lift acting vertically upward and thrust acting horizontally in the direction of flight. In addition to lift and thrust, there is weight (the downward acting force) and drag (the force opposing the motion of an airfoil through the air). [Figure 2-35]

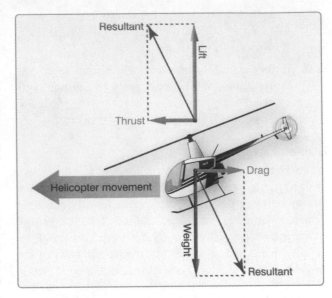

Figure 2-35. The power required to maintain a straight-and-level flight and a stabilized airspeed.

In straight-and-level (constant heading and at a constant altitude), unaccelerated forward flight, lift equals weight and thrust equals drag. If lift exceeds weight, the helicopter accelerates vertically until the forces are in balance; if thrust is less than drag, the helicopter slows until the forces are in balance. As the helicopter moves forward, it begins to lose altitude because lift is lost as thrust is diverted forward. However, as the helicopter begins to accelerate, the rotor system becomes more efficient due to the increased airflow. The result is excess power over that which is required to hover. Continued acceleration causes an even larger increase in airflow through the rotor disk and more excess power. In order to maintain unaccelerated flight, the pilot must not make any changes in power or in cyclic movement. Any such changes would cause the helicopter to climb or descend. Once straight-and-level flight is obtained, the pilot should make note of the power (torque setting) required and not make major adjustments to the flight controls. [Figure 2-36]

Translational Lift

Improved rotor efficiency resulting from directional flight is called translational lift. The efficiency of the hovering rotor system is greatly improved with each knot of incoming wind gained by horizontal movement of the aircraft or surface wind. As incoming wind produced by aircraft movement or surface wind enters the rotor system, turbulence and vortices are left behind and the flow of air becomes more horizontal. In addition, the tail rotor becomes more aerodynamically efficient during the transition from hover to forward flight. Translational thrust occurs when the tail rotor becomes more aerodynamically efficient during the transition from hover

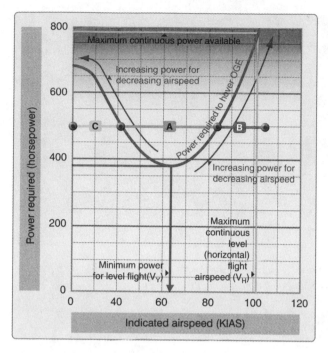

Figure 2-36. *Changing force vectors results in aircraft movement.*

to forward flight. As the tail rotor works in progressively less turbulent air, this improved efficiency produces more antitorque thrust, causing the nose of the aircraft to yaw left (with a main rotor turning counterclockwise) and forces the pilot to apply right pedal (decreasing the AOA in the tail rotor blades) in response. In addition, during this period, the airflow affects the horizontal components of the stabilizer

found on most helicopters which tends to bring the nose of the helicopter to a more level attitude. *Figure 2-37* and *Figure 2-38* show airflow patterns at different speeds and how airflow affects the efficiency of the tail rotor.

Effective Translational Lift (ETL)

While transitioning to forward flight at about 16–24 knots, the helicopter experiences effective translational lift (ETL). As mentioned earlier in the discussion on translational lift, the rotor blades become more efficient as forward airspeed increases. Between 16–24 knots, the rotor system completely outruns the recirculation of old vortices and begins to work in relatively undisturbed air. The flow of air through the rotor system is more horizontal, therefore induced flow and induced drag are reduced. The AOA is subsequently increased, which makes the rotor system operate more efficiently. This increased efficiency continues with increased airspeed until the best climb airspeed is reached, and total drag is at its lowest point.

As speed increases, translational lift becomes more effective, the nose rises or pitches up, and the aircraft rolls to the right. The combined effects of dissymmetry of lift, gyroscopic precession, and transverse flow effect cause this tendency. It is important to understand these effects and anticipate correcting for them. Once the helicopter is transitioning through ETL, the pilot needs to apply forward and left lateral cyclic input to maintain a constant rotor-disk attitude. [*Figure 2-39*]

Figure 2-37. *The airflow pattern for 1–5 knots of forward airspeed. Note how the downwind vortex is beginning to dissipate and induced flow down through the rear of the rotor system is more horizontal.*

Airflow pattern just prior to effective translational lift

10–15 knots

Figure 2-38. *An airflow pattern at a speed of 10–15 knots. At this increased airspeed, the airflow continues to become more horizontal. The leading edge of the downwash pattern is being overrun and is well back under the nose of the helicopter.*

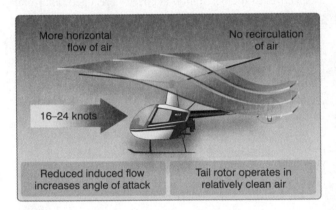

More horizontal flow of air

No recirculation of air

16–24 knots

Reduced induced flow increases angle of attack

Tail rotor operates in relatively clean air

Figure 2-39. *Effective translational lift is easily recognized in actual flight by a transient induced aerodynamic vibration and increased performance of the helicopter.*

Dissymmetry of Lift

Dissymmetry of lift is the differential (unequal) lift between advancing and retreating halves of the rotor disk caused by the different wind flow velocity across each half. This difference in lift would cause the helicopter to be uncontrollable in any situation other than hovering in a calm wind. There must be a means of compensating, correcting, or eliminating this unequal lift to attain symmetry of lift.

When the helicopter moves through the air, the relative airflow through the main rotor disk is different on the advancing side than on the retreating side. The relative wind encountered by the advancing blade is increased by the forward speed of the helicopter; while the relative windspeed acting on the retreating blade is reduced by the helicopter's forward airspeed. Therefore, as a result of the relative windspeed, the advancing blade side of the rotor disk produces more lift than the retreating blade side. *[Figure 2-40]*

Direction of Flight

Retreating Side

Advancing Side

Blade rotation

Relative wind

Blade tip speed minus helicopter speed (200 knots)

Blade tip speed plus helicopter speed (400 knots)

Relative wind

Blade rotation

Forward flight at 100 knots

Figure 2-40. *The blade tip speed of this helicopter is approximately 300 knots. If the helicopter is moving forward at 100 knots, the relative windspeed on the advancing side is 400 knots. On the retreating side, it is only 200 knots. This difference in speed causes a dissymmetry of lift.*

If this condition was allowed to exist, a helicopter with a counterclockwise main rotor blade rotation would roll to the left because of the difference in lift. In reality, the main rotor blades flap and feather automatically to equalize lift across the rotor disk. Articulated rotor systems, usually with three or more blades, incorporate a horizontal hinge (flapping hinge) to allow the individual rotor blades to move, or flap up and down as they rotate. A semirigid rotor system (two blades) utilizes a teetering hinge, which allows the blades to flap as a unit. When one blade flaps up, the other blade flaps down.

As the rotor blade reaches the advancing side of the rotor disk, it reaches its maximum upward flapping velocity. [Figure 2-41A] When the blade flaps upward, the angle between the chord line and the resultant relative wind decreases. This decreases the AOA, which reduces the amount of lift produced by the blade. At position C, the rotor blade is at its maximum downward flapping velocity. Due to downward flapping, the angle between the chord line and the resultant relative wind increases. This increases the AOA and thus the amount of lift produced by the blade.

The combination of blade flapping and slow relative wind acting on the retreating blade normally limits the maximum forward speed of a helicopter. At a high forward speed, the retreating blade stalls due to high AOA and slow relative wind speed. This situation is called "retreating blade stall" and is evidenced by a nose-up pitch, vibration, and a rolling tendency—usually to the left in helicopters with counterclockwise blade rotation.

Pilots can avoid retreating blade stall by not exceeding the never-exceed speed. This speed is designated V_{NE} and is indicated on a placard and marked on the airspeed indicator by a red line.

During aerodynamic flapping of the rotor blades as they compensate for dissymmetry of lift, the advancing blade achieves maximum upward flapping displacement over the nose and maximum downward flapping displacement over the tail. This causes the tip-path plane to tilt to the rear and is referred to as blowback. Figure 2-42 shows how the rotor disk is originally oriented with the front down following the initial cyclic input. As airspeed is gained and flapping eliminates dissymmetry of lift, the front of the disk comes

Figure 2-42. *To compensate for blowback, move the cyclic forward. Blowback is more pronounced with higher airspeeds.*

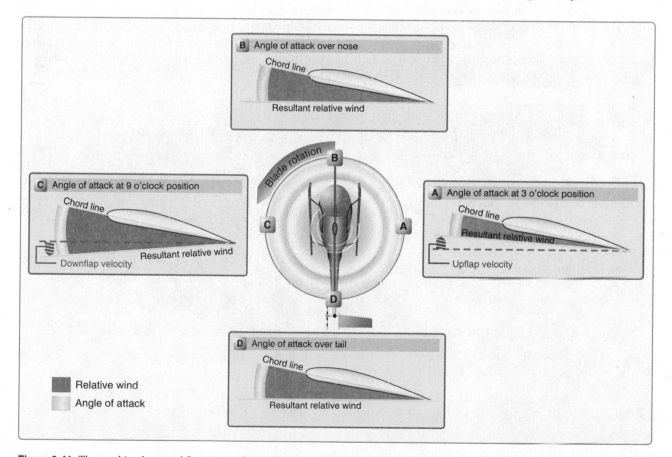

Figure 2-41. *The combined upward flapping (reduced lift) of the advancing blade and downward flapping (increased lift) of the retreating blade equalizes lift across the main rotor disk counteracting dissymmetry of lift.*

up, and the back of the disk goes down. This reorientation of the rotor disk changes the direction in which total rotor thrust acts; the helicopter's forward speed slows, but can be corrected with cyclic input. The pilot uses cyclic feathering to compensate for dissymmetry of lift allowing him or her to control the attitude of the rotor disk.

Cyclic feathering compensates for dissymmetry of lift (changes the AOA) in the following way. At a hover, equal lift is produced around the rotor system with equal pitch and AOA on all the blades and at all points in the rotor system (disregarding compensation for translating tendency). The rotor disk is parallel to the horizon. To develop a thrust force, the rotor system must be tilted in the desired direction of movement. Cyclic feathering changes the angle of incidence differentially around the rotor system. Forward cyclic movements decrease the angle of incidence at one part on the rotor system while increasing the angle at another part. Maximum downward flapping of the blade over the nose and maximum upward flapping over the tail tilt both rotor disk and thrust vector forward. To prevent blowback from occurring, the pilot must continually move the cyclic forward as the velocity of the helicopter increases. *Figure 2-42* illustrates the changes in pitch angle as the cyclic is moved forward at increased airspeeds. At a hover, the cyclic is centered and the pitch angle on the advancing and retreating blades is the same. At low forward speeds, moving the cyclic forward reduces pitch angle on the advancing blade and increases pitch angle on the retreating blade. This causes a slight rotor

tilt. At higher forward speeds, the pilot must continue to move the cyclic forward. This further reduces pitch angle on the advancing blade and further increases pitch angle on the retreating blade. As a result, there is even more tilt to the rotor than at lower speeds.

This horizontal lift component (thrust) generates higher helicopter airspeed. The higher airspeed induces blade flapping to maintain symmetry of lift. The combination of flapping and cyclic feathering maintains symmetry of lift and desired attitude on the rotor system and helicopter.

Autorotation

Autorotation is the state of flight in which the main rotor system of a helicopter is being turned by the action of air moving up through the rotor rather than engine power driving the rotor. In normal, powered flight, air is drawn into the main rotor system from above and exhausted downward, but during autorotation, air moves up into the rotor system from below as the helicopter descends. Autorotation is permitted mechanically by a freewheeling unit, which is a special clutch mechanism that allows the main rotor to continue turning even if the engine is not running. If the engine fails, the freewheeling unit automatically disengages the engine from the main rotor allowing the main rotor to rotate freely. It is the means by which a helicopter can be landed safely in the event of an engine failure; consequently, all helicopters must demonstrate this capability in order to be certificated. *[Figure 2-43]*

Figure 2-43. *During an autorotation, the upward flow of relative wind permits the main rotor blades to rotate at their normal speed. In effect, the blades are "gliding" in their rotational plane.*

Rotorcraft Controls

Swash Plate Assembly

The purpose of the swash plate is to transmit control inputs from the collective and cyclic controls to the main rotor blades. It consists of two main parts: the stationary swash plate and the rotating swash plate. *[Figure 2-44]*

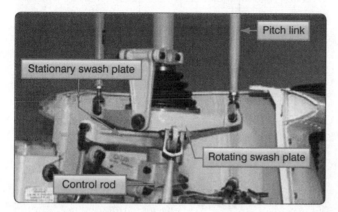

Figure 2-44. *Stationary and rotating swash plate.*

The stationary swash plate is mounted around the main rotor mast and connected to the cyclic and collective controls by a series of pushrods. It is restrained from rotating by an antidrive link but is able to tilt in all directions and move vertically. The rotating swash plate is mounted to the stationary swash plate by a uniball sleeve. It is connected to the mast by drive links and is allowed to rotate with the main rotor mast. Both swash plates tilt and slide up and down as one unit. The rotating swash plate is connected to the pitch horns by the pitch links.

There are three major controls in a helicopter that the pilot must use during flight. They are the collective pitch control, cyclic pitch control, and antitorque pedals or tail rotor control. In addition to these major controls, the pilot must also use the throttle control, which is mounted directly to the collective pitch control in order to fly the helicopter.

Collective Pitch Control

The collective pitch control is located on the left side of the pilot's seat and is operated with the left hand. The collective is used to make changes to the pitch angle of all the main rotor blades simultaneously, or collectively, as the name implies. As the collective pitch control is raised, there is a simultaneous and equal increase in pitch angle of all main rotor blades; as it is lowered, there is a simultaneous and equal decrease in pitch angle. This is done through a series of mechanical linkages, and the amount of movement in the collective lever determines the amount of blade pitch change. *[Figure 2-45]* An adjustable friction control helps prevent inadvertent collective pitch movement.

Figure 2-45. *Raising the collective pitch control increases the pitch angle by the same amount on all blades.*

Throttle Control

The function of the throttle is to regulate engine rpm. If the correlator or governor system does not maintain the desired rpm when the collective is raised or lowered, or if those systems are not installed, the throttle must be moved manually with the twist grip to maintain rpm. The throttle control is much like a motorcycle throttle, and works almost the same way; twisting the throttle to the left increases rpm, twisting the throttle to the right decreases rpm. *[Figure 2-46]*

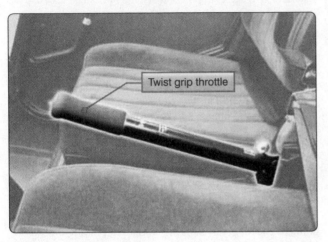

Twist grip throttle

Figure 2-46. *A twist grip throttle is usually mounted on the end of the collective lever. The throttles on some turbine helicopters are mounted on the overhead panel or on the floor in the cockpit.*

Governor/Correlator

A governor is a sensing device that senses rotor and engine rpm and makes the necessary adjustments in order to keep rotor rpm constant. Once the rotor rpm is set in normal operations, the governor keeps the rpm constant, and there is no need to make any throttle adjustments. Governors are common on all turbine helicopters (as it is a function of the fuel control system of the turbine engine), and used on some piston-powered helicopters.

A correlator is a mechanical connection between the collective lever and the engine throttle. When the collective lever is raised, power is automatically increased and when lowered, power is decreased. This system maintains rpm close to the desired value, but still requires adjustment of the throttle for fine tuning.

Some helicopters do not have correlators or governors and require coordination of all collective and throttle movements. When the collective is raised, the throttle must be increased; when the collective is lowered, the throttle must be decreased. As with any aircraft control, large adjustments of either collective pitch or throttle should be avoided. All corrections should be made with smooth pressure.

In piston helicopters, the collective pitch is the primary control for manifold pressure, and the throttle is the primary control for rpm. However, the collective pitch control also influences rpm, and the throttle also influences manifold pressure; therefore, each is considered to be a secondary control of the other's function. Both the tachometer (rpm indicator) and the manifold pressure gauge must be analyzed to determine which control to use. *Figure 2-47* illustrates this relationship.

If manifold pressure is	and rpm is	Solution
LOW	LOW	Increasing the throttle increases manifold pressure and rpm
HIGH	LOW	Lowering the collective pitch decreases manifold pressure and increases rpm
LOW	HIGH	Raising the collective pitch increases manifold pressure and decreases rpm
HIGH	HIGH	Reducing the throttle decreases manifold pressure and rpm

Figure 2-47. *Relationship between manifold pressure, rpm, collective, and throttle.*

Cyclic Pitch Control

The cyclic pitch control is mounted vertically from the cockpit floor, between the pilot's legs or, in some models, between the two pilot seats. *[Figure 2-48]* This primary flight control allows the pilot to fly the helicopter in any horizontal direction; fore, aft, and sideways. The total lift force is always perpendicular to the tip-path place of the main rotor. The purpose of the cyclic pitch control is to tilt the tip-path plane in the direction of the desired horizontal direction. The cyclic control changes the direction of this force and controls the attitude and airspeed of the helicopter.

The rotor disk tilts in the same direction the cyclic pitch control is moved. If the cyclic is moved forward, the rotor disk tilts forward; if the cyclic is moved aft, the disk tilts aft, and so on. Because the rotor disk acts like a gyro, the mechanical linkages for the cyclic control rods are rigged in such a way that they decrease the pitch angle of the rotor blade approximately 90° before it reaches the direction of cyclic displacement, and increase the pitch angle of the rotor blade approximately 90° after it passes the direction of displacement. An increase in pitch angle increases AOA; a decrease in pitch angle decreases AOA. For example, if the cyclic is moved forward, the AOA decreases as the rotor blade passes the right side of the helicopter and increases on the left side. This results in maximum downward deflection

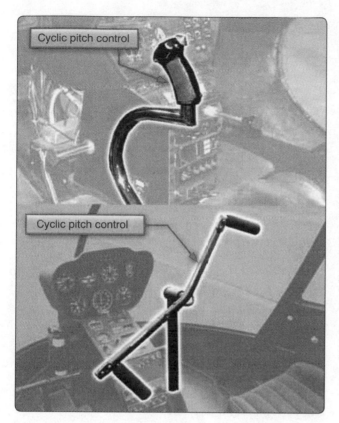

Figure 2-48. *The cyclic pitch control may be mounted vertically between the pilot's knees or on a teetering bar from a single cyclic located in the center of the helicopter. The cyclic can pivot in all directions.*

of the rotor blade in front of the helicopter and maximum upward deflection behind it, causing the rotor disk to tilt forward.

Antitorque Pedals

The antitorque pedals are located on the cabin floor by the pilot's feet. They control the pitch and, therefore, the thrust of the tail rotor blades. *[Figure 2-49]* Newton's Third Law applies to the helicopter fuselage and how it rotates in the opposite direction of the main rotor blades unless counteracted and controlled. To make flight possible and to compensate for this torque, most helicopter designs incorporate an antitorque rotor or tail rotor. The antitorque pedals allow the pilot to control the pitch angle of the tail rotor blades which in forward flight puts the helicopter in longitudinal trim and while at a hover, enables the pilot to turn the helicopter 360°. The antitorque pedals are connected to the pitch change mechanism on the tail rotor gearbox and allow the pitch angle on the tail rotor blades to be increased or decreased.

Figure 2-49. *Antitorque pedals compensate for changes in torque and control heading in a hover.*

Helicopters that are designed with tandem rotors do not have an antitorque rotor. These helicopters are designed with both rotor systems rotating in opposite directions to counteract the torque, rather than using a tail rotor. Directional antitorque pedals are used for directional control of the aircraft while in flight, as well as while taxiing with the forward gear off the ground. With the right pedal displaced forward, the forward rotor disk tilts to the right, while the aft rotor disk tilts to the left. The opposite occurs when the left pedal is pushed forward; the forward rotor disk inclines to the left, and the aft rotor disk tilts to the right. Differing combinations of pedal and cyclic application can allow the tandem rotor helicopter to pivot about the aft or forward vertical axis, as well as pivoting about the center of mass.

Stabilizer Systems

Bell Stabilizer Bar System

Arthur M. Young discovered that stability could be increased significantly with the addition of a stabilizer bar perpendicular to the two blades. The stabilizer bar has weighted ends, which cause it to stay relatively stable in the plane of rotation. The stabilizer bar is linked with the swash plate in a manner that reduces the pitch rate. The two blades can flap as a unit and, therefore, do not require lag-lead hinges (the whole rotor slows down and accelerates per turn). Two-bladed systems require a single teetering hinge and two coning hinges to permit modest coning of the rotor disk as thrust is increased. The configuration is known under multiple names, including Hiller panels, Hiller system, Bell-Hiller system, and flybar system.

Offset Flapping Hinge

The offset flapping hinge is offset from the center of the rotor hub and can produce powerful moments useful for controlling the helicopter. The distance of the hinge from the hub (the offset) multiplied by the force produced at the hinge produces a moment at the hub. Obviously, the larger the offset, the greater the moment for the same force produced by the blade.

The flapping motion is the result of the constantly changing balance between lift, centrifugal, and inertial forces. This rising and falling of the blades is characteristic of most helicopters and has often been compared to the beating of a bird's wing. The flapping hinge, together with the natural flexibility found in most blades, permits the blade to droop considerably when the helicopter is at rest and the rotor is not turning over. During flight, the necessary rigidity is provided by the powerful centrifugal force that results from the rotation of the blades. This force pulls outward from the tip, stiffening the blade, and is the only factor that keeps it from folding up.

Stability Augmentation Systems (SAS)

Some helicopters incorporate stability augmentation systems (SAS) to help stabilize the helicopter in flight and in a hover. The simplest of these systems is a force trim system, which uses a magnetic clutch and springs to hold the cyclic control in the position at which it was released. More advanced systems use electric actuators that make inputs to the hydraulic servos. These servos receive control commands from a computer that senses helicopter attitude. Other inputs, such as heading, speed, altitude, and navigation information may be supplied to the computer to form a complete autopilot system. The SAS may be overridden or disconnected by the pilot at any time.

SAS reduces pilot workload by improving basic aircraft control harmony and decreasing disturbances. These systems are very useful when the pilot is required to perform other duties, such as sling loading and search and rescue operations.

Helicopter Vibration

The following paragraphs describe the various types of vibrations. *Figure 2-50* shows the general levels into which frequencies are divided.

Extreme Low Frequency Vibration

Extreme low frequency vibration is pretty well limited to pylon rock. Pylon rocking (two to three cycles per second) is inherent with the rotor, mast, and transmission system. To keep the vibration from reaching noticeable levels, transmission mount dampening is incorporated to absorb the rocking.

Helicopter Vibration Types	
Frequency Level	Vibration
Extreme low frequency	Less than 1/rev PYLON ROCK
Low frequency	1/rev or 2/rev type vibration
Medium frequency	Generally 4, 5, or 6/rev
High frequency	Tail rotor speed or faster

Figure 2-50. *Various helicopter vibration types.*

Low Frequency Vibration

Low frequency vibrations (1/rev and 2/rev) are caused by the rotor itself. 1/rev vibrations are of two basic types: vertical or lateral. A 1/rev is caused simply by one blade developing more lift at a given point than the other blade develops at the same point.

Medium Frequency Vibration

Medium frequency vibration (4/rev and 6/rev) is another vibration inherent in most rotors. An increase in the level of these vibrations is caused by a change in the capability of the fuselage to absorb vibration, or a loose airframe component, such as the skids, vibrating at that frequency.

High Frequency Vibration

High frequency vibrations can be caused by anything in the helicopter that rotates or vibrates at extremely high speeds. The most common and obvious causes: loose elevator linkage at swashplate horn, loose elevator, or tail rotor balance and track.

Rotor Blade Tracking

Blade tracking is the process of determining the positions of the tips of the rotor blade relative to each other while the rotor head is turning, and of determining the corrections necessary to hold these positions within certain tolerances. The blades should all track one another as closely as possible. The purpose of blade tracking is to bring the tips of all blades into the same tip path throughout their entire cycle of rotation. Various methods of blade tracking are explained in the following paragraphs.

Flag and Pole

The flag and pole method, as shown in *Figure 2-51,* shows the relative positions of the rotor blades. The blade tips are marked with chalk or a grease pencil. Each blade tip should be marked with a different color so that it is easy to determine the relationship of the other tips of the rotor blades to each other. This method can be used on all types of helicopters that do not have jet propulsion at the blade tips. Refer to the applicable maintenance manual for specific procedures.

Figure 2-51. *Flag and pole blade tracking.*

Electronic Blade Tracker

The most common electronic blade tracker consists of a Balancer/Phazor, Strobex Tracker, and Vibrex Tester. *[Figures 2-52 through 2-54]* The Strobex blade tracker permits blade tracking from inside or outside the helicopter while on the ground or inside the helicopter in flight. The system uses a highly concentrated light beam flashing in sequence with the rotation of the main rotor blades so that a fixed target at the blade tips appears to be stopped. Each blade is identified by an elongated retroreflective number taped or attached to the underside of the blade in a uniform location. When viewed at an angle from inside the helicopter, the taped numbers will appear normal. Tracking can be accomplished with tracking tip cap reflectors and a strobe light. The tip caps are temporarily attached to the tip of each blade. The high-intensity strobe light flashes in time with the rotating blades. The strobe light operates from the aircraft electrical power supply. By observing the reflected tip cap image, it is possible to view the track of the rotating blades. Tracking is accomplished in a sequence of four separate steps: ground tracking, hover verification, forward flight tracking, and auto rotation rpm adjustment.

Figure 2-52. *Balancer/Phazor.*

Figure 2-53. *Strobex tracker.*

Figure 2-54. *Vibrex tracker.*

Tail Rotor Tracking

The marking and electronic methods of tail rotor tracking are explained in the following paragraphs.

Marking Method

Procedures for tail rotor tracking using the marking method, as shown in *Figure 2-55*, are as follows:

- After replacement or installation of tail rotor hub, blades, or pitch change system, check tail rotor rigging and track tail rotor blades. Tail rotor tip clearance shall be set before tracking and checked again after tracking.

Figure 2-55. *Tail rotor tracking.*

- The strobe-type tracking device may be used if available. Instructions for use are provided with the device. Attach a piece of soft rubber hose six inches long on the end of a ½ × ½ inch pine stick or other flexible device. Cover the rubber hose with Prussian blue or similar type of coloring thinned with oil.

NOTE: Ground run-up shall be performed by authorized personnel only. Start engine in accordance with applicable maintenance manual. Run engine with pedals in neutral position. Reset marking device on underside of tail boom assembly. Slowly move marking device into disk of tail rotor approximately one inch from tip. When near blade is marked, stop engine and allow rotor to stop. Repeat this procedure until tracking mark crosses over to the other blade, then extend pitch control link of unmarked blade one half turn.

Electronic Method

The electronic Vibrex balancing and tracking kit is housed in a carrying case and consists of a Model 177M-6A Balancer, a Model 135M-11 Strobex, track and balance charts, an accelerometer, cables, and attaching brackets.

The Vibrex balancing kit is used to measure and indicate the level of vibration induced by the main rotor and tail rotor of a helicopter. The Vibrex analyzes the vibration induced by out-of-track or out-of-balance rotors, and then by plotting vibration amplitude and clock angle on a chart the amount and location of rotor track or weight change is determined. In addition, the Vibrex is used in troubleshooting by measuring the vibration levels and frequencies or rpm of unknown disturbances.

Rotor Blade Preservation and Storage

Accomplish the following requirements for rotor blade preservation and storage:

- Condemn, demilitarize, and dispose of locally any blade which has incurred nonrepairable damage.

- Tape all holes in the blade, such as tree damage, or foreign object damage (FOD) to protect the interior of the blade from moisture and corrosion.

- Thoroughly remove foreign matter from the entire exterior surface of blade with mild soap and water.

- Protect blade outboard eroded surfaces with a light coating of corrosion preventive or primer coating.

- Protect blade main bolt hole bushing, drag brace retention bolt hole bushing, and any exposed bare metal (i.e., grip and drag pads) with a light coating of corrosion preventive.

- Secure blade to shock-mounted support and secure container lid.

- Place copy of manufacturer's blade records, containing information required by Title 14 of the Code of Federal Regulations (14 CFR) section 91.417(a)(2)(ii), and any other blade records in a waterproof bag and insert into container record tube.

- Obliterate old markings from the container that pertained to the original shipment or to the original item it contained. Stencil the blade National Stock Number (NSN), model, and serial number, as applicable, on the outside of the container.

Helicopter Power Systems

Powerplant

The two most common types of engines used in helicopters are the reciprocating engine and the turbine engine. Reciprocating engines, also called piston engines, are generally used in smaller helicopters. Most training helicopters use reciprocating engines because they are relatively simple and inexpensive to operate. Turbine engines are more powerful and are used in a wide variety of helicopters. They produce a tremendous amount of power for their size but are generally more expensive to operate.

Reciprocating Engine

The reciprocating engine consists of a series of pistons connected to a rotating crankshaft. As the pistons move up and down, the crankshaft rotates. The reciprocating engine gets its name from the back-and-forth movement of its internal parts. The four-stroke engine is the most common type, and refers to the four different cycles the engine undergoes to produce power. *[Figure 2-56]*

Figure 2-56. *The arrows indicate the direction of motion of the crankshaft and piston during the four-stroke cycle.*

When the piston moves away from the cylinder head on the intake stroke, the intake valve opens and a mixture of fuel and air is drawn into the combustion chamber. As the cylinder moves back toward the cylinder head, the intake valve closes, and the fuel/air mixture is compressed. When compression is nearly complete, the spark plugs fire and the compressed mixture is ignited to begin the power stroke. The rapidly expanding gases from the controlled burning of the fuel/air mixture drive the piston away from the cylinder head, thus providing power to rotate the crankshaft. The piston then moves back toward the cylinder head on the exhaust stroke where the burned gases are expelled through the opened exhaust valve. Even when the engine is operated at a fairly low speed, the four-stroke cycle takes place several hundred times each minute. In a four-cylinder engine, each cylinder operates on a different stroke. Continuous rotation of a crankshaft is maintained by the precise timing of the power strokes in each cylinder.

Turbine Engine

The gas turbine engine mounted on most helicopters is made up of a compressor, combustion chamber, turbine, and accessory gearbox assembly. The compressor draws filtered air into the plenum chamber and compresses it. The compressed air is directed to the combustion section through discharge tubes where atomized fuel is injected into it. The fuel/air mixture is ignited and allowed to expand. This combustion gas is then forced through a series of turbine wheels causing them to turn. These turbine wheels provide power to both the engine compressor and the accessory gearbox. Power is provided to the main rotor and tail rotor systems through the freewheeling unit which is attached to the accessory gearbox power output gear shaft. The combustion gas is finally expelled through an exhaust outlet. *[Figure 2-57]*

Transmission System

The transmission system transfers power from the engine to the main rotor, tail rotor, and other accessories during normal flight conditions. The main components of the transmission system are the main rotor transmission, tail rotor drive system, clutch, and freewheeling unit. The freewheeling unit, or autorotative clutch, allows the main rotor transmission to drive the tail rotor drive shaft during autorotation. Helicopter transmissions are normally lubricated and cooled with their own oil supply. A sight gauge is provided to check the oil level. Some transmissions have chip detectors located in the sump. These detectors are wired to warning lights located on the pilot's instrument panel that illuminate in the event of an internal problem. The chip detectors on modern helicopters have a "burn off" capability and attempt to correct the situation without pilot action. If the problem cannot be corrected on its own, the pilot must refer to the emergency procedures for that particular helicopter.

Main Rotor Transmission

The primary purpose of the main rotor transmission is to reduce engine output rpm to optimum rotor rpm. This reduction is different for the various helicopters. As an example, suppose the engine rpm of a specific helicopter is 2,700. A rotor speed of 450 rpm would require a 6:1 reduction. A 9:1 reduction would mean the rotor would turn at 300 rpm. Most helicopters use a dual-needle tachometer or a vertical scale instrument to show both engine and rotor rpm or a percentage of engine and rotor rpm. The rotor rpm indicator normally is used only during clutch engagement to monitor rotor acceleration, and in autorotation to maintain rpm within prescribed limits. *[Figure 2-58]*

Figure 2-57. *Many helicopters use a turboshaft engine to drive the main transmission and rotor systems. The main difference between a turboshaft and a turbojet engine is that most of the energy produced by the expanding gases is used to drive a turbine rather than producing thrust through the expulsion of exhaust gases.*

Figure 2-58. *There are various types of dual-needle tachometers; however, when the needles are superimposed, or married, the ratio of the engine rpm is the same as the gear reduction ratio.*

In helicopters with horizontally mounted engines, another purpose of the main rotor transmission is to change the axis of rotation from the horizontal axis of the engine to the vertical axis of the rotor shaft. *[Figure 2-59]*

Figure 2-59. *The main rotor transmission and gearbox reduce engine output rpm to optimum rotor rpm and change the axis of rotation of the engine output shaft to the vertical axis for the rotor shaft.*

Clutch

In a conventional airplane, the engine and propeller are permanently connected. However, in a helicopter there is a different relationship between the engine and the rotor. Because of the greater weight of a rotor in relation to the power of the engine, as compared to the weight of a propeller and the power in an airplane, the rotor must be disconnected from the engine when the starter is engaged. A clutch allows the engine to be started and then gradually pick up the load of the rotor.

On free turbine engines, no clutch is required, as the gas producer turbine is essentially disconnected from the power turbine. When the engine is started, there is little resistance from the power turbine. This enables the gas producer turbine to accelerate to normal idle speed without the load of the transmission and rotor system dragging it down. As the gas pressure increases through the power turbine, the rotor blades begin to turn, slowly at first and then gradually accelerate to normal operating rpm.

On reciprocating helicopters, the two main types of clutches are the centrifugal clutch and the belt drive clutch.

Centrifugal Clutch

The centrifugal clutch is made up of an inner assembly and an outer drum. The inner assembly, which is connected to the engine driveshaft, consists of shoes lined with material similar to automotive brake linings. At low engine speeds, springs hold the shoes in, so there is no contact with the outer drum, which is attached to the transmission input shaft. As engine speed increases, centrifugal force causes the clutch shoes to move outward and begin sliding against the outer drum. The transmission input shaft begins to rotate, causing the rotor to turn, slowly at first, but increasing as the friction increases between the clutch shoes and transmission drum. As rotor speed increases, the rotor tachometer needle shows an increase by moving toward the engine tachometer needle. When the two needles are superimposed, the engine and the rotor are synchronized, indicating the clutch is fully engaged and there is no further slippage of the clutch shoes.

Belt Drive Clutch

Some helicopters utilize a belt drive to transmit power from the engine to the transmission. A belt drive consists of a lower pulley attached to the engine, an upper pulley attached to the transmission input shaft, a belt or a series of V-belts, and some means of applying tension to the belts. The belts fit loosely over the upper and lower pulley when there is no tension on the belts. This allows the engine to be started without any load from the transmission. Once the engine is running, tension on the belts is gradually increased. When the rotor and engine tachometer needles are superimposed, the rotor and the engine are synchronized, and the clutch is then fully engaged. Advantages of this system include vibration isolation, simple maintenance, and the ability to start and warm up the engine without engaging the rotor.

Freewheeling Unit

Since lift in a helicopter is provided by rotating airfoils, these airfoils must be free to rotate if the engine fails. The freewheeling unit automatically disengages the engine from the main rotor when engine rpm is less than main rotor rpm. This allows the main rotor and tail rotor to continue turning at normal in-flight speeds. The most common freewheeling unit assembly consists of a one-way sprag clutch located between the engine and main rotor transmission. This is usually in the upper pulley in a piston helicopter or mounted on the accessory gearbox in a turbine helicopter. When the engine is driving the rotor, inclined surfaces in the sprag clutch force rollers against an outer drum. This prevents the engine from exceeding transmission rpm. If the engine fails, the rollers move inward, allowing the outer drum to exceed the speed of the inner portion. The transmission can then exceed the speed of the engine. In this condition, engine speed is less than that of the drive system, and the helicopter is in an autorotative state.

Airplane Assembly and Rigging

The primary assembly of a type certificated aircraft is normally performed by the manufacturer at the factory. The assembly includes putting together the major components, such as the fuselage, empennage, wing sections, nacelles, landing gear, and installing the powerplant. Attached to the wing and empennage are primary flight control surfaces including ailerons, elevators, and rudder. Additionally, installation of auxiliary flight control surfaces may include wing flaps, spoilers, speed brakes, slats, and leading edge flaps.

The assembly of other aircraft outside of a manufacturer's facility is usually limited to smaller size and experimental amateur-built aircraft. Typically, after a major overhaul, repair, or alteration, the reassembly of an aircraft may include reattaching wings to the fuselage, balancing of and installation of flight control surfaces, installation of the landing gear, and installation of the powerplant(s).

Rebalancing of Control Surfaces

This section is presented for familiarization purposes only. Explicit instructions for the balancing of control surfaces are given in the manufacturer's service and overhaul manuals for the specific aircraft and must be followed closely.

Any time repairs on a control surface add weight fore or aft of the hinge center line, the control surface must be rebalanced. When an aircraft is repainted, the balance of the control surfaces must be checked. Any control surface that is out of balance is unstable and does not remain in a streamlined position during normal flight. For example, an aileron that is trailing-edge heavy moves down when the wing deflects upward, and up when the wing deflects downward. Such a condition can cause unexpected and violent maneuvers of the aircraft. In extreme cases, fluttering and buffeting may develop to a degree that could cause the complete loss of the aircraft.

Rebalancing a control surface concerns both static and dynamic balance. A control surface that is statically balanced is also dynamically balanced.

Static Balance

Static balance is the tendency of an object to remain stationary when supported from its own CG. There are two ways in which a control surface may be out of static balance. They are called underbalance and overbalance.

When a control surface is mounted on a balance stand, a downward travel of the trailing edge below the horizontal position indicates underbalance. Some manufacturers indicate this condition with a plus (+) sign. An upward movement of the trailing edge, above the horizontal position indicates overbalance. This is designated by a minus (–) sign. These signs show the need for more or less weight in the correct area to achieve a balanced control surface, as shown in *Figure 2-60*.

A tail-heavy condition (static underbalance) causes undesirable flight performance and is not usually allowed. Better flight operations are gained by nose-heavy static overbalance. Most manufacturers advocate the existence of nose-heavy control surfaces.

Dynamic Balance

Dynamic balance is that condition in a rotating body wherein all rotating forces are balanced within themselves so that no vibration is produced while the body is in motion. Dynamic balance as related to control surfaces is an effort to maintain balance when the control surface is submitted to movement on the aircraft in flight. It involves the placing of weights in the correct location along the span of the surfaces. The location of the weights are, in most cases, forward of the hinge center line.

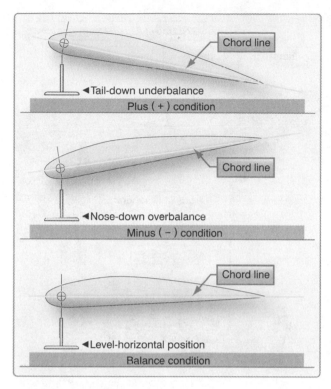

Figure 2-60. *Control surface static balance.*

Rebalancing Procedures

Repairs to a control surface or its tabs generally increase the weight aft of the hinge center line, requiring static rebalancing of the control surface system, as well as the tabs. Control surfaces to be rebalanced should be removed from the aircraft and supported, from their own points, on a suitable stand, jig, or fixture. *[Figure 2-61]*

Trim tabs on the surface should be secured in the neutral position when the control surface is mounted on the stand. The stand must be level and be located in an area free of air currents. The control surface must be permitted to rotate freely about the hinge points without binding. Balance condition is determined by the behavior of the trailing edge when the surface is suspended from its hinge points. Any excessive friction would result in a false reaction as to the overbalance or underbalance of the surface.

When installing the control surface in the stand or jig, a neutral position should be established with the chord line of the surface in a horizontal position. Use a bubble protractor to determine the neutral position before continuing balancing procedures. *[Figure 2-62]*

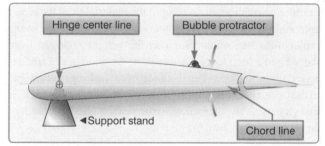

Figure 2-62. *Establishing a neutral position of the control surface.*

Figure 2-61. *Locally fabricated balancing fixture.*

Sometimes a visual check is all that is needed to determine whether the surface is balanced or unbalanced. Any trim tabs or other assemblies that are to remain on the surface during balancing procedures should be in place. If any assemblies or parts must be removed before balancing, they should be removed.

Rebalancing Methods

Several methods of balancing (rebalancing) control surfaces are in use by the various manufacturers of aircraft. The most common are the calculation method, scale method, and the balance beam method.

The calculation method of balancing a control surface has one advantage over the other methods in that it can be performed without removing the surface from the aircraft. In using the calculation method, the weight of the material from the repair area and the weight of the materials used to accomplish the repair must be known. Subtract the weight removed from the weight added to get the resulting net gain in the amount added to the surface. The distance from the hinge center line to the center of the repair area is then measured in inches. This distance must be determined to the nearest one-hundredth of an inch. *[Figure 2-63]*

Figure 2-64. *Balancing setup.*

Figure 2-63. *Calculation method measurement.*

The next step is to multiply the distance times the net weight of the repair. This results in an inch-pounds (in-lb) answer. If the in-lb result of the calculations is within specified tolerances, the control surface is considered balanced. If it is not within specified limits, consult the manufacturer's service manuals for the needed weights, material to use for weights, design for manufacture, and installation locations for addition of the weights.

The scale method of balancing a control surface requires the use of a scale that is graduated in hundredths of a pound. A support stand and balancing jigs for the surface are also required. *Figure 2-64* illustrates a control surface mounted for rebalancing purposes. Use of the scale method requires the removal of the control surface from the aircraft.

The balance beam method is used by the Cessna and Piper Aircraft companies. This method requires that a specialized tool be locally fabricated. The manufacturer's maintenance manual provides specific instructions and dimensions to fabricate the tool.

Once the control surface is placed on level supports, the weight required to balance the surface is established by moving the sliding weight on the beam. The maintenance manual indicates where the balance point should be. If the surface is found to be out of tolerance, the manual explains where to place weight to bring it into tolerance.

Aircraft manufacturers use different materials to balance control surfaces, the most common being lead or steel. Larger aircraft manufacturers may use depleted uranium because it has a heavier mass than lead. This allows the counterweights to be made smaller and still retain the same weight. Specific safety precautions must be observed when handling counterweights of depleted uranium because it is radioactive. The manufacturer's maintenance manual and service instructions must be followed and all precautions observed when handling the weights.

Aircraft Rigging

Aircraft rigging involves the adjustment and travel of movable flight controls which are attached to aircraft major surfaces, such as wings and vertical and horizontal stabilizers. Ailerons are attached to the wings, elevators are attached to the horizontal stabilizer, and the rudder is attached to the vertical stabilizer. Rigging involves setting cable tension, adjusting travel limits of flight controls, and setting travel stops.

In addition to the flight controls, rigging is also performed on various components to include engine controls, flight deck controls, and retractable landing gear component parts. Rigging also includes the safetying of the attaching hardware using various types of cotter pins, locknuts, or safety wire.

Rigging Specifications
Type Certificate Data Sheet

The Type Certificate Data Sheet (TCDS) is a formal description of an aircraft, engine, or propeller. It is issued by the Federal Aviation Administration (FAA) when the FAA determines that the product meets the applicable requirements for certification under 14 CFR. It lists the limitations and information required for type certification, including airspeed limits, weight limits, control surface movements, engine make and model, minimum crew, fuel type, thrust limits, rpm limits, etc., and the various components eligible for installation on the product.

Maintenance Manual

A maintenance manual is developed by the manufacturer of the applicable product and provides the recommended and acceptable procedures to be followed when maintaining or repairing that product. Maintenance personnel are required by regulation to follow the applicable instructions set forth by the manufacturer. The Limitations section of the manual lists "life limits" of the product or its components that must be complied with during inspections and maintenance.

Structural Repair Manual (SRM)

The structural repair manual is developed by the manufacturer's engineering department to be used as a guideline to assist in the repair of common damage to a specific aircraft structure. It provides information for acceptable repairs of specific sections of the aircraft.

Manufacturer's Service Information

Information from the manufacturer may be in the form of information bulletins, service instructions, service bulletins, service letters, etc., that the manufacturer publishes to provide instructions for product improvement. Service instructions may include a recommended modification or repair that precedes the issuance of an Airworthiness Directive (AD).

Service letters may provide more descriptive procedures or revise sections of the maintenance manuals. They may also include instructions for the installation and repair of optional equipment, not listed in the TCDS.

Airplane Assembly
Aileron Installation

The manufacturer's maintenance and illustrated parts book must be followed to ensure the correct procedures and hardware are being used for installation of the control surfaces. All of the control surfaces require specific hardware, spacers, and bearings be installed to ensure the surface does not jam or become damaged during movement. After the aileron is connected to the flight deck controls, the control system must be inspected to ensure the cables/push-pull rods are routed properly. When a balance cable is installed, check for correct attachment and operation to determine the ailerons are moving in the proper direction and opposite each other.

Flap Installation

The design, installation, and systems that operate flaps are as varied as the models of airplanes on which they are installed. As with any system on a specific aircraft, the manufacturer's maintenance manual and the illustrated parts book must be followed to ensure the correct procedures and parts are used. Simple flap systems are usually operated manually by cables and/or torque tubes. Typically, many of the smaller manufactured airplane designs have flaps that are actuated by torque tubes and chains through a gear box driven by an electric motor.

Empennage Installation

The empennage, consisting of the horizontal and vertical stabilizer, is not normally removed and installed, unless the aircraft was damaged. Elevators, rudders, and stabilators are rigged the same as any other control surface, using the instructions provided in the manufacturer's maintenance manuals.

Control Operating Systems
Cable Systems

There are various types of cable:

- Material—aircraft control cables are fabricated from carbon steel or stainless (corrosion resistant) steel. Additionally, some manufacturers use a nylon coated cable that is produced by extruding a flexible nylon coating over corrosion-resistant steel (CRES) cable. By adding the nylon coating to the corrosion resistant steel cable, it increases the service life by protecting the cable strands from friction wear, keeping dirt and grit out, and dampening vibration which can work-harden the wires in long runs of cable.

- Cable construction—the basic component of a cable is a wire. The diameter of the wire determines the total diameter of the cable. A number of wires are preformed into a helical or spiral shape and then formed into a strand. These preformed strands are laid around a straight center strand to form a cable.

- Cable designations—based on the number of strands and wires in each strand. The 7 × 19 cable is made up of seven strands of 19 wires each. Six of these strands are laid around the center strand. This cable is very flexible and is used in primary control systems and in other locations where operation over pulleys is frequent. The 7 × 7 cable consists of seven strands of seven wires each. Six of these strands are laid around the center strand. This cable is of medium flexibility and is used for trim tab controls, engine controls, and indicator controls. *[Figure 2-65]*

Figure 2-65. *Cable construction and cross-section.*

Types of control cable termination include:

- Woven splice—a hand-woven 5-tuck splice used on aircraft cable. The process is very time consuming and produces only about 75 percent of the original cable strength. The splice is rarely used except on some antique aircraft where the effort is made to keep all parts in their original configuration.

- Nicopress® process—a patented process using copper sleeves and may be used up to the full rated strength of the cable when the cable is looped around a thimble. *[Figure 2-66]* This process may also be used in place of the 5-tuck splice on cables up to and including ⅜-inch diameter. Whenever this process is used for cable splicing, it is imperative that the tools, instructions, and data supplied by Nicopress® be followed exactly to ensure the desired cable function and strength is attained. The use of sleeves that are fabricated of material other than copper requires engineering approval for the specific application by the FAA.

- Swage-type terminals—manufactured in accordance with Army-Navy (AN) and Military Standards (MS), are suitable for use in civil aircraft up to, and including, maximum cable loads. *[Figure 2-67]*

Figure 2-66. *Typical Nicopress® thimble-eye splice.*

Figure 2-67. *Swage-type terminal fittings.*

When swaging tools are used, it is imperative that all the manufacturer's instructions, including 'go' and 'no-go' dimensions, be followed exactly to avoid defective and inferior swaging. Compliance with all of the instructions should result in the terminal developing the full-rated strength of the cable. The following basic procedures are used when swaging terminals onto cable ends:

- Cut the cable to length, allowing for growth during swaging. Apply a preservative compound to the cable end before insertion into the terminal barrel. Measure the internal length of the terminal end/barrel of the fitting to determine the proper length of the cable to be inserted. Transfer that measurement to the end of the cable and mark it with a piece of masking tape wrapped around the cable. This provides a positive mark to ensure the cable did not slip during the swaging process.

    NOTE: Never solder the cable ends to prevent fraying since the solder greatly increases the tendency of the cable to pull out of the terminal.

- Insert the cable into the terminal approximately one inch and bend it toward the terminal. Then, push the cable end all the way into the terminal. The bending action puts a slight kink in the cable end and provides enough friction to hold the terminal in place until the swaging operation is performed. *[Figure 2-68]*

- Accomplish the swaging operation in accordance with the instructions furnished by the manufacturer of the swaging equipment.

- Inspect the terminal after swaging to determine that it is free of die marks and splits and is not out of round. Check the cable for slippage at the masking tape and for cut and broken wire strands.

- Using a go/no-go gauge supplied by the swaging tool manufacturer or a micrometer and swaging chart, check the terminal shank diameter for proper dimension. *[Figures 2-69 and 2-70]*

- Test the cable by proof-loading locally fabricated splices and newly installed swage terminal cable

Bend cable, then push into swaging position

Figure 2-68. *Insertion of cable into terminal.*

Figure 2-69. *Gauging terminal shank dimension after swaging.*

fittings for proper strength before installation. This is conducted by slowly applying a test load equal to 60 percent of the rated breaking strength of the cable listed in *Figure 2-71*.

Cable size (inches)	Wire strands	Before Swaging				After Swaging	
		Outside diameter	Bore diameter	Bore length	Swaging length	Minimum breaking strength (pounds)	Shank diameter *
1/16	7 x 7	0.160	0.078	1.042	0.969	480	0.138
3/32	7 x 7	0.218	0.109	1.261	1.188	920	0.190
1/8	7 x 19	0.250	0.141	1.511	1.438	2,000	0.219
5/32	7 x 19	0.297	0.172	1.761	1.688	2,800	0.250
3/16	7 x 19	0.359	0.203	2.011	1.938	4,200	0.313
7/32	7 x 19	0.427	0.234	2.261	2.188	5,600	0.375
1/4	7 x 19	0.494	0.265	2.511	2.438	7,000	0.438
9/32	7 x 19	0.563	0.297	2.761	2.688	8,000	0.500
5/16	7 x 19	0.635	0.328	3.011	2.938	9,800	0.563
3/8	7 x 19	0.703	0.390	3.510	3.438	14,400	0.625

*Use gauges in kit for checking diameters.

Figure 2-70. *Straight shank terminal dimensions.*

Nominal diameter of wire rope cable	Construction	Tolerance on diameter (plus only)	Allowable increase of diameter at cut end	Minimum Breaking Strength (Pounds)		
				MIL-W-83420 COMP A	MIL-W-83420 COMP B (CRES)	MIL-C-18375 (CRES)
INCHES		INCHES	INCHES	POUNDS	POUNDS	POUNDS
1/32	3 x 7	0.006	0.006	110	110	
3/64	7 x 7	0.008	0.008	270	270	
1/16	7 x 7	0.010	0.009	480	480	360
1/16	7 x 19	0.010	0.009	480	480	
3/32	7 x 7	0.012	0.010	920	920	700
3/32	7 x 19	0.012	0.010	1,000	920	
1/8	7 x 19	0.014	0.011	2,000	1,760	1,300
5/32	7 x 19	0.016	0.017	2,800	2,400	2,000
3/16	7 x 19	0.018	0.019	4,200	3,700	2,900
7/32	7 x 19	0.018	0.020	5,000	5,000	3,800
1/4	7 x 19	0.018	0.021	6,400	6,400	4,900
9/32	7 x 19	0.020	0.023	7,800	7,800	6,100
5/16	7 x 19	0.022	0.024	9,800	9,000	7,600
11/32	7 x 19	0.024	0.025	12,500		
3/8	7 x 19	0.026	0.027	14,400	12,000	11,000
7/16	6 x 19 IWRC	0.030	0.030	17,600	16,300	14,900
1/2	6 x 19 IWRC	0.033	0.033	22,800	22,800	19,300
9/16	6 x 19 IWRC	0.036	0.036	28,500	28,500	24,300
5/8	6 x 19 IWRC	0.039	0.039	35,000	35,000	30,100
3/4	6 x 19 IWRC	0.045	0.045	49,600	49,600	42,900
7/8	6 x 19 IWRC	0.048	0.048	66,500	66,500	58,000
1	6 x 19 IWRC	0.050	0.050	85,400	85,400	75,200
1 - 1/8	6 x 19 IWRC	0.054	0.054	106,400	106,400	
1 - 1/4	6 x 19 IWRC	0.057	0.057	129,400	129,400	
1 - 3/8	6 x 19 IWRC	0.060	0.060	153,600	153,600	
1 - 1/2	6 x 19 IWRC	0.062	0.062	180,500	180,500	

Figure 2-71. *Flexible cable construction.*

This load should be held for at least 3 minutes. Any testing of this type can be dangerous. Suitable guards should be placed over the cable during the test to prevent injury to personnel in the event of cable failure. If a proper test fixture is not available, the load test should be contracted out and performed by a properly equipped facility.

Cable Inspection

Aircraft cable systems are subject to a variety of environmental conditions and deterioration. Wire or strand breakage is easy to recognize visually. Other kinds of deterioration, such as wear, corrosion, and distortion, are not easily seen. Special attention should be given to areas where cables pass through battery compartments, lavatories, and wheel wells. These are prime areas for corrosion. Special attention should be given to critical fatigue areas. Those areas are defined as anywhere the cable runs over, under, or around a pulley, sleeve, or through a fairlead; or any section where the cable is flexed, rubbed,

or within 1 foot of a swaged-on fitting. Close inspection in these critical fatigue areas can be performed by rubbing a rag along the cable. If there are any broken strands, the rag snags on the cable. A more detailed inspection can be performed in areas that may be corroded or indicate a fatigue failure by loosing or removing the cable and bending it. This technique reveals internal broken strands not readily apparent from the outside. *[Figure 2-72]*

Cable System Installation
Cable Guides

Pulleys are used to guide cables and also to change the direction of cable movement. Pulley bearings are sealed and need no lubrication other than the lubrication done at the factory. Brackets fastened to the structure of the aircraft support the pulleys. Cables passing over pulleys are kept in place by guards. The guards are close fitting to prevent

Figure 2-72. *Cable inspection technique.*

jamming or to prevent the cables from slipping off when they slacken due to temperature variations. Pulleys should be examined to ensure proper lubrication; smooth rotation and freedom from abnormal cable wear patterns which can provide an indication of other problems in the cable system. *[Figure 2-73]*

Figure 2-73. *Pulley wear patterns.*

Fairleads may be made from a nonmetallic material, such as phenolic, or a metallic material, such as soft aluminum. The fairlead completely encircles the cable where it passes through holes in bulkheads or other metal parts. Fairleads are used to guide cables in a straight line through or between structural members of the aircraft. Fairleads should never deflect the alignment of a cable more than 3° from a straight line.

Pressure seals are installed where cables (or rods) move through pressure bulkheads. The seal grips tightly enough to prevent excess air pressure loss but not enough to hinder movement of the cable. Pressure seals should be inspected at regular intervals to determine that the retaining rings are

in place. If a retaining ring comes off, it may slide along the cable and cause jamming of a pulley. *[Figure 2-74]*

Travel Adjustment

Control surfaces should move a certain distance in either direction from the neutral position. These movements must be synchronized with the movement of the flight deck controls. The flight control system must be adjusted (rigged) to obtain these requirements. The tools for measuring surface travel primarily include protractors, rigging fixtures, contour templates, and rulers. These tools are used when rigging flight control systems to assure that the desired travel has been obtained. Generally speaking, the rigging consists of the following:

1. Positioning the flight control system in neutral and temporarily locking it there with rig pins or blocks;

2. Adjusting system cable tension and maintaining rudder, elevator, and ailerons in the neutral position; and

3. Adjusting the control stops to the aircraft manufacturer's specifications.

Cable Tension

For the aircraft to operate as it was designed, the cable tension for the flight controls must be correct. To determine the amount of tension on a cable, a tensiometer is used. When properly maintained, a tensiometer is 98 percent accurate. Cable tension is determined by measuring the amount of force needed to make an offset in the cable between two hardened steel blocks called anvils. A riser or plunger is pressed against the cable to form the offset. Several manufacturers make a variety of tensiometers, each type designed for different kinds of cable, cable sizes, and cable tensions. *[Figure 2-75]*

Rigging Fixtures

Rigging fixtures and templates are special tools (gauges) designed by the manufacturer to measure control surface travel. Markings on the fixture or template indicate desired control surface travel.

Tension Regulators

Cable tension regulators are used in some flight control systems because there is considerable difference in temperature expansion of the aluminum aircraft structure and the steel control cables. Some large aircraft incorporate tension regulators in the control cable systems to maintain a given cable tension automatically. The unit consists of a compression spring and a locking mechanism that allows the spring to make correction in the system only when the cable system is in neutral.

Figure 2-74. *Cable guides.*

Figure 2-75. *Tensiometer.*

Turnbuckles

A turnbuckle assembly is a mechanical screw device consisting of two threaded terminals and a threaded barrel. *[Figure 2-76]* Turnbuckles are fitted in the cable assembly for the purpose of making minor adjustments in cable length and for adjusting cable tension. One of the terminals has right-hand threads, and the other has left-hand threads. The barrel has matching right- and left-hand internal threads. The end of the barrel with the left-hand threads can usually be identified by a groove or knurl around that end of the barrel.

When installing a turnbuckle in a control system, it is necessary to screw both of the terminals an equal number of turns into the barrel. It is also essential that all turnbuckle terminals be screwed into the barrel until not more than three threads are exposed on either side of the turnbuckle barrel. After a turnbuckle is properly adjusted, it must be safetied. There are a number of methods to safety a turnbuckle and/ or other types of swaged cable ends that are satisfactory. A double-wrap safety wire method is preferred.

Some turnbuckles are manufactured and designed to accommodate special locking devices. A typical unit is shown in *Figure 2-77.*

Cable Connectors

In addition to turnbuckles, cable connectors are used in some systems. These connectors enable a cable length to be quickly connected or disconnected from a system. *Figure 2-78* illustrates one type of cable connector in use.

Spring-Back

With a control cable properly rigged, the flight control should hit its stops at both extremes prior to the flight deck control. The spring-back is the small extra push that is needed for the flight deck control to hit its mechanical stop.

Figure 2-76. *Typical turnbuckle assembly.*

Push Rods (Control Rods)

Push rods are used as links in the flight control system to give push-pull motion. They may be adjusted at one or both ends. *Figure 2-79* shows the parts of a push rod. Notice that it consists of a tube with threaded rod ends. An adjustable antifriction rod end, or rod end clevis, attaches at each end of the tube. The rod end, or clevis, permits attachment of the tube to flight control system parts. The checknut, when tightened, prevents the rod end or clevis from loosening. They may have adjustments at one or both ends.

The rods should be perfectly straight, unless designed to be otherwise. When installed as part of a control system, the assembly should be checked for correct alignment and free movement.

It is possible for control rods fitted with bearings to become disconnected because of failure of the peening that retains the

Figure 2-78. *Spring-type connector.*

ball races in the rod end. This can be avoided by installing the control rods so that the flange of the rod end is interposed between the ball race and the anchored end of the attaching pin or bolt as shown in *Figure 2-80*.

Figure 2-77. *Clip-type locking device and assembling in turnbuckle.*

Figure 2-79. *Push rod.*

Figure 2-80. *Attached rod end.*

Another alternative is to place a washer, having a larger diameter than the hole in the flange, under the retaining nut on the end of the attaching pin or bolt. This retains the rod on the bolt in the event of a bearing failure.

Torque Tubes

Where an angular or twisting motion is needed in a control system, a torque tube is installed. *Figure 2-81* shows how a torque tube is used to transmit motion in opposite directions. *[Figure 2-81]*

Cable Drums

Cable drums are used primarily in trim tab systems. As the trim tab control wheel is moved clockwise or counterclockwise, the cable drum winds or unwinds to actuate the trim tab cables. *[Figure 2-82]*

Rigging Checks

All aircraft assembly and rigging must be performed in accordance with the requirements prescribed by the specific aircraft and/or aircraft component manufacturer. Correctly following the procedures provides for proper operation of the components in regard to their mechanical and aerodynamic function and ensures the structural integrity of the aircraft. Rigging procedures are detailed in the applicable manufacturer's maintenance or service manuals and applicable structural repair manuals. Additionally, aircraft specification or type certificate data sheets (TCDS)

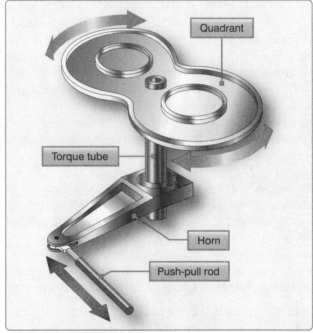

Figure 2-81. *Torque tube.*

also provide information regarding control surface movement and weight and balance limits.

The purpose of this section is to explain the methods of checking the relative alignment and adjustment of an aircraft's main structural components. It is not intended to imply that the procedures are exactly as they may be in a particular aircraft. When rigging an aircraft, always follow the procedures and methods specified by the aircraft manufacturer.

Structural Alignment

The position or angle of the main structural components is related to a longitudinal datum line parallel to the aircraft center line and a lateral datum line parallel to a line joining the wing tips. Before checking the position or angle of the main components, the aircraft must be jacked and leveled.

Figure 2-82. *Trim tab cable drum.*

Small aircraft usually have fixed pegs or blocks attached to the fuselage parallel to or coincident with the datum lines. A spirit level and a straight edge are rested across the pegs or blocks to check the level of the aircraft. This method of checking aircraft level also applies to many of the larger types of aircraft. However, the grid method is sometimes used on large aircraft. The grid plate is a permanent fixture installed on the aircraft floor or supporting structure. *[Figure 2-83]*

When the aircraft is to be leveled, a plumb bob is suspended from a predetermined position in the ceiling of the aircraft over the grid plate. The adjustments to the jacks necessary to level the aircraft are indicated on the grid scale. The aircraft is level when the plumb bob is suspended over the center point of the grid.

Certain precautions must be observed in all instances when jacking an aircraft. Normally, rigging and alignment checks should be performed in an enclosed hangar. If this cannot be accomplished, the aircraft should be positioned with the nose into the wind.

The weight and loading of the aircraft should be exactly as described in the manufacturer's manual. In all cases, the aircraft should not be jacked until it is determined that the maximum jacking weight (if applicable) specified by the manufacturer is not exceeded.

With a few exceptions, the dihedral and incidence angles of conventional modern aircraft cannot be adjusted. Some manufacturers permit adjusting the wing angle of incidence to correct for a wing-heavy condition. The dihedral and incidence angles should be checked after hard landings or after experiencing abnormal flight loads to ensure that the components are not distorted and that the angles are within the specified limits.

There are several methods for checking structural alignment and rigging angles. Special rigging boards that incorporate, or on which can be placed, a special instrument (spirit level or inclinometer) for determining the angle are used on some aircraft. On a number of aircraft, the alignment is checked using a transit and plumb bobs or a theodolite and sighting rods. The particular equipment to use is usually specified in the manufacturer's maintenance manual.

When checking alignment, a suitable sequence should be developed and followed to be certain that the checks are made at all the positions specified. The alignment checks specified usually include:

- Wing dihedral angle
- Wing incidence angle
- Verticality of the fin

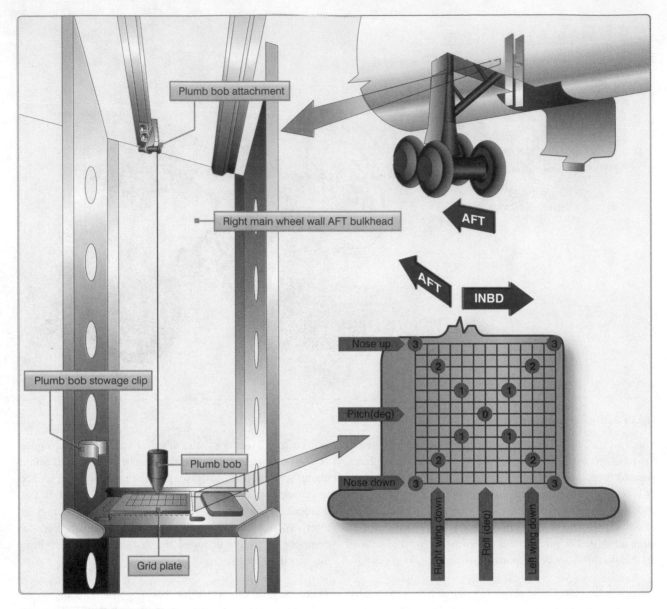

Figure 2-83. *Grid plate installed.*

- Engine alignment
- A symmetry check
- Horizontal stabilizer incidence
- Horizontal stabilizer dihedral

Checking Dihedral

The dihedral angle should be checked in the specified positions using the special boards provided by the aircraft manufacturer. If no such boards are available, a straight edge and a inclinometer can be used. The methods for checking dihedral are shown in *Figure 2-84*.

It is important that the dihedral be checked at the positions specified by the manufacturer. Certain portions of the wings or horizontal stabilizer may sometimes be horizontal or, on rare occasions, anhedral angles may be present.

Checking Incidence

Incidence is usually checked in at least two specified positions on the surface of the wing to ensure that the wing is free from twist. A variety of incidence boards are used to check the incidence angle. Some have stops at the forward edge, which must be placed in contact with the leading edge of the wing. Others are equipped with location pegs which fit into some specified part of the structure. The purpose in either case is to ensure that the board is fitted in exactly the position intended. In most instances, the boards are kept clear of the wing contour by short extensions attached to the board. A typical incidence board is shown in *Figure 2-85*.

Figure 2-84. *Checking dihedral.*

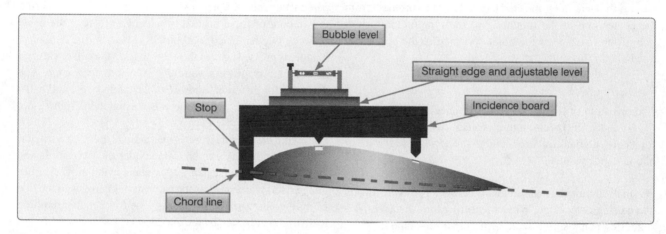

Figure 2-85. *A typical incidence board.*

When used, the board is placed at the specified locations on the surface being checked. If the incidence angle is correct, a inclinometer on top of the board reads zero, or within a specified tolerance of zero. Modifications to the areas where incidence boards are located can affect the reading. For example, if leading edge deicer boots have been installed, the position of a board having a leading edge stop is affected.

Checking Fin Verticality

After the rigging of the horizontal stabilizer has been checked, the verticality of the vertical stabilizer relative to the lateral datum can be checked. The measurements are taken from a given point on either side of the top of the fin to a given point on the left and right horizontal stabilizers. *[Figure 2-86]* The measurements should be similar within prescribed limits. When it is necessary to check the alignment of the rudder

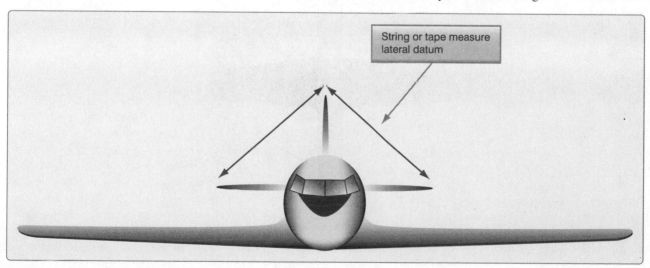

Figure 2-86. *Checking fin verticality.*

hinges, remove the rudder and pass a plumb bob line through the rudder hinge attachment holes. The line should pass centrally through all the holes. It should be noted that some aircraft have the leading edge of the vertical fin offset to the longitudinal center line to counteract engine torque.

Checking Engine Alignment

Engines are usually mounted with the thrust line parallel to the horizontal longitudinal plane of symmetry. However, this is not always true when the engines are mounted on the wings. Checking to ensure that the position of the engines, including any degree of offset is correct, depends largely on the type of mounting. Generally, the check entails a measurement from the center line of the mounting to the longitudinal center line of the fuselage at the point specified in the applicable manual. *[Figure 2-87]*

Symmetry Check

The principle of a typical symmetry check is illustrated in *Figure 2-87*. The precise figures, tolerances, and checkpoints for a particular aircraft are found in the applicable service or maintenance manual.

On small aircraft, the measurements between points are usually taken using a steel tape. When measuring long distances, it is suggested that a spring scale be used with the tape to obtain equal tension. A five-pound pull is usually sufficient.

On large aircraft, the positions at which the dimensions are to be taken are usually chalked on the floor. This is done by suspending a plumb bob from the checkpoints and marking the floor immediately under the point of each plumb bob. The measurements are then taken between the centers of each marking.

Cable Tension

When it has been determined that the aircraft is symmetrical and structural alignment is within specifications, the cable tension and control surface travel can be checked.

To determine the amount of tension on a cable, a tensiometer is used. When properly maintained, a tensiometer is 98 percent accurate. Cable tension is determined by measuring the amount of force needed to make an offset in the cable between two hardened steel blocks called anvils. A riser or plunger is pressed against the cable to form the offset. Several manufacturers make a variety of tensiometers, each type designed for different kinds of cable, cable sizes, and cable tensions. One type of tensiometer is illustrated in *Figure 2-88*.

Following the manufacturer's instructions, lower the trigger. Then, place the cable to be tested under the two anvils and close the trigger (move it up). Movement of the trigger pushes up the riser, which pushes the cable at right angles to the two clamping points under the anvils. The force that is required to do this is indicated by the dial pointer. As the sample chart beneath the illustration shows, different numbered risers are used with different size cables. Each riser has an identifying number and is easily inserted into the tensiometer.

Figure 2-87. *Typical measurements used to check aircraft symmetry.*

No. 1			Riser	No. 2		No. 3	
Diameter			Tension (lb)	5/32	3/16	7/32	1/4
1/16	3/32	1/8					
12	16	21	30	12	20		
19	23	29	40	17	26		
25	30	36	50	22	32		
31	36	43	60	26	37		
36	42	50	70	30	42		
41	48	57	80	34	47		
46	54	63	90	38	52		
51	60	69	100	42	56		
			110	46	60		
			120	50	64		

Figure 2-88. *Cable tensiometer and sample conversion chart.*

Included with each tensiometer is a conversion chart, which is used to convert the dial reading to pounds. The dial reading is converted to pounds of tension as follows. Using a No. 2 riser to measure the tension of a 5/32" diameter cable, a reading of 30 is obtained. The actual tension (see chart) of the cable is 70 lbs. Referring to the chart, also notice that a No. 1 riser is used with 1/16", 3/32", and 1/8" cable. Since the tensiometer is not designed for use in measuring 7/32" or 1/4" cable, no values are shown in the No. 3 riser column of the chart.

When actually taking a reading of cable tension in an aircraft, it may be difficult to see the dial. Therefore, a pointer lock is built in on the tensiometer. Push it in to lock the pointer, then remove the tensiometer from the cable and observe the reading. After observing the reading, pull the lock out and the pointer returns to zero.

Another variable that must be taken into account when adjusting cable tension is the ambient temperature of cable and the aircraft. To compensate for temperature variations, cable rigging charts are used when establishing cable tensions in flight control, landing gear, and other cable-operated systems. *[Figure 2-89]*

To use the chart, determine the size of the cable that is to be adjusted and the ambient air temperature. For example, assume that the cable size is 1/8" diameter, which is a 7-19 cable and the ambient air temperature is 85 °F. Follow the 85 °F line upward to where it intersects the curve for 1/8" cable. Extend a horizontal line from the point of intersection to the right edge of the chart. The value at this point indicates the tension (rigging load in pounds) to establish on the cable. The tension for this example is 70 pounds.

Control Surface Travel

In order for a control system to function properly, it must be correctly adjusted. Correctly rigged control surfaces move through a prescribed arc (surface-throw) and are synchronized with the movement of the flight deck controls. Rigging any control system requires that the aircraft manufacturer's instructions be followed as outlined in their maintenance manual.

Therefore, the explanations in this chapter are limited to the three general steps listed below:

1. Lock the flight deck control, bellcranks, and the control surfaces in the neutral position.

2. Adjust the cable tension, maintaining the rudder, elevators, or ailerons in the neutral position.

3. Adjust the control stops to limit the control surface travel to the dimensions given for the aircraft being rigged.

The range of movement of the controls and control surfaces should be checked in both directions from neutral. There are various tools used for measuring surface travel, including protractors, rigging fixtures, contour templates, and rulers. These tools are used when rigging flight control systems to ensure that the aircraft is properly rigged and the manufacturer's specifications have been complied with.

Rigging fixtures and contour templates are special tools (gauges) designed by the manufacturer to measure control surface travel. Markings on the fixture or template indicate desired control surface travel. In many instances, the aircraft manufacturer gives the travel of a particular control surface in degrees and inches. If the travel in inches is provided, a ruler can be used to measure surface travel in inches.

Protractors are tools for measuring angles in degrees. Various types of protractors are used to determine the travel of flight control surfaces. One protractor that can be used to measure

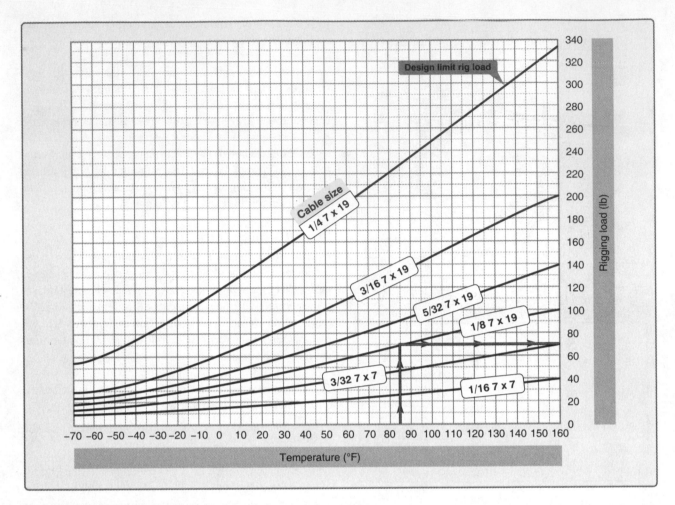

Figure 2-89. *Typical cable rigging chart.*

aileron, elevator, or wing flap travel is the universal propeller protractor shown in *Figure 2-90*.

This protractor is made up of a frame, disk, ring, and two spirit levels. The disk and ring turn independently of each other and of the frame. (The center spirit level is used to position the frame vertically when measuring propeller blade angle.) The center spirit level is used to position the disk when measuring control surface travel. A disk-to-ring lock is provided to secure the disk and ring together when the zero on the ring vernier scale and the zero on the disk degree scale align. The ring-to-frame lock prevents the ring from moving when the disk is moved. Note that they start at the same point and advance in opposite directions. A double 10-part vernier is marked on the ring.

The rigging of the trim tab systems is performed in a similar manner. The trim tab control is set to the neutral (no trim) position, and the surface tab is usually adjusted to streamline with the control surface. However, on some aircraft, the specifications may require that the trim tabs be offset a degree or two from streamline when in the neutral position. After

the tab and tab control are in the neutral position, adjust the control cable tension.

Pins, usually called rig pins, are sometimes used to simplify the setting of pulleys, levers, bellcranks, etc., in their neutral positions. A rig pin is a small metallic pin or clip. When rig pins are not provided, the neutral positions can be established by means of alignment marks, by special templates, or by taking linear measurements.

If the final alignment and adjustment of a system are correct, it should be possible to withdraw the rigging pins easily. Any undue tightness of the pins in the rigging holes indicates incorrect tensioning or misalignment of the system.

After a system has been adjusted, the full and synchronized movement of the controls should be checked. When checking the range of movement of the control surface, the controls must be operated from the flight deck and not by moving the control surfaces. During the checking of control surface travel, ensure that chains, cables, etc., have not reached

Figure 2-90. *Universal propeller protractor.*

the limit of their travel when the controls are against their respective stops.

Adjustable and nonadjustable stops (whichever the case requires) are used to limit the throw-range or travel movement of the ailerons, elevator, and rudder. Usually there are two sets of stops for each of the three main control surfaces. One set is located at the control surface, either in the snubber cylinders or as structural stops; the other, at the flight deck control. Either of these may serve as the actual limit stop. However, those situated at the control surface usually perform this function. The other stops do not normally contact each other, but are adjusted to a definite clearance when the control surface is at the full extent of its travel. These work as override stops to prevent stretching of cables and damage to the control system during violent maneuvers. When rigging control systems, refer to the applicable maintenance manual for the sequence of steps for adjusting these stops to limit the control surface travel.

Where dual controls are installed, they must be synchronized and function satisfactorily when operated from both positions.

Trim tabs and other tabs should be checked in a manner similar to the main control surfaces. The tab position indicator must be checked to see that it functions correctly. If jackscrews are used to actuate the trim tab, check to see

that they are not extended beyond the specified limits when the tab is in its extreme positions.

After determining that the control system functions properly and is correctly rigged, it should be thoroughly inspected to determine that the system is correctly assembled and operates freely over the specified range of movement.

Checking and Safetying the System

Whenever rigging is performed on any aircraft, it is good practice to have a second set of eyes inspect the control system to make certain that all turnbuckles, rod ends, and attaching nuts and bolts are correctly safetied.

As a general rule, all fasteners on an aircraft are safetied in some manner. Safetying is defined as securing by various means any nut, bolt, turnbuckle, etc., on the aircraft so that vibration does not cause it to loosen during operation.

Most aircraft manufacturers have a Standard Practices section in their maintenance manuals. These are the methods that should be used when working on a particular system of a specific aircraft. However, most standard aircraft hardware has a standard method of being safetied. The following information provides some of the most common methods used in aircraft safetying.

The most commonly used safety wire method is the double-twist, utilizing stainless steel or Monel wire in the .032 to .040-inch diameter range. This method is used on studs, cable turnbuckles, flight controls, and engine accessory attaching bolts. A single-wire method is used on smaller screws, bolts, and/or nuts when they are located in a closely spaced or closed geometrical pattern. The single-wire method is also used on electrical components and in places that are difficult to reach. *[Figure 2-91]*

Safety-of-flight emergency equipment, such as portable fire extinguishers, oxygen regulators, emergency valves, firewall shut-offs, and seals on first-aid kits, are safetied using a single copper wire (.020-inch diameter) or aluminum wire (.031-inch diameter). The wire on this emergency equipment is installed only to indicate the component is sealed or has not been actuated. It must be possible to break the wire seal by hand, without the use of any tools.

The use of safety wire pliers, or wire twisters, makes the job of safetying much easier on the mechanic's hands and produces a better finished product. *[Figure 2-92]*

The wire should have six to eight twists per inch of wire and be pulled taut while being installed. Where practicable, install the safety wire around the head of the fastener and

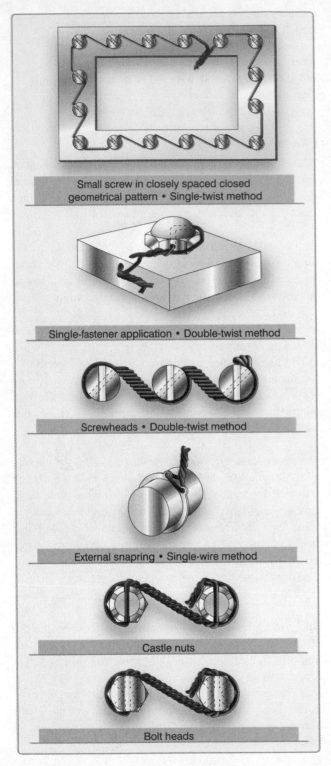

Small screw in closely spaced closed geometrical pattern • Single-twist method

Single-fastener application • Double-twist method

Screwheads • Double-twist method

External snapring • Single-wire method

Castle nuts

Bolt heads

Figure 2-91. *Double-wrap and single safety wire methods for nuts, bolts, and snap rings.*

twist it in such a manner that the loop of the wire is pulled close to the contour of the unit being safety wired, and in the direction that would have the tendency to tighten the fastener. *[Figure 2-93]*

Outer sleeve

To lock jaws

Pull knob to twist wire

Plier handles will spin when knob is pulled

Figure 2-92. *Use of safety-wire pliers or wire twisters.*

Cotter pins are used to secure such items as bolts, screws, pins, and shafts. They are used at any location where a turning or actuating movement takes place. The diameter of the cotter pin selected for any application should be the largest size that will fit consistent with the diameter of the cotter pin hole and/or the slots in the castellated nut. Cotter pins, like safety wire, should never be re-used on aircraft. *[Figure 2-94]*

Self-locking nuts are used in applications where they are not removed often. There are two types of self-locking nuts currently in use. One is all metal and the other has an insert, usually of fiber or nylon.

It is extremely important that the manufacturer's Illustrated Parts Book (IPB) be consulted for the correct type and grade of lock nut for various locations on the aircraft. The finish or plating color of the nut identifies the type of application and environment in which it can be used. For example, a cadmium-plated nut is gold in color and provides exceptionally good protection against corrosion, but should not be used in applications where the temperature may exceed 450 °F.

Repeated removal and installation causes the self-locking nut to lose its locking feature. They should be replaced when they are no longer capable of maintaining the minimum prevailing torque. *[Figure 2-95]*

| Example 1 | Example 2 | Example 3 | Example 4 | Example 5 |

Examples apply to all types of bolts, fillister-head screws, square-head plugs, and other similar parts which are wired so that the loosening tendency of either part is counteracted by tightening of the other part. The direction of twist from the second to the third unit is counterclockwise in examples to keep the loop in position against the head of the bolt. The wire entering the hole in the third unit is the lower wire, and by making a counterclockwise twist after it leaves the hole, the loop is secured in place around the head of that bolt.

Example shows methods for wiring various standard items.

NOTE: Wire may be wrapped over the unit rather than around it when wiring castellated nuts or on other items when there is clearance problem.

| Example 6 | Example 7 | Example 8 | Example 9 | Example 10 |

Correct application of single wire to closely spaced multiple group.

Fittings incorporating wire lugs shall be wired as shown in 7 and 8. Where no lock-wire lug is provided, wire should be applied as shown in 9 and 10 with caution being exerted to ensure that wire is wrapped tightly around the fitting.

| Example 6 | Example 10 |

Coupling nuts attached to straight connectors shall be wired as shown when hex is an integral part of the connector.

Coupling nuts on a tee shall be wired, as shown above, so that tension is always in the tightening direction.

Figure 2-93. *Examples of various fasteners and methods of safetying.*

Figure 2-94. *Securing hardware with cotter pins.*

Fine Thread Series	
Thread Size	Minimum Prevailing Torque
7/16 - 20	8 inch-pounds
1/2 - 20	10 inch-pounds
9/16 - 18	13 inch-pounds
5/8 - 18	18 inch-pounds
3/4 - 16	27 inch-pounds
7/8 - 14	40 inch-pounds
1 - 14	55 inch-pounds
1-1/8 - 12	73 inch-pounds
1-1/4 - 12	94 inch-pounds

Coarse Thread Series	
Thread Size	Minimum Prevailing Torque
7/16 - 14	8 inch-pounds
1/2 - 13	10 inch-pounds
9/16 - 12	14 inch-pounds
5/8 - 11	20 inch-pounds
3/4 - 10	27 inch-pounds
7/8 - 9	40 inch-pounds
1 - 8	51 inch-pounds
1-1/8 - 8	68 inch-pounds
1-1/4 - 8	68 inch-pounds

Figure 2-95. *Minimum prevailing torque values for reused self-locking unts.*

Lock washers may be used with bolts and machine screws whenever a self-locking nut or castellated nut is not applicable. They may be of the split washer spring type, or a multi-serrated internal or external star washer.

Pal nuts may be a second nut tightened against the first and used to force the primary nut thread against the bolt or screw thread. They may also be of the type that are made of stamped

spring steel and are to be used only once and replaced with new ones when removed.

Biplane Assembly and Rigging

Biplanes were some of the very first aircraft designs. The first powered heavier-than-air aircraft, the Wright brothers' Wright Flyer, successfully flown on December 17, 1903, was a biplane.

The first biplanes were designed with very thin wing sections and, consequently, the wing structure needed to be strengthened by external bracing wires. The biplane configuration allowed the two wings to be braced against one another, increasing the structural strength. When the assembly and rigging of a biplane is accomplished in accordance with the approved instructions, a stable airworthy aircraft is the result.

Whether assembling an early model vintage aircraft that may have been disassembled for repair and restoration, or constructing and assembling a new aircraft, the following are some basic alignment procedures to follow.

To start, the fuselage must be level, fore and aft and laterally. The aircraft usually has specific leveling points designated by the manufacturer or indicated on the plans. The fuselage should be blocked up off the landing gear so it is stable. A center line should be drawn on the floor the length of the fuselage and another line perpendicular to it at the firewall, for use as an additional alignment reference.

With the horizontal and vertical tail surfaces installed, the incident angle for the horizontal stabilizer should be set. The tail brace wires should be connected and tightened until the slack is removed. Alignment measurements should be checked as shown in *Figure 2-96.*

Install the elevator and rudder and clamp them in a neutral position. Verify the neutral position of the control stick and rudder pedals in the flight deck and secure them in order to simplify the connecting and final tensioning of the control cables.

If the biplane has a center section for the upper wing, it must be aligned as accurately as possible, because even the smallest error is compounded at the wing tip. Applicable cables and turnbuckles should be connected and the tension set as specified. *[Figure 2-97]* The stagger measurement can be checked as shown in *Figure 2-98.*

The lower wing sections should be individually attached to the fuselage and blocked up for support while the landing

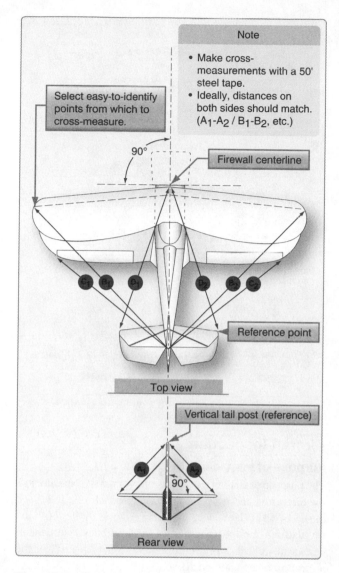

Figure 2-96. *Checking aircraft symmetry.*

Figure 2-97. *Center section alignment.*

wires are connected and adjusted to obtain the dihedral called for in the specifications or plans. *[Figure 2-99]*

Next, connect the outer "N" struts to the left and right sections of the lower wing. Now, the upper wing can be attached and the flying wires installed. The slave struts can be installed and the ailerons connected using the same alignment and adjustment procedures used for the elevator and rudder. The incidence angle can be checked, as shown in *Figure 2-100*.

Once this point is reached, it is a matter of measuring, checking angles, and adjusting the various components to obtain the overall aircraft symmetry and desired alignment, as shown in *Figure 2-96*.

Also, remember that care should be used when tightening the wing wires because extra stress can be inadvertently induced into the wings. Always loosen one wire before tightening the opposite wire. Flying and landing wires are typically set at about 600 pounds and tail brace wires at about 300 pounds of tension.

When convinced the aircraft is properly rigged, move away from it and take a good look at the finished product. Are the wings symmetrical? Does the dihedral look even? Is the tail section square with the fuselage? Are the wing attaching hardware, flying wires, and control cables safetied? And the final task, before the first flight, is to complete the maintenance record entries.

As with any aircraft maintenance or repair, the instructions and specifications from the manufacturer, or the procedures and recommendations found in the construction plans, should be the primary method to perform the assembly and rigging of the aircraft.

Figure 2-98. *Measuring stagger.*

Figure 2-99. *Measuring dihedral.*

Figure 2-100. *Checking incidence.*

Aircraft Inspection

Purpose of Inspection Programs

The purpose of an aircraft inspection program is to ensure that the aircraft is airworthy. The term airworthy is not defined in the 14 CFR. However, case law relating to the term and regulations for the issuance of a standard airworthiness certificate reveal two conditions that must be met for the aircraft to be considered airworthy:

1. *The aircraft must conform to its type certificate (TC).* Conformity to type design is considered attained when the aircraft configuration and the components installed are consistent with the drawings, specifications, and other data that are part of the TC, which includes any supplemental type certificate (STC) and field approved alterations incorporated into the aircraft.

2. *The aircraft must be in a condition for safe operation.* This refers to the condition of the aircraft relative to wear and deterioration (e.g., skin corrosion, window delamination/crazing, fluid leaks, and tire wear beyond specified limits).

When flight hours and calendar time are accumulated into the life of an aircraft, some components wear out and others deteriorate. Inspections are developed to find these items, and repair or replace them before they affect the airworthiness of the aircraft.

Perform an Airframe Conformity and Airworthiness Inspection

To establish conformity of an aircraft product, start with a Type Certificate Data Sheet (TCDS). This document is a formal description of the aircraft, the engine, or the propeller. It is issued by the Federal Aviation Administration (FAA) when they find that the product meets the applicable requirements for certification under 14 CFR.

The TCDS lists the limitations and information required for type certification of aircraft. It includes the certification basis and eligible serial numbers for the product. It lists airspeed limits, weight limits, control surface movements, engine make and models, minimum crew, fuel type, etc.; the horsepower and rpm limits, thrust limitations, size and weight for engines; and blade diameter, pitch, etc., for propellers. Additionally, it provides all the various components by make and model, eligible for installation on the applicable product.

A manufacturer's maintenance information may be in the form of service instructions, service bulletins, or service letters that the manufacturer publishes to provide instructions for product improvement or to revise and update maintenance manuals. Service bulletins are not regulatory unless:

1. All or a portion of a service bulletin is incorporated as part of an airworthiness directive.

2. The service bulletins are part of the FAA-approved airworthiness limitations section of the manufacturer's manual or part of the type certificate.

3. The service bulletins are incorporated directly or by reference into an FAA-approved inspection program, such as an approved aircraft inspection program (AAIP) or continuous aircraft maintenance program (CAMP).

4. The service bulletins are listed as an additional maintenance requirement in a certificate holder's operations specifications (Op Specs).

Airworthiness directives (ADs) are published by the FAA as amendments to 14 CFR part 39, section 39.13. They apply to the following products: aircraft, aircraft engines, propellers, and appliances. The FAA issues airworthiness directives when an unsafe condition exists in a product, and the condition is likely to exist or develop in other products of the same type design.

To perform the airframe conformity and verify the airworthiness of the aircraft, records must be checked and the aircraft inspected. The data plate on the airframe is inspected to verify its make, model, serial number, type certificate, or production certificate. Check the registration and airworthiness certificate to verify they are correct and reflect the "N" number on the aircraft.

Inspect aircraft records. Check current inspection status of aircraft, by verifying:

- The date of the last inspection and aircraft total time in service.

- The type of inspection and if it includes manufacturer's bulletins.

- The signature, certificate number, and the type of certificate of the person who returned the aircraft to service.

Identify if any major alterations or major repairs have been performed and recorded on an FAA Form 337, Major Repair and Alteration. If any STC have been added, check for flight manual supplements (FMS) in the Pilot's Operating Handbook (POH).

Check for a current weight and balance report, and the current equipment list, current status of airworthiness directives for airframe, engine, propeller, and appliances. Also, check the limitations section of the manufacturer's manual to verify the status of any life-limited components.

Obtain the latest revision of the airframe TCDS and use it as a verification document to inspect and ensure the correct engines, propellers, and components are installed on the airframe.

Required Inspections
Preflight

Preflight for the aircraft is described in the POH for that specific aircraft and should be followed with the same attention given to the checklists for takeoff, inflight, and landing checklists.

Periodic Maintenance Inspections:

Annual Inspection

With few exceptions, no person may operate an aircraft unless, within the preceding 12 calendar months, it has had an annual inspection in accordance with 14 CFR part 43 and was approved for return to service by a person authorized under section 43.7. (A certificated mechanic with an Airframe and Powerplant (A&P) rating must hold an inspection authorization (IA) to perform an annual inspection.) A checklist must be used and include as a minimum, the scope and detail of items (as applicable to the particular aircraft) in 14 CFR part 43, Appendix D.

100-hour Inspection

This inspection is required when an aircraft is operated under 14 CFR part 91 and used for hire, such as flight training. It is required to be performed every 100 hours of service in addition to the annual inspection. (The inspection may be performed by a certificated mechanic with an A & P rating.) A checklist must be used and as a minimum, the inspection must include the scope and detail of items (as applicable to the particular aircraft) in 14 CFR part 43, Appendix D.

Progressive Inspection

This inspection program can be performed under 14 CFR part 91, section 91.409(d), as an alternative to an annual inspection. However, the program requires that a written request be submitted by the registered owner or operator of an aircraft desiring to use a progressive inspection to the local FAA Flight Standards District Office (FSDO). It shall provide:

1. The name of a certificated mechanic holding an inspection authorization, a certificated airframe repair station, or the manufacturer of the aircraft to supervise or conduct the inspection.

2. A current inspection procedures manual available and readily understandable to the pilot and maintenance personnel containing in detail:

    •   An explanation of the progressive inspection, including the continuity of inspection responsibility, the making of reports, and the keeping of records and technical reference material.

    •   An inspection schedule, specifying the intervals in hours or days when routine and detailed inspections will be performed, and including instructions for exceeding an inspection interval by not more than 10 hours while en route, and for changing an inspection interval because of service experience.

    •   Sample routine and detailed inspection forms and instructions for their use.

    •   Sample reports and records and instructions for their use.

3. Enough housing and equipment for necessary disassembly and proper inspection of the aircraft.

4. Appropriate current technical information for the aircraft.

The frequency and detail of the progressive inspection program shall provide for the complete inspection of the aircraft within each 12 calendar months and be consistent with the manufacturer's recommendations and kind of operation in which the aircraft is engaged. The progressive inspection schedule must ensure that the aircraft will be airworthy at all times. A certificated A&P mechanic may perform a progressive inspection, as long as he or she is being supervised by a mechanic holding an Inspection Authorization.

If the progressive inspection is discontinued, the owner or operator must immediately notify the local FAA FSDO in writing. After discontinuance, the first annual inspection will be due within 12 calendar months of the last complete inspection of the aircraft under the progressive inspection.

Large Airplanes (over 12,500 lb)

Inspection requirements of 14 CFR part 91, section 91.409, to include paragraphs (e) and (f).

Paragraph (e) applies to large airplanes (to which 14 CFR part 125 is not applicable), turbojet multiengine airplanes, turbo propeller powered multiengine airplanes, and turbine-powered rotorcraft. Paragraph (f) lists the inspection programs that can be selected under paragraph (e).

The additional inspection requirements for these aircraft are placed on the operator because the larger aircraft typically are more complex and require a more detailed inspection program than is provided for in 14 CFR part 43, Appendix D.

An inspection program must be selected from one of the following four options by the owner or operator of the aircraft:

1. A continuous airworthiness inspection program that is part of a continuous airworthiness maintenance program currently in use by a person holding an air carrier operating certificate or an operating certificate issued under 14 CFR part 121 or 135.

2. An approved aircraft inspection program approved under 14 CFR part 135, section 135.419, and currently in use by a person holding an operating certificate issued under 14 CFR part 135.

3. A current inspection program recommended by the manufacturer.

4. Any other inspection program established by the registered owner or operator of the airplane or turbine-powered rotorcraft and approved by the FAA. This program must be submitted to the local FAA FSDO having jurisdiction of the area in which the aircraft is based. The program must be in writing and include at least the following information:

    (a) Instructions and procedures for the conduct of inspections for the particular make and model airplane or turbine-powered rotorcraft, including the necessary tests and checks. The instructions and procedures must set forth in detail the parts and areas of the airframe, engines, propellers, rotors, and appliances, including survival and emergency equipment, required to be inspected.

(b) A schedule for performing the inspections that must be performed under the program expressed in terms of the time in service, calendar time, number of system operations (cycles), or any combination of these.

This FAA approved owner/operator program can be revised at a future date by the FAA, if they find that revisions are necessary for the continued adequacy of the program. The owner/operator can petition the FAA within 30 days of notification to reconsider the notice to make changes.

Manufacturer's Inspection Program

This is a program developed by the manufacturer for their product. It is contained in the "Instructions for Continued Airworthiness" required under 14 CFR part 23, section 23.1529 and part 25, section 25.1529. It is in the form of a manual, or manuals as appropriate, for the quantity of data to be provided and including, but not limited to, the following content:

- A description of the airplane and its systems and installations, including its engines, propellers, and appliances.

- Basic information describing how the airplane components and systems are controlled and operated, including any special procedures and limitations that apply.

- Servicing information that covers servicing points, capacities of tanks, reservoirs, types of fluids to be used, pressures applicable to the various systems, lubrication points, lubricants to be used, equipment required for servicing, tow instructions, mooring, jacking, and leveling information.

- Maintenance instructions with scheduling information for the airplane and each component that provides the recommended periods at which they should be cleaned, inspected, adjusted, tested, and lubricated, and the degree of inspection and work recommended at these periods.

- The recommended overhaul periods and necessary cross references to the airworthiness limitations section of the manual.

- The inspection program that details the frequency and extent of the inspections necessary to provide for the continued airworthiness of the airplane.

- Diagrams of structural access plates and information needed to gain access for inspections when access plates are not provided.

- Details for the application of special inspection techniques, including radiographic and ultrasonic testing where such processes are specified.

- A list of special tools needed.

- An Airworthiness Limitations section that is segregated and clearly distinguishable from the rest of the document. This section must set forth—

  1. Each mandatory replacement time, structural inspection interval, and related structural inspection procedures required for type certification or approved under 14 CFR part 25, section 25.571.

  2. Each mandatory replacement time, inspection interval, related inspection procedure, and all critical design configuration control limitations approved under 14 CFR part 25, section 25.981, for the fuel tank system.

The Airworthiness Limitations section must contain a legible statement in a prominent location that reads: "The Airworthiness Limitations section is FAA approved and specifies maintenance required under 14 CFR part 43, sections 43.16 and part 91, section 91.403, unless an alternative program has been FAA-approved."

Any operator who wishes to adopt a manufacturers' inspection program should first contact their local FAA Flight Standards District Office, for further guidance.

Altimeter and Static System Inspections

Any person operating an airplane or helicopter in controlled airspace under instrument flight rules (IFR) must have had, within the preceding 24 calendar months, each static pressure system, each altimeter instrument, and each automatic pressure altitude reporting system tested and inspected and found to comply with 14 CFR part 43, Appendix E. Those test and inspections must be conducted by appropriately rated persons under 14 CFR.

Air Traffic Control (ATC) Transponder Inspections

Any person using an air traffic control (ATC) transponder must have had, within the preceding 24 calendar months, that transponder tested and inspected and found to comply with 14 CFR part 43, Appendix F. Additionally, following any installation or maintenance on an ATC transponder where data correspondence error could be introduced, the integrated system must be tested and inspected and found to comply with 14 CFR part 43, Appendix E, by an appropriately person under 14 CFR.

Emergency Locator Transmitter (ELT) Operational and Maintenance Practices in Accordance With Advisory Circular (AC) 91-44

This AC combined and updated several ACs on the subject of ELTs and receivers for airborne service.

Under the operating rules of 14 CFR part 91, most small U.S. registered civil airplanes equipped to carry more than one person must have an ELT attached to the airplane. 14 CFR part 91, section 91.207 defines the requirements of what type aircraft and when the ELT must be installed. It also states that an ELT that meets the requirements of Technical Standard Order (TSO)-C91 may not be used for new installations.* (This is the ELT that smaller general aviation aircraft have installed and they transmit on 121.5 MHz.)

The pilot in command of an aircraft equipped with an ELT is responsible for its operation and, prior to engine shutdown at the end of each flight, should tune the VHF receiver to 121.5 MHz and listen for ELT activations. Maintenance personnel are responsible for accidental activation during the actual period of their work.

Maintenance of ELTs is subject to 14 CFR part 43 and should be included in the required inspections. It is essential that the impact switch operation and the transmitter output be checked using the manufacturer's instructions. Testing of an ELT prior to installation or for maintenance reasons, should be conducted in a metal enclosure in order to avoid outside radiation by the transmitter. If this is not possible, the test should be conducted only within the first 5 minutes after any hour.

Manufacturers of ELTs are required to mark the expiration date of the battery, based on 50 percent of the useful life, on the outside of the transmitter. The batteries are required to be replaced on that date or when the transmitter has been in use for more than 1 cumulative hour. Water activated batteries, have virtually unlimited shelf life. They are not usually marked with an expiration date. They must be replaced after activation regardless of how long they were in service.

The battery replacement can be accomplished by a pilot on a portable type ELT that is readily accessible and can be removed and reinstalled in the aircraft by a simple operation. That would be considered preventive maintenance under 14 CFR part 43, section 43.3(g). Replacement batteries should be approved for the specific model of ELT and the installation performed in accordance with section 43.13.

AC 91-44 also contains additional information on:
- Airborne homing and alerting equipment for use with ELTs.
- Search and rescue responsibility.
- Alert and search procedures including various flight procedures for locating an ELT.
- The FAA Frequency Management Offices, for contacting by manufacturers when they are demonstrating and testing ELTs.

*The reason; as of January 31, 2009, the 121.5/243 MHz frequency will no longer be monitored by the COSPAS-SARSAT (Search and Rescue Satellite-Aided Tracking) search and rescue satellites.

NOTE: All new installations must be a 406 MHz digital ELT. It must meet the standards of TSO C126. When installed, the new 406 MHz ELT should be registered so that if the aircraft were to go down, search and rescue could take full advantage of the benefits the system offers. The digital circuitry of the 406 ELT can be coded with information about the aircraft type, base location, ownership, etc. This coding allows the search and rescue (SAR) coordinating centers to contact the registered owner or operator if a signal is detected to determine if the aircraft is flying or parked. This type of identification permits a rapid SAR response in the event of an accident, and will save valuable resources from a false alarm search.

Annual and 100-Hour Inspections
Preparation

An owner/operator bringing an aircraft into a maintenance facility for an annual or 100-hour inspection may not know what is involved in the process. This is the point at which the person who performs the inspection sits down with the customer to review the records and discuss any maintenance issues, repairs needed, or additional work the customer may want done. Moreover, the time spent on these items before starting the inspection usually saves time and money before the work is completed.

The work order describes the work that will be performed and the fee that the owner pays for the service. It is a contract that includes the parts, materials, and labor to complete the inspection. It may also include additional maintenance and repairs requested by the owner or found during the inspection.

Additional materials such as ADs, manufacturer's service bulletins and letters, and vendor service information must be researched to include the avionics and emergency equipment on the aircraft. The TCDS provides all the components eligible for installation on the aircraft.

The review of the aircraft records is one of the most important parts of any inspection. Those records provide the history of the aircraft. The records to be kept and how they are to be maintained are listed in 14 CFR part 91, section 91.417. Among those records that must be tracked are records of maintenance, preventive maintenance, and alteration, records of the last 100-hour, annual, or other required or approved inspections for the airframe, engine propeller, rotor, and appliances of an aircraft. The records must include:

- A description (or reference to data acceptable to the FAA) of the work performed.

- The date of completion of the work performed and the signature and certificate number of the person approving the aircraft for return to service.

- The total time in service and the current status of life-limited parts of the airframe, each engine, each propeller, and each rotor.

- The time since last overhaul of all items installed on the aircraft which are required to be overhauled on a specified time basis.

- The current inspection status of the aircraft, including the time since last inspection required by the program under which the aircraft and its appliances are maintained.

- The current status of applicable ADs including for each, the method of compliance, the AD number, and revision date. If the AD involves recurring action, the time and date when the next action is required.

- Copies of the forms prescribed by 14 CFR part 43, section 43.9, for each major alteration to the airframe and currently installed components.

The owner/operator is required to retain the records of inspection until the work is repeated, or for 1 year after the work is performed. Most of the other records that include total times and current status of life-limited parts, overhaul times, and AD status must be retained and transferred with the aircraft when it is sold.

14 CFR part 43, part 43.15, requires that each person performing a 100-hour or annual inspection shall use a checklist while performing the inspection. The checklist may be one developed by the person, one provided by the manufacturer of the equipment being inspected, or one obtained from another source. The checklist must include the scope and detail of the items contained in part 43, Appendix D.

The inspection checklist provided by the manufacturer is the preferred one to use. The manufacturer separates the areas to inspect such as engine, cabin, wing, empennage and landing gear. They typically list Service Bulletins and Service Letters for specific areas of the aircraft and the appliances that are installed.

Initial run-up provides an assessment to the condition of the engine prior to performing the inspection. The run-up should include full power and idle rpm, magneto operation, including positive switch grounding, fuel mixture check, oil and fuel pressure, and cylinder head and oil temperatures. After the engine run, check it for fuel, oil, and hydraulic leaks.

Following the checklist, the entire aircraft shall be opened by removing all necessary inspection plates, access doors, fairings, and cowling. The entire aircraft must then be cleaned to uncover hidden cracks or defects that may have been missed because of the dirt.

Following in order and using the checklist visually inspect each item, or perform the checks or tests necessary to verify the condition of the component or system. Record discrepancies when they are found. The entire aircraft should be inspected and a list of discrepancies be presented to the owner.

A typical inspection following a checklist, on a small single-engine airplane may include in part, as applicable:

- The fuselage for damage, corrosion, and attachment of fittings, antennas, and lights; for "smoking rivets" especially in the landing gear area indicating the possibility of structural movement or hidden failure.

- The flight deck and cabin area for loose equipment that could foul the controls; seats and seat belts for defects; windows and windshields for deterioration; instruments for condition, markings, and operation; flight and engine controls for proper operation.

- The engine and attached components for visual evidence of leaks; studs and nuts for improper torque and obvious defects; engine mount and vibration dampeners for cracks, deterioration, and looseness; engine controls for defects, operation, and safetying; the internal engine for cylinder compression; spark plugs for operation; oil screens and filters for metal particles or foreign matter; exhaust stacks and mufflers for leaks, cracks, and missing hardware; cooling baffles for deterioration, damage, and missing seals; and engine cowling for cracks and defects.

- The landing gear group for condition and attachment; shock absorbing devices for leaks and fluid levels; retracting and locking mechanism for defects, damage, and operation; hydraulic lines for leakage; electrical system for chafing and switches for operation; wheels and bearings for condition; tires for wear and cuts; and brakes for condition and adjustment.

- The wing and center section assembly for condition, skin deterioration, distortion, structural failure, and attachment.

- The empennage assembly for condition, distortion, skin deterioration, evidence of failure (smoking rivets), secure attachment, and component operation and installation.

- The propeller group and system components for torque and proper safetying; the propeller for nicks, cracks, and oil leaks; the anti-icing devices for defects and operation; and the control mechanism for operation, mounting, and restricted movement.

- The radios and electronic equipment for improper installation and mounting; wiring and conduits for improper routing, insecure mounting, and obvious defects; bonding and shielding for installation and condition; and all antennas for condition, mounting, and operation. Additionally, if not already inspected and serviced, the main battery inspected for condition, mounting, corrosion, and electrical charge.

- Any and all installed miscellaneous items and components that are not otherwise covered by this listing for condition and operation.

With the aircraft inspection checklist completed, the list of discrepancies should be transferred to the work order. As part of the annual and 100-hour inspections, the engine oil is drained and replaced because new filters and/or clean screens have been installed in the engine. The repairs are then completed and all fluid systems serviced.

Before approving the aircraft for return to service after the annual or 100-hour inspection, 14 CFR states that the engine must be run to determine satisfactory performance in accordance with the manufacturers recommendations. The run must include:

- Power output (static and idle rpm)

- Magnetos (for drop and switch ground)

- Fuel and oil pressure

- Cylinder and oil temperature

After the run, the engine is inspected for fluid leaks and the oil level is checked a final time before close up of the cowling.

With the aircraft inspection completed, all inspections plates, access doors, fairing and cowling that were removed, must be reinstalled. It is a good practice to visually check inside the inspection areas for tools, shop rags, etc., prior to close up. Using the checklist and discrepancy list to review areas that were repaired will help ensure the aircraft is properly returned to service.

Upon completion of the inspection, the records for each airframe, engine, propeller, and appliance must be signed off.

The record entry in accordance with 14 CFR part 43, section 43.11, must include the following information:

- The type inspection and a brief description of the extent of the inspection.

- The date of the inspection and aircraft total time in service.

- The signature, the certificate number, and kind of certificate held by the person approving or disapproving for return to service the aircraft, airframe, aircraft engine, propeller, appliance, component part, or portions thereof.

- For the annual and 100-hour inspection, if the aircraft is found to be airworthy and approved for return to service, enter the following statement: "I certify that this aircraft has been inspected in accordance with a (insert type) inspection and was determined to be in airworthy condition."

- If the aircraft is not approved for return to service because of necessary maintenance, noncompliance with applicable specifications, airworthiness directives, or other approved data, enter the following statement: "I certify that this aircraft has been inspected in accordance with a (insert type) inspection and a list of discrepancies and unairworthy items has been provided to the aircraft owner or operator."

If the owner or operator did not want the discrepancies and/or unairworthy items repaired at the location where the inspection was accomplished, they may have the option of flying the aircraft to another location with a Special Flight Permit (Ferry Permit). An application for a Special Flight Permit can be made at the local FAA FSDO.

Other Aircraft Inspection and Maintenance Programs

Aircraft operating under 14 CFR part 135, Commuter and On Demand, have additional rules for maintenance that must be followed beyond those in 14 CFR parts 43 and 91.

14 CFR part 135, section 135.411(a)(1) applies to aircraft that are type certificated for a passenger seating configuration, excluding any pilot seat, of nine seats or less. The additional rules include:

- Section 135.415—requires each certificate holder to submit a Service Difficulty Report, whenever they have an occurrence, failure, malfunction, or defect in an aircraft concerning the list detailed in this section of the regulation.

- Section 135.417—requires each certificate holder to mail or deliver a Mechanical Interruption Report, for occurrences in multi-engine aircraft, concerning unscheduled flight interruptions, and the number of propeller featherings in flight, as detailed in this section of the regulation.

- Section 135.421—requires each certificate holder to comply with the manufacturer's recommended maintenance programs, or a program approved by the FAA for each aircraft, engine, propeller, rotor, and each item of emergency required by 14 CFR part 135. This section also details requirements for single-engine IFR passenger-carrying operations.

- Section 135.422—this section applies to multi-engine airplanes and details requirements for Aging Airplane Inspections and Records review. It excludes airplanes in schedule operations between any point within the State of Alaska.

- Sections 135.423 through 135.443—the listed regulations are numerous and complex, and compliance is required; however, they are not summarized in this handbook.

Any certificated operator using aircraft with ten or more passenger seats must have the required organization and maintenance programs, along with competent and knowledgeable people to ensure a safe operation. It is their responsibility to know and comply with these and all other applicable Federal Aviation Regulations, and should contact their local FAA FSDO for further guidance.

The AAIP is an FAA-approved inspection program for aircraft of nine or less passenger seats operated under 14 CFR part 135. The AAIP is an operator developed program tailored to their particular needs to satisfy aircraft inspection requirements. This program allows operators to develop procedures and time intervals for the accomplishment of inspection tasks in accordance with the needs of the aircraft, rather than repeat all the tasks at each 100-hour interval.

The operator is responsible for the AAIP. The program must encompass the total aircraft; including all avionics equipment, emergency equipment, cargo provisions, etc. FAA Advisory Circular 135-10A provides detailed guidance to develop an approved aircraft inspection program. The following is a summary, in part, of elements that the program should include:

- A schedule of individual tasks (inspections) or groups of tasks, as well as the frequency for performing those tasks.

- Work forms designating those tasks with a signoff provision for each. The forms may be developed by the operator or obtained from another source.

- Instructions for accomplishing each task. These tasks must satisfy 14 CFR part 43, section 43.13(a), regarding methods, techniques, practices, tools, and equipment. The instructions should include adequate information in a form suitable for use by the person performing the work.

- Provisions for operator-developed revisions to referenced instructions should be incorporated in the operator's manual.

- A system for recording discrepancies and their correction.

- A means for accounting for work forms upon completion of the inspection. These forms are used to satisfy the requirements of 14 CFR part 91, section 91.417, so they must be complete, legible, and identifiable as to the aircraft and specific inspection to which they relate.

- Accommodation for variations in equipment and configurations between aircraft in the fleet.

- Provisions for transferring an aircraft from another program to the AAIP.

The development of the AAIP may come from one of the following sources:

- An adoption of an aircraft manufacturer's inspection in its entirety. However, many aircraft manufacturers' programs do not encompass avionics, emergency equipment, appliances, and related installations that must be incorporated into the AAIP. The inspection of these items and systems will require additions to the program to ensure they comply with the air carrier's operation specifications and as applicable to 14 CFR.

- A modified manufacturer's program. The operator may modify a manufacturer's inspection program to suit its needs. Modifications should be clearly identified and provide an equivalent level of safety to those in the manufacturer's approved program.

- An operator-developed program. This type of program is developed in its entirety by the operator. It should include methods, techniques, practices, and standards necessary for proper accomplishment of the program.

- An existing progressive inspection program (14 CFR part 91.409(d)) may be used as a basis for the development of an AAIP.

As part of this inspection program, the FAA strongly recommends that a Corrosion Protection Control Program and a supplemental structural inspection type program be included.

A program revision procedure should be included so that an evaluation of any revision can be made by the operator prior to submitting them to the FAA for approval.

Procedures for administering the program should be established. These should include: defining the duties and responsibilities for all personnel involved in the program, scheduling inspections, recording their accomplishment, and maintaining a file of completed work forms.

The operator's manual should include a section that clearly describes the complete program, including procedures for program scheduling, recording, and accountability for continuing accomplishment of the program. This section serves to facilitate administration of the program by the certificate holder and to direct its accomplishment by mechanics or repair stations. The operator's manual should include instructions to accomplish the maintenance/inspections tasks. It should also contain a list of the necessary tools and equipment needed to perform the maintenance and inspections.

The FAA FSDO will provide each operator with computer-generated Operations Specifications when they approve the program.

Continuous Airworthiness Maintenance Program (CAMP)

The definition of maintenance in 14 CFR part 1 includes inspection. The inspection program required for 14 CFR part 121 and part 135 air carriers is part of the Continuous Airworthiness Maintenance Program (CAMP). It is a complex program that requires an organization of experienced and knowledgeable aviation personnel to implement it.

The FAA has developed an Advisory Circular, AC 120-16D Air Carrier Aircraft Maintenance Programs, which explains the background as well as the FAA regulatory requirements for these programs. The AC applies to air carriers subject to 14 CFR parts 119, 121, and 135. For part 135, it applies only to aircraft type certificated with ten or more passenger seats.

Any person wanting to place their aircraft on this type of program should contact their local FAA FSDO for guidance.

Title 14 CFR part 125, section 125.247, Inspection Programs and Maintenance

This regulation applies to airplanes having a seating capacity of 20 or more passengers or a maximum payload capacity of 6,000 pounds or more. Inspection programs which may be approved for use under this 14 CFR part include, but are not limited to:

1. A continuous inspection program which is part of a current continuous airworthiness program approved for use by a certificate holder under 14 CFR part 121 or part 135;

2. Inspection programs currently recommended by the manufacturer of the airplane, airplane engines, propellers, appliances, or survival and emergency equipment; or

3. An inspection program developed by a certificate holder under 14 CFR part 125.

The airplane subject to this part may not be operated unless:

- The replacement times for life-limited parts specified in the aircraft type certificate data sheets, or other documents approved by the FAA are complied with;

- Defects disclosed between inspections, or as a result of inspection, have been corrected in accordance with 14 CFR part 43; and

- The airplane, including airframe, aircraft engines, propellers, appliances, and survival and emergency equipment, and their component parts, is inspected in accordance with an inspection program approved by the FAA. These inspections must include at least the following:

  o Instructions, procedures and standards for the particular make and model of airplane, including tests and checks. The instructions and procedures must set forth in detail the parts and areas of the airframe, aircraft engines, propellers, appliances, and survival and emergency equipment required to be inspected.

  o A schedule for the performance of the inspections that must be performed under the program, expressed in terms of the time in service, calendar time, number of system operations, or any combination of these.

  o The person used to perform the inspections required by 14 CFR part 125, must be authorized to perform maintenance under 14 CFR part 43. The airplane subject to part 125 may not be operated unless the installed engines have been maintained in accordance with the overhaul periods recommended by the manufacturer or a program approved by the FAA; the engine overhaul periods are specified in the inspection programs required by 14 CFR part 125, section 125.247.

Helicopter Inspections, Piston-Engine and Turbine-Powered

A piston-engine helicopter can be inspected in accordance with the scope and detail of 14 CFR part 43, Appendix D for an Annual Inspection. However, there are additional performance rules for inspections under 14 CFR part 43, section 43.15, requiring that each person performing an inspection under 14 CFR part 91 on a rotorcraft shall inspect these additional components in accordance with the maintenance manual or Instructions for Continued Airworthiness of the manufacturer concerned:

1. The drive shaft or similar systems

2. The main rotor transmission gear box for obvious defects

3. The main rotor and center section (or the equivalent area)

4. The auxiliary rotor

The operator of a turbine-powered helicopter can elect to have it inspected under 14 CFR part 91, section 91.409:

1. Annual inspection

2. 100-hour inspection

3. Applies to turbine-powered rotorcraft when operator elects to inspect in accordance with paragraph section 91.409(e), at which time (a) and (b) do not apply.

4. A progressive inspection

When performing any of the above inspections, the additional performance rules under 14 CFR part 43, section 43.15, for rotorcraft must be complied with.

Light-Sport Aircraft, Powered Parachute, and Weight-Shift Control Aircraft

When operating under an Experimental certificate issued for the purpose of Operating Light Sport Aircraft, these aircraft must have a condition inspection performed once every 12 months.

The inspection must be performed by a certificated repairman (light-sport aircraft) with a maintenance rating, an appropriately rated mechanic, or an appropriately rated repair station in accordance with the inspection procedures developed by the aircraft manufacturer or a person acceptable to the FAA. Additionally, if the aircraft is used for compensation or hire to tow a glider or unpowered ultralight vehicle, or is used by a person to conduct flight training for compensation or hire, it must have been inspected within the preceding 100 hours and returned to service in accordance with 14 CFR part 43, by one of the persons listed above.

Chapter 3
Aircraft Fabric Covering

General History

Fabric-covered aircraft play an important role in the history of aviation. The famous Wright Flyer utilized a fabric-covered wood frame in its design, and fabric covering continued to be used by many aircraft designers and builders during the early decades of production aircraft. The use of fabric covering on an aircraft offers one primary advantage: light weight. In contrast, fabric coverings have two disadvantages: flammability and lack of durability.

PK screw

Washer

Reinforcing tape

Fabric

Finely woven organic fabrics, such as Irish linen and cotton, were the original fabrics used for covering airframes, but their tendency to sag left the aircraft structure exposed to the elements. To counter this problem, builders began coating the fabrics with oils and varnishes. In 1916, a mixture of cellulose dissolved in nitric acid, called nitrate dope, came into use as an aircraft fabric coating. Nitrate dope protected the fabric, adhered to it well, and tautened it over the airframe. It also gave the fabric a smooth, durable finish when dried. The major drawback to nitrate dope was its extreme flammability.

To address the flammability issue, aircraft designers tried a preparation of cellulose dissolved in butyric acid called butyrate dope. This mixture protected the fabric from dirt and moisture, but it did not adhere as well to the fabric as nitrate dope. Eventually, a system combining the two dope coatings was developed. First, the fabric was coated with nitrate dope for its adhesion and protective qualities. Then, subsequent coats of butyrate dope were added. Since the butyrate dope coatings reduced the overall flammability of the fabric covering, this system became the standard fabric treatment system.

The second problem, lack of durability, stems from the eventual deterioration of fabric from exposure to the elements that results in a limited service life. Although the mixture of nitrate dope and butyrate dope kept out dirt and water, solving some of the degradation issue, it did not address deterioration caused by ultraviolet (UV) radiation from the sun. Ultraviolet radiation passed through the dope and degraded not only the fabric, but also the aircraft structure underneath. Attempts to paint the coated fabric proved unsuccessful, because paint does not adhere well to nitrate dope. Eventually, aluminum solids were added to the butyrate coatings. This mixture reflected the sun's rays, prevented harmful UV rays from penetrating the dope, and protected the fabric, as well as the aircraft structure.

Regardless of treatments, organic fabrics have a limited lifespan; cotton or linen covering on an actively flown aircraft lasts only about 5–10 years. Furthermore, aircraft cotton has not been available for over 25 years. As the aviation industry developed more powerful engines and more aerodynamic aircraft structures, aluminum became the material of choice. Its use in engines, aircraft frames, and coverings revolutionized aviation. As a covering, aluminum protected the aircraft structure from the elements, was durable, and was not flammable.

Although aluminum and composite aircraft dominate modern aviation, advances in fabric coverings continue to be made because gliders, home-built, and light sport aircraft, as well as some standard and utility certificated aircraft, are still

Figure 3-1. *Examples of aircraft produced using fabric skin.*

produced with fabric coverings. *[Figure 3-1]* The nitrate/butyrate dope process works well, but does not mitigate the short lifespan of organic fabrics. It was not until the introduction of polyester fabric as an aircraft covering in the 1950s that the problem of the limited lifespan of fabric covering was solved. The transition to polyester fabric had some problems because the nitrate and butyrate dope coating process is not as suitable for polyester as it is for organic fabrics. Upon initial application of the dopes to polyester, good adhesion and protection occurred; as the dopes dried, they would eventually separate from the fabric. In other words, the fabric outlasted the coating.

Eventually, dope additives were developed that minimized the separation problem. For example, plasticizers keep the dried dope flexible and nontautening dope formulas eliminate separation of the coatings from the fabric. Properly protected and coated, polyester lasts indefinitely and is stronger than cotton or linen. Today, polyester fabric coverings are the standard and use of cotton and linen on United States certificated aircraft has ceased. In fact, the long staple cotton from which grade-A cotton aircraft fabric is made is no longer produced in this country.

Re-covering existing fabric aircraft is an accepted maintenance procedure. Not all aircraft covering systems include the use of dope coating processes. Modern aircraft covering systems that include the use of nondope fabric treatments show no signs of deterioration even after decades of service. In this chapter, various fabrics and treatment systems are discussed, as well as basic covering techniques.

Fabric Terms

To facilitate the discussion of fabric coverings for aircraft, the following definitions are presented. *Figure 3-2* illustrates some of these items.

Figure 3-2. *Aircraft fabric nomenclature.*

- Warp—the direction along the length of fabric.
- Fill or weave—the direction across the width of the fabric.

- Count—the number of threads per inch in warp or filling.
- Ply—the number of yarns making up a thread.
- Bias—a cut, fold, or seam made diagonally to the warp or fill threads.
- Pinked edge—an edge which has been cut by machine or special pinking shears in a continuous series of Vs to prevent raveling.
- Selvage edge—the edge of cloth, tape, or webbing woven to prevent raveling.
- Greige—condition of polyester fabric upon completion of the production process before being heat shrunk.
- Cross coat—brushing or spraying where the second coat is applied 90° to the direction the first coat was applied. The two coats together make a single cross coat. *[Figure 3-3]*

Legal Aspects of Fabric Covering

When a fabric-covered aircraft is certificated, the aircraft manufacturer uses materials and techniques to cover the aircraft that are approved under the type certificate issued for that aircraft. The same materials and techniques must be used by maintenance personnel when replacing the aircraft fabric. Descriptions of these materials and techniques are in the manufacturer's service manual. For example, aircraft originally manufactured with cotton fabric can only be re-covered with cotton fabric unless the Federal Aviation Administration (FAA) approves an exception. Approved exceptions for alternate fabric-covering materials and procedures are common. Since polyester fabric coverings deliver performance advantages, such as lighter weight, longer life, additional strength, and lower cost, many older aircraft originally manufactured with cotton fabric have received approved alteration authority and have been re-covered with polyester fabric.

Figure 3-3. *A single cross coat is made up of two coats of paint applied 90° to each other.*

There are three ways to gain FAA approval to re-cover an aircraft with materials and processes other than those with which it was originally certificated. One is to do the work in accordance with an approved supplemental type certificate (STC). The STC must specify that it is for the particular aircraft model in question. It states in detail exactly what alternate materials must be used and what procedure(s) must be followed. Deviation from the STC data in any way renders the aircraft unairworthy. The holder of the STC typically sells the materials and the use of the STC to the person wishing to re-cover the aircraft.

The second way to gain approval to re-cover an aircraft with different materials and processes is with a field approval. A field approval is a one-time approval issued by the FAA Flight Standards District Office (FSDO) permitting the materials and procedures requested to replace those of the original manufacturer. A field approval request is made on FAA Form 337. A thorough description of the materials and processes must be submitted with proof that, when the alteration is completed, the aircraft meets or exceeds the performance parameters set forth by the original type certificate.

The third way is for a manufacturer to secure approval through the Type Certificate Data Sheet (TCDS) for a new process. For example, Piper Aircraft Co. originally covered their PA-18s in cotton. Later, they secured approval to recover their aircraft with Dacon fabric. Recovering an older PA-18 with Dacron in accordance with the TCDS would be a major repair, but not an alteration as the TCDS holder has current approval for the fabric.

Advisory Circular (AC) 43.13.1, Acceptable Methods, Techniques, and Practices—Aircraft Inspection and Repair, contains acceptable practices for covering aircraft with fabric. It is a valuable source of general and specific information on fabric and fabric repair that can be used on Form 337 to justify procedures requested for a field approval. Submitting an FAA Form 337 does not guarantee a requested field approval. The FSDO inspector considers all aspects of the procedures and their effect(s) on the aircraft for which the request is being filed. Additional data may be required for approval.

Title 14 of the Code of Federal Regulations (14 CFR) part 43, Appendix A, states which maintenance actions are considered major repairs and which actions are considered major alterations. Fabric re-covering is considered a major repair and FAA Form 337 is executed whenever an aircraft is re-covered with fabric. Appendix A also states that changing parts of an aircraft wing, tail surface, or fuselage when not listed in the aircraft specifications issued by the FAA is a major alteration. This means that replacing cotton fabric with polyester fabric is a major alteration. A properly executed FAA Form 337 also needs to be approved in order for this alteration to be legal.

FAA Form 337, which satisfies the documentation requirements for major fabric repairs and alterations, requires participation of an FAA-certificated Airframe and Powerplant (A&P) mechanic with an Inspection Authorization (IA) in the re-covering process. Often the work involved in re-covering a fabric aircraft is performed by someone else, but under the supervision of the IA (IA certification requires A&P certification). This typically means the IA inspects the aircraft structure and the re-cover job at various stages to be sure STC or field approval specifications are being followed. The signatures of the IA and the FSDO inspector are required on the approved FAA Form 337. The aircraft logbook also must be signed by the FAA-certificated A&P mechanic. It is important to contact the local FSDO before making any major repair or alteration.

Approved Materials

There are a variety of approved materials used in aircraft fabric covering and repair processes. In order for the items to legally be used, the FAA must approve the fabric, tapes, threads, cords, glues, dopes, sealants, coatings, thinners, additives, fungicides, rejuvenators, and paints for the manufacturer, the holder of an STC, or a field approval.

Fabric

A Technical Standard Order (TSO) is a minimum performance standard issued by the FAA for specified materials, parts, processes, and appliances used on civil aircraft. For example, TSO-15d, Aircraft Fabric, Grade A, prescribes the minimum performance standards that approved aircraft fabric must meet. Fabric that meets or exceeds the TSO can be used as a covering. Fabric approved to replace Grade-A cotton, such as polyester, must meet the same criteria. TSO-15d also refers to another document, Society of Automotive Engineers (SAE) Aerospace Material Specification (AMS) 3806D, which details properties a fabric must contain to be an approved fabric for airplane cloth. Lighter weight fabrics typically adhere to the specifications in TSO-C14b, which refers to SAE AMS 3804C.

When a company is approved to manufacture or sell an approved aviation fabric, it applies for and receives a Parts Manufacturing Approval (PMA). Currently, only a few approved fabrics are used for aircraft coverings, such as the polyester fabrics Ceconite™, Stits/Polyfiber™, and Superflite™. These fabrics and some of their characteristics are shown in *Figure 3-4*. The holders of the PMA for these fabrics have also developed and gained approval for the various tapes, chords, threads, and liquids that are used in the covering process. These approved materials, along with the procedures for using them, constitute the STCs for each particular fabric covering process. Only the approved materials can be used. Substitution of other materials is forbidden and results in the aircraft being unairworthy.

Approved Aircraft Fabrics					
Fabric Name or Type	Weight (oz/sq yd)	Count (warp x fill)	New Breaking Strength (lb) (warp, fill)	Minimum Deteriorated Breaking Strength	TSO
Ceconite™ 101	3.5	69 × 63	125,116	70% of original specified fabric	C-15d
Ceconite™ 102	3.16	60 × 60	106,113	70% of original specified fabric	C-15d
Polyfiber™ Heavy Duty-3	3.5	69 × 63	125,116	70% of original specified fabric	C-15d
Polyfiber™ Medium-3	3.16	60 × 60	106,113	70% of original specified fabric	C-15d
Polyfiber™ Uncertified Light	1.87	90 × 76	66,72	uncertified	
Superflight™ SF 101	3.7	70 × 51	80,130	70% of original specified fabric	C-15d
Superflight™ SF 102	2.7	72 × 64	90,90	70% of original specified fabric	C-15d
Superflight™ SF 104	1.8	94 × 91	75,55	uncertified	
Cotton (Reference Only)	4.5	80 × 84	80,80	56 lb/in (70% of New)	C-15d

Figure 3-4. *Approved fabrics for covering aircraft.*

Other Fabric Covering Materials

The following is an introduction to the supplemental materials used to complete a fabric covering job per manufacturer's instruction or a STC.

Anti-Chafe Tape

Anti-chafe tape is used on sharp protrusions, rib caps, metal seams, and other areas to provide a smoother surface to keep the fabric from being torn. It is usually self-adhesive cloth tape and is applied after the aircraft is cleaned, inspected, and primed, but before the fabric is installed.

Reinforcing Tape

Reinforcing tape is most commonly used on rib caps after the fabric covering is installed to protect and strengthen the area for attaching the fabric to the ribs.

Rib Bracing

Rib bracing tape is used on wing ribs before the fabric is installed. It is applied spanwise and alternately wrapped around a top rib cap and then a bottom rib cap progressing from rib to rib until all are braced. *[Figure 3-5]* Lacing the ribs in this manner holds them in the proper place and alignment during the covering process.

Surface Tape

Surface tape, made of polyester material and often pre-shrunk, is obtained from the STC holder. This tape, also known as finishing tape, is applied after the fabric is installed.

Figure 3-5. *Inter-rib bracing holds the ribs in place during the covering process.*

It is used over seams, ribs, patches, and edges. Surface tape can have straight or pinked edges and comes in various widths. For curved surfaces, bias cut tape is available, which allows the tape to be shaped around a radius.

Rib Lacing Cord

Rib lacing cord is used to lace the fabric to the wing ribs. It must be strong and applied as directed to safely transfer in-flight loads from the fabric to the ribs. Rib lacing cord is available in a round or flat cross-section. The round cord is easier to use than the flat lacing, but if installed properly, the flat lacing results in a smoother finish over the ribs.

Sewing Thread

Sewing of polyester fabric is rare and mostly limited to the creation of prefitted envelopes used in the envelope method covering process. When a fabric seam must be made with no structure underneath it, a sewn seam could be used. Polyester threads of various specifications are used on polyester fabric. Different thread is specified for hand sewing versus machine sewing. For hand sewing, the thread is typically a three-ply, uncoated polyester thread with a 15-pound tensile strength. Machine thread is typically four-ply polyester with a 10-pound tensile strength.

Special Fabric Fasteners

Each fabric covering job involves a method of attaching the fabric to wing and empennage ribs. The original manufacturer's method of fastening should be used. In addition to lacing the fabric to the ribs with approved rib lacing cord, special clips, screws, and rivets are employed on some aircraft. *[Figure 3-6]* The first step in using any of these fasteners is to inspect the holes into which they fit. Worn holes may have to be enlarged or re-drilled according to the manufacturer's instructions. Use of approved fasteners is mandatory. Use of unapproved fasteners can render the covering job unairworthy if substituted. Screws and rivets often incorporate the use of a plastic or aluminum washer. All fasteners and rib lacing are covered with finishing tape once installed to provide a smooth finish and airflow.

Grommets

Grommets are used to create reinforced drain holes in the aircraft fabric. Usually made of aluminum or plastic, they are glued or doped into place on the fabric surface. Once secured, a hole is created in the fabric through the center of the grommet. Often, this is done with a hot soldering pencil that also heat seals the fabric edge to prevent raveling. Seaplane grommets have a shield over the drain hole to prevent splashed water from entering the interior of the covered structure and to assist in siphoning out any water from within. *[Figure 3-7]* Drain holes using these grommets must be made before the grommets are put in place. Note that some drain holes do not require grommets if they are made through two layers of fabric.

Inspection Rings

The structure underneath an aircraft covering must be inspected periodically. To facilitate this in fabric-covered aircraft, inspection rings are glued or doped to the fabric. They provide a stable rim around an area of fabric that can be cut to allow viewing of the structure underneath. The fabric remains uncut until an inspection is desired. The rings are typically plastic or aluminum with an approximately three-inch inside diameter. Spring clip metal panel covers can be

Figure 3-6. *Clips, screws, rivets, or lace are used to attach the fabric to wing and empennage ribs.*

Figure 3-7. *Plastic, aluminum, and seaplane grommets are used to reinforce drain holes in the fabric covering.*

fitted to close the area once the fabric inside the inspection ring has been cut for access. *[Figure 3-8]* The location of the inspection rings are specified by the manufacturer. Additional rings are sometimes added to permit access to important areas that may not have been fitted originally with inspection access.

Primer

The airframe structure of a fabric covered aircraft must be cleaned, inspected, and prepared before the fabric covering process begins. The final preparation procedure involves

Figure 3-8. *Inspection rings and an inspection cover.*

priming the structure with a treatment that works with the adhesive and first coats of fabric sealant that are to be utilized. Each STC specifies which primers, or if a wood structure, which varnishes are suitable. Most often, two-part epoxy primers are used on metal structure and two-part epoxy varnishes are used on wood structure. Utilize the primer specified by the manufacturer's or STC's instructions.

Fabric Cement

Modern fabric covering systems utilize special fabric cement to attach the fabric to the airframe. There are various types of cement. *[Figure 3-9]* In addition to good adhesion qualities, flexibility, and long life, fabric cements must be compatible

Aircraft Covering Systems							
APPROVED PROPRIETARY PRODUCT NAME							
Covering System	STC #	Allowable Fabrics	Base	Cement	Filler	UV Block	Topcoats
Air-Tech	SA7965SW	Ceconite™ Poly-Fiber™ Superflite™	Urethane	UA-55	PFU 1020 PFU 1030	PFU 1020 PFU 1030	CHSM Color Coat
			Water		PFUW 1050	PFUW 1050	
Ceconite™/ Randolph System	SA4503NM	Ceconite™	Dope	New Super Seam	Nitrate Dope	Rand-O-Fill	Colored Butyrate Dope Ranthane Polyurethane
Stits/Poly-Fiber™	SA1008WE	Poly-Fiber™	Vinyl	Poly-tak	Poly-brush	Poly-spray	Vinyl Poly-tone, Aero-Thane, or Ranthane Polyurethane
Stewart System	SA01734SE	Ceconite™ Poly-Fiber™	Water-borne	EkoBond	EkoFill	EkoFlll	EkoPoly
Superflite™ • System1 • System VI	SA00478CH and others	Superflite™ 101,102	Dope	U-500	Dacproofer	SrayFil	Tinted Butyrate Dope
		Superflite™ 101,102	Urethane	U-500	SF6500	SF6500	Superflite™ CAB

Figure 3-9. *Current FAA-approved fabric covering processes.*

with the primer and the fabric sealer that are applied before and after the cement.

Fabric Sealer

Fabric sealer surrounds the fibers in the fabric with a protective coating to provide adhesion and keep out dirt and moisture. The sealer is the first coat applied to the polyester fabric after it is attached to the airframe and heat shrunk to fit snugly. Dope-based fabric coating systems utilize non-tautening nitrate dope as the primary fabric sealant. The application of tautening dope may cause the fabric to become too taut resulting in excess stress on the airframe that could damage it. Nondope coating systems use proprietary sealers that are also nontautening. *[Figure 3-9]*

Fillers

After the fabric sealer is applied, a filler is used. It is sprayed on in a number of cross coats as required by the manufacturer or the fabric covering process STC. The filler contains solids or chemicals that are included to block UV light from reaching the fabric. Proper fill coating is critical because UV light is the single most destructive element that causes polyester fabric to deteriorate. Dope-based processes use butyrate dope fillers while other processes have their own proprietary formulas. When fillers and sealers are combined, they are known as fabric primers. Aluminum pastes and powders, formerly added to butyrate dope to provide the UV protection, have been replaced by premixed formulas.

Topcoats

Once the aircraft fabric has been installed, sealed, and fill-coat protected, finishing or topcoats are applied to give the aircraft its final appearance. Colored butyrate dope is common in dope-based processes, but various polyurethane topcoats are also available. It is important to use the topcoat products and procedures specified in the applicable STC to complete an airworthy fabric re-covering job.

The use of various additives is common at different stages when utilizing the above products. The following is a short list of additional products that facilitate the proper application of the fabric coatings. Note again that only products approved under a particular STC can be used. Substitution of similar products, even though they perform the same basic function, is not allowed.

- A catalysts accelerates a chemical reaction. Catalysts are specifically designed for each product with which they are mixed. They are commonly used with epoxies and polyurethanes.

- A thinner is a solvent or mixture of solvents added to a product to give it the proper consistency for application, such as when spraying or brushing.

- A retarder is added to a product to slow drying time. Used mostly in dope processes and topcoats, a retarder allow more time for a sprayed coating to flow and level, resulting in a deeper, glossier finish. It is used when the working temperature is elevated slightly above the ideal temperature for a product. It also can be used to prevent blushing of a dope finish when high humidity conditions exist.

- An accelerators contains solvents that speed up the drying time of the product with which it is mixed. It is typically used when the application working temperature is below that of the ideal working temperature. It can also be used for faster drying when airborne contaminants threaten a coating finish.

- Rejuvenator, used on dope finishes only, contains solvents that soften coatings and allow them to flow slightly. Rejuvenator also contains fresh plasticizers that mix into the original coatings. This increases the overall flexibility and life of the coatings.

- Fungicide and mildewicide additives are important for organic fabric covered aircraft because fabrics, such as cotton and linen, are hosts for fungus and mildew. Since fungus and mildew are not concerns when using polyester fabric, these additives are not required. Modern coating formulas contain premixed anti-fungal agents, providing sufficient insurance against the problem of fungus or mildew.

Available Covering Processes

The covering processes that utilize polyester fabric are the primary focus of this chapter. The FAA-approved aircraft covering processes are listed in *Figure 3-9*. The processes can be distinguished by the chemical nature of the glue and coatings that are used. A dope-based covering process has been refined out of the cotton fabric era, with excellent results on polyester fabric. In particular, plasticizers added to the nitrate dope and butyrate dopes minimize the shrinking and tautening effects of the dope, establish flexibility, and allow esthetically pleasing tinted butyrate dope finishes that last indefinitely. Durable polyurethane-based processes integrate well with durable polyurethane topcoat finishes. Vinyl is the key ingredient in the popular Poly-Fiber covering system. Air Tech uses an acetone thinned polyurethane compatible system.

The most recent entry into the covering systems market is the Stewart Finishing System that uses waterborne technology to apply polyurethane coatings to the fabric. The glue used in the system is water-based and nonvolatile. The Stewart Finishing System is Environmental Protection Agency (EPA) compliant and STC approved. Both the Stewart and Air Tech systems operate with any of the approved polyester fabrics as stated in their covering system STCs.

All the modern fabric covering systems listed in *Figure 3-9* result in a polyester fabric covered aircraft with an indefinite service life. Individual preferences exist for working with the different approved processes. A description of basic covering procedures and techniques common to most of these systems follows later in this chapter.

Ceconite™, Polyfiber™, and Superflight™ are STC approved fabrics with processes used to install polyester fabric coverings. Two companies that do not manufacturer their own fabric have gained STC approval for covering accessories and procedures to be used with these approved fabrics. The STCs specify the fabrics and the proprietary materials that are required to legally complete the re-covering job.

The aircraft fabric covering process is a three-step process. First, select an approved fabric. Second, follow the applicable STC steps to attach the fabric to the airframe and to protect it from the elements. Third, apply the approved topcoat to give the aircraft its color scheme and final appearance.

Although Grade-A cotton can be used on all aircraft originally certificated to be covered with this material, approved aircraft cotton fabric is no longer available. Additionally, due to the shortcomings of cotton fabric coverings, most of these aircraft have been re-covered with polyester fabric. In the rare instance the technician encounters a cotton fabric covered aircraft that is still airworthy, inspection and repair procedures specified in AC 43.13-1, Chapter 2, Fabric Covering, should be followed.

Determining Fabric Condition—Repair or Recover?

Re-covering an aircraft with fabric is a major repair and should only be undertaken when necessary. Often a repair to the present fabric is sufficient to keep the aircraft airworthy. The original manufacturer's recommendations or the covering process STC should be consulted for the type of repair required for the damage incurred by the fabric covering. AC 43.13-1 also gives guidelines and acceptable practices for repairing cotton fabric, specifically when stitching is concerned.

Often a large area that needs repair is judged in reference to the overall remaining lifespan of the fabric on the aircraft. For example, if the fabric has reached the limit of its durability, it is better to re-cover the entire aircraft than to replace a large damaged area when the remainder of the aircraft would soon need to be re-covered.

On aircraft with dope-based covering systems, continued shrinkage of the dope can cause the fabric to become too tight. Overly tight fabric may require the aircraft to be re-covered

rather than repaired because excess tension on fabric can cause airframe structural damage. Loose fabric flaps in the wind during flight, affecting weight distribution and unduly stressing the airframe. It may also need to be replaced because of damage to the airframe.

Another reason to re-cover rather than repair occurs when dope coatings on fabric develop cracks. These cracks could expose the fabric beneath to the elements that can weaken it. Close observation and field testing must be used to determine if the fabrics are airworthy. If not, the aircraft must be re-covered. If the fabric is airworthy and no other problems exist, a rejuvenator can be used per manufacturer's instructions. This product is usually sprayed on and softens the coatings with very powerful solvents. Plasticizers in the rejuvenator become part of the film that fills in the cracks. After the rejuvenator dries, additional coats of aluminum-pigmented dope must be added and then final topcoats applied to finish the job. While laborious, rejuvenating a dope finish over strong fabric can save a great deal of time and money. Polyurethane-based finishes cannot be rejuvenated.

Fabric Strength

Deterioration of the strength of the present fabric covering is the most common reason to re-cover an aircraft. The strength of fabric coverings must be determined at every 100-hour and annual inspection. Minimum fabric breaking strength is used to determine if an aircraft requires re-covering.

Fabric strength is a major factor in the airworthiness of an aircraft. Fabric is considered to be airworthy until it deteriorates to a breaking strength less than 70 percent of the strength of the new fabric required for the aircraft. For example, if an aircraft was certificated with Grade-A cotton fabric that has a new breaking strength of 80 pounds, it becomes unairworthy when the fabric strength falls to 56 pounds, which is 70 percent of 80 pounds. If polyester fabric, which has a higher new breaking strength, is used to re-cover this same aircraft, it would also need to exceed 56 pounds breaking strength to remain airworthy.

In general, an aircraft is certified with a certain fabric based on its wing loading and its never exceed speed (V_{NE}). The higher the wing loading and V_{NE}, the stronger the fabric must be. On aircraft with wing loading of 9 pounds per square foot and over, or a V_{NE} of 160 miles per hour (mph) or higher, fabric equaling or exceeding the strength of Grade A cotton is required. This means the new fabric breaking strength must be at least 80 pounds and the minimum fabric breaking strength at which the aircraft becomes unairworthy is 56 pounds.

On aircraft with wing loading of 9 pounds per square foot or less, or a V_{NE} of 160 mph or less, fabric equaling or exceeding the strength of intermediate grade cotton is required. This means the new fabric breaking strength must be at least 65 pounds and the minimum fabric breaking strength at which the aircraft becomes unairworthy is 46 pounds.

Lighter weight fabric may be found to have been certified on gliders or sailplanes and may be used on many uncertificated aircraft or aircraft in the Light Sport Aircraft (LSA) category. For aircraft with wing loading less than 8 pounds per square foot or less, or V_{NE} of 135 mph or less, the fabric is considered unairworthy when the breaking strength has deteriorated to below 35 pounds (new minimum strength of 50 pounds). *Figure 3-10* summarizes these parameters.

How Fabric Breaking Strength is Determined

Manufacturer's instructions should always be consulted first for fabric strength inspection methodology. These instructions are approved data and may not require removal of a test strip to determine airworthiness of the fabric. In some cases, the manufacturer's information does not include any fabric inspection methods. It may refer the IA to AC 43.13-1, Chapter 2, Fabric Covering, which contains the approved FAA test strip method for breaking strength.

The test strip method for the breaking strength of aircraft covering fabrics uses standards published by the American Society for Testing and Materials (ASTM) for the testing of various materials. Breaking strength is determined by cutting a 1¼ inch by 4–6 inch strip of fabric from the aircraft covering. This sample should be taken from an area that is exposed to the elements—usually an upper surface. It is also wise to take the sample from an area that has a dark colored finish since this has absorbed more of the sun's UV rays and degraded faster. All coatings are then removed and the edges raveled to leave a 1-inch width. One end of the strip is clamped into a secured clamp and the other end is clamped such that a suitable container may be suspended from it. Weight is added to the container until the fabric breaks. The breaking strength of the fabric is equal to the weight of the lower clamp, the container, and the weight added to it. If the breaking strength is still in question, a sample should be sent to a qualified testing laboratory and breaking strength tests made in accordance with ASTM publication D5035.

Note that the fabric test strip must have all coatings removed from it for the test. Soaking and cleaning the test strip in methyl ethyl ketone (MEK) usually removes all the coatings.

Properly installed and maintained polyester fabric should give years of service before appreciable fabric strength degradation occurs. Aircraft owners often prefer not to have test strips cut out of the fabric, especially when the aircraft or the fabric covering is relatively new, because removal of a test strip damages the integrity of an airworthy component if the fabric passes. The test strip area then must be repaired, costing time and money. To avoid cutting a strip out of airworthy fabric, the IA makes a decision based on knowledge, experience, and available nondestructive techniques as to whether removal of a test strip is warranted to ensure that the aircraft can be returned to service.

An aircraft made airworthy under an STC is subject to the instructions for continued airworthiness in that STC. Most STCs refer to AC 43.13-1 for inspection methodology. Poly-Fiber™ and Ceconite™ re-covering process STCs contain their own instructions and techniques for determining fabric strength and airworthiness. Therefore, an aircraft covered under those STCs may be inspected in accordance with this information. In most cases, the aircraft can be approved for return to service without cutting a strip from the fabric covering.

The procedures in the Poly-Fiber™ and Ceconite™ STCs outlined in the following paragraphs are useful when inspecting any fabric covered aircraft as they add to the information gathered by the IA to determine the condition of the fabric. However, following these procedures alone on aircraft not re-covered under these STCs does not make the aircraft airworthy. The IA must add his or her own knowledge, experience, and judgment to make a final determination of the strength of the fabric and whether it is airworthy.

Fabric Performance Criteria				
IF YOUR PERFORMANCE IS. . .		FABRIC STRENGTH MUST BE. . .		
Loading	V_{NE} Speed	Type	New Breaking Strength	Minimum Breaking Strength
> 9 lb/sq ft	> 160 mph	≥ Grade A	> 80 lb	> 56
< 9 lb/sq ft	< 160 mph	≥ Intermediate	> 65 lb	> 46
< 8 lb/sq ft	< 135 mph	≥ Lightweight	> 50 lb	> 35

Figure 3-10. *Aircraft performance affects fabric selection.*

Exposure to UV radiation appreciably reduces the strength of polyester fabric and forms the basis of the Poly-Fiber™ and Ceconite™ fabric evaluation process. All approved covering systems utilize fill coats applied to the fabric to protect it from UV. If installed according to the STC, these coatings should be sufficient to protect the fabric from the sun and should last indefinitely. Therefore, most of the evaluation of the strength of the fabric is actually an evaluation of the condition of its protective coating(s).

Upon a close visual inspection, the fabric coating(s) should be consistent, contain no cracks, and be flexible, not brittle. Pushing hard against the fabric with a knuckle should not damage the coating(s). It is recommended the inspector check in several areas, especially those most exposed to the sun. Coatings that pass this test can move to a simple test that determines whether or not UV light is passing through the coatings.

This test is based on the assumption that if visible light passes through the fabric coatings, then UV light can also. To verify whether or not visible light passes through the fabric coating, remove an inspection panel from the wing, fuselage, or empennage. Have someone hold an illuminated 60-watt lamp one foot away from the exterior of the fabric. No light should be visible through the fabric. If no light is visible, the fabric has not been weakened by UV rays and can be assumed to be airworthy. There is no need to perform the fabric strip strength test. If light is visible through the coatings, further investigation is required.

Fabric Testing Devices

Mechanical devices used to test fabric by pressing against or piercing the finished fabric are not FAA approved and are used at the discretion of the FAA-certificated mechanic to form an opinion on the general fabric condition. Punch test accuracy depends on the individual device calibration, total coating thickness, brittleness, and types of coatings and fabric. If the fabric tests in the lower breaking strength range with the mechanical punch tester or if the overall fabric cover conditions are poor, then more accurate field tests may be made.

The test should be performed on exposed fabric where there is a crack or chip in the coatings. If there is no crack or chip, coatings should be removed to expose the fabric wherever the test is to be done.

The Maule punch tester, a spring-loaded device with its scale calibrated in breaking strength, tests fabric strength by pressing against it while the fabric is still on the aircraft. It roughly equates strength in pounds per square inch (psi) of resistance to breaking strength. The tester is pushed squarely against the fabric until the scale reads the amount of maximum allowable degradation. If the tester does not puncture the fabric, it may be considered airworthy. Punctures near the breaking strength should be followed with further testing, specifically the strip breaking strength test described above. Usually, a puncture indicates the fabric is in need of replacement.

A second type of punch tester, the Seyboth, is not as popular as the Maule because it punctures a small hole in the fabric when the mechanic pushes the shoulder of the testing unit against the fabric. A pin with a color-coded calibrated scale protrudes from the top of the tester and the mechanic reads this scale to determine fabric strength. Since this device requires a repair regardless of the strength of the fabric indicated, it is not widely used.

Seyboth and Maule fabric strength testers designed for cotton- and linen-covered aircraft, not to be used on modern Dacron fabrics. Mechanical devices, combined with other information and experience, help the FAA-certificated mechanic judge the strength of the fabric. *[Figure 3-11]*

Figure 3-11. *Seyboth and Maule fabric strength testers.*

General Fabric Covering Process

It is required to have an IA involved in the process of re-covering a fabric aircraft because re-covering is a major repair or major alteration. Signatures are required on FAA Form 337 and in the aircraft logbook. To ensure work progresses as required, the IA should be involved from the beginning, as well as at various stages throughout the process.

This section describes steps common to various STC and manufacturer covering processes, as well as the differences of some processes. To aid in proper performance of fabric covering and repair procedures, STC holders produce illustrated, step-by-step instructional manuals and videos that demonstrate the correct covering procedures. These training aids are invaluable to the inexperienced technician.

Since modern fabric coverings last indefinitely, a rare opportunity to inspect the aircraft exists during the re-covering process. Inspectors and owner-operators should use this opportunity to perform a thorough inspection of the aircraft before new fabric is installed.

The method of fabric attachment should be identical, as far as strength and reliability are concerned, to the method used by the manufacturer of the aircraft being recovered or repaired. Carefully remove the old fabric from the airframe, noting the location of inspection covers, drain grommets, and method of attachment. Either the envelope method or blanket method of fabric covering is acceptable, but a choice must be made prior to beginning the re-covering process.

Blanket Method vs. Envelope Method

In the blanket method of re-covering, multiple flat sections of fabric are trimmed and attached to the airframe. Certified greige polyester fabric for covering an aircraft can be up to 70 inches in width and used as it comes off the bolt. Each aircraft must be considered individually to determine the size and layout of blankets needed to cover it. A single blanket cut for each small surface (i.e., stabilizers and control surfaces) is common. Wings may require two blankets that overlap. Fuselages are covered with multiple blankets that span between major structural members, often with a single blanket for the bottom. Very large wings may require more than two blankets of fabric to cover the entire top and bottom surfaces. In all cases, the fabric is adhered to the airframe using the approved adhesives, following specific rules for the covering process being employed. *[Figure 3-12]*

Figure 3-12. *Laying out fabric during a blanket method re-covering job.*

An alternative method of re-covering, the envelope method, saves time by using precut and pre-sewn envelopes of fabric to cover the aircraft. The envelopes must be sewn with approved machine sewing thread, edge distance, fabric fold, etc., such as those specified in AC 43.13-1 or an STC. Patterns are made and fabric is cut and stitched so that each major surface, including the fuselage and wings, can be covered with a single, close-fitting envelope. Since envelopes are cut to fit, they are slid into position, oriented with the seams in the proper place, and attached with adhesive to the airframe. Envelope seams are usually located over airframe structure in inconspicuous places, such as the trailing edge structures and the very top and bottom of the fuselage, depending on airframe construction. Follow the manufacturer's or STC's instructions for proper location of the sewn seams of the envelope when using this method. *[Figure 3-13]*

Figure 3-13. *A custom-fit presewn fabric envelope is slid into position over a fuselage for the envelope method of fabric covering. Other than fitting, most steps in the covering process are the same as with the blanket covering method.*

Preparation for Fabric Covering Work

Proper preparation for re-covering a fabric aircraft is essential. First, assemble the materials and tools required to complete the job. The holder of the STC usually supplies a materials and tools list either separately or in the STC manual. Control of temperature, humidity, and ventilation is needed in the work environment. If ideal environmental conditions cannot be met, additives are available that compensate for this for most re-covering products.

Rotating work stands for the fuselage and wings provide easy, alternating access to the upper and lower surfaces while the job is in progress. *[Figure 3-14]* They can be used with sawhorses or sawhorses can be used alone to support the aircraft structure while working. A workbench or table, as well as a rolling cart and storage cabinet, are also recommended. *Figure 3-15* shows a well conceived fabric covering workshop. A paint spray booth for sprayed-on coatings and space to store components awaiting work is also recommended.

Figure 3-14. *Rotating stands and sawhorses facilitate easy access to top and bottom surfaces during the fabric covering process.*

Figure 3-15. *Some components of a work area for covering an aircraft with fabric.*

Many of the substances used in most re-covering processes are highly toxic. Proper protection must be used to avoid serious short and long term adverse health effects. Eye protection, a proper respirator, and skin protection are vital. As mentioned in the beginning of this chapter, nitrate dope is very flammable. Proper ventilation and a rated fire extinguisher should be on hand when working with this and other covering process materials. Grounding of work to prevent static electricity build-up may be required. All fabric re-covering processes also involve multiple coats of various products that are sprayed onto the fabric surface. Use of a high-volume, low-pressure (HVLP) sprayer is recommended. Good ventilation is needed for all of the processes.

Removal of Old Fabric Coverings

Removal of the old covering is the first step in replacing an aircraft fabric covering. Cut away the old fabric from the airframe with razor blades or utility knife. Care should be taken to ensure that no damage is done to the airframe. *[Figure 3-16]* To use the old covering for templates in transferring the location of inspection panels, cable guides, and other features to the new covering, the old covering should be removed in large sections. NOTE: any rib stitching fasteners, if used to attach the fabric to the structure, should be removed before the fabric is pulled free of the airframe. If fasteners are left in place, damage to the structure may occur during fabric removal.

Carefully cut away the fabric.

Gently roll the fabric back as the cut is made.

Figure 3-16. *Old fabric coverings are cut off in large pieces to preserve them as templates for locating various airframe features. Sharp blades and care must be used to avoid damaging the structure.*

Preparation of the Airframe Before Covering

Once the old fabric has been removed, the exposed airframe structure must be thoroughly cleaned and inspected. The IA collaborating on the job should be involved in this step of the process. Details of the inspection should follow the manufacturer's guidelines, the STC, or AC 43.13-1. All of the old adhesive must be completely removed from the airframe with solvent, such as MEK. A thorough inspection must be done and various components may be selected to be removed for cleaning, inspection, and testing. Any repairs that are required, including the removal and treatment of all corrosion, must be done at this time. If the airframe is steel tubing, many technicians take the opportunity to grit blast the entire airframe at this stage.

The leading edge of a wing is a critical area where airflow diverges and begins its laminar flow over the wing's surfaces, which results in the generation of lift. It is beneficial to have a smooth, regular surface in this area. Plywood leading edges must be sanded until smooth, bare wood is exposed. If oil or grease spots exist, they must be cleaned with naphtha or other specified cleaners. If there are any chips, indentations, or irregularities, approved filler may be spread into these areas and sanded smooth. The entire leading edge should be cleaned before beginning the fabric covering process.

To obtain a smooth finish on fabric-covered leading edges of aluminum wings, a sheet of felt or polyester padding may be applied before the fabric is installed. This should only be done with the material specified in the STC under which the technician is working. The approved padding ensures compatibility with the adhesives and first coatings of the covering process. When a leading edge pad is used, check the STC process instructions for permission to make a cemented fabric seam over the padding. *[Figure 3-17]*

When completely cleaned, inspected, and repaired, an approved primer, or varnish if it is a wood structure, should be applied to the airframe. This step is sometimes referred to as dope proofing. Exposed aluminum must first be acid etched. Use the product(s) specified by the manufacturer or in the STC to prepare the metal before priming. Two part epoxy primers and varnishes, which are not affected by the fabric adhesive and subsequent coatings, are usually specified. One part primers, such as zinc chromate and spar varnish, are typically not acceptable. The chemicals in the adhesives dissolve the primers, and adhesion of the fabric to the airframe is lost.

Sharp edges, metal seams, the heads of rivets, and any other feature on the aircraft structure that might cut or wear through the fabric should be covered with anti-chafe tape. As

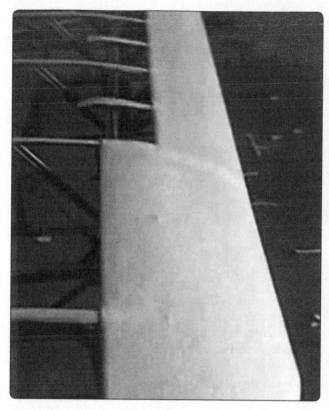

Figure 3-17. *The use of specified felt or padding over the wing leading edges before the fabric is installed results in a smooth regular surface.*

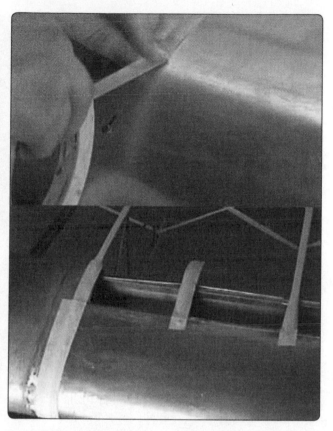

Figure 3-18. *Anti-chafe tape is applied to all features that might cut or wear through the fabric.*

described above, this cloth sticky-back tape is approved and should not be substituted with masking or any other kind of tape. Sometimes, rib cap strips need to have anti-chafe tape applied when the edges are not rounded over. *[Figure 3-18]*

Inter-rib bracing must also be accomplished before the fabric is installed. It normally does not have an adhesive attached to it and is wrapped only once around each rib. The single wrap around each rib is enough to hold the ribs in place during the covering process but allows small movements during the fabric shrinking process. *[Figure 3-19]*

Attaching Polyester Fabric to the Airframe

Inexperienced technicians are encouraged to construct a test panel upon which they can practice with the fabric and various substances and techniques to be used on the aircraft. It is often suggested to cover smaller surfaces first, such as the empennage and control surfaces. Mistakes on these can be corrected and are less costly if they occur. The techniques employed for all surfaces, including the wings and fuselage, are basically the same. Once dexterity has been established, the order in which one proceeds is often a personal choice.

When the airframe is primed and ready for fabric installation, it must receive a final inspection by an A&P with IA.

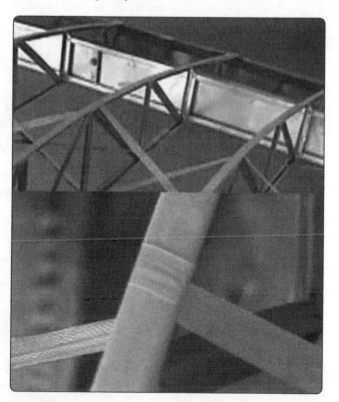

Figure 3-19. *Inter-rib bracing holds the ribs in place during the re-covering process.*

When approved, attachment of the fabric may begin. The manufacturer's or STC's instructions must be followed without deviation for the job to be airworthy. The following are the general steps taken. Each approved process has its own nuances.

Seams

During installation, the fabric is overlapped and seamed together. Primary concerns for fabric seams are strength, elasticity, durability, and good appearance. Whether using the blanket method or envelope method, position all fabric seams over airframe structure to which the fabric is to be adhered during the covering process, whenever possible. Unlike the blanket method, fabric seam overlap is predetermined in the envelope method. Seams sewn to the specifications in AC 43.13-1, the STC under which the work is being performed, or the manufacturer's instructions should perform adequately.

Most covering procedures for polyester fabric rely on doped or glued seams as opposed to sewn seams. They are simple and easy to make and provide excellent strength, elasticity, durability, and appearance. When using the blanket method, seam overlap is specified in the covering instructions and the FAA-certificated A&P mechanic must adhere to these specifications. Typically, a minimum of two to four inches of fabric overlap seam is required where ends of fabric are joined in areas of critical airflow, such as the leading edge of a wing. One to two inches of overlap is often the minimum in other areas.

When using the blanket method, options exist for deciding where to overlap the fabric for coverage. Function and the final appearance of the covering job should be considered. For example, fabric seams made on the wing's top surface of a high wing aircraft are not visible when approaching the aircraft. Seams on low wing aircraft and many horizontal stabilizers are usually made on the bottom of the wing for the same reason. *[Figure 3-20]*

Fabric Cement

A polyester fabric covering is cemented or glued to the airframe structure at all points where it makes contact. Special formula adhesives have replaced nitrate dope for adhesion in most covering processes. The adhesive (as well as all subsequent coating materials) should be mixed for optimum characteristics at the temperature at which the work is being performed. Follow the manufacturer's or STC's guidance when mixing.

To attach the fabric to the airframe, first pre-apply two coats of adhesive to the structure at all points the fabric is to contact it. (It is important to follow the manufacturer's or STC's guidance as all systems are different.) Allow these to dry. The fabric is then spread over the surface and clamped into position. It should not be pulled tighter than the relaxed but not wrinkled condition it assumes when lying on the structure. Clamps or clothespins are used to attach the fabric completely around the perimeter. The Stewart System STC does not need clamps because the glue assumes a tacky condition when precoated and dried. There is sufficient adhesion in the precoat to position the fabric.

The fabric should be positioned in all areas before undertaking final adhesion. Final adhesion often involves lifting the fabric,

Figure 3-20. *For appearance, fabric can be overlapped differently on high wing and low wing aircraft.*

applying a wet bed of cement, and pressing the fabric into the bed. An additional coat of cement over the top of the fabric is common. Depending on the process, wrinkles and excess cement are smoothed out with a squeegee or are ironed out. The Stewart System calls for heat activation of the cement precoats through the fabric with an iron while the fabric is in place. Follow the approved instructions for the covering method being used.

Fabric Heat Shrinking

Once the fabric has been glued to the structure, it can be made taut by heat shrinking. This process is done with an ordinary household iron that the technician calibrates before use. A smaller iron is also used to iron in small or tight places. *[Figure 3-21]* The iron is run over the entire surface of the fabric. Follow the instructions for the work being performed. Some processes avoid ironing seams while other processes begin ironing over structure and move to spanned fabric or visa-versa. It is important to shrink the fabric evenly. Starting on one end of a structure and progressing sequentially to the other end is not recommended. Skipping from one end to the other, and then to the middle, is more likely to evenly draw the fabric tight. *[Figure 3-22]*

The amount polyester fabric shrinks is directly related to the temperature applied. Polyester fabric can shrink nearly 5 percent at 250 °F and 10 percent at 350 °F. It is customary to shrink the fabric in stages, using a lower temperature first, before finishing with the final temperature setting. The first shrinking is used to remove wrinkles and excess fabric. The final shrinking gives the finished tautness desired. Each

Figure 3-21. *Irons used during the fabric covering process.*

process has its own temperature regime for the stages of tautening. Typically ranging from 225 °F to 350 °F, it is imperative to follow the process instructions. Not all fabric covering processes use the same temperature range and maximum temperature. Ensure irons are calibrated to prevent damage at high temperature settings.

Figure 3-22. *An example of a wing fabric ironing procedure designed to evenly taughten the fabric.*

Attaching Fabric to the Wing Ribs

Once the fabric has been tautened, covering processes vary. Some require a sealing coat be applied to the fabric at this point. It is usually put on by brush to ensure the fibers are saturated. Other processes seal the fabric later. Whatever the process, the fabric on wings must be secured to the wing ribs with more than just cement. The forces caused by the airflow over the wings are too great for cement alone to hold the fabric in place. As described in the materials section, screws, rivets, clips and lacing hold the fabric in place on manufactured aircraft. Use the same attach method as used by the original aircraft manufacturer. Deviation requires a field approval. Note that fuselage and empennage attachments may be used on some aircraft. Follow the methodology for wing rib lacing described below and the manufacturer's instructions for attach point locations and any possible variations to what is presented here.

Care must always be taken to identify and eliminate any sharp edges that might wear through the fabric. Reinforcing tape of the exact same width as the rib cap is installed before any of the fasteners. This approved sticky-back tape helps prevent the fabric from tearing. [Figure 3-23] Then, screws, rivets, and clips simply attach into the predrilled holes in the rib caps to hold the fabric to the caps. Rib lacing is a more involved process whereby the fabric is attached to the ribs with cord.

Holes are laid out and pre-punched through the skin as close to the rib caps as possible to accept the lacing cord. [Figure 3-24] This minimizes leverage the fabric could develop while trying to pull away from the structure and prevents tearing. The location of the holes is not arbitrary. The spacing between lacing holes and knots must adhere to manufacturer's instructions, if available. STC lacing guidance refers to manufacturer's instructions or to that shown on the chart in Figure 3-25 which is taken from AC 43.13-1. Notice that because of greater turbulence in the area of the propeller wash, closer spacing between the lacing is required there. This slipstream is considered to be the width of the propeller plus one additional rib. Ribs are normally laced from the leading edge to the trailing edge of the wing. Rib lacing is done with a long curved needle to guide the cord in and out of holes and through the depth of the rib. The knots are designed not to slip under the forces applied and can be made in a series out of a single strand of lacing. Stitching can begin at the leading edge or trailing edge. A square knot with a half hitch on each side is typically used for the first knot when lacing a rib. [Figure 3-26] This is followed by a series of modified seine knots until the final knot is made and secured with a half hitch. [Figure 3-27] Hidden modified seine knots are also used. These knots are placed below the fabric surface so only a single strand of lacing is visible across the rib cap. [Figure 3-28]

Figure 3-23. *Reinforcing tape the same width as the wing ribs is applied over all wing ribs.*

Figure 3-24. *A premarked location for a lacing hole, which is punched through the fabric with a pencil.*

Rib Lacing

There are two kinds of rib lacing cord. One has a round cross-section and the other flat. Which to use is a matter of preference based on ease of use and final appearance. Only approved rib lacing cord can be used. Unless a rib is unusually deep from top to bottom, rib lacing uses a single length of cord that passes completely through the wing from the upper surface to the lower surface thereby attaching the top and bottom skin to the rib simultaneously.

Structure and accessories within the wing may prevent a continuous lacing. Ending the lacing and beginning again can avoid these obstacles. Lacing that is not long enough to complete the rib may be ended and a new starting knot can be initiated at the next set of holes. The lacing can also be extended by joining it with another piece of lacing using the splice knot shown in Figure 3-29.

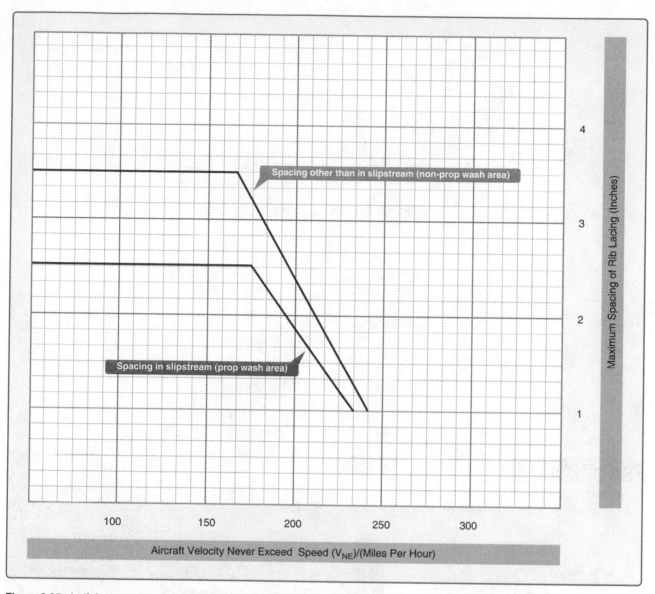

Figure 3-25. *A rib lacing spacing chart. Unless manufacturer data specifies otherwise, use the spacing indicated.*

Occasionally, lacing to just the rib cap is employed without lacing entirely through the wing and incorporating the cap on the opposite side. This is done where ribs are exceptionally deep or where through lacing is not possible, such as in an area where a fuel tank is installed. Changing to a needle with a tighter radius facilitates threading the lacing cord in these areas. Knotting procedures remain unchanged.

Technicians inexperienced at rib lacing should seek assistance to ensure the correct knots are being tied. STC holder videos are invaluable in this area. They present repeated close-up visual instruction and guidance to ensure airworthy lacing. AC 43.13-1, Chapter 2, Fabric Covering, also has in-depth instructions and diagrams as do some manufacturer's manuals and STC's instructions.

Figure 3-26. *A starter knot for rib lacing can be a square knot with a half hitch on each side.*

Modifield seine knot

Single loop lacing

Reinforcing tape (should be same width as the rib)

Capstrip

Reinforcing tape (should be same width as the rib)

Capstrip

AFT

Starting stitch

S

S

S/2

Wing leading edge fairing

S = Normal stitch spacing

Figure 3-27. *In this example of rib lacing, modified seine knots are used and shown above the fabric surface. Hidden modified seine knots are common. They are made so that the knots are pushed or pulled below the fabric surface.*

1 2 3 4

Pull tight

Push knot under fabric

Figure 3-28. *Hiding rib lacing knots below the fabric surface results in a smooth surface.*

Pull to tighten

Pull to tighten

Knot formed but not tightened

Load

Load

Knot completed

Figure 3-29. *The splice knot can be used to join two pieces of rib lacing cord.*

Rings, Grommets, and Gussets

When the ribs are laced and the fabric covering completely attached, the various inspection rings, drain grommets, reinforcing patches, and finishing tapes are applied. Inspection rings aid access to critical areas of the structure (pulleys, bell cranks, drag/anti-drag wires, etc.) once the fabric skin is in place. They are plastic or aluminum and normally cemented to the fabric using the approved cement and procedures. The area inside the ring is left intact. It is removed only when inspection or maintenance requires access through that ring. Once removed, preformed inspection panels are used to close the opening. The rings should be positioned as specified by the manufacturer. Lacking that information, they should be positioned as they were on the previous covering fabric. Additional rings should be installed by the technician if it is determined a certain area would benefit from access in the future. *[Figure 3-30]*

Figure 3-31. *Drain grommets cemented into place on the bottom side of a control surface.*

aircraft. Check the Airworthiness Directives (ADs) and Service Bulletins for the aircraft being re-covered to ensure required rings and grommets have been installed.

Cable guide openings, strut-attach fitting areas, and similar features, as well as any protrusions in the fabric covering, are reinforced with fabric gussets. These are installed as patches in the desired location. They should be cut to fit exactly around the feature they reinforce to support the original opening made in the covering fabric. *[Figure 3-32]* Gussets made to keep protrusions from coming through the fabric should overlap the area they protect. Most processes call for the gusset material to be preshrunk and cemented into place using the approved covering process cementing procedures.

Finishing Tapes

Finishing tapes are applied to all seams, edges, and over the ribs once all of the procedures above have been completed. They are used to protect these areas by providing smooth aerodynamic resistance to abrasion. The tapes are made from the same polyester material as the covering fabric. Use of lighter weight tapes is approved in some STCs. Preshrunk tapes are preferred because they react to exposure to the environment in the same way the as the fabric covering. This minimizes stress on the adhesive joint between the two. Straight edged and pinked tapes are available. The pinking provides greater surface area for adhesion of the edges and a smoother transition into the fabric covering. Only tapes approved in the STC under which work is being accomplished may be used to be considered airworthy.

Figure 3-30. *This inspection ring was cemented into place on the fabric covering. The approved technique specifies the use of a fabric overlay that is cemented over the ring and to the fabric.*

Water from rain and condensation can collect under the fabric covering and needs a way to escape. Drain grommets serve this purpose. There are a few different types as described in the materials section above. All are cemented into position in accordance with the approved process under which the work is being performed. Locations for the drain grommets should be ascertained from manufacturer's data. If not specified, AC 43.13-1 has acceptable location information. Each fabric covering STC may also give recommendations. Typically, drain grommets are located at the lowest part of each area of the structure (e.g., bottom of the fuselage, wings, empennage). *[Figure 3-31]* Each rib bay of the wings is usually drained with one or two grommets on the bottom of the trailing edge. Note that drain holes without grommets are sometimes approved in reinforced fabric.

It is possible that additional inspection rings and drain grommets have been specified after the manufacture of the

Finishing tapes from one to six inches in width are used. Typically, two inch tapes cover the rib lacing and fuselage seams. Wing leading edges usually receive the widest tape with four inches being common. *[Figure 3-33]* Bias cut tapes are often used to wrap around the curved surfaces of the airframe, such as the wing tips and empennage surface edges. They lay flat around the curves and do not require notching.

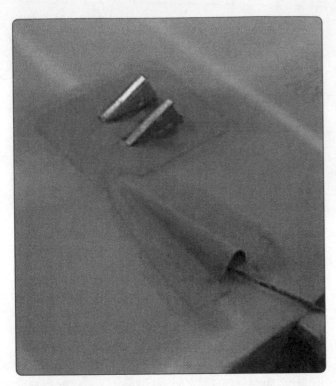

Figure 3-32. *A strut fitting and cable guide with reinforcing fabric gussets cemented in place.*

Figure 3-33. *Cement is brushed through a four-inch tape during installation over the fabric seam on a wing leading edge. Two-inch tapes cover the wing ribs and rib lacing.*

Finishing tapes are attached with the process adhesive or the nitrate dope sealer when using a dope-based process. Generally, all chordwise tapes are applied first followed by the span-wise tapes at the leading and trailing edges. Follow the manufacturer's STC or AC 43.13-1 instructions.

Coating the Fabric

The sealer coat in most fabric covering processes is applied after all finishing tapes have been installed unless it was applied prior to rib lacing as in a dope-based finishing process. This coat saturates and completely surrounds the

fibers in the polyester fabric, forming a barrier that keeps water and contaminants from reaching the fabric during its life. It is also used to provide adhesion of subsequent coatings. Usually brushed on in a cross coat application for thorough penetration, two coats of sealer are commonly used but processes vary on how many coats and whether spray coating is permitted.

With the sealer coats installed and dried, the next step provides protection from UV light, the only significant cause of deterioration of polyester fabric. Designed to prevent UV light from reaching the fabric and extend the life of the fabric indefinitely, these coating products, or fill coats, contain aluminum solids premixed into them that block the UV rays. They are sprayed on in the number of cross coats as specified in the manufacturer's STC or AC 43.13-1 instructions under which work is done. Two to four cross coats is common. Note that some processes may require coats of clear butyrate before the blocking formula is applied.

Fabric primer is a coating used in some approved covering processes that combines the sealer and fill coatings into one. Applied to fabric after the finishing tapes are installed, these fabric primers surround and seal the fabric fibers, provide good adhesion for all of the following coatings, and contain UV blocking agents. One modern primer contains carbon solids and others use chemicals that work similarly to sun block for human skin. Typically, two to four coats of fabric primer are sufficient before the top coatings of the final finish are applied. *[Figure 3-34]*

Figure 3-34. *Applying a primer with UV blocking by spraying cross coats.*

The FAA-certificated mechanic must strictly adhere to all instructions for thinning, drying times, sanding, and cleaning. Small differences in the various processes exist and what works in one process may not be acceptable and could ruin the finish of another process. STCs are issued on the basis of the holder having successfully proven the effectiveness of both the materials and the techniques involved.

When the fill coats have been applied, the final appearance of the fabric covering job is crafted with the application of various topcoats. Due to the chemical nature of the fill coating upon which topcoats are sprayed, only specified materials can be used for top coating to ensure compatibility. Colored butyrate dope and polyurethane paint finishes are most common. They are sprayed on according to instructions.

Once the topcoats are dry, the trim (N numbers, stripes, etc.) can be added. Strict observation of drying times and instructions for buffing and waxing are critical to the quality of the final finish. Also, note that STC instructions may include insight on finishing the nonfabric portions of the airframe to best match the fabric covering finish.

Polyester Fabric Repairs

Applicable Instructions

Repairs to aircraft fabric coverings are inevitable. Always inspect a damaged area to ensure the damage is confined to the fabric and does not involve the structure below. A technician who needs to make a fabric repair must first identify which approved data was used to install the covering that needs to be repaired. Consult the logbook where an entry and reference to manufacturer data, an STC, or a field approval possibly utilizing practices from AC 43.13-1 should be recorded. The source of approved data for the covering job is the same source of approved data used for a repair.

This section discusses general information concerning repairs to polyester fabric. Thorough instructions for repairs made to cotton covered aircraft can be found in AC 43.13-1. It is the responsibility of the holder of an STC to provide maintenance instructions for the STC alteration in addition to materials specifications required to do the job.

Repair Considerations

The type of repair performed depends on the extent of the damage and the process under which the fabric was installed. The size of the damaged area is often a reference for whether a patch is sufficient to do the repair or whether a new panel should be installed. Repair size may also dictate the amount of fabric-to-fabric overlap required when patching and whether finishing tapes are required over the patch. Many STC repair procedures do not require finishing tapes. Some repairs in AC 43.13-1 require the use of tape up to six inches wide.

While many cotton fabric repairs involve sewing, nearly all repairs of polyester fabric are made without sewing. It is possible to apply the sewing repair techniques outlined in AC 43.13-1 to polyester fabric, but they were developed primarily for cotton and linen fabrics. STC instructions for repairs to polyester fabric are for cemented repairs which most technicians prefer as they are generally considered easier than sewn repairs. There is no compromise to the strength of the fabric with either method.

Patching or replacing a section of the covering requires prepping the fabric area around the damage where new fabric is to be attached. Procedures vary widely. Dope-based covering systems tend toward stripping off all coatings to cement raw fabric to raw fabric when patching or seaming in a new panel. From this point, the coatings are reapplied and finished as in the original covering process. Some polyurethane-based coating processes require only a scuffing of the topcoat with sandpaper before adhering small patches that are then refinished. [Figure 3-35] Still, other processes may remove the topcoats and cement a patch into the sealer or UV blocking coating. In some repair processes, preshrunk fabric is used and in others, the fabric is shrunk after it is in place. Varying techniques and temperatures for shrinking and gluing the fabric into a repair also exist.

These deviations in procedures underscore the critical nature of identifying and strictly adhering to the correct instructions from the approved data for the fabric covering in need of repair. A patch or panel replacement technique for one covering system could easily create an unairworthy repair if used on fabric installed with a different covering process.

Large section panel repairs use the same proprietary adhesives and techniques and are only found in the instructions for the process used to install the fabric covering. A common technique for replacing any large damaged area is to replace all of the fabric between two adjacent structural members (e.g., two ribs, two longerons, between the forward and rear spars). Note that this is a major repair and carries with it the requirement to file an FAA Form 337.

Cotton-Covered Aircraft

You may encounter a cotton fabric-covered aircraft. In addition to other airworthiness criterion, the condition of the fabric under the finished surface is paramount as the cotton can deteriorate even while the aircraft is stored in a hanger. Inspection, in accordance with the manufacturer maintenance manual or AC 43.13-1, should be diligent. If the cotton covering is found to be airworthy, repairs to the fabric can be made under those specifications. This includes sewn-in and doped-in patches, as well as sewn-in and doped-in panel repairs. Due to the very limited number of airworthy aircraft that may still be covered with cotton, this handbook does not cover specific information on re-covering with cotton or

Figure 3-35. *A patch over this small hole on a polyurethane top coat is repaired in accordance with the repair instructions in the STC under which the aircraft was re-covered. It requires only a two-inch fabric overlap and scuffing into the top coat before cementing and refinishing. Other STC repair instructions may not allow this repair.*

cotton fabric maintenance and repair procedures. Refer to AC 43.13-1, Chapter 2, Fabric Covering, which thoroughly addresses these issues.

Fiberglass Coverings

References to fiberglass surfaces in aircraft covering STCs, AC 43.13-1, and other maintenance literature address techniques for finishing and maintaining this kind of surface. However, this is typically limited to fiberglass ray domes and fiberglass reinforced plywood surfaces and parts that are still in service. Use of dope-based processes on fiberglass is well established. Repair and apply coatings and finishes on fiberglass in accordance with manufacturer data, STC instructions, or AC 43.13-1 acceptable practices.

Chapter 4

Aircraft Metal Structural Repair

Aircraft Metal Structural Repair

The satisfactory performance of an aircraft requires continuous maintenance of aircraft structural integrity. It is important that metal structural repairs be made according to the best available techniques because improper repair techniques can pose an immediate or potential danger. The reliability of an aircraft depends on the quality of the design, as well as the workmanship used in making the repairs. The design of an aircraft metal structural repair is complicated by the requirement that an aircraft be as light as possible. If weight were not a critical factor, repairs could be made with a large margin of safety. In actual practice, repairs must be strong enough to carry all of the loads with the required factor of safety, but they must not have too much extra strength. For example, a joint that is too weak cannot be tolerated, but a joint that is too strong can create stress risers that may cause cracks in other locations.

As discussed in Chapter 3, Aircraft Fabric Covering, sheet metal aircraft construction dominates modern aviation. Generally, sheet metal made of aluminum alloys is used in airframe sections that serve as both the structure and outer aircraft covering, with the metal parts joined with rivets or other types of fasteners. Sheet metal is used extensively in many types of aircraft from airliners to single engine airplanes, but it may also appear as part of a composite airplane, such as in an instrument panel. Sheet metal is obtained by rolling metal into flat sheets of various thicknesses ranging from thin (leaf) to plate (pieces thicker than 6 mm or 0.25 inch). The thickness of sheet metal, called gauge, ranges from 8 to 30 with the higher gauge denoting thinner metal. Sheet metal can be cut and bent into a variety of shapes.

Damage to metal aircraft structures is often caused by corrosion, erosion, normal stress, and accidents and mishaps. Sometimes aircraft structure modifications require extensive structural rework. For example, the installation of winglets on aircraft not only replaces a wing tip with a winglet, but also requires extensive reinforcing of the wing structure to carry additional stresses.

Numerous and varied methods of repairing metal structural portions of an aircraft exist, but no set of specific repair patterns applies in all cases. The problem of repairing a damaged section is usually solved by duplicating the original part in strength, kind of material, and dimensions. To make a structural repair, the aircraft technician needs a good working knowledge of sheet metal forming methods and techniques. In general, forming means changing the shape by bending and forming solid metal. In the case of aluminum, this is usually done at room temperature. All repair parts are shaped to fit in place before they are attached to the aircraft or component.

Forming may be a very simple operation, such as making a single bend or a single curve, or it may be a complex operation, requiring a compound curvature. Before forming a part, the aircraft technician must give some thought to the complexity of the bends, the material type, the material thickness, the material temper, and the size of the part being fabricated. In most cases, these factors determine which forming method to use. Types of forming discussed in this chapter include bending, brake forming, stretch forming, roll forming, and spinning. The aircraft technician also needs a working knowledge of the proper use of the tools and equipment used in forming metal.

In addition to forming techniques, this chapter introduces the airframe technician to the tools used in sheet metal construction and repair, structural fasteners and their installation, how to inspect, classify, and assess metal structural damage, common repair practices, and types of repairs.

The repairs discussed in this chapter are typical of those used in aircraft maintenance and are included to introduce some of the operations involved. For exact information about specific repairs, consult the manufacturer's maintenance or structural repair manuals (SRM). General repair instructions are also discussed in Advisory Circular (AC) 43.13.1, Acceptable Methods, Techniques, and Practices—Aircraft Inspection and Repair.

Stresses in Structural Members

An aircraft structure must be designed so that it accepts all of the stresses imposed upon it by the flight and ground loads without any permanent deformation. Any repair made must accept the stresses, carry them across the repair, and then transfer them back into the original structure. These stresses are considered as flowing through the structure, so there must be a continuous path for them, with no abrupt changes in cross-sectional areas along the way. Abrupt changes in cross-sectional areas of aircraft structure that are subject to cycle loading or stresses result in a stress concentration that may induce fatigue cracking and eventual failure. A scratch or gouge in the surface of a highly stressed piece of metal causes a stress concentration at the point of damage and could lead to failure of the part. Forces acting on an aircraft, whether it is on the ground or in flight, introduce pulling, pushing, or twisting forces within the various members of the aircraft structure. While the aircraft is on the ground, the weight of the wings, fuselage, engines, and empennage causes forces to act downward on the wing and stabilizer tips, along the spars and stringers, and on the bulkheads and formers. These forces are passed from member to member causing bending, twisting, pulling, compression, and shearing forces.

As the aircraft takes off, most of the forces in the fuselage continue to act in the same direction; because of the motion of the aircraft, they increase in intensity. The forces on the wingtips and the wing surfaces, however, reverse direction; instead of being downward forces of weight, they become upward forces of lift. The forces of lift are exerted first against the skin and stringers, then are passed on to the ribs, and finally are transmitted through the spars to be distributed through the fuselage. The wings bend upward at their ends and may flutter slightly during flight. This wing bending cannot be ignored by the manufacturer in the original design and construction and cannot be ignored during maintenance. It is surprising how an aircraft structure composed of structural members and skin rigidly riveted or bolted together, such as a wing, can bend or act so much like a leaf spring.

The six types of stress in an aircraft are described as tension, compression, shear, bearing, bending, and torsion (or twisting). The first four are commonly called basic stresses; the last two, combination stresses. Stresses usually act in combinations rather than singly. *[Figure 4-1]*

Tension

Tension is the stress that resists a force that tends to pull apart. The engine pulls the aircraft forward, but air resistance tries to hold it back. The result is tension, which tends to stretch the aircraft. The tensile strength of a material is measured in pounds per square inch (psi) and is calculated by dividing the load (in pounds) required to pull the material apart by its cross-sectional area (in square inches).

The strength of a member in tension is determined on the basis of its gross area (or total area), but calculations

Figure 4-1. *Stresses in aircraft structures.*

involving tension must take into consideration the net area of the member. Net area is defined as the gross area minus that removed by drilling holes or by making other changes in the section. Placing rivets or bolts in holes makes no appreciable difference in added strength, as the rivets or bolts will not transfer tensional loads across holes in which they are inserted.

Compression

Compression, the stress that resists a crushing force, tends to shorten or squeeze aircraft parts. The compressive strength of a material is also measured in psi. Under a compressive load, an undrilled member is stronger than an identical member with holes drilled through it. However, if a plug of equivalent or stronger material is fitted tightly in a drilled member, it transfers compressive loads across the hole, and the member carries approximately as large a load as if the hole were not there. Thus, for compressive loads, the gross or total area may be used in determining the stress in a member if all holes are tightly plugged with equivalent or stronger material.

Shear

Shear is the stress that resists the force tending to cause one layer of a material to slide over an adjacent layer. Two riveted plates in tension subject the rivets to a shearing force. Usually, the shear strength of a material is either equal to or less than its tensile or compressive strength. Shear stress concerns the aviation technician chiefly from the standpoint of the rivet and bolt applications, particularly when attaching sheet metal, because if a rivet used in a shear application gives way, the riveted or bolted parts are pushed sideways.

Bearing

Bearing stress resists the force that the rivet or bolt places on the hole. As a rule, the strength of the fastener should be such that its total shear strength is approximately equal to the total bearing strength of the sheet material. *[Figure 4-2]*

Figure 4-2. *Bearing stress.*

Torsion

Torsion is the stress that produces twisting. While moving the aircraft forward, the engine also tends to twist it to one side, but other aircraft components hold it on course. Thus, torsion is created. The torsional strength of a material is its resistance to twisting or torque (twisting stress). The stresses arising from this action are shear stresses caused by the rotation of adjacent planes past each other around a common reference axis at right angles to these planes. This action may be illustrated by a rod fixed solidly at one end and twisted by a weight placed on a lever arm at the other, producing the equivalent of two equal and opposite forces acting on the rod at some distance from each other. A shearing action is set up all along the rod, with the center line of the rod representing the neutral axis.

Bending

Bending (or beam stress) is a combination of compression and tension. The rod in *Figure 4-1E* has been shortened (compressed) on the inside of the bend and stretched on the outside of the bend. Note that the bending stress causes a tensile stress to act on the upper half of the beam and a compressive stress on the lower half. These stresses act in opposition on the two sides of the center line of the member, which is called the neutral axis. Since these forces acting in opposite directions are next to each other at the neutral axis, the greatest shear stress occurs along this line, and none exists at the extreme upper or lower surfaces of the beam.

Tools for Sheet Metal Construction and Repair

Without modern metalworking tools and machines, the job of the airframe technician would be more difficult and tiresome, and the time required to finish a task would be much greater. These specialized tools and machines help the airframe technician construct or repair sheet metal in a faster, simpler, and better manner than possible in the past. Powered by human muscle, electricity, or compressed air, these tools are used to lay out, mark, cut, sand, or drill sheet metal.

Layout Tools

Before fitting repair parts into an aircraft structure, the new sections must be measured and marked, or laid out to the dimensions needed to make the repair part. Tools utilized for this process are discussed in this section.

Scales

Scales are available in various lengths, with the 6-inch and 12-inch scales being the most common and affordable. A scale with fractions on one side and decimals on the other side is very useful. To obtain an accurate measurement, measure with the scale held on edge from the 1-inch mark instead of the end. Use the graduation marks on the side to set a divider or compass. *[Figure 4-3]*

Combination Square

A combination square consists of a steel scale with three heads that can be moved to any position on the scale and locked in place. The three heads are a stock head that measures 90° and 45° angles, a protractor head that can

Figure 4-3. *Scales.*

measure any angle between the head and the blade, and a center head that uses one side of the blade as the bisector of a 90° angle. The center of a shaft can be found by using the center head. Place the end of the shaft in the V of the head and scribe a line along the edge of the scale. Rotate the head about 90° and scribe another line along the edge of the scale. The two lines will cross at the center of the shaft. *[Figure 4-4]*

Dividers

Dividers are used to transfer a measurement from a device to a scale to determine its value. Place the sharp points at the locations from which the measurement is to be taken. Then, place the points on a steel machinist's scale, but put one of the points on the 1-inch mark and measure from there. *[Figure 4-5]*

Rivet Spacers

A rivet spacer is used to make a quick and accurate rivet pattern layout on a sheet. On the rivet spacer, there are alignment marks for ½-inch, ¾-inch, 1-inch and 2-inch rivet spacing. *[Figure 4-6]*

Marking Tools
Pens

Fiber-tipped pens are the preferred method of marking lines and hole locations directly on aluminum, because the graphite in a No. 2 pencil can cause corrosion when used on

Figure 4-4. *Combination square.*

Figure 4-5. *Divider.*

Figure 4-6. *Rivet spacer.*

aluminum. Make the layout on the protective membrane if it is still on the material, or mark directly on the material with a fiber-tipped pen, such as a fine-point Sharpie®, or cover the material with masking tape and then mark on the tape.

Scribes

A scribe is a pointed instrument used to mark or score metal to show where it is to be cut. A scribe should only be used when marks will be removed by drilling or cutting because it makes scratches that weaken the material and could cause corrosion. *[Figure 4-7]*

Figure 4-7. *Scribe.*

Punches

Punches are usually made of carbon steel that has been hardened and tempered. Generally classified as solid or hollow, punches are designed according to their intended use. A solid punch is a steel rod with various shapes at the end for different uses. For example, it is used to drive bolts out of holes, loosen frozen or tight pins and keys, knock out rivets, pierce holes in a material, etc. The hollow punch is sharp edged and used most often for cutting out blanks. Solid punches vary in both size and point design, while hollow punches vary in size.

Prick Punch

A prick punch is primarily used during layout to place reference marks on metal because it produces a small indentation. *[Figure 4-8]* After layout is finished, the indentation is enlarged with a center punch to allow for drilling. The prick punch can also be used to transfer dimensions from a paper pattern directly onto the metal. Take the following precautions when using a prick punch:

- Never strike a prick punch a heavy blow with a hammer because it could bend the punch or cause excessive damage to the item being worked.

- Do not use a prick punch to remove objects from holes because the point of the punch spreads the object and causes it to bind even more.

Figure 4-8. *Prick punch.*

Center Punch

A center punch is used to make indentations in metal as an aid in drilling. *[Figure 4-9]* These indentations help the drill, which has a tendency to wander on a flat surface, stay on the mark as it goes through the metal. The traditional center punch is used with a hammer, has a heavier body than the prick punch, and has a point ground to an angle of about 60°. Take the following precautions when using a center punch:

- Never strike the center punch with enough force to dimple the item around the indentation or cause the metal to protrude through the other side of the sheet.

- Do not use a center punch to remove objects from holes because the point of the punch spreads the object and causes it to bind even more.

Figure 4-9. *Center punch.*

Automatic Center Punch

The automatic center punch performs the same function as an ordinary center punch, but uses a spring tension mechanism to create a force hard enough to make an indentation without the need for a hammer. The mechanism automatically strikes a blow of the required force when placed where needed and pressed. This punch has an adjustable cap for regulating the stroke; the point can be removed for replacement or sharpening. Never strike an automatic center punch with a hammer. *[Figure 4-10]*

Figure 4-10. *Automatic center punch.*

Transfer Punch

A transfer punch uses a template or existing holes in the structure to mark the locations of new holes. The punch is centered in the old hole over the new sheet and lightly tapped with a mallet. The result should be a mark that serves to locate the hole in the new sheet. *[Figure 4-11]*

Figure 4-11. *Transfer punch.*

Drive Punch

The drive punch is made with a flat face instead of a point because it is used to drive out damaged rivets, pins, and bolts that sometimes bind in holes. The size of the punch is determined by the width of the face, usually ⅛-inch to ¼-inch. *[Figure 4-12]*

Figure 4-12. *Drive punch.*

Pin Punch

The pin punch typically has a straight shank characterized by a hexagonal body. Pin punch points are sized in ⅟₃₂-inch increments of an inch and range from ⅟₁₆-inch to ⅜-inch in diameter. The usual method for driving out a pin or bolt is to start working it out with a drive punch until the shank of the punch is touching the sides of the hole. Then use a pin punch to drive the pin or bolt the rest of the way out of the hole. *[Figure 4-13]*

Figure 4-13. *Pin punch.*

Chassis Punch

A chassis punch is used to make holes in sheet metal parts for the installation of instruments and other avionics appliance, as well as lightening holes in ribs and spars. Sized in ⅟₁₆ of an inch, they are available in sizes from ½ inch to 3 inches. *[Figure 4-14]*

Figure 4-14. *Chassis punch.*

Awl

A pointed tool for marking surfaces or for punching small holes, an awl is used in aircraft maintenance to place scribe marks on metal and plastic surfaces and to align holes, such as in the installation of a deicer boot. *[Figure 4-15]*

Figure 4-15. *Awl.*

Procedures for one use of an awl:

1. Place the metal to be scribed on a flat surface. Place a ruler or straightedge on the guide marks already measured and placed on the metal.

2. Remove the protective cover from the awl.

3. Hold the straightedge firmly. Hold the awl, as shown in *Figure 4-16*, and scribe a line along the straightedge.

4. Replace the protective cover on the awl.

Figure 4-16. *Awl usage.*

Hole Duplicator

Available in a variety of sizes and styles, hole duplicators, or hole finders, utilize the old covering as a template to locate and match existing holes in the structure. Holes in a replacement sheet or in a patch must be drilled to match existing holes in the structure and the hole duplicator simplifies this process. *Figure 4-17* illustrates one type of hole duplicator. The peg on the bottom leg of the duplicator fits into the existing rivet hole. To make the hole in the replacement sheet or patch, drill through the bushing on the top leg. If the duplicator is properly made, holes drilled in this manner are in perfect alignment. A separate duplicator must be used for each diameter of rivet.

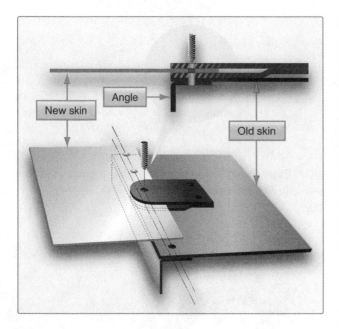

Figure 4-17. *Hole duplicator.*

Cutting Tools

Powered and nonpowered metal cutting tools available to the aviation technician include various types of saws, nibblers, shears, sanders, notchers, and grinders.

Circular-Cutting Saws

The circular cutting saw cuts with a toothed, steel disk that rotates at high speed. Handheld or table mounted and powered by compressed air, this power saw cuts metal or wood. To prevent the saw from grabbing the metal, keep a firm grip on the saw handle at all times. Check the blade carefully for cracks prior to installation because a cracked blade can fly apart during use, possibly causing serious injury.

Kett Saw

The Kett saw is an electrically operated, portable circular cutting saw that uses blades of various diameters. *[Figure 4-18]* Since the head of this saw can be turned to any desired angle, it is useful for removing damaged sections on a stringer. The advantages of a Kett saw include:

1. Can cut metal up to ³⁄₁₆-inch in thickness.

2. No starting hole is required.

3. A cut can be started anywhere on a sheet of metal.

4. Can cut an inside or outside radius.

Figure 4-18. *Kett saw.*

Pneumatic Circular Cutting Saw

The pneumatic circular cutting saw, useful for cutting out damage, is similar to the Kett saw. *[Figure 4-19]*

Figure 4-19. *Pneumatic circular saw.*

Reciprocating Saw

The versatile reciprocating saw achieves cutting action through a push and pull (reciprocating) motion of the blade. This saw can be used right sideup or upside down, a feature that makes it handier than the circular saw for working in tight or awkward spots. A variety of blade types are available for reciprocating saws; blades with finer teeth are used for cutting through metal. The portable, air-powered reciprocating saw uses a standard hacksaw blade and can cut a 360° circle or a square or rectangular hole. Unsuited for fine precision work, this saw is more difficult to control than the pneumatic circular cutting saw. A reciprocating saw should be used in such a way that at least two teeth of the saw blade are cutting at all times. Avoid applying too much downward pressure on the saw handle because the blade may break. [Figure 4-20]

Figure 4-20. *Reciprocating saw.*

Cut-off Wheel

A cut-off wheel is a thin abrasive disc driven by a high-speed pneumatic die-grinder and used to cut out damage on aircraft skin and stringers. The wheels come in different thicknesses and sizes. [Figure 4-21]

Figure 4-21. *Die grinder and cut-off wheel.*

Nibblers

Usually powered by compressed air, the nibbler is another tool for cutting sheet metal. Portable nibblers utilize a high speed blanking action (the lower die moves up and down and meets the upper stationary die) to cut the metal. [Figure 4-22] The shape of the lower die cuts out small pieces of metal approximately ¹⁄₁₆ inch wide.

Figure 4-22. *Nibbler.*

The cutting speed of the nibbler is controlled by the thickness of the metal being cut. Nibblers satisfactorily cut through sheets of metal with a maximum thickness of ¹⁄₁₆ inch. Too much force applied to the metal during the cutting operation clogs the dies (shaped metal), causing them to fail or the motor to overheat. Both electric and hand nibblers are available.

Shop Tools

Due to size, weight, and/or power source, shop tools are usually in a fixed location, and the airframe part to be constructed or repaired is brought to the tool.

Squaring Shear

The squaring shear provides the airframe technician with a convenient means of cutting and squaring sheet metal. Available as a manual, hydraulic, or pneumatic model, this shear consists of a stationary lower blade attached to a bed and a movable upper blade attached to a crosshead. [Figure 4-23]

Figure 4-23. *Power squaring shear.*

Two squaring fences, consisting of thick strips of metal used for squaring metal sheets, are placed on the bed. One squaring fence is placed on the right side and one on the left to form a 90° angle with the blades. A scale graduated in fractions of an inch is scribed on the bed for ease in placement.

To make a cut with a foot shear, move the upper blade down by placing the foot on the treadle and pushing downward. Once the metal is cut and foot pressure removed, a spring raises the blade and treadle. Hydraulic or pneumatic models utilize remote foot pedals to ensure operator safety.

The squaring shear performs three distinctly different operations:

1. Cutting to a line
2. Squaring
3. Multiple cutting to a specific size

When cutting to a line, place the sheet on the bed of the shears in front of the cutting blade with the cutting line even with the cutting edge of the bed. To cut the sheet with a foot shear, step on the treadle while holding the sheet securely in place.

Squaring requires several steps. First, one end of the sheet is squared with an edge (the squaring fence is usually used on the edge). Then, the remaining edges are squared by holding one squared end of the sheet against the squaring fence and making the cut, one edge at a time, until all edges have been squared.

When several pieces must be cut to the same dimensions, use the backstop, located on the back of the cutting edge on most squaring shears. The supporting rods are graduated in fractions of an inch and the gauge bar may be set at any point on the rods. Set the gauge bar the desired distance from the cutting blade of the shears and push each piece to be cut against the gauge bar. All the pieces can then be cut to the same dimensions without measuring and marking each one separately.

Foot-operated shears have a maximum metal cutting capacity of 0.063 inch of aluminum alloy. Use powered squaring shears for cutting thicker metals. *[Figure 4-24]*

Throatless Shear

Airframe technicians use the throatless shear to cut aluminum sheets up to 0.063 inches. This shear takes its name from the fact that metal can be freely moved around the cutting blade during cutting because the shear lacks a "throat" down which metal must be fed. *[Figure 4-25]* This feature allows great flexibility in what shapes can be cut because the metal can be turned to any angle for straight, curved, and irregular cuts. Also, a sheet of any length can be cut.

Figure 4-24. *Foot-operated squaring shear.*

Figure 4-25. *Throatless shears.*

A hand lever operates the cutting blade which is the top blade. Throatless shears made by the Beverly Shear Manufacturing Corporation, called Beverly™ shears, are often used.

Scroll Shears

Scroll shears are used for cutting irregular lines on the inside of a sheet without cutting through to the edge. *[Figure 4-26]* The upper cutting blade is stationary while the lower blade is movable. A handle connected to the lower blade operates the machine.

Rotary Punch Press

Used in the airframe repair shop to punch holes in metal parts, the rotary punch can cut radii in corners, make washers, and perform many other jobs where holes are required. *[Figure 4-27]* The machine is composed of two cylindrical turrets, one mounted over the other and supported by the frame, with both turrets synchronized to rotate together. Index pins, which ensure correct alignment at all times, may be released from their locking position by rotating a lever on the right side of the machine. This action withdraws the index pins from the tapered holes and allows an operator to turn the turrets to any size punch desired.

Figure 4-26. *Scroll shears.*

Figure 4-27. *Rotary punch press.*

When rotating the turret to change punches, release the index lever when the desired die is within 1 inch of the ram, and continue to rotate the turret slowly until the top of the punch holder slides into the grooved end of the ram. The tapered index locking pins will then seat themselves in the holes provided and, at the same time, release the mechanical locking device, which prevents punching until the turrets are aligned.

To operate the machine, place the metal to be worked between the die and punch. Pull the lever on the top of the machine toward the operator, actuating the pinion shaft, gear segment, toggle link, and the ram, forcing the punch through the metal. When the lever is returned to its original position, the metal is removed from the punch.

The diameter of the punch is stamped on the front of each die holder. Each punch has a point in its center that is placed in the center punch mark to punch the hole in the correct location.

Band Saw

A band saw consists of a toothed metal band coupled to, and continuously driven around, the circumferences of two wheels. It is used to cut aluminum, steel, and composite parts. *[Figure 4-28]* The speed of the band saw and the type and style of the blade depends on the material to be cut. Band saws are often designated to cut one type of material, and if a different material is to be cut, the blade is changed. The speed is controllable and the cutting platform can be tilted to cut angled pieces.

Figure 4-28. *Band saw.*

Disk Sander

Disk sanders have a powered abrasive-covered disk or belt and are used for smoothing or polishing surfaces. The sander unit uses abrasive paper of different grits to trim metal parts. It is much quicker to use a disk sander than to file a part to the correct dimension. The combination disk and belt sander has a vertical belt sander coupled with a disk sander and is often used in a metal shop. *[Figure 4-29]*

Figure 4-29. *Combination disk and belt sander.*

Belt Sander

The belt sander uses an endless abrasive belt driven by an electric motor to sand down metal parts much like the disk sander unit. The abrasive paper used on the belt comes in different degrees of grit or coarseness. The belt sander is available as a vertical or horizontal unit. The tension and tracking of the abrasive belt can be adjusted so the belt runs in the middle. [Figure 4-30]

Figure 4-30. *Belt sander.*

Notcher

The notcher is used to cut out metal parts, with some machines capable of shearing, squaring, and trimming metal. [Figure 4-31] The notcher consists of a top and bottom die and most often cuts at a 90° angle, although some machines can cut metal into angles up to 180°. Notchers are available in manual and pneumatic models able to cut various thicknesses of mild steel and aluminum. This is an excellent tool for quickly removing corners from sheet metal parts. [Figure 4-32]

Figure 4-31. *Notcher.*

Figure 4-32. *Power notcher.*

Wet or Dry Grinder

Grinding machines come in a variety of types and sizes, depending upon the class of work for which they are to be used. Dry and/or wet grinders are found in airframe repair shops. Grinders can be bench or pedestal mounted. A dry grinder usually has a grinding wheel on each end of a shaft that runs through an electric motor or a pulley operated by a belt. The wet grinder has a pump to supply a flow of water on a single grinding wheel. The water acts as a lubricant for faster grinding while it continuously cools the edge of the metal, reducing the heat produced by material being ground against the wheel. It also washes away any bits of metal or abrasive removed during the grinding operation. The water returns to a tank and can be re-used.

Grinders are used to sharpen knives, tools, and blades as well as grinding steel, metal objects, drill bits, and tools. *Figure 4-33* illustrates a common type bench grinder found in most airframe repair shops. It can be used to dress mushroomed heads on chisels and points on chisels, screwdrivers, and drills, as well as for removing excess metal from work and smoothing metal surfaces.

Figure 4-33. *Grinder.*

The bench grinder is generally equipped with one medium-grit and one fine-grit abrasive wheel. The medium-grit wheel is usually used for rough grinding where a considerable quantity of material is to be removed or where a smooth finish is unimportant. The fine-grit wheel is used for sharpening tools and grinding to close limits. It removes metal more slowly, gives the work a smooth finish, and does not generate enough heat to anneal the edges of cutting tools.

Before using any type of grinder, ensure that the abrasive wheels are firmly held on the spindles by the flange nuts. An abrasive wheel that comes off or becomes loose could seriously injure the operator in addition to ruining the grinder. A loose tool rest could cause the tool or piece of work to be "grabbed" by the abrasive wheel and cause the operator's hand to come in contact with the wheel, possibly resulting in severe wounds.

Always wear goggles when using a grinder, even if eyeshields are attached to the grinder. Goggles should fit firmly against the face and nose. This is the only way to protect the eyes from the fine pieces of steel. Goggles that do not fit properly should be exchanged for ones that do fit. Be sure to check the abrasive wheel for cracks before using the grinder. A cracked abrasive wheel is likely to fly apart when turning at high speeds. Never use a grinder unless it is equipped with wheel guards that are firmly in place.

Grinding Wheels

A grinding wheel is made of a bonded abrasive and provides an efficient way to cut, shape, and finish metals. Available in a wide variety of sizes and numerous shapes, grinding wheels are also used to sharpen knives, drill bits, and many other tools, or to clean and prepare surfaces for painting or plating.

Grinding wheels are removable and a polishing or buffing wheel can be substituted for the abrasive wheel. Silicon carbide and aluminum oxide are the kinds of abrasives used in most grinding wheels. Silicon carbide is the cutting agent for grinding hard, brittle material, such as cast iron. It is also used in grinding aluminum, brass, bronze, and copper. Aluminum oxide is the cutting agent for grinding steel and other metals of high tensile strength.

Hand Cutting Tools

Many types of hand cutting tools are available to cut light gauge sheet metal. Four cutting tools commonly found in the air frame repair shop are straight hand snips, aviation snips, files, and burring tools.

Straight Snips

Straight snips, or sheet metal shears, have straight blades with cutting edges sharpened to an 85° angle.

[Figure 4-34] Available in sizes ranging from 6 to 14 inches, they cut aluminum up to ¹⁄₁₆ of an inch. Straight snips can be used for straight cutting and large curves, but aviation snips are better for cutting circles or arcs.

Figure 4-34. *Straight snips.*

Aviation Snips

Aviation snips are used to cut holes, curved parts, round patches, and doublers (a piece of metal placed under a part to make it stiffer) in sheet metal. Aviation snips have colored handles to identify the direction of the cuts: yellow aviation snips cut straight, green aviation snips curve right, and red aviation snips curve left. *[Figure 4-35]*

Figure 4-35. *Aviation snips.*

Files

The file is an important but often overlooked tool used to shape metal by cutting and abrasion. Files have five distinct properties: length, contour, the form in cross section, the kind of teeth, and the fineness of the teeth. Many different types of files are available and the sizes range from 3 to 18 inches. *[Figure 4-36]*

Figure 4-36. *Files.*

The portion of the file on which the teeth are cut is called the face. The tapered end that fits into the handle is called the tang. The part of the file where the tang begins is the heel. The length of a file is the distance from the point or tip to the heel and does not include the tang. The teeth of the file do the cutting. These teeth are set at an angle across the face of the file. A file with a single row of parallel teeth is called a single-cut file. The teeth are cut at an angle of 65°-85° to the centerline, depending on the intended use of the file. Files that have one row of teeth crossing another row in a crisscross pattern are called double-cut files. The angle of the first set usually is 40°-50° and that of the crossing teeth 70°-80°. Crisscrossing produces a surface that has a very large number of little teeth that slant toward the tip of the file. Each little tooth looks like an end of a diamond point cold chisel.

Files are graded according to the tooth spacing; a coarse file has a small number of large teeth, and a smooth file has a large number of fine teeth. The coarser the teeth, the more metal is removed on each stroke of the file. The terms used to indicate the coarseness or fineness of a file are rough, coarse, bastard, second cut, smooth, and dead smooth, and the file may be either single cut or double cut. Files are further classified according to their shape. Some of the more common types are: flat, triangle, square, half round, and round.

There are several filing techniques. The most common is to remove rough edges from the finished part before it is installed. Crossfiling is used for filing the edges of metal parts that must fit tightly together. Crossfiling involves clamping the metal between two strips of wood and filing the edge to a preset line. Draw filing is used when larger surfaces need to be smoothed and squared. It is done by drawing the file over the entire surface of the work. Apply pressure on the forward stroke only except when filing very soft metals such as lead or aluminum.

To protect the teeth of a file, files should be stored separately in a plastic wrap or hung by their handles. Files kept in a toolbox should be wrapped in waxed paper to prevent rust from forming. File teeth can be cleaned with a file card.

Die Grinder

A die grinder is a handheld tool that turns a mounted cutoff wheel, rotary file, or sanding disk at high speed. *[Figure 4-37]* Usually powered by compressed air, electric die grinders are also used. Pneumatic die grinders run at 12,000 to 20,000 revolutions per minute (rpm) with the rotational speed controlled by the operator who uses a hand- or foot-operated throttle to vary the volume of compressed air. Available in straight, 45°, and 90° models, the die grinder is excellent for weld breaking, smoothing sharp edges, deburring, porting, and general high-speed polishing, grinding, and cutting.

Figure 4-37. *Die grinder.*

Burring Tool

This type of tool is used to remove a burr from an edge of a sheet or to deburr a hole. *[Figure 4-38]*

Figure 4-38. *Burring tools.*

Hole Drilling

Drilling holes is a common operation in the airframe repair shop. Once the fundamentals of drills and their uses are learned, drilling holes for rivets and bolts on light metal is not difficult. While a small portable power drill is usually the most practical tool for this common operation in airframe metalwork, sometimes a drill press may prove to be the better piece of equipment for the job.

Portable Power Drills

Portable power drills operate by electricity or compressed air. Pneumatic drill motors are recommended for use on repairs around flammable materials where potential sparks from an electric drill motor might become a fire hazard.

When using the portable power drill, hold it firmly with both hands. Before drilling, be sure to place a backup block of wood under the hole to be drilled to add support to the metal structure. The drill bit should be inserted in the chuck and tested for trueness or vibration. This may be visibly checked by running the motor freely. A drill bit that wobbles or is slightly bent should not be used since such a condition causes enlarged holes. The drill should always be held at right angles to the work regardless of the position or curvatures. Tilting the drill at any time when drilling into or withdrawing from the material may cause elongation (egg shape) of the hole. When drilling through sheet metal, small burrs are formed around the edge of the hole. Burrs must be removed to allow rivets or bolts to fit snugly and to prevent scratching. Burrs may be removed with a bearing scraper, a countersink, or a drill bit larger than the hole. If a drill bit or countersink is used, it should be rotated by hand. Always wear safety goggles while drilling.

Pneumatic Drill Motors

Pneumatic drill motors are the most common type of drill motor for aircraft repair work. *[Figure 4-39]* They are light weight and have sufficient power and good speed control. Drill motors are available in many different sizes and models. Most drill motors used for aircraft sheet metal work are rated at 3,000 rpm, but if drilling deep holes or drilling in hard materials, such as corrosion resistant steel or titanium, a drill motor with more torque and lower rpm should be selected to prevent damage to tools and materials.

Figure 4-39. *Drill motors.*

Right Angle and 45° Drill Motors

Right angle and 45° drill motors are used for positions that are not accessible with a pistol grip drill motor. Most right angle drill motors use threaded drill bits that are available in several lengths. Heavy-duty right angle drills are equipped with a chuck similar to the pistol grip drill motor. *[Figure 4-40]*

Figure 4-40. *Angle drill motors.*

Two Hole

Special drill motors that drill two holes at the same time are used for the installation of nutplates. By drilling two holes at the same time, the distance between the holes is fixed and the holes line up perfectly with the holes in the nutplate. *[Figure 4-41]*

Figure 4-41. *Nutplate drill.*

Drill Press

The drill press is a precision machine used for drilling holes that require a high degree of accuracy. It serves as an accurate means of locating and maintaining the direction of a hole that is to be drilled and provides the operator with a feed lever that makes the task of feeding the drill into the work easier. The upright drill press is the most common of the variety of drill presses available. *[Figure 4-42]*

Figure 4-42. *Drill press.*

When using a drill press, the height of the drill press table is adjusted to accommodate the height of the part to be drilled. When the height of the part is greater than the distance between the drill and the table, the table is lowered. When the height of the part is less than the distance between the drill and the table, the table is raised.

After the table is properly adjusted, the part is placed on the table and the drill is brought down to aid in positioning the metal so that the hole to be drilled is directly beneath the point of the drill. The part is then clamped to the drill press table to prevent it from slipping during the drilling operation. Parts not properly clamped may bind on the drill and start spinning, causing serious cuts on the operator's arms or body, or loss of fingers or hands. Always make sure the part to be drilled is properly clamped to the drill press table before starting the drilling operation.

The degree of accuracy that it is possible to attain when using the drill press depends to a certain extent on the condition of the spindle hole, sleeves, and drill shank. Therefore, special care must be exercised to keep these parts clean and free from nicks, dents, and warpage. Always be sure that the sleeve is securely pressed into the spindle hole. Never insert a broken drill in a sleeve or spindle hole. Be careful never to use the sleeve-clamping vise to remove a drill since this may cause the sleeve to warp.

The drill speed on a drill press is adjustable. Always select the optimum drill speed for the material to be drilled. Technically, the speed of a drill bit means its speed at the circumference, in surface feet per minute (sfm). The recommended speed for drilling aluminum alloy is from 200 to 300 sfm, and for mild steel is 30 to 50 sfm. In practice, this must be converted into rpm for each size drill. Machinist and mechanic handbooks include drill rpm charts or drill rpm may be computed by use of the formula:

$$\frac{CS \times 4}{D} = rpm$$

CS = The recommended cutting speed in sfm

D = The diameter of the drill bit in inches

Example: At what rpm should a ⅛-inch drill turn to drill aluminum at 300 sfm?

Drill Extensions and Adapters

When access to a place where drilling is difficult or impossible with a straight drill motor, various types of drill extensions and adapters are used.

Extension Drill Bits

Extension drill bits are widely used for drilling holes in locations that require reaching through small openings or past projections. These drill bits, which come in 6- to 12-inch lengths, are high speed with spring-tempered shanks. Extension drill bits are ground to a special notched point, which reduces end thrust to a minimum. When using extension drill bits always:

1. Select the shortest drill bit that will do the job. It is easier to control.

2. Check the drill bit for straightness. A bent drill bit makes an oversized hole and may whip, making it difficult to control.

3. Keep the drill bit under control. Extension drills smaller than ¼-inch must be supported by a drill guard made from a piece of tubing or spring to prevent whipping.

Straight Extension

A straight extension for a drill can be made from an ordinary piece of drill rod. The drill bit is attached to the drill rod by shrink fitting, brazing, or silver soldering.

Angle Adapters

Angle adapters can be attached to an electric or pneumatic drill when the location of the hole is inaccessible to a straight drill. Angle adapters have an extended shank fastened to the chuck of the drill. The drill is held in one hand and the adapter in the other to prevent the adapter from spinning around the drill chuck.

Snake Attachment

The snake attachment is a flexible extension used for drilling in places inaccessible to ordinary drills. Available for electric and pneumatic drill motors, its flexibility permits drilling around obstructions with minimum effort. *[Figure 4-43]*

Figure 4-43. *Snake attachment.*

Types of Drill Bits

A wide variety of drill bits including specialty bits for specific jobs are available. *Figure 4-44* illustrates the parts of the drill bit and *Figure 4-45* shows some commonly used drill bits. High speed steel (HSS) drill bits come in short shank or standard length, sometimes called jobbers length. HSS drill bits can withstand temperatures nearing the critical range of 1,400 °F (dark cherry red) without losing their hardness. The industry standard for drilling metal (aluminum, steel, etc.), these drill bits stay sharper longer.

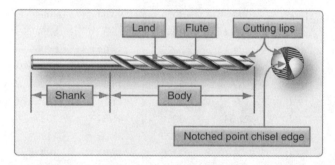

Figure 4-44. *Parts of a drill.*

Figure 4-45. *Types of drill bits.*

Step Drill Bits

Typically, the procedure for drilling holes larger than ³⁄₁₆ inch in sheet metal is to drill a pilot hole with a No. 40 or No. 30 drill bit and then to oversize with a larger drill bit to the correct size. The step drill combines these two functions into one step. The step drill bit consists of a smaller pilot drill point that drills the initial small hole. When the drill bit is advanced further into the material, the second step of the drill bit enlarges the hole to the desired size. .

Step drill bits are designed to drill round holes in most metals, plastic, and wood. Commonly used in general construction and plumbing, they work best on softer materials, such as plywood, but can be used on very thin sheet metal. Step drill bits can also be used to deburr holes left by other bits.

Cobalt Alloy Drill Bits

Cobalt alloy drill bits are designed for hard, tough metals like corrosion-resistant steel and titanium. It is important for the aircraft technician to note the difference between HSS and cobalt, because HSS drill bits wear out quickly when drilling titanium or stainless. Cobalt drill bits are excellent for drilling titanium or stainless steel, but do not produce a quality hole in aluminum alloys. Cobalt drill bits can be recognized by thicker webs and a taper at the end of the drill shank.

Twist Drill Bits

Easily the most popular drill bit type, the twist drill bit has spiral grooves or flutes running along its working length. [*Figure 4-46*] This drill bit comes in a single-fluted, two-fluted, three-fluted, and four-fluted styles. Single-fluted and two-fluted drill bits (most commonly available) are used for originating holes. Three-fluted and four-fluted drill bits are used interchangeably to enlarge existing holes. Twist drill bits are available in a wide choice of tooling materials and lengths with the variations targeting specific projects.

Figure 4-46. *Twist drill bits.*

The standard twist drill bits used for drilling aluminum are made from HSS and have a 135° split point. Drill bits for titanium are made from cobalt vanadium for increased wear resistance.

Drill Bit Sizes

Drill diameters are grouped by three size standards: number, letter, and fractional. The decimal equivalents of standard drill are shown in *Figure 4-47*.

Drill Lubrication

Normal drilling of sheet material does not require lubrication, but lubrication should be provided for all deeper drilling.

Lubricants serve to assist in chip removal, which prolongs drill life and ensures a good finish and dimensional accuracy of the hole. It does not prevent overheating. The use of a lubricant is always a good practice when drilling castings, forgings, or heavy gauge stock. A good lubricant should be thin enough to help in chip removal but thick enough to stick to the drill. For aluminum, titanium, and corrosion-resistant steel, a cetyl alcohol based lubricant is the most satisfactory. Cetyl alcohol is a nontoxic fatty alcohol chemical produced in liquid, paste, and solid forms. The solid stick and block forms quickly liquefy at drilling temperatures. For steel, sulfurized mineral cutting oil is superior. Sulfur has an affinity for steel, which aids in holding the cutting oil in place. In the case of

Drill Size	Decimal (Inches)	Drill Size	Decimal (Inches)	Drill Size	Decimal (Inches)	Drill Size	Decimal (Inches)	Drill Size	Decimal (Inches)
80	.0135	50	.0700	22	.1570	G	.2610	31/64	.4844
79	.0145	49	.0730	21	.1590	17/64	.2656	1/2	.5000
1/54	.0156	48	.0760	20	.1610	H	.2660	33/64	.5156
78	.0160	5/64	.0781	19	.1660	I	.2720	17/32	.5312
77	.0180	47	.0785	18	.1695	J	.2770	35/64	.5469
76	.0200	46	.0810	11/64	.1718	K	.2810	9/16	.5625
75	.0210	45	.0820	17	.1730	9/32	.2812	37/64	.5781
74	.0225	44	.0860	16	.1770	L	.2900	19/32	.5937
73	.0240	43	.0890	15	.1800	M	.2950	39/84	.6094
72	.0250	42	.0935	14	.1820	19/64	.2968	5/8	.6250
71	.0260	3/32	.0937	13	.1850	N	.3020	41/64	.6406
70	.0280	41	.0960	3/16	.1875	5/16	.3125	21/32	.6562
69	.0293	40	.0980	12	.1890	O	.3160	43/64	.6719
68	.0310	39	.0995	11	.1910	P	.3230	11/16	.6875
1/32	.0312	38	.1015	10	.1935	21/64	.3281	45/64	.7031
67	.0320	37	.1040	9	.1960	Q	.3320	23/32	.7187
66	.0330	36	.1065	8	.1990	R	.3390	47/64	.7344
65	.0350	7/64	.1093	7	.2010	11/32	.3437	3/4	.7500
64	.0360	35	.1100	13/64	.2031	S	.3480	49/64	.7656
63	.0370	34	.1110	6	.2040	T	.3580	25/32	.7812
62	.0380	33	.1130	5	.2055	23/64	.3593	51/64	.7969
61	.0390	32	.1160	4	.2090	U	.3680	13/16	.8125
60	.0400	31	.1200	3	.2130	3/8	.3750	53/64	.8281
59	.0410	1/8	.1250	7/32	.2187	V	.3770	27/32	.8437
58	.0420	30	.1285	2	.2210	W	.3860	55/64	.8594
57	.0430	29	.1360	1	.2280	25/64	.3906	7/8	.8750
56	.0465	28	.1405	A	.2340	X	.3970	57/64	.8906
3/64	.0468	9/64	.1406	15/64	.2343	Y	.4040	29/32	.9062
55	.0520	27	.1440	B	.2380	13/32	.4062	59/64	.9219
54	.0550	26	.1470	C	.2420	Z	.4130	15/16	.9375
53	.0595	25	.1495	D	.2460	27/64	.4219	61/64	.9531
1/16	.0625	24	.1520	1/4	.2500	7/16	.4375	31/32	.9687
52	.0635	23	.1540	E	.2500	29/64	.4531	63/64	.9844
51	.0670	5/32	.1562	F	.2570	15/32	.4687	1	1.0000

Figure 4-47. *Drill sizes and decimal equivalents.*

deep drilling, the drill should be withdrawn at intervals to relieve chip packing and to ensure the lubricant reaches the point. As a general rule, if the drill is large or the material hard, use a lubricant.

Reamers

Reamers, used for enlarging holes and finishing them smooth to a required size, are made in many styles. They can be straight or tapered, solid or expansive, and come with straight or helical flutes. *Figure 4-48* illustrates three types of reamers:

1. Three or four fluted production bullet reamers are customarily used where a finer finish and/or size is needed than can be achieved with a standard drill bit.

2. Standard or straight reamer.

3. Piloted reamer, with the end reduced to provide accurate alignment.

Figure 4-48. *Reamers.*

The cylindrical parts of most straight reamers are not cutting edges, but merely grooves cut for the full length of the reamer body. These grooves provide a way for chips to escape and a channel for lubricant to reach the cutting edge. Actual cutting is done on the end of the reamer. The cutting edges are normally ground to a bevel of 45° ± 5°.

Reamer flutes are not designed to remove chips like a drill. Do not attempt to withdraw a reamer by turning it in the reverse direction because chips can be forced into the surface, scarring the hole.

Drill Stops

A spring drill stop is a wise investment. *[Figure 4-49]* Properly adjusted, it can prevent excessive drill penetration that might damage underlying structure or injure personnel and prevent the drill chuck from marring the surface. Drill stops can be made from tubing, fiber rod, or hard rubber.

Drill Bushings and Guides

There are several types of tools available that aid in holding the drill perpendicular to the part. They consist of a hardened bushing anchored in a holder. *[Figure 4-50]*

Figure 4-49. *Drill stop.*

| Bushing holder | Arm-type bushing holder |

Figure 4-50. *Drill bushings.*

Drill bushing types:

1. Tube—hand-held in an existing hole

2. Commercial—twist lock

3. Commercial—threaded

Drill Bushing Holder Types

There are four types of drill bushing holder:

1. Standard—fine for drilling flat stock or tubing/rod; uses insert-type bushings.

2. Egg cup—improvement on standard tripod base; allows drilling on both flat and curved material; interchangeable bushings allows flexibility. *[Figure 4-51]*

3. Plate—used primarily for interchangeable production components; uses commercial bushings and self-feeding drills.

Figure 4-51. *Bushing holder.*

4. Arm—used when drilling critical structure; can be locked in position; uses interchangeable commercial bushings.

Hole Drilling Techniques

Precise location of drilled holes is sometimes required. When locating holes to close tolerances, accurately located punch marks need to be made. If a punch mark is too small, the chisel edge of the drill bit may bridge it and "walk off" the exact location before starting. If the punch mark is too heavy, it may deform the metal and/or result in a local strain hardening where the drill bit is to start cutting. The best size for a punch mark is about the width of the chisel edge of the drill bit to be used. This holds the drill point in place while starting. The procedure that ensures accurate holes follows: [Figure 4-52]

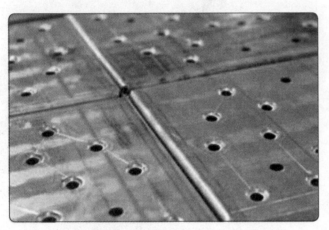

Figure 4-52. *Drilled sheet metal.*

1. Measure and lay out the drill locations carefully and mark with crossed lines.

   NOTE: The chisel edge is the least efficient operating surface element of the twist drill bit because it does not cut, but actually squeezes or extrudes the work material.

2. Use a sharp prick punch or spring-loaded center punch and magnifying glass to further mark the holes.

3. Seat a properly ground center punch (120°–135°) in the prick punch mark and, holding the center punch perpendicular to the surface, strike a firm square blow with a hammer.

4. Mark each hole with a small drill bit (1/16-inch recommended) to check and adjust the location prior to pilot drilling.

5. For holes 3/16-inch and larger, pilot drilling is recommended. Select a drill bit equal to the width of the chisel edge of the final drill bit size. Avoid using a pilot drill bit that is too large because it would cause the corners and cutting lips of the final drill bit to be dulled, burned, or chipped. It also contributes to chattering and drill motor stalling. Pilot drill at each mark.

6. Place the drill point at the center of the crossed lines, perpendicular to the surface, and, with light pressure, start drilling slowly. Stop drilling after a few turns and check to see if the drill bit is starting on the mark. It should be; if not, it is necessary to walk the hole a little by pointing the drill in the direction it should go, and rotating it carefully and intermittently until properly lined up.

7. Enlarge each pilot drilled hole to final size.

Drilling Large Holes

The following technique can be used to drill larger holes. Special tooling has been developed to drill large holes to precise tolerances. [Figure 4-53]

Figure 4-53. *Drilling large holes.*

1. Pilot drill using a drill bushing. Bushings are sized for 1/8, 3/16, or 1/4 drill bits.

2. Step drill bits are used to step the hole to approximately 1/64-inch smaller than the final hole size. The aligning step diameter matches the pilot drill bit size.

3. Finish ream to size using a step reamer. The aligning step diameter matches the core drill bit size. Reamers should be available for both clearance and interference fit hole sizes.

   NOTE: Holes can also be enlarged by using a series of step reamers.

Chip Chasers

The chip chaser is designed to remove chips and burrs lodged between sheets of metal after drilling holes for riveting. [Figure 4-54] Chip chasers have a plastic molded handle and a flexible steel blade with a hook in the end.

Figure 4-54. *Chip chaser.*

Forming Tools

Sheet metal forming dates back to the days of the blacksmith who used a hammer and hot oven to mold metal into the desired form. Today's aircraft technician relies on a wide variety of powered and hand-operated tools to precisely bend and fold sheet metal to achieve the perfect shape. Forming tools include straight line machines, such as the bar folder and press brake, as well as rotary machines, such as the slip roll former. Forming sheet metal requires a variety of tools and equipment (both powered and manual), such as the piccolo former, shrinking and stretching tools, form blocks, and specialized hammers and mallets. *[Figure 4-55]*

Figure 4-55. *Hammer and mallet forming.*

Tempered sheet stock is used in forming operations whenever possible in typical repairs. Forming that is performed in the tempered condition, usually at room temperature, is known as cold-forming. Cold forming eliminates heat treatment and the straightening and checking operations required to remove the warp and twist caused by the heat treating process. Cold-formed sheet metal experiences a phenomenon known as spring-back, which causes the worked piece to spring back

slightly when the deforming force is removed. If the material shows signs of cracking during cold forming over small radii, the material should be formed in the annealed condition.

Annealing, the process of toughening steel by gradually heating and cooling it, removes the temper from metal, making it softer and easier to form. Parts containing small radii or compound curvatures must be formed in the annealed condition. After forming, the part is heat treated to a tempered condition before use on the aircraft.

Construction of interchangeable structural and nonstructural parts is achieved by forming flat sheet stock to make channel, angle, zee, and hat section members. Before a sheet metal part is formed, a flat pattern is made to show how much material is required in the bend areas, at what point the sheet must be inserted into the forming tool, or where bend lines are located. Determination of bend lines and bend allowances is discussed in greater detail in the section on layout and forming.

Bar Folding Machine

The bar folder is designed for use in making bends or folds along edges of sheets. *[Figure 4-56]* This machine is best suited for folding small hems, flanges, seams, and edges to be wired. Most bar folders have a capacity for metal up to 22 gauge in thickness and 42 inches in length. Before using the bar folder, several adjustments must be made for thickness of material, width of fold, sharpness of fold, and angle of fold. The adjustment for thickness of material is made by adjusting the screws at each end of the folder. As this adjustment is made, place a piece of metal of the desired thickness in the folder and raise the operating handle until the small roller rests on the cam. Hold the folding blade in this position and adjust the setscrews until the metal is clamped securely and evenly the full length of the folding blade. After the folder has been adjusted, test each end of the machine separately with a small piece of metal by actually folding it.

Figure 4-56. *Bar folder.*

There are two positive stops on the folder, one for 45° folds or bends and the other for 90° folds or bends. A collar is provided that can be adjusted to any degree of bend within the capacity of the machine.

For forming angles of 45° or 90°, the appropriate stop is moved into place. This allows the handle to be moved forward to the correct angle. For forming other angles, the adjustable collar is used. This is accomplished by loosening the setscrew and setting the stop at the desired angle. After setting the stop, tighten the setscrew and complete the bend. To make the fold, adjust the machine correctly and then insert the metal. The metal goes between the folding blade and the jaw. Hold the metal firmly against the gauge and pull the operating handle toward the body. As the handle is brought forward, the jaw automatically raises and holds the metal until the desired fold is made. When the handle is returned to its original position, the jaw and blade return to their original positions and release the metal.

Cornice Brake

A brake is similar to a bar folder because it is also used for turning or bending the edges of sheet metal. The cornice brake is more useful than the bar folder because its design allows the sheet metal to be folded or formed to pass through the jaws from front to rear without obstruction. *[Figure 4-57]* In contrast, the bar folder can form a bend or edge only as wide as the depth of its jaws. Thus, any bend formed on a bar folder can also be made on the cornice brake.

Figure 4-57. *Cornice brake.*

In making ordinary bends with the cornice brake, the sheet is placed on the bed with the sight line (mark indicating line of bend) directly under the edge of the clamping bar. The clamping bar is then brought down to hold the sheet firmly in place. The stop at the right side of the brake is set for the proper angle or amount of bend and the bending leaf is raised until it strikes the stop. If other bends are to be made, the clamping bar is lifted and the sheet is moved to the correct position for bending.

The bending capacity of a cornice brake is determined by the manufacturer. Standard capacities of this machine are from 12- to 22-gauge sheet metal, and bending lengths are from 3 to 12 feet. The bending capacity of the brake is determined by the bending edge thickness of the various bending leaf bars.

Most metals have a tendency to return to their normal shape—a characteristic known as spring-back. If the cornice brake is set for a 90° bend, the metal bent probably forms an angle of about 87° to 88°. Therefore, if a bend of 90° is desired, set the cornice brake to bend an angle of about 93° to allow for spring-back.

Box and Pan Brake (Finger Brake)

The box and pan brake, often called the finger brake because it is equipped with a series of steel fingers of varying widths, lacks the solid upper jaw of the cornice brake. *[Figure 4-58]* The box and pan brake can be used to do everything that the cornice brake can do, as well as several things the cornice brake cannot do.

Figure 4-58. *Box and pan brake.*

The box and pan brake is used to form boxes, pans, and other similar shaped objects. If these shapes were formed on a cornice brake, part of the bend on one side of the box would have to be straightened in order to make the last bend. With a finger brake, simply remove the fingers that are in the way and use only the fingers required to make the bend. The fingers are secured to the upper leaf by thumbscrews. All the fingers not removed for an operation must be securely seated and firmly tightened before the brake is used. The radius of the nose on the clamping fingers is usually rather small and frequently requires nose radius shims to be custom made for the total length of the bend.

Press Brake

Since most cornice brakes and box and pan brakes are limited to a maximum forming capacity of approximately 0.090 inch annealed aluminum, 0.063-inch 7075T6, or 0.063-inch stainless steel, operations that require the forming of thicker and more complex parts use a press brake. *[Figure 4-59]* The press brake is the most common machine tool used to bend sheet metal and applies force via mechanical and/or hydraulic components to shape the sheet metal between the punch and die. Narrow U-channels (especially with long legs) and hat channel stringers can be formed on the press brake by using special gooseneck or offset dies. Special urethane lower dies are useful for forming channels and stringers. Power press brakes can be set up with back stops (some are computer controlled) for high volume production. Press brake operations are usually done manually and require skill and knowledge of safe use.

Figure 4-59. *Press brake.*

Slip Roll Former

With the exception of the brake, the slip roll is probably used more than any other machine in the shop. *[Figure 4-60]* This machine is used to form sheets into cylinders or other straight curved surfaces. It consists of right and left end frames with three solid rolls mounted in between. Gears, which are operated by either a hand crank or a power drive, connect the two gripping rolls. These rolls can be adjusted to the thickness of the metal by using the two adjusting screws located on the bottom of each frame. The two most common of these forming machines are the slip roll former and the rotary former. Available in various sizes and capabilities, these machines come in manual or powered versions.

The slip roll former in *Figure 4-60* is manually operated and consists of three rolls, two housings, a base, and a handle. The handle turns the two front rolls through a system of gears enclosed in the housing. The front rolls serve as feeding, or gripping, rolls. The rear roll gives the proper curvature to the work. When the metal is started into the machine, the rolls grip the metal and carry it to the rear roll, which curves it. The desired radius of a bend is obtained by the rear roll. The bend radius of the part can be checked as the forming operation progresses by using a circle board or radius gauge. The gauges can be made by cutting a piece of material to

Figure 4-60. *Slip roll former.*

the required finished radius and comparing it to the radius being formed by the rolling operation. On some material, the forming operation must be performed by passing the material through the rolls several times with progressive settings on the forming roll. On most machines, the top roll can be released on one end, permitting the formed sheet to be removed from the machine without distortion.

The front and rear rolls are grooved to permit forming of objects that have wired edges. The upper roll is equipped with a release that permits easy removal of the metal after it has been formed. When using the slip roll former, the lower front roll must be raised or lowered before inserting the sheet of metal. If the object has a folded edge, there must be enough clearance between the rolls to prevent flattening the fold. If a metal requiring special care (such as aluminum) is being formed, the rolls must be clean and free of imperfections.

The rear roll must be adjusted to give the proper curvature to the part being formed. There are no gauges that indicate settings for a specific diameter; therefore, trial and error settings must be used to obtain the desired curvature. The metal should be inserted between the rolls from the front of the machine. Start the metal between the rolls by rotating the operating handle in a clockwise direction. A starting edge is formed by holding the operating handle firmly with the right hand and raising the metal with the left hand. The bend of the starting edge is determined by the diameter of the part being formed. If the edge of the part is to be flat or nearly flat, a starting edge should not be formed.

Ensure that fingers and loose clothing are clear of the rolls before the actual forming operation is started. Rotate the operating handle until the metal is partially through the rolls and change the left hand from the front edge of the sheet to the upper edge of the sheet. Then, roll the remainder of the sheet through the machine. If the desired curvature is not obtained, return the metal to its starting position by rotating the handle counterclockwise. Raise or lower the rear roll and roll the metal through the rolls again. Repeat this procedure until the desired curvature is obtained, then release the upper roll and remove the metal. If the part to be formed has a tapered shape, the rear roll should be set so that the rolls are closer together on one end than on the opposite end. The amount of adjustment must be determined by experimentation. If the job being formed has a wired edge, the distance between the upper and lower rolls and the distance between the lower front roll and the rear roll should be slightly greater at the wired end than at the opposite end. [Figure 4-61]

Rotary Machine

The rotary machine is used on cylindrical and flat sheet metal to shape the edge or to form a bead along the edge.

[Figure 4-62] Various shaped rolls can be installed on the rotary machine to perform these operations. The rotary machine works best with thinner annealed materials.

Stretch Forming

In the process of stretch forming, a sheet of metal is shaped by stretching it over a formed block to just beyond the elastic limit where permanent set takes place with a minimum amount of spring-back. To stretch the metal, the sheet is rigidly clamped at two opposite edges in fixed vises. Then, the metal is stretched by moving a ram that carries the form block against the sheet with the pressure from the ram causing the material to stretch and wrap to the contour of the form block.

Stretch forming is normally restricted to relatively large parts with large radii of curvature and shallow depth, such as contoured skin. Uniform contoured parts produced at a faster speed give stretch forming an advantage over hand formed parts. Also, the condition of the material is more uniform than that obtained by hand forming.

Drop Hammer

The drop hammer forming process produces shapes by the progressive deformation of sheet metal in matched dies under the repetitive blows of a gravity-drop hammer or a power-drop hammer. The configurations most commonly formed by the process include shallow, smoothly contoured double-curvature parts, shallow-beaded parts, and parts with irregular and comparatively deep recesses. Small quantities of cup-shaped and box-shaped parts, curved sections, and contoured flanged parts are also formed. Drop hammer forming is not a precision forming method and cannot provide tolerances as close as 0.03-inch to 0.06-inch. Nevertheless, the process is often used for sheet metal parts, such as aircraft components, that undergo frequent design changes, or for which there is a short run expectancy.

Hydropress Forming

The rubber pad hydropress can be utilized to form many varieties of parts from aluminum and its alloys with relative ease. Phenolic, masonite, kirksite, and some types of hard setting moulding plastic have been used successfully as form blocks to press sheet metal parts, such as ribs, spars, fans, etc. To perform a press forming operation:

1. Cut a sheet metal blank to size and deburr edges.

2. Set the form block (normally male) on the lower press platen.

3. Place the prepared sheet metal blank (with locating pins to prevent shifting of the blank when the pressure is applied).

4. Lower or close the rubber pad-filled press head over the form block and the rubber envelope.

Figure 4-61. *Slip roll operation.*

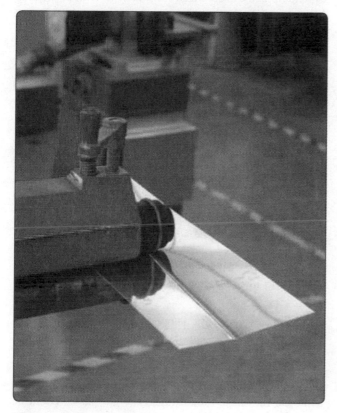

Figure 4-62. *Rotary machine.*

5. The form block forces the blank to conform to its contour.

Hydropress forming is usually limited to relatively flat parts with flanges, beads, and lightening holes. However, some types of large radii contoured parts can be formed by a combination of hand forming and pressing operations.

Spin Forming

In spin forming, a flat circle of metal is rotated at a very high speed to shape a seamless, hollow part using the combined forces of rotation and pressure. For example, a flat circular blank such as an aluminum disk, is mounted in a lathe in conjunction with a form block (usually made of hardwood). As the aircraft technician revolves the disc and form block together at high speeds, the disk is molded to the form block by applying pressure with a spinning stick or tool. It provides an economical alternative to stamping, casting, and many other metal forming processes. Propeller spinners are sometimes fabricated with this technique.

Aluminum soap, tallow, or ordinary soap can be used as a lubricant. The best adapted materials for spinning are the softer aluminum alloys, but other alloys can be used if the shape to be spun is not excessively deep or if the spinning is done in stages utilizing intermediate annealing to remove the effect of strain hardening that results from the spinning operation. Hot forming is used in some instances when spinning thicker and harder alloys. *[Figure 4-63]*

Figure 4-63. *Spin forming.*

Forming With an English Wheel

The English wheel, a popular type of metal forming tool used to create double curves in metal, has two steel wheels between which metal is formed. *[Figure 4-64]* Keep in mind that the English wheel is primarily a stretching machine, so it stretches and thins the metal before forming it into the desired shape. Thus, the operator must be careful not to over-stretch the metal.

Figure 4-64. *English wheel.*

To use the English wheel, place a piece of sheet metal between the wheels (one above and one below the metal). Then, roll the wheels against one another under a pre-adjusted pressure setting. Steel or aluminum can be shaped by pushing the metal back and forth between the wheels. Very little pressure is needed to shape the panel, which is stretched or raised to the desired shape. It is important to work slowly and gradually curve the metal into the desired shape. Monitor the curvature with frequent references to the template.

The English wheel is used for shaping low crowns on large panels and polishing or planishing (to smooth the surface of a metal by rolling or hammering it) parts that have been formed with power hammers or hammer and shot bag.

Piccolo Former

The piccolo former is used for cold forming and rolling sheet metal and other profile sections (extrusions). *[Figure 4-65]* The position of the ram is adjustable in height by means of either a handwheel or a foot pedal that permits control of the working pressure. Be sure to utilize the adjusting ring situated in the machine head to control the maximum working pressure. The forming tools are located in the moving ram and the lower tool holder. Depending on the variety of forming tools included, the operator can perform such procedures as forming edges, bending profiles, removing wrinkles, spot shrinking to remove buckles and dents, or expanding dome sheet metal. Available in either fiberglass (to prevent marring the surface) or steel (for working harder materials) faces, the tools are the quick-change type.

Figure 4-65. *Piccolo former.*

Shrinking and Stretching Tools
Shrinking Tools

Shrinking dies repeatedly clamp down on the metal, then shift inward. *[Figure 4-66]* This compresses the material between the dies, which actually slightly increases the thickness of the metal. Strain hardening takes place during this process, so it is best to set the working pressure high enough to complete the shape rather quickly (eight passes could be considered excessive).

Figure 4-66. *Shrinking and stretching tools.*

CAUTION: Avoid striking a die on the radius itself when forming a curved flange. This damages the metal in the radius and decreases the angle of bend.

Stretching Tools

Stretching dies repeatedly clamp down on the surface and then shift outward. This stretches the metal between the dies, which decreases the thickness in the stretched area. Striking the same point too many times weakens and eventually cracks the part. It is advantageous to deburr or even polish the edges of a flange that must undergo even moderate stretching to avoid crack formation. Forming flanges with existing holes causes the holes to distort and possibly crack or substantially weaken the flange.

Manual Foot-Operated Sheet Metal Shrinker

The manual foot-operated sheet metal shrinker operates very similarly to the Piccolo former though it only has two primary functions: shrinking and stretching. The only dies available are steel faced and therefore tend to mar the surface of the metal. When used on aluminum, it is necessary to gently blend out the surface irregularities (primarily in the cladding), then treat and paint the part.

Since this is a manual machine, it relies on leg power, as the operator repeatedly steps on the foot pedal. The more force is applied, the more stresses are concentrated at that single point. It yields a better part with a series of smaller stretches (or shrinks) than with a few intense ones. Squeezing the dies over the radius damages the metal and flattens out some of the bend. It may be useful to tape a thick piece of plastic or micarta to the opposite leg to shim the radius of the angle away from the clamping area of the dies.

NOTE: Watch the part change shape while slowly applying pressure. A number of small stretches works more effectively than one large one. If applying too much pressure, the metal has the tendency to buckle.

Hand-Operated Shrinker and Stretcher

The hand-operated shrinker and structure is similar to the manual foot-operated unit, except a handle is used to apply force to shrinking and stretching blocks. The dies are all metal and leave marks on aluminum that need to be blended out after the shrinking or stretching operation. *[Figure 4-67]*

Figure 4-67. *Hand-operated shrinker and stretcher unit.*

Dollies and Stakes

Sheet metal is often formed or finished (planished) over anvils, available in a variety of shapes and sizes, called dollies and stakes. These are used for forming small, odd-shaped parts, or for putting on finishing touches for which a large machine may not be suited. Dollies are meant to be held in the hand, whereas stakes are designed to be supported by a flat cast iron bench plate fastened to the workbench. *[Figure 4-68]*

Most stakes have machined, polished surfaces that have been hardened. Use of stakes to back up material when chiseling, or when using any similar cutting tool, defaces the surface of the stake and makes it useless for finish work.

Hardwood Form Blocks

Hardwood form blocks can be constructed to duplicate practically any aircraft structural or nonstructural part. The wooden block or form is shaped to the exact dimensions and contour of the part to be formed.

V-Blocks

V-blocks made of hardwood are widely used in airframe metalwork for shrinking and stretching metal, particularly angles and flanges. The size of the block depends on the work being done and on personal preference. Although any type of hardwood is suitable, maple and ash are recommended for best results when working with aluminum alloys.

Figure 4-68. *Dollies and stakes.*

Shrinking Blocks

A shrinking block consists of two metal blocks and some device for clamping them together. One block forms the base and the other is cut away to provide space where the crimped material can be hammered. The legs of the upper jaw clamp the material to the base block on each side of the crimp to prevent the material from creeping away, but remains stationary while the crimp is hammered flat (being shrunk). This type of crimping block is designed to be held in a bench vise.

Shrinking blocks can be made to fit any specific need. The basic form and principle remain the same, even though the blocks may vary considerably in size and shape.

Sandbags

A sandbag is generally used as a support during the bumping process. A serviceable bag can be made by sewing heavy canvas or soft leather to form a bag of the desired size, and filling it with sand which has been sifted through a fine mesh screen.

Before filling canvas bags with sand, use a brush to coat the inside of the bag with softened paraffin or beeswax, which forms a sealing layer and prevents the sand from working through the pores of the canvas. Bags can also be filled with shot as an alternative to sand.

Sheet Metal Hammers and Mallets

The sheet metal hammer and the mallet are metal fabrication hand tools used for bending and forming sheet metal without marring or indenting the metal. The hammer head is usually made of high carbon, heat-treated steel, while the head of the mallet, which is usually larger than that of the hammer, is made of rubber, plastic, wood, or leather. In combination with a sandbag, V-blocks, and dies, sheet metal body hammers and mallets are used to form annealed metal. *[Figure 4-69]*

Figure 4-69. *Sheet metal mallet and hammers.*

Sheet Metal Holding Devices

In order to work with sheet metal during the fabrication process, the aviation technician uses a variety of holding devices, such as clamps, vises, and fasteners to hold the work together. The type of operation being performed and the type of metal being used determine what type of the holding device is needed.

Clamps and Vises

Clamps and vises hold materials in place when it is not possible to handle a tool and the workpiece at the same time. A clamp is a fastening device with movable jaws that has opposing, often adjustable, sides or parts. An essential fastening device, it holds objects tightly together to prevent movement or separation. Clamps can be either temporary or permanent. Temporary clamps, such as the carriage clamp (commonly called the C-clamp), are used to position components while fixing them together.

C-Clamps

The C-clamp is shaped like a large C and has three main parts: threaded screw, jaw, and swivel head. *[Figure 4-70]*

Figure 4-70. *C-clamps.*

Figure 4-71. *A utility vise with swivel base and anvil.*

The swivel plate or flat end of the screw prevents the end from turning directly against the material being clamped. C-clamp size is measured by the dimension of the largest object the frame can accommodate with the screw fully extended. The distance from the center line of the screw to the inside edge of the frame or the depth of throat is also an important consideration when using this clamp. C-clamps vary in size from two inches upward. Since C-clamps can leave marks on aluminum, protect the aircraft covering with masking tape at the places where the C-clamp is used.

Vises

Vises are another clamping device that hold the workpiece in place and allow work to be done on it with tools such as saws and drills. The vise consists of two fixed or adjustable jaws that are opened or closed by a screw or a lever. The size of a vise is measured by both the jaw width and the capacity of the vise when the jaws are fully open. Vises also depend on a screw to apply pressure, but their textured jaws enhance gripping ability beyond that of a clamp.

Two of the most commonly used vises are the machinist's vise and the utility vise. *[Figure 4-71]* The machinist's vise has flat jaws and usually a swivel base, whereas the utility bench vise has scored, removable jaws and an anvil-faced back jaw. This vise holds heavier material than the machinist's vise and also grips pipe or rod firmly. The back jaw can be used as an anvil if the work being done is light. To avoid marring metal in the vise jaws, add some type of padding, such as a ready-made rubber jaw pad.

Reusable Sheet Metal Fasteners

Reusable sheet metal fasteners temporarily hold drilled sheet metal parts accurately in position for riveting or drilling. If sheet metal parts are not held tightly together, they separate while being riveted or drilled. The Cleco (also spelled Cleko) fastener is the most commonly used sheet metal holder. *[Figure 4-72]*

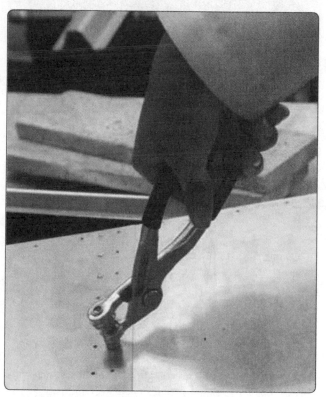

Figure 4-72. *Cleco and Cleco plier.*

Cleco Fasteners

The Cleco fastener consists of a steel cylinder body with a plunger on the top, a spring, a pair of step-cut locks, and a spreader bar. These fasteners come in six different sizes: $3/32$, $1/8$, $5/32$, $3/16$, $1/4$, and $3/8$-inch in diameter with the size stamped on the fastener. Color coding allows for easy size recognition. A special type of plier fits the six different sizes. When installed correctly, the reusable Cleco fastener keeps the holes in the separate sheets aligned.

Hex Nut and Wing Nut Temporary Sheet Fasteners

Hex nut and wing nut fasteners are used to temporarily fasten sheets of metal when higher clamp up pressure is required. [Figure 4-73] Hex nut fasteners provide up to 300 pounds of clamping force with the advantage of quick installation and removal with a hex nut runner. Wing nut sheet metal fasteners, characterized by wing shaped protrusions, not only provide a consistent clamping force from 0 to 300 pounds, but the aircraft technician can turn and tighten these fasteners by hand. Cleco hex nut fasteners are identical to Cleco wing nut fasteners, but the Cleco hex nut can be used with pneumatic Cleco installers.

Figure 4-73. *Hex nut fastener.*

Aluminum Alloys

Aluminum alloys are the most frequently encountered type of sheet metal in aircraft repair. AC 43.13.1 Chapter 4, Metal Structure, Welding, and Brazing: Identification of Metals (as revised) provides an in-depth discussion of all metal types. This section describes the aluminum alloys used in the forming processes discussed in the remainder of the chapter.

In its pure state, aluminum is lightweight, lustrous, and corrosion resistant. The thermal conductivity of aluminum is very high. It is ductile, malleable, and nonmagnetic. When combined with various percentages of other metals (generally copper, manganese, and magnesium), aluminum alloys that are used in aircraft construction are formed. Aluminum alloys are lightweight and strong. They do not possess the corrosion resistance of pure aluminum and are usually treated to prevent deterioration. Alclad™ aluminum is an aluminum alloy with a protective cladding of aluminum to improve its corrosion resistance.

To provide a visual means for identifying the various grades of aluminum and aluminum alloys, aluminum stock is usually marked with symbols such as a Government Specification Number, the temper or condition furnished, or the commercial code marking. Plate and sheet are usually marked with specification numbers or code markings in rows approximately five inches apart. Tubes, bars, rods, and extruded shapes are marked with specification numbers or code markings at intervals of three to five feet along the length of each piece.

The commercial code marking consists of a number that identifies the particular composition of the alloy. Additionally, letter suffixes designate the basic temper designations and subdivisions of aluminum alloys.

The aluminum and various aluminum alloys used in aircraft repair and construction are as follows:

- Aluminum designated by the symbol 1100 is used where strength is not an important factor, but where weight economy and corrosion resistance are desired. This aluminum is used for fuel tanks, cowlings, and oil tanks. It is also used for repairing wingtips and tanks. This material is weldable.

- Alloy 3003 is similar to 1100 and is generally used for the same purposes. It contains a small percentage of magnesium and is stronger and harder than 1100 aluminum.

- Alloy 2014 is used for heavy-duty forgings, plates, extrusions for aircraft fittings, wheels, and major structural components. This alloy is often used for applications requiring high strength and hardness, as well as for service at elevated temperatures.

- Alloy 2017 is used for rivets. This material is now in limited use.

- Alloy 2024, with or without Alclad™ coating, is used for aircraft structures, rivets, hardware, machine screw products, and other miscellaneous structural applications. In addition, this alloy is commonly used for heat-treated parts, airfoil and fuselage skins, extrusions, and fittings.

- Alloy 2025 is used extensively for propeller blades.

- Alloy 2219 is used for fuel tanks, aircraft skin, and structural components. This material has high fracture toughness and is readily weldable. Alloy 2219 is also highly resistant to stress corrosion cracking.

- Alloy 5052 is used where good workability, very good corrosion resistance, high fatigue strength, weldability, and moderate static strength are desired. This alloy is used for fuel, hydraulic, and oil lines.

- Alloy 5056 is used for making rivets and cable sheeting and in applications where aluminum comes into contact with magnesium alloys. Alloy 5056 is generally resistant to the most common forms of corrosion.

- Cast aluminum alloys are used for cylinder heads, crankcases, fuel injectors, carburetors, and landing wheels.

- Various alloys, including 3003, 5052, and 1100 aluminum, are hardened by cold working rather than by heat treatment. Other alloys, including 2017 and 2024, are hardened by heat treatment, cold working, or a combination of the two. Various casting alloys are hardened by heat treatment.

- Alloy 6061 is generally weldable by all commercial procedures and methods. It also maintains acceptable toughness in many cryogenic applications. Alloy 6061 is easily extruded and is commonly used for hydraulic and pneumatic tubing.

- Although higher in strength than 2024, alloy 7075 has a lower fracture toughness and is generally used in tension applications where fatigue is not critical. The T6 temper of 7075 should be avoided in corrosive environments. However, the T7351 temper of 7075 has excellent stress corrosion resistance and better fracture toughness than the T6 temper. The T76 temper is often used to improve the resistance of 7075 to exfoliate corrosion.

Structural Fasteners

Structural fasteners, used to join sheet metal structures securely, come in thousands of shapes and sizes with many of them specialized and specific to certain aircraft. Since some structural fasteners are common to all aircraft, this section focuses on the more frequently used fasteners. For the purposes of this discussion, fasteners are divided into two main groups: solid shank rivets and special purpose fasteners that include blind rivets.

Solid Shank Rivet

The solid shank rivet is the most common type of rivet used in aircraft construction. Used to join aircraft structures, solid shank rivets are one of the oldest and most reliable types of fastener. Widely used in the aircraft manufacturing industry, solid shank rivets are relatively low-cost, permanently installed fasteners. They are faster to install than bolts and nuts since they adapt well to automatic, high-speed installation tools. Rivets should not be used in thick materials or in tensile applications, as their tensile strengths are quite low relative to their shear strength. The longer the total grip length (the total thickness of sheets being joined), the more difficult it becomes to lock the rivet.

Riveted joints are neither airtight nor watertight unless special seals or coatings are used. Since rivets are permanently installed, they must be removed by drilling them out, a laborious task.

Description

Before installation, the rivet consists of a smooth cylindrical shaft with a factory head on one end. The opposite end is called the bucktail. To secure two or more pieces of sheet metal together, the rivet is placed into a hole cut just a bit larger in diameter than the rivet itself. Once placed in this predrilled hole, the bucktail is upset or deformed by any of several methods from hand-held hammers to pneumatically driven squeezing tools. This action causes the rivet to expand about 1½ times the original shaft diameter, forming a second head that firmly holds the material in place.

Rivet Head Shape

Solid rivets are available in several head shapes, but the universal and the 100° countersunk head are the most commonly used in aircraft structures. Universal head rivets were developed specifically for the aircraft industry and designed as a replacement for both the round and brazier head rivets. These rivets replaced all protruding head rivets and are used primarily where the protruding head has no aerodynamic significant. They have a flat area on the head, a head diameter twice the shank diameter, and a head height approximately 42.5 percent of the shank diameter. *[Figure 4-74]*

Figure 4-74. *Solid shank rivet styles.*

The countersunk head angle can vary from 60° to 120°, but the 100° has been adopted as standard because this head style provides the best possible compromise between tension/shear strength and flushness requirements. This rivet is used where flushness is required because the rivet is flat-topped and undercut to allow the head to fit into a countersunk or dimpled hole. The countersunk rivet is primarily intended for use when aerodynamics smoothness is critical, such as on the external surface of a high-speed aircraft.

Typically, rivets are fabricated from aluminum alloys, such as 2017-T4, 2024-T4, 2117-T4, 7050, and 5056. Titanium, nickel-based alloys, such as Monel® (corrosion-resistant steel), mild steel or iron, and copper rivets are also used for rivets in certain cases.

Rivets are available in a wide variety of alloys, head shapes, and sizes and have a wide variety of uses in aircraft structure. Rivets that are satisfactory for one part of the aircraft are often unsatisfactory for another part. Therefore, it is important that an aircraft technician know the strength and driving properties of the various types of rivets and how to identify them, as well as how to drive or install them.

Solid rivets are classified by their head shape, by the material from which they are manufactured, and by their size. Identification codes used are derived from a combination of the Military Standard (MS) and National Aerospace Standard (NAS) systems, as well as an older classification system known as AN for Army/Navy. For example, the prefix MS identifies hardware that conforms to written military standards. A letter or letters following the head-shaped code identify the material or alloy from which the rivet was made. The alloy code is followed by two numbers separated by a dash. The first number is the numerator of a fraction, which specifies the shank diameter in thirty-seconds of an inch. The second number is the numerator of a fraction in sixteenths of an inch and identifies the length of the rivet. Rivet head shapes and their identifying code numbers are shown in *Figure 4-75.*

Figure 4-75. *Rivet head shapes and their identifying code numbers.*

The most frequently used repair rivet is the AD rivet because it can be installed in the received condition. Some rivet alloys, such as DD rivets (alloy 2024-T4), are too hard to drive in the received condition and must be annealed before they can be installed. Typically, these rivets are annealed and stored in a freezer to retard hardening, which has led to the nickname "ice box rivets." They are removed from the freezer just prior to use. Most DD rivets have been replaced by E-type rivets which can be installed in the received condition.

The head type, size, and strength required in a rivet are governed by such factors as the kind of forces present at the point riveted, the kind and thickness of the material to be riveted, and the location of the part on the aircraft. The type of head needed for a particular job is determined by where it is to be installed. Countersunk head rivets should be used where a smooth aerodynamic surface is required. Universal head rivets may be used in most other areas.

The size (or diameter) of the selected rivet shank should correspond in general to the thickness of the material being riveted. If an excessively large rivet is used in a thin material, the force necessary to drive the rivet properly causes an undesirable bulging around the rivet head. On the other hand, if an excessively small rivet diameter is selected for thick material, the shear strength of the rivet is not great enough to carry the load of the joint. As a general rule, the rivet diameter should be at least two and a half to three times the thickness of the thicker sheet. Rivets most commonly chosen in the assembly and repair of aircraft range from ³/₃₂-inch to ³/₈-inch in diameter. Ordinarily, rivets smaller than ³/₃₂-inch in diameter are never used on any structural parts that carry stresses.

The proper sized rivets to use for any repair can also be determined by referring to the rivets (used by the manufacturer) in the next parallel row inboard on the wing or forward on the fuselage. Another method of determining the size of rivets to be used is to multiply the skin's thickness by 3 and use the next larger size rivet corresponding to that figure. For example, if the skin is 0.040 inch thick, multiply 0.040 inch by 3 to get 0.120 inch and use the next larger size of rivet, ⅛-inch (0.125 inch).

When rivets are to pass completely through tubular members, select a rivet diameter equivalent to at least ⅛ the outside diameter of the tube. If one tube sleeves or fits over another, take the outside diameter of the outside tube and use one-eighth of that distance as the minimum rivet diameter. A good practice is to calculate the minimum rivet diameter and then use the next larger size rivet.

Whenever possible, select rivets of the same alloy number as the material being riveted. For example, use 1100 and 3003 rivets on parts fabricated from 1100 and 3003 alloys, and 2117-1 and 2017-T rivets on parts fabricated from 2017 and 2024 alloys.

The size of the formed head is the visual standard of a proper rivet installation. The minimum and maximum sizes, as well as the ideal size, are shown in *Figure 4-76.*

Installation of Rivets
Repair Layout
Repair layout involves determining the number of rivets required, the proper size and style of rivets to be used, their material, temper condition and strength, the size of the holes,

Driven Rivet Standards

A, AD, B, DD Rivets

Predrive protrusion
1.33 d   1.5 d

Formed head dimension

.66 d   .5 d   .33 d
1.25 d   1.5 d   1.66 d

Minimum   Preferred   Maximum

D, E, (KE), M Rivets

Predrive protrusion
1.25 d   1.33 d

Formed head dimension

.66 d   .6 d   .5 d
1.25 d   1.4 d   1.5 d

Minimum   Preferred   Maximum

Figure 4-76. *Rivet formed head dimensions.*

the distances between the holes, and the distance between the holes and the edges of the patch. Distances are measured in terms of rivet diameter.

Rivet Length

To determine the total length of a rivet to be installed, the combined thickness of the materials to be joined must first be known. This measurement is known as the grip length. The total length of the rivet equals the grip length plus the amount of rivet shank needed to form a proper shop head. The latter equals one and a half times the diameter of the rivet shank. Where A is total rivet length, B is grip length, and C is the length of the material needed to form a shop head, this formula can be represented as A = B + C. *[Figure 4-76]*

Rivet Strength

For structural applications, the strength of the replacement rivets is of primary importance. *[Figure 4-77]* Rivets made of material that is lower in strength should not be used as replacements unless the shortfall is made up by using a larger rivet. For example, a rivet of 2024-T4 aluminum alloy should not be replaced with one of 2117-T4 or 2017-T4 aluminum alloy unless the next larger size is used.

The 2117-T rivet is used for general repair work, since it requires no heat treatment, is fairly soft and strong, and is highly corrosion resistant when used with most types of alloys. Always consult the maintenance manual for correct

Standard Rivet Alloy Code Markings

Alloy code—A
Alloy—1100 or 3003 aluminum
Head marking—None

Shear strength—10 KSI
Nonstructural uses only

Alloy code—B
Alloy—5056 aluminum
Head marking—raised cross

Shear strength—28 KSI

Alloy code—AD
Alloy—2117 aluminum
Head marking—Dimple

Shear strength—30 KSI

Alloy code—D
Alloy—2017 aluminum
Head marking—Raised dot

Shear strength—38 KSI
38 KSI When driven as received
34 KSI When re-heat treated

Alloy code—DD
Alloy—2024 aluminum
Head marking—Two bars (raised)

Shear strength—41 KSI
Must be driven in "W" condition
(Ice-Box)

Alloy code—E, [KE*] *Boeing code
Alloy—7050 aluminum
Head marking—Raised ring

Shear strength—43 KSI
Replacement for DD rivet
to be driven in "T" condition

Alloy code—E
Alloy—7050 aluminum
Head marking—raised circle

Shear strength—54 KSI

Figure 4-77. *Rivet allow strength.*

rivet type and material. The type of rivet head to select for a particular repair job can be determined by referring to the type used within the surrounding area by the manufacturer. A general rule to follow on a flush-riveted aircraft is to apply flush rivets on the upper surface of the wing and stabilizers, on the lower leading edge back to the spar, and on the fuselage back to the high point of the wing. Use universal head rivets in all other surface areas. Whenever possible, select rivets of the same alloy number as the material being riveted.

Stresses Applied to Rivets

Shear is one of the two stresses applied to rivets. The shear strength is the amount of force required to cut a rivet that holds two or more sheets of material together. If the rivet holds two parts, it is under single shear; if it holds three sheets or parts, it is under double shear. To determine the shear strength, the diameter of the rivet to be used must be found by multiplying the thickness of the skin 3. For example, a material thickness of 0.040 inch multiplied by 3 equals 0.120 inch. In this case, the rivet diameter selected would be ⅛ (0.125) inch.

Tension is the other stress applied to rivets. The resistance to tension is called bearing strength and is the amount of tension required to pull a rivet through the edge of two sheets riveted together or to elongate the hole.

Rivet Spacing

Rivet spacing otherwise known as rivet pitch is the measurement between the centers of the rivets in the same row. The minimum allowable pitch is 3D, 3 times the diameter of the rivet that is used. It is recommended that the minimum spacing between protruding head rivets not be less than 3½D and the minimum spacing between flush head rivets not be less than 4D. This allows for variations when drilling the holes for the rivets and also ensures proper pitch when the material is removed for countersinking rivets. These dimensions may be used as the minimum spacing when there is no direction given in the SRM.

Rivet Layout

On most repairs, the general practice is to use the same rivet spacing and edge distance that the manufacturer used in the area surrounding the damage. The SRM for the particular aircraft should always be consulted prior to performing any repair or alteration. Aside from these fundamental rules, there is no specific set of rules that govern the spacing of rivets in all cases. However, there are certain minimum requirements that must be observed.

When possible, rivet edge distance, rivet spacing, and distance between rows should be the same as that of the original installation.

When new sections are to be added:

- The edge distance measured from the center of the rivet should never be less than 2D.

- The distance between rivets or pitch should be at least 3D.

- The distance between rivet rows should never be less than 2½D.

Figure 4-78 illustrates acceptable ways of laying out a rivet pattern for a repair.

Figure 4-78. *Acceptable rivet patterns.*

Edge Distance

Edge distance is the distance from the center of the rivet to the edge of the sheet. It should not be less than 2D or more than 4D. It is recommended that the edge distance be 2 ½D for both protruding head and countersunk rivets. If rivets are placed too close to the edge, the sheet may crack or pull away from the rivets. If they are spaced to far from the edge, the sheet is likely to turn up at the edges. *[Figure 4-79]*

Edge Distance/Edge Margin	Minimum Edge Distance	Preferred Edge Distance
Protruding head rivets	2 D	2 D + ¹/₁₆"
Countersunk rivets	2½ D	2½ D + ¹/₁₆"

Figure 4-79. *Minimum edge distance.*

Where the smallest allowable rivet pitch is 3D, the average rivet pitch usually ranges from 4D to 6D rivet diameters and should be no larger than 12D. Rivet pitch on parts that are subject to bending moments is often closer to the minimum pitch to prevent buckling of the skin between the rivets. The recommended minimum pitch also depends on the number of rows of rivets. One-and three-row layouts have a recommended minimum pitch of 3D. Two-row layouts have a recommended 4D pitch. The pitch for countersunk rivets should be larger than for universal head rivets. If the rivet spacing is made at least 1/16 inch larger than the minimum, the rivet hole can be oversized without violating minimum rivet spacing. *[Figure 8-80]*

Where the smallest allowable edge distance is 2D, it is good practice to lay out the rivets a little further from the edge so that the rivet holes can be oversized without violating the edge distance minimum. Add 1/16 inch to the minimum edge distance or determine the edge distance using the next size up rivet diameter.

Two methods for obtaining edge distance:

- The rivet diameter of a protruding head rivet is 3/32-inch. Multiply 2 times 3/32-inch to obtain the minimum edge distance, 3/16-inch, add 1/16-inch to yield the preferred edge distance of 1/4-inch.

- The rivet diameter of a protruding head rivet is 3/32-inch. Select the next size of rivet, which is 1/8-inch. Calculate the edge distance by multiplying 2 times 1/8-inch to get 1/4-inch.

Transverse Pitch

Transverse pitch is the perpendicular distance between rivet rows. It is usually 75 percent of the rivet pitch. The smallest allowable transverse pitch is 2½ rivet diameters. The smallest allowable transverse pitch is 2½ rivet diameters. Rivet pitch and transverse pitch often have the same dimension and are simply called rivet spacing.

Rivet Layout Example

The general rules for rivet spacing, as it is applied to a straight-row layout, are quite simple. In a one-row layout,

find the edge distance at each end of the row and then lay off the rivet pitch (distance between rivets), as shown in *Figure 4-81*. In a two-row layout, lay off the first row, place the second row a distance equal to the transverse pitch from the first row, and then lay off rivet spots in the second row so that they fall midway between those in the first row. In the three-row layout, first lay off the first and third rows, then use a straightedge to determine the second row rivet spots.

When splicing a damaged tube, and the rivets pass completely through the tube, space the rivets four to seven rivet diameters apart if adjacent rivets are at right angles to each other, and space them five to seven rivet diameters apart if the rivets are parallel to each other. The first rivet on each side of the joint should be no less than 2½ rivet diameters from the end of the sleeve.

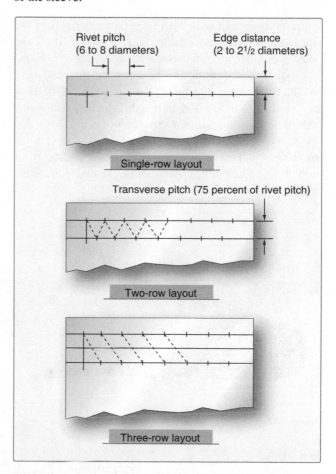

Figure 4-81. *Rivet layout.*

Rivet Spacing	Minimum Spacing	Preferred Spacing
1 and 3 rows protruding head rivet layout	3D	3D + 1/16"
2 row protruding head rivet layout	4D	4D + 1/16"
1 and 3 rows countersunk head rivet layout	3/1/2D	3/1/2D + 1/16"
2 row countersunk head rivet layout	4/1/2D	4/1/2D + 1/16"

Figure 4-80. *Rivet spacing.*

Rivet Installation Tools

The various tools needed in the normal course of driving and upsetting rivets include drills, reamers, rivet cutters or nippers, bucking bars, riveting hammers, draw sets, dimpling dies or other types of countersinking equipment, rivet guns, and squeeze riveters. C-clamps, vises, and other fasteners used to hold sheets together when riveting were discussed earlier in the chapter. Other tools and equipment needed in the installation of rivets are discussed in the following paragraphs.

Hand Tools

A variety of hand tools are used in the normal course of driving and upsetting rivets. They include rivet cutters, bucking bars, hand riveters, countersinks, and dimpling tools.

Rivet Cutter

The rivet cutter is used to trim rivets when rivets of the required length are unavailable. *[Figure 4-82]* To use the rotary rivet cutter, insert the rivet in the correct hole, place the required number of shims under the rivet head, and squeeze the cutter as if it were a pair of pliers. Rotation of the disks cuts the rivet to give the right length, which is determined by the number of shims inserted under the head. When using a large rivet cutter, place it in a vise, insert the rivet in the proper hole, and cut by pulling the handle, which shears off the rivet. If regular rivet cutters are not available, diagonal cutting pliers can be used as a substitute cutter.

Figure 4-82. *Rivet cutters.*

Bucking Bar

The bucking bar, sometimes called a dolly, bucking iron, or bucking block, is a heavy chunk of steel whose countervibration during installation contributes to proper rivet installation. They come in a variety of shapes and sizes, and their weights ranges from a few ounces to 8 or 10 pounds, depending upon the nature of the work. Bucking bars are most often made from low-carbon steel that has been case hardened or alloy bar stock. Those made of better grades of steel last longer and require less reconditioning.

Bucking faces must be hard enough to resist indentation and remain smooth, but not hard enough to shatter. Sometimes, the more complicated bars must be forged or built up by welding. The bar usually has a concave face to conform to the shape of the shop head to be made. When selecting a bucking bar, the first consideration is shape. *[Figure 4-83]* If the bar does not have the correct shape, it deforms the rivet head; if the bar is too light, it does not give the necessary bucking weight, and the material may become bulged toward the shop head. If the bar is too heavy, its weight and the bucking force may cause the material to bulge away from the shop head.

Figure 4-83. *Bucking bars.*

This tool is used by holding it against the shank end of a rivet while the shop head is being formed. Always hold the face of the bucking bar at right angles to the rivet shank. Failure to do so causes the rivet shank to bend with the first blows of the rivet gun and causes the material to become marred with the final blows. The bucker must hold the bucking bar in place until the rivet is completely driven. If the bucking bar is removed while the gun is in operation, the rivet set may be driven through the material. Allow the weight of the bucking bar to do most of the work and do not bear down too heavily on the shank of the rivet. The operator's hands merely guide the bar and supply the necessary tension and rebound action. Coordinated bucking allows the bucking bar to vibrate in unison with the gun set. With experience, a high degree of skill can be developed.

Defective rivet heads can be caused by lack of proper vibrating action, the use of a bucking bar that is too light or too heavy, and failure to hold the bucking bar at right angles to the rivet. The bars must be kept clean, smooth, and well polished. Their edges should be slightly rounded to prevent marring the material surrounding the riveting operation.

Hand Rivet Set

A hand rivet set is a tool equipped with a die for driving a particular type rivet. Rivet sets are available to fit every size and shape of rivet head. The ordinary set is made of ½-inch carbon tool steel about 6 inches in length and is knurled to prevent slipping in the hand. Only the face of the set is hardened and polished.

Sets for universal rivets are recessed (or cupped) to fit the rivet head. In selecting the correct set, be sure it provides the proper clearance between the set and the sides of the rivet head and between the surfaces of the metal and the set. Flush or flat sets are used for countersunk and flathead rivets. To seat flush rivets properly, be sure that the flush sets are at least 1 inch in diameter.

Special draw sets are used to draw up the sheets to eliminate any opening between them before the rivet is bucked. Each draw set has a hole ¹⁄₃₂-inch larger than the diameter of the rivet shank for which it is made. Occasionally, the draw set and rivet header are incorporated into one tool. The header part consists of a hole shallow enough for the set to expand the rivet and head when struck with a hammer.

Countersinking Tool

The countersink is a tool that cuts a cone-shaped depression around the rivet hole to allow the rivet to set flush with the surface of the skin. Countersinks are made with angles to correspond with the various angles of countersunk rivet heads. The standard countersink has a 100° angle, as shown in *Figure 4-84*. Special microstop countersinks (commonly called stop countersinks) are available that can be adjusted to any desired depth and have cutters to allow interchangeable holes with various countersunk angles to be made. *[Figure 4-85]* Some stop countersinks also have a micrometer set mechanism, in 0.001-inch increments, for adjusting their cutting depths.

Figure 4-84. *Countersinks.*

Dimpling Dies

Dimpling is done with a male and female die (punch and die set). The male die has a guide the size of the rivet hole and with the same degree of countersink as the rivet. The female die has a hole with a corresponding degree of countersink into which the male guide fits.

Figure 4-85. *Microstop countersink.*

Power Tools

The most common power tools used in riveting are the pneumatic rivet gun, rivet squeezers, and the microshaver.

Pneumatic Rivet Gun

The pneumatic rivet gun is the most common rivet upsetting tool used in airframe repair work. It is available in many sizes and types. *[Figure 4-86]* The manufacturer's recommended capacity for each gun is usually stamped on the barrel. Pneumatic guns operate on air pressure of 90 to 100 pounds per square inch and are used in conjunction with interchangeable rivet sets. Each set is designed to fit the specific type of rivet and the location of the work. The shank of the set is designed to fit into the rivet gun. An air-driven hammer inside the barrel of the gun supplies force to buck the rivet.

Figure 4-86. *Rivet guns.*

Slow hitting rivet guns that strike from 900 to 2,500 blows per minute are the most common type. *[Figure 4-87]* These blows are slow enough to be easily controlled and heavy enough to do the job. These guns are sized by the largest rivet size continuously driven with size often based on the Chicago Pneumatic Company's old "X" series. A 4X gun (dash 8 or ¼ rivet) is used for normal work. The less powerful 3X gun is used for smaller rivets in thinner structure. 7X guns are used for large rivets in thicker structures. A rivet gun should upset

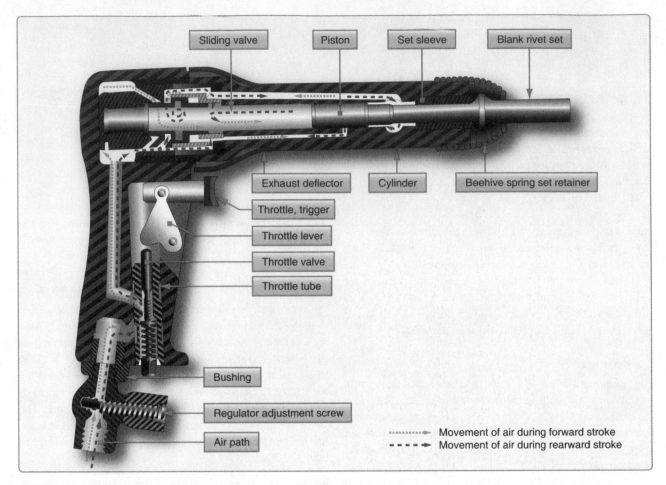

Figure 4-87. *Components of a rivet gun.*

a rivet in 1 to 3 seconds. With practice, an aircraft technician learns the length of time needed to hold down the trigger.

A rivet gun with the correct header (rivet set) must be held snugly against the rivet head and perpendicular to the surface while a bucking bar of the proper weight is held against the opposite end. The force of the gun must be absorbed by the bucking bar and not the structure being riveted. When the gun is triggered, the rivet is driven.

Always make sure the correct rivet header and the retaining spring are installed. Test the rivet gun on a piece of wood and adjust the air valve to a setting that is comfortable for the operator. The driving force of the rivet gun is adjusted by a needle valve on the handle. Adjustments should never be tested against anything harder than a wooden block to avoid header damage. If the adjustment fails to provide the best driving force, a different sized gun is needed. A gun that is too powerful is hard to control and may damage the work. On the other hand, if the gun is too light, it may work harden the rivet before the head can be fully formed.

The riveting action should start slowly and be one continued burst. If the riveting starts too fast, the rivet header might slip off the rivet and damage the rivet (smiley) or damage the skin (eyebrow). Try to drive the rivets within 3 seconds, because the rivet will work harden if the driving process takes too long. The dynamic of the driving process has the gun hitting, or vibrating, the rivet and material, which causes the bar to bounce, or countervibrate. These opposing blows (low frequency vibrations) squeeze the rivet, causing it to swell and then form the upset head.

Some precautions to be observed when using a rivet gun are:

1. Never point a rivet gun at anyone at any time. A rivet gun should be used for one purpose only: to drive or install rivets.

2. Never depress the trigger mechanism unless the set is held tightly against a block of wood or a rivet.

3. Always disconnect the air hose from the rivet gun when it is not in use for any appreciable length of time.

While traditional tooling has changed little in the past 60 years, significant changes have been made in rivet gun ergonomics. Reduced vibration rivet guns and bucking bars have been developed to reduce the incidence of carpal tunnel syndrome and enhance operator comfort.

Rivet Sets/Headers

Pneumatic guns are used in conjunction with interchangeable rivet sets or headers. Each is designed to fit the type of rivet and location of the work. The shank of the rivet header is designed to fit into the rivet gun. An appropriate header must be a correct match for the rivet being driven. The working face of a header should be properly designed and smoothly polished. They are made of forged steel, heat treated to be tough but not too brittle. Flush headers come in various sizes. Smaller ones concentrate the driving force in a small area for maximum efficiency. Larger ones spread the driving force over a larger area and are used for the riveting of thin skins.

Nonflush headers should fit to contact about the center two-thirds of the rivet head. They must be shallow enough to allow slight upsetting of the head in driving and some misalignment without eyebrowing the riveted surface. Care must be taken to match the size of the rivet. A header that is too small marks the rivet; while one too large marks the material.

Rivet headers are made in a variety of styles. *[Figure 4-88]* The short, straight header is best when the gun can be brought close to the work. Offset headers may be used to reach rivets in obstructed places. Long headers are sometimes necessary when the gun cannot be brought close to the work due to structural interference. Rivet headers should be kept clean.

Figure 4-88. *Rivet headers.*

Compression Riveting

Compression riveting (squeezing) is of limited value because this method of riveting can be used only over the edges of sheets or assemblies where conditions permit, and where the reach of the rivet squeezer is deep enough. The three types of rivet squeezers—hand, pneumatic, and pneudraulic—operate on the same principles. In the hand rivet squeezer, compression is supplied by hand pressure; in the pneumatic rivet squeezer, by air pressure; and in the pneudraulic, by a combination of air and hydraulic pressure. One jaw is stationary and serves as a bucking bar, the other jaw is movable and does the upsetting. Riveting with a squeezer is a quick method and requires only one operator.

These riveters are equipped with either a C-yoke or an alligator yoke in various sizes to accommodate any size of rivet. The working capacity of a yoke is measured by its gap and its reach. The gap is the distance between the movable jaw and the stationary jaw; the reach is the inside length of the throat measured from the center of the end sets. End sets for rivet squeezers serve the same purpose as rivet sets for pneumatic rivet guns and are available with the same type heads, which are interchangeable to suit any type of rivet head. One part of each set is inserted in the stationary jaw, while the other part is placed in the movable jaws. The manufactured head end set is placed on the stationary jaw whenever possible. During some operations, it may be necessary to reverse the end sets, placing the manufactured head end set on the movable jaw.

Microshavers

A microshaver is used if the smoothness of the material (such as skin) requires that all countersunk rivets be driven within a specific tolerance. *[Figure 4-89]* This tool has a cutter, a stop, and two legs or stabilizers. The cutting portion of the microshaver is inside the stop. The depth of the cut can be adjusted by pulling outward on the stop and turning it in either direction (clockwise for deeper cuts). The marks on

Figure 4-89. *Microshaver.*

the stop permit adjustments of 0.001 inch. If the microshaver is adjusted and held correctly, it can cut the head of a countersunk rivet to within 0.002 inch without damaging the surrounding material.

Adjustments should always be made first on scrap material. When correctly adjusted, the microshaver leaves a small round dot about the size of a pinhead on the microshaved rivet. It may occasionally be necessary to shave rivets, normally restricted to MS20426 head rivets, after driving to obtain the required flushness. Shear head rivets should never be shaved.

Riveting Procedure

The riveting procedure consists of transferring and preparing the hole, drilling, and driving the rivets.

Hole Transfer

Accomplish transfer of holes from a drilled part to another part by placing the second part over first and using established holes as a guide. Using an alternate method, scribe hole location through from drilled part onto part to be drilled, spot with a center punch, and drill.

Hole Preparation

It is very important that the rivet hole be of the correct size and shape and free from burrs. If the hole is too small, the protective coating is scratched from the rivet when the rivet is driven through the hole. If the hole is too large, the rivet does not fill the hole completely. When it is bucked, the joint does not develop its full strength, and structural failure may occur at that spot.

If countersinking is required, consider the thickness of the metal and adopt the countersinking method recommended for that thickness. If dimpling is required, keep hammer blows or dimpling pressures to a minimum so that no undue work hardening occurs in the surrounding area.

Drilling

Rivet holes in repair may be drilled with either a light power drill or a hand drill. The standard shank twist drill is most commonly used. Drill bit sizes for rivet holes should be the smallest size that permits easy insertion of the rivet, approximately 0.003-inch greater than the largest tolerance of the shank diameter. The recommended clearance drill bits for the common rivet diameters are shown in *Figure 4-90*. Hole sizes for other fasteners are normally found on work documents, prints, or in manuals.

Before drilling, center punch all rivet locations. The center punch mark should be large enough to prevent the drill from slipping out of position, yet it must not dent the surface

Rivet Diameter (in)	Drill Size	
	Pilot	Final
3/32	3/32 (0.0937)	#40 (0.098)
1/8	1/8 (0.125)	#30 (0.1285)
5/32	5/32 (0.1562)	#21 (0.159)
3/16	3/16 (0.1875)	#11 (0.191)
1/4	1/4 (0.250)	F (0.257)

Figure 4-90. *Drill sizes for standard rivets.*

surrounding the center punch mark. Place a bucking bar behind the metal during punching to help prevent denting. To make a rivet hole the correct size, first drill a slightly undersized hole (pilot hole). Ream the pilot hole with a twist drill of the appropriate size to obtain the required dimension.

To drill, proceed as follows:

1. Ensure the drill bit is the correct size and shape.

2. Place the drill in the center-punched mark. When using a power drill, rotate the bit a few turns before starting the motor.

3. While drilling, always hold the drill at a 90° angle to the work or the curvature of the material.

4. Avoid excessive pressure, let the drill bit do the cutting, and never push the drill bit through stock.

5. Remove all burrs with a metal countersink or a file.

6. Clean away all drill chips.

When holes are drilled through sheet metal, small burrs are formed around the edge of the hole. This is especially true when using a hand drill because the drill speed is slow and there is a tendency to apply more pressure per drill revolution. Remove all burrs with a burr remover or larger size drill bit before riveting.

Driving the Rivet

Although riveting equipment can be either stationary or portable, portable riveting equipment is the most common type of riveting equipment used to drive solid shank rivets in airframe repair work.

Before driving any rivets into the sheet metal parts, be sure all holes line up perfectly, all shavings and burrs have been removed, and the parts to be riveted are securely fastened with temporary fasteners. Depending on the job, the riveting process may require one or two people. In solo riveting, the riveter holds a bucking bar with one hand and operates a riveting gun with the other.

If the job requires two aircraft technicians, a shooter, or gunner, and a bucker work together as a team to install rivets.

An important component of team riveting is an efficient signaling system that communicates the status of the riveting process. This signaling system usually consists of tapping the bucking bar against the work and is often called the tap code. One tap may mean not fully seated, hit it again, while two taps may mean good rivet, and three taps may mean bad rivet, remove and drive another. Radio sets are also available for communication between the technicians.

Once the rivet is installed, there should be no evidence of rotation of rivets or looseness of riveted parts. After the trimming operation, examine for tightness. Apply a force of 10 pounds to the trimmed stem. A tight stem is one indication of an acceptable rivet installation. Any degree of looseness indicates an oversize hole and requires replacement of the rivet with an oversize shank diameter rivet. A rivet installation is assumed satisfactory when the rivet head is seated snugly against the item to be retained (0.005-inch feeler gauge should not go under rivet head for more than one-half the circumference) and the stem is proved tight.

Countersunk Rivets

An improperly made countersink reduces the strength of a flush-riveted joint and may even cause failure of the sheet or the rivet head. The two methods of countersinking commonly used for flush riveting in aircraft construction and repair are:

- Machine or drill countersinking.

- Dimpling or press countersinking.

The proper method for any particular application depends on the thickness of the parts to be riveted, the height and angle of the countersunk head, the tools available, and accessibility.

Countersinking

When using countersunk rivets, it is necessary to make a conical recess in the skin for the head. The type of countersink required depends upon the relation of the thickness of the sheets to the depth of the rivet head. Use the proper degree and diameter countersink and cut only deep enough for the rivet head and metal to form a flush surface.

Countersinking is an important factor in the design of fastener patterns, as the removal of material in the countersinking process necessitates an increase in the number of fasteners to assure the required load-transfer strength. If countersinking is done on metal below a certain thickness, a knife edge with less than the minimum bearing surface or actual enlarging of the hole may result. The edge distance required when using countersunk fasteners is greater than when universal head fasteners are used.

The general rule for countersinking and flush fastener installation procedures has been reevaluated in recent years because countersunk holes have been responsible for fatigue cracks in aircraft pressurized skin. In the past, the general rule for countersinking held that the fastener head must be contained within the outer sheet. A combination of countersinks too deep (creating a knife edge), number of pressurization cycles, fatigue, deterioration of bonding materials, and working fasteners caused a high stress concentration that resulted in skin cracks and fastener failures. In primary structure and pressurized skin repairs, some manufacturers are currently recommending the countersink depth be no more than ⅔ the outer sheet thickness or down to 0.020-inch minimum fastener shank depth, whichever is greater. Dimple the skin if it is too thin for machine countersinking. *[Figure 4-91]*

Figure 4-91. *Countersinking dimensions.*

Keep the rivet high before driving to ensure the force of riveting is applied to the rivet and not to the skin. If the rivet is driven while it is flush or too deep, the surrounding skin is work hardened.

Countersinking Tools

While there are many types of countersink tools, the most commonly used has an included angle of 100°. Sometimes types of 82° or 120° are used to form countersunk wells. *[Figure 4-84]* A six-fluted countersink works best in aluminum. There are also four- and three-fluted countersinks, but those are harder to control from a chatter standpoint. A single-flute type, such as those manufactured by the Weldon Tool Company®, works best for corrosion-resistant steel. *[Figure 4-92]*

Figure 4-92. *Single-flute countersink.*

The microstop countersink is the preferred countersinking tool. *[Figure 4-85]* It has an adjustable-sleeve cage that functions as a limit stop and holds the revolving countersink in a vertical position. Its threaded and replaceable cutters may have either a removable or an integral pilot that keeps the cutter centered in the hole. The pilot should be approximately 0.002-inch smaller than the hole size. It is recommended to test adjustments on a piece of scrap material before countersinking repair or replacement parts.

Freehand countersinking is needed where a microstop countersink cannot fit. This method should be practiced on scrap material to develop the required skill. Holding the drill motor steady and perpendicular is as critical during this operation as when drilling.

Chattering is the most common problem encountered when countersinking. Some precautions that may eliminate or minimize chatter include:

- Use sharp tooling.

- Use a slow speed and steady firm pressure.

- Use a piloted countersink with a pilot approximately 0.002-inch smaller than the hole.

- Use back-up material to hold the pilot steady when countersinking thin sheet material.

- Use a cutter with a different number of flutes.

- Pilot drill an undersized hole, countersink, and then enlarge the hole to final size.

Dimpling

Dimpling is the process of making an indentation or a dimple around a rivet hole to make the top of the head of a countersunk rivet flush with the surface of the metal. Dimpling is done with a male and female die, or forms, often called punch and die set. The male die has a guide the size of the rivet hole and is beveled to correspond to the degree of countersink of the rivet head. The female die has a hole into which the male guide fits and is beveled to a corresponding degree of countersink.

When dimpling, rest the female die on a solid surface. Then, place the material to be dimpled on the female die. Insert the male die in the hole to be dimpled and, with a hammer, strike the male die until the dimple is formed. Two or three solid hammer blows should be sufficient. A separate set of dies is necessary for each size of rivet and shape of rivet head. An alternate method is to use a countersunk head rivet instead of the regular male punch die, and a draw set instead of the female die, and hammer the rivet until the dimple is formed.

Dimpling dies for light work can be used in portable pneumatic or hand squeezers. *[Figure 4-93]* If the dies are

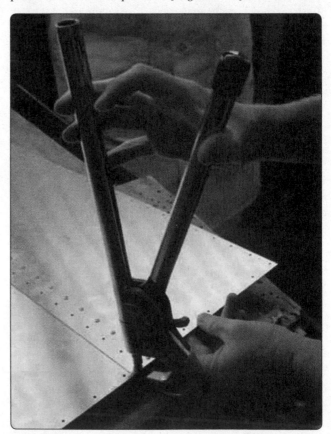

Figure 4-93. *Hand squeezers.*

used with a squeezer, they must be adjusted accurately to the thickness of the sheet being dimpled. A table riveter is also used for dimpling thin skin material and installing rivets. [Figure 4-94]

Figure 4-94. *Table riveter.*

Coin Dimpling

The coin dimpling, or coin pressing, method uses a countersink rivet as the male dimpling die. Place the female die in the usual position and back it with a bucking bar. Place the rivet of the required type into the hole and strike the rivet with a pneumatic riveting hammer. Coin dimpling should be used only when the regular male die is broken or not available. Coin pressing has the distinct disadvantage of the rivet hole needing to be drilled to correct rivet size before the dimpling operation is accomplished. Since the metal stretches during the dimpling operation, the hole becomes enlarged and the rivet must be swelled slightly before driving to produce a close fit. Because the rivet head causes slight distortions in the recess, and these are characteristic only to that particular rivet head, it is wise to drive the same rivet that was used as the male die during the dimpling process. Do not substitute another rivet, either of the same size or a size larger.

Radius Dimpling

Radius dimpling uses special die sets that have a radius and are often used with stationary or portable squeezers. Dimpling removes no metal and, due to the nestling effect, gives a stronger joint than the non-flush type. A dimpled joint reduces the shear loading on the rivet and places more load on the riveted sheets.

NOTE: Dimpling is also done for flush bolts and other flush fasteners.

Dimpling is required for sheets that are thinner than the minimum specified thickness for countersinking. However, dimpling is not limited to thin materials. Heavier parts may be dimpled without cracking by specialized hot dimpling

equipment. The temper of the material, rivet size, and available equipment are all factors to be considered in dimpling. [Figure 4-95]

Figure 4-95. *Dimpling techniques.*

Hot Dimpling

Hot dimpling is the process that uses heated dimpling dies to ensure the metal flows better during the dimpling process. Hot dimpling is often performed with large stationary equipment available in a sheet metal shop. The metal being used is an important factor because each metal presents different dimpling problems. For example, 2024-T3 aluminum alloy can be satisfactorily dimpled either hot or cold, but may crack in the vicinity of the dimple after cold dimpling because of hard spots in the metal. Hot dimpling prevents such cracking.

7075-T6 aluminum alloys are always hot dimpled. Magnesium alloys also must be hot dimpled because, like 7075-T6, they have low formability qualities. Titanium is another metal that must be hot dimpled because it is tough and resists forming. The same temperature and dwell time used to hot dimple 7075-T6 is used for titanium.

100° Combination Predimple and Countersink Method

Metals of different thicknesses are sometimes joined by a combination of dimpling and countersinking. [Figure 4-96] A countersink well made to receive a dimple is called a subcountersink. These are most often seen where a thin web is attached to heavy structure. It is also used on thin gap seals, wear strips, and repairs for worn countersinks.

Figure 4-96. *Predimple and countersink method.*

Dimpling Inspection

To determine the quality of a dimple, it is necessary to make a close visual inspection. Several features must be checked. The rivet head should fit flush and there should be a sharp break from the surface into the dimple. The sharpness of the break is affected by dimpling pressure and metal thickness. Selected dimples should be checked by inserting a fastener to make sure that the flushness requirements are met. Cracked dimples are caused by poor dies, rough holes, or improper heating. Two types of cracks may form during dimpling:

- Radial cracks—start at the edge and spread outward as the metal within the dimple stretches. They are most common in 2024-T3. A rough hole or a dimple that is too deep causes such cracks. A small tolerance is usually allowed for radial cracks.

- Circumferential cracks—downward bending into the draw die causes tension stresses in the upper portion of the metal. Under some conditions, a crack may be created that runs around the edge of the dimple. Such cracks do not always show since they may be underneath the cladding. When found, they are cause for rejection. These cracks are most common in hot-dimpled 7075 T6 aluminum alloy material. The usual cause is insufficient dimpling heat.

Evaluating the Rivet

To obtain high structural efficiency in the manufacture and repair of aircraft, an inspection must be made of all rivets before the part is put in service. This inspection consists of examining both the shop and manufactured heads and the surrounding skin and structural parts for deformities. A scale or rivet gauge can be used to check the condition of the upset rivet head to see that it conforms to the proper requirements. Deformities in the manufactured head can be detected by the trained eye alone. [Figure 4-97]

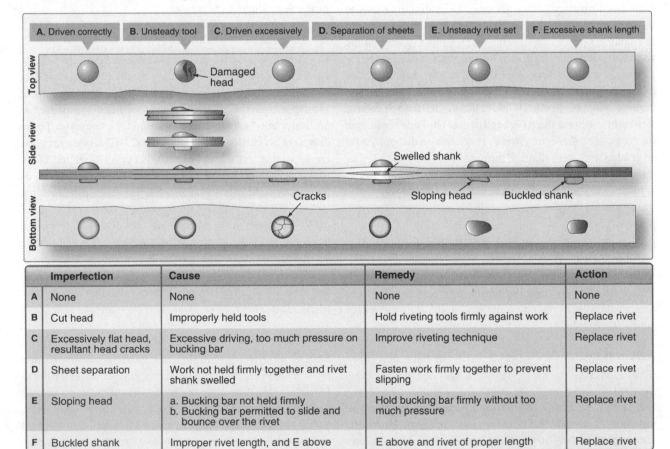

	Imperfection	Cause	Remedy	Action
A	None	None	None	None
B	Cut head	Improperly held tools	Hold riveting tools firmly against work	Replace rivet
C	Excessively flat head, resultant head cracks	Excessive driving, too much pressure on bucking bar	Improve riveting technique	Replace rivet
D	Sheet separation	Work not held firmly together and rivet shank swelled	Fasten work firmly together to prevent slipping	Replace rivet
E	Sloping head	a. Bucking bar not held firmly b. Bucking bar permitted to slide and bounce over the rivet	Hold bucking bar firmly without too much pressure	Replace rivet
F	Buckled shank	Improper rivet length, and E above	E above and rivet of proper length	Replace rivet

Figure 4-97. *Rivet defects.*

Some common causes of unsatisfactory riveting are improper bucking, rivet set slipping off or being held at the wrong angle, and rivet holes or rivets of the wrong size. Additional causes for unsatisfactory riveting are countersunk rivets not flush with the well, work not properly fastened together during riveting, the presence of burrs, rivets too hard, too much or too little driving, and rivets out of line.

Occasionally, during an aircraft structural repair, it is wise to examine adjacent parts to determine the true condition of neighboring rivets. In doing so, it may be necessary to remove the paint. The presence of chipped or cracked paint around the heads may indicate shifted or loose rivets. Look for tipped or loose rivet heads. If the heads are tipped or if rivets are loose, they show up in groups of several consecutive rivets and probably tipped in the same direction. If heads that appear to be tipped are not in groups and are not tipped in the same direction, tipping may have occurred during some previous installation.

Inspect rivets known to have been critically loaded, but that show no visible distortion, by drilling off the head and carefully punching out the shank. If, upon examination, the shank appears joggled and the holes in the sheet misaligned, the rivet has failed in shear. In that case, try to determine what is causing the shearing stress and take the necessary corrective action. Flush rivets that show head slippage within the countersink or dimple, indicating either sheet bearing failure or rivet shear failure, must be removed for inspection and replacement.

Joggles in removed rivet shanks indicate partial shear failure. Replace these rivets with the next larger size. Also, if the rivet holes show elongation, replace the rivets with the next larger size. Sheet failures such as tear-outs, cracks between rivets, and the like usually indicate damaged rivets. The complete repair of the joint may require replacement of the rivets with the next larger size.

The general practice of replacing a rivet with the next larger size ($\frac{1}{32}$-inch greater diameter) is necessary to obtain the proper joint strength of rivet and sheet when the original rivet hole is enlarged. If the rivet in an elongated hole is replaced by a rivet of the same size, its ability to carry its share of the shear load is impaired and joint weakness results.

Removal of Rivets

When a rivet has to be replaced, remove it carefully to retain the rivet hole's original size and shape. If removed correctly, the rivet does not need to be replaced with one of the next larger size. Also, if the rivet is not removed properly, the strength of the joint may be weakened and the replacement of rivets made more difficult.

When removing a rivet, work on the manufactured head. It is more symmetrical about the shank than the shop head, and there is less chance of damaging the rivet hole or the material around it. To remove rivets, use hand tools, a power drill, or a combination of both.

The procedure for universal or protruding head rivet removal is as follows:

1. File a flat area on the head of the rivet and center punch the flat surface for drilling.

   NOTE: On thin metal, back up the rivet on the upset head when center punching to avoid depressing the metal.

2. Use a drill bit one size smaller than the rivet shank to drill out the rivet head.

   NOTE: When using a power drill, set the drill on the rivet and rotate the chuck several revolutions by hand before turning on the power. This procedure helps the drill cut a good starting spot and eliminates the chance of the drill slipping off and tracking across the metal.

3. Drill the rivet to the depth of its head, while holding the drill at a 90° angle. Do not drill too deeply, as the rivet shank will then turn with the drill and tear the surrounding metal.

   NOTE: The rivet head often breaks away and climbs the drill, which is a signal to withdraw the drill.

4. If the rivet head does not come loose of its own accord, insert a drift punch into the hole and twist slightly to either side until the head comes off.

5. Drive the remaining rivet shank out with a drift punch slightly smaller than the shank diameter.

On thin metal or unsupported structures, support the sheet with a bucking bar while driving out the shank. If the shank is unusually tight after the rivet head is removed, drill the rivet about two-thirds through the thickness of the material and then drive the rest of it out with a drift punch. *Figure 4-98* shows the preferred procedure for removing universal rivets.

The procedure for the removal of countersunk rivets is the same as described above except no filing is necessary. Be careful to avoid elongation of the dimpled or the countersunk holes. The rivet head should be drilled to approximately one-half the thickness of the top sheet. The dimple in 2117–T rivets usually eliminates the necessity of filing and center punching the rivet head.

To remove a countersunk or flush head rivet, you must:

1. Select a drill about 0.003-inch smaller than the rivet shank diameter.

Rivet Removal

Remove rivets by drilling off the head and punching out the shank as illustrated.
1. File a flat area on the manufactured head of non-flush rivets.
2. Place a block of wood or a bucking bar under both flush and nonflush rivets when center punching the manufactured head.
3. Use a drill that is $^{1}/_{32}$ (0.0312) inch smaller than the rivet shank to drill through the head of the rivet. Ensure the drilling operation does not damage the skin or cut the sides of the rivet hole.
4. Insert a drift punch into the hole drilled in the rivet and tilt the punch to break off the rivet head.
5. Using a drift punch and hammer, drive out the rivet shank. Support the opposite side of the structure to prevent structural damage.

1. File a flat area on manufactured head

2. Center punch flat

3. Drill through head using drill one size smaller than rivet shank

4. Remove weakened head with machine punch

5. Punch out rivet with machine punch

Figure 4-98. *Rivet removal.*

2. Drill into the exact center of the rivet head to the approximate depth of the head.

3. Remove the head by breaking it off. Use a punch as a lever.

4. Punch out the shank. Use a suitable backup, preferably wood (or equivalent), or a dedicated backup block. If the shank does not come out easily, use a small drill and drill through the shank. Be careful not to elongate the hole.

Replacing Rivets

Replace rivets with those of the same size and strength whenever possible. If the rivet hole becomes enlarged, deformed, or otherwise damaged, drill or ream the hole for the next larger size rivet. Do not replace a rivet with a type having lower strength properties, unless the lower strength is adequately compensated by an increase in size or a greater number of rivets. It is acceptable to replace 2017 rivets of $^{3}/_{16}$-inch diameter or less, and 2024 rivets of $^{5}/_{32}$-inch diameter or less with 2117 rivets for general repairs, provided the replacement rivets are $^{1}/_{32}$-inch greater in diameter than the rivets they replace.

National Advisory Committee for Aeronautics (NACA) Method of Double Flush Riveting

A rivet installation technique known as the National Advisory Committee for Aeronautics (NACA) method has primary applications in fuel tank areas. *[Figure 4-99]* To make

Figure 4-99. *NACA riveting method.*

a NACA rivet installation, the shank is upset into a 82° countersink. In driving, the gun may be used on either the head or shank side. The upsetting is started with light blows, then the force increased and the gun or bar moved on the shank end so as to form a head inside the countersink well. If desired, the upset head may be shaved flush after driving. The optimal strength is achieved by cutting the countersink well to the dimensions given in *Figure 4-100*. Material thickness minimums must be carefully adhered to.

Rivet Size	Minimum Thickness	Countersink Diameter ± .005
3/32	.032	.141
1/8	.040	.189
5/32	.050	.236
3/16	.063	.288
1/4	.090	.400

Figure 4-100. *Material thickness minimums, in inches, for NACA riveting method using 82° countersink.*

Special Purpose Fasteners

Special purpose fasteners are designed for applications in which fastener strength, ease of installation, or temperature properties of the fastener require consideration. Solid shank rivets have been the preferred construction method for metal aircraft for many years because they fill up the hole, which results in good load transfer, but they are not always ideal. For example, the attachment of many nonstructural parts (aircraft interior furnishings, flooring, deicing boots, etc.) do not need the full strength of solid shank rivets.

To install solid shank rivets, the aircraft technician must have access to both sides of a riveted structure or structural part. There are many places on an aircraft where this access is impossible or where limited space does not permit the use of a bucking bar. In these instances, it is not possible to use solid shank rivets, and special fasteners have been designed that can be bucked from the front. *[Figure 4-101]* There are also areas of high loads, high fatigue, and bending on aircraft. Although the shear loads of riveted joints are very good, the tension, or clamp-up, loads are less than ideal.

Figure 4-101. *Assorted fasteners.*

Special purpose fasteners are sometimes lighter than solid shank rivets, yet strong enough for their intended use. These fasteners are manufactured by several corporations and have unique characteristics that require special installation tools, special installation procedures, and special removal procedures. Because these fasteners are often inserted in locations where one head, usually the shop head, cannot be seen, they are called blind rivets or blind fasteners.

Typically, the locking characteristics of a blind rivet are not as good as a driven rivet. Therefore, blind rivets are usually not used when driven rivets can be installed. Blind rivets shall not be used:

1. In fluid-tight areas.

2. On aircraft in air intake areas where rivet parts may be ingested by the engine.

3. On aircraft control surfaces, hinges, hinge brackets, flight control actuating systems, wing attachment fittings, landing gear fittings, on floats or amphibian hulls below the water level, or other heavily stressed locations on the aircraft.

NOTE: For metal repairs to the airframe, the use of blind rivets must be specifically authorized by the airframe manufacturer or approved by a representative of the Federal Aviation Administration (FAA).

Blind Rivets

The first blind fasteners were introduced in 1940 by the Cherry Rivet Company (now Cherry® Aerospace), and the aviation industry quickly adopted them. The past decades have seen a proliferation of blind fastening systems based on the original concept, which consists of a tubular rivet with a fixed head and a hollow sleeve. Inserted within the rivet's core is a stem that is enlarged or serrated on its exposed end when activated by a pulling-type rivet gun. The lower end of the stem extends beyond the inner sheet of metal. This portion contains a tapered joining portion and a blind head that has a larger diameter than the stem or the sleeve of the tubular rivet.

When the pulling force of the rivet gun forces the blind head upward into the sleeve, its stem upsets or expands the lower end of the sleeve into a tail. This presses the inner sheet upward and closes any space that might have existed between it and the outer sheet. Since the exposed head of the rivet is held tightly against the outer sheet by the rivet gun, the sheets of metal are clamped, or clinched, together.

NOTE: Fastener manufacturers use different terminology to describe the parts of the blind rivet. The terms "mandrel," "spindle," and "stem" are often used interchangeably. For clarity, the word "stem" is used in this handbook and refers to the piece that is inserted into the hollow sleeve.

Friction-Locked Blind Rivets
Standard self-plugging blind rivets consist of a hollow sleeve and a stem with increased diameter in the plug section. The blind head is formed as the stem is pulled into the sleeve. Friction-locked blind rivets have a multiple-piece construction and rely on friction to lock the stem to the sleeve. As the stem is drawn up into the rivet shank, the stem portion upsets the shank on the blind side, forming a plug in the hollow center of the rivet. The excess portion of the stem breaks off at a groove due to the continued pulling action of the rivet gun. Metals used for these rivets are 2117-T4 and 5056-F aluminum alloy. Monel® is used for special applications.

Many friction-locked blind rivet center stems fall out due to vibration, which greatly reduces its shear strength. To combat that problem, most friction-lock blind rivets are replaced by the mechanical-lock, or stem-lock, type of blind fasteners. However, some types, such as the Cherry SPR® ³⁄₃₂-inch Self-Plugging Rivet, are ideal for securing nutplates located in inaccessible and hard-to-reach areas where bucking or squeezing of solid rivets is unacceptable. *[Figure 4-102]*

Friction-lock blind rivets are less expensive than mechanical-lock blind rivets and are sometimes used for nonstructural applications. Inspection of friction-lock blind rivets is visual. A more detailed discussion on how to inspect riveted joints can be found in the section, General Repair Practices. Removal of friction-lock blind rivets consists of punching out the friction-lock stem and then treating it like any other rivet.

Mechanical-Lock Blind Rivets
The self-plugging, mechanical-lock blind rivet was developed to prevent the problem of losing the center stem due to vibration. This rivet has a device on the puller or rivet head

Figure 4-102. *Friction-lock blind rivet.*

that locks the center stem into place when installed. Bulbed, self-plugging, mechanically-locked blind rivets form a large, blind head that provides higher strength in thin sheets when installed. They may be used in applications where the blind head is formed against a dimpled sheet.

Manufacturers such as Cherry® Aerospace (CherryMAX®, CherryLOCK®, Cherry SST®) and Alcoa Fastening Systems (Huck-Clinch®, HuckMax®, Unimatic®) make many variations of this of blind rivet. While similar in design, the tooling for these rivets is often not interchangeable.

The CherryMAX® Bulbed blind rivet is one of the earlier types of mechanical-lock blind rivets developed. Their main advantage is the ability to replace a solid shank rivet size for size. The CherryMAX® Bulbed blind rivet consists of four parts:

1. A fully serrated stem with break notch, shear ring, and integral grip adjustment cone.

2. A driving anvil to ensure a visible mechanical lock with each fastener installation.

3. A separate, visible, and inspectable locking collar that mechanically locks the stem to the rivet sleeve.

4. A rivet sleeve with recess in the head to receive the locking collar.

It is called a bulbed fastener due to its large blind side bearing surface, developed during the installation process. These rivets are used in thin sheet applications and for use in materials that may be damaged by other types of blind rivets. This rivet features a safe-lock locking collar for more reliable joint integrity. The rough end of the retained stem in the center on the manufactured head must never be filed smooth because it weakens the strength of the lockring, and the center stem could fall out.

CherryMAX® bulbed rivets are available in three head styles: universal, 100° countersunk, and 100° reduced shear head styles. Their lengths are measured in increments of ¹⁄₁₆ inch. It is important to select a rivet with a length related to the grip length of the metal being joined. This blind rivet can be installed using either the Cherry® G750A or the newly released Cherry® G800 hand riveters, or either the pneumatic-hydraulic G704B or G747 CherryMAX® power tools. For installation, please refer to *Figure 4-103*.

The CherryMAX® mechanical-lock blind rivet is popular with general aviation repair shops because it features the one tool concept to install three standard rivet diameters and their oversize counterparts. *[Figure 4-104]* CherryMAX® rivets are available in four nominal diameters: ¹⁄₈, ⁵⁄₃₂, ³⁄₁₆, and ¹⁄₄-inch and three oversized diameters and four head styles: universal, 100° flush head, 120° flush head, and NAS1097 flush head. This rivet consists of a blind header, hollow rivet shell, locking (foil) collar, driving anvil, and pulling stem complete with wrapped locking collar. The rivet sleeve and the driving washer blind bulbed header takes up the extended shank and forms the bucktail.

The stem and rivet sleeve work as an assembly to provide radial expansion and a large bearing footprint on the blind side of the fastened surface. The lock collar ensures that the stem and sleeve remain assembled during joint loading and unloading. Rivet sleeves are made from 5056 aluminum, Monel® and INCO 600. The stems are made from alloy steel, CRES, and INCO® X-750. CherryMAX® rivets have an ultimate shear strength ranging from 50 KSI to 75 KSI.

Removal of Mechanically Locked Blind Rivets
Mechanically locked blind rivets are a challenge to remove because they are made from strong, hard metals. Lack of access poses yet another problem for the aviation technician. Designed for and used in difficult to reach locations means there is often no access to the blind side of the rivet or any way to provide support for the sheet metal surrounding the rivet's location when the aviation technician attempts removal.

The stem is mechanically locked by a small lock ring that needs to be removed first. Use a small center drill to provide a guide for a larger drill on top of the rivet stem and drill away the upper portion of the stem to destroy the lock. Try to remove the lock ring or use a prick punch or center punch to drive the stem down a little and remove the lock ring. After the lock ring is removed, the stem can be driven out with a drive punch. After the stem is removed, the rivet can be drilled out in the same way as a solid rivet. If possible, support the back side of the rivet with a backup block to prevent damage to the aircraft skin.

① The CherryMAX® rivet is inserted into the prepared hole. The pulling head (installation tool) is slipped over the rivet's stem. Applying a firm, steady pressure, which seats the rivet head, the installation tool is then actuated.

② The pulling head holds the rivet sleeve in place as it begins to pull the rivet stem into the rivet sleeve. This pulling action causes the stem shear ring to upset the rivet sleeve and form the bulbed blind head.

③ The continued pulling action of the installation tool causes the stem shear ring to shear from the main body of the stem as the stem continues to move through the rivet sleeve. This action allows the fastener to accommodate a minimum of ¹⁄₁₆" variation in structure thickness. The locking collar then contacts the driving anvil. As the stem continues to be pulled by the action of the installation tool, the Safe-Lock locking collar deforms into the rivet sleeve head recess.

④ The safe-lock locking collar fills the rivet sleeve head recess, locking the stem and rivet sleeve securely together. Continued pulling by the installation tool causes the stem to fracture at the break notch, providing a flush, burr-free, inspectable installation.

Figure 4-103. *CherryMax® installation procedure.*

Figure 4-104. *CherryMAX® rivet.*

Pin Fastening Systems (High-Shear Fasteners)

A pin fastening system, or high-shear pin rivet, is a two-piece fastener that consists of a threaded pin and a collar. The metal collar is swaged onto the grooved end, effecting a firm tight fit. They are essentially threadless bolts.

High-shear rivets are installed with standard bucking bars and pneumatic riveting hammers. They require the use of a special gun set that incorporates collar swaging and trimming and a discharge port through which excess collar material is discharged. A separate size set is required for each shank diameter.

Installation of High-Shear Fasteners

Prepare holes for pin rivets with the same care as for other close tolerance rivets or bolts. At times, it may be necessary to spot-face the area under the head of the pin to ensure the head of the rivet fits tightly against the material. The spot-faced area should be ¹⁄₁₆-inch larger in diameter than the head diameter. Pin rivets may be driven from either end. Procedures for driving a pin rivet from the collar end are:

1. Insert the rivet in the hole.

2. Place a bucking bar against the rivet head.

3. Slip the collar over the protruding rivet end.

4. Place previously selected rivet set and gun over the collar. Align the gun until it is perpendicular to the material.

5. Depress the trigger on the gun, applying pressure to the rivet collar. This action causes the rivet collar to swage into the groove on the rivet end.

6. Continue the driving action until the collar is properly formed and excess collar material is trimmed off.

Procedures for driving a pin rivet from the head end are:

1. Insert the rivet in the hole.

2. Slip the collar over the protruding end of rivet.

3. Insert the correct size gun rivet set in a bucking bar and place the set against the collar of the rivet.

4. Apply pressure against the rivet head with a flush rivet set and pneumatic riveting hammer.

5. Continue applying pressure until the collar is formed in the groove and excess collar material is trimmed off.

Inspection

Pin rivets should be inspected on both sides of the material. The head of the rivet should not be marred and should fit tightly against the material.

Removal of Pin Rivets

The conventional method of removing rivets by drilling off the head may be utilized on either end of the pin rivet. Center punching is recommended prior to applying drilling pressure. In some cases, alternate methods may be needed:

• Grind a chisel edge on a small pin punch to a blade width of ¹⁄₈-inch. Place this tool at right angles to the collar and drive with a hammer to split the collar down one side. Repeat the operation on the opposite side. Then, with the chisel blade, pry the collar from the rivet. Tap the rivet out of the hole.

- Use a special hollow punch having one or more blades placed to split the collar. Pry the collar from the groove and tap out the rivet.

- Sharpen the cutting blades of a pair of nippers. Cut the collar in two pieces or use nippers at right angles to the rivet and cut through the small neck.

- A hollow-mill collar cutter can be used in a power hand drill to cut away enough collar material to permit the rivet to be tapped out of the work.

The high-shear pin rivet family includes fasteners, such as the Hi-Lok®, Hi-Tigue®, and Hi-Lite® made by Hi-Shear Corporation and the CherryBUCK® 95 KSI One-Piece Shear Pin and Cherry E-Z Buck® Shear Pin made by Cherry® Aerospace.

Hi-Lok® Fastening System

The threaded end of the Hi-Lok® two-piece fastener contains a hexagonal shaped recess. *[Figure 4-105]* The hex tip of an Allen wrench engages the recess to prevent rotation of the pin while the collar is being installed. The pin is designed in two basic head styles. For shear applications, the pin is made in countersunk style and in a compact protruding head style. For tension applications, the MS24694 countersunk and regular protruding head styles are available.

Figure 4-105. *Hi-Lok®.*

The self-locking, threaded Hi-Lok® collar has an internal counterbore at the base to accommodate variations in material thickness. At the opposite end of the collar is a wrenching device that is torqued by the driving tool until it shears off during installation, leaving the lower portion of the collar seated with the proper torque without additional torque inspection. This shear-off point occurs when a predetermined preload or clamp-up is attained in the fastener during installation.

The advantages of Hi-Lok® two-piece fastener include its light weight, high fatigue resistance, high strength, and its inability to be overtorqued. The pins, made from alloy steel, corrosion resistant steel, or titanium alloy, come in many standard and oversized shank diameters. The collars are made of aluminum alloy, corrosion resistant steel, or alloy steel. The collars have wrenching flats, fracture point, threads, and a recess. The wrenching flats are used to install the collar. The fracture point has been designed to allow the wrenching flats to shear when the proper torque has been reached. The threads match the threads of the pins and have been formed into an ellipse that is distorted to provide the locking action. The recess serves as a built-in washer. This area contains a portion of the shank and the transition area of the fastener.

The hole shall be prepared so that the maximum interference fit does not exceed 0.002-inch. This avoids build up of excessive internal stresses in the work adjacent to the hole. The Hi-Lok® pin has a slight radius under its head to increase fatigue life. After drilling, deburr the edge of the hole to allow the head to seat fully in the hole. The Hi-Lok® is installed in interference fit holes for aluminum structure and a clearance fit for steel, titanium, and composite materials.

Hi-Tigue® Fastening System

The Hi-Tigue® fastener offers all of the benefits of the Hi-Lok® fastening system along with a unique bead design that enhances the fatigue performance of the structure making it ideal for situations that require a controlled interference fit. The Hi-Tigue® fastener assembly consists of a pin and collar. These pin rivets have a radius at the transition area. During installation in an interference fit hole, the radius area will "cold work" the hole. These fastening systems can be easily confused, and visual reference should not be used for identification. Use part numbers to identify these fasteners.

Hi-Lite® Fastening System

The Hi-Lite® fastener is similar in design and principle to the Hi-Lok® fastener, but the Hi-Lite® fastener has a shorter transition area between the shank and the first load-bearing thread. Hi-Lite® has approximately one less thread. All Hi-Lite® fasteners are made of titanium.

These differences reduce the weight of the Hi-Lite® fastener without lessening the shear strength, but the Hi-Lite® clamping forces are less than that of a Hi-Lok® fastener. The Hi-Lite® collars are also different and thus are not interchangeable with Hi-Lok® collars. Hi-Lite® fasteners can be replaced with Hi-Lok® fasteners for most applications, but Hi-Loks® cannot be replaced with Hi-Lites®.

CherryBUCK® 95 KSI One-Piece Shear Pin

The CherryBUCK® is a bimetallic, one-piece fastener that combines a 95 KSI shear strength shank with a ductile, titanium-columbium tail. Theses fasteners are functionally interchangeable with comparable 6AI-4V titanium alloy two-piece shear fasteners, but with a number of advantages. Their one piece design means no foreign object damage (FOD), it has a 600 °F allowable temperature, and a very low backside profile.

Lockbolt Fastening Systems

Also pioneered in the 1940s, the lockbolt is a two-piece fastener that combines the features of a high strength bolt and a rivet with advantages over each. *[Figure 4-106]* In general, a lockbolt is a nonexpanding fastener that has either a collar swaged into annular locking groves on the pin shank or a type of threaded collar to lock it in place. Available with either countersunk or protruding heads, lockbolts are permanent type fasteners assemblies and consist of a pin and a collar.

Shear and tension pull-type pins

Shear and tension stump-type pins

Figure 4-106. *Lockbolts.*

A lockbolt is similar to an ordinary rivet in that the locking collar, or nut, is weak in tension and it is difficult to remove once installed. Some of the lockbolts are similar to blind rivets and can be completely installed from one side. Others are fed into the workpiece with the manufactured head on the far side. The installation is completed on the near side with a gun similar to blind rivet gun. The lockbolt is easier and more quickly installed than the conventional rivet or bolt and eliminates the use of lockwashers, cotter pins, and special nuts. The lockbolt is generally used in wing splice fittings, landing gear fittings, fuel cell fittings, longerons, beams, skin splice plates, and other major structural attachment.

Often called huckbolts, lockbolts are manufactured by companies such as Cherry® Aerospace (Cherry® Lockbolt), Alcoa Fastening Systems (Hucktite® Lockbolt System), and SPS Technologies. Used primarily for heavily stressed structures that require higher shear and clamp-up values than can be obtained with rivets, the lockbolt and Hi-lok® are often

used for similar applications. Lockbolts are made in various head styles, alloys, and finishes.

The lockbolt requires a pneumatic hammer or pull gun for installation. Lockbolts have their own grip gauge and an installation tool is required for their installation. *[Figure 4-107]* When installed, the lockbolt is rigidly and permanently locked in place. Three types of lockbolts are commonly used: pull-type, stump-type, and blind-type.

Figure 4-107. *Lockbolt grip gauge.*

The pull-type lockbolt is mainly used in aircraft and primary and secondary structure. It is installed very rapidly and has approximately one-half the weight of equivalent AN steel bolts and nuts. A special pneumatic pull gun is required for installation of this type lockbolt, which can be performed by one operator since buckling is not required.

The stump-type lockbolt, although not having the extended stem with pull grooves, is a companion fastener to the pull-type lockbolt. It is used primarily where clearance does not permit effective installation of the pull-type lockbolt. It is driven with a standard pneumatic riveting hammer, with a hammer set attached for swaging the collar into the pin locking grooves, and a bucking bar.

The blind-type lockbolt comes as a complete unit or assembly and has exceptional strength and sheet pull-together characteristics. Blind-type lockbolts are used where only one side of the work is accessible and generally where it is difficult to drive a conventional rivet. This type lockbolt is installed in a manner similar to the pull-type lockbolt.

The pins of pull- and stump-type lockbolts are made of heat-treated alloy steel or high-strength aluminum alloy. Companion collars are made of aluminum alloy or mild steel. The blind-type lockbolt consists of a heat-treated alloy steel pin, blind sleeve, filler sleeve, mild steel collar, and carbon steel washer.

These fasteners are used in shear and tension applications. The pull type is more common and can be installed by one person. The stump type requires a two person installation. An assembly tool is used to swage the collar onto the serrated grooves in the pin and break the stem flush to the top of the collar.

The easiest way to differentiate between tension and shear pins is the number of locking grooves. Tension pins normally have four locking grooves and shear pins have two locking grooves. The installation tooling preloads the pin while swaging the collar. The surplus end of the pin, called the pintail, is then fractured.

Installation Procedure

Installation of lockbolts involves proper drilling. The hole preparation for a lockbolt is similar to hole preparation for a Hi-Lok®. An interference fit is typically used for aluminum and a clearance fit is used for steel, titanium, and composite materials. *[Figure 4-108]*

Lockbolt Inspection

After installation, a lockbolt needs to be inspected to determine if installation is satisfactory. *[Figure 4-109]* Inspect the lockbolt as follows:

1. The head must be firmly seated.

2. The collar must be tight against the material and have the proper shape and size.

3. Pin protrusion must be within limits.

Lockbolt Removal

The best way to remove a lockbolt is to remove the collar and drive out the pin. The collar can be removed with a special collar cutter attached to a drill motor that mills off the collar without damaging the skin. If this is not possible, a collar splitter or small chisel can be used. Use a backup block on the opposite side to prevent elongation of the hole.

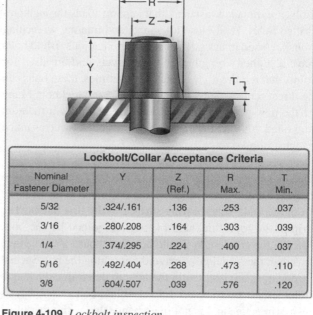

Lockbolt/Collar Acceptance Criteria				
Nominal Fastener Diameter	Y	Z (Ref.)	R Max.	T Min.
5/32	.324/.161	.136	.253	.037
3/16	.280/.208	.164	.303	.039
1/4	.374/.295	.224	.400	.037
5/16	.492/.404	.268	.473	.110
3/8	.604/.507	.039	.576	.120

Figure 4-109. *Lockbolt inspection.*

The Eddie-Bolt® 2 Pin Fastening System

The Eddie-Bolt® 2 looks similar to the Hi-Lok®, but has five flutes, equally spaced along a portion of the pin thread area. A companion threaded collar deforms into the flutes at a predetermined torque and locks the collar in place. The collar can be unscrewed using special tooling. This fastening system can be used in either clearance or interference-fit holes.

Placed the pin in the hole from the back side of the work and slip the collar on. The hold-off head must be toward the gun. This allows the gun to preload the pin before swaging. Then apply the gun; the chuck jaws engage the pull grooves of the projecting pintail. Hold the gun loosely and pull the trigger.

The initial pull draws the work up tight and pulls that portion of the shank under the head into the hole.

Further pull swages the collar into the locking grooves to form a permanent lock.

Continued force breaks the pin and ejects the tail. Anvil returns and disengages from the swaged collar.

Figure 4-108. *Lockbolt installation procedure.*

Blind Bolts

Bolts are threaded fasteners that support loads through pre-drilled holes. Hex, close-tolerance, and internal wrenching bolts are used in aircraft structural applications. Blind bolts have a higher strength than blind rivets and are used for joints that require high strength. Sometimes, these bolts can be direct replacements for the Hi-Lok® and lockbolt. Many of the new generation blind bolts are made from titanium and rated at 90 KSI shear strength, which is twice as much as most blind rivets.

Determining the correct length of the fastener is critical to correct installation. The grip length of a bolt is the distance from the underhead bearing surface to the first thread. The grip is the total thickness of material joined by the bolt. Ideally, the grip length should be a few thousands of an inch less than the actual grip to avoid bottoming the nut. Special grip gauges are inserted in the hole to determine the length of the blind bolt to be used. Every blind bolt system has its own grip gauge and is not interchangeable with other blind bolt or rivet systems.

Blind bolts are difficult to remove due to the hardness of the core bolt. A special removal kit is available from the manufacturer for removing each type of blind bolt. These kits make it easier to remove the blind bolt without damaging the hole and parent structure. Blind bolts are available in a pull type and a drive type.

Pull-Type Blind Bolt

Several companies manufacture the pull-type of blind bolt fastening systems. They may differ in some design aspects, but in general they have a similar function. The pull-type uses the drive nut concept and is composed of a nut, sleeve, and a draw bolt. Frequently used blind bolt systems include but are not limited to the Cherry Maxibolt® Blind Bolt system and the HuckBolt® fasteners which includes the Ti-Matic® Blind Bolt and the Unimatic® Advanced Bolt (UAB) blind bolt systems.

Cherry Maxibolt® Blind Bolt System

The Cherry Maxibolt® blind bolt, available in alloy steel and A-286 CRES materials, comes in four different nominal and oversized head styles. *[Figure 4-110]* One tool and pulling head installs all three diameters. The blind bolts create a larger blind side footprint and they provide excellent performance in thin sheet and nonmetallic applications. The flush breaking stem eliminates shaving while the extended grip range accommodates different application thicknesses. Cherry Maxibolts® are primarily used in structures where higher loads are required. The steel version is 112 KSI shear. The A286 version is 95 KSI shear. The Cherry® G83, G84, or G704 installation tools are required for installation.

Huck Blind Bolt System

The Huck Blind Bolt is a high strength vibration-resistant fastener. *[Figure 4-111]* These bolts have been used successfully in many critical areas, such as engine inlets and leading edge applications. All fasteners are installed with a combination of available hand, pneumatic, pneudraulic, or hydraulic pull-type tools (no threads) for ease of installation.

Huck Blind Bolts can be installed on blind side angle surfaces up to 5° without loss of performance. The stem is mechanically locked to provide vibration-resistant FOD-free installations. The locking collar is forced into a conical pocket between stem and sleeve, creating high tensile capability. The lock collar fills the sleeve lock pocket to prevent leakage or corrosion pockets (crevice corrosion).

Flush head blind bolts are designed to install with a flush stem break that often requires no trimming for aerodynamic surfaces. The Huck Blind Bolt is available in high-strength A286 CRES at 95KSI shear strength in 5/32-inch through 3/8-

During the Maxibolt® installation sequence, the Cherry® shift washer collapses into itself, leaving a solid washer that is easily retrieved.

Figure 4-110. *Maxibolt® Blind Bolt System installation.*

inch diameters in 100° flush tension and protruding head. Also available are shear flush heads in ³⁄₁₆-inch diameter. A286 CRES Huck Blind Bolts are also available in ¹⁄₆₄-inch oversize diameters for repair applications.

Figure 4-111. *Huck blind bolt system.*

Drive Nut-Type of Blind Bolt

Jo-bolts, Visu-lok®, Composi-Lok®, OSI Bolt®, and Radial-Lok® fasteners use the drive nut concept and are composed of a nut, sleeve, and a draw bolt. *[Figure 4-112]* These types of blind bolts are used for high strength applications in metals and composites when there is no access to the blind side. Available in steel and titanium alloys, they are installed with special tooling. Both powered and hand tooling is available. During installation, the nut is held stationary while the core bolt is rotated by the installation tooling. The rotation of the core bolt draws the sleeve into the installed position and continues to retain the sleeve for the life of the fastener. The bolt has left hand threads and driving flats on the threaded end. A break-off relief allows the driving portion of the bolt to break off when the sleeve is properly seated. These types of bolts are available in many different head styles, including protruding head, 100° flush head, 130° flush head, and hex head.

Figure 4-112. *Drive nut blind bolt.*

Use the grip gauge available for the type of fastener and select the bolt grip after careful determination of the material thickness. The grip of the bolt is critical for correct installation. *[Figure 4-113]*

Figure 4-113. *Drive nut blind bolt installation tool.*

Installation procedure:

1. Install the fastener into the hole, and place the installation tooling over the screw (stem) and nut.

2. Apply torque to the screw with the installation tool while keeping the drive nut stationary. The screw continues to advance through the nut body causing the sleeve to be drawn up over the tapered nose of the nut. When the sleeve forms tightly against the blind side of the structure, the screw fractures in the break groove. The stem of Jo-bolts, Visu-lok®, and Composi-Lok® II fasteners does not break off flush with the head. A screw break-off shaver tool must be used if a flush installation is required. The stem of the newer Composi-Lok3® and OSI Bolt® break off flush.

Tapered Shank Bolt

Tapered shank bolts, such as the Taper-Lok®, are lightweight, high strength shear or tension bolts. This bolt has a tapered shank designed to provide an interference fit upon installation. Tapered shank bolts can be identified by a round head (rather than a screwdriver slot or wrench flats) and a threaded shank. The Taper-Lok® is comprised of a tapered, conical-shank fastener, installed into a precision tapered hole. The use of tapered shank bolts is limited to special applications such as high stress areas of fuel tanks. It is important that a tapered bolt not be substituted for any other type of fastener in repairs. It is equally as important not to substitute any other type of fastener for a tapered bolt.

Tapered shank bolts look similar to Hi-Lok® bolts after installation, but the tapered shank bolts do not have the hex recess at the threaded end of the bolt. Tapered shank bolts are installed in precision-reamed holes, with a controlled interference fit. The interference fit compresses the material around the hole that results in excellent load transfer, fatigue resistance, and sealing. The collar used with the tapered shank bolts has a captive washer, and no extra washers are required. New tapered shank bolt installation or rework of tapered shank bolt holes needs to be accomplished by trained personnel. Properly installed, these bolts become tightly wedged and do not turn while torque is applied to the nut.

Sleeve Bolts

Sleeve bolts are used for similar purposes as tapered shank bolts, but are easier to install. Sleeve bolts, such as the two piece SLEEVbolt®, consist of a tapered shank bolt in an expandable sleeve. The sleeve is internally tapered and externally straight. The sleeve bolt is installed in a standard tolerance straight hole. During installation, the bolt is forced into the sleeve. This action expands the sleeve which fills the hole. It is easier to drill a straight tolerance hole than it is to drill the tapered hole required for a tapered shank bolt.

Rivet Nut

The rivet nut is a blind installed, internally threaded rivet invented in 1936 by the Goodrich Rubber Company for the purpose of attaching a rubber aircraft wing deicer extrusion to the leading edge of the wing. The original rivet nut is the Rivnut® currently manufactured by Bollhoff Rivnut Inc. The Rivnut® became widely used in the military and aerospace markets because of its many design and assembly advantages.

Rivet nuts are used for the installation of fairings, trim, and lightly loaded fittings that must be installed after an assembly is completed. *[Figure 4-114]* Often used for parts that are removed frequently, the rivet nut is available in two types: countersunk or flat head. Installed by crimping from one side, the rivet nut provides a threaded hole into which machine screws can be installed. Where a flush fit is required, the countersink style can be used. Rivet nuts made of alloy steel are used when increased tensile and shear strength is required.

Figure 4-114. *Rivet nut installation.*

Hole Preparation

Flat head rivet nuts require only the proper size of hole while flush installation can be made into either countersunk or dimpled skin. Metal thinner than the rivet nut head requires a dimple. The rivet nut size is selected according to the thickness of the parent material and the size of screw to be used. The part number identifies the type of rivet nut and the maximum grip length. Recommended hole sizes are shown in *Figure 4-115*.

Rivnut® Size	Drill Size	Hole Tolerance
No. 4	5/32	.155–.157
No. 6	#12	.189–.193
No. 8	#2	.221–.226

Figure 4-115. *Recommended hole sizes for rivets and nuts.*

Correct installation requires good hole preparation, removal of burrs, and holding the sheets in contact while heading. Like any sheet metal fastener, a rivet nut should fit snugly into its hole.

Blind Fasteners (Nonstructural)

Pop Rivets

Common pull-type pop rivets, produced for non-aircraft-related applications, are not approved for use on certificated aircraft structures or components. However, some homebuilt noncertificated aircraft use pull-type rivets for their structure. These types of rivets are typically made of aluminum and can be installed with hand tools.

Pull Through Nutplate Blind Rivet

Nutplate blind rivets are used where the high shear strength of solid rivets is not required or if there is no access to install a solid rivet. The ³⁄₃₂-inch diameter blind rivet is most often used. The nut plate blind rivet is available with the pull-through and self-plugging locked spindle. [Figure 4-116]

Figure 4-116. *Rivetless pull-through nutplate.*

The new Cherry® Rivetless Nut Plate, which replaces standard riveted nutplates, features a retainer that does not require flaring. This proprietary design eliminates the need for two additional rivet holes, as well as reaming, counterboring, and countersinking steps.

Forming Process

Before a part is attached to the aircraft during either manufacture or repair, it has to be shaped to fit into place. This shaping process is called forming and may be a simple process, such as making one or two holes for attaching; it may be a complex process, such as making shapes with complex curvatures. Forming, which tends to change the shape or contour of a flat sheet or extruded shape, is accomplished by either stretching or shrinking the material in a certain area to produce curves, flanges, and various irregular shapes. Since the operation involves altering the shape of the stock

material, the amount of shrinking and stretching almost entirely depends on the type of material used. Fully annealed (heated and cooled) material can withstand considerably more stretching and shrinking and can be formed at a much smaller bend radius than when it is in any of the tempered conditions.

When aircraft parts are formed at the factory, they are made on large presses or by drop hammers equipped with dies of the correct shape. Factory engineers, who designate specifications for the materials to be used to ensure the finished part has the correct temper when it leaves the machines, plan every part. Factory draftsmen prepare a layout for each part. [Figure 4-117]

Figure 4-117. *Aircraft formed at a factory.*

Forming processes used on the flight line and those practiced in the maintenance or repair shop cannot duplicate a manufacturer's resources, but similar techniques of factory metal working can be applied in the handcrafting of repair parts.

Forming usually involves the use of extremely light-gauge alloys of a delicate nature that can be readily made useless by coarse and careless workmanship. A formed part may seem outwardly perfect, yet a wrong step in the forming procedure may leave the part in a strained condition. Such a defect may hasten fatigue or may cause sudden structural failure.

Of all the aircraft metals, pure aluminum is the most easily formed. In aluminum alloys, ease of forming varies with the temper condition. Since modern aircraft are constructed chiefly of aluminum and aluminum alloys, this section deals with the procedures for forming aluminum or aluminum alloy parts with a brief discussion of working with stainless steel, magnesium, and titanium.

Most parts can be formed without annealing the metal, but if extensive forming operations, such as deep draws (large folds) or complex curves, are planned, the metal should be in the dead soft or annealed condition. During the forming of some complex parts, operations may need to be stopped and the metal annealed before the process can be continued or completed. For example, alloy 2024 in the "0" condition can be formed into almost any shape by the common forming operations, but it must be heat treated afterward.

Forming Operations and Terms

Forming requires either stretching or shrinking the metal, or sometimes doing both. Other processes used to form metal include bumping, crimping, and folding.

Stretching

Stretching metal is achieved by hammering or rolling metal under pressure. For example, hammering a flat piece of metal causes the material in the hammered area to become thinner in that area. Since the amount of metal has not been decreased, the metal has been stretched. The stretching process thins, elongates, and curves sheet metal. It is critical to ensure the metal is not stretched too much, making it too thin, because sheet metal does not rebound easily. [Figure 4-118]

Figure 4-118. *Stretch forming metal.*

Stretching one portion of a piece of metal affects the surrounding material, especially in the case of formed and extruded angles. For example, hammering the metal in the horizontal flange of the angle strip over a metal block causes its length to increase (stretched), making that section longer than the section near the bend. To allow for this difference in length, the vertical flange, which tends to keep the material near the bend from stretching, would be forced to curve away from the greater length.

Shrinking

Shrinking metal is much more difficult than stretching it. During the shrinking process, metal is forced or compressed into a smaller area. This process is used when the length of a piece of metal, especially on the inside of a bend, is to be reduced. Sheet metal can be shrunk in by hammering on a V-block or by crimping and then using a shrinking block.

To curve the formed angle by the V-block method, place the angle on the V-block and gently hammer downward against the upper edge directly over the "V." While hammering, move the angle back and forth across the V-block to compress the material along the upper edge. Compression of the material along the upper edge of the vertical flange will cause the formed angle to take on a curved shape. The material in the horizontal flange will merely bend down at the center, and the length of that flange will remain the same. [Figure 4-119]

Figure 4-119. *Shrink forming metal.*

To make a sharp curve or a sharply bent flanged angle, crimping and a shrinking block can be used. In this process, crimps are placed in the one flange, and then by hammering the metal on a shrinking block, the crimps are driven, or shrunk, one at a time.

Cold shrinking requires the combination of a hard surface, such as wood or steel, and a soft mallet or hammer because a steel hammer over a hard surface stretches the metal, as opposed to shrinking it. The larger the mallet face is, the better.

Bumping

Bumping involves shaping or forming malleable metal by hammering or tapping—usually with a rubber, plastic, or rawhide mallet. During this process, the metal is supported by a dolly, a sandbag, or a die. Each contains a depression into which hammered portions of the metal can sink. Bumping can be done by hand or by machine.

Crimping

Crimping is folding, pleating, or corrugating a piece of sheet metal in a way that shortens it or turning down a flange on a seam. It is often used to make one end of a piece of stove pipe slightly smaller so that one section may be slipped into another. Crimping one side of a straight piece of angle iron with crimping pliers causes it to curve. [Figure 4-120]

Folding Sheet Metal

Folding sheet metal is to make a bend or crease in sheets, plates, or leaves. Folds are usually thought of as sharp, angular bends and are generally made on folding machines such as the box and pan brake discussed earlier in this chapter.

Layout and Forming

Terminology

The following terms are commonly used in sheet metal forming and flat pattern layout. Familiarity with these terms aids in understanding how bend calculations are used in a bending operation. *Figure 4-121* illustrates most of these terms.

Base measurement—the outside dimensions of a formed part. Base measurement is given on the drawing or blueprint or may be obtained from the original part.

Figure 4-120. *Crimping metal.*

Leg—the longer part of a formed angle.

Flange—the shorter part of a formed angle—the opposite of leg. If each side of the angle is the same length, then each is known as a leg.

Grain of the metal—natural grain of the material is formed as the sheet is rolled from molten ingot. Bend lines should be made to lie at a 90° angle to the grain of the metal if possible.

Bend allowance (BA)—refers to the curved section of metal within the bend (the portion of metal that is curved in bending). The bend allowance may be considered as being the length of the curved portion of the neutral line.

Figure 4-121. *Bend allowance terminology.*

Bend radius—the arc is formed when sheet metal is bent. This arc is called the bend radius. The bend radius is measured from a radius center to the inside surface of the metal. The minimum bend radius depends on the temper, thickness, and type of material. Always use a Minimum Bend Radius Table to determine the minimum bend radius for the alloy that is going to be used. Minimum bend radius charts can be found in manufacturer's maintenance manuals.

Bend tangent line (BL)—the location at which the metal starts to bend and the line at which the metal stops curving. All the space between the band tangent lines is the bend allowance.

Neutral axis—an imaginary line that has the same length after bending as it had before bending. [Figure 4-122] After bending, the bend area is 10 to 15 percent thinner than before bending. This thinning of the bend area moves the neutral line of the metal in towards the radius center. For calculation purposes, it is often assumed that the neutral axis is located at the center of the material, although the neutral axis is not exactly in the center of the material. However, the amount of error incurred is so slight that, for most work, assuming it is at the center is satisfactory.

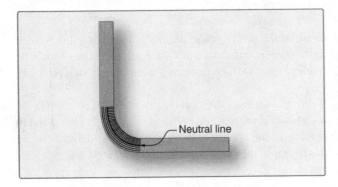

Figure 4-122. *Neutral line.*

Mold line (ML)—an extension of the flat side of a part beyond the radius.

Mold line dimension (MLD)—the dimension of a part made by the intersection of mold lines. It is the dimension the part would have if its corners had no radius.

Mold point—the point of intersection of the mold lines. The mold point would be the outside corner of the part if there were no radius.

K-Factor—the percentage of the material thickness where there is no stretching or compressing of the material, such as the neutral axis. This percentage has been calculated and is one of 179 numbers on the K chart corresponding to one of the angles between 0° and 180° to which metal can be bent.

[Figure 4-123] Whenever metal is to be bent to any angle other than 90° (K-factor of 90° equal to 1), the corresponding K-factor number is selected from the chart and is multiplied by the sum of the radius (R) and the thickness (T) of the metal. The product is the amount of setback (see next paragraph) for the bend. If no K chart is available, the K-factor can be calculated with a calculator by using the following formula: the K value is the tangent of one-half the bend angle.

Setback (SB)—the distance the jaws of a brake must be setback from the mold line to form a bend. In a 90° bend, SB = R + T (radius of the bend plus thickness of the metal). The setback dimension must be determined prior to making the bend because setback is used in determining the location of the beginning bend tangent line. When a part has more than one bend, setback must be subtracted for each bend. The majority of bends in sheet metal are 90° bends. The K-factor must be used for all bends that are smaller or larger than 90°.

SB = K(R+T)

Sight line—also called the bend or brake line, it is the layout line on the metal being formed that is set even with the nose of the brake and serves as a guide in bending the work.

Flat—that portion of a part that is not included in the bend. It is equal to the base measurement (MLD) minus the setback.

Flat = MLD – SB

Closed angle—an angle that is less than 90° when measured between legs, or more than 90° when the amount of bend is measured.

Open angle—an angle that is more than 90° when measured between legs, or less than 90° when the amount of bend is measured.

Total developed width (TDW)—the width of material measured around the bends from edge to edge. Finding the TDW is necessary to determine the size of material to be cut. The TDW is less than the sum of mold line dimensions since the metal is bent on a radius and not to a square corner as mold line dimensions indicate.

Layout or Flat Pattern Development

To prevent any waste of material and to get a greater degree of accuracy in the finished part, it is wise to make a layout or flat pattern of a part before forming it. Construction of interchangeable structural and nonstructural parts is achieved by forming flat sheet stock to make channel, angle, zee, or hat section members. Before a sheet metal part is formed, make a flat pattern to show how much material is required

Degree	K	Degree	K	Degree	K	Degree	K	Degree	K
1	0.0087	37	0.3346	73	0.7399	109	1.401	145	3.171
2	0.0174	38	0.3443	74	0.7535	110	1.428	146	3.270
3	0.0261	39	0.3541	75	0.7673	111	1.455	147	3.375
4	0.0349	40	0.3639	76	0.7812	112	1.482	148	3.487
5	0.0436	41	0.3738	77	0.7954	113	1.510	149	3.605
6	0.0524	42	0.3838	78	0.8097	114	1.539	150	3.732
7	0.0611	43	0.3939	79	0.8243	115	1.569	151	3.866
8	0.0699	44	0.4040	80	0.8391	116	1.600	152	4.010
9	0.0787	45	0.4142	81	0.8540	117	1.631	153	4.165
10	0.0874	46	0.4244	82	0.8692	118	1.664	154	4.331
11	0.0963	47	0.4348	83	0.8847	119	1.697	155	4.510
12	0.1051	48	0.4452	84	0.9004	120	1.732	156	4.704
13	0.1139	49	0.4557	85	0.9163	121	1.767	157	4.915
14	0.1228	50	0.4663	86	0.9324	122	1.804	158	5.144
15	0.1316	51	0.4769	87	0.9489	123	1.841	159	5.399
16	0.1405	52	0.4877	88	0.9656	124	1.880	160	5.671
17	0.1494	53	0.4985	89	0.9827	125	1.921	161	5.975
18	0.1583	54	0.5095	90	1.000	126	1.962	162	6.313
19	0.1673	55	0.5205	91	1.017	127	2.005	163	6.691
20	0.1763	56	0.5317	92	1.035	128	2.050	164	7.115
21	0.1853	57	0.5429	93	1.053	129	2.096	165	7.595
22	0.1943	58	0.5543	94	1.072	130	2.144	166	8.144
23	0.2034	59	0.5657	95	1.091	131	2.194	167	8.776
24	0.2125	60	0.5773	96	1.110	132	2.246	168	9.514
25	0.2216	61	0.5890	97	1.130	133	2.299	169	10.38
26	0.2308	62	0.6008	98	1.150	134	2.355	170	11.43
27	0.2400	63	0.6128	99	1.170	135	2.414	171	12.70
28	0.2493	64	0.6248	100	1.191	136	2.475	172	14.30
29	0.2586	65	0.6370	101	1.213	137	2.538	173	16.35
30	0.2679	66	0.6494	102	1.234	138	2.605	174	19.08
31	0.2773	67	0.6618	103	1.257	139	2.674	175	22.90
32	0.2867	68	0.6745	104	1.279	140	2.747	176	26.63
33	0.2962	69	0.6872	105	1.303	141	2.823	177	38.18
34	0.3057	70	0.7002	106	1.327	142	2.904	178	57.29
35	0.3153	71	0.7132	107	1.351	143	2.988	179	114.59
36	0.3249	72	0.7265	108	1.376	144	3.077	180	Inf.

Figure 4-123. *K-factor.*

in the bend areas, at what point the sheet must be inserted into the forming tool, or where bend lines are located. Bend lines must be determined to develop a flat pattern for sheet metal forming.

When forming straight angle bends, correct allowances must be made for setback and bend allowance. If shrinking or stretching processes are to be used, allowances must be made so that the part can be turned out with a minimum amount of forming.

Making Straight Line Bends

When forming straight bends, the thickness of the material, its alloy composition, and its temper condition must be considered. Generally speaking, the thinner the material is, the more sharply it can be bent (the smaller the radius of bend), and the softer the material is, the sharper the bend is. Other factors that must be considered when making straight line bends are bend allowance, setback, and brake or sight line.

The radius of bend of a sheet of material is the radius of the bend as measured on the inside of the curved material. The minimum radius of bend of a sheet of material is the sharpest curve, or bend, to which the sheet can be bent without critically weakening the metal at the bend. If the radius of bend is too small, stresses and strains weaken the metal and may result in cracking.

A minimum radius of bend is specified for each type of aircraft sheet metal. The minimum bend radius is affected by the kind of material, thickness of the material, and temper condition of the material. Annealed sheet can be bent to a radius approximately equal to its thickness. Stainless steel and 2024-T3 aluminum alloy require a fairly large bend radius.

Bending a U-Channel

To understand the process of making a sheet metal layout, the steps for determining the layout of a sample U-channel will be discussed. *[Figure 4-124]* When using bend allowance calculations, the following steps for finding the total developed length can be computed with formulas, charts, or computer-aided design (CAD) and computer-aided manufacturing (CAM) software packages. This channel is made of 0.040-inch 2024-T3 aluminum alloy.

Figure 4-124. *U-channel example.*

Step 1: Determine the Correct Bend Radius

Minimum bend radius charts are found in manufacturers' maintenance manuals. A radius that is too sharp cracks the material during the bending process. Typically, the drawing indicates the radius to use, but it is a good practice to double check. For this layout example, use the minimum radius chart in *Figure 4-125* to choose the correct bend radius for the alloy, temper, and the metal thickness. For 0.040, 2024-T3 the minimum allowable radius is 0.16-inch or 5/32-inch.

Step 2: Find the Setback

The setback can be calculated with a formula or can be found in a setback chart available in aircraft maintenance manuals or Source, Maintenance, and Recoverability books (SMRs). *[Figure 4-126]*

Using a Formula to Calculate the Setback

SB = setback

K = K-factor (K is 1 for 90° bends)

R = inside radius of the bend

T = material thickness

Since all of the angles in this example are 90° angles, the setback is calculated as follows:

$$SB = K(R+T)$$
$$SB = 1(.16+.40) = 0.56 \text{ inches}$$

NOTE: K = 1 for a 90° bend. For other than a 90° bend, use a K-factor chart.

Using a Setback Chart to Find the Setback

The setback chart is a quick way to find the setback and is useful for open and closed bends, because there is no need to calculate or find the K-factor. Several software packages and online calculators are available to calculate the setback. These programs are often used with CAD/CAM programs. *[Figure 4-126]*

- Enter chart at the bottom on the appropriate scale with the sum of the radius and material thickness.

- Read up to the bend angle.

- Find the setback from corresponding scale on the left.

Example:

- Material thickness is 0.063-inch.

- Bend angle is 135°.

- R + T = 0.183-inch.

Find 0.183 at the bottom of the graph. It is found in the middle scale.

- Read up to a bend angle of 135°.

- Locate the setback at the left hand side of the graph in the middle scale (0.435-inch). *[Figure 4-126]*

Step 3: Find the Length of the Flat Line Dimension

The flat line dimension can be found using the formula:

$$Flat = MLD - SB$$

MLD = mold line dimension

SB = setback

The flats, or flat portions of the U-channel, are equal to the mold line dimension minus the setback for each of the sides, and the mold line length minus two setbacks for the center flat. Two setbacks need to be subtracted from the center flat because this flat has a bend on either side.

MINIMUM BEND RADIUS FOR ALUMINUM ALLOYS

Thickness	5052-0 6061-0 5052-H32	7178-0 2024-0 5052-H34 6061-T4 7075-0	6061-T6	7075-T6	2024-T3 2024-T4	2024-T6
.012	.03	.03	.03	.03	.06	.06
.016	.03	.03	.03	.03	.09	.09
.020	.03	.03	.03	.12	.09	.09
.025	.03	.03	.06	.16	.12	.09
.032	.03	.03	.06	.19	.12	.12
.040	.06	.06	.09	.22	.16	.16
.050	.06	.06	.12	.25	.19	.19
.063	.06	.09	.16	.31	.22	.25
.071	.09	.12	.16	.38	.25	.31
.080	.09	.16	.19	.44	.31	.38
.090	.09	.19	.22	.50	.38	.44
.100	.12	.22	.25	.62	.44	.50
.125	.12	.25	.31	.88	.50	.62
.160	.16	.31	.44	1.25	.75	.75
.190	.19	.38	.56	1.38	1.00	1.00
.250	.31	.62	.75	2.00	1.25	1.25
.312	.44	1.25	1.38	2.50	1.50	1.50
.375	.44	1.38	1.50	2.50	1.88	1.88

Bend radius is designated to the inside of the bend. All dimensions are in inches.

Figure 4-125. *Minimum bend radius (from the Raytheon Aircraft Structural Inspection and Repair Manual).*

The flat dimension for the sample U-channel is calculated in the following manner:

Flat dimension = MLD – SB

Flat 1 = 1.00-inch – 0.56-inch = 0.44-inch

Flat 2 = 2.00-inch – (2 × 0.56-inch) = 1.44-inch

Flat 3 = 1.00-inch – 0.56-inch = 0.44-inch

Step 4: Find the Bend Allowance

When making a bend or fold in a piece of metal, the bend allowance or length of material required for the bend must be calculated. Bend allowance depends on four factors: degree of bend, radius of the bend, thickness of the metal, and type of metal used.

The radius of the bend is generally proportional to the thickness of the material. Furthermore, the sharper the radius of bend, the less the material that is needed for the bend. The type of material is also important. If the material is soft, it can be bent very sharply; but if it is hard, the radius of bend is greater, and the bend allowance is greater. The degree of bend affects the overall length of the metal, whereas the thickness influences the radius of bend.

Bending a piece of metal compresses the material on the inside of the curve and stretches the material on the outside of the curve. However, at some distance between these two extremes lies a space which is not affected by either force. This is known as the neutral line or neutral axis and occurs at a distance approximately 0.445 times the metal thickness ($0.445 × T$) from the inside of the radius of the bend. *[Figure 4-127]*

The length of this neutral axis must be determined so that sufficient material can be provided for the bend. This is called the bend allowance. This amount must be added to the overall length of the layout pattern to ensure adequate material for the bend. To save time in calculation of the bend allowance, formulas and charts for various angles, radii of bends, material thicknesses, and other factors have been developed.

Formula 1: Bend Allowance for a 90° Bend

To the radius of bend (R) add ½ the thickness of the metal (½T). This gives $R + ½T$, or the radius of the circle of the neutral axis. *[Figure 4-128]* Compute the circumference of this circle by multiplying the radius of the neutral line ($R + ½T$) by 2π (NOTE: $\pi = 3.1416$): $2\pi (R + ½T)$. Since a

Figure 4-126. *Setback chart.*

Figure 4-127. *Neutral axis and stresses resulting from bending.*

Figure 4-128. *Bend allowance for a 90° bend.*

90° bend is a quarter of the circle, divide the circumference by 4. This gives:

$$\frac{2\pi\ (R + \frac{1}{2}T)}{4}$$

This is the bend allowance for a 90° bend. To use the formula for a 90° bend having a radius of ¼ inch for material 0.051-inch thick, substitute in the formula as follows.

$$\text{Bend allowance} = \frac{(2 \times 3.1416)(0.250 + \frac{1}{2}(0.051))}{4}$$

$$= \frac{6.2832(0.250 + 0.0255)}{4}$$

$$= \frac{6.2832(0.2755)}{4}$$

$$= 0.4327$$

The bend allowance, or the length of material required for the bend, is 0.4327 or ⁷⁄₁₆-inch.

Formula 2: Bend Allowance for a 90° Bend

This formula uses two constant values that have evolved over a period of years as being the relationship of the degrees in the bend to the thickness of the metal when determining the bend allowance for a particular application. By experimentation with actual bends in metals, aircraft engineers have found that accurate bending results could be obtained by using the following formula for any degree of bend from 1° to 180°.

Bend allowance = (0.01743R + 0.0078T)N where:

R = the desired bend radius

T = the thickness of the metal

N = number of degrees of bend

To use this formula for a 90° bend having a radius of .16-inch for material 0.040-inch thick, substitute in the formula as follows:

Bend allowance =
(0.01743 × 0.16) + (0.0078 × 0.040) × 90 = 0.27 inches

Use of Bend Allowance Chart for a 90° Bend

In *Figure 4-129*, the radius of bend is shown on the top line, and the metal thickness is shown on the left hand column. The upper number in each cell is the bend allowance for a 90° bend. The lower number in the cell is the bend allowance per 1° of bend. To determine the bend allowance for a 90° bend, simply use the top number in the chart.

Example: The material thickness of the U-channel is 0.040-inch and the bend radius is 0.16-inch.

Reading across the top of the bend allowance chart, find the column for a radius of bend of .156-inch. Now, find the block in this column that is opposite the material thickness (gauge) of 0.040 in the column at the left. The upper number in the cell is (0.273), the correct bend allowance in inches for a 90° bends.

Several bend allowance calculation programs are available online. Just enter the material thickness, radius, and degree of bend and the computer program calculates the bend allowance.

Use of Chart for Other Than a 90° Bend

If the bend is to be other than 90°, use the lower number in the block (the bend allowance for 1°) and compute the bend allowance.

Metal Thickness	RADIUS OF BEND, IN INCHES													
	1/32 .031	1/16 .063	3/32 .094	1/8 .125	5/32 .156	3/16 .188	7/32 .219	1/4 .250	9/32 .281	5/16 .313	11/32 .344	3/8 .375	7/16 .438	1/2 .500
.020	.062 .000693	.113 .001251	.161 .001792	.210 .002333	.259 .002874	.309 .003433	.358 .003974	.406 .004515	.455 .005056	.505 .005614	.554 .006155	.603 .006695	.702 .007795	.799 .008877
.025	.066 .000736	.116 .001294	.165 .001835	.214 .002376	.263 .002917	.313 .003476	.362 .004017	.410 .004558	.459 .005098	.509 .005657	.558 .006198	.607 .006739	.705 .007838	.803 .008920
.028	.068 .000759	.119 .001318	.167 .001859	.216 .002400	.265 .002941	.315 .003499	.364 .004040	.412 .004581	.461 .005122	.511 .005680	.560 .006221	.609 .006762	.708 .007862	.805 .007862
.032	.071 .000787	.121 .001345	.170 .001886	.218 .002427	.267 .002968	.317 .003526	.366 .004067	.415 .004608	.463 .005149	.514 .005708	.562 .006249	.611 .006789	.710 .007889	.807 .008971
.038	.075 .00837	.126 .001396	.174 .001937	.223 .002478	.272 .003019	.322 .003577	.371 .004118	.419 .004659	.468 .005200	.518 .005758	.567 .006299	.616 .006840	.715 .007940	.812 .009021
.040	.077 .000853	.127 .001411	.176 .001952	.224 .002493	.273 .003034	.323 .003593	.372 .004134	.421 .004675	.469 .005215	.520 .005774	.568 .006315	.617 .006856	.716 .007955	.813 .009037
.051		.134 .001413	.183 .002034	.232 .002575	.280 .003116	.331 .003675	.379 .004215	.428 .004756	.477 .005297	.527 .005855	.576 .006397	.624 .006934	.723 .008037	.821 .009119
.064		.144 .001595	.192 .002136	.241 .002676	.290 .003218	.340 .003776	.389 .004317	.437 .004858	.486 .005399	.536 .005957	.585 .006498	.634 .007039	.732 .008138	.830 .009220
.072			.198 .002202	.247 .002743	.296 .003284	.436 .003842	.394 .004283	.443 .004924	.492 .005465	.542 .006023	.591 .006564	.639 .007105	.738 .008205	836 .009287
.078			.202 .002249	.251 .002790	.300 .003331	.350 .003889	.399 .004430	.447 .004963	.496 .005512	.546 .006070	.595 .006611	.644 .007152	.745 .008252	.840 .009333
.081			.204 .002272	.253 .002813	.302 .003354	.352 .003912	.401 .004453	.449 .004969	.498 .005535	.548 .006094	.598 .006635	.646 .007176	.745 .008275	.842 .009357
.091			.212 .002350	.260 .002891	.309 .003432	.359 .003990	.408 .004531	.456 .005072	.505 .005613	.555 .006172	.604 .006713	.653 .007254	.752 .008353	.849 .009435
.094			.214 .002374	.262 .002914	.311 .003455	.361 .004014	.410 .004555	.459 .005096	.507 .005637	.558 .006195	.606 .006736	.655 .007277	.754 .008376	.851 .009458
.102				.268 .002977	.317 .003518	.367 .004076	.416 .004617	.464 .005158	.513 .005699	.563 .006257	.612 .006798	.661 .007339	.760 .008439	.857 .009521
.109				.273 .003031	.321 .003572	.372 .004131	.420 .004672	.469 .005213	.518 .005754	.568 .006312	.617 .006853	.665 .008394	.764 .008493	.862 .009575
.125				.284 .003156	.333 .003697	.383 .004256	.432 .004797	.480 .005338	.529 .005678	.579 .006437	.628 .006978	.677 .007519	.776 .008618	.873 .009700
.156					.355 .003939	.405 .004497	.453 .005038	.502 .005579	.551 .006120	.601 .006679	.650 .007220	.698 .007761	.797 .008860	.895 .009942
.188					.417 .004747	.476 .005288	.525 .005829	.573 .006370	.624 .006928	.672 .007469	.721 .008010	.820 .009109	.917 .010191	
.250							.568 .006313	.617 .006853	.667 .007412	.716 .007953	.764 .008494	.863 .009593	.961 .010675	

Figure 4-129. *Bend allowance.*

Example:
The L-bracket shown in *Figure 4-130* is made from 2024-T3 aluminum alloy and the bend is 60° from flat. Note that the bend angle in the figure indicates 120°, but that is the number of degrees between the two flanges and not the bend angle from flat. To find the correct bend angle, use the following formula:

Bend Angle = 180° – Angle between flanges

Figure 4-130. *Bend allowance for bends less than 90°.*

4-66

The actual bend is 60°. To find the correct bend radius for a 60° bend of material 0.040-inches thick, use the following procedure.

1. Go to the left side of the table and find 0.040-inch.

2. Go to the right and locate the bend radius of 0.16-inch (0.156-inch).

3. Note the bottom number in the block (0.003034).

4. Multiply this number by the bend angle:

$$0.003034 \times 60 = 0.18204$$

Step 5: Find the Total Developed Width of the Material

The total developed width (TDW) can be calculated when the dimensions of the flats and the bend allowance are found. The following formula is used to calculate TDW:

TDW = Flats + (bend allowance × number of bends)

For the U-channel example, this gives:

TDW = Flat 1 + Flat 2 + Flat 3 + (2 × BA)

TDW = 0.8 + 1.6 + 0.8 + (2 × 0.27)

TDW = 3.74-inches

Note that the amount of metal needed to make the channel is less than the dimensions of the outside of the channel (total of mold line dimensions is 4 inches). This is because the metal follows the radius of the bend rather than going from mold line to mold line. It is good practice to check that the calculated TDW is smaller than the total mold line dimensions. If the calculated TDW is larger than the mold line dimensions, the math was incorrect.

Step 6: Flat Pattern Lay Out

After a flat pattern layout of all relevant information is made, the material can be cut to the correct size, and the bend tangent lines can be drawn on the material. *[Figure 4-131]*

Step 7: Draw the Sight Lines on the Flat Pattern

The pattern laid out in *Figure 4-131* is complete, except for a sight line that needs to be drawn to help position the bend tangent line directly at the point where the bend should start. Draw a line inside the bend allowance area that is one bend radius away from the bend tangent line that is placed under the brake nose bar. Put the metal in the brake under the clamp and adjust the position of the metal until the sight line is directly below the edge of the radius bar. *[Figure 4-132]* Now, clamp the brake on the metal and raise the leaf to make the bend. The bend begins exactly on the bend tangent line.

Figure 4-131. *Flat pattern layout.*

NOTE: A common mistake is to draw the sight line in the middle of the bend allowance area, instead of one radius away from the bend tangent line that is placed under the brake nose bar.

Using a J-Chart To Calculate Total Developed Width

The J-chart, often found in the SRM, can be used to determine bend deduction or setback and the TDW of a flat pattern layout when the inside bend radius, bend angle, and material thickness are known. *[Figure 4-133]* While not as accurate as the traditional layout method, the J-chart provides sufficient information for most applications. The J-chart does not require difficult calculations or memorized formulas because the required information can be found in the repair drawing or can be measured with simple measuring tools.

When using the J-chart, it is helpful to know whether the angle is open (greater than 90°) or closed (less than 90°) because the lower half of the J-chart is for open angles and the upper half is for closed angles.

How To Find the Total Developed Width Using a J-Chart

- Place a straightedge across the chart and connect the bend radius on the top scale with the material thickness on the bottom scale. *[Figure 4-133]*

- Locate the angle on the right hand scale and follow this line horizontally until it meets the straight edge.

- The factor X (bend deduction) is then read on the diagonally curving line.

- Interpolate when the X factor falls between lines.

Figure 4-132. *Sight line.*

- Add up the mold line dimensions and subtract the X factor to find the TDW.

Example 1

Bend radius = 0.22-inch

Material thickness = 0.063-inch

Bend angle = 90°

ML 1 = 2.00/ML 2 = 2.00

Use a straightedge to connect the bend radius (0.22-inch) at the top of the graph with the material thickness at the bottom (0.063-inch). Locate the 90° angle on the right hand scale and follow this line horizontally until it meets the straightedge. Follow the curved line to the left and find 0.17 at the left side. The X factor in the drawing is 0.17-inch. *[Figure 4-134]*

$$\text{Total developed width} = (\text{Mold line 1} + \text{Mold line 2}) - \text{X factor}$$

Total developed width = (2 + 2) – .17 = 3.83-inches

Example 2

Bend radius = 0.25-inch

Material thickness = 0.050-inch

Bend angle = 45°

ML 1 = 2.00/ML 2 = 2.00

Figure 4-135 illustrates a 135° angle, but this is the angle between the two legs. The actual bend from flat position is 45° (180 – 135 = 45). Use a straightedge to connect the bend radius (0.25-inch) at the top of the graph with the material thickness at the bottom (.050-inch). Locate the 45° angle on the right hand scale and follow this line horizontally until it meets the straight edge. Follow the curved line to the left

and find 0.035 at the left side. The X factor in the drawing is 0.035 inch.

$$\text{Total developed width} = (\text{Mold line 1} + \text{Mold line 2}) - \text{X factor}$$

Total developed width = (2 + 2) – .035 = 3.965-inch

Using a Sheet Metal Brake to Fold Metal

The brake set up for box and pan brakes and cornice brakes is identical. *[Figure 4-136]* A proper set up of the sheet metal brake is necessary because accurate bending of sheet metal depends on the thickness and temper of the material to be formed and the required radius of the part. Any time a different thickness of sheet metal needs to be formed or when a different radius is required to form the part, the operator needs to adjust the sheet metal brake before the brake is used to form the part. For this example, an L-channel made from 2024 –T3 aluminum alloy that is 0.032-inch thick will be bent.

Step 1: Adjustment of Bend Radius

The bend radius necessary to bend a part can be found in the part drawings, but if it is not mentioned in the drawing, consult the SRM for a minimum bend radius chart. This chart lists the smallest radius allowable for each thickness and temper of metal that is normally used. To bend tighter than this radius would jeopardize the integrity of the part. Stresses left in the area of the bend may cause it to fail while in service, even if it does not crack while bending it.

The brake radius bars of a sheet metal brake can be replaced with another brake radius bar with a different diameter. *[Figure 4-137]* For example, a 0.032-inch 2024-T3 L channel needs to be bent with a radius of ⅛-inch and a radius bar with a ⅛-inch radius must be installed. If different brake radius bars are not available, and the installed brake radius bar is

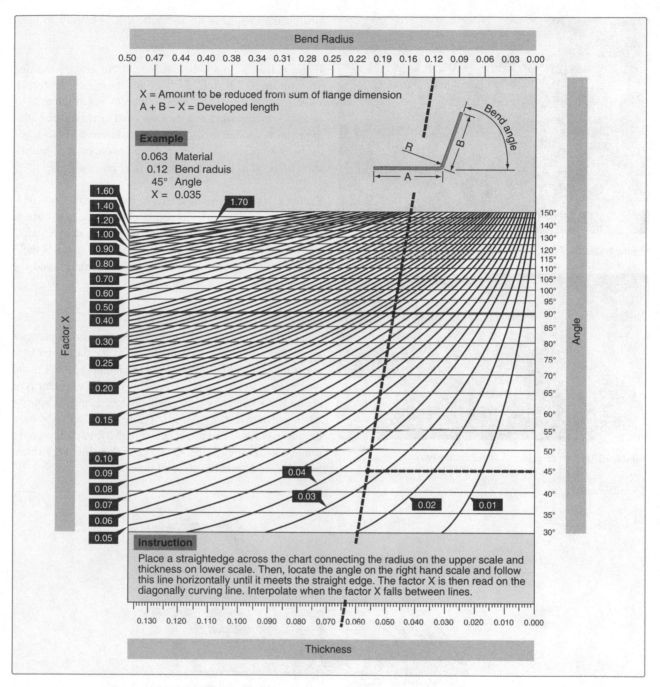

Bend Radius

0.50 0.47 0.44 0.40 0.38 0.34 0.31 0.28 0.25 0.22 0.19 0.16 0.12 0.09 0.06 0.03 0.00

X = Amount to be reduced from sum of flange dimension
A + B – X = Developed length

Example

0.063 Material
0.12 Bend raduis
45° Angle
X = 0.035

Factor X: 1.60 1.40 1.20 1.00 0.90 0.80 0.70 0.60 0.50 0.40 0.30 0.25 0.20 0.15 0.10 0.09 0.08 0.07 0.06 0.05

1.70

Angle: 150° 140° 130° 120° 115° 110° 105° 100° 95° 90° 85° 80° 75° 70° 65° 60° 55° 50° 45° 40° 35° 30°

0.04 0.03 0.02 0.01

Instruction

Place a straightedge across the chart connecting the radius on the upper scale and thickness on lower scale. Then, locate the angle on the right hand scale and follow this line horizontally until it meets the straight edge. The factor X is then read on the diagonally curving line. Interpolate when the factor X falls between lines.

0.130 0.120 0.110 0.100 0.090 0.080 0.070 0.060 0.050 0.040 0.030 0.020 0.010 0.000

Thickness

Figure 4-133. *J chart.*

Figure 4-134. *Example 1 of J chart.*

Figure 4-135. *Example 2 of J chart.*

Figure 4-136. *Brake radius nosepiece adjustment.*

Figure 4-137. *Interchangeable brake radius bars.*

smaller than required for the part, it is necessary to bend some nose radius shims. *[Figure 4-138]*

If the radius is so small that it tends to crack annealed aluminum, mild steel is a good choice of material. Experimentation with a small piece of scrap material is necessary to manufacture a thickness that increases the radius to precisely $\frac{1}{16}$-inch or $\frac{1}{8}$-inch. Use radius and fillet gauges to check this dimension. From this point on, each additional shim is added to the radius before it. *[Figure 4-139]*

Example: If the original nose was $\frac{1}{16}$-inch and a piece of .063-inch material ($\frac{1}{16}$-inch) was bent around it, the new outside radius is $\frac{1}{8}$-inch. If another .063-inch layer ($\frac{1}{16}$-inch) is added, it is now a $\frac{3}{16}$-inch radius. If a piece of .032-inch ($\frac{1}{32}$-inch) instead of .063-inch material ($\frac{1}{16}$-inch) is bent around the $\frac{1}{8}$-inch radius, a $\frac{5}{32}$-inch radius results.

Step 2: Adjusting Clamping Pressure

The next step is setting clamping pressure. Slide a piece of the material with the same thickness as the part to be bent under the brake radius piece. Pull the clamping lever toward the operator to test the pressure. This is an over center type clamp and, when properly set, will not feel springy or spongy when pulled to its fully clamped position. The operator must be able to pull this lever over center with a firm pull and have it bump its limiting stops. On some brakes, this adjustment has to be made on both sides of the brake.

Figure 4-138. *Nose radius shims may be used when the brake radius bar is smaller than required.*

Pull forward to clamp (no sponginess felt when evenly set on BOTH sides)

Radius shims

Material to be bent

Limiting stop

Lifting nut

Nut to adjust clamping pressure

Note: Bending leaf counterbalance omitted for clarity

Figure 4-139. *General brake overview including radius shims.*

Place test strips on the table 3-inch from each end and one in the center between the bed and the clamp, adjust clamp pressure until it is tight enough to prevent the work pieces from slipping while bending. The clamping pressure can be adjusted with the clamping pressure nut. *[Figure 4-140]*

Clamping pressure adjustment nut

Brake nose gap adjustment knob

Figure 4-140. *Adjust clamping pressure with the clamping pressure nut.*

Step 3: Adjusting the Nose Gap

Adjust the nose gap by turning the large brake nose gap adjustment knobs at the rear of the upper jaw to achieve its proper alignment. *[Figure 4-140]* The perfect setting is obtained when the bending leaf is held up to the angle of the finished bend and there is one material thickness between the bending leaf and the nose radius piece. Using a piece of material the thickness of the part to be bent as a feeler gauge can help achieve a high degree of accuracy. *[Figures 4-141 and 4-142]* It is essential this nose gap be perfect, even across the length of the part to be bent. Check by clamping two test strips between the bed and the clamp 3-inch from each end of the brake. *[Figure 4-143]* Bend 90° *[Figure 4-144]*, remove test strips, and place one on top of the other; they should match. *[Figure 4-145]* If they do not match, adjust the end with the sharper bend back slightly.

Folding a Box

A box can be formed the same way as the U-channel described on in the previous paragraphs, but when a sheet metal part has intersecting bend radii, it is necessary to remove material to make room for the material contained in

Figure 4-141. *Brake nose gap adjustment with piece of material same thickness as part to be formed.*

the flanges. This is done by drilling or punching holes at the intersection of the inside bend tangent lines. These holes, called relief holes and whose diameter is approximately twice the bend radius, relieve stresses in the metal as it is bent and prevent the metal from tearing. Relief holes also provide a neatly trimmed corner from which excess material may be trimmed.

The larger and smoother the relief hole is, the less likely it will be that a crack will form in the corner. Generally, the radius of the relief hole is specified on the drawing. A box and pan brake, also called a finger brake, is used to bend the box. Two opposite sides of the box are bent first. Then, the fingers of the brake are adjusted so the folded-up sides ride up in the cracks between the fingers when the leaf is raised to bend the other two sides.

Figure 4-142. *Profile illustration of brake nose gap adjustment.*

Figure 4-143. *Brake alignment with two test strips 3-inches from each end.*

Figure 4-144. *Brake alignment with two test strips bent at 90°.*

Figure 4-145. *Brake alignment by comparing test strips.*

The size of relief holes varies with thickness of the material. They should be no less than ⅛-inch in diameter for aluminum alloy sheet stock up to and including 0.064-inch thick, or ³⁄₁₆₀-inch in diameter for stock ranging from 0.072-inch to 0.128-inch thickness. The most common method of determining the diameter of a relief hole is to use the radius of bend for this dimension, provided it is not less than the minimum allowance (⅛-inch).

Relief Hole Location

Relief holes must touch the intersection of the inside bend tangent lines. To allow for possible error in bending, make the relief holes extend ¹⁄₃₂-inch to ¹⁄₁₆-inch behind the inside bend tangent lines. It is good practice to use the intersection of these lines as the center for the holes. The line on the inside of the curve is cut at an angle toward the relief holes to allow for the stretching of the inside flange.

The positioning of the relief hole is important. *[Figure 4-146]* It should be located so its outer perimeter touches the intersection of the inside bend tangent lines. This keeps any material from interfering with the bend allowance area of the other bend. If these bend allowance areas intersected with each other, there would be substantial compressive stresses that would accumulate in that corner while bending. This could cause the part to crack while bending.

Layout Method

Lay out the basic part using traditional layout procedures. This determines the width of the flats and the bend allowance. It is the intersection of the inside bend tangent lines that index the bend relief hole position. Bisect these intersected lines and move outward the distance of the radius of the hole on this line. This is the center of the hole. Drill at this point and finish by trimming off the remainder of the corner material. The trim out is often tangent to the radius and perpendicular to the edge. *[Figure 4-147]* This leaves an open corner. If the

Figure 4-146. *Relief hole location.*

Figure 4-147. *Relief hole layout.*

corner must be closed, or a slightly longer flange is necessary, then trim out accordingly. If the corner is to be welded, it is necessary to have touching flanges at the corners. The length of the flange should be one material thickness shorter than the finished length of the part so only the insides of the flanges touch.

Open and Closed Bends

Open and closed bends present unique problems that require more calculations than 90° bends. In the following 45° and a 135° bend examples, the material is 0.050-inch thick and the bend radius is ³⁄₁₆-inch.

Open End Bend (Less Than 90°)

Figure 4-148 shows an example for a 45° bend.

1. Look up K-factor in K chart. K-factor for 45° is 0.41421-inch.

2. Calculate setback.

   SB = K(R + T)

   SB = 0.41421-inch(0.1875-inch + 0.050-inch) = 0.098-inch

3. Calculate bend allowance for 45°. Look up bend allowance for 1° of bend in the bend allowance chart and multiply this by 45.

   0.003675-inch × 45 = 0.165-inch

4. Calculate flats.

   Flat = Mold line dimension – SB

   Flat 1 = .77-inch – 0.098-inch = 0.672-inch

   Flat 2 = 1.52-inch – 0.098-inch = 1.422-inch

5. Calculate TDW

   TDW = Flats + Bend allowance

   TDW = 0.672-inch + 1.422-inch + 0.165-inch = 2.259-inch.

Figure 4-148. *Open bend.*

Observe that the brake reference line is still located one radius from the bend tangent line.

Closed End Bend (More Than 90°)

Figure 4-149 shows an example of a 135° bend.

1. Look up K-factor in K chart. K-factor for 135° is 2.4142-inch.

2. Calculate SB.

   SB = K(R + T)

   SB = 2.4142-inch(0.1875-inch + 0.050-inch) = 0.57-inch

3. Calculate bend allowance for 135°. Look up bend allowance for 1° of bend in the bend allowance chart and multiply this by 135.

   0.003675-inch × 135 = 0.496-inch

4. Calculate flats.

   Flat = Mold line dimension – SB

   Flat 1 = 0.77-inch – 0.57-inch = 0.20-inch

   Flat 2 = 1.52-inch – 0.57-inch = 0.95-inch

5. Calculate TDW.

   TDW = Flats + Bend allowance

   TDW = 0.20-inch + 0.95-inch + 0.496-inch = 1.65-inch

Figure 4-149. *Closed bend.*

It is obvious from both examples that a closed bend has a smaller TDW than an open-end bend and the material length needs to be adjusted accordingly.

Hand Forming

All hand forming revolves around the processes of stretching and shrinking metal. As discussed earlier, stretching means to lengthen or increase a particular area of metal while shrinking means to reduce an area. Several methods of stretching and shrinking may be used, depending on the size, shape, and contour of the part being formed.

For example, if a formed or extruded angle is to be curved, either stretch one leg or shrink the other, whichever makes the part fit. In bumping, the material is stretched in the bulge to make it balloon, and in joggling, the material is stretched between the joggles. Material in the edge of lightening holes is often stretched to form a beveled reinforcing ridge around them. The following paragraphs discuss some of these techniques.

Straight Line Bends

The cornice brake and bar folder are ordinarily used to make straight bends. Whenever such machines are not available, comparatively short sections can be bent by hand with the aid of wooden or metal bending blocks.

After a blank has been laid out and cut to size, clamp it along the bend line between two wooden forming blocks held in a vise. The wooden forming blocks should have one edge rounded as needed for the desired radius of bend. It should also be curved slightly beyond 90° to allow for spring-back.

Bend the metal that protrudes beyond the bending block to the desired angle by tapping lightly with a rubber, plastic, or rawhide mallet. Start tapping at one end and work back and forth along the edge to make a gradual and even bend. Continue this process until the protruding metal is bent to the desired angle against the forming block. Allow for spring-back by driving the material slightly farther than the actual bend. If a large amount of metal extends beyond the forming blocks, maintain hand pressure against the protruding sheet to prevent it from bouncing. Remove any irregularities by holding a straight block of hardwood edgewise against the bend and striking it with heavy blows of a mallet or hammer. If the amount of metal protruding beyond the bending blocks is small, make the entire bend by using the hardwood block and hammer.

Formed or Extruded Angles

Both formed and extruded types of angles can be curved (not bent sharply) by stretching or shrinking either of the flanges. Curving by stretching one flange is usually preferred since the process requires only a V-block and a mallet and is easily accomplished.

Stretching With V-Block Method

In the stretching method, place the flange to be stretched in the groove of the V-block. *[Figure 4-150]* (If the flange is to be shrunk, place the flange across the V-block.) Using a round, soft-faced mallet, strike the flange directly over the V portion with light, even blows while gradually forcing it downward into the V.

Begin at one end of the flange and form the curve gradually and evenly by moving the strip slowly back and forth, distributing the hammer blows at equal spaces on the flange. Hold the strip firmly to keep it from bouncing when hammered. An overly heavy blow buckles the metal, so keep moving the flange across the V-block, but always lightly strike the spot directly above the V.

Lay out a full-sized, accurate pattern on a sheet of paper or plywood and periodically check the accuracy of the curve.

Figure 4-150. *V-block forming.*

Comparing the angle with the pattern determines exactly how the curve is progressing and just where it needs to be increased or decreased. It is better to get the curve to conform roughly to the desired shape before attempting to finish any one portion, because the finishing or smoothing of the angle may cause some other portion of the angle to change shape. If any part of the angle strip is curved too much, reduce the curve by reversing the angle strip on the V-block, placing the bottom flange up, and striking it with light blows of the mallet.

Try to form the curve with a minimum amount of hammering, for excessive hammering work-hardens the metal. Work-hardening can be recognized by a lack of bending response or by springiness in the metal. It can be recognized very readily by an experienced worker. In some cases, the part may have to be annealed during the curving operation. If so, be sure to heat treat the part again before installing it on the aircraft.

Shrinking With V-Block and Shrinking Block Methods

Curving an extruded or formed angle strip by shrinking may be accomplished by either the previously discussed V-block method or the shrinking block method. While the V-block is more satisfactory because it is faster, easier, and affects the metal less, good results can be obtained by the shrinking block method.

In the V-block method, place one flange of the angle strip flat on the V-block with the other flange extending upward. Using the process outlined in the stretching paragraphs, begin at one end of the angle strip and work back and forth making light blows. Strike the edge of the flange at a slight angle to keep the vertical flange from bending outward.

Occasionally, check the curve for accuracy with the pattern. If a sharp curve is made, the angle (cross section of the formed angle) closes slightly. To avoid such closing of the angle, clamp the angle strip to a hardwood board with the hammered flange facing upward using small C-clamps. The jaws of the C-clamps should be covered with masking tape. If the angle has already closed, bring the flange back to the correct angle with a few blows of a mallet or with the aid of a small hardwood block. If any portion of the angle strip is curved too much, reduce it by reversing the angle on the V-block and hammering with a suitable mallet, as explained in the previous paragraph on stretching. After obtaining the proper curve, smooth the entire angle by planishing with a soft-faced mallet.

If the curve in a formed angle is to be quite sharp or if the flanges of the angle are rather broad, the shrinking block method is generally used. In this process, crimp the flange that is to form the inside of the curve.

When making a crimp, hold the crimping pliers so that the jaws are about ⅛-inch apart. By rotating the wrist back and forth, bring the upper jaw of the pliers into contact with the flange, first on one side and then on the other side of the lower jaw. Complete the crimp by working a raised portion into the flange, gradually increasing the twisting motion of the pliers. Do not make the crimp too large because it will be difficult to work out. The size of the crimp depends upon the thickness and softness of the material, but usually about ¼-inch is sufficient. Place several crimps spaced evenly along the desired curve with enough space left between each crimp so that jaws of the shrinking block can easily be attached.

After completing the crimping, place the crimped flange in the shrinking block so that one crimp at a time is located between the jaws. *[Figure 4-151]* Flatten each crimp with light blows of a soft-faced mallet, starting at the apex (the closed end) of the crimp and gradually working toward the edge of the flange. Check the curve of the angle with the pattern periodically during the forming process and again after all the crimps have been worked out. If it is necessary to increase the curve, add more crimps and repeat the process. Space the additional crimps between the original ones so that the metal does not become unduly work hardened at any one point. If the curve needs to be increased or decreased slightly at any point, use the V-block.

After obtaining the desired curve, planish the angle strip over a stake or a wooden form.

Flanged Angles

The forming process for the following two flanged angles is slightly more complicated than the previously discussed

Figure 4-151. *Crimping a metal flange in order to form a curve.*

angles because the bend is shorter (not gradually curved) and necessitates shrinking or stretching in a small or concentrated area. If the flange is to point toward the inside of the bend, the material must be shrunk. If it is to point toward the outside, it must be stretched.

Shrinking

In forming a flanged angle by shrinking, use wooden forming blocks similar to those shown in *Figure 4-152* and proceed as follows:

1. Cut the metal to size, allowing for trimming after forming. Determine the bend allowance for a 90° bend and round the edge of the forming block accordingly.

2. Clamp the material in the form blocks as shown in *Figure 4-96,* and bend the exposed flange against the block. After bending, tap the blocks slightly. This induces a setting process in the bend.

3. Using a soft-faced shrinking mallet, start hammering near the center and work the flange down gradually toward both ends. The flange tends to buckle at the bend because the material is made to occupy less space. Work the material into several small buckles instead of one large one and work each buckle out gradually by hammering lightly and gradually compressing the material in each buckle. The use of a small hardwood wedge block aids in working out the buckles. *[Figure 4-153]*

4. Planish the flange after it is flattened against the form block and remove small irregularities. If the form blocks are made of hardwood, use a metal planishing hammer. If the forms are made of metal, use a soft-faced mallet. Trim the excess material away and file and polish.

Figure 4-152. *Forming a flanged angle using forming blocks.*

Figure 4-153. *Shrinking.*

Stretching

To form a flanged angle by stretching, use the same forming blocks, wooden wedge block, and mallet as used in the shrinking process and proceed as follows:

1. Cut the material to size (allowing for trim), determine bend allowance for a 90° bend, and round off the edge of the block to conform to the desired radius of bend.

2. Clamp the material in the form blocks. *[Figure 4-154]*

3. Using a soft-faced stretching mallet, start hammering near the ends and work the flange down smoothly and gradually to prevent cracking and splitting. Planish the flange and angle as described in the

Figure 4-154. *Stretching a flanged angle.*

previous procedure, and trim and smooth the edges, if necessary.

Curved Flanged Parts

Curved flanged parts are usually hand formed with a concave flange, the inside edge, and a convex flange, the outside edge.

The concave flange is formed by stretching, while the convex flange is formed by shrinking. Such parts are shaped with the aid of hardwood or metal forming blocks. *[Figure 4-155]* These blocks are made in pairs and are designed specifically for the shape of the area being formed. These blocks are made in pairs similar to those used for straight angle bends and are identified in the same manner. They differ in that they are made specifically for the particular part to be formed, they fit each other exactly, and they conform to the actual dimensions and contour of the finished article.

The forming blocks may be equipped with small aligning pins to help line up the blocks and to hold the metal in place or they may be held together by C-clamps or a vise. They also may be held together with bolts by drilling through form

Figure 4-155. *Forming blocks.*

blocks and the metal, provided the holes do not affect the strength of the finished part. The edges of the forming block are rounded to give the correct radius of bend to the part, and are undercut approximately 5° to allow for spring-back of the metal. This undercut is especially important if the material is hard or if the bend must be accurate.

The nose rib offers a good example of forming a curved flange because it incorporates both stretching and shrinking (by crimping). They usually have a concave flange, the inside edge, and a convex flange, the outside edge. Note the various types of forming represented in the following figures. In the plain nose rib, only one large convex flange is used. [*Figure 4-156*] Because of the great distance around the part and the likelihood of buckles in forming, it is rather difficult to form. The flange and the beaded (raised ridge on sheet metal used to stiffen the piece) portion of this rib provide sufficient strength to make this a good type to use.

Figure 4-156. *Plain nose rib.*

In *Figure 4-157*, the concave flange is difficult to form, but the outside flange is broken up into smaller sections by relief holes. In *Figure 4-158*, note that crimps are placed at equally spaced intervals to absorb material and cause curving, while also giving strength to the part.

Figure 4-157. *Nose rib with relief holes.*

Figure 4-158. *Nose rib with crimps.*

In *Figure 4-159*, the nose rib is formed by crimping, beading, putting in relief holes, and using a formed angle riveted on each end. The beads and the formed angles supply strength to the part. The basic steps in forming a curved flange follow: [*Figures 4-160* and *161*]

1. Cut the material to size, allowing about ¼-inch excess material for trim and drill holes for alignment pins.

2. Remove all burrs (jagged edges). This reduces the possibility of the material cracking at the edges during the forming process.

3. Locate and drill holes for alignment pins.

Figure 4-159. *Nose rib using a combination of forms.*

Figure 4-160. *Forming a concave flange.*

4. Place the material between the form blocks and clamp blocks tightly in a vise to prevent the material from moving or shifting. Clamp the work as closely as possible to the particular area being hammered to prevent strain on the form blocks and to keep the metal from slipping.

Concave Surfaces

Bend the flange on the concave curve first. This practice may keep the flange from splitting open or cracking when the metal is stretched. Should this occur, a new piece must be made. Using a plastic or rawhide mallet with a smooth, slightly rounded face, start hammering at the extreme ends of the part and continue toward the center of the bend. This procedure permits some of the metal at the ends of the part to be worked into the center of the curve where it is needed. Continue hammering until the metal is gradually worked

Figure 4-161. *Forming a convex flange.*

down over the entire flange, flush with the form block. After the flange is formed, trim off the excess material and check the part for accuracy. *[Figure 4-160]*

Convex Surfaces

Convex surfaces are formed by shrinking the material over a form block. *[Figure 4-161]* Using a wooden or plastic shrinking mallet and a backup or wedge block, start at the center of the curve and work toward both ends. Hammer the flange down over the form, striking the metal with glancing blows at an angle of approximately 45° and with a motion that tends to pull the part away from the radius of the form block. Stretch the metal around the radius bend and remove the buckles gradually by hammering on a wedge block. Use the backup block to keep the edge of the flange as nearly perpendicular to the form block as possible. The backup block also lessens the possibility of buckles, splits, or cracks. Finally, trim the flanges of excess metal, planish, remove burrs, round the corners (if any), and check the part for accuracy.

Forming by Bumping

As discussed earlier, bumping involves stretching the sheet metal by bumping it into a form and making it balloon. *[Figure 4-162]* Bumping can be done on a form block or female die, or on a sandbag.

Either method requires only one form: a wooden block, a lead die, or a sandbag. The blister, or streamlined cover plate, is an example of a part made by the form block or die method of bumping. Wing fillets are an example of parts that are usually formed by bumping on a sandbag.

Form Block or Die

The wooden block or lead die designed for form block bumping must have the same dimensions and contour as the outside of the blister. To provide enough bucking weight and bearing surface for fastening the metal, the block or die should be at least one inch larger in all dimensions than the form requires.

Follow these procedures to create a form block:

1. Hollow the block out with tools, such as saws, chisels, gouges, files, and rasps.

2. Smooth and finish the block with sandpaper. The inside of the form must be as smooth as possible, because the slightest irregularity shows up on the finished part.

3. Prepare several templates (patterns of the cross-section), as shown in *Figure 4-162* so that the form can be checked for accuracy.

4. Shape the contour of the form at points 1, 2, and 3.

5. Shape the areas between the template checkpoints to conform the remaining contour to template 4. Shaping of the form block requires particular care because the more nearly accurate it is, the less time it takes to produce a smooth, finished part.

After the form is prepared and checked, perform the bumping as follows:

1. Cut a metal blank to size allowing an extra ½ to 1-inch to permit drawing.

2. Apply a thin coat of light oil to the block and the aluminum to prevent galling (scraping on rough spots).

3. Clamp the material between the block and steel plate. Ensure it is firmly supported yet it can slip a little toward the inside of the form.

Figure 4-162. *Form block bumping.*

4. Clamp the bumping block in a bench vise. Use a soft-faced rubber mallet, or a hardwood drive block with a suitable mallet, to start the bumping near the edges of the form.

5. Work the material down gradually from the edges with light blows of the mallet. Remember, the purpose of bumping is to work the material into shape by

stretching rather than forcing it into the form with heavy blows. Always start bumping near the edge of the form. Never start near the center of the blister.

6. Before removing the work from the form, smooth it as much as possible by rubbing it with the rounded end of either a maple block or a stretching mallet.

7. Remove the blister from the bumping block and trim to size.

Sandbag Bumping

Sandbag bumping is one of the most difficult methods of hand forming sheet metal because there is no exact forming block to guide the operation. *[Figure 4-163]* In this method, a depression is made into the sandbag to take the shape of the hammered portion of the metal. The depression or pit has a tendency to shift from the hammering, which necessitates periodic readjustment during the bumping process. The degree of shifting depends largely on the contour or shape of the piece being formed, and whether glancing blows must be struck to stretch, draw, or shrink the metal. When forming by this method, prepare a contour template or some sort of a pattern to serve as a working guide and to ensure accuracy of the finished part. Make the pattern from ordinary kraft or similar paper, folding it over the part to be duplicated. Cut the paper cover at the points where it would have to be stretched to fit, and attach additional pieces of paper with masking tape to cover the exposed portions. After completely covering the part, trim the pattern to exact size.

Figure 4-163. *Sandbag bumping.*

Open the pattern and spread it out on the metal from which the part is to be formed. Although the pattern does not lie flat, it gives a fairly accurate idea of the approximate shape of the metal to be cut, and the pieced-in sections indicate where the metal is to be stretched. When the pattern has been placed on the material, outline the part and the portions to be stretched using a felt-tipped pen. Add at least 1-inch of excess metal when cutting the material to size. Trim off the excess metal after bumping the part into shape.

If the part to be formed is radially symmetrical, it is fairly easy to shape since a simple contour template can be used as a working guide. The procedure for bumping sheet metal parts on a sandbag follows certain basic steps that can be applied to any part, regardless of its contour or shape.

1. Lay out and cut the contour template to serve as a working guide and to ensure accuracy of the finished part. (This can be made of sheet metal, medium to heavy cardboard, kraft paper, or thin plywood.)

2. Determine the amount of metal needed, lay it out, and cut it to size, allowing at least ½-inch in excess.

3. Place a sandbag on a solid foundation capable of supporting heavy blows and make a pit in the bag with a smooth-faced mallet. Analyze the part to determine the correct radius the pit should have for the forming operation. The pit changes shape with the hammering it receives and must be readjusted accordingly.

4. Select a soft round-faced or bell-shaped mallet with a contour slightly smaller than the contour desired on the sheet metal part. Hold one edge of the metal in the left hand and place the portion to be bumped near the edge of the pit on the sandbag. Strike the metal with light glancing blows.

5. Continue bumping toward the center, revolving the metal, and working gradually inward until the desired shape is obtained. Shape the entire part as a unit.

6. Check the part often for accuracy of shape during the bumping process by applying the template. If wrinkles form, work them out before they become too large.

7. Remove small dents and hammer marks with a suitable stake and planishing hammer or with a hand dolly and planishing hammer.

8. Finally, after bumping is completed, use a pair of dividers to mark around the outside of the object. Trim the edge and file it smooth. Clean and polish the part.

Joggling

A joggle, often found at the intersection of stringers and formers, is the offset formed on a part to allow clearance for a sheet or another mating part. Use of the joggle maintains the smooth surface of a joint or splice. The amount of offset is usually small; therefore, the depth of the joggle is generally specified in thousandths of an inch. The thickness of the material to be cleared governs the depth of the joggle. In determining the necessary length of the joggle, allow an extra ¹⁄₁₆-inch to give enough added clearance to assure a fit between the joggled, overlapped part. The distance between the two bends of a joggle is called the allowance. This dimension is normally called out on the drawing. However, a general rule of thumb for figuring allowance is four times the thickness of the displacement of flat sheets. For 90° angles, it must be slightly more due to the stress built up at the radius while joggling. For extrusions, the allowance can be as much as 12 times the material thickness, so, it is important to follow the drawing.

There are a number of different methods of forming joggles. For example, if the joggle is to be made on a straight flange or flat piece of metal, it can be formed on a cornice break. To form the joggle, use the following procedure:

1. Lay out the boundary lines of the joggle where the bends are to occur on the sheet.

2. Insert·the sheet in the brake and bend the metal up approximately 20° to 30°.

3. Release the brake and remove the part.

4. Turn the part over and clamp it in the brake at the second bend line.

5. Bend the part up until the correct height of the joggle is attained.

6. Remove the part from the brake and check the joggle for correct dimensions and clearance.

When a joggle is necessary on a curved part or a curved flange, forming blocks or dies made of hardwood, steel, or aluminum alloy may be used. The forming procedure consists of placing the part to be joggled between the two joggle blocks and squeezing them in a vice or some other suitable clamping device. After the joggle is formed, the joggle blocks are turned over in the vice and the bulge on the opposite flange is flattened with a wooden or rawhide mallet. *[Figure 4-164]*

Since hardwood is easily worked, dies made of hardwood are satisfactory when the die is to be used only a few times. If a number of similar joggles are to be produced, use steel or aluminum alloy dies. Dies of aluminum alloy are preferred since they are easier to fabricate than those of steel and wear about as long. These dies are sufficiently soft and resilient to permit forming aluminum alloy parts on them without marring, and nicks and scratches are easily removed from their surfaces.

When using joggling dies for the first time, test them for accuracy on a piece of waste stock to avoid the possibility of ruining already fabricated parts. Always keep the surfaces of the blocks free from dirt, filings, and the like, so that the work is not marred. *[Figure 4-165]*

Lightening Holes

Lightening holes are cut in rib sections, fuselage frames, and other structural parts to decrease weight. To avoid weakening

Figure 4-164. *Forming joggle using joggle blocks.*

the member by removal of the material, flanges are often pressed around the holes to strengthen the area from which the material was removed.

Lightening holes should never be cut in any structural part unless authorized. The size of the lightening hole and the width of the flange formed around the hole are determined by design specifications. Margins of safety are considered in the specifications so that the weight of the part can be decreased and still retain the necessary strength. Lightening holes may be cut with a hole saw, a punch, or a fly cutter. The edges are·filed smooth to prevent them from cracking or tearing.

Figure 4-165. *Samples of joggled metal.*

Flanging Lightening Holes

Form the flange by using a flanging die, or hardwood or metal form blocks. Flanging dies consist of two matching parts: a female and a male die. For flanging soft metal, dies can be of hardwood, such as maple. For hard metal or for more permanent use, they should be made of steel. The pilot guide should be the same size as the hole to be flanged, and the shoulder should be the same width and angle as the desired flange.

When flanging lightening holes, place the material between the mating parts of the die and form it by hammering or squeezing the dies together in a vise or in an arbor press (a small hand operated press). The dies work more smoothly if they are coated with light machine oil. *[Figure 4-166]*

Figure 4-166. *Lightening hole die set.*

Working Stainless Steel

Corrosion-resistant-steel (CRES) sheet is used on some parts of the aircraft when high strength is required. CRES causes magnesium, aluminum, or cadmium to corrode when it touches these metals. To isolate CRES from magnesium and aluminum, apply a finish that gives protection between their mating surfaces. It is important to use a bend radius that is larger than the recommended minimum bend radius to prevent cracking of the material in the bend area.

When working with stainless steel, make sure that the metal does not become unduly scratched or marred. Also, take special precautions when shearing, punching, or drilling this metal. It takes about twice as much pressure to shear or punch stainless steel as it does mild steel. Keep the shear or punch and die adjusted very closely. Too much clearance permits the metal to be drawn over the edge of the die and causes it to become work hardened, resulting in excessive strain on the machine. When drilling stainless steel, use an HSS drill bit ground to an included angle of 135°. Keep the drill speed about one-half that required for drilling mild steel, but never exceed 750 rpm. Keep a uniform pressure on the drill so the feed is constant at all times. Drill the material on a backing plate, such as cast iron, which is hard enough to permit the drill bit to cut completely through the stock without pushing the metal away from the drill point. Spot the drill bit before turning on the power and also make sure that pressure is exerted when the power is turned on.

Working Inconel® Alloys 625 and 718

Inconel® refers to a family of nickel-chromium-iron super alloys typically used in high-temperature applications. Corrosion resistance and the ability to stay strong in high temperatures led to the frequent use of these Inconel® alloys in aircraft powerplant structures. Inconel® alloys 625 and 718 can be cold formed by standard procedures used for steel and stainless steel.

Normal drilling into Inconel® alloys can break drill bits sooner and cause damage to the edge of the hole when the drill bit goes through the metal. If a hand drill is used to drill Inconel® alloys 625 and 718, select a 135° cobalt drill bit. When hand drilling, push hard on the drill, but stay at a constant chip rate. For example, with a No. 30 hole, push the drill with approximately 50 pounds of force. Use the maximum drill rpm as illustrated in *Figure 4-167*. A cutting fluid is not necessary when hand drilling.

Drill Size	Maximum RPM
80–30	500
29–U	300
3/8	150

Figure 4-167. *Drill size and speed for drilling Inconel.*

The following drilling procedures are recommended:

- Drill pilot holes in loose repair parts with power feed equipment before preassembling them.

- Preassemble the repair parts and drill the pilot holes in the mating structure.

- Enlarge the pilot holes to their completed hole dimension.

When drilling Inconel®, autofeed-type drilling equipment is preferred.

Working Magnesium

Warning: Keep magnesium particles away from sources of ignition. Small particles of magnesium burn very easily. In sufficient concentration, these small particles can cause an explosion. If water touches molten magnesium, a steam explosion could occur. Extinguish magnesium fires with dry talc, calcium carbonate, sand, or graphite. Apply the powder on the burning metal to a depth of ½-inch or more. Do not use foam, water, carbon tetrachloride, or carbon dioxide. Magnesium alloys must not touch methyl alcohol.

Magnesium is the world's lightest structural metal. Like many other metals, this silvery-white element is not used in its pure state for stressed application. Instead, magnesium is alloyed with certain other metals (aluminum, zinc, zirconium, manganese, thorium, and rare earth metals) to obtain the strong, lightweight alloys needed for structural uses. When alloyed with these other metals, magnesium, yields alloys with excellent properties and high strength-to-weight ratios. Proper combination of these alloying constituents provide alloys suitable for sand, permanent mold and die castings, forging, extrusions, rolled sheet, and plate with good properties at room temperature, as well as at elevated temperatures.

Light weight is the best known characteristic of magnesium, an important factor in aircraft design. In comparison, aluminum weighs one and one half times more, iron and steel weigh four times more, and copper and nickel alloys weigh five times more. Magnesium alloys can be cut, drilled, and reamed with the same tools that are used on steel or brass, but the cutting edges of the tool must be sharp. Type B rivets (5056-F aluminum alloy) are used when riveting magnesium alloy parts. Magnesium parts are often repaired with clad 2024-T3 aluminum alloy.

While magnesium alloys can usually be fabricated by methods similar to those used on other metals, remember that many of the details of shop practice cannot be applied. Magnesium alloys are difficult to fabricate at room temperature; therefore, most operations must be performed at high temperatures. This requires preheating of the metal or dies, or both. Magnesium alloy sheets may be cut by blade shears, blanking dies, routers, or saws. Hand or circular saws are usually used for cutting extrusions to length. Conventional shears and nibblers should never be used for cutting magnesium alloy sheet because they produce a rough, cracked edge.

Shearing and blanking of magnesium alloys require close tool tolerances. A maximum clearance of 3 to 5 percent of the sheet thickness is recommended. The top blade of the shears should be ground with an included angle of 45° to 60°. The shear angle on a punch should be from 2° to 3°, with a 1° clearance angle on the die. For blanking, the shear angle on the die should be from 2° to 3° with a 1° clearance angle on the punch. Hold-down pressures should be used when possible. Cold shearing should not be accomplished on a hard-rolled sheet thicker than 0.064-inch or annealed sheet thicker than ⅛-inch. Shaving is used to smooth the rough, flaky edges of a magnesium sheet that has been sheared. This operation consists of removing approximately ¹⁄₃₂-inch by a second shearing.

Hot shearing is sometimes used to obtain an improved sheared edge. This is necessary for heavy sheet and plate stock. Annealed sheet may be heated to 600 °F, but hard-rolled sheet must be held under 400 °F, depending on the alloy used. Thermal expansion makes it necessary to allow for shrinkage after cooling, which entails adding a small amount of material to the cold metal dimensions before fabrication.

Sawing is the only method used in cutting plate stock more than ½-inch thick. Bandsaw raker-set blades of 4- to 6-tooth pitch are recommended for cutting plate stock or heavy extrusions. Small and medium extrusions are more easily cut on a circular cutoff saw having six teeth per inch. Sheet stock can be cut on handsaws having raker-set or straight-set teeth with an 8-tooth pitch. Bandsaws should be equipped with nonsparking blade guides to eliminate the danger of sparks igniting the magnesium alloy filings.

Cold working most magnesium alloys at room temperature is very limited, because they work harden rapidly and do not lend themselves to any severe cold forming. Some simple bending operations may be performed on sheet material, but the radius of bend must be at least 7 times the thickness of the sheet for soft material and 12 times the thickness of the sheet for hard material. A radius of 2 or 3 times the thickness of the sheet can be used if the material is heated for the forming operation.

Since wrought magnesium alloys tend to crack after they are cold-worked, the best results are obtained if the metal is heated to 450 °F before any forming operations are attempted. Parts formed at the lower temperature range are stronger because the higher temperature range has an annealing effect on the metal.

The disadvantages of hot working magnesium are:

1. Heating the dies and the material is expensive and troublesome.

2. There are problems in lubricating and handling materials at these temperatures.

The advantages to hot working magnesium are:

1. It is more easily formed when hot than are other metals.

2. Spring-back is reduced, resulting in greater dimensional accuracy.

When heating magnesium and its alloys, watch the temperature carefully as the metal is easily burned. Overheating also causes small molten pools to form within the metal. In either case, the metal is ruined. To prevent burning, magnesium must be protected with a sulfur dioxide atmosphere while being heated.

Proper bending around a short radius requires the removal of sharp corners and burrs near the bend line. Layouts should be made with a carpenter's soft pencil because any marring of the surface may result in fatigue cracks.

Press brakes can be used for making bends with short radii. Die and rubber methods should be used where bends are to be made at right angles, which complicate the use of a brake. Roll forming may be accomplished cold on equipment designed for forming aluminum. The most common method of forming and shallow drawing of magnesium is to use a rubber pad as the female die. This rubber pad is held in an inverted steel pan that is lowered by a hydraulic press ram. The press exerts pressure on the metal and bends it to the shape of the male die.

The machining characteristics of magnesium alloys are excellent, making possible the use of maximum speeds of the machine tools with heavy cuts and high feed rates. Power requirements for machining magnesium alloys are about one-sixth of those for mild steel.

Filings, shavings, and chips from machining operations should be kept in covered metal containers because of the danger of combustion. Do not use magnesium alloys in liquid deicing and water injection systems or in the integral fuel tank areas.

Working Titanium

Keep titanium particles away from sources of ignition. Small particles of titanium burn very easily. In sufficient concentration, these small particles can cause an explosion. If water touches molten titanium, a steam explosion could occur. Extinguish titanium fires with dry talc, calcium carbonate, sand, or graphite. Apply the powder on the burning metal to a depth of ½-inch or more. Do not use foam, water, carbon tetrachloride, or carbon dioxide.

Description of Titanium

Titanium in its mineral state, is the fourth most abundant structural metal in the earth's crust. It is light weight, nonmagnetic, strong, corrosion resistant, and ductile. Titanium lies between the aluminum alloys and stainless steel in modulus, density, and strength at intermediate temperatures. Titanium is 30 percent stronger than steel, but is nearly 50 percent lighter. It is 60 percent heavier than aluminum, but twice as strong.

Titanium and its alloys are used chiefly for parts that require good corrosion resistance, moderate strength up to 600 °F (315 °C), and light weight. Commercially pure titanium sheet may be formed by hydropress, stretch press, brake roll forming, drop hammer, or other similar operations. It is more difficult to form than annealed stainless steel. Titanium can also be worked by grinding, drilling, sawing, and the types of working used on other metals. Titanium must be isolated from magnesium, aluminum, or alloy steel because galvanic corrosion or oxidation of the other metals occurs upon contact.

Monel® rivets or standard close-tolerance steel fasteners should be used when installing titanium parts. The alloy sheet can be formed, to a limited extent, at room temperature. The forming of titanium alloys is divided into three classes:

• Cold forming with no stress relief

• Cold forming with stress relief

• Elevated temperature forming (built-in stress relief)

Over 5 percent of all titanium in the United States is produced in the form of the alloy Ti 6Al-4V, which is known as the workhorse of the titanium industry. Used in aircraft turbine engine components and aircraft structural components, Ti 6Al-4V is approximately 3 times stronger than pure titanium. The most widely used titanium alloy, it is hard to form.

The following are procedures for cold forming titanium 6Al-4V annealed with stress relief (room temperature forming):

1. It is important to use a minimum radius chart when forming titanium because an excessively small radius introduces excess stress to the bend area.

2. Stress relieves the part as follows: heat the part to a temperature above 1,250 °F (677 °C), but below 1,450 °F (788 °C). Keep the part at this temperature for more than 30 minutes but less than 10 hours.

3. A powerful press brake is required to form titanium parts. Regular hand-operated box and pan brakes cannot form titanium sheet material.

4.   A power slip roller is often used if the repair patch needs to be curved to fit the contour of the aircraft.

Titanium can be difficult to drill, but standard high-speed drill bits may be used if the bits are sharp, if sufficient force is applied, and if a low-speed drill motor is used. If the drill bit is dull, or if it is allowed to ride in a partially drilled hole, an overheated condition is created, making further drilling extremely difficult. Therefore, keep holes as shallow as possible; use short, sharp drill bits of approved design; and flood the area with large amounts of cutting fluid to facilitate drilling or reaming.

When working titanium, it is recommended that you use carbide or 8 percent cobalt drill bits, reamers, and countersinks. Ensure the drill or reamer is rotating to prevent scoring the side of the hole when removing either of them from a hole. Use a hand drill only when positive-power-feed drills are not available.

The following guidelines are used for drilling titanium:

*   The largest diameter hole that can be drilled in a single step is 0.1563-inch because a large force is required. Larger diameter drill bits do not cut satisfactorily when much force is used. Drill bits that do not cut satisfactorily cause damage to the hole.

*   Holes with a diameter of 0.1875-inch and larger can be hand drilled if the operator:

    -   Starts with a hole with a diameter of 0.1563-inch

    -   Increases the diameter of the hole in 0.0313-inch or 0.0625-inch increments.

*   Cobalt vanadium drill bits last much longer than HSS bits.

*   The recommended drill motor rpm settings for hand drilling titanium are listed in *Figure 4-168*.

Hole Size (inches)	Drill Speed (rpm)
0.0625	920 to 1830 rpm
0.125	460 to 920 rpm
0.1875	230 to 460 rpm

Figure 4-168. *Hole size and drill speed for drilling titanium.*

*   The life of a drill bit is shorter when drilling titanium than when drilling steel. Do not use a blunt drill bit or let a drill bit rub the surface of the metal and not cut it. If one of these conditions occurs, the titanium surface becomes work hardened, and it is very difficult to start the drill again.

*   When hand drilling two or more titanium parts at the same time, clamp them together tightly. To clamp them together, use temporary bolts, Cleco clamps, or tooling clamps. Put the clamps around the area to drill and as near the area as possible.

*   When hand drilling thin or flexible parts, put a support (such as a block of wood) behind the part.

*   Titanium has a low thermal conductivity. When it becomes hot, other metals become easily attached to it. Particles of titanium often become welded to the sharp edges of the drill bit if the drill speed is too high. When drilling large plates or extrusions, use a water soluble coolant or sulphurized oil.

NOTE: The intimate metal-to-metal contact in the metal working process creates heat and friction that must be reduced or the tools and the sheet metal used in the process are quickly damaged and/or destroyed. Coolants, also called cutting fluids, are used to reduce the friction at the interface of the tool and sheet metal by transferring heat away from the tool and sheet metal. Thus, the use of cutting fluids increases productivity, extends tool life, and results in a higher quality of workmanship.

Basic Principles of Sheet Metal Repair

Aircraft structural members are designed to perform a specific function or to serve a definite purpose. The primary objective of aircraft repair is to restore damaged parts to their original condition. Very often, replacement is the only way this can be done effectively. When repair of a damaged part is possible, first study the part carefully to fully understand its purpose or function.

Strength may be the principal requirement in the repair of certain structures, while others may need entirely different qualities. For example, fuel tanks and floats must be protected against leakage; cowlings, fairings, and similar parts must have such properties as neat appearance, streamlined shape, and accessibility. The function of any damaged part must be carefully determined to ensure the repair meets the requirements.

An inspection of the damage and accurate estimate of the type of repair required are the most important steps in repairing structural damage. The inspection includes an estimate of the best type and shape of repair patch to use; the type, size, and number of rivets needed; and the strength, thickness, and kind of material required to make the repaired member no heavier (or only slightly heavier) and just as strong as the original.

When investigating damage to an aircraft, it is necessary to make an extensive inspection of the structure. When any component or group of components has been damaged, it is essential that both the damaged members and the attaching structure be investigated, since the damaging force may have been transmitted over a large area, sometimes quite remote from the point of original damage. Wrinkled skin, elongated or damaged bolt or rivet holes, or distortion of members usually appears in the immediate area of such damage, and any one of these conditions calls for a close inspection of the adjacent area. Check all skin, dents, and wrinkles for any cracks or abrasions.

Nondestructive inspection methods (NDI) are used as required when inspecting damage. NDI methods serve as tools of prevention that allow defects to be detected before they develop into serious or hazardous failures. A trained and experienced technician can detect flaws or defects with a high degree of accuracy and reliability. Some of the defects found by NDI include corrosion, pitting, heat/stress cracks, and discontinuity of metals.

When investigating damage, proceed as follows:

- Remove all dirt, grease, and paint from the damaged and surrounding areas to determine the exact condition of each rivet, bolt, and weld.

- Inspect skin for wrinkles throughout a large area.

- Check the operation of all movable parts in the area.

- Determine if repair would be the best procedure.

In any aircraft sheet metal repair, it is critical to:

- Maintain original strength,

- Maintain original contour, and

- Minimize weight.

Maintaining Original Strength

Certain fundamental rules must be observed if the original strength of the structure is to be maintained.

Ensure that the cross-sectional area of a splice or patch is at least equal to or greater than that of the damaged part. Avoid abrupt changes in cross-sectional area. Eliminate dangerous stress concentration by tapering splices. To reduce the possibility of cracks starting from the corners of cutouts, try to make cutouts either circular or oval in shape. Where it is necessary to use a rectangular cutout, make the radius of curvature at each corner no smaller than ½-inch. If the member is subjected to compression or bending loads, the patch should be placed on the outside of the member to obtain a higher resistance to such loads. If the patch cannot be placed there, material one gauge thicker than the original shall be used for the repair.

A buckled part of a structure shall not be depended upon to carry its load. Replace buckled or bent members, or reinforce them by attaching a splice over the affected area according to guidelines specified in AC43.13 1B.

The material used in all replacements or reinforcements must be similar to that used in the original structure. If an alloy weaker than the original must be substituted for it, a heavier thickness must be used to give equivalent cross-sectional strength. A material that is stronger, but thinner, cannot be substituted for the original because one material can have greater tensile strength but less compressive strength than another, or vice versa. Also, the buckling and torsional strength of many sheet metal and tubular parts depends primarily on the thickness of the material rather than its allowable compressive and shear strengths. The manufacturer's SRM often indicates what material can be used as a substitution and how much thicker the material needs to be. *Figure 4-169* is an example of a substitution table found in an SRM.

Care must be taken when forming. Heat-treated and cold-worked aluminum alloys stand very little bending without cracking. On the other hand, soft alloys are easily formed, but they are not strong enough for primary structure. Strong alloys can be formed in their annealed (heated and allowed to cool slowly) condition, and heat treated before assembling to develop their strength.

The size of rivets for any repair can be determined by referring to the rivets used by the manufacturer in the next parallel rivet row inboard on the wing or forward on the fuselage. Another method of determining the size of rivets to be used is to multiply the thickness of the skin by three and use the next larger size rivet corresponding to that figure. For example, if the skin thickness is 0.040-inch, multiply 0.040-inch by 3, which equals 0.120-inch; use the next larger size rivet, ⅛-inch (0.125-inch). The number of rivets to be used for a repair can be found in tables in manufacturer's SRMs or in Advisory Circular (AC) 43.13-1 (as revised), Acceptable Methods, Techniques, and Practices—Aircraft Inspection and Repair. *Figure 4-170* is a table from AC 43.13-1 that is used to calculate the number of rivets required for a repair.

Extensive repairs that are made too strong can be as undesirable as repairs weaker than the original structure. All aircraft structure must flex slightly to withstand the forces imposed during takeoff, flight, and landing. If a repaired area is too strong, excessive flexing occurs at the edge of the completed repair, causing acceleration of metal fatigue.

Shape	Initial Material	Replacement Material
Sheet 0.016 to 0.125	Clad 2024–T42 Ⓕ	Clad 2024–T3 2024–T3 Clad 7075–T6 Ⓐ 7075–T6 Ⓐ
	Clad 2024–T3	2024–T3 Clad 7075–T6 Ⓐ 7075–T6 Ⓐ
	Clad 7075–T6	7075–T6
Formed or extruded section	2024–T42 Ⓕ	7075–T6 Ⓐ Ⓑ

Sheet Material To Be Replaced	Material Replacement Factor									
	7075–T6	Clad 7075–T6	2024–T3		Clad 2024–T3		Ⓕ 2024–T4 2024–T42		Ⓕ Clad 2024–T4 Clad 2024–T42	
	Ⓒ	Ⓒ Ⓗ	Ⓓ	Ⓔ	Ⓓ	Ⓔ	Ⓓ	Ⓔ	Ⓓ	Ⓔ
7075–T6	1.00	1.10	1.20	1.78	1.30	1.83	1.20	1.78	1.24	1.84
Clad 7075–T6	1.00	1.00	1.13	1.70	1.22	1.76	1.13	1.71	1.16	1.76
2024–T3	1.00 Ⓐ	1.00 Ⓐ	1.00	1.00	1.09	1.10	1.00	1.10	1.03	1.14
Clad 2024–T3	1.00 Ⓐ	1.00 Ⓐ	1.00	1.00	1.00	1.00	1.00	1.00	1.03	1.00
2024–T42	1.00 Ⓐ	1.00 Ⓐ	1.00	1.00	1.00	1.00	1.00	1.00	1.00	1.14
Clad 2024–T42	1.00 Ⓐ	1.00 Ⓐ	1.00	1.00	1.00	1.00	1.00	1.00	1.00	1.00
7178–T6	1.28	1.28	1.50	1.90	1.63	2.00	1.86	1.90	1.96	1.98
Clad 7178–T6	1.08	1.18	1.41	1.75	1.52	1.83	1.75	1.75	1.81	1.81
5052–H34 Ⓖ Ⓗ	1.00 Ⓐ	1.00 Ⓐ	1.00	1.00	1.00	1.00	1.00	1.00	1.00	1.00

Notes:
- All dimensions are in inches, unless otherwise specified.

- It is possible that more protection from corrosion is necessary when bare mineral is used to replace clad material.

- It is possible for the material replacement factor to be a lower value for a specific location on the airplane. To get that value, contact Boeing for a case-by-case analysis.

- Refer to *Figure 4-81* for minimun bend radii.

- Example:
  To refer 0.040 thick 7075–T6 with clad 7075–T6, multiply the gauge by the material replacement factor to get the replacement gauge
  0.040 x 1.10 = 0.045.

Ⓐ Cannot be used as replacement for the initial material in areas that are pressured.

Ⓑ Cannot be used in the wing interspar structure at the wing center section structure.

Ⓒ Use the next thicker standard gauge when using a formed section as a replacement for an extrusion.

Ⓓ For all gauges of flat sheet and formed sections.

Ⓔ For flat sheet < 0.071 thick.

Ⓕ For flat sheet ≥ 0.071 thick and for formed sections.

Ⓖ 2024–T4 and 2024–T42 are equivalent.

Ⓗ A compound to give protection from corrosion must be applied to bare material that is used to replace 5052–H34.

Figure 4-169. *Material substitution.*

Shear Strength and Bearing Strength

Aircraft structural joint design involves an attempt to find the optimum strength relationship between being critical in shear and critical in bearing. These are determined by the failure mode affecting the joint. The joint is critical in shear if less than the optimum number of fasteners of a given size are installed. This means that the rivets will fail, and not the sheet, if the joint fails. The joint is critical in bearing if more than the optimum number of fasteners of a given size are installed; the material may crack and tear between holes, or fastener holes may distort and stretch while the fasteners remain intact.

| Thickness "T" in inches | No. of 2117–T4 (AD) Protruding Head Rivets Required per Inch of Width "W" | | | | | No. of Bolts |
| | Rivet Size | | | | | |
	3/32	1/8	5/32	3/16	1/4	AN–3
.016	6.5	4.9	- -	- -	- -	- -
.020	6.5	4.9	3.9	- -	- -	- -
.025	6.9	4.9	3.9	- -	- -	- -
.032	8.9	4.9	3.9	3.3	- -	- -
.036	10.0	5.6	3.9	3.3	2.4	- -
.040	11.1	6.2	4.0	3.3	2.4	- -
.051	- -	7.9	5.1	3.6	2.4	3.3
.064	- -	9.9	6.5	4.5	2.5	3.3
.081	- -	12.5	8.1	5.7	3.1	3.3
.091	- -	- -	9.1	6.3	3.5	3.3
.102	- -	- -	10.3	7.1	3.9	3.3
.128	- -	- -	12.9	8.9	4.9	3.3

Notes:

    a. For stringer in the upper surface of a wing, or in a fuselage, 80 percent of the number of rivets shown in the table may be used.

    b. For intermediate frames, 60 percent of the number shown may be used.

    c. For single lap sheet joints, 75 percent of the number shown may be used.

Engineering Notes

    a. The load per inch of width of material was calculated by assuming a strip 1 inch wide in tension.

    b. Number of rivets required was calculated for 2117–T4 (AD) rivets, based on a rivet allowable shear stress equal to percent of the sheet allowable tensile stress, and a sheet allowable bearing stress equal to 160 percent of the sheet allowable tensile stress, using nominal hole diameters for rivets.

    c. Combinations of sheet thickness and rivet size above the underlined numbers are critical in (i.e., will fail by) bearing on the sheet; those below are critical in shearing of the rivets.

    d. The number of AN–3 bolts required below the underlined number was calculated based on a sheet allowable tensile stress of 55.000 psi and a bolt allowable single shear load of 2.126 pounds.

Figure 4-170. *Rivet calculation table.*

Maintaining Original Contour

Form all repairs in such a manner to fit the original contour perfectly. A smooth contour is especially desirable when making patches on the smooth external skin of high-speed aircraft.

Keeping Weight to a Minimum

Keep the weight of all repairs to a minimum. Make the size of the patches as small as practicable and use no more rivets than are necessary. In many cases, repairs disturb the original balance of the structure. The addition of excessive weight in each repair may unbalance the aircraft, requiring adjustment of the trim-and-balance tabs. In areas such as the spinner on the propeller, a repair requires application of balancing patches in order to maintain a perfect balance of the propeller. When flight controls are repaired and weight is added, it is very important to perform a balancing check to determine if the flight control is still within its balance limitations. Failure to do so could result in flight control flutter.

Flutter and Vibration Precautions

To prevent severe vibration or flutter of flight control surfaces during flight, precautions must be taken to stay within the design balance limitations when performing maintenance or repair. The importance of retaining the proper balance and rigidity of aircraft control surfaces cannot be overemphasized. The effect of repair or weight change on the balance and CG is proportionately greater on lighter surfaces than on the older heavier designs. As a general rule, repair the control surface in such a manner that the weight distribution is not affected in any way, in order to preclude the occurrence of flutter of the control surface in flight. Under certain conditions, counterbalance weight is added forward of the hinge line to maintain balance. Add or remove balance weights only when necessary in accordance with the manufacturer's instructions. Flight testing must be accomplished to ensure flutter is not a problem. Failure to check and retain control surface balance within the original or maximum allowable value could result in a serious flight hazard.

Aircraft manufacturers use different repair techniques and repairs designed and approved for one type of aircraft are not automatically approved for other types of aircraft. When repairing a damaged component or part, consult the applicable section of the manufacturer's SRM for the aircraft. Usually the SRM contains an illustration for a similar repair along with a list of the types of material, rivets and rivet spacing, and the methods and procedures to be used. Any additional knowledge needed to make a repair is also detailed. If the necessary information is not found in the SRM, attempt to find a similar repair or assembly installed by the manufacturer of the aircraft.

Inspection of Damage

When visually inspecting damage, remember that there may be other kinds of damage than that caused by impact from foreign objects or collision. A rough landing may overload one of the landing gear, causing it to become sprung; this would be classified as load damage. During inspection and sizing up of the repair job, consider how far the damage caused by the sprung shock strut extends to supporting structural members.

A shock occurring at one end of a member is transmitted throughout its length; therefore, closely inspect all rivets, bolts, and attaching structures along the complete member for any evidence of damage. Make a close examination for rivets that have partially failed and for holes that have been elongated.

Whether specific damage is suspected or not, an aircraft structure must occasionally be inspected for structural integrity. The following paragraphs provide general guidelines for this inspection.

When inspecting the structure of an aircraft, it is very important to watch for evidence of corrosion on the inside. This is most likely to occur in pockets and corners where moisture and salt spray may accumulate; therefore, drain holes must always be kept clean.

While an injury to the skin covering caused by impact with an object is plainly evident, a defect, such as distortion or failure of the substructure, may not be apparent until some evidence develops on the surface, such as canted, buckled or wrinkled covering, and loose rivets or working rivets. A working rivet is one that has movement under structural stress, but has not loosened to the extent that movement can be observed. This situation can sometimes be noted by a dark, greasy residue or deterioration of paint and primers around rivet heads. External indications of internal injury must be watched for and correctly interpreted. When found,

an investigation of the substructure in the vicinity should be made and corrective action taken.

Warped wings are usually indicated by the presence of parallel skin wrinkles running diagonally across the wings and extending over a major area. This condition may develop from unusually violent maneuvers, extremely rough air, or extra hard landings. While there may be no actual rupture of any part of the structure, it may be distorted and weakened. Similar failures may also occur in fuselages. Small cracks in the skin covering may be caused by vibration and they are frequently found leading away from rivets.

Aluminum alloy surfaces having chipped protective coating, scratches, or worn spots that expose the surface of the metal should be recoated at once, as corrosion may develop rapidly. The same principle is applied to aluminum clad (Alclad™) surfaces. Scratches, which penetrate the pure aluminum surface layer, permit corrosion to take place in the alloy beneath.

A simple visual inspection cannot accurately determine if suspected cracks in major structural members actually exist or the full extent of the visible cracks. Eddy current and ultrasonic inspection techniques are used to find hidden damage.

Types of Damage and Defects

Types of damage and defects that may be observed on aircraft parts are defined as follows:

- Brinelling—occurrence of shallow, spherical depressions in a surface, usually produced by a part having a small radius in contact with the surface under high load.

- Burnishing—polishing of one surface by sliding contact with a smooth, harder surface. Usually there is no displacement or removal of metal.

- Burr—a small, thin section of metal extending beyond a regular surface, usually located at a corner or on the edge of a hole.

- Corrosion—loss of metal from the surface by chemical or electrochemical action. The corrosion products generally are easily removed by mechanical means. Iron rust is an example of corrosion.

- Crack—a physical separation of two adjacent portions of metal, evidenced by a fine or thin line across the surface caused by excessive stress at that point. It may extend inward from the surface from a few thousandths of an inch to completely through the section thickness.

- Cut—loss of metal, usually to an appreciable depth over a relatively long and narrow area, by mechanical means, as would occur with the use of a saw blade, chisel, or sharp-edged stone striking a glancing blow.

- Dent—indentation in a metal surface produced by an object striking with force. The surface surrounding the indentation is usually slightly upset.

- Erosion—loss of metal from the surface by mechanical action of foreign objects, such as grit or fine sand. The eroded area is rough and may be lined in the direction in which the foreign material moved relative to the surface.

- Chattering—breakdown or deterioration of metal surface by vibratory or chattering action. Although chattering may give the general appearance of metal loss or surface cracking, usually, neither has occurred.

- Galling—breakdown (or build-up) of metal surfaces due to excessive friction between two parts having relative motion. Particles of the softer metal are torn loose and welded to the harder metal.

- Gouge—groove in, or breakdown of, a metal surface from contact with foreign material under heavy pressure. Usually it indicates metal loss but may be largely the displacement of material.

- Inclusion—presence of foreign or extraneous material wholly within a portion of metal. Such material is introduced during the manufacture of rod, bar or tubing by rolling or forging.

- Nick—local break or notch on an edge. Usually it involves the displacement of metal rather than loss.

- Pitting—sharp, localized breakdown (small, deep cavity) of metal surface, usually with defined edges.

- Scratch—slight tear or break in metal surface from light, momentary contact by foreign material.

- Score—deeper (than scratch) tear or break in metal surface from contact under pressure. May show discoloration from temperature produced by friction.

- Stain—a change in color, locally causing a noticeably different appearance from the surrounding area.

- Upsetting—a displacement of material beyond the normal contour or surface (a local bulge or bump). Usually it indicates no metal loss.

Classification of Damage

Damages may be grouped into four general classes. In many cases, the availabilities of repair materials and time are the most important factors in determining if a part should be repaired or replaced.

Negligible Damage

Negligible damage consists of visually apparent, surface damage that do not affect the structural integrity of the component involved. Negligible damage may be left as is or may be corrected by a simple procedure without restricting flight. In both cases, some corrective action must be taken to keep the damage from spreading. Negligible or minor damage areas must be inspected frequently to ensure the damage does not spread. Permissible limits for negligible damage vary for different components of different aircraft and should be carefully researched on an individual basis. Failure to ensure that damages within the specified limit of negligible damage may result in insufficient structural strength of the affected support member for critical flight conditions.

Small dents, scratches, cracks, and holes that can be repaired by smoothing, sanding, stop drilling, or hammering out, or otherwise repaired without the use of additional materials, fall in this classification. *[Figure 4-171]*

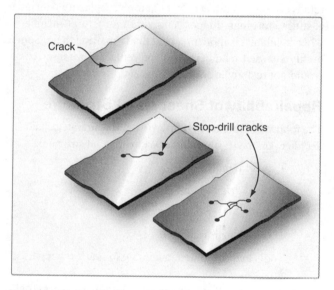

Figure 4-171. *Repair of cracks by stop-drilling.*

Damage Repairable by Patching

Damage repairable by patching is any damage exceeding negligible damage limits that can be repaired by installing splice members to bridge the damaged portion of a structural part. The splice members are designed to span the damaged areas and to overlap the existing undamaged surrounding structure. The splice or patch material used in internal riveted and bolted repairs is normally the same type of material as the damaged part, but one gauge heavier. In a patch repair, filler plates of the same gauge and type of material as that in the damaged component may be used for bearing purposes or to return the damaged part to its original contour. Structural fasteners are applied to members and the surrounding structure to restore the original load-carrying characteristics of the damaged area. The use of patching depends on the extent of the damage and the accessibility of the component to be repaired.

Damage Repairable by Insertion

Damage must be repaired by insertion when the area is too large to be patched or the structure is arranged such that repair members would interfere with structural alignment (e.g., in a hinge or bulkhead). In this type of repair, the damaged portion is removed from the structure and replaced by a member identical in material and shape. Splice connections at each end of the insertion member provide for load transfer to the original structure.

Damage Necessitating Replacement of Parts

Components must be replaced when their location or extent of damage makes repair impractical, when replacement is more economical than repair, or when the damaged part is relatively easy to replace. For example, replacing damaged castings, forgings, hinges, and small structural members, when available, is more practical than repairing them. Some highly stressed members must be replaced because repair would not restore an adequate margin of safety.

Repairability of Sheet Metal Structure

The following criteria can be used to help an aircraft technician decide upon the repairability of a sheet metal structure:

- Type of damage.

- Type of original material.

- Location of the damage.

- Type of repair required.

- Tools and equipment available to make the repair.

The following methods, procedures, and materials are only typical and should not be used as the authority for a repair.

Structural Support During Repair

During repair, the aircraft must be adequately supported to prevent further distortion or damage. It is also important that the structure adjacent to the repair is supported when it is subject to static loads. The aircraft structure can be supported adequately by the landing gear or by jacks where the work involves a repair, such as removing the control surfaces, wing panels, or stabilizers. Cradles must be prepared to hold these components while they are removed from the aircraft.

When the work involves extensive repair of the fuselage, landing gear, or wing center section, a jig (a device for holding parts in position to maintain their shape) may be constructed to distribute the loads while repairs are being

accomplished. *Figure 4-172* shows a typical aircraft jig. Always check the applicable aircraft maintenance manual for specific support requirements.

Figure 4-172. *Aircraft jig used to hold components during repairs.*

Assessment of Damage

Before starting any repair, the extent of damage must be fully evaluated to determine if repair is authorized or even practical. This evaluation should identify the original material used and the type of repair required. The assessment of the damage begins with an inspection of riveted joints and an inspection for corrosion.

Inspection of Riveted Joints

Inspection consists of examining both the shop and manufactured heads and the surrounding skin and structural parts for deformities.

During the repair of an aircraft structural part, examine adjacent parts to determine the condition of neighboring rivets. The presence of chipped or cracked paint around the heads may indicate shifted or loose rivets. If the heads are tipped or if rivets are loose, they show up in groups of several consecutive rivets and are probably tipped in the same direction. If heads that appear to be tipped are not in groups and are not tipped in the same direction, tipping may have occurred during some previous installation.

Inspect rivets that are known to have been critically loaded, but that show no visible distortion, by drilling off the head and carefully punching out the shank. If upon examination, the shank appears joggled and the holes in the sheet misaligned, the rivet has failed in shear. In that case, determine what is causing the stress and take necessary corrective action. Countersunk rivets that show head slippage within the countersink or dimple, indicating either sheet bearing failure or rivet shear failure, must be replaced.

Joggles in removed rivet shanks indicate partial shear failure. Replace these rivets with the next larger size. Also, if the rivet holes show elongation, replace the rivets with the next larger size. Sheet failures, such as tearouts, cracks between rivets, and the like, usually indicate damaged rivets, and the complete repair of the joint may require replacement of the rivets with the next larger size.

The presence of a black residue around the rivets is not an indication of looseness, but it is an indication of movement (fretting). The residue, which is aluminum oxide, is formed by a small amount of relative motion between the rivet and the adjacent surface. This is called fretting corrosion, or smoking, because the aluminum dust quickly forms a dark, dirty looking trail, like a smoke trail. Sometimes, the thinning of the moving pieces can propagate a crack. If a rivet is suspected of being defective, this residue may be removed with a general purpose abrasive hand pad, such as those manufactured by Scotch Brite™, and the surface inspected for signs of pitting or cracking. Although the condition indicates the component is under significant stress, it does not necessarily precipitate cracking. [Figure 4-173]

Figure 4-173. *Smoking rivet.*

Airframe cracking is not necessarily caused by defective rivets. It is common practice in the industry to size rivet patterns assuming one or more of the rivets is not effective. This means that a loose rivet would not necessarily overload adjacent rivets to the point of cracking.

Rivet head cracking are acceptable under the following conditions:

- The depth of the crack is less than ⅛ of the shank diameter.

- The width of the crack is less than ⅟₁₆ of the shank diameter.

- The length of the crack is confined to an area on the head within a circle having a maximum diameter of 1¼ times the shank diameter.

- Cracks should not intersect, which creates the potential for the loss of a portion of a head.

Inspection for Corrosion

Corrosion is the gradual deterioration of metal due to a chemical or electrochemical reaction with its environment. The reaction can be triggered by the atmosphere, moisture, or other agents. When inspecting the structure of an aircraft, it is important to watch for evidence of corrosion on both the outside and inside. Corrosion on the inside is most likely to occur in pockets and corners where moisture and salt spray may accumulate; therefore, drain holes must always be kept clean. Also inspect the surrounding members for evidence of corrosion.

Damage Removal

To prepare a damaged area for repair:

1. Remove all distorted skin and structure in damaged area.

2. Remove damaged material so that the edges of the completed repair match existing structure and aircraft lines.

3. Round all square corners.

4. Smooth out any abrasions and/or dents.

5. Remove and incorporate into the new repair any previous repairs joining the area of the new repair.

Repair Material Selection

The repair material must duplicate the strength of the original structure. If an alloy weaker than the original material has to be used, a heavier gauge must be used to give equivalent cross-sectional strength. A lighter gauge material should not be used even when using a stronger alloy.

Repair Parts Layout

All new sections fabricated for repairing or replacing damaged parts in a given aircraft should be carefully laid out to the dimensions listed in the applicable aircraft manual before fitting the parts into the structure.

Rivet Selection

Normally, the rivet size and material should be the same as the original rivets in the part being repaired. If a rivet hole has been enlarged or deformed, the next larger size rivet must be used after reworking the hole. When this is done, the proper edge distance for the larger rivet must be maintained. Where access to the inside of the structure is impossible and blind rivets must be used in making the repair, always consult the applicable aircraft maintenance manual for the recommended type, size, spacing, and number of rivets needed to replace either the original installed rivets or those that are required for the type of repair being performed.

Rivet Spacing and Edge Distance

The rivet pattern for a repair must conform to instructions in the applicable aircraft manual. The existing rivet pattern is used whenever possible.

Corrosion Treatment

Prior to assembly of repair or replacement parts, make certain that all existing corrosion has been removed in the area and that the parts are properly insulated one from the other.

Approval of Repair

Once the need for an aircraft repair has been established, Title 14 of the Code of Federal Regulations (14 CFR) defines the approval process. 14 CFR part 43, section 43.13(a) states that each person performing maintenance, alteration, or preventive maintenance on an aircraft, engine, propeller, or appliance shall use the methods, techniques, and practices prescribed in the current manufacturer's maintenance manual or instructions for continued airworthiness prepared by its manufacturer, or other methods, techniques, or practices acceptable to the Administrator. AC 43.13-1 contains methods, techniques, and practices acceptable to the Administrator for the inspection and repair of nonpressurized areas of civil aircraft, only when there are no manufacturer repair or maintenance instructions. This data generally pertains to minor repairs. The repairs identified in this AC may only be used as a basis for FAA approval for major repairs. The repair data may also be used as approved data, and the AC chapter, page, and paragraph listed in block 8 of FAA Form 337 when:

a. The user has determined that it is appropriate to the product being repaired;

b. It is directly applicable to the repair being made; and

c. It is not contrary to manufacturer's data.

Engineering support from the aircraft manufacturer is required for repair techniques and methods that are not described in the aircraft maintenance manual or SRM.

FAA Form 337, Major Repair and Alteration, must be completed for repairs to the following parts of an airframe and repairs of the following types involving the strengthening, reinforcing, splicing, and manufacturing of primary structural members or their replacement, when replacement is by fabrication, such as riveting or welding. *[Figure 4-174]*

- Box beams
- Monocoque or semimonocoque wings or control surfaces
- Wing stringers or chord members
- Spars
- Spar flanges

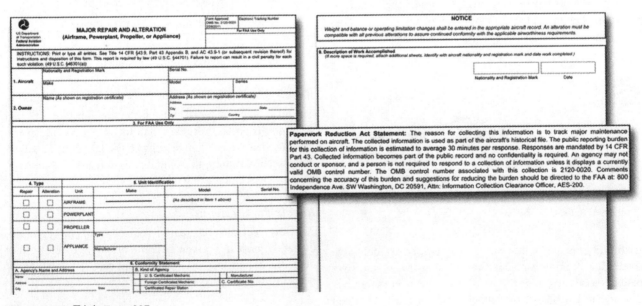

Figure 4-174. FAA *Form 337.*

- Members of truss-type beams
- Thin sheet webs of beams
- Keel and chine members of boat hulls or floats
- Corrugated sheet compression members that act as flange material of wings or tail surfaces
- Wing main ribs and compression members
- Wing or tail surface brace struts, fuselage longerons
- Members of the side truss, horizontal truss, or bulkheads
- Main seat support braces and brackets
- Landing gear brace struts
- Repairs involving the substitution of material
- Repair of damaged areas in metal or plywood stressed covering exceeding six inches in any direction
- Repair of portions of skin sheets by making additional seams
- Splicing of thin sheets
- Repair of three or more adjacent wing or control surface ribs or the leading edge of wings and control surfaces between such adjacent ribs

For major repairs made in accordance with a manual or specifications acceptable to the Administrator, a certificated repair station may use the customer's work order upon which the repair is recorded in place of the FAA Form 337.

Repair of Stressed Skin Structure

In aircraft construction, stressed skin is a form of construction in which the external covering (skin) of an aircraft carries part or all of the main loads. Stressed skin is made from high strength rolled aluminum sheets. Stressed skin carries a large portion of the load imposed upon an aircraft structure. Various specific skin areas are classified as highly critical, semicritical, or noncritical. To determine specific repair requirements for these areas, refer to the applicable aircraft maintenance manual.

Minor damage to the outside skin of the aircraft can be repaired by applying a patch to the inside of the damaged sheet. A filler plug must be installed in the hole made by the removal of the damaged skin area. It plugs the hole and forms a smooth outside surface necessary for aerodynamic smoothness of the aircraft. The size and shape of the patch is determined in general by the number of rivets required in the repair. If not otherwise specified, calculate the required number of rivets by using the rivet formula. Make the patch plate of the same material as the original skin and of the same thickness or of the next greater thickness.

Patches

Skin patches may be classified as two types:

- Lap or scab patch
- Flush patch

Lap or Scab Patch

The lap or scab type of patch is an external patch where the edges of the patch and the skin overlap each other. The overlapping portion of the patch is riveted to the skin. Lap patches may be used in most areas where aerodynamic smoothness is not important. *Figure 4-175* shows a typical patch for a crack and or for a hole.

Figure 4-175. *Lap or scab patch (crack).*

When repairing cracks or small holes with a lap or scab patch, the damage must be cleaned and smoothed. In repairing cracks, a small hole must be drilled in each end and sharp bend of the crack before applying the patch. These holes relieve the stress at these points and prevent the crack from spreading. The patch must be large enough to install the required number of rivets. It may be cut circular, square, or rectangular. If it is cut square or rectangular, the corners are rounded to a radius no smaller than ¼-inch. The edges must be chamfered to an angle of 45° for ½ the thickness of the material, and bent down 5° over the edge distance to seal the edges. This reduces the chance that the repair is affected by the airflow over it. These dimensions are shown in *Figure 4-176*.

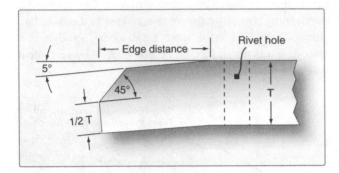

Figure 4-176. *Lap patch edge preparation.*

Flush Patch

A flush patch is a filler patch that is flush to the skin when applied it is supported by and riveted to a reinforcement plate which is, in turn, riveted to the inside of the skin. *Figure 4-177* shows a typical flush patch repair. The doubler is inserted through the opening and rotated until it slides in place under the skin. The filler must be of the same gauge and material as the original skin. The doubler should be of material one gauge heavier than the skin.

Open and Closed Skin Area Repair

The factors that determine the methods to be used in skin repair are accessibility to the damaged area and the instructions found in the aircraft maintenance manual. The skin on most areas of an aircraft is inaccessible for making the repair from the inside and is known as closed skin. Skin that is accessible from both sides is called open skin. Usually, repairs to open skin can be made in the conventional manner using standard rivets, but in repairing closed skin, some type of special fastener must be used. The exact type to be used depends on the type of repair being made and the recommendations of the aircraft manufacturer.

Design of a Patch for a Nonpressurized Area

Damage to the aircraft skin in a non-pressurized area can be repaired by a flush patch if a smooth skin surface is required or by an external patch in noncritical areas. *[Figure 4-178]* The first step is to remove the damage. Cut the damage to a round, oval, or rectangular shape. Round all corners of a rectangular patch to a minimum radius of 0.5-inch. The minimum edge distance used is 2 times the diameter and the rivet spacing

Figure 4-177. *Typical flush patch repair.*

is typically between 4-6 times the diameter. The size of the doubler depends on the edge distance and rivet spacing. The doubler material is of the same material as the damaged skin, but of one thickness greater than the damaged skin. The size of the doubler depends on the edge distance and rivet spacing. The insert is made of the same material and thickness as the damaged skin. The size and type of rivets should be the same as rivets used for similar joints on the aircraft. The SRM indicates what size and type of rivets to use.

Figure 4-178. *Repair patch for a non-pressurized area.*

Typical Repairs for Aircraft Structures

This section describes typical repairs of the major structural parts of an airplane. When repairing a damaged component or part, consult the applicable section of the manufacturer's SRM for the aircraft. Normally, a similar repair is illustrated, and the types of material, rivets, and rivet spacing and the methods and procedures to be used are listed. Any additional knowledge needed to make a repair is also detailed. If the necessary information is not found in the SRM, attempt to find a similar repair or assembly installed by the manufacturer of the aircraft.

Floats

To maintain the float in an airworthy condition, periodic and frequent inspections should be made because of the rapidity of corrosion on metal parts, particularly when the aircraft is operated in salt water. Inspection of floats and hulls involves examination for damage due to corrosion, collision with other objects, hard landings, and other conditions that may lead to failure.

NOTE: Blind rivets should not be used on floats or amphibian hulls below the water line.

Sheet-metal floats should be repaired using approved practices; however, the seams between sections of sheet metal should be waterproofed with suitable fabric and sealing compound. A float that has undergone hull repairs should be tested by filling it with water and allowing it to stand for at least 24 hours to see if any leaks develop. *[Figure 4-179]*

Corrugated Skin Repair

Some of the flight controls of smaller general aviation aircraft have beads in their skin panels. The beads give some stiffness to the thin skin panels. The beads for the repair patch can be formed with a rotary former or press brake. *[Figure 4-180]*

Replacement of a Panel

Damage to metal aircraft skin that exceeds repairable limits requires replacement of the entire panel. *[Figure 4-181]* A panel must also be replaced when there are too many previous repairs in a given section or area.

In aircraft construction, a panel is any single sheet of metal covering. A panel section is the part of a panel between adjacent stringers and bulk heads. Where a section of skin is damaged to such an extent that it is impossible to install a standard skin repair, a special type of repair is necessary. The particular type of repair required depends on whether the damage is repairable outside the member, inside the member, or to the edges of the panel.

Outside the Member

For damage that, after being trimmed, has 8½ rivet diameters or more of material, extend the patch to include the manufacturer's row of rivets and add an extra row inside the members.

Inside the Member

For damage that, after being trimmed, has less than 8½ manufacturer's rivet diameters of material inside the members, use a patch that extends over the members and an extra row of rivets along the outside of the members.

Edges of the Panel

For damage that extends to the edge of a panel, use only one row of rivets along the panel edge, unless the manufacturer used more than one row. The repair procedure for the other edges of the damage follows the previously explained methods.

Figure 4-179. *Float repair.*

Figure 4-180. *Beaded skin repair on corrugated surfaces.*

The procedures for making all three types of panel repairs are similar. Trim out the damaged portion to the allowances mentioned in the preceding paragraphs. For relief of stresses at the corners of the trim-out, round them to a minimum radius of ½-inch. Lay out the new rivet row with a transverse pitch of approximately five rivet diameters and stagger the rivets with those put in by the manufacturer. Cut the patch plate from material of the same thickness as the original or the next greater thickness, allowing an edge distance of 2½ rivet diameters. At the corners, strike arcs having the radius equal to the edge distance.

Chamfer the edges of the patch plate for a 45° angle and form the plate to fit the contour of the original structure. Turn the edges downward slightly so that the edges fit closely. Place the patch plate in its correct position, drill one rivet hole, and temporarily fasten the plate in place with a fastener. Using a hole finder, locate the position of a second hole, drill it, and insert a second fastener. Then, from the back side and through the original holes, locate and drill the remaining holes. Remove the burrs from the rivet holes and apply corrosion protective material to the contacting surfaces before riveting the patch into place.

Repair seam same as strongest parallel adjacent seam.

Repair seam same as strongest parallel adjacent seam. Use original holes and add as needed.

Additional Rivets

Trimmed hole radiused corners

● 3/16"   ● 5/32"   ▲ 1/8"

Figure 4-181. *Replacement of an entire panel.*

Repair of Lightening Holes

As discussed earlier, lightening holes are cut in rib sections, fuselage frames, and other structural parts to reduce the weight of the part. The holes are flanged to make the web stiffer. Cracks can develop around flanged lightening holes, and these cracks need to be repaired with a repair plate. The damaged area (crack) needs to be stop drilled or the damage must be removed. The repair plate is made of the same material and thickness as the damaged part. Rivets are the same as in surrounding structure and the minimum edge distance is 2 times the diameter and spacing is between four to six times the diameter. *Figure 4-182* illustrates a typical lightening hole repair.

Repairs to a Pressurized Area

The skin of aircraft that are pressurized during flight is highly stressed. The pressurization cycles apply loads to the skin, and the repairs to this type of structure requires more rivets than a repair to a nonpressurized skin. *[Figure 4-183]*

1. Remove the damaged skin section.

2. Radius all corners to 0.5-inch.

3. Fabricate a doubler of the same type of material as, but of one size greater thickness than, the skin. The size of the doubler depends on the number of rows, edge distance, and rivets spacing.

4. Fabricate an insert of the same material and same thickness as the damaged skin. The skin to insert clearance is typically 0.015-inch to 0.035-inch.

5. Drill the holes through the doubler, insertion, and original skin.

6. Spread a thin layer of sealant on the doubler and secure the doubler to the skin with Clecos.

7. Use the same type of fastener as in the surrounding area, and install the doubler to the skin and the insertion to the doubler. Dip all fasteners in the sealant before installation.

Stringer Repair

The fuselage stringers extend from the nose of the aircraft to the tail, and the wing stringers extend from the fuselage to the wing tip. Surface control stringers usually extend the

Figure 4-182. *Repair of lightening holes.*

length of the control surface. The skin of the fuselage, wing, or control surface is riveted to stringers.

Stringers may be damaged by vibration, corrosion, or collision. Because stringers are made in many different shapes, repair procedures differ. The repair may require the use of preformed or extruded repair material, or it may require material formed by the airframe technician. Some repairs may need both kinds of repair material. When repairing a stringer, first determine the extent of the damage and remove the rivets from the surrounding area. *[Figure 4-184]* Then, remove the damaged area by using a hacksaw, keyhole saw, drill, or file. In most cases, a stringer repair requires the use of insert and splice angle. When locating the splice angle on the stringer during repair, be sure to consult the applicable structural repair manual for the repair piece's position. Some stringers are repaired by placing the splice angle on the inside, whereas others are repaired by placing it on the outside.

Extrusions and preformed materials are commonly used to repair angles and insertions or fillers. If repair angles and fillers must be formed from flat sheet stock, use the brake. It may be necessary to use bend allowance and sight lines when making the layout and bends for these formed parts. For repairs to curved stringers, make the repair parts so that they fit the original contour.

Figure 4-185 shows a stringer repair by patching. This repair is permissible when the damage does not exceed two-thirds of the width of one leg and is not more than 12-inch long. Damage exceeding these limits can be repaired by one of the following methods.

Figure 4-186 illustrates repair by insertion where damage exceeds two-thirds of the width of one leg and after a portion of the stringer is removed. *Figure 4-187* shows repair by insertion when the damage affects only one stringer and

Figure 4-183. *Pressurized skin repair.*

exceeds 12-inch in length. *Figure 4-188* illustrates repair by an insertion when damage affects more than one stringer.

Former or Bulkhead Repair

Bulkheads are the oval-shaped members of the fuselage that give form to and maintain the shape of the structure. Bulkheads or formers are often called forming rings, body frames, circumferential rings, belt frames, and other similar names. They are designed to carry concentrated stressed loads.

There are various types of bulkheads. The most common type is a curved channel formed from sheet stock with stiffeners added. Others have a web made from sheet stock with extruded angles riveted in place as stiffeners and flanges. Most of these members are made from aluminum alloy. Corrosion-resistant steel formers are used in areas that are exposed to high temperatures.

Bulkhead damages are classified in the same manner as other damages. Specifications for each type of damage are established by the manufacturer and specific information is given in the maintenance manual or SRM for the aircraft. Bulkheads are identified with station numbers that are very helpful in locating repair information. *Figure 4-189* is an example of a typical repair for a former, frame section, or bulkhead repair.

Figure 4-184. *Stringer repair.*

1. Stop drill the crack ends with a No. 40 size drill.

2. Fabricate a doubler of the same material but one size thicker than the part being repaired. The doubler should be of a size large enough to accommodate ⅛-inch rivet holes spaced one inch apart, with a minimum edge distance of 0.30-inch and 0.50-inch spacing between staggered rows. *[Figure 4-190]*

3. Attach the doubler to the part with clamps and drill holes.

4. Install rivets.

Most repairs to bulkheads are made from flat sheet stock if spare parts are not available. When fabricating the repair from flat sheet, remember the substitute material must provide

Figure 4-185. *Stringer repair by patching.*

Figure 4-186. *Stringer repair by insertion when damage exceeds two-thirds of one leg in width.*

cross-sectional tensile, compressive, shear, and bearing strength equal to the original material. Never substitute material that is thinner or has a cross-sectional area less than the original material. Curved repair parts made from flat sheet must be in the "0" condition before forming, and then must be heat treated before installation.

Longeron Repair

Generally, longerons are comparatively heavy members that serve approximately the same function as stringers. Consequently, longeron repair is similar to stringer repair. Because the longeron is a heavy member and more strength is needed than with a stringer, heavy rivets are used in the repair. Sometimes bolts are used to install a longeron repair, due to the need for greater accuracy, they are not as suitable as rivets. Also, bolts require more time for installation.

If the longeron consists of a formed section and an extruded angle section, consider each section separately. A longeron repair is similar to a stringer repair, but keep the rivet pitch between 4 and 6 rivet diameters. If bolts are used, drill the bolt holes for a light drive fit.

Spar Repair

The spar is the main supporting member of the wing. Other components may also have supporting members called spars that serve the same function as the spar does in the wing. Think of spars as the hub, or base, of the section in which they are located, even though they are not in the center. The spar is usually the first member located during the construction of the section, and the other components are fastened directly or indirectly to it. Because of the load the spar carries, it is very important that particular care be taken when repairing this member to ensure the original strength of the structure is not impaired. The spar is constructed so that two general classes of repairs, web repairs and cap strip repairs, are usually necessary.

Figures 4-190 and *4-191* are examples of typical spar repairs. The damage to the spar web can be repaired with a round or rectangular doubler. Damage smaller than 1-inch is typically repaired with a round doubler and larger damage is repaired with a rectangular doubler.

1. Remove the damage and radius all corners to 0.5-inch.

2. Fabricate doubler; use same material and thickness. The doubler size depends on edge distance (minimum of 2D) and rivet spacing (4-6D).

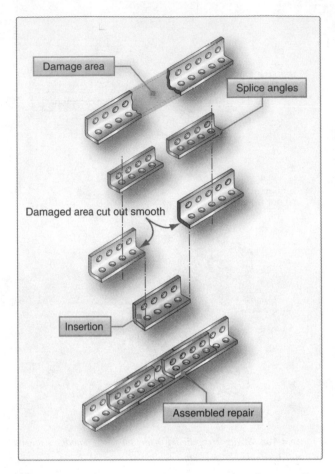

Figure 4-187. *Stringer repair by insertion when damage affects only one stringer.*

3. Drill through the doubler and the original skin and secure doubler with Clecos.

4. Install rivets.

Rib and Web Repair

Web repairs can be classified into two types:

1. Those made to web sections considered critical, such as those in the wing ribs.

2. Those considered less critical, such as those in elevators, rudders, flaps, and the like.

Web sections must be repaired in such a way that the original strength of the member is restored. In the construction of a member using a web, the web member is usually a light gauge aluminum alloy sheet forming the principal depth of the member. The web is bounded by heavy aluminum alloy extrusions known as cap strips. These extrusions carry the loads caused by bending and also provide a foundation for attaching the skin. The web may be stiffened by stamped beads, formed angles, or extruded sections riveted at regular intervals along the web.

Figure 4-188. *Stringer repair by insertion when damage affects more than one stringer.*

The stamped beads are a part of the web itself and are stamped in when the web is made. Stiffeners help to withstand the compressive loads exerted upon the critically stressed web members. Often, ribs are formed by stamping the entire piece from sheet stock. That is, the rib lacks a cap strip, but does have a flange around the entire piece, plus lightening holes in the web of the rib. Ribs may be formed with stamped beads for stiffeners, or they may have extruded angles riveted on the web for stiffeners.

Figure 4-189. *Bulkhead repair.*

Most damages involve two or more members, but only one member may be damaged and need repairing. Generally, if the web is damaged, cleaning out the damaged area and installing a patch plate are all that is required.

The patch plate should be of sufficient size to ensure room for at least two rows of rivets around the perimeter of the damage that includes proper edge distance, pitch, and transverse pitch for the rivets. The patch plate should be of material having the same thickness and composition as the original member. If any forming is necessary when making the patch plate, such as fitting the contour of a lightening hole, use material in the "0" condition and then heat treat it after forming.

Damage to ribs and webs, that require a repair larger than a simple plate, probably needs a patch plate, splice plates, or angles and an insertion. *[Figure 4-192]*

Leading Edge Repair

The leading edge is the front section of a wing, stabilizer, or other airfoil. The purpose of the leading edge is to streamline the forward section of the wings or control surfaces to ensure effective airflow. The space within the leading edge is sometimes used to store fuel. This space may also house extra equipment, such as landing lights, plumbing lines, or thermal anti-icing systems.

The construction of the leading edge section varies with the type of aircraft. Generally, it consists of cap strips, nose ribs, stringers, and skin. The cap strips are the main lengthwise extrusions, and they stiffen the leading edges and furnish a base for the nose ribs and skin. They also fasten the leading edge to the front spar.

The nose ribs are stamped from aluminum alloy sheet or machined parts. These ribs are U-shaped and may have their web sections stiffened. Regardless of their design, their purpose is to give contour to the leading edge. Stiffeners are used to stiffen the leading edge and supply a base for fastening the nose skin. When fastening the nose skin, use only flush rivets.

Leading edges constructed with thermal anti-icing systems consist of two layers of skin separated by a thin air space. The inner skin, sometimes corrugated for strength, is perforated to conduct the hot air to the nose skin for anti-icing purposes. Damage can be caused by contact with other objects, namely, pebbles, birds, and hail. However, the major cause of damage is carelessness while the aircraft is on the ground.

A damaged leading edge usually involves several structural parts. FOD probably involves the nose skin, nose ribs, stringers, and possibly the cap strip. Damage involving all of these members necessitates installing an access door to make the repair possible. First, the damaged area has to be removed and repair procedures established. The repair needs insertions and splice pieces. If the damage is serious enough, it may require repair of the cap strip and stringer, a new nose rib, and a skin panel. When repairing a leading edge, follow the procedures prescribed in the appropriate repair manual for this type of repair. *[Figure 4-193]* Repairs to leading edges are more difficult to accomplish than repairs to flat and straight structures because the repair parts need to be formed to fit the existing structure.

Trailing Edge Repair

A trailing edge is the rearmost part of an airfoil found on the wings, ailerons, rudders, elevators, and stabilizers. It is

Figure 4-190. *Wing spar repair.*

usually a metal strip that forms the shape of the edge by tying the ends of a rib section together and joining the upper and lower skins. Trailing edges are not structural members, but they are considered to be highly stressed in all cases.

Damage to a trailing edge may be limited to one point or extended over the entire length between two or more rib sections. Besides damage resulting from collision and careless handling, corrosion damage is often present. Trailing edges are particularly subject to corrosion because moisture collects or is trapped in them.

Thoroughly inspect the damaged area before starting repairs, and determine the extent of damage, the type of repair required, and the manner in which the repair should be performed. When making trailing edge repairs, remember that the repaired area must have the same contour and be made of material with the same composition and temper as the original section. The repair must also be made to retain the design characteristics of the airfoil. *[Figure 4-194]*

Figure 4-191. *Wing spar repair.*

If web stiffener is within ½" of hole and is not damaged. Drill out stiffener rivets. After repair is made, rivet stiffener at original location. Add new stiffener if stiffener is damaged.

Reinforcement material—same as original and of same gauge or one gauge heavier.

Pick up rivets along flange— add reinforcing rivets spaced ³/₄" as shown, maintaining 2½ times rivet diameter for proper edge

Rib

Original damaged web area

Clean holes smooth

Reinforcement plate

Figure 4-192. *Wing rib repair.*

Specialized Repairs

Figures 4-195 through *4-199* are examples of repairs for various structural members. Specific dimensions are not included since the illustrations are intended to present the basic design philosophy of general repairs rather than be used as repair guidelines for actual structures. Remember to consult the SRM for specific aircraft to obtain the maximum allowable damage that may be repaired and the suggested method for accomplishing the repair.

Inspection Openings

If it is permitted by the applicable aircraft maintenance manual, installation of a flush access door for inspection purposes sometimes makes it easier to repair the internal structure as well as damage to the skin in certain areas. This installation consists of a doubler and a stressed cover plate. A single row of nut plates is riveted to the doubler, and the doubler is riveted to the skin with two staggered rows of rivets. *[Figure 4-200]* The cover plate is then attached to the doubler with machine screws.

Figure 4-193. *Leading edge repair.*

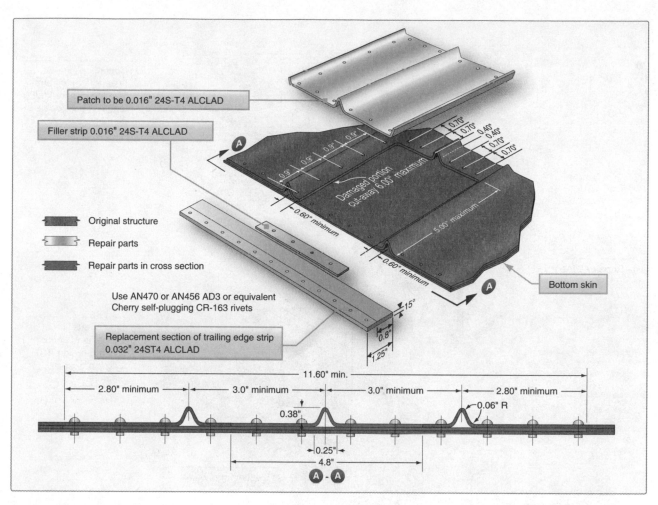

Figure 4-194. *Trailing edge repair.*

Remaining portions of existing member

Trimmed damage

Continuous line of fasteners at uniform spacing required full length to join repair element

Repair element

Trimmed damage

Continuous line of fasteners at uniform spacing required full length or repair element

Existing member

Repair element

The required quantity of fasteners used to install the repair element is equal on both sides of the trimmed damage.

Figure 4-195. *C-channel repair.*

Figure 4-196. *Primary Z-section repair.*

Figure 4-197. *U-channel repair.*

Figure 4-198. *Channel repair by patching.*

Figure 4-199. *Channel repair by insertion.*

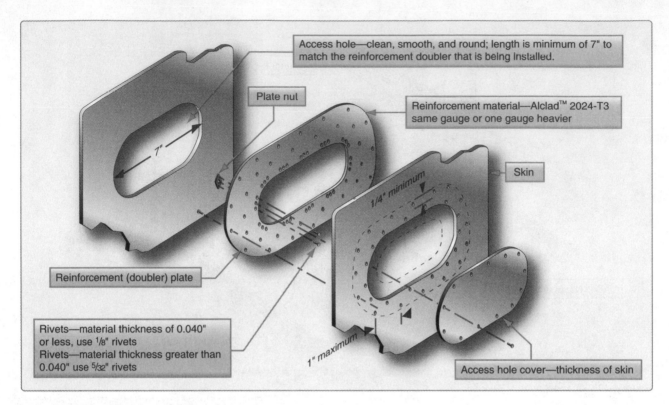

Figure 4-200. *Inspection hole.*

4-114

Chapter 5

Aircraft Welding

Introduction

Welding can be traced back to the Bronze Age, but it was not until the 19th century that welding as we know it today was invented. Some of the first successful commercially manufactured aircraft were constructed from welded steel tube frames.

As the technology and manufacturing processes evolved in the aircraft and aerospace industry, lighter metals, such as aluminum, magnesium, and titanium, were used in their construction. New processes and methods of welding these metals were developed. This chapter provides some of the basic information needed to understand and initiate the various welding methods and processes.

Traditionally, welding is defined as a process that joins metal by melting or hammering the work pieces until they are united together. With the right equipment and instruction, almost anyone with some basic mechanical skill, dexterity, and practice can learn to weld.

There are three general types of welding: gas, electric arc, and electric resistance. Each type of welding has several variations, some of which are used in the construction of aircraft. Additionally, there are some new welding processes that have been developed in recent years that are highlighted for the purpose of information.

This chapter addresses the welding equipment, methods, and various techniques used during the repair of aircraft and fabrication of component parts, including the processes of brazing and soldering of various metals.

Types of Welding

Gas Welding

Gas welding is accomplished by heating the ends or edges of metal parts to a molten state with a high temperature flame. The oxy-acetylene flame, with a temperature of approximately 6,300 °Fahrenheit (F), is produced with a torch burning acetylene and mixing it with pure oxygen. Hydrogen may be used in place of acetylene for aluminum welding, but the heat output is reduced to about 4,800 °F. Gas welding was the method most commonly used in production on aircraft materials under 3/16-inch in thickness until the mid 1950s, when it was replaced by electric welding for economic (not engineering) reasons. Gas welding continues to be a very popular and proven method for repair operations.

Nearly all gas welding in aircraft fabrication is performed with oxy-acetylene welding equipment consisting of:

- Two cylinders, acetylene and oxygen.

- Acetylene and oxygen pressure regulators and cylinder pressure gauges.

- Two lengths of colored hose (red for acetylene and green for oxygen) with adapter connections for the regulators and torch.

- A welding torch with an internal mixing head, various size tips, and hose connections.

- Welding goggles fitted with appropriate colored lenses.

- A flint or spark lighter.

- Special wrench for acetylene tank valve if needed.

- An appropriately-rated fire extinguisher.

The equipment may be permanently installed in a shop, but most welding outfits are of the portable type. *[Figure 5-1]*

Figure 5-1. *Portable oxy-acetylene welding outfit.*

Electric Arc Welding

Electric arc welding is used extensively by the aircraft industry in both the manufacture and repair of aircraft. It can be used satisfactorily to join all weldable metals, provided that the proper processes and materials are used. The four types of electric arc welding are addressed in the following paragraphs.

Shielded Metal Arc Welding (SMAW)

Shielded metal arc welding (SMAW) is the most common type of welding and is usually referred to as "stick" welding. The equipment consists of a metal wire rod coated with a welding flux that is clamped in an electrode holder that is connected by a heavy electrical cable to a low voltage and high current in either alternating current (AC) or direct current (DC), depending on the type of welding being done. An arc is struck between the rod and the work and produces heat in excess of 10,000 °F, which melts both the material and the rod. The welding circuit consists of a welding machine, two leads, an electrode holder, an electrode, and the work to be welded. *[Figure 5-2]*

When the electrode is touched to the metal to be welded, the circuit is complete and the current flows. The electrode is then withdrawn from the metal approximately 1/4-inch to form an air gap between the metal and the electrode. If the correct gap is maintained, the current bridges the gap to form a sustained electric spark called the arc. This action melts the electrode and the coating of flux.

As the flux melts, it releases an inert gas that shields the molten puddle from oxygen in the air to prevent oxidation. The molten flux covers the weld and hardens to an airtight

Figure 5-2. *Typical arc welding circuit.*

slag that protects the weld bead as it cools. Some aircraft manufacturers, such as Stinson, used this process for the welding of 4130 steel fuselage structures. This was followed by heat treatment in an oven to stress relieve and normalize the structure. Shown in *Figure 5-3* is a typical arc welding machine with cables, ground clamp, and electrode holder.

Figure 5-3. *Stick welder–Shielded Metal Arc Welder (SMAW).*

Gas Metal Arc Welding (GMAW)

Gas metal arc welding (GMAW) was formerly called metal inert gas (MIG) welding. It is an improvement over stick welding because an uncoated wire electrode is fed into and through the torch and an inert gas, such as argon, helium, or carbon dioxide, flows out around the wire to protect the puddle from oxygen. The power supply is connected to the

torch and the work, and the arc produces the intense heat needed to melt the work and the electrode. *[Figure 5-4]*

Low-voltage high-current DC is typically used with GMAW welding. *Figure 5-5* shows the equipment required for a typical MIG welding setup.

This method of welding can be used for large volume manufacturing and production work; it is not well suited to repair work because weld quality cannot be easily determined without destructive testing. *Figure 5-6* depicts a typical power source used for MIG welding.

Gas Tungsten Arc Welding (GTAW)

Gas tungsten arc welding (GTAW) is a method of electric arc welding that fills most of the needs in aircraft maintenance and repair when proper procedures and materials are used. It is the preferred method to use on stainless steel, magnesium, and most forms of thick aluminum. It is more commonly known as Tungsten Inert Gas (TIG) welding and by the trade names of Heliarc or Heliweld. These names were derived from the inert helium gas that was originally used.

The first two methods of electric arc welding that were addressed used a consumable electrode that produced the filler for the weld. In TIG welding, the electrode is a tungsten rod that forms the path for the high amperage arc between it and the work to melt the metal at over 5,400 °F. The electrode is not consumed and used as filler so a filler rod is manually fed into the molten puddle in almost the same manner as when using an oxy-acetylene torch. A stream of inert gas, such as argon or helium, flows out around the electrode and envelopes the arc thereby preventing the formation of oxides in the molten puddle. *[Figure 5-7]*

Figure 5-4. *Metal inert gas (MIG) welding process.*

Figure 5-5. *MIG welding equipment.*

The versatility of a TIG welder is increased by the choice of the power supply being used. DC of either polarity or AC may be used. *[Figure 5-8]*

Figure 5-6. *MIG welder–gas metal arc welder (GMAW).*

Figure 5-7. *Tungsten inert gas (TIG) welding process.*

- Either select the welder setting to DC straight polarity (the work being the positive and the torch being negative) when welding mild steel, stainless steel, and titanium; or

- Select AC for welding aluminum and magnesium.

Figure 5-9 is a typical power source for TIG welding along with a torch, foot operated current control, regulator for inert gas, and assorted power cables.

Electric Resistance Welding

Electric resistance welding, either spot welding or seam welding, is typically used to join thin sheet metal components during the manufacturing process.

Figure 5-9. *TIG welder–gas tungsten arc welder (GTAW).*

Figure 5-8. *Typical setup for TIG welding.*

Spot Welding

Two copper electrodes are held in the jaws of the spot welding machine, and the material to be welded is clamped between them. Pressure is applied to hold the electrodes tightly together and electrical current flows through the electrodes and the material. The resistance of the material being welded is so much higher than that of the copper electrodes that enough heat is generated to melt the metal. The pressure on the electrodes forces the molten spots in the two pieces of metal to unite, and this pressure is held after the current stops flowing long enough for the metal to solidify. The amount of current, pressure, and dwell time are all carefully controlled and matched to the type of material and the thickness to produce the correct spot welds. *[Figure 5-10]*

Figure 5-10. *Spot welding thin sheet metal.*

Seam Welding

Rather than having to release the electrodes and move the material to form a series of spot welds, a seam-welding machine is used to manufacture fuel tanks and other components where a continuous weld is needed. Two copper wheels replace the bar-shaped electrodes. The metal to be welded is moved between them, and electric pulses create spots of molten metal that overlap to form the continuous seam.

Plasma Arc Welding (PAW)

Plasma arc welding (PAW) was developed in 1964 as a method of bringing better control to the arc welding process. PAW provides an advanced level of control and accuracy using automated equipment to produce high quality welds in miniature and precision applications. Furthermore, PAW is equally suited to manual operation and can be performed by a person using skills similar to those for GTAW.

In the plasma welding torch, a nonconsumable tungsten electrode is located within a fine-bore copper nozzle. A pilot arc is initiated between the torch electrode and nozzle tip. This arc is then transferred to the metal being welded. *[Figure 5-11]*

Figure 5-11. *The plasma welding process.*

By forcing the plasma gas and arc through a constricted orifice, the torch delivers a high concentration of heat to a small area. The plasma process produces exceptionally high quality welds. *[Figure 5-12.]*

Figure 5-12. *Plasma arc.*

Plasma gas is normally argon. The torch also uses a secondary gas, such as argon/helium or argon/nitrogen, that assists in shielding the molten weld puddle and minimizing oxidation of the weld.

Like GTAW, the PAW process can be used to weld most commercial metals, and it can be used for a wide variety of metal thicknesses. On thin material, from foil to ⅛-inch, the process is desirable because of the low heat input. The process provides relatively constant heat input because arc length variations are not very critical. On material thicknesses greater than ⅛-inch, and using automated equipment, a keyhole technique is often used to produce full penetration single-path welds. In the keyhole technique, the plasma completely penetrates the work piece. The molten weld metal flows to the rear of the keyhole and solidifies as the torch moves on. The high quality welds produced are characterized by deep, narrow penetration and a small weld face.

When PAW is performed manually, the process requires a high degree of welding skills similar to that required for GTAW. However, the equipment is more complex and requires a high degree of knowledge to set up and use. The equipment required for PAW includes a welding machine, a special plasma arc control system, the plasma welding torch (water-cooled), the source of plasma and shielding gas, and filler material, when required. Because of the cost associated with this equipment, this process is very limited outside of manufacturing facilities.

Plasma Arc Cutting

When a plasma cutting torch is used, the gas is usually compressed air. The plasma cutting machine works by constricting an electrical arc in a nozzle and forcing the ionized gas through it. This heats the gas that melts the metal which is blown away by the air pressure. By increasing air pressure and intensifying the arc with higher voltages, the cutter is capable of blasting through thicker metals and blowing away the dross with minimal cleanup.

Plasma arc systems can cut all electrically conductive metals, including aluminum and stainless steel. These two metals cannot be cut by oxy-fuel cutting systems because they have an oxide layer that prevents oxidation from occurring. Plasma cutting works well on thin metals and can successfully cut brass and copper in excess of two inches thick.

Plasma cutting machines can rapidly and precisely cut through, gouge, or pierce any electrically conductive metal without preheating. The plasma cutter produces a precise kerf (cut) width and a small heat-affected zone (HAZ) that prevents warping and damage.

Gas Welding and Cutting Equipment

Welding Gases

Acetylene

This is the primary fuel for oxy-fuel welding and cutting. It is chemically very unstable, and is stored in special cylinders designed to keep the gas dissolved. The cylinders are packed with a porous material and then saturated with acetone. When the acetylene is added to the cylinder, it dissolves; in this solution, it becomes stable. Pure acetylene stored in a free state explodes from a slight shock at 29.4 pounds per square inch (psi). The acetylene pressure gauge should never be set higher than 15 psi for welding or cutting.

Argon

Argon is a colorless, odorless, tasteless, and nontoxic inert gas. Inert gas cannot combine with other elements. It has a very low chemical reactivity and low thermal conductivity. It is used as a gas shield for the electrode in MIG, TIG, and plasma welding equipment.

Helium

Helium is a colorless, odorless, tasteless, and nontoxic inert gas. Its boiling and melting points are the lowest of the elements and it normally exists only in gas form. It is used as a protective gas shield for many industrial uses including electric arc welding.

Hydrogen

Hydrogen is a colorless, odorless, tasteless, and highly flammable gas. It can be used at a higher pressure than acetylene and is used for underwater welding and cutting. It also can be used for aluminum welding using the oxy-hydrogen process.

Oxygen

Oxygen is a colorless, odorless, and nonflammable gas. It is used in the welding process to increase the combustion rate which increases the flame temperature of flammable gas.

Pressure Regulators

A pressure regulator is attached to a gas cylinder and is used to lower the cylinder pressure to the desired working pressure. Regulators have two gauges, one indicating the pressure in the cylinder and the second showing the working pressure. By turning the adjustment knob in or out, a spring operating a flexible diaphragm opens or closes a valve in the regulator. Turning the knob in causes the flow and pressure to increase; backing it out decreases the flow and pressure.

There are two types of regulators: single stage and two stage. They perform the same function but the two-stage regulator maintains a more constant outlet pressure and flow as the cylinder volume and pressure drops. Two-stage regulators can be identified by a larger, second pressure chamber under the regulator knob. *[Figures 5-13 and 5-14]*

Figure 5-13. *Single-stage acetylene regulator. Note the maximum 15-psi working pressure. The notched groove cylinder connection nut indicates a left hand thread.*

Figure 5-14. *Two-stage oxygen regulator. No groove on the cylinder connection nut indicates a right hand thread.*

Welding Hose

A welding hose connects the regulators to the torch. It is typically a double hose joined together during manufacture. The acetylene hose is red and has left hand threads indicated by a groove cut into the connection nut. The oxygen hose is green and has right hand threads indicated by the absence of a groove on the connection nut.

Welding hoses are produced in different sizes from ¼-inch to ½-inch inside diameter (ID). The hose should be marked for light, standard, and heavy duty service plus a grade indicating whether it has an oil- and/or flame-resistant cover. The hose should have the date of manufacture, maximum working pressure of 200 psi, and indicate that it meets specification IP-90 of the Rubber Manufacturers Association and the Compressed Gas Association for rubber welding hoses. Grade-R hose should only be used with acetylene gas. A T-grade hose must be used with propane, MAPP®, and all other fuel gases.

Check Valves and Flashback Arrestors

The check valve stops the reverse flow of the gas and can be installed either between the regulator and the hose or the hose and the torch. *[Figure 5-15]* Excessive overheating of cutting, welding, and heating tips can cause flashback conditions. A flashback can be caused when a tip is overheated and the gas ignites before passing out of the tip. The flame is then burning internally rather than on the outside of the tip and is usually identified by a shrill hissing or squealing noise.

Figure 5-15. *Check valves.*

A flashback arrestor installed on each hose prevents a high pressure flame or oxygen-fuel mixture from being pushed back into either cylinder causing an explosion. The flashback arrestors incorporate a check valve that stops the reverse flow of gas and the advancement of a flashback fire. *[Figure 5-16]*

Figure 5-16. *Flashback arrestors.*

Figure 5-17. *Torch handle with cutting, heating, and welding tips.*

Torches

Equal Pressure Torch

The equal pressure torch is the most commonly used torch for oxy-acetylene welding. It has a mixing chamber and uses acetylene fuel at 1–15 psi. The flame is easy to adjust and there is less chance of flashback with this torch. There are several small lightweight torches of this type that are ideal for aviation welding projects. The Smith Airline™ and the Meco Midget™ torches are small enough to be used in close confined areas, lightweight enough to reduce fatigue during long welding sessions yet, with the appropriate tips, are capable of welding 0.250-inch steel.

Injector Torch

The injector torch uses fuel gas at pressures between just above 0 and 2 psi. This torch is typically used with propane and propylene gas. High-pressure oxygen comes through a small nozzle inside the torch head and pulls the fuel gas along with it via a venturi effect. The low-pressure injector torch is more prone to flashback.

Cutting Torch

The cutting torch is an attachment added to the torch handle that allows the cutting of metal. The cutting process is fundamentally the rapid burning or oxidizing of the metal in a localized area. The metal is heated to a bright red color (1,400 °F to 1,600 °F), which is the kindling temperature, using only the preheat jets. Then, a jet of high pressure oxygen released by the lever on the cutting attachment is directed against the heated metal. This oxygen blast combines with the hot metal and forms an intensely hot oxide. The molten oxide is blown down the sides of the cut, heating the metal in its path to the kindling temperature as the torch is moved along the line of the desired cut. The heated metal also burns to an oxide that is blown away on the underside of the piece. *[Figure 5-17]*

Torch Tips

The torch tip delivers and controls the final flow of gases. It is important that you use the correct tip with the proper gas pressures for the work to be welded satisfactorily. The size of the tip opening—not the temperature—determines the amount of heat applied to the work. If an excessively small tip is used, the heat provided is insufficient to produce penetration to the proper depth. If the tip is too large, the heat is too great, and holes are burned in the metal.

Torch tip sizes are designated by numbers. The manufacturer can provide a chart with recommended sizes for welding specific thicknesses of metal. With use, a torch tip becomes clogged with carbon deposits. If it is allowed to contact the molten pool, particles of slag may clog the tip. This may cause a backfire, which is a momentary backward flow of the gases at the torch tip. A backfire is rarely dangerous, but molten metal may be splattered when the flame pops. Tips should be cleaned with the proper size tip cleaner to avoid enlarging the tip opening.

Welding Eyewear

Protective eyewear for use with oxy-fuel welding outfits is available in several styles and must be worn to protect the welder's eyes from the bright flame and flying sparks. This eyewear is not for use with arc welding equipment.

Some of the styles available have individual lenses and include goggles that employ a head piece and/or an elastic head strap to keep them snug around the eyes for protection from the occasional showering spark. *[Figure 5-18]* Another popular style is the rectangular eye shield that takes a standard 2-inch by 4.25-inch lens. This style is available with an elastic strap but is far more comfortable and better fitting when attached to a proper fitting adjustable headgear. It

Figure 5-18. *Welding goggles.*

can be worn over prescription glasses, provides protection from flying sparks, and accepts a variety of standard shade and color lenses. A clear safety glass lens is added in front of the shaded lens to protect it from damage. *[Figure 5-19]*

Figure 5-19. *Gas welding eye shield attached to adjustable headgear.*

It was standard practice in the past to select a lens shade for gas welding based on the brightness of flame emitting from the torch. The darkest shade of lens showing a clear definition of the work was normally the most desirable. However, when flux was used for brazing and welding, the torch heat caused the sodium in the flux to give off a brilliant yellow-orange flare, hiding a clear view of the weld area and causing many eye problems.

Various types of lens and colors were tried for periods of time without much success. It was not until the late 1980s that TM Technologies developed and patented a new green glass designed especially for aluminum oxy-fuel welding. It not only eliminated the sodium orange flare completely, but also provided the necessary protection from ultraviolet, infrared, and blue light, and impact to meet the requirements of the American National Standards Institute (ANSI) Z87-1989 Safety Standards for a special purpose lens. This lens can be used for welding and brazing all metals using an oxy-fuel torch.

Torch Lighters
Torch lighters are called friction lighters or flint strikers. The lighter consists of a file-shaped piece of steel, usually recessed in a cuplike device, and a replaceable flint, which, when drawn across the steel, produces a shower of sparks to light the fuel gas. An open flame or match should never be used

to light a torch because accumulated gas may envelop the hand and, when ignited, cause a severe burn. *[Figure 5-20]*

Figure 5-20. *Torch lighter.*

Filler Rod
The use of the proper type of filler rod is very important for oxy-acetylene welding. This material adds not only reinforcement to the weld area, but also desired properties to the finished weld. By selecting the proper rod, tensile strength or ductility can be secured in a weld. Similarly, the proper rod can help retain the desired amount of corrosion resistance. In some cases, a suitable rod with a lower melting point helps to avoid cracks caused by expansion and contraction.

Welding rods may be classified as ferrous or nonferrous. Ferrous rods include carbon and alloy steel rods, as well as cast-iron rods. Nonferrous rods include brass, aluminum, magnesium, copper, silver, and their various alloys.

Welding rods are manufactured in standard 36-inch lengths and in diameters from $\frac{1}{16}$-inch to $\frac{3}{8}$-inch. The diameter of the rod to be used is governed by the thickness of the metals to be joined. If the rod is too small, it cannot conduct heat away from the puddle rapidly enough, and a burned hole results. A rod too large in diameter draws heat away and chills the puddle, resulting in poor penetration of the joined metal. All filler rods should be cleaned prior to use.

Equipment Setup
Setting up acetylene welding equipment in preparation for welding should be accomplished in a systematic and definite order to avoid costly damage to equipment and compromising the safety of personnel.

Gas Cylinders
All cylinders should be stored and transported in the upright position, especially acetylene cylinders, because they contain an absorbent material saturated with liquid acetone. If the cylinder were laid on its side, allowing the acetone to enter and contaminate the regulator, hose, and torch, fuel starvation and a resultant flashback in the system could result. If an acetylene cylinder must be placed on its side for a period of

time, it must be stored in the upright position for at least twice as long before being used. Gas cylinders should be secured, usually with a chain, in a permanent location or in a suitable mobile cart. The cylinder's protective steel cap should not be removed until the cylinder is put into service.

Regulators

Prior to installing the regulator on a gas cylinder, open the cylinder shutoff valve for an instant to blow out any foreign material that may be lodged in the outlet. Close the valve and wipe off the connection with a clean oil-free cloth. Connect the acetylene pressure regulator to the acetylene cylinder and tighten the left hand nut. Connect the oxygen pressure regulator to the oxygen cylinder and tighten the right hand nut. The connection fittings are brass and do not require a lot of torque to prevent them from leaking. At this time, check to ensure the adjusting screw on each pressure regulator is backed out by turning counterclockwise until it turns freely.

Hoses

Connect the red hose with the left hand threads to the acetylene pressure regulator and the green hose with the right hand threads to the oxygen pressure regulator. This is the location, between the regulator and hose, in which flashback arrestors should be installed. Again, because the fittings are brass and easily damaged, tighten only enough to prevent leakage.

Stand off to the side away from the face of the gauges. Now, very slowly open the oxygen cylinder valve and read the cylinder gauge to check the contents in the tank. The oxygen cylinder shutoff valve has a double seat valve and should be opened fully against its stop to seat the valve and prevent a leak. The acetylene cylinder shutoff valve should be slowly opened just enough to get the cylinder pressure reading on the regulator and then one half of a turn more. This allows a quick shutoff, if needed.

NOTE: As a recommended safety practice, the cylinders should not be depleted in content below 20 psi. This prevents the possible reverse flow of gas from the opposite tank.

Both hoses should be blown out before attaching to the torch. This is accomplished for each cylinder by turning the pressure adjusting screw in (clockwise) until the gas escapes, and then quickly backing the screw out (counterclockwise) to shut off the flow. This should be done in a well ventilated open space, free from sparks, flames, or other sources of ignition.

Connecting Torch

Connect the red hose with the left hand thread connector nut to the left hand thread fitting on the torch. Connect the green hose with the right hand thread connector nut to the right hand thread fitting on the torch. Close the valves on the torch handle and check all connections for leaks, as follows:

- Turn in the adjusting screw on the oxygen pressure regulator until the working pressure indicates 10 psi. Turn in the adjusting screw on the acetylene pressure regulator until the working pressure indicates 5 psi.

- Back out both adjusting screws on the regulators and verify that the working pressure remains steady. If it drops and pressure is lost, a leak is indicated between the regulator and the torch.

- A general tightening of all connections should fix the leak. Repeat a check of the system.

- If a leak is still indicated by a loss in working pressure, a mixture of soapy water on all the connections reveals the source of the leak. Never check for a leak with a flame because a serious explosion could occur.

Select the Tip Size

Welding and cutting tips are available in a variety of sizes for almost any job, and are identified by number. The higher the number is, the bigger the hole in the tip is allowing more heat to be directed onto the metal and allowing thicker metal to be welded or cut.

Welding tips have one hole and cutting tips have a number of holes. The cutting tip has one large hole in the center for the cutting oxygen and a number of smaller holes around it that supply fuel, gas, and oxygen for the preheating flame. The selection of the tip size is very important, not only for the quality of the weld and/or the efficiency of the cutting process, but for the overall operation of the welding equipment and safety of the personnel using it.

Starvation occurs if torch tips are operated at less than the required volume of gas, leading to tip overheating and possible flashbacks. Incorrect tip size and obstructed tip orifices can also cause overheating and/or flashback conditions.

All fuel cylinders have a limited capacity to deliver gas to the tip. That capacity is further limited by the gas contents remaining in the cylinder and the temperature of the cylinder.

The following provides some recommended procedures to guard against overheating and flashbacks:

- Refer to the manufacturer's recommendations for tip size based on the metal's thickness.

- Use the recommended gas pressure settings for the tip size being used.

- Provide the correct volume of gas as recommended for each tip size.

- Do not use an excessively long hose, one with multiple splices, or one that may be too small in diameter and restrict the flow of gas.

NOTE: Acetylene is limited to a maximum continuous withdrawal rate of one-seventh of the cylinder's rated capacity when full. For example, an acetylene cylinder that has a capacity of 330 cubic feet has a maximum withdrawal of 47 cubic feet per hour. This is determined by dividing 330 (cylinder capacity) by 7 (one-seventh of the cylinder capacity).

As a safety precaution, it is recommended that flashback arrestors be installed between the regulators and the gas supply hoses of all welding outfits. *Figure 5-21* shows recommended tip sizes of different manufacturers, for welding various thickness of metals.

Welding Tip Size Conversion Chart									
Wire Drill	Decimal Inch	Metric Equiv. (mm)	Smiths™ AW1A	Henrob/ Dillion	Harris 15	Victor J Series	Meco N Midget™	Aluminum Thickness (in)	Steel Thickness (in)
97	0.0059	0.150						Foil	Foil
85	0.0110	0.279							
80	0.0135	0.343		#00			#00		
76	0.0200	0.508	AW200				#0		
75	0.0220	0.559		#0	#0	#000			.015
74	0.0225	0.572	AW20					.025	
73	0.0240	0.610					0.5		
72	0.0250	0.635		0.5					
71	0.0260	0.660	AW201		1				
70	0.0280	0.711				#00	1		.032
69	0.0292	0.742	AW202						
67	0.0320	0.813	AW203				1.5	.040	
66	0.0340	0.864		1					
65	0.0350	0.889			2	#0	2	.050	.046
63	0.0370	0.940	AW204				2.5		
60	0.0400	1.016				1			
59	0.0410	1.041		1.5					
58	0.0420	1.067			3		3		.062
57	0.0430	1.092	AW205						
56	0.0465	1.181	AW206			2	4	.063	
55	0.0520	1.321		2	4				.093
54	0.0550	1.397	AW207				4.5		
53	0.0595	1.511			5	3			.125
52	0.0635	1.613	AW208				5	.100	
51	0.0670	1.702			6				.187
49	0.0730	1.854	AW209	2.5		4	5.5		
48	0.0760	1.930			7			.188	.250
47	0.0780	1.981					6		
45	0.0820	2.083			8				.312
44	0.0860	2.184	AW210				6.5	.25	
43	0.0890	2.261			9	5	7		.375
42	0.0930	2.362		3					
40	0.0980	2.489			10				
36	0.1060	2.692				6			
35	0.1100	2.794			13				

Figure 5-21. *Chart of recommended tip sizes for welding various thicknesses of metal.*

Adjusting the Regulator Working Pressure

The working pressure should be set according to the manufacturer's recommendation for the tip size that is being used to weld or cut. This is a recommended method that works for most welding and cutting operations.

In a well ventilated area, open the acetylene valve on the torch and turn the adjusting screw on the acetylene pressure regulator clockwise until the desired pressure is set. Close the acetylene valve on the torch. Then, set the oxygen pressure in the same manner by opening the oxygen valve on the torch and turning the adjusting screw clockwise on the oxygen regulator until desired pressure is set. Then, close the oxygen valve on the torch handle. With the working pressures set, the welding or cutting operation can be initiated.

Lighting and Adjusting the Torch

With the proper working pressures set for the acetylene and oxygen, open the torch acetylene valve a quarter to a half turn. Direct the torch away from the body and ignite the acetylene gas with the flint striker. Open the acetylene valve until the black sooty smoke disappears from the flame. The pure acetylene flame is long, bushy, and has a yellowish color. Open the torch oxygen valve slowly and the flame shortens and turns to a bluish-white color that forms a bright inner luminous cone surrounded by an outer flame envelope. This is a neutral flame that should be set before either a carburizing or oxidizing flame mixture is set.

Different Flames

The three types of flame commonly used for welding are neutral, carburizing, and oxidizing. Each serves a specific purpose. *[Figure 5-22]*

Figure 5-22. *Oxy-acetylene flames.*

Neutral Flame

The neutral flame burns at approximately 5,850 °F at the tip of the inner luminous cone and is produced by a balanced mixture of acetylene and oxygen supplied by the torch. The neutral flame is used for most welding because it does not alter the composition of the base metal. When using this flame on steel, the molten metal puddle is quiet and clear, and the metal flows to give a thoroughly fused weld without burning or sparking.

Carburizing Flame

The carburizing flame burns at approximately 5,700 °F at the tip of the inner core. It is also referred to as a reducing flame because it tends to reduce the amount of oxygen in the iron oxides. The flame burns with a coarse rushing sound, and has a bluish-white inner cone, a white center cone, and a light blue outer cone.

The flame is produced by burning more acetylene than oxygen, and can be recognized by the greenish feathery tip at the end of the cone. The longer the feather, the more acetylene is in the mix. For most welding operations, the length of the feather should be about twice the length of the inner cone.

The carburizing flame is best used for welding high-carbon steels, for hard facing, and for welding such nonferrous alloys as aluminum, nickel, and Monel.

Oxidizing Flame

The oxidizing flame burns at approximately 6,300 °F and is produced by burning an excess of oxygen. It takes about two parts of oxygen to one part acetylene to produce this flame. It can be identified by the shorter outer flame and the small, white, inner cone. To obtain this flame, start with a neutral flame and then open the oxygen valve until the inner cone is about one-tenth of its original length. The oxidizing flame makes a hissing sound, and the inner cone is somewhat pointed and purplish in color at the tip.

The oxidizing flame does have some specific uses. A slightly oxidizing flame is used for bronze welding (brazing) of steel and cast iron. A stronger oxidizing flame is used for fusion welding of brass and bronze. If an oxidizing flame is used on steel, it causes the molten metal to foam, give off sparks, and burn.

Soft or Harsh Flames

With each size of tip, a neutral, carburizing, or oxidizing flame can be obtained. It is also possible to obtain a soft or harsh flame by decreasing or increasing the working pressure of both gases (observing the maximum working pressure of 15 psi for acetylene gas).

For some work, it may be desirable to have a soft or low velocity flame without a reduction of thermal output. This can be achieved by reducing the working pressure using a larger tip and closing the torch valves until the neutral flame is quiet and steady. It is especially desirable to use a soft flame when welding aluminum to avoid blowing holes in the metal when the puddle is formed.

Handling of the Torch

It should be cautioned that improper adjustment or handling of the torch may cause the flame to backfire or, in rare cases, to flashback. A backfire is a momentary backward flow of gases at the torch tip that causes the flame to go out. A backfire may be caused by touching the tip against the work, overheating the tip, by operating the torch at other than recommended pressures, by a loose tip or head, or by dirt or slag in the end of the tip, and may cause molten metal to be splattered when the flame pops.

A flashback is dangerous because it is the burning of gases within the torch. It is usually caused by loose connections, improper pressures, or overheating of the torch. A shrill hissing or squealing noise accompanies a flashback, and unless the gases are turned off immediately, the flame may burn back through the hose and regulators causing great damage and personal injury. The cause of the flashback should always be determined and the problem corrected before relighting the torch. All gas welding outfits should have a flashback arrestor.

Oxy-acetylene Cutting

Cutting ferrous metals by the oxy-acetylene process is primarily the rapid burning or oxidizing of the metal in a localized area. This is a quick and inexpensive way to cut iron and steel where a finished edge is not required.

Figure 5-23 shows an example of a cutting torch. It has the conventional oxygen and acetylene valves in the torch handle that control the flow of the two gases to the cutting head. It also has an oxygen valve below the oxygen lever on the cutting head so that a finer adjustment of the flame can be obtained.

Figure 5-23. *Cutting torch with additional tools.*

The size of the cutting tip is determined by the thickness of the metal to be cut. Set the regulators to the recommended working pressures for the cutting torch based on the tip size selected. Before beginning any cutting operation, the area should be clear of all combustible material and the proper protective equipment should be worn by personnel engaged in the cutting operation.

The flame for the torch in *Figure 5-23* is set by first closing the oxygen valve below the cutting lever and fully opening the oxygen valve on the handle. (This supplies the high pressure oxygen blast when the cutting lever is actuated.) The acetylene valve on the handle is then opened and the torch is lit with a striker. The acetylene flame is increased until the black soot is gone. Then, open the oxygen valve below the cutting lever and adjust the flame to neutral. If more heat is needed, open the valves to add more acetylene and oxygen. Actuate the cutting lever and readjust the preheat flame to neutral if necessary.

The metal is heated to a bright red color (1,400 °F–1,600 °F, which is the kindling or ignition temperature) by the preheat orifices in the tip of the cutting torch. Then, a jet of high-pressure oxygen is directed against it by pressing the oxygen lever on the torch. This oxygen blast combines with the red-hot metal and forms an intensely hot molten oxide that is blown down the sides of the cut. As the torch is moved along the intended cut line, this action continues heating the metal in its path to the kindling temperature. The metal, thus heated, also burns to an oxide that is blown away to the underside of the piece.

Proper instruction and practice provides the knowledge and skill to become proficient in the technique needed to cut with a torch. Hold the torch in either hand, whichever is most comfortable. Use the thumb of that hand to operate the oxygen cutting lever. Use the other hand to rest the torch on and steady it along the cut line.

Begin at the edge of the metal and hold the tip perpendicular to the surface, preheating until the spot turns bright red. Lightly depress the cutting lever to allow a shower of sparks and molten metal to blow through the cut. Fully depress the cutting lever and move the torch slowly in the direction of the intended cut.

Practice and experience allow the technician to learn how to judge the speed at which to move the torch. It should be just fast enough to allow the cut to penetrate completely without excessive melting around the cut. If the torch is moved too fast, the metal will not be preheated enough, and the cutting action stops. If this happens, release the cutting lever, preheat the cut to bright red, depress the lever, and continue with the cut.

Shutting Down the Gas Welding Equipment

Shutting down the welding equipment is fairly simple when some basic steps are followed:

- Turn off the flame by closing the acetylene valve on the torch first. This shuts the flame off quickly. Then, close the oxygen valve on the torch handle. Also, close oxygen valve on cutting torch, if applicable.

- If the equipment is not used in the immediate future (approximately the next 30 minutes), the valves on the acetylene and oxygen cylinders should be closed and pressure relieved from the hoses.

- In a well-ventilated area, open the acetylene valve on the torch and allow the gas to escape to the outside atmosphere, and then close the valve.

- Open the oxygen valve on the torch, allow the gas to escape, and then close the valve.

- Close both the acetylene and oxygen regulators by backing out the adjusting screw counterclockwise until loose.

- Carefully coil the hose to prevent kinking and store it to prevent damage to the torch and tip.

Gas Welding Procedures and Techniques

The material to be welded, the thickness of the metal, the type of joint, and the position of the weld dictates the procedure and technique to be used.

When light-gauge metal is welded, the torch is usually held with the hose draped over the wrist. *[Figure 5-24]* To weld heavy materials, the more common grip may provide better control of the torch. *[Figure 5-25]*

The torch should be held in the most comfortable position that allows the tip to be in line with the joint to be welded, and inclined between 30° and 60° from the perpendicular. This position preheats the edges just ahead of the molten puddle. The best angle depends on the type of weld, the amount of preheating required, and the thickness and type of metal. The thicker the metal, the more vertical the torch must be for proper heat penetration. The white cone of the flame should be held about ⅛-inch from the surface of the metal.

Welding can be performed by pointing the torch flame in the direction that the weld is progressing. This is referred to as forehand welding, and is the most commonly used method for lighter tubing and sheet metal. The filler rod is kept ahead of the tip in the direction the weld is going and is added to the puddle.

Figure 5-24. *Hand position for light-gauge materials.*

For welding thick metals or heavy plate, a technique called backhand welding can be used. In this method, the torch flame is pointed back toward the finished weld and the filler rod is added between the flame and the weld. This method provides a greater concentration of heat for welding thicker metals and would rarely be used in aircraft maintenance.

Puddle

If the torch is held in the correct position, a small puddle of molten metal forms. The puddle should be centered in the joint and composed of equal parts of those pieces being welded. After the puddle appears, the tip should be moved in a semicircular arc or circular motion equally between the pieces to ensure an even distribution of heat.

Adding Filler Rod to the Puddle

As the metal melts and the puddle forms, filler rod is needed to replace the metal that flows out from around the joint. The rod is added to the puddle in the amount that provides for the completed fillet to be built up about one-fourth the thickness of the base metal. The filler rod selected should be compatible with the base metal being welded.

Figure 5-25. *Hand position for heavy-gauge materials.*

Correct Forming of a Weld

The form of the weld metal has considerable bearing upon the strength and fatigue resistance of a joint. The strength of an improperly made weld is usually less than the strength for which the joint was designed. Low-strength welds are generally the result of insufficient penetration; undercutting of the base metal at the toe of the weld; poor fusion of the weld metal with the base metal; trapped oxides, slag, or gas pockets in the weld; overlap of the weld metal on the base metal; too much or too little reinforcement; or overheating of the weld.

Characteristics of a Good Weld

A completed weld should have the following characteristics:

1. The seam should be smooth, the bead ripples evenly spaced, and of a uniform thickness.

2. The weld should be built up, slightly convex, thus providing extra thickness at the joint.

3. The weld should taper off smoothly into the base metal.

4. No oxide should be formed on the base metal close to the weld.

5. The weld should show no signs of blowholes, porosity, or projecting globules.

6. The base metal should show no signs of burns, pits, cracks, or distortion.

Although a clean, smooth weld is desirable, this characteristic does not necessarily mean that the weld is a good one; it may be dangerously weak inside. However, when a weld is rough, uneven, and pitted, it is almost always unsatisfactory inside. Welds should never be filed to give them a better appearance, since filing deprives the weld of part of its strength. Welds should never be filled with solder, brazing material, or filler of any sort.

When it is necessary to reweld a joint, all old weld material must be removed before the operation is begun. It must be remembered that reheating the area may cause the base metal to lose some of its strength and become brittle. This should not be confused with a postweld heat treatment that does not raise the metal to a high enough temperature to cause harm to the base material.

Oxy-Acetylene Welding of Ferrous Metals

Steel (Including SAE 4130)

Low-carbon steel, low-alloy steel (e.g., 4130), cast steel, and wrought iron are easily welded with the oxy-acetylene flame. Low-carbon and low-alloy steels are the ferrous materials that are gas welded most frequently. As the carbon content of steel increases, it may be repaired by welding using specific procedures for various alloy types. Factors involved are the carbon content and hardenability. For corrosion-resistant and heat-resistant nickel chromium steels, the allowed weldability depends upon their stability, carbon content, and reheat treatment.

The Society of Automotive Engineers (SAE) and the American Iron and Steel Institute (AISI) provide a designation system that is an accepted standard for the industry. SAE 4130 is an alloy steel that is an ideal material for constructing fuselages and framework on small aircraft; it is also used for motorcycle and high-end bicycle frames and race car frames and roll cages. The tubing has high tensile strength, malleability, and is easy to weld.

The number '4130' is also an AISI 4-digit code that defines the approximate chemical composition of the steel. The '41' indicates a low-alloy steel containing chromium and molybdenum (chromoly) and the '30' designates a carbon content of 0.3 percent. 4130 steel also contains small amounts of manganese, phosphorus, sulfur, and silicon, but like all steels, it contains mostly iron.

In order to make a good weld, the carbon content of the steel must not be altered to any appreciable degree, nor can other atmospheric chemical constituents be added to or subtracted from the base metal without seriously altering the properties of the metal. However, many welding filler wires do contain constituents different from the base material for specific reasons, which is perfectly normal and acceptable if approved materials are used. Molten steel has a great affinity for carbon, oxygen, and nitrogen combining with the molten puddle to form oxides and nitrates, both of which lower the strength of steel. When welding with an oxy-acetylene flame, the inclusion of impurities can be minimized by observing the following precautions:

- Maintain an exact neutral flame for most steels and a slight excess of acetylene when welding alloys with a high nickel or chromium content, such as stainless steel.

- Maintain a soft flame and control the puddle.

- Maintain a flame sufficient to penetrate the metal and manipulate it so that the molten metal is protected from the air by the outer envelope of flame.

- Keep the hot end of the welding rod in the weld pool or within the flame envelope.

- When the weld is complete and still in the red heat, circle the outer envelope of the torch around the entire weldment to bring it evenly to a dull red. Slowly back the torch away from the weldment to ensure a slow cooling rate.

Chrome Molybdenum

The welding technique for chrome molybdenum (chrome-moly) is practically the same as that for carbon steels, except for sections over ³⁄₁₆-inch thick. The surrounding area must be preheated to a temperature between 300 °F and 400 °F before beginning to weld. If this is not done, the sudden quenching of the weld area after the weld is complete may cause a brittle grain structure of untempered martensite that must be eliminated with post-weld heat treatments. Untempered martensite is a glass-like structure that takes the place of the normally ductile steel structure and makes the steel prone to cracking, usually near the edge of the weld. This preheating also helps to alleviate some of the distortion caused by welding along with using proper practices found in other sections of this chapter.

A soft neutral flame should be used for welding and must be maintained during the process. If the flame is not kept neutral, an oxidizing flame may cause oxide inclusions and fissures. A carburizing flame makes the metal more hardenable by raising the carbon content. The volume of the flame must be sufficient to melt the base metal, but not hot enough to overheat the base metal and cause oxide inclusions or a loss of metal thickness. The filler rod should be compatible with the base metal. If the weld requires high strength, special low-alloy filler is used, and the piece is heat treated after welding.

It may be advantageous to TIG weld 4130 chrome-moly sections over 0.093-inch thickness followed by a proper postweld heat treatment as this can result in less overall distortion. However, do not eliminate the postweld heat treatment as doing so could severely limit the fatigue life of the weldment due to the formed martensitic grain structure.

Stainless Steel

The procedure for welding stainless steel is basically the same as that for carbon steels. There are, however, some special precautions you must take to obtain the best results.

Only stainless steel used for nonstructural members of aircraft can be welded satisfactorily. The stainless steel used for structural components is cold worked or cold rolled and, if heated, loses some of its strength. Nonstructural stainless steel is obtained in sheet and tubing form and is often used for exhaust collectors, stacks, or manifolds. Oxygen combines very readily with this metal in the molten state, and you must take extreme care to prevent this from occurring.

A slightly carburizing flame is recommended for welding stainless steel. The flame should be adjusted so that a feather of excess acetylene, about ¹⁄₁₆-inch long, forms around the inner cone. Too much acetylene, however, adds carbon to the metal and causes it to lose its resistance to corrosion. The torch tip size should be one or two sizes smaller than that prescribed for a similar gauge of low carbon steel. The smaller tip lessens the chances of overheating and subsequent loss of the corrosion-resistant qualities of the metal.

To prevent the formation of chromium oxide, a specially compounded flux for stainless steel, should be used. The flux, when mixed with water, can be spread on the underside of the joint and on the filler rod. Since oxidation must be avoided as much as possible, use sufficient flux. The filler rod used should be of the same composition as the base metal.

When welding, hold the filler rod within the envelope of the torch flame so that the rod is melted in place or melted at the same time as the base metal. Add the filler rod by allowing it to flow into the molten pool. Do not stir the weld pool, because air enters the weld and increases oxidation. Avoid rewelding any portion or welding on the reverse side of the weld, which results in warping and overheating of the metal.

Another method used to keep oxygen from reaching the metal is to surround the weld with a blanket of inert gas. This is done by using a TIG welder to perform welding of stainless steel. It is a recommended method for excellent weld results and does not require the application of flux and its subsequent cleanup.

Oxy-Acetylene Welding of Nonferrous Metals

Nonferrous metals are those that contain no iron. Examples of nonferrous metals are lead, copper, silver, magnesium, and the most important in aircraft construction, aluminum. Some of these metals are lighter than the ferrous metals, but in most cases, they are not as strong. Aluminum manufacturers have compensated for the lack of strength of pure aluminum by alloying it with other metals or by cold working it. For still greater strength, some aluminum alloys are also heat treated.

Aluminum Welding

Gas welding of certain aluminum alloys can be accomplished successfully, but it requires some practice and the appropriate equipment to produce a successful weld. Before attempting to weld aluminum for the first time, become familiar with how the metal reacts under the welding flame.

A good example for practice and to see how aluminum reacts to a welding flame, heat a piece of aluminum sheet on a welding bench. Hold a torch with a neutral flame perpendicular to the sheet and bring the tip of the inner cone almost in contact with the metal. Observe that the metal suddenly melts away, almost without any indication, and leaves a hole in the metal. Now repeat the operation, only this time hold the torch at an angle of about 30° to the surface. This allows for better control of the heat and allows the surface metal to melt without forming a hole. Practice by slowly moving the flame along the surface until the puddle can be controlled without melting holes. Once that is mastered, practice on flanged joints by tacking and welding without filler rod. Then, try welding a butt joint using flux and filler rod. Practice and experience provides the visual indication of the melting aluminum so that a satisfactory weld can be performed.

Aluminum gas welding is usually confined to material between 0.031-inch and 0.125-inch in thickness. The weldable aluminum alloys used in aircraft construction are 1100, 3003, 4043, and 5052. Alloy numbers 6053, 6061, and 6151 can also be welded, but since these alloys are in the heat-treated condition, welding should not be done unless the parts can be reheat treated.

Proper preparation prior to welding any metal is essential to produce a satisfactory weld. This preparation is especially critical during oxy-acetylene welding of aluminum. Select the proper torch tip for the thickness of metal being welded. Tip selection for aluminum is always one size larger than one would normally choose for the same thickness in a steel sheet. A rule of thumb: ¾ metal thickness = tip orifice.

Set the proper regulator pressure using the following method for oxy-acetylene welding of aluminum. This method has been used by all aircraft factories since World War II. Start by slowly opening the valve on the oxygen cylinder all the way until it stops to seat the upper packing. Now, barely crack open the acetylene cylinder valve until the needle on the gauge jumps up, then open one-quarter turn more. Check the regulators to ensure the adjusting screws are turned counterclockwise all the way out and loose. Now, open both torch valves wide open, about two full turns (varies with the torch model). Turn the acetylene regulator by adjusting the screw until the torch blows a light puff at a two-inch distance. Now, hold the torch away from the body and light it with the striker, adjusting the flame to a bright yellow bushy flame with the regulator screw. Add oxygen by slowly turning in the oxygen regulator screw to get a loud blue flame with a bright inner cone, perhaps a bit of the "fuel-rich" feather or carburizing secondary cone. By alternately turning in each of the torch valves a little bit, the flame setting can be lowered to what is needed to either tack or weld.

Special safety eyewear must also be used to protect the welder and provide a clear view through the yellow-orange flare given off by the incandescing flux. Special purpose green-glass lens have been designed and patented especially for aluminum oxy-fuel welding by TM Technologies. These lenses cut the sodium orange flare completely and provide the necessary protection from ultraviolet, infrared, blue light, and impact. They meet safety standard ANSI Z87-1989 for a special-purpose lens.

Apply flux either to the material, the filler, or both if needed. The aluminum welding flux is a white powder mixed one part powder to two parts clean spring or mineral water. (Do not use distilled water.) Mix a paste that can be brushed on the metal. Heating the filler or the part with the torch before applying the flux helps the flux dry quickly and not pop off when the torch heat approaches. Proper safety precautions, such as eye protection, adequate ventilation, and avoiding the fumes, are recommended.

The material to be welded must be free of oil or grease. It should be cleaned with a solvent; the best being denatured isopropyl (rubbing) alcohol. A stainless toothbrush should be used to scrub off the invisible aluminum oxide film just prior to welding, but after cleaning with alcohol. Always clean the filler rod or filler wire prior to use with alcohol and a clean cloth.

Make the best possible fit-up for joints to avoid large gaps and select the appropriate filler metal that is compatible with the base metal. The filler should not be a larger diameter than the pieces to be welded. *[Figure 5-26]*

Filler Metal Selection Chart					
Base Metals	1100 3003	5005	5052	5086 DO NOT GAS WELD	6061
6061	4043 (a) 4047	4043 (a) 5183 5356 5556 5554 (d) 5654 (c)	5356 5183 5554 5556 5654 (d) 4043 (a)	5356 5183 5356 5556 5654 (c)	4043 (a) 4047 5556 5183 5554 (d)
5086 DO NOT GAS WELD	5356 4043 (a)	5356 5183 5556	5356 5183 5556	5356 5183 5556	
5052	5183 5356 5556 4043 (a,b)	4043 (a) 5183 5356 5556 4047	5654 (c) 5183 5356 5556 5554 (d) 4043 (a)		
5005	5183 5356 5556 4043 (a,b)	5183 5356 4043 (a,b)			
1100 3003	1110 4043 (a)				
For explanation of (a. b. c. d) see below					

Copyright © 1997 TM Technologies

(a) 4043, because of its Si content, is less susceptible to hot cracking but has less ductility and may crack when planished.
(b) For applications at sustained temperatures above 150F because of intergranular corrosion.
(c) Low temperature service at 150F and below.
(d) 5554 is suitable for elevated temperatures.

NOTE: When choosing between 5356, 5183, 5556, be aware that 5356 is the weakest and 5556 is the strongest, with 5183 in between. Also, 4047 has more Si than 4043, therefore less sensitivity to hot cracking, slightly higher weld shear strength, and less ductility.

Figure 5-26. *Filler metal selection chart.*

Begin by tacking the pieces. The tacks should be applied 1–1½-inches apart. Tacks are done hot and fast by melting the edges of the metal together, if they are touching, or by adding filler to the melting edges when there is a gap. Tacking requires a hotter flame than welding. So, if the thickness of the metal being welded is known, set the length of the inner cone of the flame roughly three to four metal thicknesses in length for tacking. (Example: .063 aluminum sheet = ³⁄₁₆–¼ inch inner cone.)

Once the edges are tacked, begin welding by either starting at the second tack and continuing on, or starting the weld one inch in from the end and then welding back to the edge of the sheet. Allow this initial skip-weld to chill and solidify. Then, begin to weld from the previous starting point and continue all the way to the end. Decrease the heat at the end of the seam to allow the accumulated heat to dissipate. The last inch or so is tricky and must be dabbed to prevent blow-through. (Dabbing is the adding of filler metal in the molten pool while controlling the heat on the metal by raising and lowering the torch.)

Weld bead appearance, or making ringlets, is caused by the movement of the torch and dabbing the filler metal. If the torch and add filler metal is moved at the same time, the ringlet is more pronounced. A good weld has a bead that is not too proud and has penetration that is complete.

Immediately after welding, the flux must be cleaned by using hot (180 °F) water and the stainless steel brush, followed by liberal rinsing with fresh water. If only the filler was fluxed, the amount of cleanup is minimal. All flux residues must be removed from voids and pinholes. If any particular area is suspect to hidden flux, pass a neutral flame over it and a yellow-orange incandescence will betray hiding residues.

Proper scrubbing with an etching solution and waiting no longer than 20 minutes to prime and seal avoids the lifting, peeling, or blistering of the finished topcoat.

Magnesium Welding

Gas welding of magnesium is very similar to welding aluminum using the same equipment. Joint design also follows similar practice to aluminum welding. Care must be taken to avoid designs that may trap flux after the welding is completed, with butt and edge welds being preferred. Of special interest is the high expansion rate of magnesium-based alloys, and the special attention that must be given to avoid stresses being set up in the parts. Rigid fixtures should be avoided; use careful planning to eliminate distortion.

In most cases, filler material should match the base material in alloy. When welding two different magnesium alloys together, the material manufacturer should be consulted for recommendations. Aluminum should never be welded to magnesium. As in aluminum welding, a flux is required to break down the surface oxides and ensure a sound weld. Fluxes sold specifically for the purpose of fusion welding magnesium are available in powder form and are mixed with water in the same manner as for aluminum welding. Use the minimum amount of flux necessary to reduce the corrosive effects and cleaning time required after the weld is finished. The sodium-flare reducing eye protection used for aluminum welding is of the same benefit on magnesium welding.

Welding is done with a neutral flame setting using the same tip size for aluminum welding. The welding technique follows the same pattern as aluminum with the welding being completed in a single pass on sheet gauge material. Generally, the TIG process has replaced gas welding of magnesium due to the elimination of the corrosive flux and its inherent limitations on joint design.

Brazing and Soldering

Torch Brazing of Steel

The definition of joining two pieces of metal by brazing typically meant using brass or bronze as the filler metal. However, that definition has been expanded to include any metal joining process in which the bonding material is a nonferrous metal or alloy with a melting point higher than 800 °F, but lower than that of the metals being joined.

Brazing requires less heat than welding and can be used to join metals that may be damaged by high heat. However, because the strength of a brazed joint is not as great as that of a welded joint, brazing is not used for critical structural repairs on aircraft. Also, any metal part that is subjected to a sustained high temperature should not be brazed.

Brazing is applicable for joining a variety of metals, including brass, copper, bronze and nickel alloys, cast iron, malleable iron, wrought iron, galvanized iron and steel, carbon steel, and alloy steels. Brazing can also be used to join dissimilar metals, such as copper to steel or steel to cast iron.

When metals are joined by brazing, the base metal parts are not melted. The brazing metal adheres to the base metal by molecular attraction and intergranular penetration; it does not fuse and amalgamate with them.

In brazing, the edges of the pieces to be joined are usually beveled as in welding steel. The surrounding surfaces must be cleaned of dirt and rust. Parts to be brazed must be securely fastened together to prevent any relative movement. The strongest brazed joint is one in which the molten filler metal is drawn in by capillary action, requiring a close fit.

A brazing flux is necessary to obtain a good union between the base metal and the filler metal. It destroys the oxides and floats them to the surface, leaving a clean metal surface free from oxidation. A brazing rod can be purchased with a flux coating already applied, or any one of the numerous fluxes available on the market for specific application may be used. Most fluxes contain a mixture of borax and boric acid.

The base metal should be preheated slowly with a neutral soft flame until it reaches the flowing temperature of the filler metal. If a filler rod that is not precoated with flux is used, heat about 2 inches of the rod end with the torch to a dark purple color and dip it into the flux. Enough flux adheres to the rod that it is unnecessary to spread it over the surface of the metal. Apply the flux-coated rod to the red-hot metal with a brushing motion, using the side of the rod; the brass flows freely into the steel. Keep the torch heat on the base metal to melt the filler rod. Do not melt the rod with the torch. Continue to add the rod as the brazing progresses, with a rhythmic dipping action so that the bead is built to a uniform width and height. The job should be completed rapidly and with the fewest possible passes of the rod and torch.

Notice that some metals are good conductors of heat and dissipate the heat more rapidly away from the joint. Other metals are poor conductors that tend to retain the heat and overheat readily. Controlling the temperature of the base metal is extremely important. The base metal must be hot enough for the brazing filler to flow, but never overheated to the filler boiling point. This causes the joint to be porous and brittle.

The key to even heating of the joint area is to watch the appearance of the flux. The flux should change appearance uniformly when even heat is being applied. This is especially important when joining two metals of different mass or conductivity.

The brazing rod melts when applied to the red-hot base metal and runs into the joint by capillary attraction. (Note that molten brazing filler metal tends to flow toward the area of higher temperature.) In a torch heated assembly, the outer metal surfaces are slightly hotter than the interior joint surfaces. The filler metal should be deposited directly adjacent to the joint. Where possible, the heat should be applied to the assembly on the side opposite to where the filler is applied because the filler metal tends to flow toward the source of greater heat.

After the brazing is complete, the assembly or component must be cleaned. Since most brazing fluxes are water soluble, a hot water rinse (120 °F or hotter) and a wire brush remove the flux. If the flux was overheated during the brazing process, it usually turns green or black. In this case, the flux needs to be removed with a mild acid solution recommended by the manufacturer of the flux in use.

Torch Brazing of Aluminum

Torch brazing of aluminum is done using similar methods as brazing of other materials. The brazing material itself is an aluminum/silicon alloy having a slightly lower melting temperature than the base material. Aluminum brazing occurs at temperatures over 875 °F, but below the melting point of the parent metal. This is performed with a specific aluminum brazing flux. Brazing is best suited to joint configurations that have large surface areas in contact, such as the lap, or for fitting fuel tank bungs and fittings. Either acetylene or hydrogen may be used as fuel gas, both being used for production work for many years. Using eye protection that reduces the sodium flare, such as the TM2000 lens, is recommended.

When using acetylene, the tip size is usually the same, or one size smaller than that used for welding of aluminum. A 1–2X reducing flame is used to form a slightly cooler flame, and the torch is held back at a greater distance using the outer envelope as the heat source rather than the inner cone. Prepare the flux and apply in the same manner as the aluminum welding flux, fluxing both the base metal and filler material. Heat the parts with the outer envelope of the flame, watching for the flux to begin to liquefy; the filler may be applied at that point. The filler should flow easily. If the part gets overheated, the flux turns brown or grey. If this happens, reclean and re-flux the part before continuing. Brazing is more easily accomplished on 1100, 3003, and 6061 aluminum alloys. 5052 alloy is more difficult; proper cleaning and practice are vital. There are brazing products sold that have the flux contained in hollow spaces in the filler metal itself, which typically work only on 1100, 3003, and 6061 alloys as the flux is not strong enough for use on 5052. Cleaning after brazing is accomplished the same as with oxy-fuel welding of aluminum, using hot water and a clean stainless brush. The flux is corrosive, so every effort should be made to remove it thoroughly and quickly after the brazing is completed.

Soldering

Soft solder is chiefly used to join copper and brass where a leak proof joint is desired, and sometimes for fitting joints to promote rigidity and prevent corrosion. Soft soldering is generally performed only in minor repair jobs. Soft solder is also used to join electrical connections. It forms a strong union with low electrical resistance.

Soft soldering does not require the heat of an oxy-fuel gas torch and can be performed using a small propane or MAPP® torch, an electrical soldering iron, or in some cases, a soldering copper, that is heated by an outside source, such as an oven or torch. The soft solders are chiefly alloys of tin and lead. The percentages of tin and lead vary considerably in the various solders with a corresponding change in their melting points ranging from 293 °F to 592 °F. Half-and-half (50/50) is the most common general-purpose solder. It contains equal portions of tin and lead and melts at approximately 360 °F.

To get the best results for heat transfer when using an electrical soldering iron or a soldering copper, the tip must be clean and have a layer of solder on it. This is usually referred to as being tinned. The hot iron or copper should be fluxed and the solder wiped across the tip to form a bright, thin layer of solder.

Flux is used with soft solder for the same reasons as with brazing. It cleans the surface area to be joined and promotes the flow by capillary action into the joint. Most fluxes should be cleaned away after the job is completed because they cause corrosion. Electrical connections should be soldered only with soft solder containing rosin. Rosin does not corrode the electrical connection.

Aluminum Soldering

The soldering of aluminum is much like the soldering of other metals. The use of special aluminum solders is required, along with the necessary flux. Aluminum soldering occurs at temperatures below 875 °F. Soldering can be accomplished using the oxy-acetylene, oxy-hydrogen, or even an air-propane torch setup. A neutral flame is used in the case of either oxy-acetylene or oxy-hydrogen. Depending on the solder and flux type, most common aluminum alloys can be soldered. Being of lower melting temperature, a tip one or two sizes smaller than required for welding is used, along with a soft flame setting.

Joint configurations for aluminum soldering follow the same guidelines as any other base material. Lap joints are preferred to tee or butt joints due to the larger surface contact area. However parts, such as heat exchanger tubes, are a common exception to this.

Normally, the parts are cleaned as for welding or brazing, and the flux is applied according to manufacturer's instructions. The parts are evenly heated with the outer envelope of the flame to avoid overheating the flux, and the solder is applied in a fashion similar to that for other base metals. Cleaning after soldering may not be required to prevent oxidation because some fluxes are not corrosive. However, it is always advisable to remove all flux residues after soldering.

Aluminum soldering is commonly used in such applications as the repair of heat exchanger or radiator cores originally using a soldered joint. It is not, however, to be used as a direct replacement repair for brazing or welding.

Silver Soldering

The principle use of silver solder in aircraft work is in the fabrication of high-pressure oxygen lines and other parts that must withstand vibration and high temperatures.

Silver solder is used extensively to join copper and its alloys, nickel and silver, as well as various combinations of these metals and thin steel parts. Silver soldering produces joints of higher strength than those produced by other brazing processes.

Flux must be used in all silver soldering operations to ensure the base metal is chemically clean. The flux removes the film of oxide from the base metal and allows the silver solder to adhere to it.

All silver solder joints must be physically, as well as chemically, clean. The joint must be free of dirt, grease, oil, and/or paint. After removing the dirt, grease, etc., any oxide (rust and/or corrosion) should be removed by grinding or filing the piece until bright metal can be seen. During the soldering operation, the flux continues to keep the oxide away from the metal and aid in the flow of the solder.

The three recommended types of joint for silver soldering are lap, flanged, and edge. With these, the metal is formed to furnish a seam wider than the base metal thickness and provide the type of joint that holds up under all types of loads. *[Figure 5-27]*

Figure 5-27. *Silver solder joints.*

The oxy-acetylene flame for silver soldering should be a soft neutral or slightly reducing flame. That is, a flame with a slight excess of acetylene. During both preheating and application of the solder, the tip of the inner cone of the flame should be held about ½-inch from the work. The flame should be kept moving so that the metal does not overheat.

When both parts of the base metal are at the correct temperature, the flux flows and solder can be applied directly adjacent to the edge of the seam. It is necessary to simultaneously direct the flame over the seam and keep it moving so that the base metal remains at an even temperature.

Gas Metal Arc Welding (TIG Welding)

The TIG process as it is known today is a combination of the work done by General Electric in the 1920s to develop the basic process, the work done by Northrop in the 1940s to develop the torch itself, and the use of helium shielding gas and a tungsten electrode. The process was developed for welding magnesium in the Northrop XP-56 flying wing to eliminate the corrosion and porosity issues with the atomic hydrogen process they had been using with a boron flux. It was not readily used on other materials until the late 1950s when it found merit in welding space-age super alloys. It was also later used on other metals, such as aluminum and steel, to a much greater degree.

Modern TIG welding machines are offered in DC, AC, or with AC/DC configurations, and use either transformer or inverter-based technology. Typically, a machine capable of AC output is required for aluminum. The TIG torch itself has changed little since the first Northrop patent. TIG welding is similar to oxy-fuel welding in that the heat source (torch) is manipulated with one hand, and the filler, if used, is manipulated with the other. A distinct difference is to control the heat input to the metal. The heat control may be preset and fixed by a machine setting or variable by use of a foot pedal or torch mounted control.

Several types of tungsten electrode are used with the TIG welder. Thoriated and zirconiated electrodes have better electron emission characteristics than pure tungsten, making them more suitable for DC operations on transformer-based machines, or either AC or DC with the newer inverter-based machines. Pure tungsten provides a better current balance with AC welding with a transformer based machine, which is advantageous when welding aluminum and magnesium. The equipment manufacturers' suggestions for tungsten type and form should be followed as this is an ever changing part of the TIG technology.

The shape of the electrode used in the TIG welding torch is an important factor in the quality and penetration of the weld. The tip of the electrode should be shaped on a dedicated grinding stone or a special-purpose tungsten grinder to avoid contaminating the electrode. The grinding should be done longitudinally, not radially, with the direction of stone travel away from the tip. *Figure 5-28* shows the effects of a sharp versus blunt electrode with transformer-based machines.

Sharper Electrode	Blunter Electrode
Easy arc starting	Usually harder to start the arc
Handles less amperage	Handles more amperage
Wider arc shape	Narrower arc shape
Good arc stability	Potential for arc wander
Less weld penetration	Better weld penetration
Shorter electrode life	Longer electrode life

Figure 5-28. *Effects of sharp and blunt electrodes.*

When in doubt, consult the machine manufacturer for the latest up-to-date suggestions on tungsten preparation or if problems arise.

The general guidelines for weld quality, joint fit prior to welding, jigging, and controlling warp all apply to this process in the same regard as any other welding method. Of particular note are the additional process steps that sometimes must be taken to perform a quality weld; these are dealt within their appropriate sections.

TIG Welding 4130 Steel Tubing

Welding 4130 with TIG is not much different than welding other steels as far as technique is concerned. The following information generally addresses material under 0.120-inch thick.

Clean the steel of any oil or grease and use a stainless steel wire brush to clean the work piece prior to welding. This is to prevent porosity and hydrogen embrittlement during the welding process. The TIG process is highly susceptible to these problems, much more so than oxy-acetylene welding, so care must be taken to ensure all oils and paint are removed from all surfaces of the parts to be welded.

Use a TIG welder with high-frequency starting to eliminate arc strikes. Do not weld where there is any breeze or draft; the welds should be allowed to cool slowly. Preheating is not necessary for tubing of less than 0.120-inch wall thickness; however, postweld tempering (stress relieving) is still recommended to prevent the possible brittleness of the area surrounding the weld due to the untempered martensite formations caused by the rapid cooling of the weld inherent to the TIG process.

If you use 4130 filler rod, preheat the work before welding and heat treat afterward to avoid cracking. In a critical situation such as this, engineering should be done to determine preheat and postweld heat treatment needed for the particular application.

Weld at a slower speed, make sufficiently large fillets, and make them flat or slightly convex, not concave. After the welding is complete, allow the weldment to cool to room temperature. Using an oxy-acetylene torch set to a neutral flame, heat the entire weldment evenly to 1,100 °F–1,200 °F; hold this temperature for about 45 minutes per inch of metal thickness. The temperature is generally accepted to be a dull red in ambient lighting. Note that for most tubing sections, the temperature needs to be held for only a minute or two. This process is found in most materials engineering handbooks written by The Materials Information Society (ASM) and other engineering sources. When working on a critical component, seek engineering help if there is any doubt.

TIG Welding Stainless Steel

Stainless steels, or more precisely, corrosion-resisting steels, are a family of iron-based metals that contain chromium in amounts ranging from 10 percent to about 30 percent. Nickel is added to some of the stainless steels, which reduces the thermal conductivity and decreases the electrical conductivity. The chromium-nickel steels belong in the AISI 300 series of stainless steels. They are nonmagnetic and have austenitic microstructure. These steels are used extensively in aircraft in which strength or resistance to corrosion at high temperature is required.

All of the austenitic stainless steels are weldable with most welding processes, with the exception of AISI 303, which contains high sulfur, and AISI 303Se, which contains selenium to improve its machinability.

The austenitic stainless steels are slightly more difficult to weld than mild-carbon steel. They have lower melting temperatures, and a lower coefficient of thermal conductivity, so welding current can be lower. This helps on thinner materials because these stainless steels have a higher coefficient of thermal expansion, requiring special precautions and procedures to be used to reduce warping and distortion. Any of the distortion-reducing techniques, such as skip welding or back-step welding, should be used. Fixtures and/or jigs should be used where possible. Tack welds should be applied twice as often as normal.

The selection of the filler metal alloy for welding the stainless steel is based on the composition of the base metal. Filler metal alloys for welding austenitic type stainless include AISI No. 309, 310, 316, 317, and 347. It is possible to weld several different stainless base metals with the same filler metal alloy. Follow the manufacturer's recommendations.

Clean the base metal just prior to welding to prevent the formation of oxides. Clean the surface and joint edges with a nonchlorinated solvent, and brush with a stainless steel wire brush to remove the oxides. Clean the filler material in the same manner.

To form a weld bead, move the torch along the joint at a steady speed using the forehand method. Dip the filler metal into the center of the weld puddle to ensure adequate shielding from the gas.

The base metal needs protection during the welding process by either an inert gas shield, or a backing flux, on both sides of the weld. Back purging uses a separate supply of shielding gas to purge the backside of the weld of any ambient air. Normally, this requires sealing off the tubular structures or using other various forms of shields and tapes to contain the shielding gas. A special flux may also be used on the inside of tubular structures in place of a back purge. This is especially advantageous with exhaust system repairs in which sealing off the entire system is time consuming. The flux is the same as is used for the oxy-acetylene welding process on stainless materials.

TIG Welding Aluminum

TIG welding of aluminum uses similar techniques and filler materials as oxy-fuel welding. Consult with the particular welding machine manufacturer for recommendations on tungsten type and size, as well as basic machine settings for a particular weldment because this varies with specific machine types. Typically, the machine is set to an AC output waveform because it causes a cleaning action that breaks up surface oxides. Argon or helium shielding gas may be used, but argon is preferred because it uses less by volume than helium. Argon is a heavier gas than helium, providing better cover, and it provides a better cleaning action when welding aluminum.

Filler metal selection is the same as used with the oxy-fuel process; however, the use of a flux is not needed as the shielding gas prevents the formation of aluminum oxide on the surface of the weld pool, and the AC waveform breaks up any oxides already on the material. Cleaning of the base metal and filler follows the same guidelines as for oxy-fuel welding. When welding tanks of any kind, it is a good practice to back-purge the inside of the tank with a shielding gas. This promotes a sound weld with a smooth inner bead profile that can help lessen pinhole leaks and future fatigue failures.

Welding is done with similar torch and filler metal angles as in oxy-fuel welding. The tip on the tungsten is held a short distance (1/16–1/8-inch) from the surface of the material, taking care not to ever let the molten pool contact the tungsten and contaminate it. Contamination of the tungsten must be dealt with by removal of the aluminum from the tungsten and re-grinding the tip to the factory recommended profile.

TIG Welding Magnesium

Magnesium alloys can be welded successfully using the same type joints and preparation that are used for steel or aluminum. However, because of its high thermal conductivity and coefficient of thermal expansion, which combine to cause severe stresses, distortion, and cracking, extra precautions must be taken. Parts must be clamped in a fixture or jig. Smaller welding beads, faster welding speed, and the use of a lower melting point and lower shrinkage filler rods are recommended.

DC, both straight or reverse polarity, and AC, with superimposed high frequency for arc stabilization, are commonly used for welding magnesium. DC reverse polarity provides better cleaning action of the metal and is preferred for manual welding operations.

AC power sources should be equipped with a primary contactor operated by a control switch on the torch or a foot control for starting or stopping the arc. Otherwise, the arcing that occurs while the electrode approaches or draws away from the work piece may result in burned spots on the work.

Argon is the most common used shielding gas for manual welding operations. Helium is the preferred gas for automated welding because it produces a more stable arc than argon and permits the use of slightly longer arc lengths. Zirconiated, thoriated, and pure tungsten electrodes are used for TIG welding magnesium alloys.

The welding technique for magnesium is similar to that used for other non-ferrous metals. The arc should be maintained at about 5/16-inch. Tack welds should be used to maintain fit and prevent distortion. To prevent weld cracking, weld from the middle of a joint towards the end, and use starting and run off plates to start and end the weld. Minimize the number of stops during welding. After a stop, the weld should be restarted about 1/2-inch from the end of the previous weld. When possible, make the weld in one uninterrupted pass.

TIG Welding Titanium

The techniques for welding titanium are similar to those required for nickel-based alloys and stainless steels. To produce a satisfactory weld, emphasis is placed on the surface cleanliness and the use of inert gas to shield the weld area. A clean environment is one of the requirements to weld titanium.

TIG welding of titanium is performed using DC straight polarity. A water-cooled torch, equipped with a ¾-inch ceramic cup and a gas lens, is recommended. The gas lens provides a uniform, nonturbulent inert gas flow. Thoriated tungsten electrodes are recommended for TIG welding of titanium. The smallest diameter electrode that can carry the required current should be used. A remote contactor controlled by the operator should be employed to allow the arc to be broken without removing the torch from the cooling weld metal, allowing the shielding gas to cover the weld until the temperature drops.

Most titanium welding is performed in an open fabrication shop. Chamber welding is still in use on a limited basis, but field welding is common. A separate area should be set aside and isolated from any dirt producing operations, such as grinding or painting. Additionally, the welding area should be free of air drafts and the humidity should be controlled.

Molten titanium weld metal must be totally shielded from contamination by air. Molten titanium reacts readily with oxygen, nitrogen, and hydrogen; exposure to these elements in air or in surface contaminants during welding can adversely affect titanium weld properties and cause weld embrittlement. Argon is preferred for manual welding because of better arc stability characteristics. Helium is used in automated welding and when heavier base metals or deeper penetration is required.

Care must be taken to ensure that the heat affected zones and the root side of the titanium welds are shielded until the weld metal temperature drops below 800 °F. This can be accomplished using shielding gas in three separate gas streams during welding.

1. The first shielding of the molten puddle and adjacent surfaces is provided by the flow of gas through the torch. Manufacturer recommendations should be followed for electrodes, tip grinding, cup size, and gas flow rates.

2. The secondary, or trailing, shield of gas protects the solidified weld metal and the heat affected zone until the temperature drops. Trailing shields are custom-made to fit a specific torch and a particular welding operation.

3. The third, or backup, flow is provided by a shielding device that can take many forms. On straight seam welds, it may be a grooved copper backing bar clamped behind the seam allowing the gas flow in the groove and serving as a heat sink. Irregular areas may be enclosed with aluminum tents taped to the backside of welds and purged with the inert gas.

Titanium weld joints are similar to those employed with other metals. Before welding, the weld joint surfaces must be cleaned and remain free of any contamination during the welding operation. Detergent cleaners and nonchlorinated cleaners, such as denatured isopropyl alcohol, may be used. The same requirements apply to the filler rod, it too must be cleaned and free of all contaminates. Welding gloves, especially the one holding the filler, must be contaminate free.

A good indication and measure of weld quality for titanium is the weld color. A bright silver weld indicates that the shielding is satisfactory and the heat affected zone and backup was properly purged until weld temperatures dropped. Straw-colored films indicate slight contamination, unlikely to affect mechanical properties; dark blue films or white powdery oxide on the weld would indicate a seriously deficient purge. A weld in that condition must be completely removed and rewelded.

Arc Welding Procedures, Techniques, and Welding Safety Equipment

Arc welding, also referred to as stick welding, has been performed successfully on almost all types of metals. This section addresses the procedures as they may apply to fusion welding of steel plate and provides the basic steps and procedures required to produce an acceptable arc weld. Additional instruction and information pertaining to arc welding of other metals can be obtained from training institutions and the various manufacturers of the welding equipment.

The first step in preparing to arc weld is to make certain that the necessary equipment is available and that the welding machine is properly connected and in good working order. Particular attention should be given to the ground connection, since a poor connection results in a fluctuating arc, that is difficult to control.

When using a shielded electrode, the bare end of the electrode should be clamped in its holder at a 90° angle to the jaws. (Some holders allow the electrode to be inserted at a 45° angle when needed for various welding positions.)

Before starting to weld, the following typical list of items should be checked:

• Is the proper personal safety equipment being used, including a welding helmet, welding gloves, protective clothing, and footwear; if not, in an adequately ventilated area, appropriate breathing equipment?

• Has the ground connection been properly made to the work piece and is it making a good connection?

- Has the proper type and size electrode been selected for the job?

- Is the electrode properly secured in the holder?

- Does the polarity of the machine coincide with that of the electrode?

- Is the machine in good working order and is it adjusted to provide the necessary current for the job?

The welding arc is established by touching the base metal plate with the electrode and immediately withdrawing it a short distance. At the instant the electrode touches the plate, a rush of current flows through the point of contact. As the electrode is withdrawn, an electric arc is formed, melting a spot on the plate and at the end of the electrode.

Correctly striking an arc takes practice. The main difficulty in confronting a beginner in striking the arc is sticking the electrode to the work. If the electrode is not withdrawn promptly upon contact with the metal, the high amperage flows through the electrode causing it to stick or freeze to the plate and practically short circuits the welding machine. A quick roll of the wrist, either right or left, usually breaks the electrode loose from the work piece. If that does not work, quickly unclamp the holder from the electrode, and turn off the machine. A small chisel and hammer frees the electrode from the metal so it can be regripped in the holder. The welding machine can then be turned back on.

There are two essentially similar methods of striking the arc. One is the tough or tapping method. When using this method, the electrode should be held in a vertical position and lowered until it is an inch or so above the point where the arc is to be struck. Then, the electrode is lightly tapped on the work piece and immediately lifted to form an arc approximately ¼-inch in length. [Figure 5-29]

Figure 5-29. *Touch method of starting an arc.*

The second (and usually easier to master) is a scratch or sweeping method. To strike the arc by the scratch method, the electrode is held just above the plate at an angle of 20°–25°. The arc should be struck by sweeping the electrode with a wrist motion and lightly scratching the plate. The electrode is then lifted immediately to form an arc. [Figure 5-30]

Figure 5-30. *Scratch/sweeping method of starting the arc.*

Either method takes some practice, but with time and experience, it becomes easy. The key is to raise the electrode quickly, but only about ¼-inch from the base or the arc is lost. If it is raised too slowly, the electrode sticks to the plate.

To form a uniform bead, the electrode must be moved along the plate at a constant speed in addition to the downward feed of the electrode. If the rate of advance is too slow, a wide overlapping bead forms with no fusion at the edges. If the rate is too fast, the bead is too narrow and has little or no fusion at the plate.

The proper length of the arc cannot be judged by looking at it. Instead, depend on the sound that the short arc makes. This is a sharp cracking sound, and it should be heard during the time the arc is being moved down to and along the surface of the plate.

A good weld bead on a flat plate should have the following characteristics:

- Little or no splatter on the surface of the plate.

- An arc crater in the bead of approximately 1⁄16-inch when the arc has been broken.

- The bead should be built up slightly, without metal overlap at the top surface.

- The bead should have a good penetration of approximately 1⁄16-inch into the base metal.

Figure 5-31 provides examples of operator's technique and welding machine settings.

Examples of Good and Bad Stick Welds
Good weld
Travel too fast
Travel too slow
Arc too short
Arc too long
Amperage too high
Amperage too low

Figure 5-31. *Examples of good and bad stick welds.*

When advancing the electrode, it should be held at an angle of about 20° to 25° in the direction of travel moving away from the finished bead. *[Figure 5-32]*

If the arc is broken during the welding of a bead and the electrode is removed quickly, a crater is formed at the point where the arc ends. This shows the depth of penetration or fusion that the weld is getting. The crater is formed by the pressure of the gases from the electrode tip forcing the weld metal toward the edges of the crater. If the electrode is removed slowly, the crater is filled.

Figure 5-32. *Angle of electrode.*

If you need to restart an arc of an interrupted bead, start just ahead of the crater of the previous weld bead. Then, the electrode should be returned to the back edge of the crater. From this point, the weld may be continued by welding right through the crater and down the line of weld as originally planned. *[Figure 5-33]*

Figure 5-33. *Re-starting the arc.*

Once a bead has been formed, every particle of slag must be removed from the area of the crater before restarting the arc. This is accomplished with a pick hammer and wire brush and prevents the slag from becoming trapped in the weld.

Multiple Pass Welding

Grove and fillet welds in heavy metals often require the deposit of a number of beads to complete a weld. It is important that the beads be deposited in a predetermined sequence to produce the soundest welds with the best proportions. The number of beads is determined by the thickness of the metal being welded.

Plates from ⅛-inch to ¼-inch can be welded in one pass, but they should be tacked at intervals to keep them aligned. Any weld on a plate thicker than ¼-inch should have the edges beveled and multiple passes.

The sequence of the bead deposits is determined by the kind of joint and the position of the metal. All slag must be removed from each bead before another bead is deposited. Typical multiple-pass grove welding of butt joints is shown in *Figure 5-34*.

Techniques of Position Welding

Each time the position of a welded joint or the type of joint is changed, it may be necessary to change any one or a combination of the following:

- Current value
- Electrode
- Polarity
- Arc length
- Welding technique

Current values are determined by the electrode size, as well as the welding position. Electrode size is governed by the thickness of the metal and the joint preparation. The electrode type is determined by the welding position. Manufacturers specify the polarity to be used with each electrode. Arc length is controlled by a combination of the electrode size, welding position, and welding current.

Since it is impractical to cite every possible variation occasioned by different welding conditions, only the information necessary for the commonly used positions and welds is discussed here.

Flat Position Welding

There are four types of welds commonly used in flat position welding: bead, groove, fillet, and lap joint. Each type is discussed separately in the following paragraphs.

Bead Weld

The bead weld utilizes the same technique that is used when depositing a bead on a flat metal surface. *[Figure 5-35]* The only difference is that the deposited bead is at the butt joint of two steel plates, fusing them together. Square butt joints may be welded in one or multiple passes. If the thickness of the metal is such that complete fusion cannot be obtained by welding from one side, the joint must be welded from both sides. Most joints should first be tack-welded to ensure alignment and reduce warping.

Groove Weld

Groove welding may be performed on a butt joint or an outside corner joint. Groove welds are made on butt joints where the metal to be welded is ¼-inch or more in thickness. The butt joint can be prepared using either a single or double groove depending on the thickness of the plate. The number of passes required to complete a weld is determined by the thickness of the metal being welded and the size of the electrode being used.

Any groove weld made in more than one pass must have the slag, spatter, and oxide carefully removed from all previous weld deposits before welding over them. Some of the common types of groove welds performed on butt joints in the flat position are shown in *Figure 5-36*.

Fillet Weld

Fillet welds are used to make tee and lap joints. The electrode should be held at an angle of 45° to the plate surface. The electrode should be tilted at an angle of about 15° in the

First pass-string bead, second, and third weave pattern.

Notice the variations of edge preparation and bead patterns as stock becomes progressively larger.

On plate thicknesses ¾" or more, double vee the edges and use multiple-pass welding.

Figure 5-34. *Multiple-pass groove welding of butt joints.*

Figure 5-35. *Proper bead weld.*

Figure 5-36. *Groove welds on butt joints in the flat position.*

Figure 5-37. *Tee joint fillet weld.*

Figure 5-38. *Typical lap joint fillet weld.*

direction of welding. Thin plates should be welded with little or no weaving motion of the electrode and the weld is made in one pass. Fillet welding of thicker plates may require two or more passes using a semicircular weaving motion of the electrode. *[Figure 5-37]*

Lap Joint Weld

The procedure for making fillet weld in a lap joint is similar to that used in the tee joint. The electrode is held at about a 30° angle to the vertical and tilted to an angle of about 15° in the direction of welding when joining plates of the same thickness. *[Figure 5-38]*

Vertical Position Welding

Vertical positing welding includes any weld applied to a surface inclined more than 45° from the horizontal. Welding in the vertical position is more difficult than welding in the flat position because of the force of gravity. The molten metal has the tendency to run down. To control the flow of molten metal, the voltage and current adjustments of the welding machine must be correct.

The current setting, or amperage, is less for welding in the vertical position than for welding in the flat position for similar size electrodes. Additionally, the current used for welding upward should be set slightly higher than the current used for welding downward on the same work piece. When welding up, hold the electrode 90° to the vertical, and weld moving the bead upward. Focus on welding the sides of the joint and the middle takes care of itself. In welding downward, with the hand below the arc and the electrode tilted about 15° upward, the weld should move downward.

Overhead Position Welding

Overhead position welding is one of the most difficult in welding since a very short arc must be constantly maintained to control the molten metal. The force of gravity tends to cause the molten metal to drop down or sag from the plate, so it is important that protective clothing and head gear be worn at all times when performing overhead welding.

For bead welds in an overhead position, the electrode should be held at an angle of 90° to the base metal. In some cases where it is desirable to observe the arc and the crater of the weld, the electrode may be held at an angle of 15° in the direction of welding.

When making fillet welds on overhead tee or lap joints, a short arc should be held, and there should be no weaving of the electrode. The arc motion should be controlled to secure good penetration to the root of the weld and good fusion to the plates. If the molten metal becomes too fluid and tends to sag, the electrode should be whipped away quickly from the center ahead of the weld to lengthen the arc and allow the metal to solidify. The electrode should then be returned immediately to the crater of the weld and the welding continued.

Anyone learning or engaged in arc welding should always have a good view of the weld puddle. Otherwise there is no way to ensure that the welding is in the joint and keeping the arc on the leading edge of the puddle. For the best view, the welder should keep their head off to the side and out of the fumes so they can see the puddle.

Expansion and Contraction of Metals

The expansion and contraction of metal is a factor taken into consideration during the design and manufacturing of all aircraft. It is equally important to recognize and allow for the dimensional changes and metal stress that may occur during any welding process.

Heat causes metals to expand; cooling causes them to contract. Therefore, uneven heating causes uneven expansion, and uneven cooling causes uneven contraction. Under such conditions, stresses are set up within the metal. These forces must be relieved, and unless precautions are taken, warping or buckling of the metal takes place. Likewise, on cooling, if nothing is done to take up the stress set up by the contraction forces, further warping may result; or if the metal is too heavy to permit this change in shape, the stresses remain within the metal itself.

The coefficient of linear expansion of a metal is the amount in inches that a one inch piece of metal expands when its temperature is raised 1 °F. The amount that a piece of metal expands when heat is applied is found by multiplying the coefficient of linear expansion by the temperature rise and multiplying that product by the length of the metal in inches.

Expansion and contraction have a tendency to buckle and warp thin sheet metal ⅛-inch or thinner. This is the result of having a large surface area that spreads heat rapidly and dissipates it soon after the source of heat is removed. The most effective method of alleviating this situation is to remove the heat from the metal near the weld, preventing it from spreading across the whole surface area. This can be done by placing heavy pieces of metal, known as chill bars, on either side of the weld; to absorb the heat and prevent it from spreading. Copper is most often used for chill bars because of its ability to absorb heat readily. Welding fixtures sometimes use this same principle to remove heat from the base metal. Expansion can also be controlled by tack welding at intervals along the joint.

The effect of welding a seam longer than 10 or 12 inches is to draw the seam together as the weld progresses. If the edges of the seam are placed in contact with each other throughout their length before welding starts, the far ends of the seam actually overlap before the weld is completed. This tendency can be overcome by setting the pieces to be welded with the seam spaced correctly at one end and increasing the space at the opposite end. *[Figure 5-39]*

Figure 5-39. *Allowance for a straight butt weld when joining steel sheets.*

The amount of space allowed depends on the type of material, the thickness of the material, the welding process being used, and the shape and size of the pieces to be welded. Instruction and/or welding experience dictates the space needed to produce a stress-free joint.

The weld is started at the correctly spaced end and proceeds toward the end that has the increased gap. As the seam is welded, the space closes and should provide the correct gap at the point of welding. Sheet metal under 1/16-inch can be handled by flanging the edges, tack welding at intervals, and then by welding between the tacks.

There are fewer tendencies for plate stock over ⅛-inch to warp and buckle when welded because the greater thickness limits the heat to a narrow area and dissipates it before it travels far on the plate.

Preheating the metal before welding is another method of controlling expansion and contraction. Preheating is especially important when welding tubular structures and castings. Great stress can be set up in tubular welds by contraction. When welding two members of a tee joint, one tube tends to draw up because of the uneven contraction. If the metal is preheated before the welding operation begins, contraction still takes place in the weld, but the accompanying contraction in the rest of the structure is at almost the same rate, and internal stress is reduced.

Welded Joints Using Oxy-Acetylene Torch

Figure 5-40 shows various types of basic joints.

Figure 5-40. *Basic joints.*

Butt Joints

A butt joint is made by placing two pieces of material edge to edge, without overlap, and then welding. A plain butt joint is used for metals from ¹⁄₁₆-inch to ⅛-inch in thickness. A filler rod is used when making this joint to obtain a strong weld.

The flanged butt joint can be used in welding thin sheets, ¹⁄₁₆-inch or less. The edges are prepared for welding by turning up a flange equal to the thickness of the metal. This type of joint is usually made without the use of a filler rod.

If the metal is thicker than ⅛-inch, it may be necessary to bevel the edges so that the heat from the torch can completely penetrate the metal. These bevels may be either single or double-bevel type or single or double-V type. A filler rod is used to add strength and reinforcement to the weld. *[Figure 5-41]*

Repair of cracks by welding may be considered just another type of butt joint. The crack should be stop drilled at either end and then welded like a plain butt joint using filler rod. In most cases, the welding of the crack does not constitute

Figure 5-41. *Types of butt joints.*

a complete repair and some form of reinforcement is still required, as described in following sections.

Tee Joints

A tee joint is formed when the edge or end of one piece is welded to the surface of another. *[Figure 5-42]* These joints are quite common in aircraft construction, particularly in tubular structures. The plain tee joint is suitable for most thicknesses of metal used in aircraft, but heavier thicknesses require the vertical member to be either single or double-beveled to permit the heat to penetrate deeply enough. The dark areas in *Figure 5-42* show the depth of heat penetration and fusion required. It is a good practice to leave a gap between the parts, about equal to the metal thickness to aid full penetration of the weld. This is common when welding from only one side with tubing clusters. Tight fitment of the parts prior to welding does not provide for a proper weldment unless full penetration is secured, and this is much more difficult with a gapless fitment.

Figure 5-42. *Types of tee joints showing filler penetration.*

Edge Joints

An edge joint is used when two pieces of sheet metal must be fastened together and load stresses are not important. Edge joints are usually made by bending the edges of one or both parts upward, placing the two ends parallel to each other, and welding along the outside of the seam formed by the two joined edges. The joint shown in *Figure 5-43A*, requires no filler rod since the edges can be melted down to fill the seam.

The joint shown in *Figure 5-43B,* being thicker material, must be beveled for heat penetration; filler rod is added for reinforcement.

Figure 5-43. *Edge joints.*

Corner Joints

A corner joint is made when two pieces of metal are brought together so that their edges form a corner of a box or enclosure. *[Figure 5-44]* The corner joint shown in *Figure 5-44A* requires no filler rod, since the edges fuse to make the weld. It is used where the load stress is not important. The type shown in *Figure 5-44B* is used on heavier metals, and filler rod is added for roundness and strength. If a higher stress is to be placed on the corner, the inside is reinforced with another weld bead. *[Figure 5-44C]*

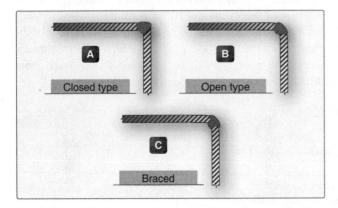

Figure 5-44. *Corner joints.*

Lap Joints

The lap joint is seldom used in aircraft structures when welding with oxy-acetylene, but is commonly used and joined by spot welding. The single lap joint has very little resistance to bending, and cannot withstand the shearing stress to which the weld may be subjected under tension or compression loads. The double lap joint offers more strength, but requires twice the amount of welding required on the simpler, more efficient butt weld. *[Figure 5-45]*

Figure 5-45. *Single and double lap joints.*

Repair of Steel Tubing Aircraft Structure by Welding

Dents at a Cluster Weld

Dents at a cluster weld can be repaired by welding a formed steel patch plate over the dented area and surrounding tubes. Remove any existing finish on the damaged area and thoroughly clean prior to welding.

To prepare the patch plate, cut a section from a steel sheet of the same material and thickness as the heaviest tube damaged. Fashion the reinforcement plate so that the fingers extend over the tubes a minimum of 1½ times the respective tube diameter. The plate may be cut and formed prior to welding or cut and tack welded to the cluster, then heated and formed around the joint to produce a snug smooth contour. Apply sufficient heat to the plate while forming so there is a gap of no more than ¹⁄₁₆-inch from the contour of the joint to the plate.

In this operation, avoid unnecessary heating and exercise care to prevent damage at the point of the angle formed by any two adjacent fingers of the plate. After the plate is formed and tack welded to the joint, weld all the plate edges to the cluster joint. *[Figure 5-46]*

Dents Between Clusters

A damaged tubular section can be repaired using welded split sleeve reinforcement. The damaged member should be carefully straightened and should be stop drilled at the ends of any cracks with a No. 40 drill bit.

Select a length of steel tube of the same material and at least the same wall thickness having an inside diameter approximately equal to the outside diameter of the damaged tube.

Diagonally cut the selected piece at a 30° angle on both ends so the minimum distance of the sleeve from the edge of the crack or dent is not less than 1½ times the diameter of the damaged tube. Then, cut through the entire length of the sleeve and separate the half sections as shown in *Figure 5-47.* Clamp the two sleeve sections in the proper position on the damaged area of the tube. Weld the reinforcement sleeve along the length of the two sides, and weld both ends of the sleeve to the damaged tube.

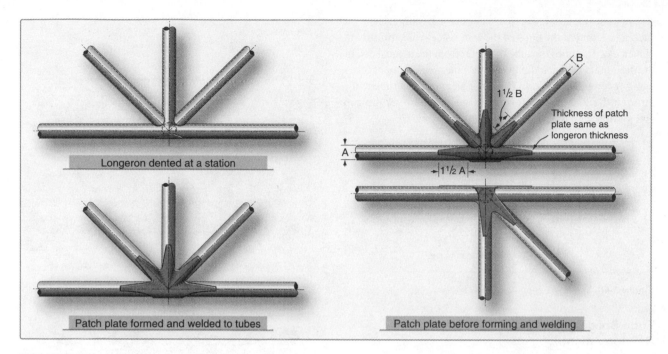

Figure 5-46. *Repair of tubing dented at a cluster.*

Figure 5-47. *Repair using welded sleeve.*

Tube Splicing with Inside Sleeve Reinforcement

If a partial replacement of the tube is necessary, do an inner sleeve splice, especially where you want a smooth tube surface.

Make a diagonal cut to remove the damaged section of the tube, and remove the burrs from the inner and outer cut edges with a file or similar means. Diagonally cut a replacement steel tube of the same material, diameter, and wall thickness to match the length of the removed section of the damaged tube. The replacement tube should allow a ⅛-inch gap for welding at each end to the stubs of the original tube.

Select a length of steel tubing of the same material and at least the same wall thickness with an outside diameter equal to the inside diameter of the damaged tube. From this inner sleeve tube material, cut two sections of tubing, each of such a length that the ends of the inner sleeve is a minimum distance of 1½ times the tube diameter from the nearest end of the diagonal cut. Tack the outer and inner replacement tubes using rosette welds. Weld the inner sleeve to the tube stubs through the ⅛-inch gap forming a weld bead over the gap and joining with the new replacement section. *[Figure 5-48]*

Figure 5-48. *Splicing with inner sleeve method.*

Tube Splicing with Outer Split Sleeve Reinforcement

If partial replacement of a damaged tube is necessary, make the outer sleeve splice using a replacement tube of the same diameter and material. *[Figures 5-49 and 5-50]*

To perform the outer sleeve repair, remove the damaged section of the tube, utilizing a 90° cut at either end. Cut a replacement steel tube of the same material, diameter, and at least the same wall thickness to match the length of the removed portion of the damaged tube. The replacement tube must bear against the stubs of the original tube with a tolerance of ±¹⁄₆₄-inch. The material selected for the outer sleeve must be of the same material and at least the same wall thickness as the original tube. The clearance between the inside diameter of the sleeve and the outside diameter of the original tube may not exceed ¹⁄₁₆-inch.

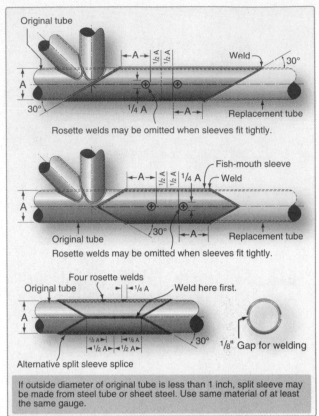

Figure 5-49. *Splicing by the outer sleeve method.*

From this outer sleeve tube material, either cut diagonally or fishmouth two sections of tubing, each of such a length that the nearest end of the outer sleeve is a minimum distance of 1½ tube diameters from the end of the cut on the original tube. Use the fish mouth sleeve wherever possible. Remove all burrs from the edges of the replacement tube, sleeves, and the original tube stubs.

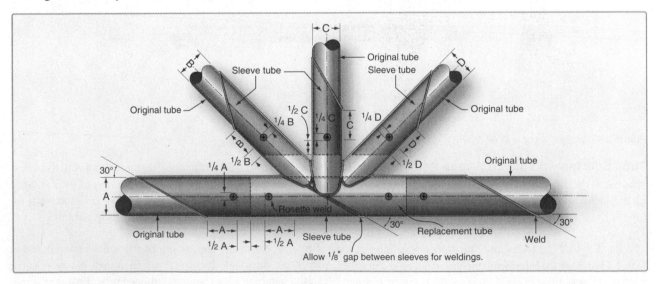

Figure 5-50. *Tube replacement at a cluster by outer sleeve method.*

Slip the two sleeves over the replacement tube, align the replacement tube with the original tube stubs, and slip the sleeves over the center of each joint. Adjust the sleeves to the area to provide maximum reinforcement.

Tack weld the two sleeves to the replacement tube in two places before welding ends. Apply a uniform weld around both ends of one of the reinforcement sleeves and allow the weld to cool. Then, weld around both ends of the remaining reinforcement tube. Allow one sleeve weld to cool before welding the remaining tube to prevent undue warping.

Landing Gear Repairs

Some components of a landing gear may be repaired by welding while others, when damaged, may require replacement. Representative types of repairable and nonrepairable landing gear assemblies are shown in *Figure 5-51*.

The landing gear types shown in A, B, and C of this figure are repairable axle assemblies. They are formed from steel tubing and may be repaired by any of the methods described in this chapter or in FAA Advisory Circular (AC) 43.13-1, Acceptable Methods, Techniques, and Practices—Aircraft Inspection and Repair. However, it must be determined if

Figure 5-51. *Representative types of repairable and nonrepairable landing gear assemblies.*

the assemblies were heat treated. Assemblies originally heat treated must be reheat treated after a welding repair.

The landing gear assembly type D is generally nonrepairable for the following reasons:

1. The lower axle stub is usually made from a highly heat-treated nickel alloy steel and machined to close tolerances. It should be replaced when damaged.

2. During manufacture, the upper oleo section of the assembly is heat treated and machined to close tolerances to assure proper functioning of the shock absorber. These parts would be distorted by any welding repair and should be replaced if damaged to ensure the part was airworthy.

The spring-steel leaf, shown as type E, is a component of a standard main landing gear on many light aircraft. The spring-steel part is, in general, nonrepairable, should not be welded on, and should be replaced when it is excessively sprung or otherwise damaged.

Streamline tubing, used for some light aircraft landing gear, may be repaired using a round insert tube of the same material and having a wall thickness of one gauge thicker than the original streamline tube and inserting and welding as shown in *Figure 5-52*.

A = Slot width (original tube)
B = Outside diameter (insert tube)
C = Streamline tube length of major axis

S.L. size	A	B	C	6A
1"	0.380	0.560	1.340	0.496
1 1/4"	0.380	0.690	1.670	0.619
1 1/2"	0.500	0.875	2.005	0.743
1 3/4"	0.500	1.000	2.339	0.867
2"	0.500	1.125	2.670	0.991
2 1/4"	0.500	1.250	3.008	1.115
2 1/2"	0.500	1.380	3.342	1.239

Round insert tube (B) should be of same material and one gauge thicker than original streamline tube (C).

Figure 5-52. *Streamline landing gear repair using round tube.*

The streamline landing gear tube may also be repaired by inserting a tube of the same streamline original tubing and welding. This can be accomplished by cutting off the trailing edge of the insert and fitting it into the original tube. Once fitted, remove the insert, weld the trailing edge back together, and reinsert into the original tube. Use the figures and weld as indicated in *Figure 5-53*.

Insert tube is of same streamline tubing as original.
A = 2/3" B
B = minor axis length of original streamline tube
C = major axis length of original streamline tube

S.L. size	A	B	C	6A
1"	0.382	0.572	1.340	5.160
1 1/4"	0.476	0.714	1.670	6.430
1 1/2"	0.572	0.858	2.005	7.720
1 3/4"	0.667	1.000	2.339	9.000
2"	0.763	1.144	2.670	10.300
2 1/4"	0.858	1.286	3.008	11.580
2 1/2"	0.954	1.430	3.342	12.880

Figure 5-53. *Streamline tube splice using split insert.*

Engine Mount Repairs

All welding on an engine mount should be performed by an experienced welder and be of the highest quality, since vibration tends to accentuate any minor defect.

The preferred method to repair an engine mount member is by using a larger diameter replacement tube telescoped over the stub of the original member using fish-mouth and rosette welds. 30° scarf welds are also acceptable in place of the fish-mouth welds.

One of the most important aspects to keep in mind when repairing an engine mount is that the alignment of the structure must be maintained. This can be accomplished by attaching to a fixture designed for that purpose, or bolting the mount to an engine and/or airframe before welding.

All cracked welds should be ground out and only high-grade filler rod of the appropriate material should be used.

If all members of the mount are out of alignment, the mount should be replaced with one supplied by the manufacturer or with one built to conform to the manufacturer's drawings and specifications.

Minor damage, such as a crack adjacent to an engine attachment lug, can be repaired by rewelding the ring and extending a gusset or a mounting lug past the damaged area. Engine mount rings that are extensively damaged must not be repaired unless the method of repair is specifically approved by FAA Engineering, a Designated Engineering Representative (DAR), or the repair is accomplished in accordance with FAA-approved instructions.

If the manufacturer stress relieved the engine mount after welding, the engine mount should again be stress relieved after weld repairs are made.

Rosette Welding

Rosette welds are used on many of the type repairs that were previously discussed. They are holes, typically one-fourth the diameter of the original tube, drilled in the outer splice and welded around the circumference for attachment to the inner replacement tube or original tube structure.

Chapter 6

Aircraft Wood and Structural Repair

Aircraft Wood and Structural Repair

Wood was among the first materials used to construct aircraft. Most of the airplanes built during World War I (WWI) were constructed of wood frames with fabric coverings. Wood was the material of choice for aircraft construction into the 1930s. Part of the reason was the slow development of strong, lightweight, metal aircraft structures and the lack of suitable corrosion-resistant materials for all-metal aircraft.

In the late 1930s, the British airplane company DeHavilland designed and developed a bomber named the Mosquito. Well into the late 1940s, DeHavilland produced more than 7,700 airplanes made of spruce, birch plywood, and balsa wood. *[Figure 6-1]*

Figure 6-1. *British DeHavilland Mosquito bomber.*

During the early part of WWII, the U.S. government put out a contract to build three flying boats. Hughes Aircraft ultimately won the contract with the mandate to use only materials not critical to the war, such as aluminum and steel. Hughes designed the aircraft to be constructed out of wood.

After many delays and loss of government funding, Howard Hughes continued construction, using his own money and completing one aircraft. On November 2, 1947, during taxi tests in the harbor at Long Beach, California, Hughes piloted the Spruce Goose for over a mile at an altitude of 70 feet, proving it could fly.

This was the largest seaplane and the largest wooden aircraft ever constructed. Its empty weight was 300,000 pounds with a maximum takeoff weight of 400,000 pounds. The entire airframe, surface structures, and flaps were composed of laminated wood with fabric covered primary control surfaces. It was powered by eight Pratt & Whitney R-4360 radial engines, each producing 3,000 horsepower. *[Figure 6-2]*

Figure 6-2. *Hughes Flying Boat, H-4 Hercules named the Spruce Goose.*

As the aircraft design and manufacturing evolved, the development of lightweight metals and the demand for increased production moved the industry away from aircraft constructed entirely of wood. Some general aviation aircraft were produced with wood spars and wings, but today only a limited number of wood aircraft are produced. Most of those are built by their owners for education or recreation and not for production.

Quite a number of airplanes in which wood was used as the primary structural material still exist and are operating, including certificated aircraft that were constructed during the 1930s and later. With the proper maintenance and repair procedures, these older aircraft can be maintained in an airworthy condition and kept operational for many years.

Wood Aircraft Construction and Repairs

The information presented in this chapter is general in nature and should not be regarded as a substitute for specific instructions contained in the aircraft manufacturer's maintenance and repair manuals. Methods of construction vary greatly with different types of aircraft, as do the various repair and maintenance procedures required to keep them airworthy.

When specific manufacturer's manuals and instructions are not available, the Federal Aviation Administration (FAA) Advisory Circular (AC) 43.13-1, Acceptable Methods, Techniques, and Practices—Aircraft Inspection and Repair, can be used as reference for inspections and repairs. The AC details in the first paragraph, Purpose, the criteria necessary for its use. In part, it stipulates that the use of the AC is acceptable to the FAA for the inspection and minor repair of nonpressurized areas of civil aircraft.

It also specifies that the repairs identified in the AC may also be used as a basis for FAA approval of major repairs when listed in block 8 of FAA Form 337, Major Repair and Alteration, when:

1. The user has determined that it is appropriate to the product being repaired;

2. It is directly applicable to the repair being made; and

3. It is not contrary to manufacturer's data.

Certificated mechanics that have the experience of working on wooden aircraft are becoming rare. Title 14 of the Code of Federal Regulations (14 CFR) part 65 states in part that a certificated mechanic may not perform any work for which he or she is rated unless he or she has performed the work concerned at an earlier date. This means that if an individual does not have the previous aviation woodworking experience performing the repair on an aircraft, regulation requires a certificated and appropriately rated mechanic or repairman who has had previous experience in the operation concerned to supervise that person.

The ability to inspect wood structures and recognize defects (dry rot, compression failures, etc.) can be learned through experience and instruction from knowledgeable certificated mechanics and appropriately qualified technical instructors.

Inspection of Wood Structures

To properly inspect an aircraft constructed or comprised of wood components, the aircraft must be dry. It should be placed in a dry, well-ventilated hanger with all inspection covers, access panels, and removable fairings opened and removed. This allows interior sections and compartments to thoroughly dry. Wet, or even damp, wood causes swelling and makes it difficult to make a proper determination of the condition of the glue joints.

If there is any doubt that the wood is dry, a moisture meter should be utilized to verify the percentage of moisture in the structure. Nondestructive meters are available that check moisture without making holes in the surface. The ideal range is 8–12 percent, with any reading over 20 percent providing an environment for the growth of fungus in the wood.

External and Internal Inspection

The inspection should begin with an examination of the external surface of the aircraft. This provides a general assessment of the overall condition of the wood and structure. The wings, fuselage, and empennage should be inspected for undulation, warping, or any other disparity from the original shape. Where the wings, fuselage, or empennage structure and skins form stressed structures, no departure from the original contour or shape is permissible. *[Figure 6-3]*

Where light structures using single plywood covering are concerned, some slight sectional undulation or bulging between panels may be permissible if the wood and glue are sound. However, where such conditions exist, a careful check must be made of the attachment of the plywood to its supporting structure. A typical example of a distorted single plywood structure is illustrated in *Figure 6-4*.

The contours and alignment of leading and trailing edges are of particular importance. A careful check should be made for any deviation from the original shape. Any distortion of these light plywood and spruce structures is indicative of deterioration, and a detailed internal inspection has to be made for security of these parts to the main wing structure. If deterioration is found in these components, the main wing structure may also be affected.

Figure 6-3. *Cross sectional view of a stressed skin structure.*

Figure 6-4. *A distorted single plywood structure.*

Splits in the fabric covering on plywood surfaces must be investigated to ascertain whether the plywood skin beneath is serviceable. In all cases, remove the fabric and inspect the plywood, since it is common for a split in the plywood skin to initiate a similar defect in the protective fabric covering.

Although a preliminary inspection of the external structure can be useful in assessing the general condition of the aircraft, note that wood and glue deterioration can often take place inside a structure without any external indications. Where moisture can enter a structure, it seeks the lowest point, where it stagnates and promotes rapid deterioration. A musty or moldy odor apparent as you remove the access panels during the initial inspection is a good indication of moisture, fungal growth, and possible decay.

Glue failure and wood deterioration are often closely related, and the inspection of glued joints must include an examination of the adjacent wood structure. NOTE: Water need not be present for glue deterioration to take place.

The inspection of a complete aircraft for glue or wood deterioration requires scrutiny of parts of the structure that may be known, or suspected, trouble spots. In many instances, these areas are boxed in or otherwise inaccessible. Considerable dismantling may be required. It may be necessary to cut access holes in some of the structures to facilitate the inspection. Do such work only in accordance with approved drawings or instructions in the maintenance manual for the aircraft concerned. If drawings and manuals are not available, engineering review may be required before cutting access holes.

Glued Joint Inspection

The inspection of glued joints in wooden aircraft structures presents considerable difficulties. Even where access to the joint exists, it is still difficult to positively assess the integrity of the joint. Keep this in mind when inspecting any glue joint.

Some common factors in premature glue deterioration include:

- Chemical reactions of the glue caused by aging or moisture, extreme temperatures, or a combination of these factors, and

- Mechanical forces caused mainly by wood shrinkage, and

- Development of fungal growths.

An aircraft painted in darker colors experiences higher skin temperatures and heat buildup within its structure. Perform a more detailed inspection on a wooden aircraft structure immediately beneath the upper surfaces for signs of deteriorating adhesives.

Aircraft that are exposed to large cyclic changes of temperature and humidity are especially prone to wood shrinkage that may lead to glue joint deterioration. The amount of movement of a wooden member due to these changes varies with the size of each member, the rate of growth of the tree from which it was cut, and the way the wood was converted in relation to the grain.

This means that two major structural members joined to each other by glue are not likely to have identical characteristics. Over a period of time, differential loads are transmitted across the glue joint because the two members do not react identically. This imposes stresses in the glue joint that can normally be accommodated when the aircraft is new and for some years afterwards. However, glue tends to deteriorate with age, and stresses at the glued joints may cause failure of the joints. This is a fact even when the aircraft is maintained under ideal conditions.

The various cuts of lumber from a tree have tendency to shrink and warp in the direction(s) indicated in the yellow area around each cut in *Figure 6-5*.

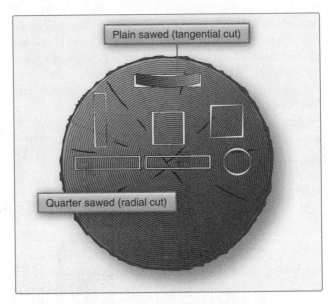

Figure 6-5. *Effects of shrinkage on the various shapes during drying from the green condition.*

When checking a glue line (the edge of the glued joint) for condition, all protective coatings of paint should be removed by careful scraping. It is important to ensure that the wood is not damaged during the scraping operation. Scraping should cease immediately when the wood is revealed in its natural state and the glue line is clearly discernible. At this point in the inspection, it is important that the surrounding wood is dry; otherwise, you will get a false indication of the integrity of the glue line due to swelling of the wood and subsequent closing of the joint.

Inspect the glue line using a magnifying glass. Where the glue line tends to part, or where the presence of glue cannot be detected or is suspect, probe the glue line with a thin feeler gauge. If any penetration is observed, the joint is defective. The structure usually dictates the feeler gauge thickness, but use the thinnest feeler gauge whenever possible. The illustration indicates the points a feeler gauge should probe. [Figure 6-6]

Pressure exerted on a joint either by the surrounding structure or by metal attachment devices, such as bolts or screws, can cause a false appearance of the glue condition. The joint must be relieved of this pressure before the glue line inspection is performed.

A glued joint may fail in service as a result of an accident or because of excessive mechanical loads having been imposed upon it. Glued joints are generally designed to take shear loads. If a joint is expected to take tension loads, it is secured by a number of bolts or screws in the area of tension loading. In all cases of glued joint failure, whatever the direction of loading, there should be a fine layer of wood fibers adhering to the glue. The presence of fibers usually indicates that the joint itself is not at fault.

Examination of the glue under magnification that does not reveal any wood fibers, but shows an imprint of the wood grain, indicates that the cause of the failure was the predrying of the glue before applying pressure during the manufacture of the joint. If the glue exhibits an irregular appearance with star-shaped patterns, this is an indication that precuring of the glue occurred before pressure was applied, or that pressure

had been incorrectly applied or maintained on the joint. If there is no evidence of wood fiber adhesion, there may also be glue deterioration.

Wood Condition

Wood decay and dry rot are usually easy to detect. Decay may be evident as either a discoloration or a softening of the wood. Dry rot is a term loosely applied to many types of decay, but especially to a condition that, in an advanced stage, permits the wood to be crushed to a dry powder. The term is actually a misnomer for any decay, since all fungi require considerable moisture for growth.

Dark discolorations of the wood or gray stains running along the grain are indicative of water penetration. If such discoloration cannot be removed by light scraping, replace the part. Disregard local staining of the wood by dye from a synthetic adhesive hardener.

In some instances where water penetration is suspected, a few screws removed from the area in question reveal, by their degree of corrosion, the condition of the surrounding joint. [Figure 6-7]

Another method of detecting water penetration is to remove the bolts holding the fittings at spar root-end joints, aileron hinge brackets, etc. Corrosion on the surface of such bolts and wood discoloration provide a useful indication of water penetration.

Plain brass screws are normally used for reinforcing glued wooden members. For hardwoods, such as mahogany or ash,

Figure 6-6. *Inspection points for laminated glue joints.*

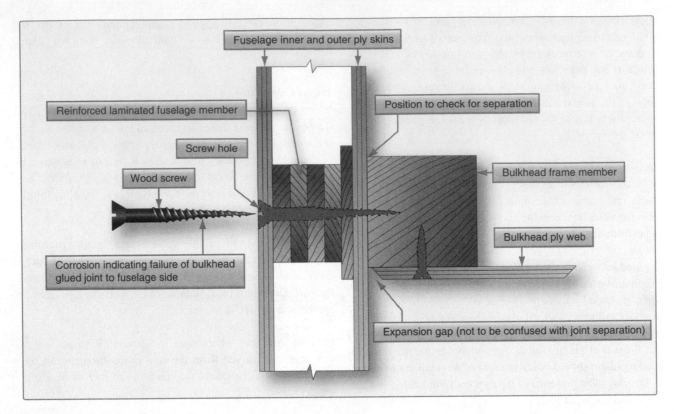

Figure 6-7. *Checking a glued joint for water penetration.*

steel screws may be used. Unless specified by the aircraft manufacturer, replace removed screws with new screws of identical length, but one gauge larger in diameter.

Inspection experience with a particular type of aircraft provides insight to the specific areas most prone to water penetration and moisture entrapment. Wooden aircraft are more prone to the damaging effects of water, especially without the protection of covered storage. Control system openings, fastener holes, cracks or breaks in the finish, and the interfaces of metal fittings and the wood structure are points that require additional attention during an inspection. Additionally, windshield and window frames, the area under the bottom of entrance and cargo doors, and the lower sections of the wing and fuselage are locations that require detailed inspections for water damage and corrosion on all aircraft.

The condition of the fabric covering on plywood surfaces provides an indication of the condition of the wood underneath. If there is any evidence of poor adhesion, cracks in the fabric, or swelling of the wood, remove the fabric to allow further inspection. The exposed surface shows water penetration by the existence of dark gray streaks along the grain and dark discoloration at ply joints or screw holes.

Cracks in wood spars are often hidden under metal fittings or metal rib flanges and leading edge skins. Any time a reinforcement plate exists that is not feathered out on its ends, a stress riser exists at the ends of the plate. A failure of the primary structure can be expected at this point. *[Figure 6-8]*

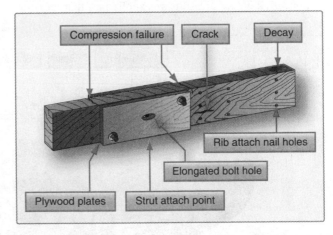

Figure 6-8. *Areas likely to incur structural damage.*

As part of the inspection, examine the structure for other defects of a mechanical nature, including any location where bolts secure fittings that take load-carrying members, or where the bolts are subject to landing or shear loads. Remove the bolts and examine the holes for elongation or surface crushing of the wood fibers. It is important to ensure the bolts are a good fit in the holes. Check for evidence of bruises or crushing of the structural member, which can be caused by overtorquing of the bolts.

Check all metal fittings that are attached to a wood structure for looseness, corrosion, cracks, or bending. Areas of particular concern are strut attach fittings, spar butt fittings, aileron and flap hinges, jury strut fittings, compression struts, control cable pulley brackets, and landing gear fittings. All exposed end grain wood, particularly the spar butts, should be inspected for cracking or checking.

Inspect structural members for compression failures, which is indicated by rupture across the wood fibers. This is a serious defect that can be difficult to detect. If a compression failure is suspected, a flashlight beam shown along the member, and running parallel to the grain, will assist in revealing it. The surface will appear to have minute ridges or lines running across the grain. Particular attention is necessary when inspecting any wooden member that has been subjected to abnormal bending or compression loads during a hard landing. If undetected, compression failures of the spar may result in structural failure of the wing during flight. *[Figure 6-9]*

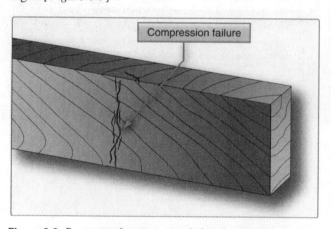

Figure 6-9. *Pronounced compression failure in wood beam.*

When a member has been subjected to an excessive bending load, the failure appears on the surface that has been compressed. The surface subject to tension normally shows no defects. In the case of a member taking an excessive direct compression load, the failure is apparent on all surfaces.

The front and rear spars should be checked for longitudinal cracks at the ends of the plywood reinforcement plates where the lift struts attach. *[Figure 6-8]* Check the ribs on either side of the strut attach points for cracks where the cap strips pass over and under the spars, and for missing or loose

rib-to-spar attach nails. All spars, those in the wing(s) and empennage, should be inspected on the face and top surface for compression cracks. A borescope can be utilized by accessing existing inspection holes.

Various mechanical methods can be employed to enhance the visual inspection of wood structures. Tapping the subject area with a light plastic hammer or screwdriver handle should produce a sharp solid sound. If the suspected area sounds hollow and dull, further inspection is warranted. Use a sharp metal awl or thin-bladed screwdriver to probe the area. The wood structure should be solid and firm. If the area is soft and mushy, the wood is rotted and disassembly and repair of the structure is necessary.

Repair of Wood Aircraft Structures

The standard for any repair is that it should return the aircraft or component to its original condition in strength, function, and aerodynamic shape. It should also be accomplished in accordance with the manufacturer's specifications and/or instructions, or other approved data.

The purpose of repairing all wood structural components is to obtain a structure as strong as the original. Major damage probably requires replacement of the entire damaged assembly, but minor damage can be repaired by removing or cutting away the damaged members and replacing them with new sections. This replacement may be accomplished by gluing, glue and nails, or glue and screw-reinforced splicing.

Materials

Several forms of wood are commonly used in aircraft.

- Solid wood or the adjective "solid" used with such nouns as "beam" or "spar" refers to a member consisting of one piece of wood.

- Laminated wood is an assembly of two or more layers of wood that have been glued together with the grain of all layers or laminations approximately parallel.

- Plywood is an assembled product of wood and glue that is usually made of an odd number of thin plies, or veneers, with the grain of each layer placed 90° with the adjacent ply or plies.

- High-density material includes compreg, impreg, or similar commercially made products, heat-stabilized wood, or any of the hardwood plywoods commonly used as bearing or reinforcement plates.

Suitable Wood

The various species of wood listed in *Figure 6-10* are acceptable for structural purposes when used for the repair of aircraft. Spruce is the preferred choice and the standard by which the other wood is measured. *Figure 6-10* provides a comparison of other wood that may be suitable for aircraft repair. It lists the strength and characteristics of the wood in comparison to spruce. The one item common to all the species is that the slope of the grain cannot be steeper than 1:15.

All solid wood and plywood used for the construction and repair of aircraft should be of the highest quality and grade. For certificated aircraft, the wood should have traceability to a source that can provide certification to a military specification (MIL-SPEC). The term "aircraft quality" or "aircraft grade" is referred to and specified in some repair documents, but that grade wood cannot be purchased from a local lumber company. To purchase the material, contact one of the specialty aircraft supply companies and request a certification document with the order. The MIL-SPEC for solid spruce is MIL-S-6073 and for plywood it is MIL-P-6070B.

When possible, fabricated wood components should be purchased from the aircraft manufacturer, or someone who may have a Parts Manufacturer Approval (PMA) to produce replacement parts for the aircraft. With either of these sources supplying the wood components, the mechanic can be assured of installing approved material. At the completion of the repair, as always, it is the responsibility of the person returning the aircraft to service to determine the quality of the replacement wood and the airworthiness of the subsequent repair.

Species of Wood	Strength Properties (as compared to spruce)	Maximum Permissible Grain Deviation (slope of grain)	Remarks
1	2	3	4
Spruce (Picea) Sitka (P. sitchensis) Red (P. rubra) White (P. glauca)	100%	1.15	Excellent for all uses. Considered standard for this table.
Douglas fir (Pseudotsuga taxifolia)	Exceeds spruce	1.15	May be used as substitute for spruce in same sizes or in slightly reduced sizes if reductions are substantiated. Difficult to work with hand tools. Some tendency to split and splinter during fabrication and much greater care in manufacture is necessary. Large solid pieces should be avoided due to inspection difficulties. Satisfactory for gluing .
Noble fir (Abies procera, also known as Abies nobilis)	Slightly exceeds spruce except 8% deficient in shear	1.15	Satisfactory characteristics of workability, warping, and splitting. May be used as direct substitute for spruce in same sizes if shear does not become critical. Hardness somewhat less than spruce. Satisfactory for gluing.
Western hemlock (Tsuga heterophylla)	Slightly exceeds spruce	1.15	Less uniform in texture than spruce. May be used as direct substitute for spruce. Upland growth superior to lowland growth. Satisfactory for gluing.
Northern white pine, also known as Eastern white pine (Pinus strobus)	Properties between 85% and 96% those of spruce	1.15	Excellent working qualities and uniform in properties, but somewhat low in hardness and shock-resistance. Cannot be used as substitute for spruce without increase in sizes to compensate for lesser strength. Satisfactory for gluing.
Port Orford white cedar (Chamaecyparis lawsoniana)	Exceeds spruce	1.15	May be used as substitute for spruce in same sizes or in slightly reduced sizes if reductions are substantiated. Easy to work with hand tools. Gluing is difficult, but satisfactory joints can be obtained if suitable precautions are taken.
Yellow poplar (Liriodendron tulipifera)	Slightly less than spruce except in compression (crushing) and shear	1.15	Excellent working qualities. Should not be used as a direct substitute for spruce without carefully accounting for slightly reduced strength properties. Somewhat low in shock-resistance. Satisfactory for gluing.

Figure 6-10. *Selection and properties of wood for aircraft repairs.*

To help determine the suitability of the wood, inspect it for defects that would make it unsuitable material to repair or construct an aircraft. The type, location, and amount or size of the defects grade the wood for possible use. All woods used for structural repair of aircraft are classified as softwood. Softwood is typically used for construction and is graded based on strength, load carrying ability, and safety. Hardwoods, on the other hand, are typically appearance woods and are graded based on the number and size of clear cuttings from the tree.

Defects Permitted

The following defects are permitted in the wood species used for aircraft repair that are identified in *Figure 6-10:*

1. Cross grain—Spiral grain, diagonal grain, or a combination of the two is acceptable if the grain does not diverge from the longitudinal axis of the material more than specified in *Figure 6-10* column 3. A check of all four faces of the board is necessary to determine the amount of divergence. The direction of free-flowing ink frequently assists in determining grain direction.

2. Wavy, curly, and interlocked grain—Acceptable, if local irregularities do not exceed limitations specified for spiral and diagonal grain.

3. Hard knots—Sound, hard knots up to ⅜-inch in diameter are acceptable if: (1) they are not projecting portions of I-beams, along the edges of rectangular or beveled unrouted beams, or along the edges of flanges of box beams (except in portions of low stress); (2) they do not cause grain divergence at the edges of the board or in the flanges of a beam more than specified in *Figure 6-10* column 3; and (3) they are in the center third of the beam and not closer than 20-inches to another knot or other defect (pertains to ⅜-inch knots; smaller knots may be proportionately closer). Knots greater than ¼-inch must be used with caution.

4. Pin knot clusters—small clusters are acceptable if they produce only a small effect on grain direction.

5. Pitch pockets—Acceptable in center portion of a beam if they are at least 14-inches apart when they lie in the same growth ring and do not exceed 1½-inches in length by ⅛-inch width by ⅛-inch depth, and if they are not along the projecting portions of I-beams, along the edges of rectangular or beveled unrouted beams, or along the edges of the flanges of box beams.

6. Mineral streaks—acceptable if careful inspection fails to reveal any decay.

Defects Not Permitted

The following defects are not permitted in wood used for aircraft repair. If a defect is listed as unacceptable, please refer to the previous section, Defects Permitted, for acceptable conditions.

1. Cross grain—unacceptable.

2. Wavy, curly, and interlocked grain – unacceptable.

3. Hard knots—unacceptable.

4. Pin knot clusters—unacceptable, if they produce large effect on grain direction.

5. Spike knots—knots running completely through the depth of a beam perpendicular to the annual rings and appear most frequently in quarter-sawed lumber. Reject wood containing this defect.

6. Pitch pockets—unacceptable.

7. Mineral streaks—unacceptable, if accompanied by decay.

8. Checks, shakes, and splits—checks are longitudinal cracks extending, in general, across the annual rings. Shakes are longitudinal cracks usually between two annual rings. Splits are longitudinal cracks caused by artificially induced stress. Reject wood containing these defects.

9. Compression—very detrimental to strength and is difficult to recognize readily, compression wood is characterized by high specific gravity, has the appearance of an excessive growth of summer wood, and in most species shows little contrast in color between spring wood and summer wood. If in doubt, reject the material or subject samples to toughness machine test to establish the quality of the wood. Reject all material containing compression wood.

10. Compression failures—caused from overstress in compression due to natural forces during the growth of the tree, felling trees on rough or irregular ground, or rough handling of logs or lumber. Compression failures are characterized by a buckling of the fibers that appears as streaks substantially at right angles to the grain on the surface of the piece, and vary from pronounced failures to very fine hairlines that require close inspection to detect. Reject wood containing obvious failures. If in doubt, reject the wood or make a further inspection in the form of microscopic examination or toughness test, the latter being more reliable.

11. Tension—forming on the upper side of branches and leaning trunks of softwood trees, tension wood is caused by the natural overstressing of trying to pull the branches and leaning trunk upright. It is typically harder, denser, and may be darker in color than normal wood, and is a serious defect, having higher than usual longitudinal shrinkage that may break down due to uneven shrinkage. When in doubt, reject the wood.

12. Decay—rot, dote, red heart, purple heart, etc., must not appear on any piece. Examine all stains and discoloration carefully to determine whether or not they are harmless or in a stage of preliminary or advanced decay.

Glues (Adhesives)

Because adhesives play a critical role in the bonding of aircraft structure, the mechanic must employ only those types of adhesives that meet all of the performance requirements necessary for use in certificated aircraft. The product must be used strictly in accordance with the aircraft and adhesive manufacturer's instructions. All instructions must be followed exactly, including the mixing ratios, the ambient and surface temperatures, the open and closed assembly times, the gap-filling ability, or glue line thickness, the spread of the adhesive, whether one or two surfaces, and the amount of clamping pressure and time required for full cure of the adhesive.

AC 43.13-1 provides information on the criteria for identifying adhesives that are acceptable to the FAA. It stipulates the following:

1. Refer to the aircraft maintenance or repair manual for specific instructions on acceptable adhesive selection for use on that type aircraft.

2. Adhesives meeting the requirements of a MIL-SPEC, Aerospace Material Specification (AMS), or Technical Standard Order (TSO) for wooden aircraft structures are satisfactory, providing they are found to be compatible with existing structural materials in the aircraft and fabrication methods to be used in the repair.

New adhesives have been developed in recent years, and some of the older ones are still in use. Some of the more common adhesives that have been used in aircraft construction and repair include casein glue, plastic resin glue, resorcinol glue, and epoxy adhesives.

Casein glue should be considered obsolete for all aircraft repairs. The adhesive deteriorates when exposed to moisture and temperature variations that are part of the normal operating environment of any aircraft.

NOTE: Some modern adhesives are incompatible with casein adhesive. If a joint that has previously been bonded with casein is to be reglued using another type adhesive, all traces of the casein must be scraped off before a new adhesive is applied. If any casein adhesive is left, residual alkalinity may cause the new adhesive to fail to cure properly.

Plastic resin glue, also known as a urea-formaldehyde adhesive, came on the market in the middle to late 1930s. Tests and practical applications have shown that exposure to moist conditions, and particularly to a warm humid environment, under swell-shrink stress, leads to deterioration and eventual failure of the bond. For these reasons, plastic resin glue should be considered obsolete for all aircraft repairs. Discuss any proposed use of this type adhesive on aircraft with FAA engineering prior to use.

Resorcinol glue, or resorcinol-formaldehyde glue, is a two-component synthetic adhesive consisting of resin and a catalyst. It was first introduced in 1943 and almost immediately found wide application in the wood boat-building and wood aircraft industry in which the combination of high durability and moderate-temperature curing was extremely important. It has better wet-weather and ultraviolet (UV) resistance than other adhesives. This glue meets all strength and durability requirements if the fit of the joint and proper clamping pressure results in a very thin and uniform bond line.

The manufacturer's product data sheets must be followed regarding mixing, usable temperature range, and the open and close assembly times. It is very important that this type of glue is used at the recommended temperatures because the full strength of the joint cannot be relied on if assembly and curing temperatures are below 70 °F. With that in mind, higher temperatures shorten the working life because of a faster cure rate, and open and closed assembly times must be shortened.

Epoxy adhesive is a two-part synthetic resin product that depends less on joint quality and clamping pressure. However, many epoxies have not exhibited joint durability in the presence of moisture and elevated temperatures and are not recommended for structural aircraft bonding unless they meet the acceptable standards set forth by the FAA in AC 43.13-1, as referenced earlier in this chapter.

Definition of Terms Used in the Glue Process

• Close contact adhesive—a non-gap-filling adhesive (e.g., resorcinol-formaldehyde glue) suitable for use only in those joints where the surfaces to be joined can be brought into close contact by means of adequate pressure, to allow a glue line of no more than 0.005-inch gap.

- Gap-filling adhesive—an adhesive suitable for use in those joints in which the surfaces to be joined may not be close or in continuous contact (e.g., epoxy adhesives) due either to the impracticability of applying adequate pressure or to the slight inaccuracies of fabricating the joint.

- Glue line—resultant layer of adhesive joining any two adjacent wood layers in the assembly.

- Single spread—spread of adhesive to one surface only.

- Double spread—spread of adhesive to both surfaces and equally divided between the two surfaces to be joined.

- Open assembly time—period of time between the application of the adhesive and the assembly of the joint components.

- Closed assembly time—time elapsing between the assembly of the joints and the application of pressure.

- Pressing or clamping time—time during which the components are pressed tightly together under recommended pressure until the adhesive cures (may vary from 10 to 150 pounds per square inch (psi) for softwoods, depending on the viscosity of the glue).

- Caul—a clamping device, usually two rigid wooden bars, to keep an assembly of flat panel boards aligned during glue-up. It is assembled with long bolts and placed on either side of the boards, one on top and another below, and parallel with the pipe/bar clamps. A caul is usually finished and waxed before each use to keep glue from adhering to it.

- Adhesive pot life—time elapsed from the mixing of the adhesive components until the mixture must be discarded, because it no longer performs to its specifications. The manufacturer's product data sheet may define this as working time or useful life; once expired, the adhesive must not be used. It lists the specific temperature and quantity at which the sample amount can be worked. Pot life is a product of time and temperature. The cooler the mix is kept, within the recommended temperature range, the longer it is usable.

Preparation of Wood for Gluing

Satisfactory glue joints in aircraft should develop the full strength of the wood under all conditions of stress. To produce this result, the conditions involved in the gluing operation must be carefully controlled to obtain a continuous, thin, uniform film of solid glue in the joint with adequate adhesion to both surfaces of the wood. These conditions required:

1. Proper and equal moisture content of wood to be joined (8 to 12 percent).

2. Properly prepared wood surfaces that are machined or planed, and not sanded or sawed.

3. Selection of the proper adhesive for the intended task, which is properly prepared and of good quality.

4. The application of good gluing techniques, including fitment, recommended assembly times, and adequate equal pressure applied to the joint.

5. Performing the gluing operation under the recommended temperature conditions.

The surfaces to be joined must be clean, dry, and free from grease, oil, wax, paint, etc. Keep large prepared surfaces covered with a plastic sheet or masking paper prior to the bonding operation. It is advisable to clean all surfaces with a vacuum cleaner just prior to adhesive application.

Smooth even surfaces produced on planers and joiners with sharp knives and correct feed adjustments are the best surfaces for gluing solid wood. The use of sawn surfaces for gluing has been discouraged for aircraft component assembly because of the difficulty in producing a surface free of crushed fibers. Glue joints made on surfaces that are covered with crushed fibers do not develop the normal full strength of the wood.

Some of the surface changes in plywood, such as glazing and bleed-through, that occur in manufacture and may interfere with the adhesion of glue in secondary gluing are easily recognized. A light sanding of the surface with 220-grit sandpaper in the direction of the grain restores the surface fibers to their original condition, removes the gloss, and improves the adhesion of the glue. In contrast to these recognized surface conditions, wax deposits from cauls used during hot pressing produce unfavorable gluing surfaces that are not easily detected.

Wetting tests are a useful means of detecting the presence of wax. A finely sprayed mist or drops of water on the surface of wax-coated plywood bead and do not wet the wood. This test may also give an indication of the presence of other materials or conditions that would degrade a glue joint. Only a proper evaluation of the adhesion properties, using gluing tests, determines the gluing characteristics of the plywood surfaces.

Preparing Glues for Use

The manufacturer's directions should be followed for the preparation of any glue or adhesive. Unless otherwise specified by the glue manufacturer, clear, cool water should be used with glues that require mixing with water. The recommended proportions of glue, catalyst, and water or other solvent should be determined by the weight of each component. Mixing can be either by hand or machine. Whatever method is used, the glue should be thoroughly mixed and free of air bubbles, foam, and lumps of insoluble material.

Applying the Glue/Adhesive

To make a satisfactorily bonded joint, it is generally desirable to apply adhesive to both surfaces and join in a thin even layer. The adhesive can be applied with a brush, glue spreader, or a grooved rubber roller. Follow the adhesive manufacturer's application instructions for satisfactory results.

Be careful to ensure the surfaces make good contact and the joint is positioned correctly before applying the adhesive. Keep the open assembly time as short as possible and do not exceed the recommended times indicated in the product data sheet.

Pressure on the Joint

To ensure the maximum strength of the bonded surfaces, apply even force to the joint. Non-uniform gluing pressure commonly results in weak areas and strong areas in the same joint. The results of applied pressure are illustrated in *Figure 6-11.*

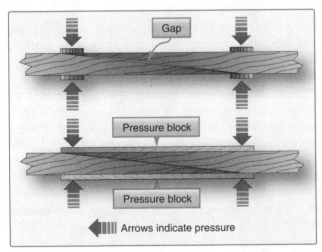

Figure 6-11. *Even distribution of gluing pressure creates a strong, gap-free joint.*

Use pressure to squeeze the glue out into a thin continuous film between the wood layers, to force air from the joint, to bring the wood surfaces into intimate contact with the glue, and to hold them in this position during the setting of the glue.

Pressure may be applied by means of clamps, elastic straps, weight, vacuum bags, or other mechanical devices. Other methods used to apply pressure to joints in aircraft gluing operations range from the use of brads, nails, and screws to the use of electric and hydraulic power presses.

The amount of pressure required to produce strong joints in aircraft assembly operations may vary from 10 to 150 psi for softwoods and as high as 200 psi for hardwoods. Insufficient pressure to poorly machined or fitted wood joints usually results in a thick glue line, indicating a weak joint, and should be carefully avoided.

High clamping pressure is neither essential nor desirable, provided good contact between the surfaces being joined is obtained. When pressure is applied, a small quantity of glue should be squeezed from the joint. This excess should be removed before it sets. It is important that full pressure be maintained on the joint for the entire cure time of the adhesive because the adhesive does not chemically relink and bond if it is disturbed before it is fully cured.

The full curing time of the adhesive is dependent on the ambient temperature; therefore, it is very important to follow the manufacturer's product data sheets for all phases of the gluing operation from the shelf life to the moisture content of the wood to the proper mixing of the adhesive to the application, and especially to the temperature. The successful assembly and fabrication depends on the workmanship and quality of the joints and following the glue manufacturer's instructions.

All gluing operations should be performed above 70 °F for proper performance of the adhesive. Higher temperatures shorten the assembly times, as does coating the pieces of wood with glue and exposing openly to the air. This open assembly promotes a more rapid thickening of the glue than pieces being mated together as soon as the spreading of the glue is completed.

Figure 6-12 provides an example of resorcinol resin glue and the allowable assembly times and gluing pressure when in the open and closed assembly condition. All examples are for an ambient temperature of 75 °F.

Figure 6-13 provides examples of strong and weak glue joints resulting from different gluing conditions. A is a well glued joint with a high percentage of wood failure made under proper conditions; B is a glue-starved joint resulting from the application of excessive pressure with thin glues; C is a dried glue joint resulting from an excessively long assembly time and/or insufficient pressure.

Glue	Gluing Pressure	Type of Assembly	Maximum Assembly Time
Resorcinol resins	100–250 psi	Closed	Up to 50 minutes
	100–250 psi	Open	Up to 12 minutes
	Less than 100 psi	Closed	Up to 40 minutes
	Less than 100 psi	Open	Up to 10 minutes

Figure 6-12. *Examples of differences for open and closed assembly times.*

Figure 6-13. *Strong and weak glue joints.*

Testing Glued Joints

Satisfactory glue joints in aircraft should develop the full strength of the wood under all conditions of stress. Tests should be made by the mechanic prior to gluing a joint of a major repair, such as a wing spar. Whenever possible, perform tests using pieces cut from the actual wood used for the repair under the same mechanical and environmental conditions that the repair will undergo.

Perform a sample test using two pieces of scrap wood from the intended repair, each cut approximately 1" × 2" × 4". The pieces should be joined by overlapping each approximately 2 inches. The type of glue, pressure, and curing time should be the same as used for the actual repair. After full cure, place the test sample in a bench vise and break the joint by exerting pressure on the overlapping member. The fractured glue faces should show a high percentage of at least 75 percent of the wood fibers evenly distributed over the fractured glue surface. *[Figure 6-14]*

Figure 6-14. *An example of good glue joint.*

Repair of Wood Aircraft Components
Wing Rib Repairs

Ribs that have sustained damage may be repaired or replaced, depending upon the type of damage and location in the aircraft. If new parts are available from the aircraft manufacturer or the holder of a PMA for the part, it is advisable to replace the part rather than to repair it.

If you make a repair to a rib, do the work in such a manner and using materials of such quality that the completed repair is at least equal to the original part in aerodynamic function, structural strength, deterioration, and other qualities affecting airworthiness, such as fit and finish. When manufacturer's repair manuals or instructions are not available, acceptable methods of repairing damaged ribs are described in AC 43.13-1 under Wood Structure Repairs.

When necessary, a rib can be fabricated and installed using the same materials and dimensions from a manufacturer-approved drawing or by reference to an original rib. However, if you fabricated it from an existing rib, you must provide evidence to verify that the dimensions are accurate and the materials are correct for the replacement part.

You can repair a cap strip of a wood rib using a scarf splice. The repair is reinforced on the side opposite the wing covering by a spruce block that extends beyond the scarf joint not less than three times the thickness of the strips being repaired. Reinforce the entire splice, including the spruce reinforcing block, on each side with a plywood side plate.

The scarf length bevel is 10 times dimension A (thickness of the rib cap strip) with the spruce reinforcement block being 16 times dimension A (the scarf length plus extension on either end of the scarf). The plywood splice plates should be of the same material and thickness as the original plates used to fabricate the rib. The spruce block should have a 5:1 bevel on each end. [Figure 6-15]

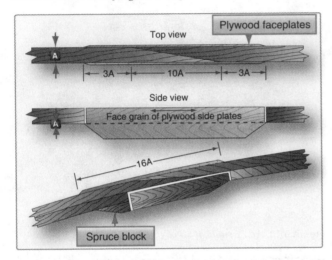

Figure 6-15. *A rib cap strip repair.*

These specific rib repairs describing the use of one scarf splice implies that either the entire forward or aft portion of the cap strip beyond the damage can be replaced to complete the repair and replace the damaged section. Otherwise, replacement of the damaged section may require a splice repair at both ends of the replaced section of the cap strip using the indicated dimensions for cutting and reinforcing of each splice.

When a cap strip is to be repaired at a point where there is a joint between it and cross members of the rib, make the repair by reinforcing the scarf joint with plywood gussets, as shown in *Figure 6-16*.

If a cap strip must be repaired where it crosses a spar, reinforce the joint with a continuous gusset extending over the spar, as shown in *Figure 6-17*.

Figure 6-16. *Cap strip repair at cross member.*

Figure 6-17. *Cap strip repair at a spar.*

The scarf joints referred to in the rib repairs are the most satisfactory method of fabricating an end joint between two solid wood members. When the scarf splice is used to repair a solid wood component, the mechanic must be aware of the direction and slope of the grain. To ensure the full strength of the joint, the scarf cut is made in the general direction of the grain on both connecting ends of the wood and then correctly oriented to each other when glued. [Figure 6-18]

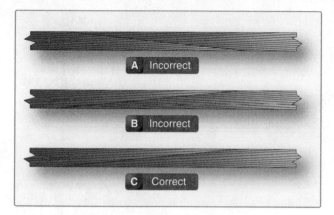

Figure 6-18. *Relationship of scarf slope to grain slope.*

The trailing edge of a rib can be replaced and repaired by removing the damaged portion of the cap strip and inserting a softwood block of white pine, spruce, or basswood. The entire repair is then reinforced with plywood gussets and nailed and glued, as shown in *Figure 6-19*.

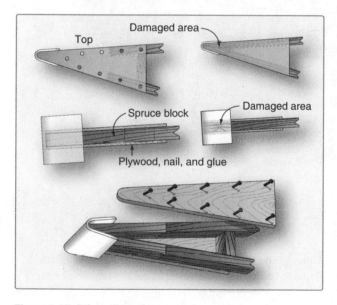

Figure 6-19. *Rib trailing edge repair.*

Compression ribs are of many different designs, and the proper method of repairing any part of this type of rib is specified by the manufacturer. All repairs should be performed using recommended or approved practices, materials and adhesives.

Figure 6-20A illustrates the repair of a compression rib of the I section type (i.e., wide, shallow cap strips, and a center plywood web with a rectangular compression member on each side of the web). The rib damage suggests that the upper and lower cap strips, the web member, and the compression members are cracked completely through. To facilitate this repair, cut the compression members as shown in *Figure 6-20D* and repair as recommended using replacement sections to the rear spar. Cut the damaged cap strips and repair as shown in *Figure 6-20*, replacing the aft section of the cap strips. Plywood side plates are then bonded on each side diagonally to reinforce the damaged web as shown in *Figure 6-20, A-A*.

Figure 6-20B illustrates a compression rib of the type that is a standard rib with rectangle compression members added to one side and a plywood web to the other side. The method used in this repair is essentially the same as in *Figure 6-20A*, except that the plywood reinforcement plate, shown in *Figure 6-20B-B*, is continued the full distance between the spars.

Figure 6-20C illustrates a compression rib of the I type with a rectangular vertical member on each side of the web. The method of repair is essentially the same as in *Figure 6-20A*, except the plywood reinforcement plates on each side, shown in *Figure 6-20C-C*, are continued the full distance between the spars.

Wing Spar Repairs

Wood wing spars are fabricated in various designs using solid wood, plywood, or a combination of the two. [Figure 6-21]

When a spar is damaged, the method of repair must conform to the manufacturer's instructions and recommendations. In the absence of manufacturer's instructions, contact the FAA for advice and approval before making repairs to the spar and following recommendations in AC 43.13-1. If instructions are not available for a specific type of repair, it is highly recommended that you request appropriate engineering

Figure 6-20. *Typical compression rib repair.*

assistance to evaluate and provide guidance for the intended repair.

Shown in *Figure 6-22* is a recommended method to repair either a solid or laminated rectangle spar. The slope of the scarf in any stressed part, such as a spar, should not be steeper than 15 to 1.

Unless otherwise specified by the aircraft manufacturer, a damaged spar may be spliced at almost any point except at wing attachment fittings, landing gear fittings, engine mount fittings, or lift-and-interplane strut fittings. These fittings may not overlap any part of the splice. The reinforcement plates of the splice should not interfere with the proper attachment or alignment of the fittings. Taper reinforcement plates on the ends at a 5:1 slope *[Figure 6-23]*.

Figure 6-21. *Typical splice repair of solid rectangular spar.*

Figure 6-22. *Typical splice repair of solid rectangular spar.*

The use of a scarf joint to repair a spar or any other component of an aircraft is dependent on the accessibility to the damaged section. It may not be possible to utilize a scarf repair where recommended, so the component may have to be replaced. A scarf must be precisely cut on both adjoining pieces to ensure an even thin glue line; otherwise, the joint may not achieve full strength. The primary difficulty encountered in making this type of joint is obtaining the same bevel on each piece. *[Figure 6-24]*

Figure 6-23. *Tapered faceplate.*

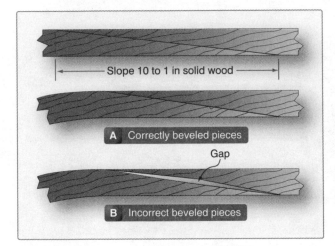

Figure 6-24. *Beveled scarf joint.*

Figure 6-25. *Making a scarf joint.*

Figure 6-26. *Scarf cutting fixture.*

The mating surfaces of the scarf must be smooth. You can machine smooth a saw cut using any of a variety of tools, such as a plane, a joiner, or a router. For most joints, you need a beveled fixture set at the correct slope to complete the cut. *Figure 6-25* illustrates one method of producing an accurate scarf joint.

Once the two bevels are cut for the intended splice, clamp the pieces to a flat guide board of similar material. Then, work a sharp, fine-tooth saw all the way through the joint. Remove the saw, decrease pressure, and tap one of the pieces on the end to close the gap. Work the saw again through the joint. Continue this procedure until the joint is perfectly parallel with matching surfaces. Then, make a light cut with the grain, using a sharp plane, to smooth both mating surfaces.

Another method of cutting a scarf uses a simple scarf-cutting fixture that you can also fabricate for use with a router. Extend the work piece beyond the edge so the finished cut results in a feathered edge across the end of the scarf. *[Figure 6-26]*

There are numerous tools made by individuals, and there are commercial plans for sale with instructions for building scarf-cutting tools. Most of them work, but some are better than others. The most important requirement for the tool is that it produces a smooth, repeatable cut at the appropriate angle.

Local damage to the top or bottom edge of a solid spar may be repaired by removing the damaged portion and fabricating a replacement filler block of the same material as the spar. Full width doublers are fabricated as shown and then all three pieces are glued and clamped to the spar. Nails or screws should not be used in spar repairs. A longitudinal crack in a solid spar may be repaired using doublers made from the proper thickness plywood. Care must be taken to ensure the doublers extend the minimum distance beyond the crack. *[Figure 6-27]*

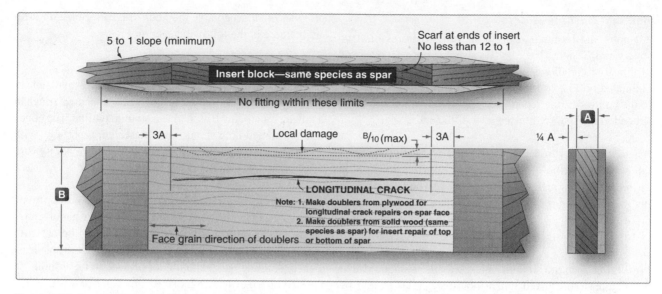

Figure 6-27. *A method to repair damage to solid spar.*

A typical repair to a built-up I spar is illustrated using plywood reinforcement plates with solid wood filler blocks. As with all repairs, the reinforcement plate ends should be feathered out to a 5:1 slope. *[Figure 6-28]*

Repair methods for the other types of spar illustrated at the start of this section all follow the basic steps of repair. The wood used should be of the same type and size as the original spar. Always splice and reinforce plywood webs with the same type of plywood as the original. Do not use solid wood to replace plywood webs because plywood is stronger in shear than solid wood of the same thickness. The splices and scarf cuts must be of the correct slope for the repair with the face grain running in the same direction as the original member. Not more than two splices should be made in any one spar.

When a satisfactory repair to a spar cannot be accomplished, the spar should be replaced. New spars may be obtained from the manufacturer or the holder of a PMA for that part. An owner-produced spar may be installed provided it is made from a manufacturer-approved drawing. Care should be taken to ensure that any replacement spars accurately match the manufacturer's original design.

Figure 6-28. *Repairs to a built-up I spar.*

Bolt and Bushing Holes

All bolts and bushings used in aircraft structures must fit snugly into the holes. If the bolt or bushing is loose, movement of the structure allows it to enlarge the hole. In the case of elongated bolt holes in a spar or cracks in close proximity to the bolt holes, the repair may require a new section to be spliced in the spar, or replacement of the entire spar.

All holes drilled in a wood structure to receive bolts or bushings should be of such size that inserting the bolt or bushing requires a light tapping with a wood or rawhide mallet. If the hole is so tight that heavy blows are necessary, deformation of the wood may cause splitting or unequal load distribution.

For boring accurate smooth holes, it is recommended that a drill press be utilized where possible. Holes should be drilled with sharp bits using slow steady pressure. Standard twist drills can be used in wood when sharpened to a 60° angle. However, a better designed drill was developed for wood boring called a lip and spur or brad point. The center of the drill has a spur with a sharp point and four sharp corners to center and cut rather than walk as a conventional drill sometimes does. It has the outside corner of the cutting edges leading, so that it cuts the periphery of the hole first and maximizes the chance that the wood fibers cut cleanly, leaving a smooth bore.

Forstner bits bore precise, flat bottomed holes in wood, in any orientation with respect to the wood grain. They must be used in a drill press because more force is needed for their cutting action. Also, they are not designed to clear chips from the hole and must be pulled out periodically to do this. A straight, accurate bore-through hole can be completed by drilling through the work piece and into a piece of wood backing the work piece.

All holes bored for bolts that are to hold fittings in place should match the hole diameter in the fitting. Bushings made of steel, aluminum, or plastic are sometimes used to prevent crushing the wood when bolts are tightened. Holes drilled in the wood structure should be sealed after being drilled. This can be accomplished by application of varnish or other acceptable sealer into the open hole. The sealer must be allowed to dry or cure thoroughly prior to the bolts or bushings being installed.

Plywood Skin Repairs

Plywood skin can be repaired using a number of different methods depending on the size of the hole and its location on the aircraft. Manufacturer's instructions, when available, should be the first source of a repair scheme. AC 43.13-1 provides other acceptable methods of repair. Some of those are featured in the following section.

Fabric patch

A fabric patch is the simplest method to repair a small hole in plywood. This repair is used on holes not exceeding 1-inch in diameter after being trimmed to a smooth outline. The edges of the trimmed hole should first be sealed, preferably with a two-part epoxy varnish. This varnish requires a long cure time, but it provides the best seal on bare wood.

The fabric used for the patch should be of an approved material using the cement recommended by the manufacturer of the fabric system. The fabric patch should be cut with pinking shears and overlap the plywood skin by at least 1-inch. A fabric patch should not be used to repair holes in the leading edge of a wing, in the frontal area of the fuselage, or nearer than 1-inch to any frame member.

Splayed Patch

A splayed patch is a flush patch. The term splayed denotes that the edges of the patch are tapered, with the slope cut at a 5:1 ratio to the thickness of the skin. This may be used for small holes where the largest dimension of the hole to be repaired is not more than 15 times the skin thickness and the skin is not more than $\frac{1}{10}$-inch thick. This calculates to nothing larger than a 1½-inch trimmed hole in very thin plywood.

Using the sample $\frac{1}{10}$-inch thick plywood and a maximum trimmed hole size of 1½-inches, and cutting a 5:1 scarf, results in a 2½-inches round section to be patched. The patch should be fabricated with a 5:1 scarf, from the same type and thickness plywood as the surface being repaired.

Glue is applied to the beveled edges and the patch is set with the grain parallel to the surface being repaired. A pressure plate of thicker plywood cut to the exact size of the patch is centered over the patch covered with waxed paper. A suitable weight is used for pressure until the glue has set. The repair is then sanded and finished to match the original surface. [Figure 6-29]

Surface Patch

Plywood skins not over $\frac{1}{8}$-inch thick that are damaged between or along framing members may be repaired with a surface or overlay patch. Surface patches located aft of the 10 percent chord line, or which wrap around the leading edge and terminate aft of the 10 percent chord line, are permissible. You can use surface patches to patch trimmed holes up to a 50-inch perimeter, and may cover an area as large as one frame or rib space.

Figure 6-29. *Splayed patch.*

Trim the damaged area to a rectangle or triangular shape with rounded corners. The radius of the corners must be at least 5 times the skin thickness. Doublers made of plywood at least ¼-inch thick are reinforcements placed under the edge of the hole inside the skin. Nail and glue the doublers in place. Extend the doublers from one framing member to another and strengthen at the ends by saddle gussets attached to the framing members. *[Figure 6-30]*

The surface patch is sized to extend beyond the cutout as indicated. All edges of the patch are beveled, but the leading edge of the patch should be beveled at an angle at least 4:1 of the skin thickness. The face-grain direction of the patch must be in the same direction of the original skin. Where possible, weights are used to apply pressure to a surface patch until the glue has dried. If the location of the patch precludes the use of weight, small round head wood screws can be used to apply glue pressure to secure the patch. After a surface patch has dried, the screws can be removed and the holes filled. The patch should be covered with fabric that overlaps the original surface by at least 2-inches. The fabric should be from one of the approved fabric covering systems using the procedures recommended by the manufacturer to cement and finish the fabric.

Plug Patch

Two types of plug patch, oval and round, may be used on plywood skins. Because the plug patch is only a skin repair,

use it only for damage that does not involve the supporting structure under the skin.

Cut the edges of a plug patch at right angles to the surface of the skin. Cut the skin also to a clean round or oval hole with edges at right angles to the surface. Cut the patch to the exact size of the hole; when installed, the edge of the patch forms a butt joint with the edge of the hole.

You can use a round plug patch where the cutout repair is no larger than 6-inches in diameter. Sample dimensions for holes of 4-inches and 6-inches in diameter appear in *Figure 6-31*.

The following steps provide a method for making a round plug patch:

1. Cut a round patch large enough to cover the intended repair. If applicable for size, use the sample dimensions in *Figure 6-31*. The patch must be of the same material and thickness as the original skin.

2. Place the patch over the damaged spot and mark a circle of the same size as the patch.

3. Cut the skin inside the marked circle so that the plug patch fits snugly into the hole around the entire perimeter.

4. Cut a doubler of soft quarter-inch plywood, such as poplar. A small patch is cut so that its outside radius

Figure 6-30. *Surfaces patches.*

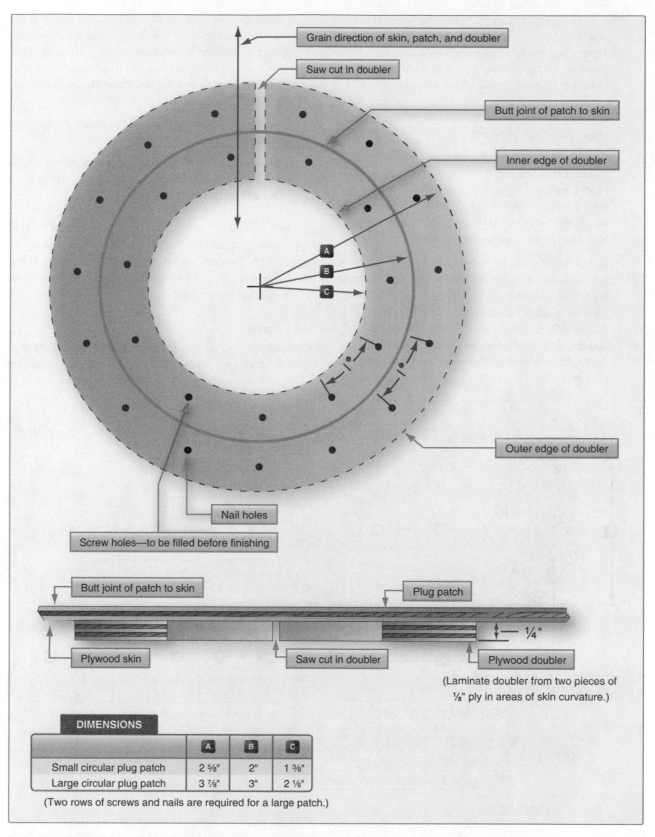

Grain direction of skin, patch, and doubler

Saw cut in doubler

Butt joint of patch to skin

Inner edge of doubler

Outer edge of doubler

Nail holes

Screw holes—to be filled before finishing

Butt joint of patch to skin

Plug patch

Plywood skin

Saw cut in doubler

Plywood doubler

1/4"

(Laminate doubler from two pieces of 1/8" ply in areas of skin curvature.)

DIMENSIONS	A	B	C
Small circular plug patch	2 5/8"	2"	1 3/8"
Large circular plug patch	3 7/8"	3"	2 1/8"

(Two rows of screws and nails are required for a large patch.)

Figure 6-31. *Round plug patch assembly.*

is ⅝-inch greater than the hole to be patched and the inside radius is ⅝-inch less. For a large patch the dimensions would be increased to ⅞-inch each. If the curvature of the skin surface is greater than a rise of ⅛-inch in 6-inches, the doubler should be preformed to the curvature using hot water or steam. As an alternative, the doubler may be laminated from two pieces of ⅛-inch plywood.

5. Cut the doubler through one side so that it can be inserted through the hole to the back of the skin. Place the patch plug centered on the doubler and mark around its perimeter. Apply a coat of glue outside the line to the outer half of the doubler surface that will bear against the inner surface of the skin.

6. Install the doubler by slipping it through the cutout hole and place it so that the mark is concentric with the hole. Nail it in place with nailing strips, while holding a bucking bar or similar object under the doubler for backup. Place waxed paper between the nailing strips and the skin. Cloth webbing under the nailing strips facilitates removal of the strips and nails after the glue dries.

7. After the glue has set for the installed doubler, and you have removed the nail strips, apply glue to the inner half of the doubler and to the patch plug. Drill holes around the plug's circumference to accept No. 4 round head wood screws. Insert the plug with the grain aligned to the surface wood.

8. Apply the pressure to the patch by means of the wood screws. No other pressure is necessary.

9. After the glue has set, remove the screws and fill the nail and screw holes. Sand and finish to match the original surface.

The steps for making an oval plug patch are identical to those for making the round patch. The maximum dimensions for large oval patches are 7-inches long and 5-inches wide. Oval patches must be cut, so when installed, the face grain matches the direction of the original surface. [Figure 6-32]

Scarf Patch

A properly prepared and installed scarf patch is the best repair for damaged plywood and is preferred for most skin

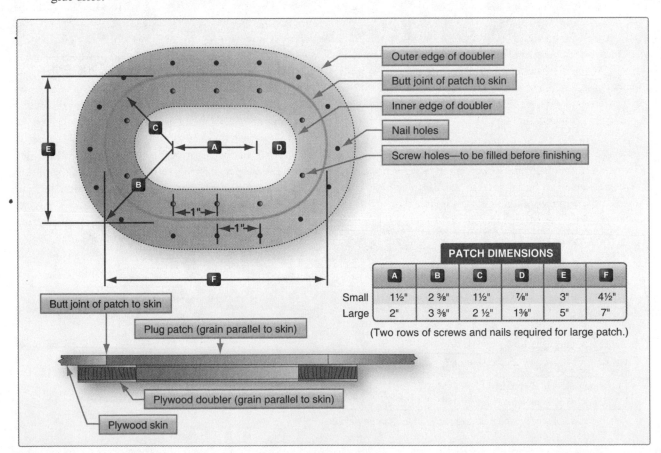

	Outer edge of doubler
	Butt joint of patch to skin
	Inner edge of doubler
	Nail holes
	Screw holes—to be filled before finishing

PATCH DIMENSIONS

	A	B	C	D	E	F
Small	1½"	2 ⅜"	1½"	⅞"	3"	4½"
Large	2"	3 ⅜"	2 ½"	1⅜"	5"	7"

(Two rows of screws and nails required for large patch.)

Butt joint of patch to skin

Plug patch (grain parallel to skin)

Plywood doubler (grain parallel to skin)

Plywood skin

Figure 6-32. *An oval plug patch.*

repairs. The scarf patch has edges beveled at a 12:1 slope; the splayed patch is beveled at a 5:1 slope. The scarf patch also uses reinforcements under the patch at the glue joints.

Much of the outside surface of a plywood aircraft is curved. If the damaged plywood skin has a radius of curvature not greater than 100 times the skin thickness, you can install a scarf patch. However, it may be necessary to soak or steam the patch, to preform it prior to gluing it in place. Shape backing blocks or other reinforcements to fit the skin curvature.

You can make scarf cuts in plywood with various tools, such as a hand plane, spoke shave, a sharp scraper, or sanding block. Sawn or roughly filed surfaces are not recommended because they are normally inaccurate and do not form the best glue joint.

The Back of the Skin is Accessible for Repair

When the back of a damaged plywood skin is accessible, such as a fuselage skin, repair it with scarf patches cut and installed with the grain parallel to the surface skin. Details for this type of repair are shown in *Figure 6-33*.

Figure 6-33, Section A-A, shows methods of support for a scarf between frame members using permanent backing and gussets. When the damage follows or extends to a framing member, support the scarf as shown in section B-B. When the scarf does not quite extend to a frame member, support the patch as shown in section C-C.

Damage that does not exceed 25 times the skin thickness (3⅛-inches for ⅛-inch thick skin) after being trimmed to a circular shape can be repaired as shown in section D-D, provided the trimmed opening is not nearer than 15 times the skin thickness to a frame member (1⅞-inches for ⅛-inch thick skin).

A temporary backing block is carefully shaped from solid wood and fitted to the inside surface of the skin. A piece of waxed paper or plastic wrap is placed between the block and the underside of the skin. The scarf patch is installed and temporarily attached to the backing block, being held together in place with nailing strips. When the glue sets, remove the nails and block, leaving a flush surface on both sides of the repaired skin.

The Back of the Skin Is Not Accessible for Repair

To repair a section of the skin with a scarf patch when access to the back side is not possible, use the following steps to facilitate a repair, as shown in *Figure 6-34*.

Cut out and remove the damaged section. Carefully mark and cut the scarf around the perimeter of the hole. Working through the cutout, install backing strips along all edges that are not fully backed by a rib or spar. To prevent warping of the skin, fabricate backing strips from soft-textured plywood, such as yellow poplar or spruce, rather than a piece of solid wood.

Use nailing strips to hold backing strips in place while the glue sets. Use a bucking bar, where necessary, to provide support for nailing. A saddle gusset of plywood should support the end of the backing strip at all junctions between the backing strips and ribs or spars. If needed, nail and bond the new gusset plate to the rib or spar. It may be necessary to remove and replace an old gusset plate with a new saddle gusset, or nail a new gusset over the original.

Unlike some of the other type patches that are glued and installed as one process, this repair must wait for the glue to set on the backing strips and gussets. At that point, the scarf patch can be cut and fit to match the grain, and glued, using weight for pressure on the patch as appropriate. When dry, fill and finish the repair to match the original surface.

Figure 6-33. *Scarf patches, back of skin accessible.*

Figure 6-34. *Scarf patches, back of skin not accessible.*

Chapter 7
Advanced Composite Materials

Description of Composite Structures

Introduction

Composite materials are becoming more important in the construction of aerospace structures. Aircraft parts made from composite materials, such as fairings, spoilers, and flight controls, were developed during the 1960s for their weight savings over aluminum parts. New generation large aircraft are designed with all composite fuselage and wing structures, and the repair of these advanced composite materials requires an in-depth knowledge of composite structures, materials, and tooling. The primary advantages of composite materials are their high strength, relatively low weight, and corrosion resistance.

Laminated Structures

Composite materials consist of a combination of materials that are mixed together to achieve specific structural properties. The individual materials do not dissolve or merge completely in the composite, but they act together as one. Normally, the components can be physically identified as they interface with one another. The properties of the composite material are superior to the properties of the individual materials from which it is constructed.

An advanced composite material is made of a fibrous material embedded in a resin matrix, generally laminated with fibers oriented in alternating directions to give the material strength and stiffness. Fibrous materials are not new; wood is the most common fibrous structural material known to man.

Applications of composites on aircraft include:

- Fairings
- Flight control surfaces
- Landing gear doors
- Leading and trailing edge panels on the wing and stabilizer
- Interior components
- Floor beams and floor boards
- Vertical and horizontal stabilizer primary structure on large aircraft
- Primary wing and fuselage structure on new generation large aircraft
- Turbine engine fan blades
- Propellers

Major Components of a Laminate

An isotropic material has uniform properties in all directions. The measured properties of an isotropic material are independent of the axis of testing. Metals such as aluminum and titanium are examples of isotropic materials.

A fiber is the primary load carrying element of the composite material. The composite material is only strong and stiff in the direction of the fibers. Unidirectional composites have predominant mechanical properties in one direction and are said to be anisotropic, having mechanical and/or physical properties that vary with direction relative to natural reference axes inherent in the material. Components made from fiber-reinforced composites can be designed so that the fiber orientation produces optimum mechanical properties, but they can only approach the true isotropic nature of metals, such as aluminum and titanium.

A matrix supports the fibers and bonds them together in the composite material. The matrix transfers any applied loads to the fibers, keeps the fibers in their position and chosen orientation, gives the composite environmental resistance, and determines the maximum service temperature of a composite.

Strength Characteristics

Structural properties, such as stiffness, dimensional stability, and strength of a composite laminate, depend on the stacking sequence of the plies. The stacking sequence describes the distribution of ply orientations through the laminate thickness. As the number of plies with chosen orientations increases, more stacking sequences are possible. For example, a symmetric eight-ply laminate with four different ply orientations has 24 different stacking sequences.

Fiber Orientation

The strength and stiffness of a composite buildup depends on the orientation sequence of the plies. The practical range of strength and stiffness of carbon fiber extends from values as low as those provided by fiberglass to as high as those provided by titanium. This range of values is determined by the orientation of the plies to the applied load. Proper selection of ply orientation in advanced composite materials is necessary to provide a structurally efficient design. The part might require 0° plies to react to axial loads, ±45° plies to react to shear loads, and 90° plies to react to side loads. Because the strength design requirements are a function of the applied load direction, ply orientation and ply sequence have to be correct. It is critical during a repair to replace each damaged ply with a ply of the same material and ply orientation.

The fibers in a unidirectional material run in one direction and the strength and stiffness is only in the direction of the fiber. Pre-impregnated (prepreg) tape is an example of a unidirectional ply orientation.

The fibers in a bidirectional material run in two directions, typically 90° apart. A plain weave fabric is an example of a bidirectional ply orientation. These ply orientations have strength in both directions but not necessarily the same strength. *[Figure 7-1]*

The plies of a quasi-isotropic layup are stacked in a 0°, –45°, 45°, and 90° sequence or in a 0°, –60°, and 60° sequence. *[Figure 7-2]* These types of ply orientation simulate the properties of an isotropic material. Many aerospace composite structures are made of quasi-isotropic materials.

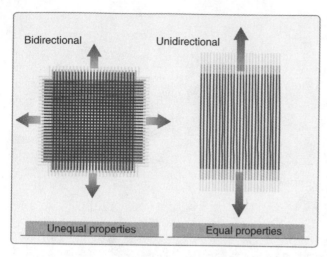

Figure 7-1. *Bidirectional and unidirectional material properties.*

Figure 7-2. *Quasi-isotropic material lay-up.*

Warp Clock

Warp indicates the longitudinal fibers of a fabric. The warp is the high strength direction due to the straightness of the fibers. A warp clock is used to describe direction of fibers on a diagram, spec sheet, or manufacturer's sheets. If the warp clock is not available on the fabric, the orientation is defaulted to zero as the fabric comes off the roll. Therefore, 90° to zero is the width of the fabric across. *[Figure 7-3]*

Fiber Forms

All product forms generally begin with spooled unidirectional raw fibers packaged as continuous strands. An individual fiber is called a filament. The word strand is also used to identify an individual glass fiber. Bundles of filaments are identified as tows, yarns, or rovings. Fiberglass yarns are twisted, while Kevlar® yarns are not. Tows and rovings do not have any twist. Most fibers are available as dry fiber that needs to be impregnated (impreg) with a resin before use or prepreg materials where the resin is already applied to the fiber.

Figure 7-3. *A warp clock.*

Roving

A roving is a single grouping of filament or fiber ends, such as 20-end or 60-end glass rovings. All filaments are in the same direction and they are not twisted. Carbon rovings are usually identified as 3K, 6K, or 12K rovings, K meaning 1,000 filaments. Most applications for roving products utilize mandrels for filament winding and then resin cure to final configuration.

Unidirectional (Tape)

Unidirectional prepreg tapes have been the standard within the aerospace industry for many years, and the fiber is typically impregnated with thermosetting resins. The most common method of manufacture is to draw collimated raw (dry) strands into the impregnation machine where hot melted resins are combined with the strands using heat and pressure. Tape products have high strength in the fiber direction and virtually no strength across the fibers. The fibers are held in place by the resin. Tapes have a higher strength than woven fabrics. *[Figure 7-4]*

Bidirectional (Fabric)

Most fabric constructions offer more flexibility for layup of complex shapes than straight unidirectional tapes offer. Fabrics offer the option for resin impregnation either by solution or the hot melt process. Generally, fabrics used for structural applications use like fibers or strands of the same weight or yield in both the warp (longitudinal) and fill (transverse) directions. For aerospace structures, tightly woven fabrics are usually the choice to save weight, minimizing resin void size, and maintaining fiber orientation during the fabrication process.

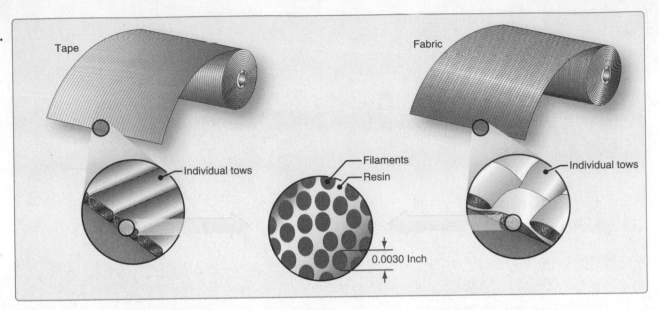

Figure 7-4. *Tape and fabric products.*

Woven structural fabrics are usually constructed with reinforcement tows, strands, or yarns interlocking upon themselves with over/under placement during the weaving process. The more common fabric styles are plain or satin weaves. The plain weave construction results from each fiber alternating over and then under each intersecting strand (tow, bundle, or yarn). With the common satin weaves, such as 5 harness or 8 harness, the fiber bundles traverse both in warp and fill directions changing over/under position less frequently.

These satin weaves have less crimp and are easier to distort than a plain weave. With plain weave fabrics and most 5 or 8 harness woven fabrics, the fiber strand count is equal in both warp and fill directions. Example: 3K plain weave often has an additional designation, such as 12 x 12, meaning there are twelve tows per inch in each direction. This count designation can be varied to increase or decrease fabric weight or to accommodate different fibers of varying weight. *[Figure 7-5]*

Nonwoven (Knitted or Stitched)

Knitted or stitched fabrics can offer many of the mechanical advantages of unidirectional tapes. Fiber placement can be straight or unidirectional without the over/under turns of woven fabrics. The fibers are held in place by stitching with fine yarns or threads after preselected orientations of one or more layers of dry plies. These types of fabrics offer a wide range of multi-ply orientations. Although there may be some added weight penalties or loss of some ultimate reinforcement fiber properties, some gain of interlaminar shear and toughness properties may be realized. Some common stitching yarns are polyester, aramid, or thermoplastics. *[Figure 7-6]*

Types of Fiber
Fiberglass

Fiberglass is often used for secondary structure on aircraft, such as fairings, radomes, and wing tips. Fiberglass is also used for helicopter rotor blades. There are several types of fiberglass used in the aviation industry. Electrical glass, or E-glass, is identified as such for electrical applications. It has high resistance to current flow. E-glass is made from borosilicate glass. S-glass and S2-glass identify structural fiberglass that have a higher strength than E-glass. S-glass is produced from magnesia-alumina-silicate. Advantages of fiberglass are lower cost than other composite materials, chemical or galvanic corrosion resistance, and electrical properties (fiberglass does not conduct electricity). Fiberglass has a white color and is available as a dry fiber fabric or prepreg material.

Kevlar®

Kevlar® is DuPont's name for aramid fibers. Aramid fibers are light weight, strong, and tough. Two types of Aramid fiber are used in the aviation industry. Kevlar® 49 has a high stiffness and Kevlar® 29 has a low stiffness. An advantage of aramid fibers is their high resistance to impact damage, so they are often used in areas prone to impact damage. The main disadvantage of aramid fibers is their general weakness in compression and hygroscopy. Service reports have indicated that some parts made from Kevlar® absorb up to 8 percent of their weight in water. Therefore, parts made from aramid fibers need to be protected from the environment. Another disadvantage is that Kevlar® is difficult to drill and cut. The fibers fuzz easily and special scissors are needed to cut the

8 harness satin weave
Example:
Style 3K-135-8H carbon

Plain weave
Example:
Style 3K-70-P carbon

4 shaft satin weave
Example:
Style 120 fiberglass

8 shaft satin weave
Example:
Style 1581 fiberglass

Crowfoot satin weave
Example:
Style 285 Kevlar®

5 harness satin weave
Example:
Style 1K-50-5H carbon

8 shaft satin weave
Example:
Style 181 fiberglass

Figure 7-5. *Typical fabric weave styles.*

Figure 7-6. *Nonwoven material (stitched).*

material. Kevlar® is often used for military ballistic and body armor applications. It has a natural yellow color and is available as dry fabric and prepreg material. Bundles of aramid fibers are not sized by the number of fibers like carbon or fiberglass but by the weight.

Carbon/Graphite

One of the first distinctions to be made among fibers is the difference between carbon and graphite fibers, although the terms are frequently used interchangeably. Carbon and graphite fibers are based on graphene (hexagonal) layer networks present in carbon. If the graphene layers, or planes, are stacked with three dimensional order, the material is defined as graphite. Usually extended time and temperature processing is required to form this order, making graphite fibers more expensive. Bonding between planes is weak. Disorder frequently occurs such that only two-dimensional ordering within the layers is present. This material is defined as carbon.

Carbon fibers are very stiff and strong, 3 to 10 times stiffer than glass fibers. Carbon fiber is used for structural aircraft applications, such as floor beams, stabilizers, flight controls, and primary fuselage and wing structure. Advantages include its high strength and corrosion resistance. Disadvantages include lower conductivity than aluminum; therefore, a lightning protection mesh or coating is necessary for aircraft parts that are prone to lightning strikes. Another disadvantage of carbon fiber is its high cost. Carbon fiber is gray or black in color and is available as dry fabric and prepreg material. Carbon fibers have a high potential for causing galvanic corrosion when used with metallic fasteners and structures. *[Figure 7-7]*

Figure 7-7. *Fiberglass (left), Kevlar® (middle), and carbon fiber material (right).*

Boron

Boron fibers are very stiff and have a high tensile and compressive strength. The fibers have a relatively large diameter and do not flex well; therefore, they are available only as a prepreg tape product. An epoxy matrix is often used with the boron fiber. Boron fibers are used to repair cracked aluminum aircraft skins, because the thermal expansion of boron is close to aluminum and there is no galvanic corrosion potential. The boron fiber is difficult to use if the parent material surface has a contoured shape. The boron fibers are very expensive and can be hazardous for personnel. Boron fibers are used primarily in military aviation applications.

Ceramic Fibers

Ceramic fibers are used for high-temperature applications, such as turbine blades in a gas turbine engine. The ceramic fibers can be used to temperatures up to 2,200 °F.

Lightning Protection Fibers

An aluminum airplane is quite conductive and is able to dissipate the high currents resulting from a lightning strike. Carbon fibers are 1,000 times more resistive than aluminum to current flow, and epoxy resin is 1,000,000 times more resistive (i.e., perpendicular to the skin). The surface of an external composite component often consists of a ply or layer of conductive material for lightning strike protection because composite materials are less conductive than aluminum. Many different types of conductive materials are used ranging from nickel-coated graphite cloth to metal meshes to aluminized fiberglass to conductive paints. The materials are available for wet layup and as prepreg.

In addition to a normal structural repair, the technician must also recreate the electrical conductivity designed into the part. These types of repair generally require a conductivity test to be performed with an ohmmeter to verify minimum electrical resistance across the structure. When repairing these types of structures, it is extremely important to use only the approved materials from authorized vendors, including such items as potting compounds, sealants, adhesives, and so forth. *[Figures 7-8 and 7-9]*

Figure 7-8. *Copper mesh lightning protection material.*

Figure 7-9. *Aluminum mesh lightning protection material.*

Matrix Materials
Thermosetting Resins
Resin is a generic term used to designate the polymer. The resin, its chemical composition, and physical properties fundamentally affect the processing, fabrication, and ultimate properties of a composite material. Thermosetting resins are the most diverse and widely used of all man-made materials. They are easily poured or formed into any shape, are compatible with most other materials, and cure readily (by heat or catalyst) into an insoluble solid. Thermosetting resins are also excellent adhesives and bonding agents.

Polyester Resins
Polyester resins are relatively inexpensive, fast processing resins used generally for low cost applications. Low smoke producing polyester resins are used for interior parts of the aircraft. Fiber-reinforced polyesters can be processed by many methods. Common processing methods include matched metal molding, wet layup, press (vacuum bag) molding, injection molding, filament winding, pultrusion, and autoclaving.

Vinyl Ester Resin
The appearance, handling properties, and curing characteristics of vinyl ester resins are the same as those of conventional polyester resins. However, the corrosion resistance and mechanical properties of vinyl ester composites are much improved over standard polyester resin composites.

Phenolic Resin
Phenol-formaldehyde resins were first produced commercially in the early 1900s for use in the commercial market. Urea-formaldehyde and melamine-formaldehyde appeared in the 1920–1930s as a less expensive alternative for lower temperature use. Phenolic resins are used for interior components because of their low smoke and flammability characteristics.

Epoxy
Epoxies are polymerizable thermosetting resins and are available in a variety of viscosities from liquid to solid. There are many different types of epoxy, and the technician should use the maintenance manual to select the correct type for a specific repair. Epoxies are used widely in resins for prepreg materials and structural adhesives. The advantages of epoxies are high strength and modulus, low levels of volatiles, excellent adhesion, low shrinkage, good chemical resistance, and ease of processing. Their major disadvantages are brittleness and the reduction of properties in the presence of moisture. The processing or curing of epoxies is slower than polyester resins. Processing techniques include autoclave molding, filament winding, press molding, vacuum bag molding, resin transfer molding, and pultrusion. Curing temperatures vary from room temperature to approximately 350 °F (180 °C). The most common cure temperatures range between 250° and 350 °F (120–180 °C). *[Figure 7-10]*

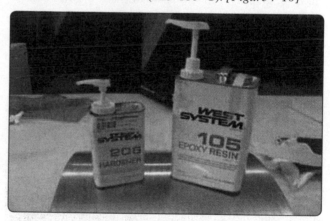
Figure 7-10. *Two part wet layup epoxy resin system with pump dispenser.*

Polyimides
Polyimide resins excel in high-temperature environments where their thermal resistance, oxidative stability, low coefficient of thermal expansion, and solvent resistance benefit the design. Their primary uses are circuit boards and hot engine and airframe structures. A polyimide may be either a thermoset resin or a thermoplastic. Polyimides require high cure temperatures, usually in excess of 550 °F (290 °C). Consequently, normal epoxy composite bagging materials are not usable, and steel tooling becomes a necessity. Polyimide bagging and release films, such as Kapton® are used. It is extremely important that Upilex® replace the lower cost nylon bagging and polytetrafluoroethylene (PTFE) release films common to epoxy composite processing. Fiberglass

fabrics must be used for bleeder and breather materials instead of polyester mat materials due to the low melting point of polyester.

Polybenzimidazoles (PBI)

Polybenzimidazole resin is extremely high temperature resistant and is used for high temperature materials. These resins are available as adhesive and fiber.

Bismaleimides (BMI)

Bismaleimide resins have a higher temperature capability and higher toughness than epoxy resins, and they provide excellent performance at ambient and elevated temperatures. The processing of bismaleimide resins is similar to that for epoxy resins. BMIs are used for aero engines and high temperature components. BMIs are suitable for standard autoclave processing, injection molding, resin transfer molding, and sheet molded compound (SMC) among others.

Thermoplastic Resins

Thermoplastic materials can be softened repeatedly by an increase of temperature and hardened by a decrease in temperature. Processing speed is the primary advantage of thermoplastic materials. Chemical curing of the material does not take place during processing, and the material can be shaped by molding or extrusion when it is soft.

Semicrystalline Thermoplastics

Semicrystalline thermoplastics possess properties of inherent flame resistance, superior toughness, good mechanical properties at elevated temperatures and after impact, and low moisture absorption. They are used in secondary and primary aircraft structures. Combined with reinforcing fibers, they are available in injection molding compounds, compression-moldable random sheets, unidirectional tapes, prepregs fabricated from tow (towpreg), and woven prepregs. Fibers impregnated in semicrystalline thermoplastics include carbon, nickel-coated carbon, aramid, glass, quartz, and others.

Amorphous Thermoplastics

Amorphous thermoplastics are available in several physical forms, including films, filaments, and powders. Combined with reinforcing fibers, they are also available in injection molding compounds, compressive moldable random sheets, unidirectional tapes, woven prepregs, etc. The fibers used are primarily carbon, aramid, and glass. The specific advantages of amorphous thermoplastics depend upon the polymer. Typically, the resins are noted for their processing ease and speed, high temperature capability, good mechanical properties, excellent toughness and impact strength,

and chemical stability. The stability results in unlimited shelf life, eliminating the cold storage requirements of thermoset prepregs.

Polyether Ether Ketone (PEEK)

Polyether ether ketone, better known as PEEK, is a high-temperature thermoplastic. This aromatic ketone material offers outstanding thermal and combustion characteristics and resistance to a wide range of solvents and proprietary fluids. PEEK can also be reinforced with glass and carbon.

Curing Stages of Resins

Thermosetting resins use a chemical reaction to cure. There are three curing stages, which are called A, B, and C.

- A stage: The components of the resin (base material and hardener) have been mixed but the chemical reaction has not started. The resin is in the A stage during a wet layup procedure.

- B stage: The components of the resin have been mixed and the chemical reaction has started. The material has thickened and is tacky. The resins of prepreg materials are in the B stage. To prevent further curing the resin is placed in a freezer at 0 °F. In the frozen state, the resin of the prepreg material stays in the B stage. The curing starts when the material is removed from the freezer and warmed again.

- C stage: The resin is fully cured. Some resins cure at room temperature and others need an elevated temperature cure cycle to fully cure.

Pre-Impregnated Products (Prepregs)

Prepreg material consists of a combination of a matrix and fiber reinforcement. It is available in unidirectional form (one direction of reinforcement) and fabric form (several directions of reinforcement). All five of the major families of matrix resins can be used to impregnate various fiber forms. The resin is then no longer in a low-viscosity stage, but has been advanced to a B stage level of cure for better handling characteristics. The following products are available in prepreg form: unidirectional tapes, woven fabrics, continuous strand rovings, and chopped mat. Prepreg materials must be stored in a freezer at a temperature below 0 °F to retard the curing process. Prepreg materials are cured with an elevated temperature. Many prepreg materials used in aerospace are impregnated with an epoxy resin and they are cured at either 250 °F or 350 °F. Prepreg materials are cured with an autoclave, oven, or heat blanket. They are typically purchased and stored on a roll in a sealed plastic bag to avoid moisture contamination. [Figure 7-11]

Figure 7-11. *Tape and fabric prepreg materials.*

Dry Fiber Material

Dry fiber materials, such as carbon, glass, and Kevlar®, are used for many aircraft repair procedures. The dry fabric is impregnated with a resin just before the repair work starts. This process is often called wet layup. The main advantage of using the wet layup process is that the fiber and resin can be stored for a long time at room temperature. The composite can be cured at room temperature or an elevated temperature cure can be used to speed up the curing process and increase the strength. The disadvantage is that the process is messy and reinforcement properties are less than prepreg material properties. *[Figure 7-12]*

Figure 7-12. *Dry fabric materials (top to bottom: aluminum lightning protection mess, Kevlar®, fiberglass, and carbon fiber).*

Thixotropic Agents

Thixotropic agents are gel-like at rest but become fluid when agitated. These materials have high static shear strength and low dynamic shear strength at the same time to lose viscosity under stress.

Adhesives
Film Adhesives

Structural adhesives for aerospace applications are generally supplied as thin films supported on a release paper and stored under refrigerated conditions (–18 °C, or 0 °F). Film adhesives are available using high temperature aromatic amine or catalytic curing agents with a wide range of flexibilizing and toughening agents. Rubber-toughened epoxy film adhesives are widely used in aircraft industry. The upper temperature limit of 121–177 °C (250–350 °F) is usually dictated by the degree of toughening required and by the overall choice of resins and curing agents. In general, toughening of a resin results in a lower usable service temperature. Film materials are frequently supported by fibers that serve to improve handling of the films prior to cure, control adhesive flow during bonding, and assist in bond line thickness control. Fibers can be incorporated as short-fiber mats with random orientation or as woven cloth. Commonly encountered fibers are polyesters, polyamides (nylon), and glass. Adhesives containing woven cloth may have slightly degraded environmental properties because of wicking of water by the fiber. Random mat scrim cloth is not as efficient for controlling film thickness as woven cloth because the unrestricted fibers move during bonding. Spun-bonded nonwoven scrims do not move and are, therefore, widely used. *[Figures 7-13 and 7-14]*

Paste Adhesives

Paste adhesives are used as an alternative to film adhesive. These are often used to secondary bond repair patches to damaged parts and also used in places where film adhesive is difficult to apply. Paste adhesives for structural bonding are made mostly from epoxy. One part and two part systems are available. The advantages of paste adhesives are that they can be stored at room temperature and have a long shelf life. The disadvantage is that the bond line thickness is hard to control, which affects the strength of the bond. A scrim

Figure 7-13. *The use of film adhesive mess, Kevlar®, fiberglass, and carbon fiber.*

Figure 7-14. *A roll of film adhesive.*

Figure 7-15. *Two-part paste adhesive.*

cloth can be used to maintain adhesive in the bondline when bonding patches with paste adhesive. *[Figure 7-15]*

Foaming Adhesives

Most foaming adhesives are 0.025-inch to 0.10-inch thick sheets of B staged epoxy. Foam adhesives cure at 250 °F or 350 °F. During the cure cycle, the foaming adhesives expand. Foaming adhesives need to be stored in the freezer just like prepregs, and they have only a limited storage life. Foaming adhesives are used to splice pieces of honeycomb together in a sandwich construction and to bond repair plugs to the existing core during a prepreg repair. *[Figure 7-16]*

Description of Sandwich Structures

Theory A sandwich construction is a structural panel concept that consists in its simplest form of two relatively thin, parallel face sheets bonded to and separated by a relatively thick, lightweight core. The core supports the face sheets against buckling and resists out-of-plane shear loads. The core must have high shear strength and compression stiffness. Composite sandwich construction is most often fabricated using autoclave cure, press cure, or vacuum bag cure. Skin laminates may be precured and subsequently bonded to core, co-cured to core in one operation, or a combination of the

Figure 7-16. *The use of foaming adhesives.*

two methods. Examples of honeycomb structure are: wing spoilers, fairings, ailerons, flaps, nacelles, floor boards, and rudders. *[Figure 7-17]*

Figure 7-17. *Honeycomb sandwich construction.*

Properties

Sandwich construction has high bending stiffness at minimal weight in comparison to aluminum and composite laminate construction. Most honeycombs are anisotropic; that is, properties are directional. *Figure 7-18* illustrates the advantages of using a honeycomb construction. Increasing the core thickness greatly increases the stiffness of the honeycomb construction, while the weight increase is minimal. Due to the high stiffness of a honeycomb construction, it is not necessary to use external stiffeners, such as stringers and frames. *[Figure 7-18]*

	Solid Material	Core Thickness t	Core Thickness 3t
	t	2t	4t
Thickness	1.0	7.0	37.0
Flexural Strength	1.0	3.5	9.2
Weight	1.0	1.03	1.06

Figure 7-18. *Strength and stiffness of honeycomb sandwich material compared to a solid laminate.*

Facing Materials

Most honeycomb structures used in aircraft construction have aluminum, fiberglass, Kevlar®, or carbon fiber face sheets. Carbon fiber face sheets cannot be used with aluminum honeycomb core material, because it causes the aluminum to corrode. Titanium and steel are used for specialty applications in high temperature constructions. The face sheets of many components, such as spoilers and flight controls, are very thin—sometimes only 3 or 4 plies. Field reports have indicated that these face sheets do not have a good impact resistance.

Core Materials

Honeycomb

Each honeycomb material provides certain properties and has specific benefits. *[Figure 7-19]* The most common core material used for aircraft honeycomb structures is aramid paper (Nomex® or Korex®). Fiberglass is used for higher strength applications.

• Kraft paper—relatively low strength, good insulating properties, is available in large quantities, and has a low cost.

Figure 7-19. *Honeycomb core materials.*

- Thermoplastics—good insulating properties, good energy absorption and/or redirection, smooth cell walls, moisture and chemical resistance, are environmentally compatible, aesthetically pleasing, and have a relatively low cost.

- Aluminum—best strength-to-weight ratio and energy absorption, has good heat transfer properties, electromagnetic shielding properties, has smooth, thin cell walls, is machinable, and has a relatively low cost.

- Steel—good heat transfer properties, electromagnetic shielding properties, and heat resistant.

- Specialty metals (titanium)—relatively high strength-to-weight ratio, good heat transfer properties, chemical resistance, and heat resistant to very high temperatures.

- Aramid paper—flame resistant, fire retardant, good insulating properties, low dielectric properties, and good formability.

- Fiberglass—tailorable shear properties by layup, low dielectric properties, good insulating properties, and good formability.

- Carbon—good dimensional stability and retention, high-temperature property retention, high stiffness, very low coefficient of thermal expansion, tailorable thermal conductivity, relatively high shear modulus, and very expensive.

- Ceramics—heat resistant to very high temperatures, good insulating properties, is available in very small cell sizes, and very expensive. *[Figure 7-19]*

Honeycomb core cells for aerospace applications are usually hexagonal. The cells are made by bonding stacked sheets at special locations. The stacked sheets are expanded to form hexagons. The direction parallel to the sheets is called ribbon direction.

Bisected hexagonal core has another sheet of material cutting across each hexagon. Bisected hexagonal honeycomb is stiffer and stronger than hexagonal core. Overexpanded core is made by expanding the sheets more than is needed to make hexagons. The cells of overexpanded core are rectangular. Overexpanded core is flexible perpendicular to the ribbon direction and is used in panels with simple curves. Bell-shaped core, or flexicore, has curved cell walls, that make it flexible in all directions. Bell-shaped core is used in panels with complex curves.

Honeycomb core is available with different cell sizes. Small sizes provide better support for sandwich face sheets. Honeycomb is also available in different densities. Higher density core is stronger and stiffer than lower density core. *[Figure 7-20]*

Figure 7-20. *Honeycomb density.*

Foam

Foam cores are used on homebuilts and lighter aircraft to give strength and shape to wing tips, flight controls, fuselage sections, wings, and wing ribs. Foam cores are not commonly used on commercial type aircraft. Foams are typically heavier than honeycomb and not as strong. A variety of foams can be used as core material including:

- Polystyrene (better known as styrofoam)—aircraft grade styrofoam with a tightly closed cell structure and no voids between cells; high compressive strength and good resistance to water penetration; can be cut with a hot wire to make airfoil shapes.

- Phenolic—very good fire-resistant properties and can have very low density, but relatively low mechanical properties.

- Polyurethane—used for producing the fuselage, wing tips, and other curved parts of small aircraft; relatively inexpensive, fuel resistant, and compatible with most adhesives; do not use a hot wire to cut polyurethane foam; easily contoured with a large knife and sanding equipment.

- Polypropylene—used to make airfoil shapes; can be cut with a hot wire; compatible with most adhesives and epoxy resins; not for use with polyester resins, dissolves in fuels and solvents.

- Polyvinyl chloride (PVC) (Divinycell, Klegecell, and Airex)—a closed cell medium- to high-density foam with high compression strength, durability, and excellent fire resistance; can be vacuum formed to compound shapes and be bent using heat; compatible with polyester, vinyl ester, and epoxy resins.

- Polymethacrylimide (Rohacell)—a closed-cell foam used for lightweight sandwich construction; excellent mechanical properties, high dimensional stability under heat, good solvent resistance, and outstanding creep compression resistance; more expensive than the other types of foams, but has greater mechanical properties.

Balsa Wood

Balsa is a natural wood product with elongated closed cells; it is available in a variety of grades that correlate to the structural, cosmetic, and physical characteristics. The density of balsa is less than one-half of the density of conventional wood products. However, balsa has a considerably higher density than the other types of structural cores.

Manufacturing and In-Service Damage

Manufacturing Defects

Manufacturing defects include:

- Delamination
- Resin starved areas
- Resin rich areas
- Blisters, air bubbles
- Wrinkles
- Voids
- Thermal decomposition

Manufacturing damage includes anomalies, such as porosity, microcracking, and delaminations resulting from processing discrepancies. It also includes such items as inadvertent edge cuts, surface gouges and scratches, damaged fastener holes, and impact damage. Examples of flaws occurring in manufacturing include a contaminated bondline surface or inclusions, such as prepreg backing paper or separation film, that is inadvertently left between plies during layup. Inadvertent (nonprocess) damage can occur in detail parts or components during assembly or transport or during operation.

A part is resin rich if too much resin is used, for nonstructural applications this is not necessarily bad, but it adds weight. A part is called resin starved if too much resin is bled off during the curing process or if not enough resin is applied during the wet layup process. Resin-starved areas are indicated by fibers that show to the surface. The ratio of 60:40 fiber to resin ratio is considered optimum. Sources of manufacturing defects include:

- Improper cure or processing
- Improper machining
- Mishandling
- Improper drilling
- Tool drops
- Contamination
- Improper sanding
- Substandard material
- Inadequate tooling
- Mislocation of holes or details

Damage can occur at several scales within the composite material and structural configuration. This ranges from damage in the matrix and fiber to broken elements and failure of bonded or bolted attachments. The extent of damage controls repeated load life and residual strength and is critical to damage tolerance.

Fiber Breakage

Fiber breakage can be critical because structures are typically designed to be fiber dominant (i.e., fibers carry most of the loads). Fortunately, fiber failure is typically limited to a zone near the point of impact and is constrained by the impact object size and energy. Only a few of the service-related events listed in the previous section could lead to large areas of fiber damage.

Matrix Imperfections

Matrix imperfections usually occur on the matrix-fiber interface or in the matrix parallel to the fibers. These imperfections can slightly reduce some of the material properties but are seldom critical to the structure, unless the matrix degradation is widespread. Accumulation of matrix cracks can cause the degradation of matrix-dominated properties. For laminates designed to transmit loads with their fibers (fiber dominant), only a slight reduction of properties is observed when the matrix is severely damaged. Matrix cracks, or microcracks, can significantly reduce properties dependent on the resin or the fiber-resin interface, such as interlaminar shear and compression strength. Micro-cracking can have a very negative effect on properties of high-temperature resins. Matrix imperfections may develop into delaminations, which are a more critical type of damage.

Delamination and Debonds

Delaminations form on the interface between the layers in the laminate. Delaminations may form from matrix cracks that grow into the interlaminar layer or from low-energy impact. Debonds can also form from production nonadhesion along the bondline between two elements and initiate delamination in adjacent laminate layers. Under certain conditions, delaminations or debonds can grow when subjected to repeated loading and can cause catastrophic failure when the laminate is loaded in compression. The criticality of delaminations or debonds depend on:

• Dimensions.

• Number of delaminations at a given location.

• Location—in the thickness of laminate, in the structure, proximity to free edges, stress concentration region, geometrical discontinuities, etc.

• Loads—behavior of delaminations and debonds depend on loading type. They have little effect on the response of laminates loaded in tension. Under compression or shear loading, however, the sublaminates adjacent to the delaminations or debonded elements may buckle and cause a load redistribution mechanism that leads to structural failure.

Combinations of Damages

In general, impact events cause combinations of damages. High-energy impacts by large objects (e.g., turbine blades) may lead to broken elements and failed attachments. The resulting damage may include significant fiber failure, matrix cracking, delamination, broken fasteners, and debonded elements. Damage caused by low-energy impact is more contained, but may also include a combination of broken fibers, matrix cracks, and multiple delaminations.

Flawed Fastener Holes

Improper hole drilling, poor fastener installation, and missing fasteners may occur in manufacturing. Hole elongation can occur due to repeated load cycling in service.

In-Service Defects

In-service defects include:

• Environmental degradation

• Impact damage

• Fatigue

• Cracks from local overload

• Debonding

• Delamination

• Fiber fracturing

• Erosion

Many honeycomb structures, such as wing spoilers, fairings, flight controls, and landing gear doors, have thin face sheets which have experienced durability problems that could be grouped into three categories: low resistance to impact, liquid ingression, and erosion. These structures have adequate stiffness and strength but low resistance to a service environment in which parts are crawled over, tools dropped, and service personnel are often unaware of the fragility of thin-skinned sandwich parts. Damages to these components, such as core crush, impact damages, and disbonds, are quite often easy to detect with a visual inspection due to their thin face sheets. However, they are sometimes overlooked or damaged by service personnel who do not want to delay aircraft departure or bring attention to their accidents, which might reflect poorly on their performance record. Any damage to composite structure should be inspected, evaluated and repaired in accordance with manufacturer's recommendations or accepted industry practices. Nondurable design details (e.g., improper core edge close-outs) also lead to liquid ingression.

The repair of parts due to liquid ingression can vary depending on the liquid, most commonly water or Skydrol (hydraulic fluid). Water tends to create additional damage in repaired parts when cured unless all moisture is removed from the part. Most repair material systems cure at temperatures above the boiling point of water, which can cause a disbond at the skin-to-core interface wherever trapped water resides. For this reason, core drying cycles are typically included prior to performing any repair. Some operators take the extra step of placing a damaged but unrepaired part in the autoclave to dry to preclude any additional damage from occurring during the cure of the repair. Skydrol presents a different problem. Once the core of a sandwich part is saturated, complete removal of Skydrol is almost impossible. The part continues to weep the liquid even in cure until bondlines can become contaminated and full bonding does not occur. Removal of contaminated core and adhesive as part of the repair is highly recommended. *[Figure 7-21]*

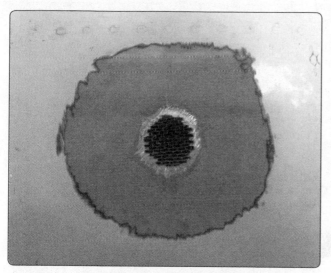

Figure 7-21. *Damage to radome honeycomb sandwich structure.*

Erosion capabilities of composite materials have been known to be less than that of aluminum and, as a result, their application in leading-edge surfaces has been generally avoided. However, composites have been used in areas of highly complex geometry, but generally with an erosion coating. The durability and maintainability of some erosion coatings are less than ideal. Another problem, not as obvious as the first, is that edges of doors or panels can erode if they are exposed to the air stream. This erosion can be attributed to improper design or installation/fit-up. On the other hand, metal structures in contact or in the vicinity of these composite parts may show corrosion damage due to inappropriate choice of aluminum alloy, damaged corrosion sealant of metal parts during assembly or at splices, or insufficient sealant and/or lack of glass fabric isolation plies at the interfaces of spars, ribs, and fittings. *[Figure 7-22]*

Corrosion

Many fiberglass and Kevlar® parts have a fine aluminum mesh for lightning protection. This aluminum mesh often corrodes around the bolt or screw holes. The corrosion affects the electrical bonding of the panel, and the aluminum mesh needs to be removed and new mesh installed to restore the electrical bonding of the panel. *[Figure 7-23]*

Ultraviolet (UV) light affects the strength of composite materials. Composite structures need to be protected by a top coating to prevent the effects of UV light. Special UV primers and paints have been developed to protect composite materials.

Nondestructive Inspection (NDI) of Composites

Visual Inspection

A visual inspection is the primary inspection method for in-service inspections. Most types of damage scorch, stain, dent, penetrate, abrade, or chip the composite surface, making the damage visible. Once damage is detected, the affected area needs to be inspected closer using flashlights, magnifying glasses, mirrors, and borescopes. These tools are used to magnify defects that otherwise might not be seen easily and to allow visual inspection of areas that are not readily accessible. Resin starvation, resin richness, wrinkles, ply bridging, discoloration (due to overheating, lightning strike, etc.), impact damage by any cause, foreign matter, blisters, and disbonding are some of the discrepancies that can be detected with a visual inspection. Visual inspection cannot find internal flaws in the composite, such as delaminations, disbonds, and matrix crazing. More sophisticated NDI techniques are needed to detect these types of defects.

Figure 7-22. *Erosion damage to wingtip.*

Figure 7-23. *Corrosion of aluminum lightning protection mesh.*

Audible Sonic Testing (Coin Tapping)

Sometimes referred to as audio, sonic, or coin tap, this technique makes use of frequencies in the audible range (10 Hz to 20 Hz). A surprisingly accurate method in the hands of experienced personnel, tap testing is perhaps the most common technique used for the detection of delamination and/or disbond. The method is accomplished by tapping the inspection area with a solid round disk or lightweight hammer-like device and listening to the response of the structure to the hammer. *[Figure 7-24]* A clear, sharp, ringing sound is indicative of a well-bonded solid structure, while a dull or thud-like sound indicates a discrepant area.

The tapping rate needs to be rapid enough to produce enough sound for any difference in sound tone to be discernable to the ear. Tap testing is effective on thin skin to stiffener bondlines, honeycomb sandwich with thin face sheets, or even near the surface of thick laminates, such as rotorcraft blade supports. Again, inherent in the method is the possibility that changes within the internal elements of the structure might produce pitch changes that are interpreted as defects, when in fact they are present by design. This inspection should be accomplished in as quiet an area as possible and by experienced personnel familiar with the part's internal configuration. This method is not reliable for structures with more than four plies. It is often used to map out the damage on thin honeycomb facesheets. *[Figure 7-24]*

Automated Tap Test

This test is very similar to the manual tap test except that a solenoid is used instead of a hammer. The solenoid produces multiple impacts in a single area. The tip of the impactor has a transducer that records the force versus time signal of the impactor. The magnitude of the force depends on the impactor, the impact energy, and the mechanical properties of the structure. The impact duration (period) is not sensitive

Tap hammer

25 – 38 mm
(1.00 – 1.50 in)
(approximately)

38 mm
(1.50 in)
(approximately)

Panel surface

Figure 7-24. *Tap test with tap hammer.*

to the magnitude of the impact force; however, this duration changes as the stiffness of the structure is altered. Therefore, the signal from an unflawed region is used for calibration, and any deviation from this unflawed signal indicates the existence of damage.

Ultrasonic Inspection

Ultrasonic inspection has proven to be a very useful tool for the detection of internal delaminations, voids, or inconsistencies in composite components not otherwise discernable using visual or tap methodology. There are many ultrasonic techniques; however, each technique uses sound wave energy with a frequency above the audible range. *[Figure 7-25]* A high-frequency (usually several MHz) sound wave is introduced into the part and may be directed to travel normal to the part surface, or along the surface of the part, or at some predefined angle to the part surface. You may need to try different directions to locate the flow. The introduced sound is then monitored as it travels its assigned route through the part for any significant change. Ultrasonic sound waves have properties similar to light waves. When an ultrasonic wave strikes an interrupting object, the wave or energy is either absorbed or reflected back to the surface. The disrupted or diminished sonic energy is then picked up by a receiving transducer and converted into a display on an oscilloscope or a chart recorder. The display allows the operator to evaluate

the discrepant indications comparatively with those areas known to be good. To facilitate the comparison, reference standards are established and utilized to calibrate the ultrasonic equipment.

The repair technician must realize that the concepts outlined here work fine in the repetitive manufacturing environment, but are likely to be more difficult to implement in a repair environment given the vast number of different composite components installed on the aircraft and the relative complexity of their construction. The reference standards would also have to take into account the transmutations that take place when a composite component is exposed to an in-service environment over a prolonged period or has been the subject of repair activity or similar restorative action. The four most common ultrasonic techniques are discussed next.

Through Transmission Ultrasonic Inspection

Through transmission ultrasonic inspection uses two transducers, one on each side of the area to be inspected. The ultrasonic signal is transmitted from one transducer to the other transducer. The loss of signal strength is then measured by the instrument. The instrument shows the loss as a percent of the original signal strength or the loss in decibels. The signal loss is compared to a reference standard. Areas with a greater loss than the reference standard indicate a defective area.

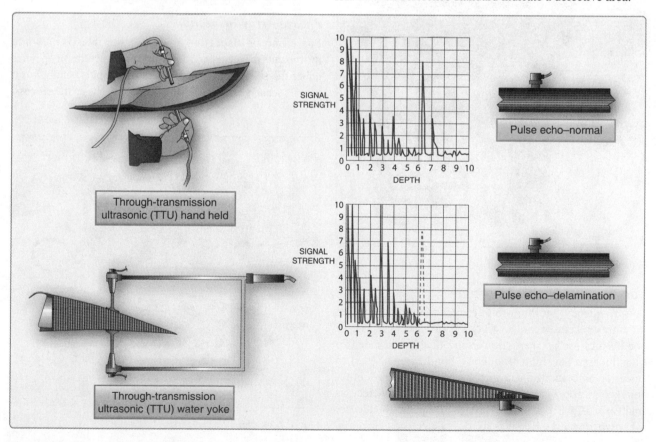

Figure 7-25. *Ultrasonic testing methods.*

Pulse Echo Ultrasonic Inspection

Single-side ultrasonic inspection may be accomplished using pulse echo techniques. In this method, a single search unit is working as a transmitting and a receiving transducer that is excited by high voltage pulses. Each electrical pulse activates the transducer element. This element converts the electrical energy into mechanical energy in the form of an ultrasonic sound wave. The sonic energy travels through a Teflon® or methacrylate contact tip into the test part. A waveform is generated in the test part and is picked up by the transducer element. Any change in amplitude of the received signal, or time required for the echo to return to the transducer, indicates the presence of a defect. Pulse echo inspections are used to find delaminations, cracks, porosity, water, and disbonds of bonded components. Pulse echo does not find disbonds or defects between laminated skins and honeycomb core. *[Figure 7-26]*

Figure 7-26. *Pulse echo test equipment.*

Ultrasonic Bondtester Inspection

Low-frequency and high-frequency bondtesters are used for ultrasonic inspections of composite structures. These bondtesters use an inspection probe that has one or two transducers. The high-frequency bondtester is used to detect delaminations and voids. It cannot detect a skin-to-honeycomb core disbond or porosity. It can detect defects as small as 0.5-inch in diameter. The low-frequency bondtester uses two transducers and is used to detect delamination,

voids, and skin to honeycomb core disbands. This inspection method does not detect which side of the part is damaged, and cannot detect defects smaller than 1.0-inch. *[Figure 7-27]*

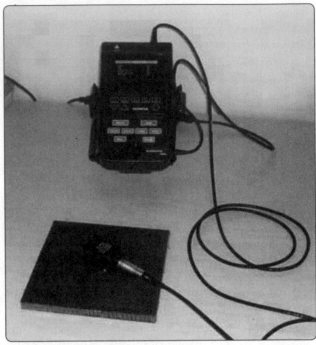

Figure 7-27. *Bond tester.*

Phased Array Inspection

Phased array inspection is one of the latest ultrasonic instruments to detect flaws in composite structures. It operates under the same principle of operation as pulse echo, but it uses 64 sensors at the same time, which speeds up the process. *[Figure 7-28]*

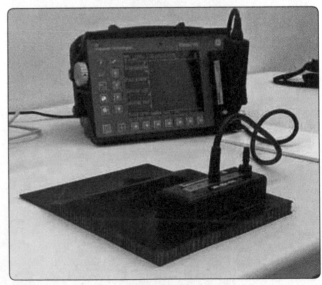

Figure 7-28. *Phased array testing equipment.*

Radiography

Radiography, often referred to as X-ray, is a very useful NDI method because it essentially allows a view into the interior of the part. This inspection method is accomplished by passing X-rays through the part or assembly being tested while recording the absorption of the rays onto a film sensitive to X-rays. The exposed film, when developed, allows the inspector to analyze variations in the opacity of the exposure recorded onto the film, in effect creating a visualization of the relationship of the component's internal details. Since the method records changes in total density through its thickness, it is not a preferred method for detecting defects such as delaminations that are in a plane that is normal to the ray direction. It is a most effective method, however, for detecting flaws parallel to the X-ray beam's centerline. Internal anomalies, such as delaminations in the corners, crushed core, blown core, water in core cells, voids in foam adhesive joints, and relative position of internal details, can readily be seen via radiography. Most composites are nearly transparent to X-rays, so low energy rays must be used. Because of safety concerns, it is impractical to use around aircraft. Operators should always be protected by sufficient lead shields, as the possibility of exposure exists either from the X-ray tube or from scattered radiation. Maintaining a minimum safe distance from the X-ray source is always essential.

Thermography

Thermal inspection comprises all methods in which heat-sensing devices are used to measure temperature variations for parts under inspection. The basic principle of thermal inspection consists of measuring or mapping of surface temperatures when heat flows from, to, or through a test object. All thermographic techniques rely on differentials in thermal conductivity between normal, defect free areas, and those having a defect. Normally, a heat source is used to elevate the temperature of the part being examined while observing the surface heating effects. Because defect free areas conduct heat more efficiently than areas with defects, the amount of heat that is either absorbed or reflected indicates the quality of the bond. The type of defects that affect the thermal properties include debonds, cracks, impact damage, panel thinning, and water ingress into composite materials and honeycomb core. Thermal methods are most effective for thin laminates or for defects near the surface.

Neutron Radiography

Neutron radiography is a nondestructive imaging technique that is capable of visualizing the internal characteristics of a sample. The transmission of neutrons through a medium is dependent upon the neutron cross sections for the nuclei in the medium. Differential attenuation of neutrons through a medium may be measured, mapped, and then visualized.

The resulting image may then be utilized to analyze the internal characteristics of the sample. Neutron radiography is a complementary technique to X-ray radiography. Both techniques visualize the attenuation through a medium. The major advantage of neutron radiography is its ability to reveal light elements such as hydrogen found in corrosion products and water.

Moisture Detector

A moisture meter can be used to detect water in sandwich honeycomb structures. A moisture meter measures the RF power loss caused by the presence of water. The moisture meter is often used to detect moisture in nose radomes. *[Figure 7-29] Figure 7-30* provides a comparison of NDI testing equipment.

Figure 7-29. *Moisture tester equipment.*

Composite Repairs

Layup Materials
Hand Tools

Prepreg and dry fabrics can be cut with hand tools, such as scissors, pizza cutters, and knives. Materials made from Kevlar® are more difficult to cut than fiberglass or carbon and tools wear quicker. A squeegee and a brush are used to impregnate dry fibers with resin for wet layup. Markers, rulers, and circle templates are used to make a repair layout. *[Figure 7-31]*

Method of Inspection	Type of Defect							
	Disbond	Delamination	Dent	Crack	Hole	Water Ingestion	Overheat and Burns	Lightning Strike
Visual	X (1)	X (1)	X	X	X		X	X
X-Ray	X (1)	X (1)		X (1)		X		
Ultrasonic TTU	X	X						
Ultrasonic pulse echo		X				X		
Ultrasonic bondtester	X	X						
Tap test	X (2)	X (2)						
Infrared thermography	X (3)	X (3)				X		
Dye penetrant				X (4)				
Eddy current				X (4)				
Shearography	X (3)	X (3)						

Notes:
(1) For defects that open to the surface
(2) For thin structure (3 plies or less)
(3) The procedures for this type of inspection are being developed
(4) This procedure is not recommended

Figure 7-30. *Comparison of NDI testing equipment.*

Figure 7-31. *Hand tools for laminating.*

Figure 7-32. *Air tools used for composite repair.*

Air Tools

Air-driven power tools, such as drill motors, routers, and grinders, are used for composite materials. Electric motors are not recommended, because carbon is a conductive material that can cause an electrical short circuit. If electric tools are used, they need to be of the totally enclosed type. [Figure 7-32]

Caul Plate

A caul plate made from aluminum is often used to support the part during the cure cycle. A mold release agent, or parting film, is applied to the caul plate so that the part does not attach to the caul plate. A thin caul plate is also used on top of the repair when a heat bonder is used. The caul plate provides a more uniform heated area and it leaves a smoother finish of the composite laminate.

Support Tooling and Molds

Certain repairs require tools to support the part and/or maintain surface contour during cure. A variety of materials can be used to manufacture these tools. The type of material depends on the type of repair, cure temperature, and whether it is a temporary or permanent tool. Support tooling is necessary for oven and autoclave cure due to the high cure temperature. The parts deform if support tooling is not used. There are many types of tooling material available. Some are molded to a specific part contour and others are used as rigid supports to maintain the contour during cure. Plaster is an inexpensive and easy material for contour tooling. It can be filled with fiberglass, hemp, or other material. Plaster is not very durable, but can be used for temporary tools. Often, a layer of fiberglass-reinforced epoxy is placed on the tool side surface to improve the finish quality. Tooling resins are used to impregnate fiberglass, carbon fiber, or other reinforcements to make permanent tools. Complex parts are made from metal or high-temperature tooling boards that are machined with 5-axis CNC equipment to make master tools that can be used to fabricate aircraft parts. *[Figures 7-33 and 7-34]*

Figure 7-33. *Five-axis CNC equipment for tool and mold making.*

Figure 7-34. *A mold of an inlet duct.*

Vacuum Bag Materials

Repairs of composite aircraft components are often performed with a technique known as vacuum bagging. A plastic bag is sealed around the repair area. Air is then removed from the bag, which allows repair plies to be drawn together with no air trapped in between. Atmospheric pressure bears on the repair and a strong, secure bond is created.

Several processing materials are used for vacuum bagging a part. These materials do not become part of the repair and are discarded after the repair process.

Release Agents

Release agents, also called mold release agents, are used so that the part comes off the tool or caul plate easily after curing.

Bleeder Ply

The bleeder ply creates a path for the air and volatiles to escape from the repair. Excess resin is collected in the bleeder. Bleeder material could be made of a layer of fiberglass, nonwoven polyester, or it could be a perforated Teflon® coated material. The structural repair manual (SRM) indicates what type and how many plies of bleeder are required. As a general rule, the thicker the laminate, the more bleeder plies are required.

Peel Ply

Peel plies are often used to create a clean surface for bonding purposes. A thin layer of fiberglass is cured with the repair part. Just before the part is bonded to another structure, the peel ply is removed. The peel ply is easy to remove and leaves a clean surface for bonding. Peel plies are manufactured from polyester, nylon, flouronated ethylene propylene (FEP), or coated fiberglass. They can be difficult to remove if overheated. Some coated peel plies can leave an undesirable contamination on the surface. The preferred peel ply material is polyester that has been heat-set to eliminate shrinkage.

Layup Tapes

Vacuum bag sealing tape, also called sticky tape, is used to seal the vacuum bag to the part or tool. Always check the temperature rating of the tape before use to ensure that you use appropriately rated tape.

Perforated Release Film

Perforated parting film is used to allow air and volatiles out of the repair, and it prevents the bleeder ply from sticking to the part or repair. It is available with different size holes and hole spacing depending on the amount of bleeding required.

Solid Release Film

Solid release films are used so that the prepreg or wet layup plies do not stick to the working surface or caul plate. Solid release film is also used to prevent the resins from bleeding through and damaging the heat blanket or caul plate if they are used.

Breather Material

The breather material is used to provide a path for air to get out of the vacuum bag. The breather must contact the bleeder. Typically, polyester is used in either 4-ounce or 10-ounce weights. Four ounces is used for applications below 50 pounds per square inch (psi) and 10 ounces is used for 50–100 psi.

Vacuum Bag

The vacuum bag material provides a tough layer between the repair and the atmosphere. The vacuum bag material is available in different temperature ratings, so make sure that the material used for the repair can handle the cure temperature. Most vacuum bag materials are one time use, but material made from flexible silicon rubber is reusable. Two small cuts are made in the bagging material so that the vacuum probe valve can be installed. The vacuum bag is not very flexible and plies need to be made in the bag if complex shapes are to be bagged. Sometimes, an envelope type bag is used, but the disadvantage of this method is that the vacuum pressure might crush the part. Reusable bags made from silicon rubber are available that are more flexible. Some have a built-in heater blanket that simplifies the bagging task. *[Figures 7-35, 7-36, and 7-37]*

Figure 7-35. *Bagging materials.*

Figure 7-36. *Bagging of complex part.*

Figure 7-37. *Self-sealing vacuum bag with heater element.*

Vacuum Equipment

A vacuum pump is used to evacuate air and volatiles from the vacuum bag so that atmospheric pressure consolidates the plies. A dedicated vacuum pump is used in a repair shop. For repairs on the aircraft, a mobile vacuum pump could be used. Most heat bonders have a built-in vacuum pump. Special air hoses are used as vacuum lines, because regular air hoses might collapse when a vacuum is applied. The vacuum lines that are used in the oven or autoclave need to be able to withstand the high temperatures in the heating device. A vacuum pressure regulator is sometimes used to lower the vacuum pressure during the bagging process.

Vacuum Compaction Table

A vacuum compaction table is a convenient tool for debulking composite layups with multiple plies. Essentially a reusable vacuum bag, a compaction table consists of a metal table surface with a hinged cover. The cover includes a solid frame, a flexible membrane, and a vacuum seal. Repair plies are laid up on the table surface and sealed beneath the cover with vacuum to remove entrapped air. Some compaction tables are heated but most are not.

Heat Sources
Oven

Composite materials can be cured in ovens using various pressure application methods. *[Figure 7-38]* Typically, vacuum bagging is used to remove volatiles and trapped air and utilizes atmospheric pressure for consolidation. Another method of pressure application for oven cures is the use of shrink wrapping or shrink tape. The oven uses heated air circulated at high speed to cure the material system. Typical oven cure temperatures are 250 °F and 350 °F. Ovens have a temperature sensor to feed temperature data back to the oven controller. The oven temperature can differ from the actual part temperature depending upon the location of the oven sensor and the location of the part in the oven. The thermal mass of the part in the oven is generally greater

Figure 7-38. *Walk-in curing oven.*

than the surrounding oven and during rise to temperature, the part temperature can lag the oven temperature by a considerable amount. To deal with these differences, at least two thermocouples must be placed on the part and connected to a temperature-sensing device (separate chart recorder, hot bonder, etc.) located outside the oven. Some oven controllers can be controlled by thermocouples placed on the repair part.

Autoclave

An autoclave system allows a complex chemical reaction to occur inside a pressure vessel according to a specified time, temperature, and pressure profile in order to process a variety of materials. *[Figure 7-39]* The evolution of materials and processes has taken autoclave operating conditions from 120 °C (250 °F) and 275 kPa (40 psi) to well over 760 °C (1,400 °F) and 69,000 kPa (10,000 psi). Autoclaves that are operated at lower temperatures and pressures can be pressurized by air, but if higher temperatures and pressures are required for the cure cycle, a 50/50 mixture of air and nitrogen or 100 percent nitrogen should be used to reduce the change of an autoclave fire.

The major elements of an autoclave system are a vessel to contain pressure, sources to heat the gas stream and circulate it uniformly within the vessel, a subsystem to apply vacuum to parts covered by a vacuum bag, a subsystem to control operating parameters, and a subsystem to load the molds into the autoclave. Modern autoclaves are computer controlled and the operator can write and monitor all types of cure cycle programs. The most accurate way to control the cure cycle is to control the autoclave controller with thermocouples that are placed on the actual part.

Most parts processed in autoclaves are covered with a vacuum bag that is used primarily for compaction of laminates and to provide a path for removal of volatiles. The bag allows the part to be subjected to differential pressure in the autoclave without being directly exposed to the autoclave atmosphere. The vacuum bag is also used to apply varying levels of vacuum to the part.

Heat Bonder and Heat Lamps

Typical on-aircraft heating methods include electrical resistance heat blankets, infrared heat lamps, and hot air devices. All heating devices must be controlled by some means so that the correct amount of heat can be applied. This is particularly important for repairs using prepreg material and adhesives, because controlled heating and cooling rates are usually prescribed.

Figure 7-39. *Autoclave.*

Heat Bonder

A heat bonder is a portable device that automatically controls heating based on temperature feedback from the repair area. Heat bonders also have a vacuum pump that supplies and monitors the vacuum in the vacuum bag. The heat bonder controls the cure cycle with thermocouples that are placed near the repair. Some repairs require up to 10 thermocouples. Modern heat bonders can run many different types of cure programs and cure cycle data can be printed out or uploaded to a computer. *[Figure 7-40]*

Figure 7-40. *Heat bonder equipment.*

Heat Blanket

A heat blanket is a flexible heater. It is made of two layers of silicon rubber with a metal resistance heater between the two layers of silicon. Heat blankets are a common method of applying heat for repairs on the aircraft. Heat blankets may be controlled manually; however, they are usually used in conjunction with a heat bonder. Heat is transferred from the blanket via conduction. Consequently, the heat blanket must conform to and be in 100 percent contact with the part, which is usually accomplished using vacuum bag pressure. *[Figure 7-41]*

Figure 7-41. *Heat blankets.*

Heat Lamp

Infrared heat lamps can also be used for elevated temperature curing of composites if a vacuum bag is not utilized. However, they are generally not effective for producing curing temperatures above 150 °F, or for areas larger than two square feet. It is also difficult to control the heat applied with a lamp, and lamps tend to generate high-surface temperatures quickly. If controlled by thermostats, heat lamps can be useful in applying curing heat to large or irregular surfaces. Heat bonders can be used to control heat lamps.

Hot Air System

Hot air systems can be used to cure composite repairs, and are mainly restricted to small repairs and for drying the repair area. A heat generator supplies hot air that is directed into an insulated enclosure set up around the repair area after vacuum bagging has been deployed. The hot air surrounds the repair for even temperature rise.

Heat Press Forming

During the press forming process, flat stacked thermoplastic prepreg is heated to above melt temperature (340–430 °C, or 645–805 °F) in an oven, rapidly (1-10 seconds) shuttled to a forming die, pressed to shape, and consolidated and cooled under pressure (700–7,000 kPa, or 100–1,000 psi). *[Figure 7-42]* In production, press forming dies usually are matched male-female sets constructed of steel or aluminum. However, rubber, wood, phenolics, and so on can be used during prototyping. The die set can be maintained at room temperature throughout the forming-consolidation cycle. But, the use of a hot die (120–200 °C, or 250–390 °F) allows control of the cooling-down rate (avoiding part warpage and controlling morphology in semicrystalline thermoplastic prepreg, such as PEEK and polyphenylene sulfide) and extends the forming window promoting better ply slip.

Figure 7-42. *Heat press.*

The main disadvantage with this method is that the press only applies pressure in one direction, and hence, it is difficult to make complex-shaped (e.g., beads, closed corners) parts or parts with legs that approach vertical. Since the temperature of the die set need not be cycled with each part, rapid forming times of between 10 minutes and 2 hours are achievable with press forming.

Thermocouples

A thermocouple (TC) is a thermoelectric device used to accurately measure temperatures. It may be connected to a simple temperature reading device, or connected to a hot bonder, oven, or other type of controller that regulates the amount of heat. TCs consist of a wire with two leads of dissimilar metals that are joined at one end. Heating the joint produces an electric current, which is converted to a temperature reading with a TC monitor. Select the type of wire (J or K) and the type of connector that are compatible with the local temperature monitoring equipment (hot bonder, oven, autoclave, etc.). TC wire is available with different types of insulation; check the manufacturer's product data sheets to ensure the insulation withstands the highest cure temperature. Teflon-insulated wire is generally good for 390 °F and lower cures; Kapton-insulated wire should be used for higher temperatures.

Thermocouple Placement

Thermocouple placement is the key in obtaining proper cure temperatures throughout the repair. In general, the thermocouples used for temperature control should be placed as close as possible to the repair material without causing it to become embedded in the repair or producing indentations in the repair. They should also be placed in strategic hot or cold locations to ensure the materials are adequately cured but not exposed to excessively high temperatures that could degrade the material structural properties. The thermocouples should be placed as close as practical to the area that needs to be monitored. The following steps should be taken when using thermocouples:

- Never use fewer than three thermocouples to monitor a heating cycle.

- If bonding a precured patch, place the thermocouple near the center of the patch.

- A control thermocouple may be centered over a low-temperature (200 °F or lower) co-cured patch as long as it is placed on top of a thin metallic sheet to prevent a thermocouple indentation onto the patch. This may allow for a more accurate control of the patch temperature.

- The thermocouples installed around the perimeter of the repair patch should be placed approximately 0.5 inch away from the edge of the adhesive line.

- Place flash tape below and above the thermocouple tips to protect them from resin flash and to protect the control unit from electrical shorts.

- Do not place the thermocouple under the vacuum port as the pressure may damage the lead and cause erroneous readings to occur.

- Do not place thermocouple wires adjacent to or crossing the heat blanket power cord to prevent erroneous temperature readings caused by magnetic flux lines.

- Do not place any control thermocouple beyond the heat blanket's two-inch overlap of the repair to prevent the controller from trying to compensate for the lower temperature.

- Always leave slack in the thermocouple wire under the vacuum bag to prevent the thermocouple from being pulled away from the area to be monitored as vacuum is applied.

Thermal Survey of Repair Area

In order to achieve maximum structural bonded composite repair, it is essential to cure these materials within the recommended temperature range. Failure to cure at the correct temperatures can produce weak patches and/or bonding surfaces and can result in a repair failure during service. A thermal survey should be performed prior to installing the repair to ensure proper and uniform temperatures can be achieved. The thermal survey determines the heating and insulation requirements, as well as TC locations for the repair area. The thermal survey is especially useful for determining the methods of heating (hot air modules, heat lamps, heat blanket method and monitoring requirements in cases where heat sinks (substructure for instance) exist in the repair area). It should be performed for all types of heating methods to preclude insufficient, excessive, or uneven heating of the repair area.

Temperature Variations in Repair Zone

Thermal variations in the repair area occur for many reasons. Primary among these are material type, material thickness, and underlying structure in the repair zone. For these reasons, it is important to know the structural composition of the area to be repaired. Substructure existing in the repair zone conducts heat away from the repair area, resulting in a cold spot directly above the structure. Thin skins heat quickly and can easily be overheated. Thick skin sections absorb heat slowly and take longer to reach soak temperature. The thermal survey identifies these problem areas and allows the technician to develop the heat and insulation setup required for even heating of the repair area.

Thermal Survey

During the thermal survey process, try to determine possible hot and cold areas in the repair zone. Temporarily attach a patch of the same material and thickness, several thermal couples, heating blanket, and a vacuum bag to the repair area. Heat the area and, after the temperature is stabilized, record the thermocouple temperatures. Add insulation if the temperature of the thermocouple varies more than 10 degrees from average. The areas with a stringer and rib indicate a lower temperature than the middle of the patch because they act as a heat sink. Add insulation to these areas to increase the temperature. *[Figure 7-43]*

Solutions to Heat Sink Problems

Additional insulation can be placed over the repair area. This insulation can also be extended beyond the repair area to minimize heat being conducted away. Breather materials and fiberglass cloths work well, either on top of the vacuum bag or within the vacuum bag or on the accessible backside of the structure. Place more insulation over cool spots and less insulation over hot spots. If access is available to the backside of the repair area, additional heat blankets could be placed there to heat the repair area more evenly.

Types of Layups
Wet Layups

During the wet layup process, a dry fabric is impregnated with a resin. Mix the resin system just before making the repair. Lay out the repair plies on a piece of fabric and impregnate the fabric with the resin. After the fabric is impregnated, cut the repair plies, stack in the correct ply orientation, and vacuum bag. Wet layup repairs are often used with fiberglass for nonstructural applications. Carbon and Kevlar® dry fabric could also be used with a wet layup resin system. Many resin systems used with wet layup cure at room temperature, are easy to accomplish, and the materials can be stored at room temperature for long period of times. The disadvantage of room temperature wet layup is that it does not restore the strength and durability of the original structure and parts that were cured at 250 °F or 350 °F during manufacturing. Some wet layup resins use an elevated temperature cure and have improved properties. In general, wet layup properties are less than properties of prepreg material.

Epoxy resins may require refrigeration until they are used. This prevents the aging of the epoxy. The label on the container states the correct storage temperature for each component. The typical storage temperature is between 40 °F and 80 °F for most epoxy resins. Some resin systems require storage below 40 °F.

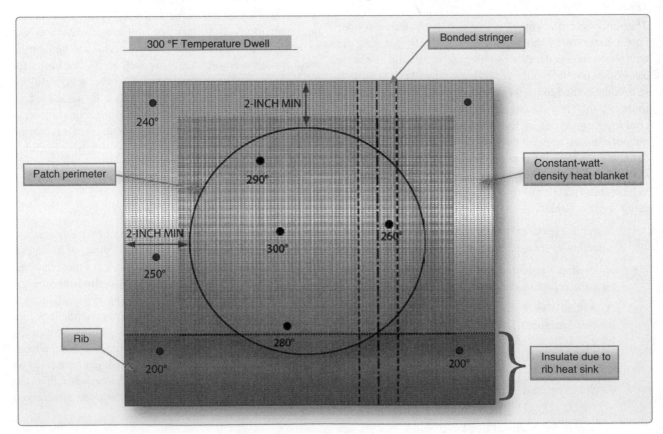

Figure 7-43. *Thermal survey example.*

Prepreg

Prepreg is a fabric or tape that is impregnated with a resin during the manufacturing process. The resin system is already mixed and is in the B stage cure. Store the prepreg material in a freezer below 0 °F to prevent further curing of the resin. The material is typically placed on a roll and a backing material is placed on one side of the material so that the prepreg does not stick together. The prepreg material is sticky and adheres to other plies easily during the stack-up process. You must remove the prepreg from the freezer and let the material thaw, which might take 8 hours for a full roll. Store the prepreg materials in a sealed, moisture proof bag. Do not open these bags until the material is completely thawed, to prevent contamination of the material by moisture.

After the material is thawed and removed from the backing material, cut it in repair plies, stack in the correct ply orientation, and vacuum bag. Do not forget to remove the backing material when stacking the plies. Cure prepregs at an elevated cure cycle; the most common temperatures used are 250 °F and 350 °F. Autoclaves, curing ovens, and heat bonders can be used to cure the prepreg material.

Consolidation is necessary if parts are made from several layers of prepreg, because large quantities of air can be trapped between each prepreg layer. Remove this trapped air by covering the prepreg with a perforated release film and a breather ply, and apply a vacuum bag. Apply the vacuum for 10 to 15 minutes at room temperature. Typically, attach the first consolidated ply to the tool face and repeat this process after every 3 or 5 layers depending on the prepreg thickness and component shape.

Store prepreg, film adhesive, and foaming adhesives in a freezer at a temperature below 0 °F. If these types of materials need to be shipped, place them in special containers filled with dry ice. The freezer must not be of the automatic defrost type; the auto-defrost cycle periodically warms the inside of the freezer, which can reduce the shelf life and consume the allowable out-time of the composite material. Freezers must be capable of maintaining 0 °F or below; most household freezers meet this level. Walk-in freezers can be used for large volume cold storage. If usage is small, a chest-type freezer may suffice. Refrigerators are used to store laminating and paste adhesives and should be kept near 40 °F. [Figure 7-44]

Uncured prepreg materials have time limits for storage and use. [Figure 7-45] The maximum time allowed for storing of a prepreg at low temperature is called the storage life, which is typically 6 months to a year. The material can be tested, and the storage life could be extended by the material

Figure 7-44. *Walk-in freezer for storing prepreg materials.*

Figure 7-45. *Storage life for prepreg materials.*

manufacturer. The maximum time allowed for material at room temperature before the material cures is called the mechanical life. The recommended time at room temperature to complete layup and compaction is called the handling life. The handling life is shorter than the mechanical life. The mechanical life is measured from the time the material is removed from the freezer until the time the material is returned to the freezer. The operator must keep records of the time in and out of the freezer. Material that exceeds the mechanical life needs to be discarded.

Many repair facilities cut the material in smaller kits and store them in moisture-proof bags that thaw quicker when removed from the freezer. This also limits the time out of the freezer for a big roll.

All frozen prepreg materials need to be stored in moisture proof back to avoid moisture contamination. All prepreg material should be protected from dust, oil, vapors, smoke, and other contaminants. A clean room for repair layup would be best, but if a clean room is not available, the prepreg should be protected by storing them in bags or keeping them covered with plastic. Before starting the layup, cover the unprotected sides of the prepreg with parting film, and clean the area being repaired immediately before laying up the repair plies.

Prepreg material is temperature sensitive. Excessively high temperatures cause the material to begin curing, and excessively low temperatures make the material difficult to handle. For repairs on aircraft in very cold or very hot climates, the area should be protected by a tent around the repair area. Prepare the prepreg repair plies in a controlled-temperature environment and bring them to the repair area immediately before using them.

Co-curing

Co-curing is a process wherein two parts are simultaneously cured. The interface between the two parts may or may not have an adhesive layer. Co-curing often results in poor panel surface quality, which is prevented by using a secondary surfacing material co-cured in the standard cure cycle or a subsequent fill-and-fair operation. Co-cured skins may also have poorer mechanical properties, requiring the use of reduced design values.

A typical co-cure application is the simultaneous cure of a stiffener and a skin. Adhesive film is frequently placed into the interface between the stiffener and the skin to increase fatigue and peel resistance. Principal advantages derived from the co-cure process are excellent fit between bonded components and guaranteed surface cleanliness.

Secondary Bonding

Secondary bonding utilizes precured composite detail parts, and uses a layer of adhesive to bond two precured composite parts. Honeycomb sandwich assemblies commonly use a secondary bonding process to ensure optimal structural performance. Laminates co-cured over honeycomb core may have distorted plies that have dipped into the core cells. As a result, compressive stiffness and strength can be reduced as much as 10 and 20 percent, respectively.

Precured laminates undergoing secondary bonding usually have a thin nylon or fiberglass peel ply cured onto the bonding surfaces. While the peel ply sometimes hampers nondestructive inspection of the precured laminate, it has been found to be the most effective means of ensuring surface cleanliness prior to bonding. When the peel ply is stripped away, a pristine surface becomes available. Light scuff sanding removes high resin peak impressions produced by the peel ply weave which, if they fracture, create cracks in the bondline.

Composite materials can be used to structurally repair, restore, or enhance aluminum, steel, and titanium components. Bonded composite doublers have the ability to slow or stop fatigue crack growth, replace lost structural area due to corrosion grind-outs, and structurally enhance areas with small and negative margins. This technology has often been referred to as a combination of metal bonding and conventional on-aircraft composite bonded repair. Boron prepreg tape with an epoxy resin is most often used for this application.

Co-bonding

In the co-bonding process, one of the detail parts is precured with the mating part being cured simultaneously with the adhesive. Film adhesive is often used to improve peel strength.

Layup Process (Typical Laminated Wet Layup)
Layup Techniques

Read the SRM and determine the correct repair material, number of plies required for the repair, and the ply orientation. Dry the part, remove the damage, and taper sand the edges of damaged area. Use a piece of thin plastic, and trace the size of each repair ply from the damaged area. Indicate the ply orientation of each ply on the trace sheet. Copy the repair ply information to a piece of repair material that is large enough to cut all plies. Impregnate the repair material with resin, place a piece of transparent release film over the fabric, cut out the plies, and lay up the plies in the damaged area. The plies are usually placed using the smallest ply first taper layup sequence, but an alternative method is to use the largest ply first layup sequence. In this sequence, the first layer of reinforcing fabric completely covers the work area, followed by successively smaller layers, and then is finished with an extra outer layer or two extending over the patch and onto the sound laminate for some distance. Both methods are illustrated in *Figures 7-46* and *7-47*.

Figure 7-46. *Repair layup process.*

Figure 7-47. *Different lay-up techniques.*

Figure 7-48. *Vacuum bagging of contoured part.*

Bleedout Technique

The traditional bleedout using a vacuum bag technique places a perforated release film and a breather/bleeder ply on top of the repair. The holes in the release film allow air to breath and resin to bleed off over the entire repair area. The amount of resin bled off depends on the size and number of holes in the perforated release film, the thickness of the bleeder/breather cloth, the resin viscosity and temperature, and the vacuum pressure.

Controlled bleed allows a limited amount of resin to bleed out in a bleeder ply. Place a piece of perforated release film on top of the prepreg material, a bleeder ply on top of the perforated release film, and a solid release film on top of the bleeder. Use a breather and a vacuum bag to compact the repair. The breather allows the air to escape. The bleeder can only absorb a limited amount of resin, and the amount of resin that is bled can be controlled by using multiple bleeder plies. Too many bleeder plies can result in a resin-starved repair. Always consult the maintenance manual or manufacturer tech sheets for correct bagging and bleeding techniques.

No Bleedout

Prepreg systems with 32 to 35 percent resin content are typically no-bleed systems. These prepregs contain exactly the amount of resin needed in the cured laminate; therefore, resin bleedoff is not desired. Bleedout of these prepregs results in a resin-starved repair or part. Many high-strength prepregs in use today are no-bleed systems. No bleeder is used, and the resin is trapped/sealed so that none bleeds away. Consult the maintenance manual to determine if bleeder plies are required for the repair. A sheet of solid release film (no holes) is placed on top of the prepreg and taped off at the edges with flash tape. Small openings are created at the edges of the tape so that air can escape. A breather and vacuum bag are installed to compact the prepreg plies. The air can escape on the edge of the repair but no resin can bleed out. *[Figure 7-48]*

Horizontal (or edge) bleedout is used for small room temperature wet layup repairs. A 2-inch strip of breather cloth is placed around the repair or part (edge breather). There is no need for a release film because there is no bleeder/breather cloth on top of the repair. The part is impregnated with resin, and the vacuum bag is placed over the repair. A vacuum is applied and a squeegee is used to remove air and excess resin to the edge breather.

Ply Orientation Warp Clock

In order to minimize any residual thermal stresses caused during cure of the resin, it is always good practice to design a symmetrical, or balanced, laminate. Examples of balance laminates are presented in *Figure 7-49*. The first example uses unidirectional tape, and examples 2 and 3 are typical quasi-isotropic laminates fabricated from woven cloth.

Example	Lamina	Written as
1	±45°, −45°, 0°, 0°, −45°, +45°	(+45, −45, 0) S
2	±45°, 0°/90°, ±45°, 0°/90°, 0°/90°, ±45°, 0°/90°, ±45°	(±45, 0/90)2S
3	±45°, ±45°, 0°/90°, 0°/90°, ±45°, ±45°	([±45] 2, 0/90) S

Figure 7-49. *Examples of balance laminates.*

Figure 7-50 presents examples of the effects caused by nonsymmetrical laminates. These effects are most pronounced in laminates that are cured at high temperature in an autoclave or oven due to the thermal stresses developed in the laminate as the laminate cools down from the cure temperature to room temperature. Laminates cured at room temperature using typical wet layup do not exhibit the same degree of distortion due to the much smaller thermal stresses.

Type	Example	Comments
Symmetrical, balanced	(+45, −45, 0, 0, −45, +45)	Flat, constant midplane stress
Nonsymmetrical, balanced	(90, +45, 0, 90, −45, 0)	Induces curvature
Symmetrical, nonbalanced	(−45, 0, 0, −45)	Induces twist
Nonsymmetrical, nonbalanced	(90, −45, 0, 90, −45, 0)	Induces twist and curvature

Figure 7-50. *Examples of the effects caused by nonsymmetrical laminates.*

The strength and stiffness of a composite buildup depends on the ply orientation. The practical range of strength and stiffness of carbon epoxy extends from values as low as those provided by fiberglass to as high as those provided by titanium. This range of values is determined by the orientation of the plies to the applied load. Because the strength design requirement is a function of the applied load direction, ply orientation and ply sequence must be correct. It is critical during a repair operation to replace each damaged ply with a ply of the same material and orientation or an approved substitute.

Warp is the longitudinal fibers of a fabric. The warp is the high-strength direction due to the straightness of the fibers. A warp clock is used to describe direction of fibers on a diagram, spec sheet, or manufacturer's sheets. If the warp clock is not available on the fabric, the orientation is defaulted to zero as the fabric comes off the roll. Therefore, 90° to zero is across the width of the fabric. 90° to zero is also called the fill direction.

Mixing Resins

Epoxy resins, like all multipart materials, must be thoroughly mixed. Some resin systems have a dye added to aid in seeing how well the material is mixed. Since many resin systems do not have a dye, the resin must be mixed slowly and fully for three minutes. Air enters into the mixture if the resin is mixed too fast. If the resin system is not fully mixed, the resin may not cure properly. Make sure to scrape the edges and bottom of the mixing cup to ensure that all resin is mixed correctly.

Do not mix large quantities of quick curing resin. These types of resins produce heat after they are mixed. Smoke can burn or poison you when the resin overheats. Mix only the amount of material that is required. Mix more than one batch if more material is needed than the maximum batch size.

Saturation Techniques

For wet layup repair, impregnate the fabric with resin. It is important to put the right amount of resin on the fabric. Too much or too little resin affects the strength of the repair. Air that is put into the resin or not removed from the fabric also reduces the repair strength.

Fabric Impregnation With a Brush or Squeegee

The traditional way of impregnating the fabric is by using a brush or squeegee. The technician puts a mold release compound or a release film on a caul plate so that the plies will not adhere to the caul plate. Place a sheet of fabric on the caul plate and apply resin in the middle of the sheet. Use a brush or squeegee to thoroughly wet the fabric. More plies of fabric and resin are added and the process is repeated until all plies are impregnated. A vacuum bag will be used to consolidate the plies and to bleed off excess resin and volatiles. Most wet layup processes have a room temperature cure but extra heat, up to 150 °F, are used to speed up the curing process. *[Figure 7-51]*

Fabric Impregnation Using a Vacuum Bag

The vacuum-assisted impregnation method is used to impregnate repair fabric with a two-part resin while enclosed inside a vacuum bag. This method is preferred for tight-knit weaves and when near optimum resin-to-fiber ratio is required. Compared to squeegee impregnation, this process reduces the level of entrapped air within the fabric and offers a more controlled and contained configuration for completing the impregnation process.

Vacuum-assisted impregnation consists of the following steps:

1. Place vacuum bag sealing tape on the table surface around the area that is used to impregnate the material. The area should be at least 4 inches larger than the material to be impregnated.

2. Place an edge breather cloth next to the vacuum bag sealing tape. The edge breather should be 1–2 inches wide.

3. Place a piece of solid parting film on the table. The sheet should be 2-inches larger than the material to be impregnated.

4. Weigh the fabric to find the amount of resin mix that is necessary to impregnate the material.

5. Lay the fabric on the parting film.

6. Put a piece of breather material between the fabric and the edge breather to provide an air path.

Figure 7-51. *Fabric impregnation with a brush or squeegee: A) wet layup materials; B) fabric placement; C) fabric impregnation; D) squeegee used to thoroughly wet the fabric.*

7. Pour the resin onto the fabric. The resin should be a continuous pool in the center area of the fabric.

8. Put vacuum probes on the edge breather.

9. Place a second piece of solid parting film over the fabric. This film should be the same size or larger than the first piece.

10. Place and seal the vacuum bag, and apply vacuum to the bag.

11. Allow 2 minutes for the air to be removed from the fabric.

12. Sweep the resin into the fabric with a squeegee. Slowly sweep the resin from the center to the edge of the fabric. The resin should be uniformly distributed over all of the fabric.

13. Remove the fabric and cut the repair plies.

Vacuum Bagging Techniques

Vacuum bag molding is a process in which the layup is cured under pressure generated by drawing a vacuum in the space between the layup and a flexible sheet placed over it and sealed at the edges. In the vacuum bag molding process, the plies are generally placed in the mold by hand layup using prepreg or wet layup. High-flow resins are preferred for vacuum bag molding.

Single Side Vacuum Bagging

This is the preferred method if the repair part is large enough for a vacuum bag on one side of the repair. The vacuum bag is taped in place with tacky tape and a vacuum port is placed through the bag to create the vacuum.

Envelope Bagging

Envelope bagging is a process in which the part to be repaired is completely enclosed in a vacuum bag or the bag is wrapped around the end of the component to obtain an adequate seal. It is frequently used for removable aircraft parts, such as flight controls, access panels, etc., and when a part's geometry and/or the repair location makes it very difficult to properly vacuum bag and seal the area in a vacuum. In some cases, a part may be too small to allow installation of a single-side bag vacuum. Other times, the repair is located on the end of a large component that must have a vacuum bag wrapped around the ends and sealed all the way around. [*Figure 7-52*]

Figure 7-52. *Envelope bagging of repair.*

Alternate Pressure Application
Shrink Tape
Another method of pressure application for oven cures is the use of shrink wrapping or shrink tape. This method is commonly used with parts that have been filament wound, because some of the same rules for application apply. The tape is wrapped around the completed layup, usually with only a layer of release material between the tape and the layup. Heat is applied to the tape, usually using a heat gun to make the tape shrink, a process that can apply a tremendous amount of pressure to the layup. After shrinking, the part is placed in the oven for cure. High quality parts can be made inexpensively using shrink tape.

C-Clamps
Parts can also be pressed together with clamps. This technique is used for solid laminate edges of honeycomb panels. Clamps (e.g., C-clamps and spring clamps) are used for pressing together the edges of components and/or repair details. Always use clamps with pressure distribution pads because damage to the part may occur if the clamping force is too high. Spring clamps can be used in applications where resin squeeze-out during cure would require C-clamps to be retightened periodically.

Shotbags and Weights
Shotbags and weights can be used also to provide pressure, but their use is limited due to the low level of pressure imposed.

Curing of Composite Materials
A cure cycle is the time/temperature/pressure cycle used to cure a thermosetting resin system or prepreg. The curing of a repair is as important as the curing of the original part material. Unlike metal repairs in which the materials are premanufactured, composite repairs require the technician to manufacture the material. This includes all storage, processing, and quality control functions. An aircraft repair's cure cycle starts with material storage. Materials that are stored incorrectly can begin to cure before they are used for a repair. All time and temperature requirements must be met and documented. Consult the aircraft structural repair manual to determine the correct cure cycle for the part that needs to be repaired.

Room Temperature Curing
Room temperature curing is the most advantageous in terms of energy savings and portability. Room temperature cure wet layup repairs do not restore either the strength or the durability of the original 250 °F or 350 °F cure components and are often used for wet layup fiberglass repairs for noncritical components. Room temperature cure repairs can be accelerated by the application of heat. Maximum properties are achieved at 150 °F. A vacuum bag can be used to consolidate the plies and to provide a path for air and volatiles to escape.

Elevated Temperature Curing
All prepreg materials are cured with an elevated temperature cure cycle. Some wet layup repairs use an elevated cure cycle as well to increase repair strength and to speed up the curing process. The curing oven and heat bonder uses a vacuum bag to consolidate the plies and to provide a path for air and volatiles to escape. The autoclave uses vacuum and positive pressure to consolidate the plies and to provide a path for air and volatiles to escape. Most heating devices use a programmable computer control to run the cure cycles. The operator can select from a menu of available cure cycles or write his or her own program. Thermocouples are placed near the repair, and they provide temperature feedback for the heating device. Typical curing temperature for composite materials is 250 °F or 350 °F. The temperature of large parts that are cured in an oven or autoclave might be different from that of an oven or autoclave during the cure cycle, because they act like a heat sink. The part temperature is most important for a correct cure, so thermocouples are placed on the part to monitor and control part temperature. The oven or autoclave air temperature probe that measures oven or autoclave temperature is not always a reliable device to determine part curing temperature. The oven temperature and the part temperature can be substantially different if the part or tool acts as a heat sink.

The elevated cure cycle consists of at least three segments:

- Ramp up: The heating device ramps up at a set temperature typically between 3 °F to 5 °F per minute.

- Hold or soak: The heating device maintains the temperature for a predetermined period.

- Cool down: The heating device cools down at a set temperature. Cool down temperatures are typically below 5 °F per minute. When the heating device is below 125 °F, the part can be removed. When an autoclave is used for curing parts, make sure that the pressure in the autoclave is relieved before the door is opened. *[Figure 7-53]*

The curing process is accomplished by the application of heat and pressure to the laminate. The resin begins to soften and flow as the temperature is increased. At lower temperatures, very little reaction occurs. Any volatile contaminants, such as air and/or water, are drawn out of the laminate with vacuum during this time. The laminate is compacted by applying pressure, usually vacuum (atmospheric pressure); autoclaves apply additional pressure, typically 50–100 psi. As the temperature approaches the final cure temperature, the rate of reaction greatly increases, and the resin begins to gel and harden. The hold at the final cure lets the resin finish curing and attain the desired structural properties.

Composite Honeycomb Sandwich Repairs

A large proportion of current aerospace composite components are light sandwich structures that are susceptible to damage and are easily damaged. Because sandwich structure is a bonded construction and the face sheets are thin, damage to sandwich structure is usually repaired by

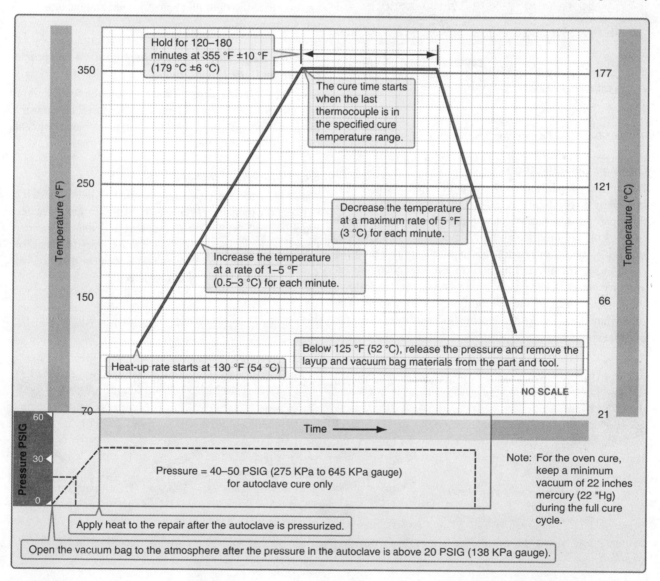

Figure 7-53. *Autoclave cure.*

bonding. Repairs to sandwich honeycomb structure use similar techniques for the most common types of face sheet materials, such as fiberglass, carbon, and Kevlar®. Kevlar® is often repaired with fiberglass. *[Figure 7-54]*

Figure 7-54. *Typical repairs for honeycomb sandwich structure.*

Damage Classification

A temporary repair meets the strength requirements, but is limited by time or flight cycles. At the end of the repair's life, the repair must be removed and replaced. An interim repair restores the required strength to the component. However, this repair does not restore the required durability to the component. Therefore, it has a different inspection interval and/or method. A permanent repair is a repair that restores the required strength and durability to the component. The repair has the same inspection method and interval as the original component.

Sandwich Structures
Minor Core Damage (Filler and Potting Repairs)

A potted repair can be used to repair damage to a sandwich honeycomb structure that is smaller than 0.5 inches. The honeycomb material could be left in place or could be removed and is filled up with a potting compound to restore some strength. Potted repairs do not restore the full strength of the part.

Potting compounds are most often epoxy resins filled with hollow glass, phenolic or plastic microballoons, cotton, flox, or other materials. The potting compound can also be used as filler for cosmetic repairs to edges and skin panels. Potting compounds are also used in sandwich honeycomb panels as hard points for bolts and screws. The potting compound is heavier than the original core and this could affect flight control balance. The weight of the repair must be calculated and compared with flight control weight and balance limits set out in the SRM.

Damage Requiring Core Replacement and Repair to One or Both Faceplates

Note: the following steps are not a substitution for the aircraft specific Structural Repair Manual (SRM). Do not assume that the repair methods used by one manufacturer are applicable to another manufacturer.

Step 1: Inspect the Damage

Thin laminates can be visually inspected and tap tested to map out the damage. *[Figure 7-55]* Thicker laminates need more in-depth NDI methods, such as ultrasonic inspection. Check in the vicinity of the damage for entry of water, oil, fuel, dirt, or other foreign matter. Water can be detected with X-ray, back light, or a moisture detector.

Figure 7-55. *Tap testing techniques.*

Step 2: Remove Water From Damaged Area

Water needs to be removed from the core before the part is repaired. *[Figure 7-56]* If the water is not removed, it boils during the elevated temperature cure cycle and the face sheets blow off the core, resulting in more damage. Water in the honeycomb core could also freeze at the low temperatures that exist at high altitudes, which could result in disbonding of the face sheets.

Step 3: Remove the Damage

Trim out the damage to the face sheet to a smooth shape with rounded corners, or a circular or oval shape. Do not damage the undamaged plies, core, or surrounding material. If the core is damaged as well, remove the core by trimming to the same outline as the skin. *[Figure 7-57]*

Step 4: Prepare the Damaged Area

Use a flexible disk sander or a rotating pad sander to taper sand a uniform taper around the cleaned up damage. Some manufacturers give a taper ratio, such as 1:40, and others prescribe a taper distance like a 1-inch overlap for each existing ply of the face sheet. Remove the exterior finish, including conductive coating for an area that is at least 1 inch larger than the border of the taper. Remove all sanding dust with dry compressed air and a vacuum cleaner. Use a clean cloth moistened with approved solvent to clean the damaged area. *[Figure 7-58]*

Figure 7-56. *Vacuum bag method for drying parts.*

Figure 7-57. *Core damage removal.*

Figure 7-58. *Taper sanding of repair area.*

Step 5: Installation of Honeycomb Core (Wet Layup)

Use a knife to cut the replacement core. The core plug must be of the same type, class, and grade of the original core. The direction of the core cells should line up with the honey comb of the surrounding material. The plug must be trimmed to the right length and be solvent washed with an approved cleaner.

For a wet layup repair, cut two plies of woven fabric that fit on the inside surface of the undamaged skin. Impregnate the fabric plies with a resin and place in the hole. Use potting compound around the core and place it in the hole. For a prepreg repair, cut a piece of film adhesive that fits the hole and use a foaming adhesive around the plug. The plug should touch the sides of the hole. Line up the cells of the plug with the original material. Vacuum bag the repair area and use an oven, autoclave, or heat blanket to cure the core replacement. The wet layup repair can be cured at a room temperature up to 150 °F. The prepreg repair must be cured at 250 °F or 350 °F. Usually, the core replacement is cured with a separate curing cycle and not co-cured with the patch. The plug must be sanded flush with the surrounding area after the cure. *[Figure 7-59]*

Step 6: Prepare and Install the Repair Plies

Consult the repair manual for the correct repair material and the number of plies required for the repair. Typically, one more ply than the original number of plies is installed. Cut the plies to the correct size and ply orientation. The repair plies must be installed with the same orientation as that of the original plies being repaired. Impregnate the plies with resin for the wet layup repair, or remove the backing material from the prepreg material. The plies are usually placed using the smallest ply first taper layup sequence. *[Figure 7-60]*

Step 7: Vacuum Bag the Repair

Once the ply materials are in place, vacuum bagging is used to remove air and to pressurize the repair for curing. Refer to *Figure 7-61* for bagging instructions.

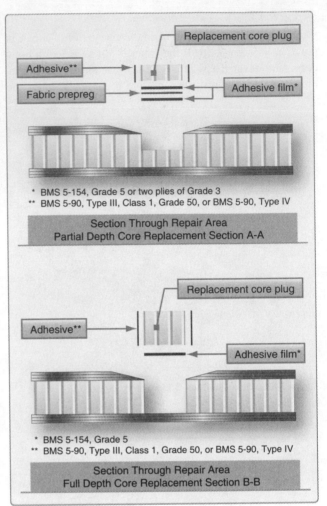

Figure 7-59. *Core replacement.*

Step 8: Curing the Repair

The repair is cured at the required cure cycle. Wet layup repairs can be cured at room temperature. An elevated temperature up to 150 °F can be used to speed up the cure. The prepreg repair needs to be cured at an elevated cure cycle. *[Figure 7-62]* Parts that can be removed from the aircraft could be cured in a hot room, oven, or autoclave. A heating blanket is used for on-aircraft repairs.

Remove the bagging materials after curing and inspect the repair. The repair should be free from pits, blisters, resin-rich and resin-starved areas. Lightly sand the repair patch to produce a smooth finish without damaging the fibers. Apply top finish and conductive coating (lighting protection).

Step 9: Post Repair Inspection

Use visual, tap, and/or ultrasonic inspection to inspect the repair. Remove the repair patch if defects are found. *[Figure 7-63]*

Figure 7-60. *Repair ply installation.*

Figure 7-61. *Vacuum processing.*

Perform a balance check if a repair to a flight control surface was made, and ensure that the repaired flight control is within limits of the SRM. Failure to do so could result in flight control flutter, and safety of flight could be affected.

Solid Laminates
Bonded Flush Patch Repairs

New generation aircraft have fuselage and wing structures made from solid laminates that are externally stiffened with co-cured or co-bonded stringers. These solid laminates have many more plies than the face sheets of honeycomb sandwich structures. The flush repair techniques for solid laminate structures are similar for fiberglass, Kevlar®, and graphite with minor differences.

A flush repair can be stepped or, more commonly, scarved (tapered). The scarf angles are usually small to ease the load into the joint and to prevent the adhesive from escaping. This translates into thickness-to-length ratios of 1:10 to 1:70. Because inspection of bonded repairs is difficult, bonded repairs, as contrasted with bolted repairs, require a higher commitment to quality control, better trained personnel, and cleanliness.

The scarf joint is more efficient from the viewpoint of load transfer as it reduces load eccentricity by closely aligning the neutral axis of the parent and the patch. However, this configuration has many drawbacks in making the repair. First, to maintain a small taper angle, a large quantity of

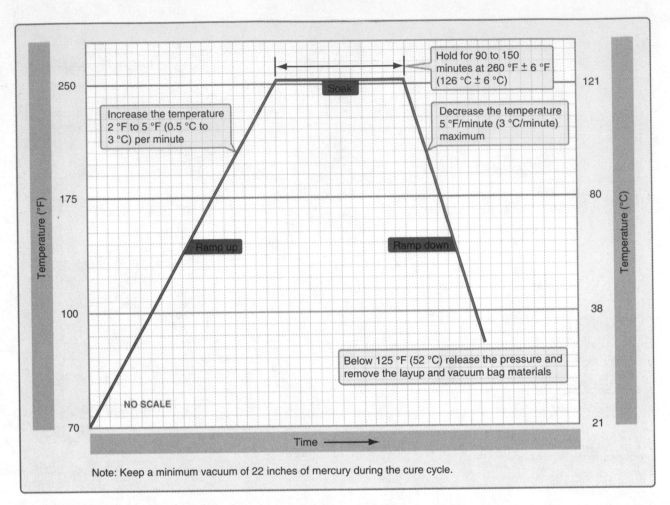

Increase the temperature 2 °F to 5 °F (0.5 °C to 3 °C) per minute

Hold for 90 to 150 minutes at 260 °F ± 6 °F (126 °C ± 6 °C)

Decrease the temperature 5 °F/minute (3 °C/minute) maximum

Soak

Ramp up

Ramp down

Below 125 °F (52 °C) release the pressure and remove the layup and vacuum bag materials

NO SCALE

Time

Note: Keep a minimum vacuum of 22 inches of mercury during the cure cycle.

Figure 7-62. *Curing the repair.*

Heat affected area

Repair

Heat blanket area

Figure 7-63. *Postrepair inspection.*

sound material must be removed. Second, the replacement plies must be very accurately laid up and placed in the repair joint. Third, curing of replacement plies can result in significantly reduced strength if not cured in the autoclave. Fourth, the adhesive can run to the bottom of the joint, creating a nonuniform bond line. This can be alleviated by approximating the scarf with a series of small steps. For these reasons, unless the part is lightly loaded, this type of repair is usually performed at a repair facility where the part can be inserted into the autoclave, which can result in part strength as strong as the original part.

There are several different repair methods for solid laminates. The patch can be precured and then secondarily bonded to the parent material. This procedure most closely approximates the bolted repair. *[Figure 7-64]* The patch can be made from prepreg and then co-cured at the same time as the adhesive. The patch can also be made using a wet layup repair. The curing cycle can also vary in length of time, cure temperature, and cure pressure, increasing the number of possible repair combinations.

Figure 7-64. *A precured patch can be secondarily bound to the parent material.*

Scarf repairs of composite laminates are performed in the sequence of steps described below.

Step 1: Inspection and Mapping of Damage

The size and depth of damage to be repaired must be accurately surveyed using appropriate nondestructive evaluation (NDE) techniques. A variety of NDE techniques can be used to inspect for damage in composite structures. The simplest technique is visual inspection, in which whitening due to delamination and/or resin cracking can be used to indicate the damage area in semitransparent composites, such as glass-polyester and glass-vinyl ester laminates.

Visual inspection is not an accurate technique because not all damage is detectable to the eye, particularly damage hidden by paint, damage located deep below the surface, and damage in nontransparent composites, such as carbon and aramid laminates. A popular technique is tap testing, in which a lightweight object, such as a coin or hammer, is used to locate damage. The main benefits of tap testing are that it is simple and it can be used to rapidly inspect large areas. Tap testing can usually be used to detect delamination damage close to the surface, but becomes increasingly less reliable the deeper the delamination is located below the surface. Tap testing is not useful for detecting other types of damage, such as resin cracks and broken fibers.

More advanced NDE techniques for inspecting composites are impedance testing, x-ray radiography, thermography, and ultrasonics. Of these techniques, ultrasonics is arguably the most accurate and practical and is often used for surveying damage. Ultrasonics can be used to detect small delaminations located deep below the surface, unlike visual inspection and tap testing.

Step 2: Removal of Damaged Material

Once the scope of the damaged area to be repaired has been determined, the damaged laminate must be removed. The edges of the sound laminate are then tapered back to a shallow angle. The taper slope ratio, also known as the scarf angle, should be less than 12 to 1 (< 5°) to minimize

the shear strains along the bond line after the repair patch is applied. The shallow angle also compensates for some errors in workmanship and other shop variables that might diminish patch adhesion. *[Figure 7-65]*

Figure 7-65. *Scarf patch of solid laminate.*

Step 3: Surface Preparation

The laminate close to the scarf zone should be lightly abraded with sandpaper, followed by the removal of dust and contaminates. It is recommended that, if the scarf zone has been exposed to the environment for any considerable period of time, it should be cleaned with a solvent to remove contamination.

Step 4: Molding

A rigid backing plate having the original profile of the composite structure is needed to ensure the repair has the same geometry as the surrounding structure.

Step 5: Laminating

Laminated repairs are usually done using the smallest ply-first taper sequence. While this repair is acceptable, it produces relatively weak, resin-rich areas at each ply edge at the repair interface. The largest ply first laminate sequence, where the first layer of reinforcing fabric completely covers the work area, produces a stronger interface joint. Follow the manufacturer's SRM instructions.

Selection of the reinforcing material is critical to ensuring the repair has acceptable mechanical performance. The reinforcing fabric or tape should be identical to the reinforcement material used in the original composite. Also, the fiber orientation of the reinforcing layers within the repair laminate should match those of the original part laminate, so that the mechanical properties of the repair are as close to original as possible.

Step 6: Finishing

After the patch has cured, a conducting mesh and finish coat should be applied if needed.

Trailing Edge and Transition Area Patch Repairs

Trailing edges of control panels are highly vulnerable to damage. The aft 4 inches are especially subject to ground collision and handling, as well as to lightning strike. Repairs in this region can be difficult because both the skins and the trailing edge reinforcement may be involved. The repairs to a honeycomb core on a damaged edge or panel are similar to the repair of a sandwich honeycomb structure discussed in the Damage Requiring Core Replacement and Repair to One or Both Faceplate Repair sections. Investigate the damage, remove damaged plies and core, dry the part, install new core, layup the repair plies, curing and post inspection. A typical trail edge repair is shown in *Figure 7-66*.

Figure 7-66. *Trailing edge repair.*

Resin Injection Repairs

Resin injection repairs are used on lightly loaded structures for small damages to a solid laminate due to delamination. Two holes are drilled on the outside of the delamination area and a low-viscosity resin is injected in one hole until it flows

out the other hole. Resin injection repairs are sometimes used on sandwich honeycomb structure to repair a facesheet disbond. Disadvantages of the resin injection method are that the fibers are cut as a result of drilling holes, it is difficult to remove moisture from the damaged area, and it is difficult to achieve complete infusion of resin. *[Figure 7-67]*

Figure 7-67. *Resin injection repair.*

Composite Patch Bonded to Aluminum Structure

Composite materials can be used to structurally repair, restore, or enhance aluminum, steel, and titanium components. Bonded composite doublers have the ability to slow or stop fatigue crack growth, replace lost structural area due to corrosion grindouts, and structurally enhance areas with small and negative margins.

Boron epoxy, GLARE®, and graphite epoxy materials have been used as composite patches to restore damaged metallic wing skins, fuselage sections, floor beams, and bulkheads. As a crack growth inhibitor, the stiff bonded composite materials constrain the cracked area, reduce the gross stress in the metal, and provide an alternate load path around the crack. As a structural enhancement or blendout filler, the high modulus fiber composites offer negligible aerodynamic resistance and tailorable properties.

Surface preparation is very important to achieve the adhesive strength. Grit blast silane and phosphoric acid anodizing are used to prepare aluminum skin. Film adhesives using a 250 °F (121 °C) cure are used routinely to bond the doublers to the metallic structure. Critical areas of the installation process include a good thermal cure control, having and maintaining water free bond surfaces, and chemically and physically prepared bond surfaces.

Secondarily bonded precured doublers and in-situ cured doublers have been used on a variety of structural geometries ranging from fuselage frames to door cutouts to blade stiffeners. Vacuum bags are used to apply the bonding and curing pressure between the doubler and metallic surface.

Fiberglass Molded Mat Repairs

Fiberglass molded mats consists of short fibers, and the strength is much less than other composite products that use continuous fibers. Fiberglass molded mats are not used for structural repair applications, but could be used for non-structural applications. The fiberglass molded mat is typically used in combination with fiberglass fabric. The molded mats are impregnated with resin just like a wet layup for fiberglass fabric. The advantage of the molded mat is the lower cost and the ease of use.

Radome Repairs

Aircraft radomes, being an electronic window for the radar, are often made of nonconducting honeycomb sandwich structure with only three or four plies of fiberglass. The skins are so thin so that they do not block the radar signals. The thin structure, combined with the location in front of the aircraft, makes the radome vulnerable to hail damage, bird strikes, and lightning strikes. Low-impact damage could lead to disbonds and delamination. Often, water is found in the radome structure due to impact damage or erosion. The moisture collects in the core material and begins a freeze-thaw cycle each time the airplane is flown. This eventually breaks down the honeycomb material causing a soft spot on the radome itself. Damage to a radome needs to be repaired quickly to avoid further damage and radar signal obstructions. Trapped water or moisture can produce a shadow on the radar image and severely degrade the performance of the radar. To detect water ingression in radomes, the available NDE techniques include x-ray radiography, infrared thermography, and a radome moisture meter that measures the RF power loss caused by the presence of water. The repairs to radomes are similar to repairs to other honeycomb structures, but the technician needs to realize that repairs could affect the radar performance. A special tool is necessary to repair severely damaged radomes. [Figure 7-68]

Figure 7-68. *Radome repair tool.*

Transmissivity testing after radome repair ensures that the radar signal is transmitted properly through the radome. Radomes have lightning protections strips bonded to the outside of the radome to dissipate the energy of a lighting strike. It is important that these lightning protection strips are in good condition to avoid damage to the radome structure. Typical failures of lightning protection strips that are found during inspection are high resistance caused by shorts in the strips or attaching hardware and disbonding of the strips from the radome surface. [Figures 7-69]

Figure 7-69. *Lightning protection strips on a radome.*

External Bonded Patch Repairs

Repairs to damaged composite structures can be made with an external patch. The external patch repair could be made with prepreg, a wet layup, or a precured patch. External patches are usually stepped to reduce the stress concentration at the edge of the patch. The disadvantages of the external patch are the eccentricity of the loading that causes peel stresses and the protrusion of the patch in the air stream. The advantage of the external patch is that it is easier to accomplish than a flush scarf-type repair.

External Bonded Repair With Prepreg Plies

The repair methods for carbon, fiberglass, and Kevlar® are similar. Fiberglass is sometimes used to repair Kevlar® material. The main steps in repairing damage with an external patch are investigating and mapping the damage, removal of the damage, layup of the repair plies, vacuum bagging, curing, and finish coating.

Step 1: Investigating and Mapping the Damage
Use the tap test or ultrasonic test to map out the damage.

Step 2: Damage Removal
Trim out the damage to a smooth round or oval shape. Use scotch or sand paper to rough up the parent surface at least 1 inch larger than the patch size. Clean the surface with an approved solvent and cheese cloth.

Step 3: Layup of the Repair Plies

Use the SRM to determine the number, size, and orientation of the repair plies. The repair ply material and orientation must be the same as the orientation of the parent structure. The repair can be stepped to reduce peel stresses at the edges.

Step 4: Vacuum Bagging

A film adhesive is placed over the damaged area and the repair layup is placed on top of the repair. The vacuum bagging materials are placed on top of the repair (see Prepreg Layup and Controlled Bleed Out) and a vacuum is applied.

Step 5: Curing the Repair

The prepreg patch can be cured with a heater blanket that is placed inside the vacuum bag, oven, or autoclave when the part can be removed from the aircraft. Most prepregs and film adhesives cure at either 250 °F or 350 °F. Consult the SRM for the correct cure cycle.

Step 6: Applying Top Coat

Remove the vacuum bag from the repair after the cure and inspect the repair, remove the patch if the repair is not satisfactory. Lightly sand the repair and apply a protective topcoating.

External Repair Using Wet Layup and Double Vacuum Debulk Method (DVD)

Generally, the properties of a wet layup repair are not as good as a repair with prepreg material; but by using a DVD method, the properties of the wet layup process can be improved. The DVD process is a technique to remove entrapped air that causes porosity in wet layup laminates. The DVD process is often used to make patches for solid laminate structures for complex contoured surfaces. The wet layup patch is prepared in a DVD tool and then secondary bonded to the aircraft structure. *[Figure 7-70]* The laminating process is similar to a standard wet layup process. The difference is how the patch is cured.

Double Vacuum Debulk Principle

The double vacuum bag process is used to fabricate wet layup or prepreg repair laminates. Place the impregnated fabric within the debulking assembly, shown in *Figure 7-70*. To begin the debulking process, evacuate the air within the inner flexible vacuum bag. Then, seal the rigid outer box onto the inner vacuum bag, and evacuate the volume of air between the rigid outer box and inner vacuum bag. Since the outer box is rigid, the second evacuation prevents atmospheric pressure from pressing down on the inner vacuum bag over the patch. This subsequently prevents air bubbles from being pinched off within the laminate and facilitates air removal by the inner vacuum. Next, heat the laminate to a predetermined debulking temperature in order to reduce the resin viscosity and further improve the removal of air and volatiles from the laminate. Apply the heat through a heat blanket that is controlled with thermocouples placed directly on the heat blanket. Once the debulking cycle is complete, compact the laminate to consolidate the plies by venting the vacuum source attached to the outer rigid box, allowing atmospheric pressure to reenter the box and provide positive pressure against the inner vacuum bag. Upon completion of the compaction cycle, remove the laminate from the assembly and prepare for cure.

DVD tools can be purchased commercially but can also be fabricated locally from wood two by fours and sheets of plywood, as illustrated in *Figure 7-70*.

Patch Installation on the Aircraft

After the patch comes out of the DVD tool, it is still possible to form it to the contour of the aircraft, but the time is typically limited to 10 minutes. Place a film adhesive, or paste adhesive, on the aircraft skin and place the patch on the aircraft. Use a vacuum bag and heater blanket to cure the adhesive. *[Figures 7-71 and 7-72]*

Figure 7-70. *DVD tool made from wood two by fours and plywood.*

1. Insulation
2. Heat blanket
3. Caul plate
4. Nonporous film
5. Porous film
6. Patch laminate
7. Bagging materials
8. Bagging film
V1: Inner vacuum
V2: Outer vacuum

Vacuum port

Rigid outer box

V2

V1

Bottom plate

Vacuum port

Figure 7-71. *Double vacuum debulk schematic.*

External Repair Using Precured Laminate Patches

Precured patches are not very flexible and cannot be used on highly curved or compound curved surfaces. The repair steps are similar as in External Bonded Repair With Prepreg Plies, except step 3 and 4 that follow.

Step 3: A Precured Patch

Consult the SRM for correct size, ply thickness, and orientation. You can laminate and cure the precured patch in the repair shop and secondary bond to the parent structure, or obtain standard precured patches. *[Figure 7-73]*

Figure 7-73. *Precured patches.*

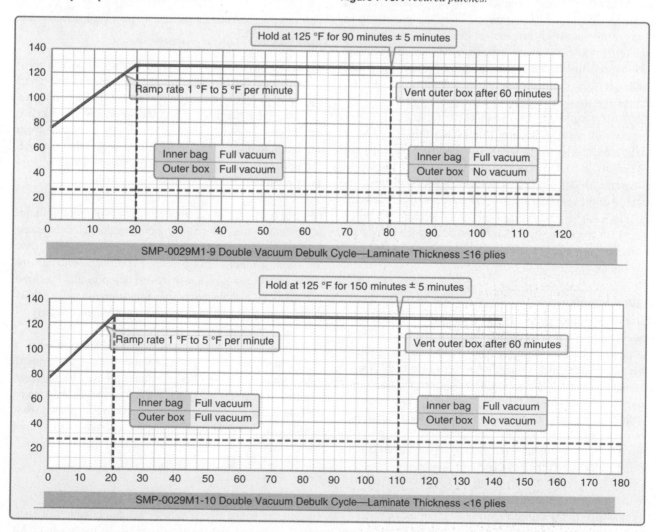

Hold at 125 °F for 90 minutes ± 5 minutes

Ramp rate 1 °F to 5 °F per minute

Vent outer box after 60 minutes

| Inner bag | Full vacuum |
| Outer box | Full vacuum |

| Inner bag | Full vacuum |
| Outer box | No vacuum |

SMP-0029M1-9 Double Vacuum Debulk Cycle—Laminate Thickness ≤16 plies

Hold at 125 °F for 150 minutes ± 5 minutes

Ramp rate 1 °F to 5 °F per minute

Vent outer box after 60 minutes

| Inner bag | Full vacuum |
| Outer box | Full vacuum |

| Inner bag | Full vacuum |
| Outer box | No vacuum |

SMP-0029M1-10 Double Vacuum Debulk Cycle—Laminate Thickness <16 plies

Figure 7-72. *DVD cure cycle.*

Step 4: For a Precured Patch

Apply film adhesive or paste adhesive to the damaged area and place the precured patch on top. Vacuum bag the repair and cure at the correct temperature for the film adhesive or paste adhesive. Most film adhesive cure at either 250 °F or 350 °F. Some paste adhesives cure at room temperature although an elevated temperature could be used to speed the curing process.

Bonded versus Bolted Repairs

Bonded repair concepts have found applicability in both types of manufacturing assembly methods. They have the advantage of not introducing stress concentrations by drilling fastener holes for patch installation and can be stronger than original part material. The disadvantage of bonded repairs is that most repair materials require special storage, handling, and curing procedures.

Bolted repairs are quicker and easier to fabricate than bonded repairs. They are normally used on composite skins thicker than 0.125-inch to ensure sufficient fastener bearing area is available for load transfer. They are prohibited in honeycomb sandwich assemblies due to the potential for moisture intrusion from the fastener holes and the resulting core degradation. Bolted repairs are heavier than comparable bonded repairs, limiting their use on weight-sensitive flight control surfaces.

Honeycomb sandwich parts often have thin face sheets and are most effectively repaired by using a bonded scarf type repair. A bonded external step patch can be used as an alternative. Bolted repairs are not effective for thin laminates because of the low bearing stress of the composite laminate. Thicker solid laminates used on larger aircraft can be up to an inch thick in highly loaded areas and these types of laminates cannot be effectively repaired using a bonded scarf type repair. *[Figure 7-74]*

Bolted Repairs

Aircraft designed in the 1970s used composite sandwich honeycomb structure for lightly loaded secondary structure, but new large aircraft use thick solid laminates for primary structure instead of sandwich honeycomb. These thick solid laminate structures are quite different from the traditional sandwich honeycomb structures used for flight controls, landing gear doors, flaps, and spoilers of today's aircraft. They present a challenge to repair and are difficult to repair with a bonded repair method. Bolted repair methods have been developed to repair thicker solid laminates.

Bolted repairs are not desirable for honeycomb sandwich structure due to the limited bearing strength of the thin face sheets and weakened honeycomb structure from drilling

Bonded versus bolted repair	Bolted	Bonded
Lightly loaded structures – laminate thickness less than 0.1"		X
Highly loaded structures – laminate thickness between 0.125" – 0.5"	X	X
Highly loaded structures – laminate thickness larger than 0.5"	X	
High peeling stresses	X	
Honeycomb structure		X
Dry surfaces	X	X
Wet and/or contaminated surfaces	X	
Disassembly required	X	
Restore unnotched strength		X

Figure 7-74. *Bolted versus bonded repair.*

holes. The advantage of a bolted repair is that you need to select only patch material and fasteners, and the repair method is similar to a sheet metal repair. There is no need for curing the repair and storing the prepreg repair material and film adhesives in a freezer. Patches may be made from aluminum, titanium, steel, or precured composite material. Composite patches are often made from carbon fiber with an epoxy resin or fiberglass with an epoxy resin.

You can repair a carbon fiber structure with an aluminum patch, but you must place a layer of fiberglass cloth between the carbon part and the aluminum patch to prevent galvanic corrosion. Titanium and precured composite patches are preferred for repair of highly loaded components. Precured carbon/epoxy patches have the same strength and stiffness as the parent material as they are usually cured similarly.

Titanium or stainless steel fasteners are used for bolted repairs of a carbon fiber structure. Aluminum fasteners corrode if used with carbon fiber. Rivets cannot be used because the installation of rivets using a rivet gun introduce damage to the hole and surrounding structure and rivets expand during installation, which is undesirable for composite structures because it could cause delimination of the composite material.

Repair Procedures
Step 1: Inspection of the Damage
The tap test is not effective to detect delamination in thick laminates unless the damage is close to the surface. An

ultrasonic inspection is necessary to determine the damage area. Consult the SRM to find an applicable NDI procedure.

Step 2: Removal of the Damage

The damaged area needs to be trimmed to a round or rectangular hole with large smooth radii to prevent stress concentrations. Remove the damage with a sander, router, or similar tool.

Step 3: Patch Preparation

Determine the size of the patch based on repair information found in the SRM. Cut, form, and shape the patch before attaching the patch to the damaged structure. It is easier to make the patch a little bigger than calculated and trim to size after drilling all fastener holes. In some cases, the repair patches are stocked preshaped and predrilled. If cutting is to be performed, standard shop procedures should be used that are suitable for the patch material. Titanium is hard to work and requires a large powerful slip roller to curve the material. Metal patches require filing to prevent crack initiation around the cut edges. When drilling pilot holes in the composite, the holes for repair fasteners must be a minimum of four diameters from existing fasteners and have a minimum edge distance of three fastener diameters. This is different from the standard practice for aluminum of allowing a two diameter distance. Specific pilot hole sizes and drill types to be used should follow specific SRM instructions. *[Figure 7-75]*

Step 4: Hole Pattern Lay Out

To locate the patch on the damaged area, draw two perpendicular centerlines on the parent structure and on the patch material that define the principal load or geometric directions. Then, lay out hole pattern on the patch and drill

pilot holes in the patch material. Align the two perpendicular centerlines of the patch with the lines on the parent structure and transfer the pilot holes to the parent material. Use clecos to keep the patch in place. Mark the edges of the patch so that it can be returned to the same location easily.

Step 5: Drilling and Reaming Holes in Patch and Parent Structure

Composite skins should be backed up to prevent splitting. Enlarge the pilot holes in the patch and parent materials with a drill $\frac{1}{64}$ undersize and then ream all holes to the correct size. A tolerance of +0.0025/–0.000-inch is usually recommended for aircraft parts. For composites, this means interference fasteners are not used.

Step 6: Fastener Installation

Once fastener holes are drilled full size and reamed, permanent fasteners are installed. Before installation, measure the fastener grip length for each fastener using a grip length gauge. As different fasteners are required for different repairs, consult the SRM for permissible fastener type and installation procedure. However, install all fasteners wet with sealant and with proper torque for screws and bolts.

Step 7: Sealing of Fasteners and Patch

Sealants are applied to bolted repairs for prevention of water/ moisture intrusion, chemical damage, galvanic corrosion, and fuel leaks. They also provide contour smoothness. The sealant must be applied to a clean surface. Masking tape is usually placed around the periphery of the patch, parallel with the patch edges and leaving a small gap between the edge of the patch and the masking tape. Sealing compound is applied into this gap.

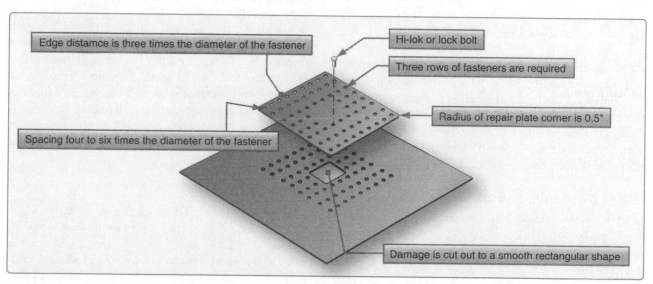

Figure 7-75. *Repair layout for bolted repair of composite structure.*

Step 8: Application of Finish Coat and Lightening Protection Mesh

The repair needs to be sanded, primed, and painted with an approved paint system. A lightning protection mesh needs to be applied if composite patches are used in an area that is prone to lightening strikes.

Fasteners Used with Composite Laminates

Many companies make specialty fasteners for composite structures and several types of fasteners are commonly used: threaded fasteners, lock bolts, blind bolts, blind rivets, and specialty fasteners for soft structures, such as honeycomb panels. The main differences between fasteners for metal and composite structures are the materials and the footprint diameter of nuts and collars.

Corrosion Precautions

Neither fiberglass nor Kevlar® fiber reinforced composites cause corrosion problems when used with most fastener materials. Composites reinforced with carbon fibers, however, are quite cathodic when used with materials, such as aluminum or cadmium, the latter of which is a common plating used on fasteners for corrosion protection.

Fastener Materials

Titanium alloy Ti-6Al-4V is the most common alloy for fasteners used with carbon fiber reinforced composite structures. Austenitic stainless steels, superalloys (e.g., A286), multiphase alloys (e.g., MP35N or MP159), and nickel alloys (e.g., alloy 718) also appear to be very compatible with carbon fiber composites.

Fastener System for Sandwich Honeycomb Structures (SPS Technologies Comp Tite)

The adjustable sustain preload (ASP) fastening system provides a simplified method of fastening composite, soft core, metallic or other materials, which are sensitive to fastener clamp-up or installation force conditions. Clamping force can be infinitely adjustable within maximum recommended torque limits and no further load is applied during installation of the lock collar. The fastener is available in two types. The Asp® has full shank and the 2Asp® has a pilot type shank. *[Figures 7-76 and 7-77]*

Hi-Lok® and Huck-Spin® Lockbolt Fasteners

Most composite primary structures for the aircraft industry are fastened with Hi-Loks® (Hi-Shear Corp.) or Huck-Spin® lockbolts for permanent installations. The Hi-Lok® is a threaded fastener that incorporates a hex key in the threaded end to react to the torque applied to the collar during installation. The collar includes a frangible portion that separates at a predetermined torque value. *[Figure 7-78]*

Figure 7-76. *ASP fastener system.*

The Lockbolt incorporates a collar that is swaged into annular grooves. It comes in two types: pull and stump. The pull-type is the most common, where a frangible pintail is used to react the axial load during the swaging of the collar. When the swaging load reaches a predetermined limit, the pintail breaks away at the breakneck groove. The installation of the Hi-Lok® and the pull-type Huck-Spin® lockbolt can be performed by one technician from one side of the structure. The stump-type Lockbolt, on the other hand, requires support on the head side of the fastener to react the swage operation. This method is usually reserved for automated assembly of detail structure in which access is not a problem.

The specific differences in these fasteners for composite structure in contrast to metal structure are small. For the Hi-Lok®, material compatibility is the only issue; aluminum collars are not recommended. Standard collars of A286, 303 stainless steel, and titanium alloy are normally used. The Huck-Spin® lockbolt requires a hat-shaped collar that incorporates a flange to spread the high bearing loads during installation. The Lockbolt pin designed for use in composite structure has six annular grooves as opposed to five for metal structure. *[Figures 7-79 and 7-80]*

Eddie-Bolt® Fasteners

Eddie-Bolt® fasteners (Alcoa) are similar in design to Hi-Loks® and are a natural choice for carbon fiber composite structures. The Eddie-Bolt® pin is designed with flutes in the threaded portion, which allow a positive lock to be made during installation using a specially designed mating nut or collar. The mating nut has three lobes that serve as driving ribs. During installation, at a predetermined preload, the lobes

Figure 7-77. *ASP fastener system installation sequence.*

Figure 7-78. *Hi-Lok® installation.*

HLH 103, HLH 104, HLH 110, HLH 111 or HLH 500 installation tool

Large 130 flush shear head

Lock grooves

CP titanium flanged collar

Pull grooves

Figure 7-79. *Huck-Spin® lockbolt.*

compress the nut material into the flutes of the pin and form the locking feature. The advantage for composite structure is that titanium alloy nuts can be used for compatibility and weight saving without the fear of galling. The nuts spin on freely, and the locking feature is established at the end of the installation cycle. *[Figure 7-81]*

Cherry's E-Z Buck® (CSR90433) Hollow Rivet

The Cherry Hollow End E-Z Buck® rivet is made from titanium/columbium alloy and has a shear strength of 40 KSI. The E-Z Buck® rivet is designed to be used in a double flush application for fuel tanks. The main advantage of this type of rivet is that it takes less than half the force of a solid rivet of the same material. The rivets are installed with automated riveting equipment or a rivet squeezer. Special optional dies ensure that the squeezer is always centered during installation, avoiding damage to the structure. *[Figure 7-82]*

Blind Fasteners

Composite structures do not require as many fasteners as metal aircraft because stiffeners and doublers are co-cured with the skins, eliminating many fasteners. The size of panels on aircraft has increased in composite structures, which causes backside inaccessibility. Therefore, blind fasteners or screws and nutplates must be used in these areas. Many manufacturers make blind fasteners for composite structures; a few are discussed below.

1. Tool engages lockbolt pintail

2. Gap closes, collar swage begins

3. Swage process complete

4. Pintail fractures at the break notch

5. Tool anvil reverses off swaged collar

6. Installation complete

Figure 7-80. *Huck-Spin® installation sequence.*

Figure 7-81. *Eddie Bolts®.*

Blind Bolts

The Cherry Maxibolt® is available in titanium for compatibility with composite structures. The shear strength of the Maxibolt® is 95 KSI. It can be installed from one side with a G-83 or equivalent pneumatic-hydraulic installation tool, and is available in 100° flush head, 130° flush head and protruding head styles. *[Figure 7-83]*

The Alcoa UAB™ blind bolt system is designed for composite structures and is available in titanium and stainless steel. The UAB™ blind bolt system is available in 100° flush head, 130° flush head, and protruding head styles.

The Accu-Lok™ Blind Fastening System is designed specifically for use in composite structures in which access is limited to one side of the structure. It combines high joint preload with a large diameter footprint on the blind side. The large footprint enables distribution of the joint preload over a larger area, virtually eliminating the possibility of delaminating the composite structure. The shear strength of the Accu-Lok™ is 95 KSI, and it is available in 100° flush head, 130° flush head, and protruding head styles. A similar fastener designed by Monogram is called the Radial-Lok®. *[Figure 7-84]*

Fiberlite

The fiberlite fastening system uses composite materials for a wide range of aerospace hardware. The strength of fiberlite fasteners is equivalent to aluminum at two-thirds the weight. The composite fastener provides good material compatibility with carbon fiber and fiberglass.

Screws and Nutplates in Composite Structures

The use of screws and nutplates in place of Hi-Loks® or blind fasteners is recommended if a panel must be removed periodically for maintenance. Nutplates used in composite structures usually require three holes: two for attachment of the nutplate and one for the removable screw, although rivetless nut plates and adhesive bonded nutplates are available that do not require drilling and countersinking two extra holes.

Rivet Diameter	A REF	CSR 90433			
		B REF	C1 DIA	C2 DIA	D DIA
1/8 (−4)	0.028	0.028	0.195 / 0.189	0.195 / 0.189	0.132 / 0.129
5/32 (−5)	0.037	0.037	0.247 / 0.242	0.247 / 0.242	0.162 / 0.159
3/16 (−6)	0.046	0.046	0.302 / 0.297	0.302 / 0.297	0.195 / 0.191
7/32 (−7)	0.046	0.046	0.328 / 0.323	0.328 / 0.323	0.227 / 0.224

Hollow End E-Z Buck® Nominal Diameter	Upset Load (Lb) + 200 Lb
1/8" (−4)	2,500
5/32" (−5)	2,700
3/16" (−6)	3,000
7/32" (−7)	3,750

Cherry Flaring Snap Die Part Numbers

Rivet Diameter	3/16" Diameter Mount	1/4" Diameter Mount
1/8"	839B1-4	839B10-4
5/32"	839B1-5	839B10-5
3/16"	839B1-6	839B10-6
7/32"	839B1-7	839B10-7

Figure 7-82. *Cherry's E-Z buck hollow rivet.*

Machining Processes and Equipment
Drilling

Hole drilling in composite materials is different from drilling holes in metal aircraft structures. Different types of drill bits, higher speeds, and lower feeds are required to drill precision holes. Structures made from carbon fiber and epoxy resin are very hard and abrasive, requiring special flat flute drills or similar four-flute drills. Aramid fiber (Kevlar®)/epoxy composites are not as hard as carbon but are difficult to drill unless special cutters are used because the fibers tend to fray or shred unless they are cut clean while embedded in the epoxy. Special drill bits with clothes pin points and fish-tail points have been developed that slice the fibers prior to pulling them out of the drilled hole. If the Kevlar®/epoxy part is sandwiched between two metal parts, standard twist drills can be used.

Equipment

Air-driven tools are used for drilling holes in composite materials. Drill motors with free speed of up to 20,000 rpm are used. A general rule for drilling composites is to use high speed and a low feed rate (pressure). Drilling equipment with a power feed control produces better hole quality than drill motors without power feed control. Drill guides are recommended, especially for thicker laminates.

Do not use standard twist drill bits for drilling composite structures. Standard high-speed steel is unacceptable, because it dulls immediately, generates excessive heat, and causes ply delamination, fiber tear-out, and unacceptable hole quality.

Drill bits used for carbon fiber and fiberglass are made from diamond-coated material or solid carbide because the fibers

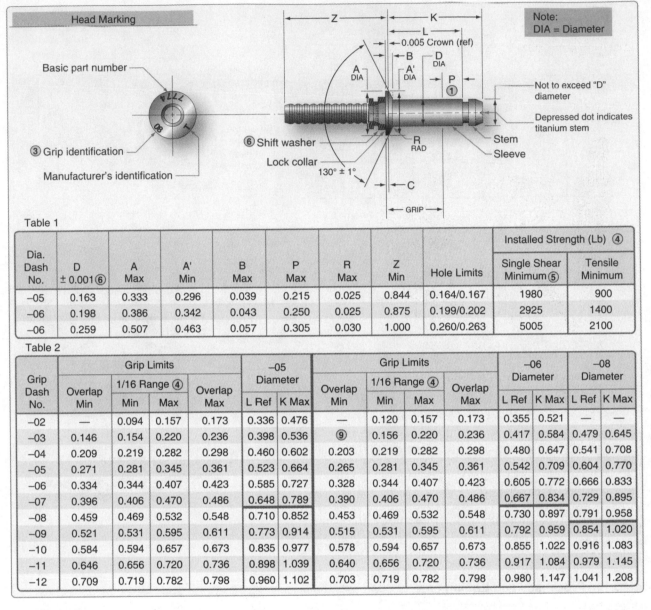

Figure 7-83. *Cherry's titanium Maxibolt.*

Table 1

Dia. Dash No.	D ± 0.001 ⑥	A Max	A' Min	B Max	P Max	R Max	Z Min	Hole Limits	Installed Strength (Lb) ④ Single Shear Minimum ⑤	Tensile Minimum
–05	0.163	0.333	0.296	0.039	0.215	0.025	0.844	0.164/0.167	1980	900
–06	0.198	0.386	0.342	0.043	0.250	0.025	0.875	0.199/0.202	2925	1400
–06	0.259	0.507	0.463	0.057	0.305	0.030	1.000	0.260/0.263	5005	2100

Table 2

Grip Dash No.	Grip Limits Overlap Min	1/16 Range ④ Min	1/16 Range ④ Max	Overlap Max	–05 Diameter L Ref	–05 Diameter K Max	Grip Limits Overlap Min	1/16 Range ④ Min	1/16 Range ④ Max	Overlap Max	–06 Diameter L Ref	–06 Diameter K Max	–08 Diameter L Ref	–08 Diameter K Max
–02	—	0.094	0.157	0.173	0.336	0.476	—	0.120	0.157	0.173	0.355	0.521	—	—
–03	0.146	0.154	0.220	0.236	0.398	0.536	⑨	0.156	0.220	0.236	0.417	0.584	0.479	0.645
–04	0.209	0.219	0.282	0.298	0.460	0.602	0.203	0.219	0.282	0.298	0.480	0.647	0.541	0.708
–05	0.271	0.281	0.345	0.361	0.523	0.664	0.265	0.281	0.345	0.361	0.542	0.709	0.604	0.770
–06	0.334	0.344	0.407	0.423	0.585	0.727	0.328	0.344	0.407	0.423	0.605	0.772	0.666	0.833
–07	0.396	0.406	0.470	0.486	0.648	0.789	0.390	0.406	0.470	0.486	0.667	0.834	0.729	0.895
–08	0.459	0.469	0.532	0.548	0.710	0.852	0.453	0.469	0.532	0.548	0.730	0.897	0.791	0.958
–09	0.521	0.531	0.595	0.611	0.773	0.914	0.515	0.531	0.595	0.611	0.792	0.959	0.854	1.020
–10	0.584	0.594	0.657	0.673	0.835	0.977	0.578	0.594	0.657	0.673	0.855	1.022	0.916	1.083
–11	0.646	0.656	0.720	0.736	0.898	1.039	0.640	0.656	0.720	0.736	0.917	1.084	0.979	1.145
–12	0.709	0.719	0.782	0.798	0.960	1.102	0.703	0.719	0.782	0.798	0.980	1.147	1.041	1.208

Figure 7-84. *Accu-Lok ™ installation.*

are so hard that standard high-speed steel (HSS) drill bits do not last long. Typically, twist drills are used, but brad point drills are also available. The Kevlar® fibers are not as hard as carbon, and standard HSS drill bits can be used. The hole quality can be poor if standard drill bits are used and the preferred drill style is the sickle-shaped Klenk drill. This drill first pulls on the fibers and then shears them, which results in a better quality hole. Larger holes can be cut with diamond-coated hole saws or fly cutters, but only use fly cutters in a drill press, and not in a drill motor. [*Figures 7-85, 7-86,* and *7-87*]

Figure 7-85. *Klenk-type drill for drilling Kevlar®.*

Figure 7-86. *Drilling and cutting tools for composite materials.*

Figure 7-87. *Autofeed drill.*

Processes and Precautions

Composite materials are drilled with drill motors operating between 2,000 and 20,000 rpm and a low feed rate. Drill motors with a hydraulic dash pod or other type of feed control are preferred because they restrict the surging of the drill as it exits the composite materials. This reduces breakout damage and delaminations. Parts made from tape products are especially susceptible to breakout damage; parts made from fabric material have experienced less damage. The composite structure needs to be backed with a metal plate or sheet to avoid breakout. Holes in composite structures are often predrilled with a small pilot hole, enlarged with a diamond-coated or carbide drill bit and reamed with a carbide reamer to final hole size.

Back counterboring is a condition that can occur when carbon/epoxy parts mate metal substructure parts. The back edge of the hole in the carbon/epoxy part can be eroded or radiused by metal chips being pulled through the composite. The condition is more prevalent when there are gaps between the parts or when the metal debris is stringy rather than small chips. Back counterboring can be minimized or eliminated by changing feeds and speeds, cutter geometry, better part clamp-up adding a final ream pass, using a peck drill, or combination of these.

When drilling combinations of composite parts with metal parts, the metal parts may govern the drilling speed. For example, even though titanium is compatible with carbon/epoxy material from a corrosion perspective, lower drilling speeds are required in order to ensure no metallurgical damage occurs to the titanium. Titanium is drilled with low speed and high feed. Drill bits suitable for titanium might not be suitable for carbon or fiberglass. Drill bits that are used for drilling titanium are often made from cobalt-vanadium; drill bits used for carbon fiber are made from carbide or are diamond coated to increase drill life and to produce an accurate hole. Small-diameter high-speed steel (HSS) drill bits, such as No. 40 drill, which are used to manually drill pilot holes, are typically used because carbide drills are relatively brittle and are easily broken. The relatively low cost of these small HSS drill bits offsets the limited life expectancy. High-speed steel drill bits may last for only one hole.

The most common problem with carbide cutters used in hand-drill operations is handling damage (chipped edges) to the cutters. A sharp drill with a slow constant feed can produce a 0.1 mm (0.004-inch) tolerance hole through carbon/epoxy plus thin aluminum, especially if a drill guide is used. With hard tooling, tighter tolerances can be maintained. When the structure under the carbon/epoxy is titanium, drills can pull titanium chips through the carbon/epoxy and enlarge the hole. In this case, a final ream operation may be required to hold tight hole tolerances. Carbide reamers are needed for holes through carbon/epoxy composite structure. In addition, the exit end of the hole needs good support to prevent splintering and delaminations when the reamer removes more than about 0.13 mm (0.005-inch) on the diameter. The support can be the substructure or a board held firmly against the back surface. Typical reaming speeds are about one-half of the drilling speed.

Cutting fluids are not normally used or recommended for drilling thin (less than 6.3 mm, or 0.25-inch thick) carbon/epoxy structure. It is good practice to use a vacuum while drilling in composite materials to avoid that carbon dust freely floats around the work area.

Countersinking

Countersinking a composite structure is required when flush head fasteners are to be installed in the assembly. For metallic structures, a 100° included angle shear or tension head fastener has been the typical approach. In composite structures, two types of fastener are commonly used: a 100° included angle tension head fastener or a 130° included angle head fastener. The advantage of the 130° head is that the fastener head can have about the same diameter as a tension head 100° fastener with the head depth of a shear-type head 100° fastener. For seating flush fasteners in composite parts, it is recommended that the countersink cutters be designed to produce a controlled radius between the hole and the countersink to accommodate the head-to-shank fillet radius on the fasteners. In addition, a chamfer operation or a washer may be required to provide proper clearance for protruding head fastener head-to-shank radii. Whichever head style is used, a matching countersink/chamfer must be prepared in the composite structure.

Carbide cutters are used for producing a countersink in carbon/epoxy structure. These countersink cutters usually have straight flutes similar to those used on metals. For Kevlar® fiber/epoxy composites, S-shaped positive rake cutting flutes are used. If straight-fluted countersink cutters are used, a special thick tape can be applied to the surface to allow for a clean cutting of the Kevlar® fibers, but this is not as effective as the S-shaped fluted cutters. Use of a piloted countersink cutter is recommended because it ensures better concentricity between the hole and the countersink and decreases the possibility of gaps under the fasteners due to misalignment or delaminations of the part.

Use a microstop countersink gauge to produce consistent countersink wells. Do not countersink through more than 70 percent of the skin depth because a deeper countersink well reduces material strength. When a piloted countersink cutter is used, the pilot must be periodically checked for wear, as wear can cause reduction of concentricity between the hole and countersink. This is especially true for countersink cutters with only one cutting edge. For piloted countersink cutters, position the pilot in the hole and bring the cutter to full rpm before beginning to feed the cutter into the hole and preparing the countersink. If the cutter is in contact with the composite before triggering the drill motor, you may get splintering.

Cutting Processes and Precautions

Cutters that work well for metals would either have a short life or produce a poorly cut edge if used for composite materials. The cutters that are used for composites vary with the composite material that is being cut. The general rule for cutting composites is high speed and slow feed.

- Carbon fiber reinforced plastics: Carbon fiber is very hard and quickly wears out high speed steel cutters. For most trimming and cutting tasks, diamond grit cutters are best. Aluminum-oxide or silicon-carbide sandpaper or cloth is used for sanding. Silicon-carbide lasts longer then aluminum-oxide. Router bits can also be made from solid carbide or diamond coated.

- Glass fiber reinforced plastics: Glass fibers, like carbon, are very hard and quickly wear out high-speed steel cutters. Fiberglass is drilled with the same type and material drill bits as carbon fiber.

- Aramid (Kevlar®) fiber-reinforced plastics: Aramid fiber is not as hard as carbon and glass fiber, and cutters made from high-speed steel can be used. To prevent loose fibers at the edge of aramid composites, hold the part and then cut with a shearing action. Aramid composites need to be supported with a plastic backup plate. The aramid and backup plate are cut through at the same time. Aramid fibers are best cut by being held in tension and then sheared. There are specially shaped cutters that pull on the fibers and then shear them. When using scissors to cut aramid fabric or prepreg, they must have a shearing edge on one blade and a serrated or grooved surface on the other. These serrations hold the material from slipping. Sharp blades should always be used as they minimize fiber damage. Always clean the scissor serrations immediately after use so the uncured resin does not ruin the scissors.

Always use safety glasses and other protective equipment when using tools and equipment.

Cutting Equipment

The bandsaw is the equipment that is most often used in a repair shop for cutting composite materials. A toothless carbide or diamond-coated saw blade is recommended. A typical saw blade with teeth does not last long if carbon fiber or fiberglass is cut. *[Figure 7-88]* Air-driven hand tools, such as routers, saber saws, die grinders, and cut-off wheels can be used to trim composite parts. Carbide or diamond-coated cutting tools produce a better finish and they last much longer. Specialized shops have ultrasonic, waterjet, and laser cutters. These types of equipment are numerical controlled (NC) and produce superior edge and hole quality. A waterjet cutter cannot be used for honeycomb structure because it introduces water in the part. Do not cut anything else on equipment that is used for composites because other materials can contaminate the composite material.

Figure 7-88. *Bandsaw.*

Prepreg materials can be cut with a CNC Gerber table. The use of this equipment speeds up the cutting process and optimizes the use of the material. Design software is available that calculates how to cut plies for complex shapes. *[Figures 7-89]*

Figure 7-89. *Gerber cutting table.*

Repair Safety

Advanced composite materials including prepreg, resin systems, cleaning solvents, and adhesives could be hazardous, and it is important that you use personal protection equipment. It is important to read and understand the Material Safety Data Sheets (MSDS) and handle all chemicals, resins, and fibers correctly. The MSDS lists the hazardous chemicals in the material system, and it outlines the hazards. The material could be a respiratory irritant or carcinogenic, or another kind of dangerous substance.

Eye Protection

Always protect eyes from chemicals and flying objects. Wear safety glasses at all times and, when mixing or pouring acids, wear a face shield. Never wear corrective contact lenses in a shop, even with safety glasses. Some of the chemical solvents can melt the lenses and damage eyes. Dust can also get under the lenses, causing damage.

Respiratory Protection

Do not breathe carbon fiber dust and always ensure that there is a good flow of air where the work is performed. Always use equipment to assist in breathing when working in a confined space. Use a vacuum near the source of the dust to remove the dust from the air. When sanding or applying paint, you need a dust mask or a respirator. A properly fitted dust mask provides the protection needed. For application of paints, a sealed respirator with the correct filters or a fresh air supply respirator is required.

Downdraft Tables

A downdraft table is an efficient and economical device for protecting workers from harmful dust caused by sanding and grinding operations. The tables are also useful housekeeping tools because the majority of particulate material generated by machining operations is immediately collected for disposal. Downdraft tables should be sized and maintained to have an average face velocity between 100 and 150 cubic feet per minute. The downdraft table draws contaminants like dust and fibers away from the operator's material. Downdraft tables should be monitored and filters changed on a regular basis to provide maximum protection and particulate collection.

Skin Protection

During composite repair work, protect your skin from hazardous materials. Chemicals could remain on hands that burn sensitive skin. Always wear gloves and clothing that offer protection against toxic materials. Use only approved gloves that protect skin and do not contaminate the composite material. Always wash hands prior to using the toilet or eating. Damaged composite components should be handled with care. Single fibers can easily penetrate the skin, splinter off, and become lodged in the skin.

Fire Protection

Most solvents are flammable. Close all solvent containers and store in a fireproof cabinet when not in use. Make sure that solvents are kept away from areas where static electricity can occur. Static electricity can occur during sanding operations or when bagging material is unrolled. It is preferable to use air-driven tools. If electric tools are used, ensure that they are the enclosed type. Do not mix too much resin. The resin could overheat and start smoking caused by the exothermic process. Ensure that a fire extinguisher is always nearby.

Transparent Plastics

Plastics cover a broad field of organic synthetic resin and may be divided into two main classifications: thermoplastics and thermosetting plastics.

a. Thermoplastics—may be softened by heat and can be dissolved in various organic solvents. Acrylic plastic is commonly used as a transparent thermoplastic material for windows, canopies, etc. Acrylic plastics are known by the trade names of Lucite® or Plexiglas® and by the British as Perspex®, and meet the military specifications of MIL-P-5425 for regular acrylic and MIL-P-8184 for craze-resistant acrylic.

b. Thermosetting plastics—do not soften appreciably under heat but may char and blister at temperatures of 240–260 °C (400–500 °F). Most of the molded products of synthetic resin composition, such as phenolic, urea-formaldehyde, and melamine formaldehyde resins, belong to the thermosetting group. Once the plastic becomes hard, additional heat does not change it back into a liquid as it would with a thermoplastic.

Optical Considerations

Scratches and other types of damage that obstruct the vision of the pilots are not acceptable. Some types of damage might be acceptable at the edges of the windshield.

Identification
Storage and Handling

Because transparent thermoplastic sheets soften and deform when they are heated, they must be stored where the temperature never becomes excessive. Store them in a cool, dry location away from heating coils, radiators, or steam pipes, and away from such fumes as are found in paint spray booths or paint storage areas.

Keep paper-masked transparent sheets out of the direct rays of the sun, because sunlight accelerates deterioration of the adhesive, causing it to bond to the plastic, and making it difficult to remove.

Store plastic sheets with the masking paper in place, in bins that are tilted at a 10° angle from the vertical to prevent buckling. If the sheets are stored horizontally, take care to avoid getting dirt and chips between them. Stacks of sheets must never be over 18 inches high, with the smallest sheets stacked on top of the larger ones so there is no unsupported overhang. Leave the masking paper on the sheets as long as possible, and take care not to scratch or gouge the sheets by sliding them against each other or across rough or dirty tables.

Store formed sections with ample support so they do not lose their shape. Vertical nesting should be avoided. Protect formed parts from temperatures higher than 120 °F (49 °C), and leave their protective coating in place until they are installed on the aircraft.

Forming Procedures and Techniques

Transparent acrylic plastics get soft and pliable when they are heated to their forming temperatures and can be formed to almost any shape. When they cool, they retain the shape to which they were formed. Acrylic plastic may be cold-bent into a single curvature if the material is thin and the bending radius is at least 180 times the thickness of the sheet. Cold bending beyond these limits impose so much stress on the surface of the plastic that tiny fissures or cracks, called crazing, form.

Heating

Wear cotton gloves when handling the plastic to eliminate finger marks on the soft surface. Before heating any transparent plastic material, remove all of the masking paper and adhesive from the sheet. If the sheet is dusty or dirty, wash it with clean water and rinse it well. Dry the sheet thoroughly by blotting it with soft absorbent paper towels.

For the best results when hot forming acrylics, adhere to the temperatures recommended by the manufacturer. Use a forced-air oven that can operate over a temperature range of 120–374 °F (49–190 °C). If the part gets too hot during the forming process, bubbles may form on the surface and impair the optical qualities of the sheet.

For uniform heating, it is best to hang the sheets vertically by grasping them by their edges with spring clips and suspending the clips in a rack. [Figure 7-90] If the piece is too small to hold with clips, or if there is not enough trim area, lay the sheets on shelves or racks covered with soft felt or flannel. Be sure there is enough open space to allow the air to circulate around the sheet and heat it evenly.

Figure 7-90. *Hanging an acrylic sheet.*

Small forming jobs, such as landing light covers, may be heated in a kitchen baking oven. Infrared heat lamps may be used if they are arranged on 7 to 8-inch centers and enough of them are used in a bank to heat the sheet evenly. Place the lamps about 18-inches from the material.

Never use hot water or steam directly on the plastic to heat it because this likely causes the acrylic to become milky or cloudy.

Forms

Heated acrylic plastic molds with almost no pressure, so the forms used can be of very simple construction. Forms made of pressed wood, plywood, or plaster are adequate to form simple curves, but reinforced plastic or plaster may be needed to shape complex or compound curves. Since hot plastic conforms to any waviness or unevenness, the form used must be completely smooth. To ensure this, sand the form and cover it with soft cloth, such as outing flannel or billiard felt. The mold should be large enough to extend beyond the trim line of the part, and provisions should be made for holding the hot plastic snug against the mold as it cools.

A mold can be made for a complex part by using the damaged part itself. If the part is broken, tape the pieces together, wax or grease the inside so the plaster does not stick to it, and support the entire part in sand. Fill the part with plaster and allow it to harden, and then remove it from the mold. Smooth out any roughness and cover it with soft cloth. It is now ready to use to form the new part.

Forming Methods

Simple Curve Forming

Heat the plastic material to the recommended temperature, remove it from the heat source, and carefully drape it over the prepared form. Carefully press the hot plastic to the form and either hold or clamp the sheet in place until it cools. This process may take from 10–30 minutes. Do not force cool it.

Compound Curve Forming

Compound curve forming is normally used for canopies or complex wingtip light covers, and it requires a great deal of specialized equipment. There are four commonly used methods, each having its advantages and disadvantages.

Stretch Forming

Preheated acrylic sheets are stretched mechanically over the form in much the same way as is done with the simple curved piece. Take special care to preserve uniform thickness of the material, since some parts must stretch more than others.

Male and Female Die Forming

Male and female die forming requires expensive matching male and female dies. The heated plastic sheet is placed between the dies that are then mated. When the plastic cools, the dies are opened.

Vacuum Forming Without Forms

Many aircraft canopies are formed by this method. In this process, a panel, which has cut into it the outline of the desired shape, is attached to the top of a vacuum box. The heated and softened sheet of plastic is then clamped on top of the panel. When the air in the box is evacuated, the outside air pressure forces the hot plastic through the opening and forms the concave canopy. It is the surface tension of the plastic that shapes the canopy.

Vacuum Forming With a Female Form

If the shape needed is other than that which would be formed by surface tension, a female mold, or form must be used. It is placed below the plastic sheet and the vacuum pump is connected. When air from the form is evacuated, the outside air pressure forces the hot plastic sheet into the mold and fills it.

Sawing and Drilling

Sawing

Several types of saws can be used with transparent plastics; however, circular saws are the best for straight cuts. The blades should be hollow ground or have some set to prevent binding. After the teeth are set, they should be side dressed to produce a smooth edge on the cut. Band saws are recommended for cutting flat acrylic sheets when the cuts must be curved or where the sheet is cut to a rough dimension to be trimmed later. Close control of size and shape may be obtained by band sawing a piece to within 1/16-inch of the desired size, as marked by a scribed line on the plastic, and then sanding it to the correct size with a drum or belt sander.

Drilling

Unlike soft metal, acrylic plastic is a very poor conductor of heat. Make provisions for removing the heat when drilling. Deep holes need cooling, and water-soluble cutting oil is a satisfactory coolant since it has no tendency to attack the plastic.

The drill used on acrylics must be carefully ground and free from nicks and burrs that would affect the surface finish. [Figure 7-91] Grind the drill with a greater included angle than would be used for soft metal. The rake angle should be zero in order to scrape, and not cut.

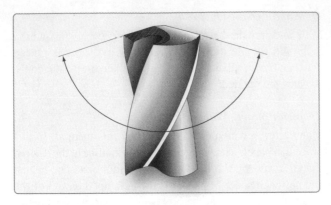

Figure 7-91. *A twist drill with an included angle of 150° is used to drill acrylic plastics.*

The patented Unibit® is good for drilling small holes in aircraft windshields and windows. *[Figure 7-92]* It can cut holes from ⅛ to ½-inch in 1/32-inch increments and produces good smooth holes with no stress cracks around their edges.

Figure 7-92. *Unibit® drill for drilling acrylic plastics.*

Cementing

Polymerizable cements are those in which a catalyst is added to an already thick monomer-polymer syrup to promote rapid hardening. Cement PS-30® and Weld-On 40® are polymerizable cements of this type. They are suitable for cementing all types of plexiglas acrylic cast sheet and parts molded from plexiglas molding pellets. At room temperature, the cements harden (polymerize) in the container in about 45 minutes after mixing the components. They harden more rapidly at higher temperatures. The cement joints are usually hard enough for handling within 4 hours after assembly. The joints may be machined within 4 hours after assembly, but it is better to wait 24 hours.

Application of Cement

PS-30® and Weld-On 40® joints retain excellent appearance and color stability after outdoor exposure. These cements produce clear, transparent joints and should be used when the color and appearance of the joints are important.

PS-30® and Weld-On 40® should be used at temperatures no lower than 65 °F. If cementing is done in a room cooler than 65 °F, it requires a longer time to harden and the joint strength is reduced.

The cement should be prepared with the correct proportions of components as given in the manufacturer's instructions and thoroughly mixed, making sure neither the mixing container nor mixing paddle adds color or effects the hardening of the cement. Clean glass or polyethylene mixing containers are preferred. Because of their short pot life (approximately 45 minutes), Cement PS-30® and Weld-On 40® must be used quickly once the components are mixed. Time consumed in preparation shortens the effective working time, making it necessary to have everything ready to be cemented before the cements are mixed. For better handling, pour cement within 20 minutes of mixing. For maximum joint strength, the final cement joint should be free of bubbles. It is usually sufficient to allow the mixed cement to stand for 10 minutes before cementing to allow bubbles to rise to the surface. The gap joint technique can only be used with colorless plexiglas acrylic or in cases where joints are hidden. If inconspicuous joints in colored plexiglas acrylic are needed, the parts must be fitted closely, using closed V groove, butt, or arc joints.

Cement forms, or dams, may be made with masking tape as long as the adhesive surface does not contact the cement. This is easily done with a strip of cellophane tape placed over the masking tape adhesive. The tape must be chosen carefully. The adhesive on ordinary cellophane tape prevents the cure of PS-30® and Weld-On 40®. Before actual fabrication of parts, sample joints should be tried to ensure that the tape system used does not harm the cement. Since it is important for all of the cement to remain in the gap, only contact pressure should be used.

Bubbles tend to float to the top of the cement bead in a gap joint after the cement is poured. These cause no problem if the bead is machined off. A small wire (not copper) or similar object may be used to lift some bubbles out of the joint; however, the cement joint should be disturbed as little as possible.

Polymerizable cements shrink as the cement hardens. Therefore, the freshly poured cement bead should be left above the surfaces being cemented to compensate for the shrinkage. If it is necessary for appearances, the bead may be machined off after the cement has set.

Repairs

Whenever possible, replace, rather than repair, extensively damaged transparent plastic. A carefully patched part is not the equal of a new section, either optically or structurally. At the first sign of crack development, drill a small hole with a # 30 or a ⅛-inch drill at the extreme ends of the cracks. *[Figure 7-93]* This serves to localize the cracks and to prevent further splitting by distributing the strain over a large area. If the cracks are small, stopping them with drilled holes usually suffices until replacement or more permanent repairs can be made.

Cleaning

Plastics have many advantages over glass for aircraft use, but they lack the surface hardness of glass and care must be exercised while servicing the aircraft to avoid scratching or otherwise damaging the surface. Clean the plastic by washing it with plenty of water and mild soap, using a clean, soft, grit-free cloth, sponge, or bare hands. Do not use gasoline, alcohol, benzene, acetone, carbon tetrachloride, fire extinguisher or deicing fluids, lacquer thinners, or window cleaning sprays. These soften the plastic and cause crazing.

Plastics should not be rubbed with a dry cloth since it is likely to cause scratches and to build up an electrostatic charge that attracts dust particles to the surface. If, after removing dirt and grease, no great amount of scratching is visible, finish the plastic with a good grade of commercial wax. Apply the wax in a thin even coat and bring to a high polish by rubbing lightly with a soft cloth.

Polishing

Do not attempt hand polishing or buffing until the surface is clean. A soft, open-type cotton or flannel buffing wheel is suggested. Minor scratches may be removed by vigorously rubbing the affected area by hand, using a soft clean cloth dampened with a mixture of turpentine and chalk, or by applying automobile cleanser with a damp cloth. Remove the cleaner and polish with a soft, dry cloth. Acrylic and cellulose acetate plastics are thermoplastic. Friction created by buffing or polishing too long in one spot can generate sufficient heat to soften the surface. This condition produces visual distortion and should be avoided.

Windshield Installation

Use material equivalent to that originally used by the manufacturer of the aircraft for replacement panels. There are many types of transparent plastics on the market. Their properties vary greatly, particularly expansion characteristics, brittleness under low temperatures, resistance to discoloration when exposed to sunlight, surface checking, etc. Information on these properties is in MIL-HDBK-17, Plastics for Flight Vehicles, Part II Transparent Glazing Materials, available from the Government Printing Office (GPO). These properties are considered by aircraft manufacturers in selecting materials to be used in their designs and the use of substitutes having different characteristics may result in subsequent difficulties.

Installation Procedures

When installing a replacement panel, use the same mounting method employed by the manufacturer of the aircraft. While the actual installation varies from one type of aircraft to another, consider the following major principles when installing any replacement panel.

1. Never force a plastic panel out of shape to make it fit a frame. If a replacement panel does not fit easily into the mounting, obtain a new replacement or heat the whole panel and re-form. When possible, cut and fit a new panel at ordinary room temperature.

2. In clamping or bolting plastic panels into their mountings, do not place the plastic under excessive compressive stress. It is easy to develop more than 1,000 psi on the plastic by overtorquing a nut and bolt. Tighten each nut to a firm fit, and then back the nut off one full turn (until they are snug and can still be rotated with the fingers).

All the strains that originally caused the crack are concentrated at point **A** tending to extend the crack. Therefore, with a #30 or 1/8" drill bit, drill a small hole **A1** at the end of the crack point to distribute the strain over a wider area.

Each crack occurring at any hole or tear is drilled in the same manner.

Figure 7-93. *Stop drilling of cracks.*

3. In bolted installations, use spacers, collars, shoulders, or stop-nuts to prevent tightening the bolt excessively. Whenever such devices are used by the aircraft manufacturer, retain them in the replacement installation. It is important that the original number of bolts, complete with washers, spacers, etc., be used. When rivets are used, provide adequate spacers or other satisfactory means to prevent excessive tightening of the frame to the plastic.

4. Mount plastic panels between rubber, cork, or other gasket material to make the installation waterproof, to reduce vibration, and to help to distribute compressive stresses on the plastic.

5. Plastics expand and contract considerably more than the metal channels in which they are mounted. Mount windshield panels to a sufficient depth in the channel to prevent it from falling out when the panel contracts at low temperatures or deforms under load. When the manufacturer's original design permits, mount panels to a minimum depth of 1⅛-inches, and with a clearance of ⅛-inch between the plastic and bottom of the channel.

6. In installations involving bolts or rivets, make the holes through the plastic oversize by ⅛-inch and center so that the plastic does not bind or crack at the edge of the holes. The use of slotted holes is also recommended.

Chapter 8
Aircraft Painting and Finishing

Introduction

Paint, or more specifically its overall color and application, is usually the first impression that is transmitted to someone when they look at an aircraft for the first time. Paint makes a statement about the aircraft and the person who owns or operates it. The paint scheme may reflect the owner's ideas and color preferences for an amateur-built aircraft project, or it may be colors and identification for the recognition of a corporate or air carrier aircraft.

	Nitrate	Nitrate dope	Butyrate dope	Nitro-cellulose lacquer	Poly-tone Poly-brush Poly-spray	Synthetic enamel	Acrylic lacquer	Acrylic enamel	Ure ena
Methanol	S	IS	IS	IS					
Toluol (Toluene)	IS	IS	IS	IS	PS	IS	PS		
MEK (Methyl ethyl ketone)	S	S	S	S	IS	S	ISW	IS	
Isopropanol	IS	IS		S	ISW	S	ISW	IS	
Methylene chloride	SS	IS	IS	IS	IS	S	ISW	IS	
	VS	S	VS	IS	S	IS	IS		
				ISW	S	IS			
						ISW	ISW		IS

Dial

Locking bolt

Spreader adjustment valve

Fluid needle valve

Air valve

Gun body

Dial at 0

Dial at 2

Dial at 4

Dial at 6

Paint is more than aesthetics; it affects the weight of the aircraft and protects the integrity of the airframe. The topcoat finish is applied to protect the exposed surfaces from corrosion and deterioration. Also, a properly painted aircraft is easier to clean and maintain because the exposed surfaces are more resistant to corrosion and dirt, and oil does not adhere as readily to the surface.

A wide variety of materials and finishes are used to protect and provide the desired appearance of the aircraft. The term "paint" is used in a general sense and includes primers, enamels, lacquers, and the various multipart finishing formulas. Paint has three components: resin as coating material, pigment for color, and solvents to reduce the mix to a workable viscosity.

Internal structure and unexposed components are finished to protect them from corrosion and deterioration. All exposed surfaces and components are finished to provide protection and to present a pleasing appearance. Decorative finishing includes trim striping, the addition of company logos and emblems, and the application of decals, identification numbers, and letters.

Finishing Materials

A wide variety of materials are used in aircraft finishing. Some of the more common materials and their uses are described in the following paragraphs.

Acetone

Acetone is a fast-evaporating colorless solvent. It is used as an ingredient in paint, nail polish, and varnish removers. It is a strong solvent for most plastics and is ideal for thinning fiberglass resin, polyester resins, vinyl, and adhesives. It is also used as a superglue remover. Acetone is a heavy-duty degreaser suitable for metal preparation and removing grease from fabric covering prior to doping. It should not be used as a thinner in dope because of its rapid evaporation, which causes the doped area to cool and collect moisture. This absorbed moisture prevents uniform drying and results in blushing of the dope and a flat no-gloss finish.

Alcohol

Butanol, or butyl alcohol, is a slow-drying solvent that can be mixed with aircraft dope to retard drying of the dope film on humid days, thus preventing blushing. A mixture of dope solvent containing 5 to 10 percent of butyl alcohol is usually sufficient for this purpose. Butanol and ethanol alcohol are mixed together in ratios ranging from 1:1 to 1:3 to use to dilute wash coat primer for spray applications because the butyl alcohol retards the evaporation rate.

Ethanol or denatured alcohol is used to thin shellac for spraying and as a constituent of paint and varnish remover. It can also be used as a cleaner and degreaser prior to painting.

Isopropyl, or rubbing alcohol, can be used as a disinfectant. It is used in the formulation of oxygen system cleaning solutions. It can be used to remove grease pencil and permanent marker from smooth surfaces, or to wipe hand or fingerprint oil from a surface before painting.

Benzene

Benzene is a highly flammable, colorless liquid with a sweet odor. It is a product used in some paint and varnish removers. It is an industrial solvent that is regulated by the Environmental Protection Agency (EPA) because it is an extremely toxic chemical compound when inhaled or absorbed through the skin. It has been identified as a Class A carcinogen known to cause various forms of cancer. It should be avoided for use as a common cleaning solvent for paint equipment and spray guns.

Methyl Ethyl Ketone (MEK)

Methyl ethyl ketone (MEK), also referred to as 2-Butanone, is a highly flammable, liquid solvent used in paint and varnish removers, paint and primer thinners, in surface coatings, adhesives, printing inks, as a catalyst for polyester resin hardening, and as an extraction medium for fats, oils, waxes, and resins. Because of its effectiveness as a quickly evaporating solvent, MEK is used in formulating high solids coatings that help to reduce emissions from coating operations. Persons using MEK should use protective gloves and have adequate ventilation to avoid the possible irritation effects of skin contact and breathing of the vapors.

Methylene Chloride

Methylene Chloride is a colorless, volatile liquid completely miscible with a variety of other solvents. It is widely used in paint strippers and as a cleaning agent/degreaser for metal parts. It has no flash point under normal use conditions and can be used to reduce the flammability of other substances.

Toluene

Referred to as toluol or methylbenzene, toluene is a clear, water-insoluble liquid with a distinct odor similar to that of benzene. It is a common solvent used in paints, paint thinners, lacquers, and adhesives. It has been used as a paint remover in softening fluorescent-finish, clear-topcoat sealing materials. It is also an acceptable thinner for zinc chromate primer. It has been used as an antiknocking additive in gasoline. Prolonged exposure to toluene vapors should be avoided because it may be linked to brain damage.

Turpentine

Turpentine is obtained by distillation of wood from certain pine trees. It is a flammable, water-insoluble liquid solvent used as a thinner and quick-drier for varnishes, enamels, and other oil-based paints. Turpentine can be used to clean paint equipment and paint brushes used with oil-based paints.

Mineral Spirits

Sometimes referred to as white spirit, Stoddard solvent, or petroleum spirits, mineral spirits is a petroleum distillate used as a paint thinner and mild solvent. The reference to the name Stoddard came from a dry cleaner who helped to develop it in the 1920s as a less volatile dry cleaning solvent and as an alternative to the more volatile petroleum solvents that were being used for cleaning clothes. It is the most widely used solvent in the paint industry, used in aerosols, paints, wood preservatives, lacquers, and varnishes. It is also commonly used to clean paint brushes and paint equipment. Mineral spirits are used in industry for cleaning and degreasing machine tools and parts because it is very effective in removing oils and greases from metal. It has low odor, is less flammable, and less toxic than turpentine.

Naphtha

Naphtha is one of a wide variety of volatile hydrocarbon mixtures that is sometimes processed from coal tar but more often derived from petroleum. Naphtha is used as a solvent for various organic substances, such as fats and rubber, and in the making of varnish. It is used as a cleaning fluid and is incorporated into some laundry soaps. Naphtha has a low flashpoint and is used as a fuel in portable stoves and lanterns. It is sold under different names around the world and is known as white gas, or Coleman fuel, in North America.

Linseed Oil

Linseed oil is the most commonly used carrier in oil paint. It makes the paint more fluid, transparent, and glossy. It is used to reduce semipaste oil colors, such as dull black stenciling paint and insignia colors, to a brushing consistency. Linseed oil is also used as a protective coating on the interior of metal tubing. Linseed oil is derived from pressing the dried ripe flax seeds of the flax plant to obtain the oil and then using a process called solvent extraction. Oil obtained without the solvent extraction process is marketed as flaxseed oil. The term "boiled linseed oil" indicates that it was processed with additives to shorten its drying time.

A note of caution is usually added to packaging of linseed oil with the statement, "Risk of Fire from Spontaneous Combustion Exists with this Product." Linseed oil generates heat as it dries. Oily materials and rags must be properly disposed after use to eliminate the possible cause of spontaneous ignition and fire.

Thinners

Thinners include a plethora of solvents used to reduce the viscosity of any one of the numerous types of primers, subcoats, and topcoats. The types of thinner used with the various coatings is addressed in other sections of this chapter.

Varnish

Varnish is a transparent protective finish primarily used for finishing wood. It is available in interior and exterior grades. The exterior grade does not dry as hard as the interior grade, allowing it to expand and contract with the temperature changes of the material being finished. Varnish is traditionally a combination of a drying oil, a resin, and a thinner or solvent. It has little or no color, is transparent, and has no added pigment. Varnish dries slower than most other finishes. Resin varnishes dry and harden when the solvents in them evaporate. Polyurethane and epoxy varnishes remain liquid after the evaporation of the solvent but quickly begin to cure through chemical reactions of the varnish components.

Primers

The importance of primers in finishing and protection is generally misunderstood and underestimated because it is invisible after the topcoat finish is applied. A primer is the foundation of the finish. Its role is to bond to the surface, inhibit corrosion of metal, and provide an anchor point for the finish coats. It is important that the primer pigments be either anodic to the metal surface or passivate the surface should moisture be present. The binder must be compatible with the finish coats. Primers on nonmetallic surfaces do not require sacrificial or passivating pigments. Some of the various primer types are discussed below.

Wash Primers

Wash primers are water-thin coatings of phosphoric acid in solutions of vinyl butyral resin, alcohol, and other ingredients. They are very low in solids with almost no filling qualities. Their functions are to passivate the surface, temporarily provide corrosion resistance, and provide an adhesive base for the next coating, such as a urethane or epoxy primer. Wash primers do not require sanding and have high corrosion protection qualities. Some have a very small recoat time frame that must be considered when painting larger aircraft. The manufacturers' instructions must be followed for satisfactory results.

Red Iron Oxide

Red oxide primer is an alkyd resin-based coating that was developed for use over iron and steel located in mild environmental conditions. It can be applied over rust that is free of loose particles, oil, and grease. It has limited use in the aviation industry.

Gray Enamel Undercoat

This is a single component, nonsanding primer compatible with a wide variety of topcoats. It fills minor imperfections, dries fast without shrinkage, and has high corrosion resistance. It is a good primer for composite substrates.

Urethane

This is a term that is misused or interchanged by painters and manufacturers alike. It is typically a two-part product that uses a chemical activator to cure by linking molecules together to form a whole new compound. Polyurethane is commonly used when referring to urethane, but not when the product being referred to is acrylic urethane.

Urethane primer, like the urethane paint, is also a two-part product that uses a chemical activator to cure. It is easy to sand and fills well. The proper film thickness must be observed, because it can shrink when applied too heavily. It is typically applied over a wash primer for best results. Special precautions must be taken by persons spraying because the activators contain isocyanates (discussed further in the Protective Equipment section at the end of this chapter).

Epoxy

Epoxy is a synthetic, thermosetting resin that produces tough, hard, chemical-resistant coatings and adhesives. It uses a catalyst to chemically activate the product, but it is not classified as hazardous because it contains no isocyanates. Epoxy can be used as a nonsanding primer/sealer over bare metal and it is softer than urethane, so it has good chip resistance. It is recommended for use on steel tube frame aircraft prior to installing fabric covering.

Zinc Chromate

Zinc chromate is a corrosion-resistant pigment that can be added to primers made of different resin types, such as epoxy, polyurethane, and alkyd. Older type zinc chromate is distinguishable by its bright yellow color when compared to the light green color of some of the current brand primers. Moisture in the air causes the zinc chromate to react with the metal surface, and it forms a passive layer that prevents corrosion. Zinc chromate primer was, at one time, the standard primer for aircraft painting. Environmental concerns and new formula primers have all but replaced it.

Identification of Paints

Dope

When fabric-covered aircraft ruled the sky, dope was the standard finish used to protect and color the fabric. The dope imparted additional qualities of increased tensile strength, airtightness, weather-proofing, ultraviolet (UV) protection, and tautness to the fabric cover. Aircraft dope is essentially a colloidal solution of cellulose acetate or nitrate combined with plasticizers to produce a smooth, flexible, homogeneous film.

Dope is still used on fabric covered aircraft as part of a covering process. However, the type of fabric being used to cover the aircraft has changed. Grade A cotton or linen was the standard covering used for years, and it still may be used if it meets the requirements of the Federal Aviation Administration (FAA), Technical Standard Order (TSO) C-15d/AMS 3806c.

Polyester fabric coverings now dominate in the aviation industry. These new fabrics have been specifically developed for aircraft and are far superior to cotton and linen. The protective coating and topcoat finishes used with the Ceconite® polyester fabric covering materials are part of a Supplemental Type Certificate (STC) and must be used as specified when covering any aircraft with a Standard Airworthiness Certificate. The Ceconite® covering procedures use specific brand name, nontautening nitrate and butyrate dope as part of the STC.

The Poly-Fiber® system also uses a special polyester fabric covering as part of its STC, but it does not use dope. All the liquid products in the Poly-Fiber® system are made from vinyl, not from cellulose dope. The vinyl coatings have several real advantages over dope: they remain flexible, they do not shrink, they do not support combustion, and they are easily removed from the fabric with MEK, which simplifies most repairs.

Synthetic Enamel

Synthetic enamel is an oil-based single-stage paint (no clear coat) that provides durability and protection. It can be mixed with a hardener to increase the durability and shine while decreasing the drying time. It is one of the more economical types of finish.

Lacquers

The origin of lacquer dates back thousands of years to a resin obtained from trees indigenous to China. In the early 1920s, nitrocellulose lacquer was developed from a process using cotton and wood pulp.

Nitrocellulose lacquers produce a hard, semiflexible finish that can be polished to a high sheen. The clear variety yellows as it ages, and it can shrink over time to a point that the surface crazes. It is easy to spot repair because each new coat of lacquer softens and blends into the previous coat. This was one of the first coatings used by the automotive industry in mass production, because it reduced finishing times from almost two weeks to two days.

Acrylic lacquers were developed to eliminate the yellowing problems and crazing of the nitrocellulose lacquers. General Motors started using acrylic lacquer in the mid-1950s, and they used it into the 1960s on some of their premium model cars. Acrylics have the same working properties but dry to a less brittle and more flexible film than nitrocellulose lacquer.

Lacquer is one of the easiest paints to spray, because it dries quickly and can be applied in thin coats. However, lacquer is not very durable; bird droppings, acid rain, and gasoline spills actually eat down into the paint. It still has limited use on collector and show automobiles because they are usually kept in a garage, protected from the environment.

The current use of lacquer for an exterior coating on an aircraft is almost nonexistent because of durability and environmental concerns. Upwards of 85 percent of the volatile organic compounds (VOCs) in the spray gun ends up in the atmosphere, and some states have banned its use.

There are some newly developed lacquers that use a catalyst, but they are used mostly in the woodworking and furniture industry. They have the ease of application of nitrocellulose lacquer with much better water, chemical, and abrasion resistance. Additionally, catalyzed lacquers cure chemically, not solely through the evaporation of solvents, so there is a reduction of VOCs released into the atmosphere. It is activated when the catalyst is added to the base mixture.

Polyurethane

Polyurethane is at the top of the list when compared to other coatings for abrasion-, stain-, and chemical-resistant properties. Polyurethane was the coating that introduced the wet look. It has a high degree of natural resistance to the damaging effects of UV rays from the sun. Polyurethane is usually the first choice for coating and finishing the corporate and commercial aircraft in today's aviation environment.

Urethane Coating

The term urethane applies to certain types of binders used for paints and clear coatings. (A binder is the component that holds the pigment together in a tough, continuous film and provides film integrity and adhesion.) Typically, urethane is a two-part coating that consists of a base and catalyst that, when mixed, produces a durable, high-gloss finish that is abrasion and chemical resistant.

Acrylic Urethanes

Acrylic simply means plastic. It dries to a harder surface but is not as resistant to harsh chemicals as polyurethane. Most acrylic urethanes need additional UV inhibitors added when subject to the UV rays of the sun.

Methods of Applying Finish

There are several methods of applying aircraft finish. Among the most common are dipping, brushing, and spraying.

Dipping

The application of finishes by dipping is generally confined to factories or large repair stations. The process consists of dipping the part to be finished in a tank filled with the finishing material. Primer coats are frequently applied in this manner.

Brushing

Brushing has long been a satisfactory method of applying finishes to all types of surfaces. Brushing is generally used for small repair work and on surfaces where it is not practicable to spray paint.

The material to be applied should be thinned to the proper consistency for brushing. A material that is too thick has a tendency to pull or rope under the brush. If the materials are too thin, they are likely to run or not cover the surface adequately. Proper thinning and substrate temperature allows the finish to flow-out and eliminates the brush marks.

Spraying

Spraying is the preferred method for a quality finish. Spraying is used to cover large surfaces with a uniform layer of material, which results in the most cost effective method of application. All spray systems have several basic similarities. There must be an adequate source of compressed air, a reservoir or feed tank to hold a supply of the finishing material, and a device for controlling the combination of the air and finishing material ejected in an atomized cloud or spray against the surface to be coated.

A self-contained, pressurized spray can of paint meets the above requirements and satisfactory results can be obtained painting components and small areas of touchup. However, the aviation coating materials available in cans is limited, and this chapter addresses the application of mixed components through a spray gun.

There are two main types of spray equipment. A spray gun with an integral paint container is adequate for use when painting small areas. When large areas are painted, pressure-feed equipment is more desirable since a large supply of finishing material can be applied without the interruption of having to stop and refill a paint container. An added bonus is the lighter overall weight of the spray gun and the flexibility of spraying in any direction with a constant pressure to the gun.

The air supply to the spray gun must be entirely free of water or oil in order to produce the optimum results in the finished product. Water traps, as well as suitable filters to remove any trace of oil, must be incorporated in the air pressure supply line. These filters and traps must be serviced on a regular basis.

Finishing Equipment
Paint Booth
A paint booth may be a small room in which components of an aircraft are painted, or it can be an aircraft hangar big enough to house the largest aircraft. Whichever it is, the location must be able to protect the components or aircraft from the elements. Ideally, it would have temperature and humidity controls; but, in all cases, the booth or hangar must have good lighting, proper ventilation, and be dust free.

A simple paint booth can be constructed for a small aircraft by making a frame out of wood or polyvinyl chloride (PVC) pipe. It needs to be large enough to allow room to walk around and maneuver the spray gun. The top and sides can be covered with plastic sheeting stapled or taped to the frame. An exhaust fan can be added to one end with a large air-conditioning filter placed on the opposite end to filter incoming air. Lights should be large enough to be set up outside of the spray booth and shine through the sheeting or plastic windows. The ideal amount of light would be enough to produce a glare off of all the surfaces to be sprayed. This type of temporary booth can be set up in a hangar, a garage, or outside on a ramp, if the weather and temperature are favorable.

Normally, Environmental Protection Agency (EPA) regulations do not apply to a person painting one airplane. However, anyone planning to paint an aircraft should be aware that local clean air regulations may be applicable to an airplane painting project. When planning to paint an aircraft at an airport, it would be a good idea to check with the local airport authority before starting.

Air Supply
The air supply for paint spraying using a conventional siphon feed spray gun should come from an air compressor with a storage tank big enough to provide an uninterrupted supply of air with at least 90 pounds per square inch (psi) providing 10 cubic feet per minute (CFM) of air to the spray gun.

The compressor needs to be equipped with a regulator, water trap, air hose, and an adequate filter system to ensure that clean, dry, oil-free air is delivered to the spray gun.

If using one of the newer high-volume low-pressure (HVLP) spray guns and using a conventional compressor, it is better to use a two stage compressor of at least a 5 horsepower (hp)

that operates at 90 psi and provides 20 CFM to the gun. The key to the operation of the newer HVLP spray guns is the air volume, not the pressure.

If purchasing a new complete HVLP system, the air supply is from a turbine compressor. An HVLP turbine has a series of fans, or stages, that move a lot of air at low pressure. The more stages provide greater air output (rated in CFM) that means better atomization of the coating being sprayed. The intake air is also the cooling air for the motor. This air is filtered from dirt and dust particles prior to entering the turbine. Some turbines also have a second filter for the air supply to the spray gun. The turbine does not produce oil or water to contaminate the air supply, but the air supply from the turbine heats up, causing the paint to dry faster, so you may need an additional length of hose to reduce the air temperature at the spray gun.

Spray Equipment
Air Compressors
Piston–type compressors are available with one-stage and multiple-stage compressors, various size motors, and various size supply tanks. The main requirement for painting is to ensure the spray gun has a continuous supplied volume of air. Piston-type compressors compress air and deliver it to a storage tank. Most compressors provide over 100 psi, but only the larger ones provide the volume of air needed for an uninterrupted supply to the gun. The multistage compressor is a good choice for a shop when a large volume of air is needed for pneumatic tools. When in doubt about the size of the compressor, compare the manufacturer's specifications and get the largest one possible. *[Figure 8-1]*

Figure 8-1. *Standard air compressor.*

Large Coating Containers

For large painting projects, such as spraying an entire aircraft, the quantity of mixed paint in a pressure tank provides many advantages. The setup allows a greater area to be covered without having to stop and fill the cup on a spray gun. The painter is able to keep a wet paint line, and more material is applied to the surface with less overspray. It provides the flexibility of maneuvering the spray gun in any position without the restriction and weight of an attached paint cup. Remote pressure tanks are available in sizes from 2 quarts to over 60 gallons. *[Figure 8-2]*

Figure 8-2. *Pressure paint tank.*

System Air Filters

The use of a piston-type air compressor for painting requires that the air supply lines include filters to remove water and oil. A typical filter assembly is shown in *Figure 8-3*.

Miscellaneous Painting Tools and Equipment

Some tools that are available to the painter include:

- Masking paper/tape dispenser that accommodates various widths of masking paper. It includes a masking tape dispenser that applies the tape to one edge of the paper as it is rolled off to facilitate one person applying the paper and tape in a single step.

- Electronic and magnetic paint thickness gauges to measure dry paint thickness.

- Wet film gauges to measure freshly applied wet paint.

- Infrared thermometers to measure coating and substrate surfaces to verify that they fall in the recommended temperature range prior to spraying.

Figure 8-3. *Air line filter assembly.*

Spray Guns

A top quality spray gun is a key component in producing a quality finish in any coating process. It is especially important when painting an aircraft because of the large area and varied surfaces that must be sprayed.

When spray painting, it is of utmost importance to follow the manufacturer's recommendations for correct sizing of the air cap, fluid tip, and needle combinations. The right combination provides the best coverage and the highest quality finish in the shortest amount of time.

All of the following examples of the various spray guns (except the airless) are of the air atomizing type. They are the most capable of providing the highest quality finish.

Siphon Feed Gun

The siphon feed gun is a conventional spray gun familiar to most people, with a one quart paint cup located below the gun. Regulated air passes through the gun and draws (siphons) the paint from the supply cup. This is an external mix gun, which means the air and fluid mix outside the air cap. This gun applies virtually any type coating and provides a high quality finish. *[Figure 8-4]*

Gravity-Feed Gun

A gravity-feed gun provides the same high-quality finish as a siphon-feed gun, but the paint supply is located in a cup on top of the gun and supplied by gravity. The operator can make fine adjustments between the atomizing pressure and fluid flow and utilize all material in the cup. This also is an external mix gun. *[Figure 8-5]*

The HVLP production spray gun is an internal mix gun. The air and fluid is mixed inside the air cap. Because of the low pressure used in the paint application, it transfers at least 65

Figure 8-4. *Siphon-feed spray gun.*

Figure 8-5. *Gravity-feed spray gun.*

Figure 8-6. *A High Volume Low Pressure (HVLP) spray gun.*

spray gun under high hydraulic pressure (500 to 4,500 psi) to atomize the fluid. The fluid is then released through an orifice in the spray nozzle. This system increases transfer efficiency and production speed with less overspray than conventional air atomized spray systems. It is used for production work but does not provide the fine finish of air atomized systems. *[Figure 8-7]*

Figure 8-7. *Airless spray gun.*

Fresh Air Breathing Systems

Fresh air breathing systems should be used whenever coatings are being sprayed that contain isocyanides. This includes

percent and upwards of 80 percent of the finish material to the surface. HVLP spray guns are available with a standard cup located underneath or in a gravity-feed model with the cup on top. The sample shown can be connected with hoses to a remote paint material container holding from 2 quarts to 60 gallons. *[Figure 8-6]*

Because of more restrictive EPA regulations, and the fact that more paint is being transferred to the surface with less waste from overspray, a large segment of the paint and coating industry is switching to HVLP spray equipment.

Airless spraying does not directly use compressed air to atomize the coating material. A pump delivers paint to the all polyurethane coatings. The system incorporates a high-capacity electric air turbine that provides a constant source of fresh air to the mask. The use of fresh air breathing systems is also highly recommended when spraying chromate primers and chemical stripping aircraft. The system provides cool filtered breathing air with up to 200 feet of hose, which allows the air pump intake to be placed in an area of fresh air, well outside of the spraying area. *[Figure 8-8]*

Figure 8-8. *Breathe-Cool II® supplied air respirator system with Tyvek® hood.*

A charcoal-filtered respirator should be used for all other spraying and sanding operations to protect the lungs and respiratory tract. The respirator should be a double-cartridge, organic vapor type that provides a tight seal around the nose and mouth. The cartridges can be changed separately, and should be changed when detecting odor or experiencing nose or throat irritation. The outer prefilters should be changed if experiencing increased resistance to breathing. *[Figure 8-9]*

Figure 8-9. *Charcoal-filtered respirator.*

Viscosity Measuring Cup

This is a small cup with a long handle and a calibrated orifice in the bottom, that allows the liquid in the cup to drain out at a specific timed rate. Coating manufacturers recommend spraying their product at a specific pressure and viscosity. That viscosity is determined by measuring the efflux (drain) time of the liquid coating through the cup orifice. The time (in seconds) is listed on most paint manufacturers' product/technical data pages. The measurement determines if the mixed coating meets the recommended viscosity for spraying.

There are different manufacturers of the viscosity measuring devices, but the most common one listed and used for spray painting is known as a Zahn cup. The orifice number must correspond to the one listed on the product/technical data sheet. For most primers and topcoats, the #2 or #3 Zahn cup is the one recommended. *[Figure 8-10]*

Figure 8-10. *A Zahncup viscosity measuring cup.*

To perform an accurate viscosity measurement, it is very important that the temperature of the sample material be within the recommended range of 73.5 °F ± 3.5 °F (23 °C ± 2 °C), and then proceed as follows:

1. Thoroughly mix the sample with minimum bubbles.

2. Dip the Zahn cup vertically into the sample being tested, totally immersing the cup below the surface.

3. With a stopwatch in one hand, briskly lift the cup out of the sample. As the top edge of the cup breaks the surface, start the stopwatch.

4. Stop the stopwatch when the first break in the flow of the liquid is observed at the orifice exit. The number in seconds is referred to as the efflux time.

5. Record the time on the stopwatch and compare it to the coating manufacturer's recommendation. Adjust the viscosity, if necessary, but be aware not to thin the coating below recommendations that could result in the release of VOCs into the atmosphere above the regulated limitations.

Mixing Equipment

Use a paint shaker for all coatings within 5 days of application to ensure the material is thoroughly mixed. Use a mechanical paint stirrer to mix larger quantities of material. If a mechanical stirrer is driven by a drill, the drill should be pneumatic, instead of electric. The sparks from an electric drill can cause an explosion from the paint vapors.

Preparation

Surfaces

The most important part of any painting project is the preparation of the substrate surface. It takes the most work and time, but with the surface properly prepared, the results are a long-lasting, corrosion-free finish. Repainting an older aircraft requires more preparation time than a new paint job because of the additional steps required to strip the old paint, and then clean the surface and crevices of paint remover. Paint stripping is discussed in another section of this chapter.

It is recommended that all the following procedures be performed using protective clothing, rubber gloves, and goggles, in a well-ventilated area, at temperatures between 68 °F and 100 °F.

Aluminum surfaces are the most common on a typical aircraft. The surface should be scrubbed with Scotch-Brite® pads using an alkaline aviation cleaner. The work area should be kept wet and rinsed with clean water until the surface is water break free. This means that there are no beads or breaks in the water surface as it flows over the aluminum surface.

The next step is to apply an acid etch solution to the surface. Following manufacturers' suggestions, this is applied like a wash using a new sponge and covering a small area while keeping it wet and allowing it to contact the surface for between 1 and 2 minutes. It is then rinsed with clean water without allowing the solution to dry on the surface. Continue this process until all the aluminum surfaces are washed and rinsed. Extra care must be taken to thoroughly rinse this solution from all the hidden areas that it may penetrate. It provides a source for corrosion to form if not completely removed.

When the surfaces are completely dry from the previous process, the next step is to apply Alodine® or another type of an aluminum conversion coating. This coating is also applied like a wash, allowing the coating to contact the surface and keeping it wet for 2 to 5 minutes without letting it dry. It then must be thoroughly rinsed with clean water to remove all chemical salts from the surface. Depending on the brand, the conversion coating may color the aluminum a light gold or green, but some brands are colorless. When the surface is thoroughly dry, the primer should be applied as soon as possible as recommended by the manufacturer.

The primer should be one that is compatible with the topcoat finish. Two-part epoxy primers provide excellent corrosion resistance and adhesion for most epoxy and urethane surfaces and polyurethane topcoats. Zinc chromate should not be used under polyurethane paints.

Composite surfaces that need to be primed may include the entire aircraft if it is constructed from those materials, or they may only be components of the aircraft, such as fairings, radomes, antennas, and the tips of the control surfaces.

Epoxy sanding primers have been developed that provide an excellent base over composites and can be finish sanded with 320 grit using a dual action orbital sander. They are compatible with two-part epoxy primers and polyurethane topcoats.

Topcoats must be applied over primers within the recommended time window, or the primer may have to be scuff sanded before the finish coat is applied. Always follow the recommendations of the coating manufacturer.

Primer and Paint

Purchase aircraft paint for the aviation painting project. Paint manufacturers use different formulas for aircraft and automobiles because of the environments they operate in. The aviation coatings are formulated to have more flexibility and chemical resistance than the automotive paint.

It is also highly recommended that compatible paints of the same brand are used for the entire project. The complete system (of a particular brand) from etching to primers and reducers to the finish topcoat are formulated to work together. Mixing brands is a risk that may ruin the entire project.

When purchasing the coatings for a project, always request a manufacturer's technical or material data and safety data sheets, for each component used. Before starting to spray, read the sheets. If the manufacturer's recommendations are not followed, a less than satisfactory finish or a hazard to personal safety or the environment may result. It cannot be emphasized enough to follow the manufacturer's recommendations. The finished result is well worth the effort.

Before primer or paint is used for any type application, it must be thoroughly mixed. This is done so that any pigment that may have settled to the bottom of the container is brought into suspension and distributed evenly throughout the paint. Coatings now have shelf lives listed in their specification sheets. If a previously opened container is found to have a skin or film formed over the primer or paint, the film must be completely removed before mixing. The material should not be used if it has exceeded its shelf life and/or has become thick or jelled.

Mechanical shaking is recommended for all coatings within 5 days of use. After opening, a test with a hand stirrer should be made to ensure that all the pigment has been brought into suspension. Mechanical stirring is recommended for all two-part coatings. When mixing any two-part paint, the catalyst/activator should always be added to the base or pigmented component. The technical or material data sheet of the coating manufacturer should be followed for recommended times of induction (the time necessary for the catalyst to react with the base prior to application). Some coatings do not require any induction time after mixing, and others need 30 minutes of reaction time before being applied.

Thinning of the coating material should follow the recommendations of the manufacturer. The degree of thinning depends on the method of application. For spray application, the type of equipment, air pressure, and atmospheric conditions guide the selection and mixing ratios for the thinners. Because of the importance of accurate thinning to the finished product, use a viscosity measuring (flow) cup. Material thinned using this method is the correct viscosity for the best application results.

Thin all coating materials and mix in containers separate from the paint cup or pot. Then, filter the material through a paint strainer recommended for the type coating you are spraying as you pour it into the cup or supply pot.

Spray Gun Operation

Adjusting the Spray Pattern

To obtain the correct spray pattern, set the recommended air pressure on the gun, usually 40 to 50 psi for a conventional gun. Test the pattern of the gun by spraying a piece of masking paper taped to the wall. Hold the gun square to the wall approximately 8 to 10 inches from the surface. (With hand spread, it is the distance from the tip of the thumb to the tip of the little finger.)

All spray guns (regardless of brand name) have the same type of adjustments. The upper control knob proportions the air flow, adjusting the spray pattern of the gun. *[Figure 8-11]*

The lower knob adjusts the fluid passing the needle, which in turn controls the amount or volume of paint being delivered through the gun.

Pull the trigger lever fully back. Move the gun across the paper, and alternately adjust between the two knobs to obtain a spray fan of paint that is wet from top to bottom (somewhat like the pattern at dial 10.) Turning in (to the right) on the lower, or fluid knob, reduces the amount of paint going through the gun. Turning out increases the volume of paint. Turning out (to the left) on the upper, or pattern control knob, widens the spray pattern. Turning in reduces it to a cone shape (as shown with dial set at 0).

Once the pattern is set on the gun, the next step is to follow the correct spraying technique for applying the coating to the surface.

Applying the Finish

If the painter has never used a spray gun to apply a finish coat of paint, and the aircraft has been completely prepared, cleaned, primed, and ready for the topcoat, he or she may need to pause for some practice. Reading a book or an instruction manual is a good start as it provides the basic knowledge about the movement of the spray gun across the surface. Also, if available, the opportunity to observe an aircraft being painted is well worth the time.

At this point in the project, the aircraft has already received its primer coats. The difference between the primer and the finish topcoat is that the primer is flat (no gloss) and the finish coat has a glossy surface (some more than others, depending on the paint). The flat finish of the primer is obtained by paying attention to the basics of trigger control distance from the surface and consistent speed of movement of the spray gun across the surface.

Figure 8-11. *Adjustable spray pattern.*

Primer is typically applied using a crosscoat spray pattern. A crosscoat is one pass of the gun from left to right, followed by another pass moving up and down. The starting direction does not matter as long as the spraying is accomplished in two perpendicular passes. The primer should be applied in light coats as cross-coating is the application of two coats of primer.

Primer does not tend to run because it is applied in light coats. The gloss finish requires a little more experience with the gun. A wetter application produces the gloss, but the movement of the gun, overlap of the spray pattern, and the distance from the surface all affect the final product. It is very easy to vary one or another, yielding runs or dry spots and a less than desirable finish. Practice not only provides some experience, but also provides the confidence needed to produce the desired finish.

Start the practice by spraying the finish coat material on a flat, horizontal panel. The spray pattern has been already adjusted by testing it on the masking paper taped to the wall. Hold the gun 8–10 inches away from and perpendicular to the surface. Pull the trigger enough for air to pass through the cap and start a pass with the gun moving across the panel. As it reaches the point to start painting, squeeze the trigger fully back and continue moving the gun about one foot per second across the panel until the end is reached. Then, release the trigger enough to stop the paint flow but not the air flow. *[Figure 8-12]*

The constant air flow through the gun maintains a constant pressure, rather than a buildup of pressure each time that the trigger is released. This would cause a buildup of paint at the end of each pass, causing runs and sags in the finish. Repeat the sequence of the application, moving back in the opposite direction and overlapping the first pass by 50 percent. This is accomplished by aiming the center of the spray pattern at the outer edge of the first pass and continuing the overlap with each successive pass of the gun.

Once the painter has mastered spraying a flat horizontal panel, practice next on a panel that is positioned vertically against a wall. This is the panel that shows the value of applying a light tack coat before spraying on the second coat. The tack coat holds the second coat from sagging and runs. Practice spraying this test panel both horizontally with overlapping passes and then rotate the air cap 90° on the gun and practice spraying vertically with the same 50 percent overlapping passes.

Practice cross-coating the paint for an even application. Apply two light spray passes horizontally, overlapping each by 50 percent, and allowing it to tack. Then, spray vertically with overlapping passes, covering the horizontal sprayed area. When practice results in a smooth, glossy, no-run application on the vertical test panel, you are ready to try your skill on the actual project.

Common Spray Gun Problems

A quick check of the spray pattern can be verified before using the gun by spraying some thinner or reducer, compatible with the finish used, through the gun. It is not of the same viscosity as the coating, but it indicates if the gun is working properly before the project is started.

Figure 8-12. *Proper spray application.*

If the gun is not working properly, use the following information to troubleshoot the problem:

- A pulsating, or spitting, fan pattern may be caused by a loose nozzle, clogged vent hole on the supply cup, or the packing may be leaking around the needle.

- If the spray pattern is offset to one side or the other, the air ports in the air cap or the ports in the horns may be plugged.

- If the spray pattern is heavy on the top or the bottom, rotate the air cap 180°. If the pattern reverses, the air cap is the problem. If it stays the same, the fluid tip or needle may be damaged.

- Other spray pattern problems may be a result of improper air pressure, improper reducing of the material, or wrong size spray nozzle.

Sequence for Painting a Single-Engine or Light Twin Airplane

As a general practice on any surface being painted, spray each application of coating in a different direction to facilitate even and complete coverage. After you apply the primer, apply the tack coat and subsequent top coats in opposite directions, one coat vertically and the next horizontally, as appropriate.

Start by spraying all the corners and gaps between the control surfaces and fixed surfaces. Paint the leading and trailing edges of all surfaces. Spray the landing gear and wheel wells, if applicable, and paint the bottom of the fuselage up the sides to a horizontal break, such as a seam line. Paint the underside of the horizontal stabilizer. Paint the vertical stabilizer and the rudder, and then move to the top of the horizontal stabilizer. Spray the top and sides of the fuselage down to the point of the break from spraying the underside of the fuselage. Then, spray the underside of the wings. Complete the job by spraying the top of the wings.

The biggest challenge is to control the overspray and keep the paint line wet. The ideal scenario would be to have another experienced painter with a second spray gun help with the painting. It is much easier to keep the paint wet and the job is completed in half the time.

Common Paint Troubles

Common problems that may occur during the painting of almost any project but are particularly noticeable and troublesome on the surfaces of an aircraft include poor adhesion, blushing, pinholes, sags and/or runs, "orange peel," fisheyes, sanding scratches, wrinkling, and spray dust.

Poor Adhesion

- Improper cleaning and preparation of the surface to be finished.

- Application of the wrong primer.

- Incompatibility of the topcoat with the primer. [Figure 8-13]

- Improper thinning of the coating material or selection of the wrong grade reducer.

- Improper mixing of materials.

- Contamination of the spray equipment and/or air supply.

Figure 8-13. *Example of poor adhesion.*

Correction for poor adhesion requires a complete removal of the finish, a determination and correction of the cause, and a complete refinishing of the affected area.

Blushing

Blushing is the dull milky haze that appears in a paint finish. *[Figure 8-14]* It occurs when moisture is trapped in the paint. Blushing forms when the solvents quickly evaporate from the sprayed coating, causing a drop in temperature that is enough to condense the water in the air. It usually forms when the humidity is above 80 percent. Other causes include:

- Incorrect temperature (below 60 °F or above 95 °F).

- Incorrect reducer (fast drying) being used.

- Excessively high air pressure at the spray gun.

If blushing is noticed during painting, a slow-drying reducer can sometimes be added to the paint mixture, and then the area resprayed. If blushing is found after the finish has dried, the area must be sanded down and repainted.

Figure 8-14. *Example of blushing.*

Pinholes

Pinholes are tiny holes, or groups of holes, that appear in the surface of the finish as a result of trapped solvents, air, or moisture. *[Figure 8-15]* Examples include:

- Contaminants in the paint or air lines.

- Poor spraying techniques that allow excessively heavy or wet paint coats, which tend to trap moisture or solvent under the finish.

- Use of the wrong thinner or reducer, either too fast by quick drying the surface and trapping solvents or too slow and trapping solvents by subsequent topcoats.

Figure 8-15. *Example of pinholes.*

If pinholes occur during painting, the equipment and painting technique must be evaluated before continuing. When dry, sand the surface smooth and then repaint.

Sags and Runs

Sags and runs are usually caused by applying too much paint to an area, by holding the spray gun too close to the surface, or moving the gun too slowly across the surface. *[Figure 8-16]*

Figure 8-16. *Example of sags and runs.*

Other causes include:

- Too much reducer in the paint (too thin).

- Incorrect spray gun setting of air-paint mixture.

Sags and runs can be avoided by following the recommended thinning instructions for the coatings being applied and taking care to use the proper spray gun techniques, especially on vertical surfaces and projected edges. Dried sags and runs must be sanded out and the surface repainted.

Orange Peel

"Orange peel" refers to the appearance of a bumpy surface, much like the skin of an orange. *[Figure 8-17]* It can be the result of a number of factors with the first being the improper adjustment of the spray gun. Other causes include:

- Not enough reducer (too thick) or the wrong type reducer for the ambient temperature.

- Material not uniformly mixed.

- Forced drying method, either with fans or heat, is too quick.

Figure 8-17. *Example of orange peel.*

- Too little flash time between coats.
- Spray painting when the ambient or substrate temperature is either too hot or too cold.

Light orange peel can be wet sanded or buffed out with polishing compound. In extreme cases, it has to be sanded smooth and resprayed.

Fisheyes

Fisheyes appear as small holes in the coating as it is being applied, which allows the underlying surface to be seen. *[Figure 8-18]* Usually, it is due to the surface not being cleaned of all traces of silicone wax. If numerous fisheyes appear when spraying a surface, stop spraying and clean off all the wet paint. Then, thoroughly clean the surface to remove all traces of silicone with a silicone wax remover.

Figure 8-18. *Example of fisheyes.*

The most effective way to eliminate fisheyes is to ensure that the surface about to be painted is clean and free from any type of contamination. A simple and effective way to check this is referred to as a water break test. Using clean water, spray, pour, or gently hose down the surface to be painted. If the water beads up anywhere on the surface, it is not clean. The water should flatten out and cover the area with an unbroken film.

If the occasional fisheye appears when spraying, wait until the first coat sets up and then add a recommended amount of fisheye eliminator to the subsequent finish coats. Fisheyes may appear during touchup of a repair. A coat of sealer may help, but completed removal of the finish may be the only solution.

One last check before spraying is to ensure that the air compressor has been drained of water, the regulator cleaned, and the system filters are clean or have been replaced so that this source of contamination is eliminated.

Sanding Scratches

Sanding scratches appear in the finish paint when the surface has not been properly sanded and/or sealed prior to spraying the finish coats. *[Figure 8-19]* This usually shows up in nonmetal surfaces. Composite cowling, wood surfaces, and plastic fairings must be properly sanded and sealed before painting. The scratches may also appear if on overly rapid quick-drying thinner is used.

The only fix after the finish coat has set up is to sand down the affected areas using a finer grade of sandpaper, follow with a recommended sealer, and then repaint.

Figure 8-19. *Example of sanding scratches.*

Wrinkling

Wrinkling is usually caused by trapped solvents and unequal drying of the paint finish due to excessively thick or solvent-heavy paint coats. *[Figure 8-20]* Fast reducers can also contribute to wrinkling if the sprayed coat is not allowed to dry thoroughly. Thick coatings and quick-drying reducers allow the top surface of the coating to dry, trapping the

Figure 8-20. *Example of wrinkling.*

solvents underneath. If another heavy coat is applied before the first one dries, wrinkles may result. It may also have the effect of lifting the coating underneath, almost with the same result as a paint stripper.

Rapid changes in ambient temperatures while spraying may cause an uneven release of the solvents, causing the surface to dry, shrink, and wrinkle. Making the mistake of using an incompatible thinner, or reducer, when mixing the coating materials may cause not only wrinkles but other problems as well. Wrinkled paint must be completely removed and the surface refinished.

Spray Dust

Spray dust is caused by the atomized spray particles from the gun becoming dry before reaching the surface being painted, thus failing to flow into a continuous film. *[Figure 8-21]* This may be caused by:

- Incorrect spray gun setting of air pressure, paint flow, or spray pattern.

- Spray gun being held too far from the surface.

- Material being improperly thinned or the wrong reducers being used with the finish coats.

The affected area needs to be sanded and recoated.

Figure 8-21. *Example of spray dust.*

Painting Trim and Identification Marks
Masking and Applying the Trim

At this point in the project, the entire aircraft has been painted with the base color and all the masking paper and tape carefully removed. Refer again to the coating manufacturer's technical data sheet for "dry and recoat" times for the appropriate temperatures and "dry to tape" time that must elapse before safe application and removal of tape on new paint without it lifting.

Masking Materials

When masking for the trim lines, use 3M® Fine Line tape. It is solvent proof, available in widths of ⅛–1 inch and, when applied properly, produces a sharp edge paint line. A good quality masking tape should be used with masking paper to cover all areas not being trimmed to ensure the paper does not lift and allow overspray on the basecoat. Do not use newspaper to mask the work as paint penetrates newspaper. Using actual masking paper is more efficient, especially if with a masking paper/tape dispenser as part of the finishing equipment.

Masking for the Trim

After the base color has dried and cured for the recommended time shown in the manufacturer's technical data sheet, the next step is to mask for the trim. The trim design can be simple, with one or two color stripes running along the fuselage, or it can be an elaborate scheme covering the entire aircraft. Whichever is chosen, the basic masking steps are the same.

If unsure of a design, there are numerous websites that provide the information and software to do a professional job. If electing to design a personalized paint scheme, the proposed design should be portrayed on a silhouette drawing of the aircraft as close to scale as possible. It is much easier to change a drawing than to remask the aircraft.

Start by identifying a point on the aircraft from which to initiate the trim lines using the Fine Line tape. If the lines are straight and/or have large radius curves, use ¾-inch or one-inch tape and keep it pulled tight. The wider tape is much easier to control when masking a straight line. Smaller radius curves may require ½-inch or even ¼-inch tape. Try and use the widest tape that lays flat and allows for a smooth curve. Use a small roller (like those used for wallpaper seams) to go back over and roll the tape edges firmly onto the surface to ensure they are flat.

Finish masking the trim lines on one side of the aircraft, to include the fuselage, vertical fin and rudder, the engine nacelles and wing(s). Once complete, examine the lines. If adjustments are needed to the placement or design, now is the time to correct it. With one side of the aircraft complete, the entire design and placement can be transferred to the opposite side.

Different methods can be employed to transfer the placement of the trim lines from one side of the aircraft to the other. One method is to trace the design on paper and then apply it to the other side, starting at the same point opposite the first starting point. Another method is to use the initial starting point and apply the trim tape using sheet metal or rivet lines as reference, along with measurements, to position the tape in the correct location.

When both sides are completed, a picture can be taken of each side and a comparison made to verify the tape lines on each side of the aircraft are identical.

With the Fine Line taping complete, some painters apply a sealing strip of ¾-inch or 1-inch masking tape covering half and extending over the outside edge of the Fine Line tape. This provides a wider area to apply the masking paper and adds an additional seal to the Fine Line tape. Now, apply the masking paper using 1-inch tape, placing half the width of the tape on the paper and half on the masked trim tape.

Use only masking paper made for painting and a comparable quality masking tape. With all the trim masking complete, cover the rest of the exposed areas of the aircraft to prevent overspray from landing on the base color. Tape the edges of the covering material to ensure the spray does not drift under it.

Now, scuff-sand all the area of trim to be painted to remove the gloss of the base paint. The use of 320-grit for the main area and a fine mesh Scotch-Brite pad next to the tape line should be sufficient. Then, blow all the dust and grit off the aircraft, and wipe down the newly sanded trim area with a degreaser and a tack cloth. Press or roll down the trim tape edges one more time before painting.

There are some various methods used by painters to ensure that a sharp defined tape line is attained upon removal of the tape. The basic step is to first use the 3M® Fine Line tape to mask the trim line. Some painters then spray a light coat of the base color or clear coat just prior to spraying the trim color. This will seal the tape edge line and ensure a clean sharp line when the tape is removed.

If multiple colors are used for the trim, cover the trim areas not to be sprayed with masking paper. When the first color is sprayed and dried, remove the masking paper from the next trim area to spray and cover the trim area that was first sprayed, taking care not to press the masking paper or tape into the freshly dried paint.

With all the trim completed, the masking paper should be removed as soon as the last trimmed area is dry to the touch. Carefully remove the Fine Line trim edge tape by slowly pulling it back onto itself at a sharp angle. Remove all trim

and masking tape from the base coat as soon as possible to preclude damage to the paint.

As referenced previously, use compatible paint components from the same manufacturer when painting trim over the base color. This reduces the possibility of an adverse reaction between the base coat and the trim colors.

Display of Nationality and Registration Marks

The complete regulatory requirement for identification and marking of a U.S.-registered aircraft can be found in Title 14 of the Code of Federal Regulations (14 CFR), Part 45, Identification and Registration Marking.

In summary, the regulation states that the marks must:

- Be painted on the aircraft or affixed by other means to insure a similar degree of permanence;

- Have no ornamentation;

- Contrast in color with the background; and

- Be legible.

The letters and numbers may be taped off and applied at the same time and using the same methods as when the trim is applied, or they may be applied later as decals of the proper size and color.

Display of Marks

Each operator of an aircraft shall display on the aircraft marks consisting of the Roman capital letter "N" (denoting United States registration) followed by the registration number of the aircraft. Each suffix letter must also be a Roman capital letter.

Location and Placement of Marks

On fixed-wing aircraft, marks must be displayed on either the vertical tail surfaces or the sides of the fuselage. If displayed on the vertical tail surfaces, they shall be horizontal on both surfaces of a single vertical tail or on the outer surfaces of a multivertical tail. If displayed on the fuselage surfaces, then horizontally on both sides of the fuselage between the trailing edge of the wing and the leading edge of the horizontal stabilizer. Exceptions to the location and size requirement for certain aircraft can be found in 14 CFR part 45.

On rotorcraft, marks must be displayed horizontally on both surfaces of the cabin, fuselage, boom, or tail. On airships, balloons, powered parachutes, and weight-shift control aircraft, display marks as required by 14 CFR part 45.

Size Requirements for Different Aircraft

Almost universally for U.S.-registered, standard certificated, fixed-wing aircraft, the marks must be at least 12 inches high. A glider may display marks at least 3 inches high.

In all cases, the marks must be of equal height, two-thirds as wide as they are high, and the characters must be formed by solid lines one-sixth as wide as they are high. The letters "M" and "W" may be as wide as they are high.

The spacing between each character may not be less than one-fourth of the character width. The marks required by 14 CFR part 45 for fixed-wing aircraft must have the same height, width, thickness, and spacing on both sides of the aircraft.

The marks must be painted or, if decalcomanias (decals), be affixed in a permanent manner. Other exceptions to the size and location of the marks are applicable to aircraft with Special Airworthiness certificates and those penetrating ADIZ and DEWIZ airspace. The current 14 CFR part 45 should be consulted for a complete copy of the rules.

Decals

Markings are placed on aircraft surfaces to provide servicing instructions, fuel and oil specifications, tank capacities, and to identify lifting and leveling points, walkways, battery locations, or any areas that should be identified. These markings can be applied by stenciling or by using decals.

Decals are used instead of painted instructions because they are usually less expensive and easier to apply. Decals used on aircraft are usually of three types: paper, metal, or vinyl film. These decals are suitable for exterior and interior surface application.

To assure proper adhesion of decals, clean all surfaces thoroughly with aliphatic naphtha to remove grease, oil, wax, or foreign matter. Porous surfaces should be sealed and rough surfaces sanded, followed by cleaning to remove any residue.

The instructions to be followed for applying decals are usually printed on the reverse side of each decal. A general application procedure for each type of decal is presented in the following paragraphs to provide familiarization with the techniques involved.

Paper Decals

Immerse paper decals in clean water for 1 to 3 minutes. Allowing decals to soak longer than 3 minutes causes the backing to separate from the decal while immersed. If decals are allowed to soak less than 1 minute, the backing does not separate from the decal.

Place one edge of the decal on the prepared receiving surface and press lightly, then slide the paper backing from beneath the decal. Perform any minor alignment with the fingers. Remove water by gently blotting the decal and adjacent area with a soft, absorbent cloth. Remove air or water bubbles trapped under the decal by wiping carefully toward the nearest edge of the decal with a cloth. Allow the decal to dry.

Metal Decals with Cellophane Backing

Apply metal decals with cellophane backing adhesive as follows:

1. Immerse the decal in clean, warm water for 1 to 3 minutes.

2. Remove it from the water and dry carefully with a clean cloth.

3. Remove the cellophane backing, but do not touch adhesive.

4. Position one edge of the decal on the prepared receiving surface. On large foil decals, place the center on the receiving surface and work outward from the center to the edges.

5. Remove all air pockets by rolling firmly with a rubber roller, and press all edges tightly against the receiving surface to ensure good adhesion.

Metal Decals With Paper Backing

Metal decals with a paper backing are applied similarly to those having a cellophane backing. However, it is not necessary to immerse the decal in water to remove the backing. It may be peeled from the decal without moistening. Follow the manufacturer's recommendation for activation of the adhesive, if necessary, before application. The decal should be positioned and smoothed out following the procedures given for cellophane-backed decals.

Metal Decals with No Adhesive

Apply decals with no adhesive in the following manner:

1. Apply one coat of cement, Military Specification MIL-A-5092, to the decal and prepared receiving surface.

2. Allow cement to dry until both surfaces are tacky.

3. Apply the decal and smooth it down to remove air pockets.

4. Remove excess adhesive with a cloth dampened with aliphatic naphtha.

Vinyl Film Decals

To apply vinyl film decals, separate the paper backing from the plastic film. Remove any paper backing adhering to the adhesive by rubbing the area gently with a clean cloth saturated with water. Remove small pieces of remaining paper with masking tape.

1. Place vinyl film, adhesive side up, on a clean porous surface, such as wood or blotter paper.

2. Apply recommended activator to the adhesive in firm, even strokes to the adhesive side of decal.

3. Position the decal in the proper location, while adhesive is still tacky, with only one edge contacting the prepared surface.

4. Work a roller across the decal with overlapping strokes until all air bubbles are removed.

Removal of Decals

Paper decals can be removed by rubbing the decal with a cloth dampened with lacquer thinner. If the decals are applied over painted or doped surfaces, use lacquer thinner sparingly to prevent removing the paint or dope.

Remove metal decals by moistening the edge of the foil with aliphatic naphtha and peeling the decal from the adhering surface. Work in a well-ventilated area.

Vinyl film decals are removed by placing a cloth saturated with MEK on the decal and scraping with a plastic scraper. Remove the remaining adhesive by wiping with a cloth dampened with a dry-cleaning solvent.

Paint System Compatibility

The use of several different types of paint, coupled with several proprietary coatings, makes repair of damaged and deteriorated areas particularly difficult. Paint finishes are not necessarily compatible with each other. The following general rules for coating compatibility are included for information and are not necessarily listed in order of importance:

1. Old type zinc chromate primer may be used directly for touchup of bare metal surfaces and for use on interior finishes. It may be overcoated with wash primers if it is in good condition. Acrylic lacquer finishes do not adhere to this material.

2. Modified zinc chromate primer does not adhere satisfactorily to bare metal. It must never be used over a dried film of acrylic nitrocellulose lacquer.

3. Nitrocellulose coatings adhere to acrylic finishes, but the reverse is not true. Acrylic nitrocellulose lacquers may not be used over old nitrocellulose finishes.

4. Acrylic nitrocellulose lacquers adhere poorly to bare metal and both nitrocellulose and epoxy finishes. For best results, the lacquers must be applied over fresh, successive coatings of wash primer and modified zinc

chromate. They also adhere to freshly applied epoxy coatings (dried less than 6 hours).

5. Epoxy topcoats adhere to any paint system that is in good condition, and may be used for general touchup, including touchup of defects in baked enamel coatings.

6. Old wash primer coats may be overcoated directly with epoxy finishes. A new second coat of wash primer must be applied if an acrylic finish is to be applied.

7. Old acrylic finishes may be refinished with new acrylic if the old coating is softened using acrylic nitrocellulose thinner before touchup.

8. Damage to epoxy finishes can best be repaired by using more epoxy, since neither of the lacquer finishes stick to the epoxy surface. In some instances, air-drying enamels may be used for touchup of epoxy coatings if edges of damaged areas are abraded with fine sandpaper.

Paint Touchup

Paint touchup may be required on an aircraft following repair to the surface substrate. Touchup may also be used to cover minor topcoat damage, such as scratches, abrasions, permanent stains, and fading of the trim colors. One of the first steps is to identify the paint that needs to be touched up.

Identification of Paint Finishes

Existing finishes on current aircraft may be any one of several types, a combination of two or more types, or combinations of general finishes with special proprietary coatings.

Any of the finishes may be present at any given time, and repairs may have been made using material from several different type coatings. Some detailed information for the identification of each finish is necessary to ensure the topcoat application does not react adversely with the undercoat. A simple test can be used to confirm the nature of the coatings present.

The following procedure aids in identification of the paint finish. Apply a coating of engine oil (MIL SPEC, MIL-PRF-7808, turbine oil, or equivalent) to a small area of the surface to be checked. Old nitrocellulose finishes soften within a period of a few minutes. Acrylic and epoxy finishes show no effects.

If still not identified, wipe a small area of the surface in question with a rag wet with MEK. The MEK picks up the pigment from an acrylic finish, but has no effect on an epoxy coating. Just wipe the surface, and do not rub. Heavy rubbing picks up even epoxy pigment from coatings that are not thoroughly cured. Do not use MEK on nitrocellulose finishes. *Figure 8-22* provides a solvent test to identify the coating on an aircraft.

Surface Preparation for Touchup

In the case of a repair and touchup, once the aircraft paint coating has been identified, the surface preparation follows some basic rules.

The first rule, as with the start of any paint project, is to wash and wipe down the area with a degreaser and silicone wax remover, before starting to sand or abrade the area.

If a whole panel or section within a seam line can be refinished during a touchup, it eliminates having to match and blend the topcoat to an existing finish. The area of repair should be stripped to a seam line and the finish completely redone from wash primer to the topcoat, as applicable. The paint along the edge of the stripped area should be hand-sanded wet and feathered with a 320 grade paper.

For a spot repair that requires blending of the coating, an area about three times the area of the actual repair will need to be prepared for blending of the paint. If the damaged area is through the primer to the substrate, the repair area should be abraded with 320 aluminum oxide paper on a double-action (D/A) air sander. Then, the repair and the surrounding area should be wet sanded using the air sander fitted with 1500 wet paper. The area should then be wiped with a tack cloth prior to spraying.

Apply a crosscoat of epoxy primer to the bare metal area, following the material data sheet for drying and recoat times. Abrade the primer area lightly with 1500 wet or dry, and then abrade the unsanded area around the repair with cutting compound. Clean and wipe the area with a degreasing solvent, such as isopropyl alcohol, and then a tack cloth.

Mix the selected topcoat paint that is compatible for the repair. Apply two light coats over the sanded repair area, slightly extending the second coat beyond the first. Allow time for the first coat to flash before applying the second coat. Then, thin the topcoat by one-third to one-half with a compatible reducer and apply one more coat, extending beyond the first two coats. Allow to dry according to the material data sheet before buffing and polishing the blended area.

If the damage did not penetrate the primer, and only the topcoat is needed for the finish, complete the same steps that would follow a primer coat.

Paint touchup procedures generally are the same for almost any repair. The end result, however, is affected by numerous variables, which include the preparation, compatibility of the finishing materials, color match, selection of reducers and/or retarders based on temperature, and experience and expertise of the painter.

Stripping the Finish

The most experienced painter, the best finishing equipment, and newest coatings, do not produce the desired finish on an aircraft if the surface was not properly prepared prior to refinishing. Surface preparation for painting of an entire aircraft typically starts with the removal of the paint. This is done not only for the weight reduction that is gained by stripping the many gallons of topcoats and primers, but for the opportunity to inspect and repair corrosion or other defects uncovered by the removal of the paint.

Before any chemical stripping can be performed, all areas of the aircraft not being stripped must be protected. The stripper manufacturer can recommend protective material for this purpose. This normally includes all window material,

3–5 Minute Contact With Cotton Wad Saturated With Test Solvent

Hitrate	Nitrate dope	Butyrate dope	Nitro-cellulose lacquer	Poly-tone Poly-brush Poly-spray	Synthetic enamel	Acrylic lacquer	Acrylic enamel	Urethane enamel	Epoxy paint
Methanol	S	IS	IS	IS	PS	IS	PS	IS	IS
Toluol (Toluene)	IS	IS	IS	S	IS	S	ISW	IS	IS
MEK (Methyl ethyl ketone)	S	S	S	S	ISW	S	ISW	IS	IS
Isopropanol	IS	IS	IS	IS	IS	S	IS	IS	IS
Methylene chloride	SS	VS	S	VS	ISW	S	ISW	ISW	ISW

IS – Insoluble
ISW – Insoluble, film wrinkles
PS – Penetrate film, slight softening without wrinkling

S – Soluble
SS – Slightly Soluble
VS – Very Soluble

Figure 8-22. *Chart for solvent test of coating.*

vents and static ports, rubber seals and tires, and composite components that may be affected by the chemicals.

The removal of paint from an aircraft, even a small single-engine model, involves not only the labor but a concern for the environment. You should recognize the impact and regulatory requirements that are necessary to dispose of the water and coating materials removed from the aircraft.

Chemical Stripping

At one time, most chemical strippers contained methylene chloride, considered an environmentally acceptable chemical until 1990. It was very effective in removing multiple layers of paint. However, in 1990, it was listed as a toxic air contaminant that caused cancer and other medical problems and was declared a Hazardous Air Pollutant (HAP) by the EPA in the Clean Air Act Amendments of 1990.

Since then, other substitute chemical strippers were tested, from formic acid to benzyl alcohol. None of them were found to be particularly effective in removing multiple layers of paint. Most of them were not friendly to the environment.

One of the more recent entries into the chemical stripping business is an environmentally friendly product known as EFS-2500, which works by breaking the bond between the substrate and primer. This leads to a secondary action that causes the paint to lift both primer and top coat off the surface as a single film. Once the coating is lifted, it is easily removed with a squeegee or high-pressure water.

This product differs from conventional chemical strippers by not melting the coatings. Cleanup is easier, and the product complies with EPA rules on emissions. Additionally, it passed Boeing testing specifications related to sandwich corrosion, immersion corrosion, and hydrogen embrittlement. EFS-2500 has no chlorinated components, is non-acidic, nonflammable, nonhazardous, biodegradable, and has minimal to no air pollution potential.

The stripper can be applied using existing common methods, such as airless spraying, brushing, rolling, or immersion in a tank. It works on all metals, including aluminum, magnesium, cadmium plate, titanium, wood, fiberglass, ceramic, concrete, plaster, and stone.

Plastic Media Blasting (PMB)

Plastic media blasting (PMB) is one of the stripping methods that reduces and may eliminate a majority of environmental pollution problems that can be associated with the earlier formulations of some chemical stripping. PMB is a dry abrasive blasting process designed to replace chemical paint stripping operations. PMB is similar to conventional sand blasting except that soft, angular plastic particles are used as the blasting medium. The process has minimum effect on the surface under the paint because of the plastic medium and relatively low air pressure used in the process. The media, when processed through a reclamation system, can be reused up to 10 times before it becomes too small to effectively remove the paint.

PMB is most effective on metal surfaces, but it has been used successfully on composite surfaces after it was found to produce less visual damage than removing the paint by sanding.

New Stripping Methods

Various methods and materials for stripping paint and other coatings are under development and include:

- A laser stripping process used to remove coatings from composites.

- Carbon dioxide pellets (dry ice) used in conjunction with a pulsed flashlamp that rapidly heats a thin layer of paint, which is then blasted away by the ice pellets.

Safety in the Paint Shop

All paint booths and shops must have adequate ventilation systems installed that not only remove the toxic air but, when properly operating, reduce and/or eliminate overspray and dust from collecting on the finish. All electric motors used in the fans and exhaust system should be grounded and enclosed to eliminate sparks. The lighting systems and all bulbs should be covered and protected against breakage.

Proper respirators and fresh-air breathing systems must be available to all personnel involved in the stripping and painting process. When mixing any paint or two-part coatings, eye protection and respirators should be worn.

An appropriate number and size of the proper class fire extinguishers should be available in the shop or hangar during all spraying operations. They should be weighed and certified, as required, to ensure they work in the event they are needed. Fireproof containers should be available for the disposal of all paint and solvent soaked rags.

Storage of Finishing Materials

All chemical components that are used to paint an aircraft burn in their liquid state. They should be stored away from all sources of heat or flames. The ideal place would be in fireproof metal cabinets located in a well ventilated area.

Some of the finishing components have a shelf life listed in the material or technical data sheet supplied by the coating manufacturer. Those materials should be marked on the container, with a date of purchase, in the event that they are not used immediately.

Protective Equipment for Personnel

The process of painting, stripping, or refinishing an aircraft requires the use of various coatings, chemicals, and procedures that may be hazardous if proper precautions are not utilized to protect personnel involved in their use.

The most significant hazards are airborne chemicals inhaled either from the vapors of opened paint containers or atomized mist resulting from spraying applications. There are two types of devices available to protect against airborne hazards: respirators and forced-air breathing systems.

A respirator is a device worn over the nose and mouth to filter particles and organic vapors from the air being inhaled. The most common type incorporate double charcoal-filtered cartridges with replaceable dust filters that fits to the face over the nose and mouth with a tight seal. When properly used, this type of respirator provides protection against the inhalation of organic vapors, dust, mists of paints, lacquers, and enamels. A respirator does not provide protection against paints and coatings containing isocyanates (polyurethane paint).

A respirator must be used in an area of adequate ventilation. If breathing becomes difficult, there is a smell or taste the contaminant(s), or an individual becomes dizzy or feel nauseous, they should leave the area and seek fresh air and assistance as necessary. Carefully read the warnings furnished with each respirator describing the limits and materials for which they provide protection.

A forced-air breathing system must be used when spraying any type of polyurethane or any coating that contains isocyanates. It is also recommended for all spraying and stripping of any type, whether chemical or media blasting. The system provides a constant source of fresh air for breathing, which is pumped into the mask through a hose from an electric turbine pump.

Protective clothing, such as Tyvek® coveralls, should be worn that not only protects personnel from the paint but also help keep dust off the painted surfaces. Rubber gloves must be worn when any stripper, etching solution, conversion coatings, and solvent is used.

When solvents are used for cleaning paint equipment and spray guns, the area must be free of any open flame or other heat source. Solvent should not be randomly sprayed into the atmosphere when cleaning the guns. Solvents should not be used to wash or clean paint and other coatings from bare hands and arms. Use protective gloves and clothing during all spraying operations.

In most states, there are Occupational Safety Hazard Administration (OSHA) regulations in effect that may require personnel to be protected from vapors and other hazards while on the job. In any hangar or shop, personnel must be vigilant and provide and use protection for safety.

Chapter 9
Aircraft Electrical System

Introduction

The satisfactory performance of any modern aircraft depends to a very great degree on the continuing reliability of electrical systems and subsystems. Improperly or carelessly installed or maintained wiring can be a source of both immediate and potential danger. The continued proper performance of electrical systems depends on the knowledge and technique of the mechanic who installs, inspects, and maintains the electrical system wires and cables.

Tightening nut

Iron ring

Mica V-ring

Front V-ring

Commutator bar

Mica

Iron shell

Commutator bars

Mica insulation between bars

Slots

Back V-ring with mica inner and outer rings for insulation

A. Voltage and current are in phase

B. Two voltage waves, 90° out of phase

C. Two voltage waves, 180° out of phase

Ohm's Law

Ohm's Law describes the basic mathematical relationships of electricity. The law was named after German Physicist George Simon Ohm (1789–1854). Basically, Ohm's Law states that the current (electron flow) through a conductor is directly proportional to the voltage (electrical pressure) applied to that conductor and inversely proportional to the resistance of the conductor. The unit used to measure resistance is called the ohm. The symbol for the ohm is the Greek letter omega (Ω). In mathematical formulas, the capital letter R refers to resistance. The resistance of a conductor and the voltage applied to it determine the number of amperes of current flowing through the conductor. Thus, 1 ohm of resistance limits the current flow to 1 ampere in a conductor to which a voltage of 1 volt is applied. The primary formula derived from Ohm's Law is: $E = I \times R$ (E = electromotive force measured in volts, I = current flow measured in amps, and R = resistance measured in ohms). This formula can also be written to solve for current or resistance:

$$I = \frac{E}{R}$$

$$R = \frac{E}{I}$$

Ohm's Law provides a foundation of mathematical formulas that predict how electricity responds to certain conditions. *[Figure 9-1]* For example, Ohm's Law can be used to calculate that a lamp of 12 Ohms (Ω) passes a current of 2 amps when connected to a 24-volt direct current (DC) power source.

Figure 9-1. *Ohm's Law used to calculate how much current a lamp will pass when connected to a 24-volt DC power source.*

Example 1

A 28-volt landing light circuit has a lamp with 4 ohms of resistance. Calculate the total current of the circuit.

$$I = \frac{E}{R}$$

$$I = \frac{28 \text{ volts}}{4\Omega}$$

$$I = 7 \text{ amps}$$

Example 2

A 28-volt deice boot circuit has a current of 6.5 amps. Calculate the resistance of the deice boot.

$$R = \frac{E}{I}$$

$$R = \frac{28 \text{ volts}}{6.5 \text{ amps}}$$

$$R = 4.31\Omega$$

Example 3

A taxi light has a resistance of 4.9 Ω and a total current of 2.85 amps. Calculate the system voltage.

$$E = I \times R$$

$$E = 2.85 \times 4.9\Omega$$

$$E = 14 \text{ volts}$$

Whenever troubleshooting aircraft electrical circuits, it is always valuable to consider Ohm's Law. A good understanding of the relationship between resistance and current flow can help one determine if a circuit contains an open or a short. Remembering that a low resistance means increased current can help explain why circuit breakers pop or fuses blow. In almost all cases, aircraft loads are wired in parallel to each other; therefore, there is a constant voltage supplied to all loads and the current flow through a load is a function of that load's resistance.

Figure 9-2 illustrates several ways of using Ohm's Law for the calculation of current, voltage, and resistance.

Current

Electrical current is the movement of electrons. This electron movement is referred to as current, flow, or current flow. In practical terms, this movement of electrons must take place within a conductor (wire). Current is typically measured in amps. The symbol for current is I and the symbol for amps is A.

The current flow is actually the movement of the free electrons found within conductors. Common conductors

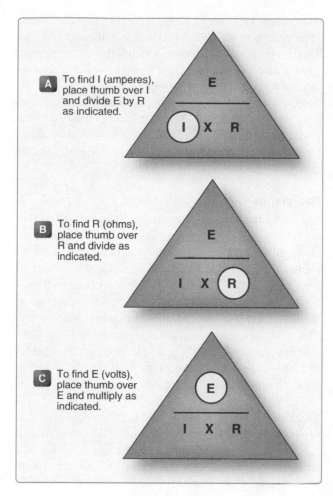

A. To find I (amperes), place thumb over I and divide E by R as indicated.

B. To find R (ohms), place thumb over R and divide as indicated.

C. To find E (volts), place thumb over E and multiply as indicated.

Figure 9-2. *Ohm's Law chart.*

include copper, silver, aluminum, and gold. The term "free electron" describes a condition in some atoms where the outer electrons are loosely bound to their parent atom. These loosely bound electrons are easily motivated to move in a given direction when an external source, such as a battery, is applied to the circuit. These electrons are attracted to the positive terminal of the battery, while the negative terminal is the source of the electrons. So, the measure of current is actually the number of electrons moving through a conductor in a given amount of time.

The internationally accepted unit for current is the ampere (A). One ampere (A) of current is equivalent to 1 coulomb (C) of charge passing through a conductor in 1 second. One coulomb of charge equals 6.28×10^{18} electrons. Obviously, the unit of amperes is a much more convenient term to use than coulombs. The unit of coulombs is simply too small to be practical.

When current flow is in one direction, it is called direct current (DC). Later in the text, the form of current that periodically oscillates back and forth within the circuit is discussed. The present discussion is concerned only with the use of DC. It should be noted that as with the movement of any mass, electron movement (current flow) only occurs when there is a force present to push the electrons. This force is commonly called voltage (described in more detail in the next section). When a voltage is applied across the conductor, an electromotive force creates an electric field within the conductor, and a current is established. The electrons do not move in a straight direction, but undergo repeated collisions with other nearby atoms within a conductor. These collisions usually knock other free electrons from their atoms, and these electrons move on toward the positive end of the conductor with an average velocity called the drift velocity, which is relatively low speed. To understand the nearly instantaneous speed of the effect of the current, it is helpful to visualize a long tube filled with steel balls. *[Figure 9-3]*

Figure 9-3. *Electron flow.*

It can be seen that a ball introduced in one end of the tube, which represents the conductor, immediately causes a ball to be emitted at the opposite end of the tube. Thus, electric current can be viewed as instantaneous, even though it is the result of a relatively slow drift of electrons.

Conventional Current Theory and Electron Theory

There are two competing schools of thought regarding the flow of electricity. The two explanations are the conventional current theory and the electron theory. Both theories describe the movement of electrons through a conductor. They simply explain the direction current moves. Typically during troubleshooting or the connection of electrical circuits, the use of either theory can be applied as long as it is used consistently. The Federal Aviation Administration (FAA) officially defines current flow using electron theory (negative to positive).

The conventional current theory was initially advanced by Benjamin Franklin, who reasoned that current flowed out of a positive source into a negative source or an area that lacked an abundance of charge. The notation assigned to the electric charges was positive (+) for the abundance of charge and negative (−) for a lack of charge. It then seemed natural to visualize the flow of current as being from the positive (+) to the negative (−). Later discoveries were made that proved that just the opposite is true. Electron theory describes what actually happens in the case of an abundance of electrons flowing out of the negative (−) source to an area that lacks electrons or the positive (+) source. Both conventional flow and electron flow are used in industry.

Electromotive Force (Voltage)

Voltage is most easily described as electrical pressure force. It is the electromotive force (EMF), or the push or pressure from one end of the conductor to the other, that ultimately moves the electrons. The symbol for EMF is the capital letter E. EMF is always measured between two points and voltage is considered a value between two points. For example, across the terminals of the typical aircraft battery, voltage can be measured as the potential difference of 12 volts or 24 volts. That is to say that between the two terminal posts of the battery, there is a voltage available to push current through a circuit. Free electrons in the negative terminal of the battery move toward the excessive number of positive charges in the positive terminal. The net result is a flow or current through a conductor. There cannot be a flow in a conductor unless there is an applied voltage from a battery, generator, or ground power unit. The potential difference, or the voltage across any two points in an electrical system, can be determined by:

$$V_1 - V_2 = V_{Drop}$$

Example

The voltage at one point is 14 volts. The voltage at a second point in the circuit is 12.1 volts. To calculate the voltage drop, use the formula above to get a total voltage drop of 1.9 volts.

Figure 9-4 illustrates the flow of electrons of electric current. Two interconnected water tanks demonstrate that when a difference of pressure exists between the two tanks, water flows until the two tanks are equalized. *Figure 9-4* shows the level of water in tank A to be at a higher level, reading 10 pounds per square inch (psi) (higher potential energy), than the water level in tank B, reading 2 psi (lower potential energy). Between the two tanks, there is 8 psi potential difference. If the valve in the interconnecting line between the tanks is opened, water flows from tank A into tank B until the level of water (potential energy) of both tanks is equalized. It is important to note that it was not the pressure in tank A

that caused the water to flow; rather, it was the difference in pressure between tank A and tank B that caused the flow. This comparison illustrates the principle that electrons move, when a path is available, from a point of excess electrons (higher potential energy) to a point deficient in electrons (lower potential energy). The force that causes this movement is the potential difference in electrical energy between the two points. This force is called the electrical pressure (voltage), the potential difference, or the electromotive force (electron moving force).

Resistance

The two fundamental properties of current and voltage are related by a third property known as resistance. In any electrical circuit, when voltage is applied to it, a current results. The resistance of the conductor determines the amount of current that flows under the given voltage. In general, the greater the circuit resistance, the less the current. If the resistance is reduced, then the current will increase. This relation is linear in nature and is known as Ohm's Law. An example would be if the resistance of a circuit is doubled, and the voltage is held constant, then the current through the resistor is cut in half.

There is no distinct dividing line between conductors and insulators; under the proper conditions, all types of material conduct some current. Materials offering a resistance to current flow midway between the best conductors and the poorest conductors (insulators) are sometimes referred to as semiconductors and find their greatest application in the field of transistors.

The best conductors are materials, chiefly metals, that possess a large number of free electrons. Conversely, insulators are materials having few free electrons. The best conductors are silver, copper, gold, and aluminum, but some nonmetals, such as carbon and water, can be used as conductors. Materials such as rubber, glass, ceramics, and plastics are such poor conductors that they are usually used as insulators. The current flow in some of these materials is so low that it is usually considered zero.

Factors Affecting Resistance

The resistance of a metallic conductor is dependent on the type of conductor material. It has been pointed out that certain metals are commonly used as conductors because of the large number of free electrons in their outer orbits. Copper is usually considered the best available conductor material, since a copper wire of a particular diameter offers a lower resistance to current flow than an aluminum wire of the same diameter. However, aluminum is much lighter than copper, and for this reason, as well as cost considerations, aluminum is often used when the weight factor is important.

Figure 9-4. *Difference of pressure.*

The resistance of a metallic conductor is directly proportional to its length. The longer the length of a given size of wire, the greater the resistance. *Figure 9-5* shows two wire conductors of different lengths. If 1 volt of electrical pressure is applied across the two ends of the conductor that is 1 foot in length and the resistance to the movement of free electrons is assumed to be 1 ohm, the current flow is limited to 1 ampere. If the same size conductor is doubled in length, the same electrons set in motion by the 1 volt applied now find twice the resistance.

Figure 9-5. *Resistance varies with length of conductor.*

Electromagnetic Generation of Power

Electrical energy can be produced through a number of methods. Common methods include the use of light, pressure, heat, chemical, and electromagnetic induction. Of these processes, electromagnetic induction is most responsible for the generation of the majority of the electrical power used by humans. Virtually all mechanical devices (generators and alternators) that produce electrical power employ the process of electromagnetic induction. The use of light, pressure, heat, and chemical sources for electrical power is found on aircraft but produce a minimal amount of all the electrical power consumed during a typical flight.

In brief, light can produce electricity using a solar cell (photovoltaic cell). These cells contain a certain chemical that converts light energy into voltage/current.

Using pressure to generate electrical power is commonly known as the piezoelectric effect. The piezoelectric effect (piezo or piez taken from Greek: to press; pressure; to squeeze) is a result of the application of mechanical pressure on a dielectric or nonconducting crystal.

Chemical energy can be converted into electricity, most commonly in the form of a battery. A primary battery produces electricity using two different metals in a chemical solution like alkaline electrolyte. A chemical reaction exists between the metals which frees more electrons in one metal than in the other.

Heat used to produce electricity creates the thermoelectric effect. When a device called a thermocouple is subjected to heat, a voltage is produced. A thermocouple is a junction between two different metals that produces a voltage related to a temperature difference. If the thermocouple is connected to a complete circuit, a current also flows. Thermocouples are often found on aircraft as part of a temperature monitoring system, such as a cylinder head temperature gauge.

Electromagnetic induction is the process of producing a voltage (EMF) by moving a magnetic field in relationship to a conductor. As shown in *Figure 9-6,* when a conductor (wire) is moved through a magnetic field, an EMF is produced in the conductor. If a complete circuit is connected to the conductor, the voltage also produces a current flow.

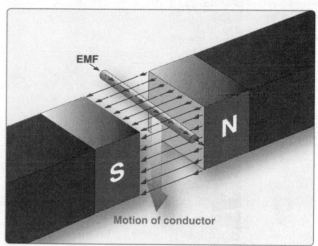

Figure 9-6. *Inducing an EMF in a conductor.*

One single conductor does not produce significant voltage/current via electromagnetic induction. *[Figure 9-6]* In practice, instead of a single wire, a coil of wire is moved through the magnetic field of a strong magnet. This produces a greater electrical output. In many cases, the magnetic field is created by using a powerful electromagnet. This allows for the production of a greater voltage/current due to the stronger magnetic field produced by the electromagnet when compared to an ordinary magnet.

Please note that this text often refers to voltage/current in regards to electrical power. Remember voltage (electrical pressure) must be present to produce a current (electron flow). Hence, the output energy generated through the process of electromagnetic induction always consists of voltage.

Current also results when a complete circuit is connected to that voltage. Electrical power is produced when there is both electrical pressure E (EMF) and current (I). Power = Current × Voltage (P = I × E)

It is the relative motion between a conductor and a magnetic field that causes current to flow in the conductor. Either the conductor or magnet can be moving or stationary. When a magnet and its field are moved through a coiled conductor, as shown in *Figure 9-7*, a DC voltage with a specific polarity is produced. The polarity of this voltage depends on the direction in which the magnet is moved and the position of the north and south poles of the magnetic field. The generator left-hand rule can be used to determine the direction of current flow within the conductor. *[Figure 9-8]* Of course, the direction of current flow is a function of the polarity of the voltage induced in to the conductor.

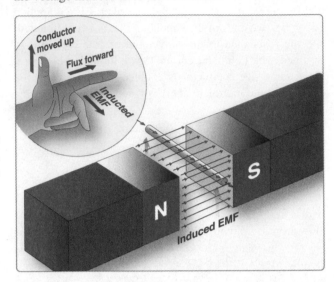

Figure 9-8. *An application of the generator left-hand rule.*

In practice, producing voltage/current using the process of electromagnetic induction requires a rotating machine. Generally speaking, on all aircraft, a generator or alternator employs the principles of electromagnetic induction to create electrical power for the aircraft. Either the magnetic field can rotate or the conductor can rotate. *[Figure 9-9]* The rotating component is driven by a mechanical device, such as an aircraft engine.

Figure 9-9. *Voltage induced in a loop.*

During the process of electromagnetic induction, the value of the induced voltage/current depends on three basic factors:

1. Number of turns in the conductor coil (more loops equals greater induced voltage)

Figure 9-7. *Inducing a current flow.*

2. Strength of the electromagnet (the stronger the magnetic field, the greater the induced voltage)

3. Speed of rotation of the conductor or magnet (the faster the rotation, the greater the induced voltage)

Figure 9-10 illustrates the basics of a rotating machine used to produce voltage. The simple generating device consists of a rotating loop, marked A and B, placed between two magnetic poles, N and S. The ends of the loop are connected to two metal slip rings (collector rings), C1 and C2. Current is taken from the collector rings by brushes. If the loop is considered as separate wires, A and B, and the left-hand rule for generators is applied, then it can be observed that as wire B moves up across the field, a voltage is induced that causes the current to flow towards the reader. As wire A moves down across the field, a voltage is induced that causes the current to flow away from the reader. When the wires are formed into a loop, the voltages induced in the two sides of the loop are combined. Therefore, for explanatory purposes, the action of either conductor, A or B, while rotating in the magnetic field is similar to the action of the loop.

Figure 9-11 illustrates the generation of alternating current (AC) with a simple loop conductor rotating in a magnetic field. As it is rotated in a counterclockwise direction, varying voltages are induced in the conductive loop.

Position 1

The conductor A moves parallel to the lines of force. Since it cuts no lines of force, the induced voltage is zero. As the

conductor advances from position 1 to position 2, the induced voltage gradually increases.

Position 2

The conductor is now moving in a direction perpendicular to the flux and cuts a maximum number of lines of force; therefore, a maximum voltage is induced. As the conductor moves beyond position 2, it cuts a decreasing amount of flux, and the induced voltage decreases.

Position 3

At this point, the conductor has made half a revolution and again moves parallel to the lines of force, and no voltage is induced in the conductor. As the A conductor passes position 3, the direction of induced voltage now reverses since the A conductor is moving downward, cutting flux in the opposite direction. As the A conductor moves across the south pole, the induced voltage gradually increases in a negative direction until it reaches position 4.

Position 4

Like position 2, the conductor is again moving perpendicular to the flux and generates a maximum negative voltage. From position 4 to position 5, the induced voltage gradually decreases until the voltage is zero, and the conductor and wave are ready to start another cycle.

Position 5

The curve shown at position 5 is called a sine wave. It represents the polarity and the magnitude of the instantaneous

A side of loop   B side of loop   ⊕ Current flow is toward the reader   ⊙ Current flow is away from reader

Figure 9-10. *Simple generator.*

Figure 9-11. *Generation of a sine wave.*

values of the voltages generated. The horizontal baseline is divided into degrees, or time, and the vertical distance above or below the baseline represents the value of voltage at each particular point in the rotation of the loop.

The specific operating principles of both alternators and generators as they apply to aircraft is presented later in this text.

Within the figure:

Magnetic field

Zero voltage

Position 1
Rotating conductors moving parallel to magnetic field, cutting minimum lines of force.

Maximum positive voltage

Position 2 Quarter turn completed
Conductors cutting directly across the magnetic field as conductor A passes across the north magnetic pole and B passes across the S pole.

Voltage drops to zero

Position 3 One half turn completed
Conductor again moving parallel to magnetic field, cutting minimum lines of force.

Maximum negative voltage

Position 4 Three quarters turn completed
Conductors again moving directly across magnetic field A passes across south magnetic pole and B across N magnetic pole.

Zero voltage

Position 5 Full turn completed
Conductor A has made one complete cycle and is in same position as in position A. The generator has generated one complete cycle of alternating voltage or current.

Alternating Current (AC) Introduction

Alternating current (AC) electrical systems are found on most multi-engine, high performance turbine powered aircraft and transport category aircraft. AC is the same type of electricity used in industry and to power our homes. Direct current (DC) is used on systems that must be compatible with battery power, such as on light aircraft and automobiles. There are many benefits of AC power when selected over DC power for aircraft electrical systems.

AC can be transmitted over long distances more readily and more economically than DC, since AC voltages can be increased or decreased by means of transformers. Because more and more units are being operated electrically in airplanes, the power requirements are such that a number of advantages can be realized by using AC (especially with large transport category aircraft). Space and weight can be saved since AC devices, especially motors, are smaller and simpler than DC devices. In most AC motors, no brushes are required, and they require less maintenance than DC motors. Circuit breakers operate satisfactorily under loads at high altitudes in an AC system, whereas arcing is so excessive on DC systems that circuit breakers must be replaced frequently. Finally, most airplanes using a 24-volt DC system have special equipment that requires a certain amount of 400 cycle AC current. For these aircraft, a unit called an inverter is used to change DC to AC. Inverters are discussed later in this book.

AC is constantly changing in value and polarity, or as the name implies, alternating. *Figure 9-12* shows a graphic comparison of DC and AC. The polarity of DC never changes, and the polarity and voltage constantly change in AC. It should also be noted that the AC cycle repeats at given intervals. With AC, both voltage and current start at zero, increase, reach a peak, then decrease and reverse polarity. If one is to graph this concept, it becomes easy to see the alternating wave form. This wave form is typically referred to as a sine wave.

Definitions

Values of AC

There are three values of AC that apply to both voltage and current. These values help to define the sine wave and are called instantaneous, peak, and effective. It should be noted that during the discussion of these terms, the text refers to voltage. But remember, the values apply to voltage and current in all AC circuits.

Instantaneous

An instantaneous voltage is the value at any instant in time along the AC wave. The sine wave represents a series of these values. The instantaneous value of the voltage varies from zero at 0° to maximum at 90°, back to zero at 180°, to maximum in the opposite direction at 270°, and to zero again at 360°. Any point on the sine wave is considered the instantaneous value of voltage.

Peak

The peak value is the largest instantaneous value, often referred to as the maximum value. The largest single positive value occurs after a certain period of time when the sine wave reaches 90°, and the largest single negative value occurs when the wave reaches 270°. Although important in the understanding of the AC sine wave, peak values are seldom used by aircraft technicians.

Effective

The effective values for voltage are always less than the peak (maximum) values of the sine wave and approximate DC voltage of the same value. For example, an AC circuit of 24 volts and 2 amps should produce the same heat through a resistor as a DC circuit of 24 volts and 2 amps. The effective value is also known as the root mean square, or RMS value, which refers to the mathematical process by which the value is derived.

Most AC meters display the effective value of the AC. In almost all cases, the voltage and current ratings of a system

Figure 9-12. *DC and AC voltage curves.*

or component are given in effective values. In other words, the industry ratings are based on effective values. Peak and instantaneous values, used only in very limited situations, would be stated as such. In the study of AC, any values given for current or voltage are assumed to be effective values unless otherwise specified. In practice, only the effective values of voltage and current are used.

The effective value is equal to .707 times the peak (maximum) value. Conversely, the peak value is 1.41 times the effective value. Thus, the 110 volt value given for AC is only 0.707 of the peak voltage of this supply. The maximum voltage is approximately 155 volts (110 × 1.41 = 155 volts maximum).

How often the AC waveform repeats is known as the AC frequency. The frequency is typically measured in cycles per second (CPS) or hertz (Hz). One Hz equals one CPS. The time it takes for the sine wave to complete one cycle is known as period (P). Period is a value or time period and typically measured in seconds, milliseconds, or microseconds. It should be noted that the time period of a cycle can change from one system to another; it is always said that the cycle completes in 360° (related to the 360° of rotation of an AC alternator). *[Figure 9-13]*

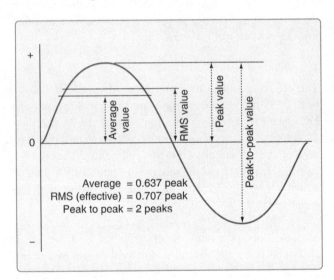

Figure 9-13. *Values of AC.*

Cycle Defined

A cycle is a completion of a pattern. Whenever a voltage or current passes through a series of changes, returns to the starting point, and then repeats the same series of changes, the series is called a cycle. When the voltage values are graphed, as in *Figure 9-14*, the complete AC cycle is displayed. One complete cycle is often referred to as the sine wave and said to be 360°. It is typical to start the sine wave where the voltage is zero. The voltage then increases to a maximum positive value, decreases to a value of zero, then

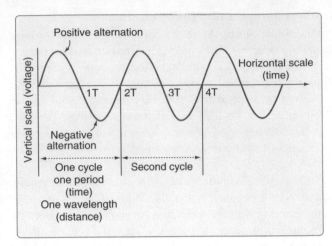

Figure 9-14. *Cycle of voltage.*

increases to a maximum negative value, and again decreases to zero. The cycle repeats until the voltage is no longer available. There are two alternations in a complete cycle: the positive alternation and the negative. It should be noted that the polarity of the voltage reverses for each half cycle. Therefore, during the positive half cycle, the electron flow is considered to be in one direction; during the negative half cycle, the electrons reverse direction and flow the opposite way through the circuit.

Frequency Defined

The frequency is the number of cycles of AC per second (CPS). The standard unit of frequency measurement is the Hz. *[Figure 9-15]* In a generator, the voltage and current pass through a complete cycle of values each time a coil or conductor passes under a north and south pole of the magnet. The number of cycles for each revolution of the coil or conductor is equal to the number of pairs of poles.

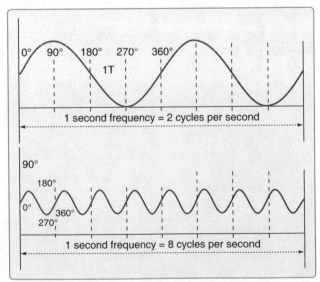

Figure 9-15. *Frequency in cycles per second.*

The frequency, then, is equal to the number of cycles in one revolution multiplied by the number of revolutions per second.

Period Defined

The time required for a sine wave to complete one full cycle is called a period (P). A period is typically measured in seconds, milliseconds, or microseconds. *[Figure 9-14]* The period of a sine wave is inversely proportional to the frequency. That is to say that the higher the frequency, the shorter the period. The mathematical relationship between frequency and period is given as:

Period

$$P = \frac{1}{f}$$

Frequency

$$F = \frac{1}{P}$$

Wavelength Defined

The distance that a waveform travels during a period is commonly referred to as a wavelength and is indicated by the Greek letter lambda (λ). Wavelength is related to frequency by the formula:

$$\frac{\text{wave speed}}{\text{frequency}} = \text{wavelength}$$

The higher the frequency is, the shorter the wavelength is. The measurement of wavelength is taken from one point on the waveform to a corresponding point on the next waveform. *[Figure 9-14]* Since wavelength is a distance, common units of measure include meters, centimeters, millimeters, or nanometers. For example, a sound wave of frequency 20 Hz would have wavelength of 17 meters and a visible red light wave of $4.3 \times 10 -12$ Hz would have a wavelength of roughly 700 nanometers. Keep in mind that the actual wavelength depends on the media through which the waveform must travel.

Phase Relationships

Phase is the relationship between two sine waves, typically measured in angular degrees. For example, if there are two different alternators producing power, it would be easy to compare their individual sine waves and determine their phase relationship. In *Figure 9-16B*, there is a 90° phase difference between the two voltage waveforms. A phase relationship can be between any two sine waves. The phase relationship can be measured between two voltages of different alternators or the current and voltage produced by the same alternator.

Figure 9-16. *In-phase and out-of-phase conditions.*

Figure 9-16A shows a voltage signal and a current signal superimposed on the same time axis. Notice that when the voltage increases in the positive alternation that the current also increases. When the voltage reaches its peak value, so does the current. Both waveforms then reverse and decrease back to a zero magnitude, then proceed in the same manner in the negative direction as they did in the positive direction. When two waves are exactly in step with each other, they are said to be in phase. To be in phase, the two waveforms must go through their maximum and minimum points at the same time and in the same direction.

When two waveforms go through their maximum and minimum points at different times, a phase difference exists between the two. In this case, the two waveforms are said to be out of phase with each other. The terms lead and lag are often used to describe the phase difference between waveforms. The waveform that reaches its maximum or minimum value first is said to lead the other waveform. *Figure 9-16B* shows this relationship. On the other hand, the second waveform is said to be lagging the first source. When a waveform is said to be leading or lagging, the difference in degrees is usually stated. If the two waveforms differ by 360°, they are said to be in phase with each other. If there is a 180° difference between the two signals, then they are still out of phase even though they are both reaching their minimum and maximum values at the same time. *[Figure 9-16C]*

Opposition to Current Flow of AC

There are three factors that can create an opposition to the flow of electrons (current) in an AC circuit. Resistance, similar to resistance of DC circuits, is measured in ohms and has a direct influence on AC regardless of frequency. Inductive reactance and capacitive reactance, on the other hand, oppose current flow only in AC circuits, not in DC circuits. Since AC constantly changes direction and intensity, inductors and capacitors may also create an opposition to current flow in AC circuits. It should also be noted that inductive reactance and capacitive reactance may create a phase shift between the voltage and current in an AC circuit. Whenever analyzing an AC circuit, it is very important to consider the resistance, inductive reactance, and the capacitive reactance. All three have an effect on the current of that circuit.

Resistance

As mentioned, resistance creates an opposition to current in an AC circuit similar to the resistance of a DC circuit. The current through a resistive portion of an AC circuit is inversely proportional to the resistance and directly proportional to the voltage applied to that circuit or portion of the circuit. The equations $I = E / R$ & $E = I \times R$ show how current is related to both voltage and resistance. It should be noted that resistance in an AC circuit does not create a phase shift between voltage and current.

Figure 9-17 shows how a circuit of 10 ohms allows 11.5 amps of current flow through an AC resistive circuit of 115 volts.

$$I = \frac{E}{R}$$

$$I = \frac{115V}{10\Omega}$$

$$I = 11.5 \text{ Amps}$$

Figure 9-17. *Resistance.*

Inductive Reactance

When moving a magnet through a coil of wire, a voltage is induced across the coil. If a complete circuit is provided, then a current will also be induced. The amount of induced voltage is directly proportional to the rate of change of the magnetic field with respect to the coil. Conversely, current flowing through a coil of wire produces a magnetic field. When this wire is formed into a coil, it then becomes a basic inductor.

The primary effect of a coil is its property to oppose any change in current through it. This property is called inductance. When current flows through any conductor, a magnetic field starts to expand from the center of the wire. As the lines of magnetic force grow outward through the conductor, they induce an EMF in the conductor itself. The induced voltage is always in the direction opposite to the direction of the applied current flow. The effects of this countering EMF are to oppose the applied current. This effect is only a temporary condition. Once the current reaches a steady value in the conductor, the lines of magnetic force are no longer expanding and the countering EMF is no longer present. Since AC is constantly changing in value, the inductance repeats in a cycle always opposite the applied voltage. It should be noted that the unit of measure for inductance is the henry (H).

The physical factors that affect inductance are:

1. Number of turns—doubling the number of turns in a coil produces a field twice as strong if the same current is used. As a general rule, the inductance varies with the square of the number of turns.

2. Cross-sectional area of the coil—the inductance of a coil increases directly as the cross-sectional area of the core increases. Doubling the radius of a coil increases the inductance by a factor of four.

3. Length of a coil—doubling the length of a coil, while keeping the same number of turns, reduces inductance by one-half.

4. Core material around which the coil is formed—coils are wound on either magnetic or nonmagnetic materials. Some nonmagnetic materials include air, copper, plastic, and glass. Magnetic materials include nickel, iron, steel, and cobalt, which have a permeability that provides a better path for the magnetic lines of force and permit a stronger magnetic field.

Since AC is in a constant state of change, the magnetic fields within an inductor are also continuously changing and create an inducted voltage/current. This induced voltage opposes the applied voltage and is known as the counter EMF. This opposition is called inductive reactance, symbolized by XL, and is measured in ohms. This characteristic of the inductor may also create a phase shift between voltage and current of the circuit. The phase shift created by inductive reactance always causes voltage to lead current. That is, the voltage of an inductive circuit reaches its peak values before the current reaches peak values. Additional discussions related to phase shift are presented later in this chapter.

Inductance is the property of a circuit to oppose any change in current and is measured in henries. Inductive reactance is a measure of how much the countering EMF in the circuit opposes the applied current. The inductive reactance of a component is directly proportional to the inductance of the component and the applied frequency to the circuit. By increasing either the inductance or applied frequency, the inductive reactance likewise increases and presents more opposition to current in the circuit. This relationship is given as XL = 2πfL Where XL = inductive reactance in ohms, L = inductance in henries, f = frequency in cycles per second, and π = 3.1416

In *Figure 9-18*, an AC series circuit is shown in which the inductance is 0.146 henry and the voltage is 110 volts at a frequency of 60 cycles per second. Inductive reactance is determined by the following method.

$$X_L = 2\pi \times f \times L$$

$$X_L = 6.28 \times 60 \times 0.146$$

$$X_L = 55\,\Omega$$

Figure 9-18. *AC circuit containing inductance.*

In AC series circuits, inductive reactance is added like resistances in series in a DC circuit. *[Figure 9-19]* The total reactance in the illustrated circuit equals the sum of the individual reactances.

Figure 9-19. *Inductances in series.*

$$X_L = X_{L1} + X_{L2}$$

$$X_L = 10\,\Omega + 15\,\Omega$$

$$X_{LT} = 25\,\Omega$$

The total reactance of inductors connected in parallel is found the same way as the total resistance in a parallel circuit. *[Figure 9-20]* Thus, the total reactance of inductances connected in parallel, as shown, is expressed as:

$$X_{LT} = \cfrac{1}{\cfrac{1}{X_{L1}} + \cfrac{1}{X_{L2}} + \cfrac{1}{X_{L3}}}$$

$$X_{LT} = \cfrac{1}{\cfrac{1}{15} + \cfrac{1}{15} + \cfrac{1}{15}}$$

$$X_{LT} = 5\,\Omega$$

Figure 9-20. *Inductances in parallel.*

Capacitive Reactance

Capacitance is the ability of a body to hold an electric charge. In general, a capacitor is constructed of two parallel plates separated by an insulator. The insulator is commonly called the dielectric. The capacitor's plates have the ability to store electrons when charged by a voltage source. The capacitor discharges when the applied voltage is no longer present and the capacitor is connected to a current path. In an electrical circuit, a capacitor serves as a reservoir or storehouse for electricity.

The basic unit of capacitance is the farad and is given by the letter F. By definition, one farad is one coulomb of charge stored with one volt across the plates of the capacitor. In practical terms, one farad is a large amount of capacitance. Typically, in electronics, much smaller units are used. The two more common smaller units are the microfarad (μF), which is 10^{-6} farad and the picofarad (pF), which is 10^{-12} farad.

Capacitance is a function of the physical properties of the capacitor:

1. The capacitance of parallel plates is directly proportional to their area. A larger plate area produces a larger capacitance, and a smaller area produces less capacitance. If we double the area of the plates, there is room for twice as much charge.

2. The capacitance of parallel plates is inversely proportional to the distance between the plates.

3. The dielectric material effects the capacitance of parallel plates. The dielectric constant of a vacuum is defined as 1, and that of air is very close to 1. These values are used as a reference, and all other materials have values relative to that of air (vacuum).

When an AC is applied in the circuit, the charge on the plates constantly changes. *[Figure 9-21]* This means that electricity must flow first from Y clockwise around to X, then from X counterclockwise around to Y, then from Y clockwise around to X, and so on. Although no current flows through the insulator between the plates of the capacitor, it constantly flows in the remainder of the circuit between X and Y. As this current alternates to and from the capacitor, a certain time lag is created. When a capacitor charges or discharges through a resistance, a certain amount of time is required for a full charge or discharge. The voltage across the capacitor does not change instantaneously. The rate of charging or discharging is determined by the time constant of the circuit. This rate of charge and discharge creates an opposition to current flow in AC circuits known as capacitive reactance. Capacitive reactance is symbolized by X_C and is measured in ohms. This characteristic of a capacitor may also create a phase shift between voltage and current of the circuit. The phase shift created by capacitive reactance always causes current to lead voltage. That is, the current of a capacitive circuit reaches its peak values before the voltage reaches peak values.

Figure 9-21. *Capacitor in an AC circuit.*

Capacitive reactance is a measure of how much the capacitive circuit opposes the applied current flow. Capacitive reactance is measured in ohms. The capacitive reactance of a circuit is indirectly proportional to the capacitance of the circuit and the applied frequency to the circuit. By increasing either the capacitance or applied frequency, the capacitive reactance decreases, and vice versa. This relationship is given as:

$$X_C = \frac{1}{2\pi fC}$$

Where: X_C = capacitive reactance in ohms, C = capacitance in farads, f = frequency in cycles per second, and π = 3.1416.

In *Figure 9-21,* a series circuit is shown in which the applied voltage is 110 volts at 400 cps, and the capacitance of a condenser is 80 mf. Find the capacitive reactance and the current flow.

To find the capacitive reactance, the following equation:

$$X_C = \frac{1}{2\pi fC}$$

First, the capacitance, 80 µf, is changed to farads by dividing 80 by 1,000,000, since 1 million microfarads is equal to 1 farad. This quotient equals 0.000080 farad. This is substituted in the equation:

$$X_C = \frac{1}{2\pi fC}$$

$$X_C = \frac{1}{2\pi(400)(0.000080)}$$

$$X_C = 4.97\Omega$$

Impedance

The total opposition to current flow in an AC circuit is known as impedance and is represented by the letter Z. The combined effects of resistance, inductive reactance, and capacitive reactance make up impedance (the total opposition to current flow in an AC circuit). In order to accurately calculate voltage and current in AC circuits, the effect of inductance and capacitance along with resistance must be considered. Impedance is measured in ohms.

The rules and equations for DC circuits apply to AC circuits only when that circuit contains resistance alone and no inductance or capacitance. In both series and parallel circuits, if an AC circuit consists of resistance only, the value of the impedance is the same as the resistance, and Ohm's law for an AC circuit, I = E/Z, is exactly the same as for a DC circuit. *Figure 9-22* illustrates a series circuit containing a heater element with 11 ohms resistance connected across a 110-volt source. To find how much current flows if 110 volts AC is applied, the following example is solved:

$$I = \frac{E}{Z}$$

$$I = \frac{110V}{11\Omega}$$

I = 10 Amps

Figure 9-22. *Applying DC and AC to a circuit.*

If there are two resistance values in parallel connected to an AC voltage, as seen in *Figure 9-23*, impedance is equal to the total resistance of the circuit. Once again, the calculations would be handled the same as if it were a DC circuit and the following would apply:

$$R_T = \frac{1}{\frac{1}{R_1} + \frac{1}{R_2}}$$

$$R_T = \frac{1}{\frac{1}{20} + \frac{1}{20}}$$

$$R_T = 10\Omega$$

Since this is a pure resistive circuit $R_T = Z$ (resistance = Impedance)

$$Z_T = R_T$$

$$Z_T = 10\Omega$$

To determine the current flow in the circuit use the equation:

$$I = \frac{E}{Z}$$

$$I = \frac{50V}{10\Omega}$$

I = 5 Amps

Figure 9-23. *Two resistance values in parallel connected to an AC voltage. Impedance is equal to the total resistance of the circuit.*

Impedance is the total opposition to current flow in an AC circuit. If a circuit has inductance or capacitance, one must take into consideration resistance (R), inductive reactance (X_L), and/or capacitive reactance (X_C) to determine impedance (Z). In this case, Z does not equal R_T. Resistance and reactance (inductive or capacitive) cannot be added directly, but they can be considered as two forces acting at right angles to each other. Thus, the relation between resistance, reactance, and impedance may be illustrated by a right triangle. *[Figure 9-24]* Since these quantities may be related to the sides of a right triangle, the formula for finding the impedance can be found using the Pythagorean Theorem. It states that the square of the hypotenuse is equal to the sum of the squares of the other two sides. Thus, the value of any side of a right triangle can be found if the other two sides are known.

Figure 9-25. *A circuit containing resistance and inductance.*

coil with an inductance of 0.021 henry. What is the value of the impedance and the current through the circuit?

Solution:
First, the inductive reactance of the coil is computed:

$$X_L = 2\pi \times f \times L$$

$$X_L = 6.28 \times 60 \times 0.021$$

$$X_L = 8 \text{ ohms inductive reactance}$$

Next, the total impedance is computed:

$$Z = \sqrt{R^2 + X_L^2}$$

$$Z = \sqrt{6^2 + 8^2}$$

$$Z = \sqrt{36 + 64}$$

$$Z = \sqrt{100}$$

$$Z = 10\Omega$$

Remember when making calculations for Z always use inductive reactance not inductance, and use capacitive reactance, not capacitance.

Once impedance is found, the total current can be calculated.

$$I = \frac{E}{Z}$$

$$I = \frac{110V}{10\Omega}$$

$$I = 11 \text{ Amps}$$

Since this circuit is resistive and inductive, there is a phase shift where voltage leads current.

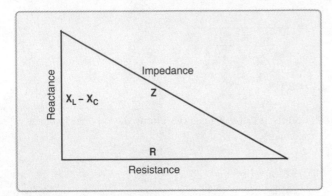

Figure 9-24. *Impedance triangle.*

In practical terms, if a series AC circuit contains resistance and inductance, as shown in *Figure 9-25*, the relation between the sides can be stated as:

$$Z^2 = R^2 + (X_L - X_C)^2$$

The square root of both sides of the equation gives:

$$Z = \sqrt{R^2 + (X_L - X_C)^2}$$

This formula can be used to determine the impedance when the values of inductive reactance and resistance are known. It can be modified to solve for impedance in circuits containing capacitive reactance and resistance by substituting X_C in the formula in place of X_L. In circuits containing resistance with both inductive and capacitive reactance, the reactances can be combined; but because their effects in the circuit are exactly opposite, they are combined by subtraction (the smaller number is always subtracted from the larger):

$$Z = X_L - X_C$$

or

$$X = X_C - X_L$$

Figure 9-25 shows example 1. Here, a series circuit containing a resistor and an inductor are connected to a source of 110 volts at 60 cycles per second. The resistive element is a simple measuring 6 ohms, and the inductive element is a

Example 2 is a series circuit illustrated in which a capacitor of 200 µf is connected in series with a 10 ohm resistor. *[Figure 9-26]* What is the value of the impedance, the current flow, and the voltage drop across the resistor?

Figure 9-26. *A circuit containing resistance and capacitance.*

Solution:

First, the capacitance is changed from microfarads to farads. Since 1 million microfarads equal 1 farad, then 200 µf = 0.000200 farads

Next solve for capacitive reactance:

$$X_C = \frac{1}{2\pi fC}$$

$$X_C = \frac{1}{2\pi(60)(.00020)}$$

$$X_C = \frac{1}{0.07536}$$

$$X_C = 13\Omega$$

To find the impedance,

$$Z = \sqrt{R^2 + X_C^2}$$

$$Z = \sqrt{10^2 + 13^2}$$

$$Z = 16.4\Omega$$

Since this circuit is resistive and capacitive, there is a phase shift where current leads voltage:

To find the current:

$$I_T = \frac{E}{Z}$$

$$I_T = \frac{110V}{16.4\Omega}$$

$$I_T = 6.7 \text{ Amps}$$

To find the voltage drop across the resistor (E_R):

$$E_R = I \times R$$

$$E_R = 6.7A \times 10\Omega$$

$$E_R = 67 \text{ Volts}$$

To find the voltage drop over the capacitor (E_C):

$$E_C = I \times X_C$$

$$E_C = 6.7A \times 13\Omega$$

$$E_C = 86.1 \text{ Volts}$$

The sum of these two voltages does not equal the applied voltage, since the current leads the voltage. Use the following formula to find the applied voltage:

$$E = \sqrt{(E_R)^2 + (E_C)2}$$

$$E = \sqrt{67^2 + 86.1^2}$$

$$E = \sqrt{4,489 + 7,413}$$

$$E = \sqrt{11,902}$$

$$E = 110 \text{ Volts}$$

When the circuit contains resistance, inductance, and capacitance, the following equation is used to find the impedance.

$$Z = \sqrt{R^2 + (X_L - X_C)^2}$$

Example 3: What is the impedance of a series circuit consisting of a capacitor with a capacitive reactance of 7 ohms, an inductor with an inductive reactance of 10 ohms, and a resistor with a resistance of 4 ohms? [Figure 9-27]

Figure 9-27. *A circuit containing resistance, inductance, and capacitance.*

Solution:

$$Z = \sqrt{R^2 + (X_L - X_C)^2}$$

$$Z = \sqrt{4^2 + (10 - 7)^2}$$

$$Z = \sqrt{25}$$

$$Z = 5\Omega$$

To find total current:

$$I_T = \frac{E_T}{Z}$$

$$I_T = \frac{110V}{5\Omega}$$

$$I_T = 22 \text{ Amps}$$

Remember that inductive and capacitive reactances can cause a phase shift between voltage and current. In this example, inductive reactance is larger than capacitive reactance, so the voltage leads current.

It should be noted that since inductive reactance, capacitive reactance, and resistance affect each other at right angles, the voltage drops of any series AC circuit should be added using vector addition. *Figure 9-28* shows the voltage drops over the series AC circuit described in example 3 above.

Figure 9-28. *Voltage drops.*

To calculate the individual voltage drops, simply use the equations:

$$E_R = I \times R$$

$$E_{X_L} = I \times X_L$$

$$E_{X_C} = I \times X_C$$

To determine the total applied voltage for the circuit, each individual voltage drop must be added using vector addition.

$$E_T = \sqrt{E_R^2 + (E_L - E_C)^2}$$

$$E_T = \sqrt{88^2 + (220 - 154)^2}$$

$$E_T = \sqrt{88^2 + 66^2}$$

$$E_T = \sqrt{12,100}$$

$$E_T = 110 \text{ Volts}$$

Parallel AC Circuits

When solving parallel AC circuits, one must also use a derivative of the Pythagorean Theorem. The equation for finding impedance in an AC circuit is as follows:

$$Z = \sqrt{\left(\frac{1}{R}\right)^2 + \left(\frac{1}{X_L} - \frac{1}{X_C}\right)^2}$$

To determine the total impedance of the parallel circuit shown in *Figure 9-29*, one would first determine the capacitive and inductive reactances. (Remember to convert microfarads to farads.)

Figure 9-29. *Total impedance of parallel circuit.*

$$X_L = 2\pi FL$$

$$X_L = 2\pi(400)(0.02)$$

$$X_L = 50\Omega$$

$$X_C = \frac{1}{2\pi FC}$$

$$100\mu f = 0.0001F$$

$$X_C = \frac{1}{2\pi(400)(0.0001)}$$

$$X_C = 4\Omega$$

Next, the impedance can be found:

$$Z = \frac{1}{\sqrt{\left(\frac{1}{R}\right)^2 + \left(\frac{1}{X_L} - \frac{1}{X_C}\right)^2}}$$

$$Z = \frac{1}{\sqrt{\left(\frac{1}{50}\right)^2 + \left(\frac{1}{50} - \frac{1}{4}\right)^2}}$$

$$Z = \frac{1}{\sqrt{(.02)^2 + (.02 - .25)^2}}$$

$$Z = \frac{1}{\sqrt{.0004 + .0529}}$$

$$Z = \frac{1}{.23}$$

$$Z = 4.33\Omega$$

To determine the current flow in the circuit:

$$I_T = \frac{E_T}{Z}$$

$$I_T = \frac{100V}{4.33\Omega}$$

$$I_T = 23.09 \text{ Amps}$$

To determine the current flow through each parallel path of the circuit, calculate I_R, I_L, and I_C.

$$I_R = \frac{E}{R}$$

$$I_R = \frac{100V}{50\Omega}$$

$$I_R = 2 \text{ Amps}$$

$$I_L = \frac{E}{X_L}$$

$$I_L = \frac{100V}{50\Omega}$$

$$I_L = 2 \text{ Amps}$$

$$I_C = \frac{E}{X_C}$$

$$I_C = \frac{100V}{4\Omega}$$

$$I_C = 25 \text{ Amps}$$

It should be noted that the total current flow of parallel circuits is found by using vector addition of the individual current flows as follows:

$$I_T = \sqrt{I_R^2 + (I_L - I_C)^2}$$

$$I_T = \sqrt{2^2 + (2 - 25)^2}$$

$$I_T = \sqrt{2^2 + 23^2}$$

$$I_T = \sqrt{4 + 529}$$

$$I_T = \sqrt{533}$$

$$I_T = 23 \text{ Amps}$$

Power in AC Circuits

Since voltage and current determine power, there are similarities in the power consumed by both AC and DC circuits. In AC however, current is a function of both the resistance and the reactance of the circuit. The power consumed by any AC circuit is a function of the applied voltage and both circuit's resistance and reactance. AC circuits have two distinct types of power, one created by the resistance of the circuit and one created by the reactance of the circuit.

True Power

True power of any AC circuit is commonly referred to as the working power of the circuit. True power is the power consumed by the resistance portion of the circuit and is measured in watts (W). True power is symbolized by the letter P and is indicated by any wattmeter in the circuit. True power is calculated by the formula:

$P = I^2 \times Z$

Apparent Power

Apparent power in an AC circuit is sometimes referred to as the reactive power of a circuit. Apparent power is the power consumed by the entire circuit, including both the resistance and the reactance. Apparent power is symbolized by the letter S and is measured in volt-amps (VA). Apparent power is a product of the effective voltage multiplied by the effective current. Apparent power is calculated by the formula:

$S = E \times I$

Power Factor

As seen in *Figure 9-30,* the resistive power and the reactive power effect the circuit at right angles to each other. The power factor in an AC circuit is created by this right angle effect.

Power factor can be defined as the mathematical difference between true power and apparent power. Power factor (PF) is a ratio and always a measurement between 0 and 100. The power factor is directly related to the phase shift of a circuit. The greater the phase shift of a circuit the lower the power factor. For example, an AC circuit that is purely inductive (contains reactance only and no resistance) has a phase shift of 90° and a power factor of 0.0. An AC circuit that is purely resistive (has no reactance) has a phase shift of 0 and a power factor of 100. Power factor is calculated by using the following formula:

$$PF = \frac{\text{True Power (Watts)}}{\text{Apparent Power (VA)}} \times 100$$

Example of calculating PF: *Figure 9-31* shows an AC load connected to a 50 volt power supply. The current draw of the circuit is 5 amps and the total resistance of the circuit is 8 ohms. Determine the true power, the apparent power, and the power factor for this circuit.

Figure 9-31. *AC load connected to a 50-volt power supply.*

Solution:

$P = I^2 \times R$

$P = 5^2 \times 8$

$P = 200 \text{ Watts}$

$S = E \times I$

$S = 50 \times 5$

$S = 250 \text{VA}$

$PF = \frac{TP}{S} \times 100$

$PF = \frac{200}{250} \times 100$

$PF = 80$

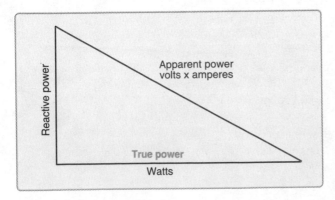

Figure 9-30. *Power relations in AC circuit.*

Power factor can also be represented as a percentage. Using a percentage to show power factor, the circuit in the previous example would have a power factor of 80 percent.

It should be noted that a low power factor is undesirable. Circuits with a lower power factor create excess load on the power supply and produce inefficiency in the system. Aircraft AC alternators must typically operate with a power factor between 90 percent and 100 percent. It is therefore very important to carefully consider power factor when designing the aircraft electrical system.

Aircraft Batteries

Aircraft batteries are used for many functions (e.g., ground power, emergency power, improving DC bus stability, and fault clearing). Most small private aircraft use lead-acid batteries. Most commercial and corporate aircraft use nickel-cadmium (NiCd) batteries. However, other lead acid types of batteries are becoming available, such as the valve-regulated lead-acid (VRLA) batteries. The battery best suited for a particular application depends on the relative importance of several characteristics, such as weight, cost, volume, service or shelf life, discharge rate, maintenance, and charging rate. Any change of battery type may be considered a major alteration.

Type of Batteries

Aircraft batteries are usually identified by the material used for the plates. The two most common types of battery used are lead-acid and NiCd batteries.

Lead-Acid Batteries

Dry Charged Cell Lead Acid Batteries

Dry charged cell lead-acid batteries, also known as flooded or wet batteries, are assembled with electrodes (plates) that have been fully charged and dried. The electrolyte is added to the battery when it is placed in service, and battery life begins when the electrolyte is added. An aircraft storage battery consists of 6 or 12 lead-acid cells connected in series. The open circuit voltage of the 6 cell battery is approximately 12 volts, and the open circuit voltage of the 12-cell battery is approximately 24 volts. Open circuit voltage is the voltage of the battery when it is not connected to a load. When flooded (vented) batteries are on charge, the oxygen generated at the positive plates escapes from the cell. Concurrently, at the negative plates, hydrogen is generated from water and escapes from the cell. The overall result is the gassing of the cells and water loss. Therefore, flooded cells require periodic water replenishment. [Figure 9-32]

Figure 9-32. *Lead acid battery installation.*

Valve-Regulated Lead-Acid Batteries (VRLA)

VRLA batteries contain all electrolyte absorbed in glass-mat separators with no free electrolyte and are sometimes referred to as sealed batteries. [Figure 9-33] The electrochemical reactions for VRLA batteries are the same as flooded batteries, except for the gas recombination mechanism that is predominant in VRLA batteries. These types of battery are used in general aviation and turbine powered aircraft and are sometimes authorized replacements for NiCd batteries.

Figure 9-33. *Valve-regulated lead-acid battery (sealed battery).*

When VRLA batteries are on charge, oxygen combines chemically with the lead at the negative plates in the presence of H_2SO_4 to form lead sulfate and water. This oxygen recombination suppresses the generation of hydrogen at the negative plates. Overall, there is no water loss during charging. A very small quantity of water may be lost as a result of self-discharge reactions; however, such loss is so small that no provisions are made for water replenishment. The battery cells have a pressure relief safety valve that may vent if the battery is overcharged.

NiCd Batteries

A NiCd battery consists of a metallic box, usually stainless steel, plastic-coated steel, painted steel, or titanium containing a number of individual cells. *[Figure 9-34]* These cells are connected in series to obtain 12 volts or 24 volts. The cells are connected by highly conductive nickel copper links. Inside the battery box, the cells are held in place by partitions, liners, spacers, and a cover assembly. The battery has a ventilation system to allow the escape of the gases produced during an overcharge condition and provide cooling during normal operation.

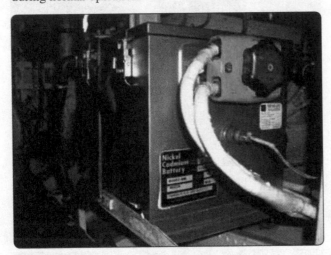

Figure 9-34. *NiCd battery installation.*

NiCd cells installed in an aircraft battery are typical of the vented cell type. The vented cells have a vent or low pressure release valve that releases any generated oxygen and hydrogen gases when overcharged or discharged rapidly. This also means the battery is not normally damaged by excessive rates of overcharge, discharge, or even negative charge. The cells are rechargeable and deliver a voltage of 1.2 volts during discharge.

Aircraft that are outfitted with NiCd batteries typically have a fault protection system that monitors the condition of the battery. The battery charger is the unit that monitors the condition of the battery and the following conditions are monitored.

1. Overheat condition
2. Low temperature condition (below –40 °F)
3. Cell imbalance
4. Open circuit
5. Shorted circuit

If the battery charger finds a fault, it turns off and sends a fault signal to the Electrical Load Management System (ELMS).

NiCd batteries are capable of performing to its rated capacity when the ambient temperature of the battery is in the range of approximately 60–90 °F. An increase or decrease in temperature from this range results in reduced capacity. NiCd batteries have a ventilation system to control the temperature of the battery. A combination of high battery temperature (in excess of 160 °F) and overcharging can lead to a condition called thermal runaway. *[Figure 9-35]* The temperature of the battery has to be constantly monitored to ensure safe operation. Thermal runaway can result in a NiCd chemical fire and/or explosion of the NiCd battery under recharge by a constant-voltage source and is due to cyclical, ever-increasing temperature and charging current. One or more shorted cells or an existing high temperature and low charge can produce the following cyclical sequence of events:

1. Excessive current,
2. Increased temperature,
3. Decreased cell(s) resistance,
4. Further increased current, and
5. Further increased temperature.

Figure 9-35. *Thermal runaway damage.*

This does not become a self-sustaining thermal-chemical action if the constant-voltage charging source is removed before the battery temperature is in excess of 160 °F.

Capacity

Capacity is measured quantitatively in ampere-hours delivered at a specified discharge rate to a specified cut-off voltage at room temperature. The cut-off voltage is 1.0 volt per cell. Battery available capacity depends upon several factors including such items as:

1. Cell design (cell geometry, plate thickness, hardware, and terminal design govern performance under specific usage conditions of temperature, discharge rate, etc.).

2. Discharge rate (high current rates yield less capacity than low rates).

3. Temperature (capacity and voltage levels decrease as battery temperature moves away from the 60 °F (16 °C) to 90 °F (32 °C) range toward the high and low extremes).

4. Charge rate (higher charge rates generally yield greater capacity).

Aircraft Battery Ratings by Specification

The one-hour rate is the rate of discharge a battery can endure for 1 hour with the battery voltage at or above 1.67 volts per cell, or 20 volts for a 24-volt lead-acid battery, or 10 volts for a 12-volt lead-acid battery. The one-hour capacity, measured in ampere hours (Ah), is the product of the discharge rate and time (in hours) to the specified end voltage.

The emergency rate is the total essential load, measured in amperes, required to support the essential bus for 30 minutes. This is the rate of discharge a battery can endure for 30 minutes with the battery voltage at or above 1.67 volts per cell, or 20 volts for a 24 volt lead-acid battery, or 10 volts for a 12 volt lead-acid battery.

Storing and Servicing Facilities

Separate facilities for storing and/or servicing flooded electrolyte lead-acid and NiCd batteries must be maintained. Introduction of acid electrolyte into alkaline electrolyte causes permanent damage to vented (flooded electrolyte) NiCd batteries and vice versa. However, batteries that are sealed can be charged and capacity checked in the same area. Because the electrolyte in a valve-regulated lead-acid battery is absorbed in the separators and porous plates, it cannot contaminate a NiCd battery even when they are serviced in the same area.

WARNING: It is extremely dangerous to store or service lead-acid and NiCd batteries in the same area. Introduction of acid electrolytes into alkaline electrolyte destroys the NiCd, and vice versa.

Battery Freezing

Discharged lead-acid batteries exposed to cold temperatures are subject to plate damage due to freezing of the electrolyte. To prevent freezing damage, maintain each cell's specific gravity at 1.275 or, for sealed lead-acid batteries, check open circuit voltage. *[Figure 9-36]* NiCd battery electrolyte is not as susceptible to freezing because no appreciable chemical change takes place between the charged and discharged states. However, the electrolyte freezes at approximately −75 °F.

Specific Gravity	Freezing Point		State of Charge (SOC) for Sealed Lead-Acid Batteries at 70°		
	°C	°F	SOC	12 volt	24 volt
1.300	−70	−95	100%	12.9	25.8
1.275	−62	−80	75%	12.7	25.4
1.250	−52	−62	50%	12.4	24.8
1.225	−37	−35	25%	12.0	24.0
1.200	−26	−16			
1.175	−20	−04			
1.150	−15	+05			
1.125	−10	+13			
1.100	−08	+19			

Figure 9-36. *Lead-acid battery electrolyte freezing points.*

NOTE: Only a load check determines overall battery condition.

Temperature Correction

U.S.-manufactured lead-acid batteries are considered fully charged when the specific gravity reading is between 1.275 and 1.300. A ⅓ discharged battery reads about 1.240 and a ⅔ discharged battery shows a specific gravity reading of about 1.200 when tested by a hydrometer at an electrolyte temperature of 80 °F. However, to determine precise specific gravity readings, a temperature correction should be applied to the hydrometer indication. *[Figure 9-37]* As an example, for a hydrometer reading of 1.260 and electrolyte temperature of 40 °F, the corrected specific gravity reading of the electrolyte is 1.244.

Electrolyte Temperature		Points to Subtract From or Add to Specific Gravity Readings
°C	°F	12 volt
+60	+140	+0.024
+55	+130	+0.020
+49	+120	+0.016
+43	+110	+0.012
+38	+100	+0.008
+33	+90	+0.004
+27	+80	0
+23	+70	−0.004
+15	+60	−0.008
+10	+50	−0.012
+05	+40	−0.016
−02	+30	−0.020
−07	+20	−0.024
−13	+10	−0.028
−18	0	−0.032
−23	−10	−0.036
−28	−20	−0.040
−35	−30	−0.044

Figure 9-37. *Sulfuric acid temperature correction.*

Battery Charging

Operation of aircraft batteries beyond their ambient temperature or charging voltage limits can result in excessive cell temperatures leading to electrolyte boiling, rapid deterioration of the cells, and battery failure. The relationship between maximum charging voltage and the number of cells in the battery is also significant. This determines (for a given ambient temperature and state of charge) the rate at which energy is absorbed as heat within the battery. For lead-acid batteries, the voltage per cell must not exceed 2.35 volts. In the case of NiCd batteries, the charging voltage limit varies with design and construction. Values of 1.4 and 1.5 volts per cell are generally used. In all cases, follow the recommendations of the battery manufacturer.

Constant Voltage Charging (CP)

The battery charging system in an airplane is of the constant voltage type. An engine-driven generator, capable of supplying the required voltage, is connected through the aircraft electrical system directly to the battery. A battery switch is incorporated in the system so that the battery may be disconnected when the airplane is not in operation.

The voltage of the generator is accurately controlled by means of a voltage regulator connected in the field circuit of the generator. For a 12-volt system, the voltage of the generator is adjusted to approximately 14.25. On 24-volt systems, the adjustment should be between 28 and 28.5 volts. When these conditions exist, the initial charging current through the battery is high. As the state of charge increases, the battery voltage also increases, causing the current to taper down. When the battery is fully charged, its voltage is almost equal to the generator voltage, and very little current flows into the battery. When the charging current is low, the battery may remain connected to the generator without damage.

When using a constant-voltage system in a battery shop, a voltage regulator that automatically maintains a constant voltage is incorporated in the system. A higher capacity battery (e.g., 42 Ah) has a lower resistance than a lower capacity battery (e.g., 33 Ah). Hence, a high-capacity battery draws a higher charging current than a low-capacity battery when both are in the same state of charge and when the charging voltages are equal. The constant voltage method is the preferred charging method for lead-acid batteries.

Constant Current Charging

Constant current charging is the most convenient for charging batteries outside the airplane because several batteries of varying voltages may be charged at once on the same system. A constant current charging system usually consists of a rectifier to change the normal AC supply to DC. A transformer is used to reduce the available 110-volt or 220-volt AC supply to the desired level before it is passed through the rectifier. If a constant current charging system is used, multiple batteries may be connected in series, provided that the charging current is kept at such a level that the battery does not overheat or gas excessively.

The constant current charging method is the preferred method for charging NiCd batteries. Typically, a NiCd battery is constant current charged at a rate of 1CA until all the cells have reached at least 1.55V. Another charge cycle follows at 0.1CA, again until all cells have reached 1.55V. The charge is finished with an overcharge or top-up charge, typically for not less than 4 hours at a rate of 0.1CA. The purpose of the overcharge is to expel as much, if not all the gases collected on the electrodes, hydrogen on the anode, and oxygen on the cathode; some of these gases recombine to form water that, in turn, raises the electrolyte level to its highest level after which it is safe to adjust the electrolyte levels. During the overcharge or top-up charge, the cell voltages go beyond 1.6V and then slowly start to drop. No cell should rise above 1.71V (dry cell) or drop below 1.55V (gas barrier broken).

Charging is done with vent caps loosened or open. A stuck vent might increase the pressure in the cell. It also allows for refilling of water to correct levels before the end of the top-up charge while the charge current is still on. However, cells should be closed again as soon as the vents have been cleaned and checked since carbon dioxide dissolved from outside air carbonates the cells and ages the battery.

Battery Maintenance

Battery inspection and maintenance procedures vary with the type of chemical technology and the type of physical construction. Always follow the battery manufacturer's approved procedures. Battery performance at any time in a given application depends upon the battery's age, state of health, state of charge, and mechanical integrity, which you can determine according to the following:

- To determine the life and age of the battery, record the install date of the battery on the battery. During normal battery maintenance, battery age must be documented either in the aircraft maintenance log or in the shop maintenance log.

- Lead-acid battery state of health may be determined by duration of service interval (in the case of vented batteries), by environmental factors (such as excessive heat or cold), and by observed electrolyte leakage (as evidenced by corrosion of wiring and connectors or accumulation of powdered salts). If the battery needs to be refilled often, with no evidence of external leakage, this may indicate a poor state of the battery, the battery charging system, or an overcharge condition.

- Use a hydrometer to determine the specific gravity of the lead-acid battery electrolyte, which is the weight of the electrolyte compared to the weight of pure water. Take care to ensure the electrolyte is returned to the cell from which it was extracted. When a specific gravity difference of 0.050 or more exists between cells of a battery, the battery is approaching the end of its useful life and replacement should be considered. Electrolyte level may be adjusted by the addition of distilled water. Do not add electrolyte.

- Battery state of charge is determined by the cumulative effect of charging and discharging the battery. In a normal electrical charging system, the aircraft generator or alternator restores a battery to full charge during a flight of 1 hour to 90 minutes.

- Proper mechanical integrity involves the absence of any physical damage, as well as assurance that hardware is correctly installed and the battery is properly connected. Battery and battery compartment venting system tubes, nipples, and attachments, when required, provide a means of avoiding the potential buildup of explosive gases, and should be checked periodically to ensure that they are securely connected and oriented in accordance with the maintenance manual's installation procedures. Always follow procedures approved for the specific aircraft and battery system to ensure that the battery system is capable of delivering specified performance.

Battery and Charger Characteristics

The following information is provided to acquaint the user with characteristics of the more common aircraft battery and battery charger types. *[Figure 9-38]* Products may vary from these descriptions due to different applications of available technology. Consult the manufacturer for specific performance data.

Figure 9-38. *Battery charger.*

NOTE: Never connect a lead-acid battery to a charger, unless properly serviced.

Lead-Acid Batteries

Lead-acid vented batteries have a two volt nominal cell voltage. Batteries are constructed so that individual cells cannot be removed. Occasional addition of water is required to replace water loss due to overcharging in normal service. Batteries that become fully discharged may not accept recharge. Lead-acid sealed batteries are similar in most respects to lead-acid vented batteries, but do not require the addition of water.

The lead-acid battery is economical and has extensive application but is heavier than an equivalent performance battery of another type. The battery is capable of a high rate of discharge and low-temperature performance. However, maintaining a high rate of discharge for a period of time usually warps the cell plates, shorting out the battery. Its electrolyte has a moderate specific gravity, and state of charge can be checked with a hydrometer.

Lead-acid batteries are usually charged by regulated DC voltage sources. This allows maximum accumulation of charge in the early part of recharging.

NiCd Batteries

NiCd vented batteries have a 1.2-volt nominal cell voltage. Occasional addition of distilled water is required to replace water loss due to overcharging in normal service. Cause of failure is usually shorting or weakening of a cell. After replacing the bad cell with a good cell, the battery's life can be extended for 5 or more years. Full discharge is not harmful to this type of battery.

NiCd sealed batteries are similar in most respects to NiCd vented batteries, but do not normally require the addition of water. Fully discharging the battery (to zero volts) may cause irreversible damage to one or more cells, leading to eventual battery failure due to low capacity.

The state of charge of a NiCd battery cannot be determined by measuring the specific gravity of the potassium hydroxide electrolyte. The electrolyte specific gravity does not change with the state of charge. The only accurate way to determine the state of charge of a NiCd battery is by a measured discharge with a NiCd battery charger and following the manufacturer's instructions. After the battery has been fully charged and allowed to stand for at least 2 hours, the fluid level may be adjusted, if necessary, using distilled or demineralized water. Because the fluid level varies with the state of charge, water should never be added while the battery is installed in the aircraft. Overfilling the battery results in electrolyte spewage during charging. This causes corrosive effects on the cell links, self-discharge of the battery, dilution of the electrolyte density, possible blockage of the cell vents, and eventual cell rupture.

Constant current battery chargers are usually provided for NiCd batteries because the NiCd cell voltage has a negative temperature coefficient. With a constant voltage charging source, a NiCd battery having a shorted cell might overheat due to excessive overcharge and undergo a thermal runaway, destroying the battery and creating a possible safety hazard to the aircraft. Pulsed-current battery chargers are sometimes provided for NiCd batteries.

CAUTION: It is important to use the proper charging procedures for batteries under test and maintenance. These charging regimes for reconditioning and charging cycles are defined by the aircraft manufacturer and should be closely followed.

Aircraft Battery Inspection

Aircraft battery inspection consists of the following items:

1. Inspect battery sump jar and lines for condition and security.

2. Inspect battery terminals and quickly disconnect plugs and pins for evidence of corrosion, pitting, arcing, and burns. Clean as required.

3. Inspect battery drain and vent lines for restriction, deterioration, and security.

4. Routine preflight and postflight inspection procedures should include observation for evidence of physical damage, loose connections, and electrolyte loss.

Ventilation Systems

Modern airplanes are equipped with battery ventilating systems. The ventilating system removes gasses and acid fumes from the battery in order to reduce fire hazards and to eliminate damage to airframe parts. Air is carried from a scoop outside the airplane through a vent tube to the interior of the battery case. After passing over the top of the battery, air, battery gasses, and acid fumes are carried through another tube to the battery sump. This sump is a glass or plastic jar of at least one pint capacity. In the jar is a felt pad about 1 inch thick saturated with a 5-percent solution of bicarbonate of soda and water. The tube carrying fumes to the sump extends into the jar to within about ¼ inch of the felt pad. An overboard discharge tube leads from the top of the sump

jar to a point outside the airplane. The outlet for this tube is designed so there is negative pressure on the tube whenever the airplane is in flight. This helps to ensure a continuous flow of air across the top of the battery through the sump and outside the airplane. The acid fumes going into the sump are neutralized by the action of the soda solution, thus preventing corrosion of the aircraft's metal skin or damage to a fabric surface.

Installation Practices

- External surface—Clean the external surface of the battery prior to installation in the aircraft.

- Replacing lead-acid batteries—When replacing lead-acid batteries with NiCd batteries, a battery temperature or current monitoring system must be installed. Neutralize the battery box or compartment and thoroughly flush with water and dry. A flight manual supplement must also be provided for the NiCd battery installation. Acid residue can be detrimental to the proper functioning of a NiCd battery, as alkaline is to a lead-acid battery.

- Battery venting—Battery fumes and gases may cause an explosive mixture or contaminated compartments and should be dispersed by adequate ventilation. Venting systems often use ram pressure to flush fresh air through the battery case or enclosure to a safe overboard discharge point. The venting system pressure differential should always be positive and remain between recommended minimum and maximum values. Line runs should not permit battery overflow fluids or condensation to be trapped and prevent free airflow.

- Battery sump jars—A battery sump jar installation may be incorporated in the venting system to dispose of battery electrolyte overflow. The sump jar should be of adequate design and the proper neutralizing agent used. The sump jar must be located only on the discharge side of the battery venting system.

- Installing batteries—When installing batteries in an aircraft, exercise care to prevent inadvertent shorting of the battery terminals. Serious damage to the aircraft structure (frame, skin and other subsystems, avionics, wire, fuel, etc.) can be sustained by the resultant high discharge of electrical energy. This condition may normally be avoided by insulating the terminal posts during the installation process. Remove the grounding lead first for battery removal, then the positive lead. Connect the grounding lead of the battery last to minimize the risk of shorting the hot terminal of the battery during installation.

- Battery hold down devices—Ensure that the battery hold down devices are secure, but not so tight as to exert excessive pressure that may cause the battery to buckle causing internal shorting of the battery.

- Quick-disconnect type battery—If a quick-disconnect type of battery connector that prohibits crossing the battery lead is not employed, ensure that the aircraft wiring is connected to the proper battery terminal. Reverse polarity in an electrical system can seriously damage a battery and other electrical components. Ensure that the battery cable connections are tight to prevent arcing or a high resistance connection.

Troubleshooting

See *Figure 9-39* for a troubleshooting chart.

DC Generators and Controls

DC generators transform mechanical energy into electrical energy. As the name implies, DC generators produce direct current and are typically found on light aircraft. In many cases, DC generators have been replaced with DC alternators. Both devices produce electrical energy to power the aircraft's electrical loads and charge the aircraft's battery. Even though they share the same purpose, the DC alternator and DC generator are very different. DC generators require a control circuit in order to ensure the generator maintains the correct voltage and current for the current electrical conditions of the aircraft. Typically, aircraft generators maintain a nominal output voltage of approximately 14 volts or 28 volts.

Generators

The principles of electromagnetic induction were discussed earlier in this chapter. These principles show that voltage is induced in the armature of a generator throughout the entire 360° rotation of the conductor. The armature is the rotating portion of a DC generator. As shown, the voltage being induced is AC. *[Figure 9-40]*

Since the conductor loop is constantly rotating, some means must be provided to connect this loop of wire to the electrical loads. As shown in *Figure 9-41,* slip rings and brushes can be used to transfer the electrical energy from the rotating loop to the stationary aircraft loads. The slip rings are connected to the loop and rotate; the brushes are stationary and allow a current path to the electrical loads. The slip rings are typically a copper material and the brushes are a soft carbon substance.

It is important to remember that the voltage being produced by this basic generator is AC, and AC voltage is supplied to the slip rings. Since the goal is to supply DC loads, some means must be provided to change the AC voltage to a DC voltage. Generators use a modified slip ring arrangement, known as a commutator, to change the AC produced in the generator loop into a DC voltage. The action of the commutator allows the generator to produce a DC output.

By replacing the slip rings of the basic AC generator with two half cylinders (the commutator), a basic DC generator is obtained. In *Figure 9-42*, the red side of the coil is connected to the red segment and the amber side of the coil to the amber segment. The segments are insulated from each other. The two stationary brushes are placed on opposite sides of the commutator and are so mounted that each brush contacts each segment of the commutator as the commutator revolves simultaneously with the loop. The rotating parts of a DC generator (coil and commutator) are called an armature.

As seen in the very simple generator of *Figure 9-42*, as the loop rotates the brushes make contact with different segments of the commutator. In positions A, C, and E, the brushes touch the insulation between the brushes; when the loop is in these positions, no voltage is being produced. In position B, the positive brush touches the red side of the conductor loop. In position D, the positive brush touches the amber side of the armature conductor. This type of connection reversal changes the AC produced in the conductor coil into DC to power the aircraft. An actual DC generator is more complex, having several loops of wire and commutator segments.

Because of this switching of commutator elements, the red brush is always in contact with the coil side moving downward, and the amber brush is always in contact with the coil side moving upward. Though the current actually reverses its direction in the loop in exactly the same way as in the AC generator, commutator action causes the current to flow always in the same direction through the external circuit or meter.

The voltage generated by the basic DC generator in *Figure 9-42* varies from zero to its maximum value twice for each revolution of the loop. This variation of DC voltage is called ripple and may be reduced by using more loops, or coils, as shown in *Figure 9-43*.

As the number of loops is increased, the variation between maximum and minimum values of voltage is reduced *[Figure 9-43]*, and the output voltage of the generator approaches a steady DC value. For each additional loop in the rotor, another two commutator segments is required. A photo of a typical DC generator commutator is shown in *Figure 9-44*.

Trouble	Probable Cause	Corrective Action
Apparent loss of capacity	Very common when recharging on a constant potential bus, as in aircraft	Reconditioning will alleviate this condition.
	Usually indicates imbalance between cells because of difference in temperature, charge efficiency, self-discharge rate, etc., in the cells	
	Electrolyte level too low Battery not fully charged	Charge. Adjust electrolyte level. Check aircraft voltage regulator. If OK, reduce maintenance interval.
Complete failure to operate	Defective connection in equipment circuitry in which battery is installed, such as broken lead, inoperative relay, or improper receptacle installation	Check and correct external circuitry.
	End terminal connector loose or diengaged Poor intercell connections	Clean and retighten hardware using proper torque values.
	Open circuit or dry cell	Replace defective cell.
Excessive spewage of electrolyte	High charge voltage High temperature during charge Electrolyte level too high	Clean battery, charge, and adjust electrolyte level.
	Loose or damaged vent cap	Clean battery, tighten or replace cap, charge and adjust electrolyte level.
	Damaged cell and seal	Short out all cells to 0 volts, clean battery, replace defective cell, charge, and adjust electrolyte level.
Failure of one or more cells to rise to the required 1.55 volts at the end of charge	Negative electrode not fully charged Cellophane separator damage	Discharge battery and recharge. If the cell still fails to rise to 1.55 volts or if the cell's voltage rises to 1.55 volts or above and then drops, remove cell and replace.
Distortion of cell case to cover	Overcharged, overdischarged, or overheated cell with internal short	Discharge battery and disassemble. Replace defective cell. Recondition battery.
	Plugged vent cap	Replace vent cap.
	Overheated battery	Check voltage regulator: treat battery as above, replacing battery case and cover and all other defective parts.
Foreign material within the cell case	Introduced into cell through addition of impure water or water contaminated with acid	Discharge battery and disassemble, remove cell and replace, recondition battery.
Frequent addition of water	Cell out of balance	Recondition battery.
	Damaged "O" ring, vent cap	Replace damaged parts.
	Leaking cell	Discharge battery and disassemble. Replace defective cell, recondition battery.
	Charge voltage too high	Adjust voltage regulator.
Corrosion of top hardware	Acid flumes or spray or other corrosive atmosphere	Replace parts. Battery should be kept clean and kept away from such environments.

Figure 9-39. *Battery troubleshooting guide.*

Trouble	Probable Cause	Corrective Action
Discolored or burned end connectors or intercell connectors	Dirty connections Loose connection Improper mating of parts	Clean parts: replace if necessary. Retighten hardware using proper torque values. Check to see that parts are properly mated.

Distortion of battery case and/or cover	Explosion caused by:
	  Dry cells
	  Charger failure
	  High charge voltage
	  Plugged vent caps
	  Loose intercell connectors
		Discharge battery and disassemble. Replace damaged parts and recondition.

Figure 9-39. *Battery troubleshooting guide (continued).*

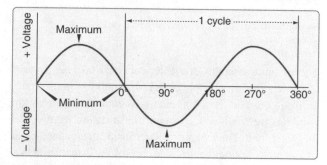

Figure 9-40. *Output of an elementary generator.*

Construction Features of DC Generators

The major parts, or assemblies, of a DC generator are a field frame, a rotating armature, and a brush assembly. The parts of a typical aircraft generator are shown in *Figure 9-45.*

Field Frame

The frame has two functions: to hold the windings needed to produce a magnetic field, and to act as a mechanical support for the other parts of the generator. The actual electromagnet conductor is wrapped around pieces of laminated metal called field poles. The poles are typically bolted to the inside of the frame and laminated to reduce eddy current losses and serve

Figure 9-41. *Generator slip rings and loop rotate; brushes are stationary.*

the same purpose as the iron core of an electromagnet; they concentrate the lines of force produced by the field coils. The field coils are made up of many turns of insulated wire and are usually wound on a form that fits over the iron core of the pole to which it is securely fastened. *[Figure 9-46]*

Figure 9-42. *A two-piece slip ring, or commutator, allows brushes to transfer current that flows in a single direction (DC).*

Figure 9-44. *Typical DC generator commutator.*

Armature

The armature assembly of a generator consists of two primary elements: the wire coils (called windings) wound around an iron core and the commutator assembly. The armature windings are evenly spaced around the armature and mounted on a steel shaft. The armature rotates inside the magnetic field produced by the field coils. The core of the armature acts as an iron conductor in the magnetic field and, for this reason, is laminated to prevent the circulation of eddy currents. A typical armature assembly is shown in *Figure 9-47.*

Figure 9-43. *Increasing the number of coils reduces the ripple in the voltage.*

A DC current is fed to the field coils to produce an electromagnetic field. This current is typically obtained from an external source that provides voltage and current regulation for the generator system. Generator control systems are discussed later in this chapter.

Figure 9-45. *Typical 24-volt aircraft generator.*

Figure 9-46. *Generator field frame.*

Figure 9-47. *A drum-type armature.*

Commutators

Figure 9-48 shows a cross-sectional view of a typical commutator. The commutator is located at the end of an armature and consists of copper segments divided by a thin insulator. The insulator is often made from the mineral mica. The brushes ride on the surface of the commutator forming the electrical contact between the armature coils and the external circuit. A flexible, braided copper conductor, commonly called a pigtail, connects each brush to the external circuit. The brushes are free to slide up and down in their holders in order to follow any irregularities in the surface of the commutator. The constant making and breaking of electrical connections

between the brushes and the commutator segments, along with the friction between the commutator and the brush, causes brushes to wear out and need regular attention or replacement. For these reasons, the material commonly used for brushes is high-grade carbon. The carbon must be soft enough to prevent undue wear of the commutator and yet hard enough to provide reasonable brush life. Since the contact resistance of carbon is fairly high, the brush must be quite large to provide a current path for the armature windings.

The commutator surface is highly polished to reduce friction as much as possible. Oil or grease must never be used on a

Figure 9-48. *Commutator with portion removed to show construction.*

commutator, and extreme care must be used when cleaning it to avoid marring or scratching the surface.

Types of DC Generators

There are three types of DC generator: series wound, parallel (shunt) wound, and series-parallel (or compound wound). The appropriate generator is determined by the connections to the armature and field circuits with respect to the external circuit. The external circuit is the electrical load powered by the generator. In general, the external circuit is used for charging the aircraft battery and supplying power to all electrical equipment being used by the aircraft. As their names imply, windings in series have characteristics different from windings in parallel.

Series Wound DC Generators

The series generator contains a field winding connected in series with the external circuit. *[Figure 9-49]* Series generators have very poor voltage regulation under changing load, since the greater the current is through the field coils to the external circuit, the greater the induced EMF's and the greater the output voltage is. When the aircraft electrical load is increased, the voltage increases; when the load is decreased, the voltage decreases.

Figure 9-49. *Diagram of a series wound generator.*

Since the series wound generator has such poor voltage and current regulation, it is never employed as an airplane generator. Generators in airplanes have field windings, that are connected either in shunt or in compound formats.

Parallel (Shunt) Wound DC Generators

A generator having a field winding connected in parallel with the external circuit is called a shunt generator. *[Figure 9-50]* It should be noted that, in electrical terms, shunt means

Figure 9-50. *Shunt wound generator.*

parallel. Therefore, this type of generator could be called either a shunt generator or a parallel generator.

In a shunt generator, any increase in load causes a decrease in the output voltage, and any decrease in load causes an increase output voltage. This occurs since the field winding is connected in parallel to the load and armature, and all the current flowing in the external circuit passes only through the armature winding (not the field).

As shown in *Figure 9-50A*, the output voltage of a shunt generator can be controlled by means of a rheostat inserted in series with the field windings. As the resistance of the field circuit is increased, the field current is reduced; consequently, the generated voltage is also reduced. As the field resistance is decreased, the field current increases and the generator output increases. In the actual aircraft, the field rheostat would be replaced with an automatic control device, such as a voltage regulator.

Compound Wound DC Generators

A compound wound generator employs two field windings one in series and another in parallel with the load. *[Figure 9-51]* This arrangement takes advantage of both the series and

Figure 9-51. *Compound wound generator.*

parallel characteristics described earlier. The output of a compound wound generator is relatively constant, even with changes in the load.

Generator Ratings

A DC generator is typically rated for its voltage and power output. Each generator is designed to operate at a specified voltage, approximately 14 or 28 volts. It should be noted that aircraft electrical systems are designed to operate at one of these two voltage values. The aircraft's voltage depends on which battery is selected for that aircraft. Batteries are either 12 or 24 volts when fully charged. The generator selected must have a voltage output slightly higher than the battery voltage. Hence, the 14-or 28-volt rating is required for aircraft DC generators.

The power output of any generator is given as the maximum number of amperes the generator can safely supply. Generator rating and performance data are stamped on the nameplate attached to the generator. When replacing a generator, it is important to choose one of the proper ratings.

The rotation of generators is termed either clockwise or counterclockwise, as viewed from the driven end. The direction of rotation may also be stamped on the data plate. It is important that a generator with the correct rotation be used;

otherwise, the polarity of the output voltage is reversed. The speed of an aircraft engine varies from idle rpm to takeoff rpm; however, during the major portion of a flight, it is at a constant cruising speed. The generator drive is usually geared to turn the generator between 1⅛ and 1½ times the engine crankshaft speed. Most aircraft generators have a speed at which they begin to produce their normal voltage. Called the "coming in" speed, it is usually about 1,500 rpm.

DC Generator Maintenance

The following information about the inspection and maintenance of DC generator systems is general in nature because of the large number of differing aircraft generator systems. These procedures are for familiarization only. Always follow the applicable manufacturer's instructions for a given generator system. In general, the inspection of the generator installed in the aircraft should include the following items:

1. Security of generator mounting.

2. Condition of electrical connections.

3. Dirt and oil in the generator. If oil is present, check engine oil seals. Blow out any dirt with compressed air.

4. Condition of generator brushes.

5. Generator operation.

6. Voltage regulator operation.

Sparking of brushes quickly reduces the effective brush area in contact with the commutator bars. The degree of such sparking should be determined. Excessive wear warrants a detailed inspection and possible replacement of various components. *[Figure 9-52]*

Figure 9-52. *Wear areas of commutator and brushes.*

Manufacturers usually recommend the following procedures to seat brushes that do not make good contact with slip rings or commutators. Lift the brush sufficiently to permit

9-33

the insertion of a strip of extra-fine 000 (triple aught) grit, or finer, sandpaper under the brush, rough side towards the carbon brush. [Figure 9-53]

Figure 9-53. *Seating brushes with sandpaper.*

Pull the sandpaper in the direction of armature rotation, being careful to keep the ends of the sandpaper as close to the slip ring or commutator surface as possible in order to avoid rounding the edges of the brush. When pulling the sandpaper back to the starting point, raise the brush so it does not ride on the sandpaper. Sand the brush only in the direction of rotation. Carbon dust resulting from brush sanding should be thoroughly cleaned from all parts of the generators after a sanding operation.

After the generator has run for a short period, brushes should be inspected to make sure that pieces of sand have not become embedded in the brush. Under no circumstances should emery cloth or similar abrasives be used for seating brushes (or smoothing commutators), since they contain conductive materials that cause arcing between brushes and commutator bars. It is important that the brush spring pressure be correct. Excessive pressure causes rapid wear of brushes. Too little pressure, however, allows bouncing of the brushes, resulting in burned and pitted surfaces. The pressure recommended by the manufacturer should be checked by the use of a spring scale graduated in ounces. Brush spring tension on some generators can be adjusted. A spring scale is used to measure the pressure that a brush exerts on the commutator.

Flexible low-resistance pigtails are provided on most heavy current carrying brushes, and their connections should be securely made and checked at frequent intervals. The pigtails should never be permitted to alter or restrict the free motion of the brush. The purpose of the pigtail is to conduct the current from the armature, through the brushes, to the external circuit of the generator.

Generator Controls
Theory of Generator Control

All aircraft are designed to operate within a specific voltage range (for example 13.5–14.5 volts). And since aircraft operate at a variety of engine speeds (remember, the engine drives the generator) and with a variety of electrical demands, all generators must be regulated by some control system. The generator control system is designed to keep the generator output within limits for all flight variables. Generator control systems are often referred to as voltage regulators or generator control units (GCU).

Aircraft generator output can easily be adjusted through control of the generator's magnetic field strength. Remember, the strength of the magnetic field has a direct effect on generator output. More field current means more generator output and vice versa. *Figure 9-54* shows a simple generator control used to adjust field current. When field current is controlled, generator output is controlled. Keep in mind, this system is manually adjusted and would not be suitable for aircraft. Aircraft systems must be automatic and are therefore a bit more complex.

Figure 9-54. *Regulation of generator voltage by field rheostat.*

There are two basic types of generator controls: electro-mechanical and solid-state (transistorized). The electromechanical type controls are found on older aircraft and tend to require regular inspection and maintenance. Solid-state systems are more modern and typically considered to have better reliability and more accurate generator output control.

Functions of Generator Control Systems

Most generator control systems perform a number of functions related to the regulation, sensing, and protection of the DC generation system. Light aircraft typically require a less complex generator control system than larger multiengine aircraft. Some of the functions listed below are not found on light aircraft.

Voltage Regulation

The most basic of the GCU functions is that of voltage regulation. Regulation of any kind requires the regulation unit to take a sample of a generator output and compare that sample to a known reference. If the generator's output voltage falls outside of the set limits, then the regulation unit must provide an adjustment to the generator field current. Adjusting field current controls generator output.

Overvoltage Protection

The overvoltage protection system compares the sampled voltage to a reference voltage. The overvoltage protection circuit is used to open the relay that controls the field excitation current. It is typically found on more complex generator control systems.

Parallel Generator Operations

On multiengine aircraft, a paralleling feature must be employed to ensure all generators operate within limits. In general, paralleling systems compare the voltages between two or more generators and adjust the voltage regulation circuit accordingly.

Overexcitation Protection

When one generator in a paralleled system fails, one of the generators can become overexcited and tends to carry more than its share of the load, if not all of the loads. Basically, this condition causes the generator to produce too much current. If this condition is sensed, the overexcited generator must be brought back within limits, or damage occurs. The overexcitation circuit often works in conjunction with the overvoltage circuit to control the generator.

Differential Voltage

This function of a control system is designed to ensure all generator voltage values are within a close tolerance before being connected to the load bus. If the output is not within the specified tolerance, then the generator contactor is not allowed to connect the generator to the load bus.

Reverse Current Sensing

If the generator cannot maintain the required voltage level, it eventually begins to draw current instead of providing it. This situation occurs, for example, if a generator fails. When a generator fails, it becomes a load to the other operating generators or the battery. The defective generator must be removed from the bus. The reverse current sensing function monitors the system for a reverse current. Reverse current indicates that current is flowing to the generator not from the generator. If this occurs, the system opens the generator relay and disconnects the generator from the bus.

Generator Controls for High Output Generators

Most modern high output generators are found on turbine powered corporate-type aircraft. These small business jets and turboprop aircraft employ a generator and starter combined into one unit. This unit is referred to as a starter-generator. A starter-generator has the advantage of combining two units into one housing, saving space and weight. Since the starter-generator performs two tasks, engine starting and generation of electrical power, the control system for this unit is relatively complex.

A simple explanation of a starter-generator shows that the unit contains two sets of field windings. One field is used to start the engine and one used for the generation of electrical power. *[Figure 9-55]*

Figure 9-55. *Starter-generator.*

During the start function, the GCU must energize the series field and the armature causes the unit to act like a motor. During the generating mode, the GCU must disconnect the series field, energize the parallel field, and control the current produced by the armature. At this time, the starter-generator acts like a typical generator. Of course, the GCU must perform all the functions described earlier to control voltage and protect the system. These functions include voltage regulation, reverse current sensing, differential voltage, overexcitation protection, overvoltage protection, and parallel generator operations. A typical GCU is shown in *Figure 9-56.*

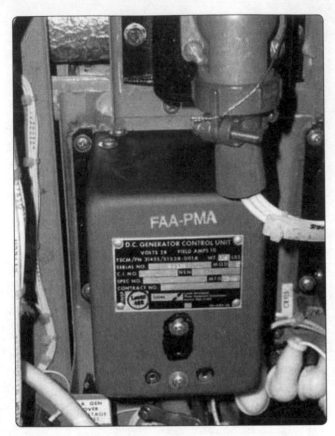

Figure 9-56. *Generator control unit (GCU).*

In general, modern GCUs for high-output generators employ solid-state electronic circuits to sense the operations of the generator or starter-generator. The circuitry then controls a series of relays and/or solenoids to connect and disconnect the unit to various distribution busses. One unit found in almost all voltage regulation circuitry is the zener diode. The zener diode is a voltage sensitive device that is used to monitor system voltage. The zener diode, connected in conjunction to the GCU circuitry, then controls the field current, which in turn controls the generator output.

Generator Controls for Low-Output Generators

A typical generator control circuit for low-output generators modifies current flow to the generator field to control generator output power. As flight variables and electrical loads change, the GCU must monitor the electrical system and make the appropriate adjustments to ensure proper system voltage and current. The typical generator control is referred to as a voltage regulator or a GCU.

Since most low-output generators are found on older aircraft, the control systems for these systems are electromechanical devices. (Solid-state units are found on more modern aircraft that employ DC alternators and not DC generators.) The two most common types of voltage regulator are the carbon pile regulator and the three-unit regulator. Each of these

units controls field current using a type of variable resistor. Controlling field current then controls generator output. A simplified generator control circuit is shown in *Figure 9-57*.

Figure 9-57. *Voltage regulator for low-output generator.*

Carbon Pile Regulators

The carbon pile regulator controls DC generator output by sending the field current through a stack of carbon disks (the carbon pile). The carbon disks are in series with the generator field. If the resistance of the disks increases, the field current decreases and the generator output goes down. If the resistance of the disks decreases, the field current increases and generator output goes up. As seen in *Figure 9-58*, a voltage coil is installed in parallel with the generator output leads. The voltage coil acts like an electromagnet that increases or decrease strength as generator output voltage changes. The magnetism of the voltage coil controls the pressure on the carbon stack. The pressure on the carbon stack controls the resistance of the carbon; the resistance of the carbon controls field current and the field current controls generator output.

Figure 9-58. *Carbon pile regulator.*

Carbon pile regulators require regular maintenance to ensure accurate voltage regulation; therefore, most have been replaced on aircraft with more modern systems.

Three-Unit Regulators

The three-unit regulator used with DC generator systems is made of three distinct units. Each of these units performs a specific function vital to correct electrical system operation. A typical three-unit regulator consists of three relays mounted in a single housing. Each of the three relays monitors generator outputs and opens or closes the relay contact points according to system needs. A typical three-unit regulator is shown in *Figure 9-59*.

Figure 9-59. *The three relays found on this regulator are used to regulate voltage, limit current, and prevent reverse current flow.*

Voltage Regulator

The voltage regulator section of the three-unit regulator is used to control generator output voltage. The voltage regulator monitors generator output and controls the generator field current as needed. If the regulator senses that system voltage is too high, the relay points open and the current in the field circuit must travel through a resistor. This resistor lowers field current and therefore lowers generator output. Remember, generator output goes down whenever generator field current goes down.

As seen in *Figure 9-60*, the voltage coil is connected in parallel with the generator output, and it therefore measures the voltage of the system. If voltage gets beyond a predetermined limit, the voltage coil becomes a strong magnet and opens the contact points. If the contact points are open, field current must travel through a resistor and therefore field current goes down. The dotted arrow shows the current flow through the voltage regulator when the relay points are open.

Since this voltage regulator has only two positions (points open and points closed), the unit must constantly be in adjustment to maintain accurate voltage control. During normal system operation, the points are opening and closing at regular intervals. The points are in effect vibrating. This type of regulator is sometimes referred to as a vibrating-type regulator. As the points vibrate, the field current raises and lowers and the field magnetism averages to a level that

Figure 9-60. *Voltage regulator.*

maintains the correct generator output voltage. If the system requires more generator output, the points remain closed longer and vice versa.

Current Limiter

The current limiter section of the three-unit regulator is designed to limit generator output current. This unit contains a relay with a coil wired in series with respect to the generator output. As seen in *Figure 9-61,* all the generator output current must travel through the current coil of the relay. This creates a relay that is sensitive to the current output of the generator. That is, if generator output current increases, the relay points open and vice versa. The dotted line shows the current flow to the generator field when the current limiter points are open. It should be noted that, unlike the voltage regulator relay, the current limiter is typically closed during normal flight. Only during extreme current loads must the current limiter points open; at that time, field current is lowered and generator output is kept within limits.

Figure 9-61. *Current limiter.*

Reverse-Current Relay

The third unit of a three-unit regulator is used to prevent current from leaving the battery and feeding the generator. This type of current flow would discharge the battery and is opposite of normal operation. It can be thought of as a reverse current situation and is known as reverse current relay. The simple reverse current relay shown in *Figure 9-62* contains both a voltage coil and a current coil.

Figure 9-62. *Reverse-current relay.*

The voltage coil is wired in parallel to the generator output and is energized any time the generator output reaches its operational voltage. As the voltage coil is energized, the contact points close and the current is then allowed to flow to the aircraft electrical loads, as shown by the dotted lines. The diagram shows the reverse current relay in its normal

operating position; the points are closed and current is flowing from the generator to the aircraft electrical loads. As current flows to the loads, the current coil is energized and the points remain closed. If there is no generator output due to a system failure, the contact points open because magnetism in the relay is lost. With the contact points open, the generator is automatically disconnected from the aircraft electrical system, which prevents reverse flow from the load bus to the generator. A typical three-unit regulator for aircraft generators is shown in *Figure 9-63*.

As seen in *Figure 9-63*, all three units of the regulator work together to control generator output. The regulator monitors generator output and controls power to the aircraft loads as needed for flight variables. Note that the vibrating regulator just described was simplified for explanation purposes. A typical vibrating regulator found on an aircraft would probably be more complex.

DC Alternators and Controls

DC alternators (like generators) change mechanical energy into electrical energy by the process of electromagnetic induction. In general, DC alternators are lighter and more efficient than DC generators. DC alternators and their related controls are found on modern, light, piston-engine aircraft. The alternator is mounted in the engine compartment driven by a v-belt, or drive gear mechanism, which receives power from the aircraft engine. *[Figure 9-64]* The control system of a DC alternator is used to automatically regulate alternator output power and ensure the correct system voltage for various flight parameters.

Figure 9-63. *Three-unit regulator for variable speed generators.*

Figure 9-64. *DC alternator installation.*

DC Alternators

DC alternators contain two major components: the armature winding and the field winding. The field winding (which produces a magnetic field) rotates inside the armature and, using the process of electromagnetic induction, the armature produces a voltage. This voltage produced by the armature is fed to the aircraft electrical bus and produces a current to power the electrical loads. *Figure 9-65* shows a basic diagram of a typical alternator.

Figure 9-65. *Diagram of a typical alternator.*

The armature used in DC alternators actually contains three coils of wire. Each coil receives current as the magnetic field rotates inside the armature. The resulting output voltage consists of three distinct AC sine waves, as shown in *Figure 9-66*. The armature winding is known as a three-phase armature, named after the three different voltage waveforms produced.

Figure 9-67 shows the two common methods used to connect the three phase armature windings: the delta winding and the Y winding. For all practical purposes, the two windings produce the same results in aircraft DC alternators.

Figure 9-66. *Sine waves.*

Figure 9-67. *Three-phase armature windings: Y on the left and delta winding on the right.*

Since the three-phase voltage produced by the alternators armature is AC, it is not compatible with typical DC electrical loads and must be rectified (changed to DC). Therefore, the armature output current is sent through a rectifier assembly that changes the three-phase AC to DC. *[Figure 9-67]* Each phase of the three-phase armature overlaps when rectified, and the output becomes a relatively smooth ripple DC. *[Figure 9-68]*

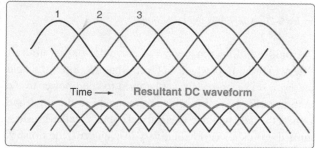

Figure 9-68. *Relatively smooth ripple DC.*

The invention of the diode has made the development of the alternator possible. The rectifier assembly is comprised of six diodes. This rectifier assembly replaces the commutator and brushes found on DC generators and helps to make the alternator more efficient. *Figure 9-69* shows the inside of a typical alternator; the armature assembly is located on the outer edges of the alternator and the diodes are mounted to the case.

Figure 9-69. *Diode assembly.*

The field winding, shown in *Figure 9-70*, is mounted to a rotor shaft so it can spin inside of the armature assembly.

Figure 9-70. *Alternator field winding.*

The field winding must receive current from an aircraft battery in order to produce an electromagnet. Since the field rotates, a set of brushes must be used to send power to the rotating field. Two slip rings are mounted to the rotor and connect the field winding to electrical contacts called brushes. Since the brushes carry relatively low current, the brushes of an alternator are typically smaller than those found inside a DC generator. *[Figure 9-71]* DC alternator brushes last longer and require less maintenance than those found in a DC generator.

The alternator case holds the alternator components inside a compact housing that mounts to the engine. Aircraft alternators either produce a nominal 14-volt output or a 26-volt output. The physical size of the alternator is typically a function of the alternator's amperage output. Common alternators for light aircraft range in output form 60–120 amps.

Figure 9-71. *Alternator brushes.*

Alternator Voltage Regulators

Voltage regulators for DC alternators are similar to those found on DC generators. The general concepts are the same in that adjusting alternator field current controls alternator output. Regulators for most DC alternators are either the vibrating-relay type or solid-state regulators, which are found on most modern aircraft. Vibrating-relay regulators are similar to those discussed in the section on generator regulators. As the points of the relay open, the field current is lowered and alternator output is lowered and vice versa.

Solid-State Regulators

Solid-state regulators for modern light aircraft are often referred to as alternator control units (ACUs). These units contain no moving parts and are generally considered to be more reliable and provide better system regulation than vibrating-type regulators. Solid-state regulators rely on transistor circuitry to control alternator field current and alternator output. The regulator monitors alternator output voltage/current and controls alternator field current accordingly. Solid-state regulators typically provide additional protection circuitry not found in vibrating-type regulators. Protection may include over- or under-voltage protection, overcurrent protection, as well as monitoring the alternator for internal defects, such as a defective diode. In many cases, the ACU also provides a warning indication to the pilot if a system malfunction occurs.

A key component of any solid-state voltage regulator is known as the zener diode. *Figure 9-72* shows the schematic diagram symbol of a zener diode, as well as one installed in an ACU.

The operation of a zener diode is similar to a common diode in that the zener only permits current flow in one direction. This is true until the voltage applied to the zener reaches a certain level. At that predetermined voltage level, the zener then permits current flow with either polarity. This is known as the breakdown or zener voltage.

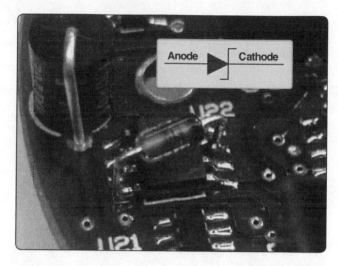

Figure 9-72. *Zener diode.*

As an ACU monitors alternator output, the zener diode is connected to system voltage. When the alternator output reaches the specific zener voltage, the diode controls a transistor in the circuit, which in turn controls the alternator field current. This is a simplified explanation of the complete circuitry of an ACU. *[Figure 9-73]* However, it is easy to see how the zener diode and transistor circuit are used in place of an electromechanical relay in a vibrating-type regulator. The use of solid-state components creates a more accurate regulator that requires very little maintenance. The solid-state ACU is, therefore, the control unit of choice for modern aircraft with DC alternators.

Figure 9-73. *ACU circuitry.*

Power Systems

Since certain electrical systems operate only on AC, many aircraft employ a completely AC electrical system, as well as a DC system. The typical AC system would include an AC alternator (generator), a regulating system for that alternator, AC power distribution busses, and related fuses and wiring. Note that when referring to AC systems, the terms "alternator" and "generator" are often used interchangeably. This chapter uses the term "AC alternator."

AC power systems are becoming more popular on modern aircraft. Light aircraft tend to operate most electrical systems using DC, therefore the DC battery can easily act as a backup power source. Some modern light aircraft also employ a small AC system. In this case, the light aircraft probably uses an AC inverter to produce the AC needed for this system.

Inverters are commonly used when only a small amount of AC is required for certain systems. Inverters may also be used as a backup AC power source on aircraft that employ an AC alternator. *Figure 9-74* shows a typical inverter that might be found on modern aircraft.

Figure 9-74. *Inverter.*

A modern inverter is a solid-state device that converts DC power into AC power. The electronic circuitry within an inverter is quite complex; however, for an aircraft technician's purposes, the inverter is simply a device that uses DC power, then feeds power to an AC distribution bus. Many inverters supply both 26-volt AC, as well as 115-volt AC. The aircraft can be designed to use either voltage or both simultaneously. If both voltages are used, the power must be distributed on separate 26-and 115-volt AC busses.

AC Alternators

AC alternators are found only on aircraft that use a large amount of electrical power. Virtually all transport category aircraft, such as the Boeing 757 or the Airbus A-380, employ one AC alternator driven by each engine. These aircraft also have an auxiliary AC alternator driven by the auxiliary power unit. In most cases, transport category aircraft also have at least one more AC backup power source, such as an AC inverter or a small AC alternator driven by a ram-air turbine (RAT).

AC alternators produce a three-phase AC output. For each revolution of the alternator, the unit produces three separate voltages. The sine waves for these voltages are separated by 120°. [Figure 9-75] This wave pattern is similar to those produced internally by a DC alternator; however, in this case, the AC alternator does not rectify the voltage and the output of the unit is AC.

Figure 9-75. *AC alternator sine waves.*

The modern AC alternator does not utilize brushes or slip rings and is often referred to as a brushless AC alternator. This brushless design is extremely reliable and requires very little maintenance. In a brushless alternator, energy to or from the alternator's rotor is transferred using magnetic energy. In other words, energy from the stator to the rotor is transferred using magnetic flux energy and the process of electromagnetic induction. A typical large aircraft AC alternator is shown in *Figure 9-76*.

Figure 9-76. *Large aircraft AC alternator.*

As seen in *Figure 9-77*, the brushless alternator actually contains three generators: the Exciter generator (armature and permanent magnet field), the Pilot exciter generator (armature and fields windings), and the main AC alternator (armature winding and field windings. The need for brushes is eliminated by using a combination of these three distinct generators.

The exciter is a small AC generator with a stationary field made of a permanent magnet and two electromagnets. The exciter armature is three phase and mounted on the rotor shaft. The exciter armature output is rectified and sent to the pilot exciter field and the main generator field.

The pilot exciter field is mounted on the rotor shaft and is connected in series with the main generator field. The pilot exciter armature is mounted on the stationary part of the assembly. The AC output of the pilot exciter armature is supplied to the generator control circuitry where it is rectified, regulated, and then sent to the exciter field windings. The current sent to the exciter field provides the voltage regulation for the main AC alternator. If greater AC alternator output is needed, there is more current sent to the exciter field and vice versa.

In short, the exciter permanent magnet and armature starts the generation process, and the output of the exciter armature is rectified and sent to the pilot exciter field. The pilot exciter field creates a magnetic field and induces power in the pilot exciter armature through electromagnetic induction. The output of the pilot exciter armature is sent to the main alternator control unit and then sent back to the exciter field. As the rotor continues to turn, the main AC alternator field generates power into the main AC alternator armature, also using electromagnetic induction. The output of the main AC armature is three-phase AC and used to power the various electrical loads.

Some alternators are cooled by circulating oil through the internal components of the alternator. The oil used for cooling is supplied from the constant speed drive assembly and often cooled by an external oil cooler assembly. Located in the flange connecting the generator and drive assemblies, ports make oil flow between the constant speed drive and the generator possible. This oil level is critical and typically checked on a routine basis.

Alternator Drive

The unit shown in *Figure 9-78* contains an alternator assembly combined with an automatic drive mechanism. The automatic drive controls the alternator's rotational speed which allows the alternator to maintain a constant 400-Hz AC output.

All AC alternators must rotate at a specific rpm to keep the frequency of the AC voltage within limits. Aircraft AC alternators should produce a frequency of approximately 400 Hz. If the frequency strays more than 10 percent from this value, the electrical systems do not operate correctly. A unit called a constant-speed drive (CSD) is used to ensure the alternator rotates at the correct speed to ensure a 400-

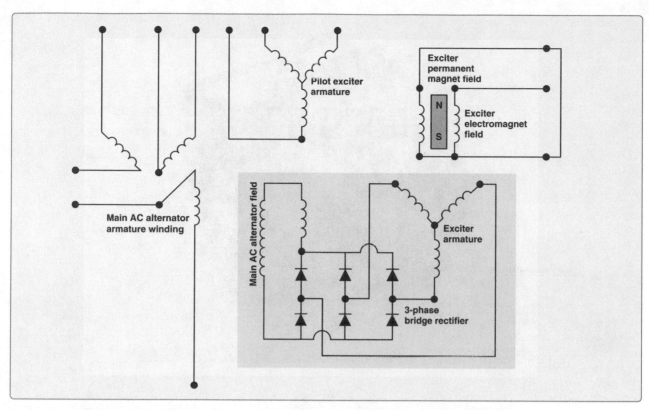

Figure 9-77. *Schematic of an AC alternator.*

Hz frequency. The CSD can be an independent unit or mounted within the alternator housing. When the CSD and the alternator are contained within one unit, the assembly is known as an integrated drive generator (IDG).

The CSD is a hydraulic unit similar to an automatic transmission found in a modern automobile. The engine of the automobile can change rpm while the speed of the car remains constant. This is the same process that occurs for an aircraft AC alternator. If the aircraft engine changes speed, the alternator speed remains constant. A typical hydraulic-type drive is shown in *Figure 9-79*. This unit can be controlled either electrically or mechanically. Modern aircraft employ an electronic system. The constant-speed drive enables the alternator to produce the same frequency at slightly above engine idle rpm as it does at maximum engine rpm.

The hydraulic transmission is mounted between the AC alternator and the aircraft engine. Hydraulic oil or engine oil is used to operate the hydraulic transmission, which creates a constant output speed to drive the alternator. In some cases, this same oil is used to cool the alternator as shown in the CSD cutaway view of *Figure 9-79*. The input drive shaft is powered by the aircraft engine gear case. The output drive shaft, on the opposite end of the transmission, engages the drive shaft of the alternator. The CSD employs a hydraulic pump assembly, a mechanical speed control, and a hydraulic drive. Engine rpm drives the hydraulic pump, the hydraulic

drive turns the alternator. The speed control unit is made up of a wobble plate that adjusts hydraulic pressure to control output speed.

Figure 9-80 shows a typical electrical circuit used to control alternator speed. The circuit controls the hydraulic assembly found in a typical CSD. As shown, the alternator input speed is monitored by a tachometer (tach) generator. The tach generator signal is rectified and sent to the valve assembly. The valve assembly contains three electromagnetic coils that operate the valve. The AC alternator output is sent through a control circuit that also feeds the hydraulic valve assembly. By balancing the force created by the three electromagnets, the valve assembly controls the flow of fluid through the automatic transmission and controls the speed of the AC alternator.

It should be noted that an AC alternator also produces a constant 400 Hz if that alternator is driven directly by an engine that rotates at a constant speed. On many aircraft, the auxiliary power unit operates at a constant rpm. AC alternators driven by these APUs are typically driven directly by the engine, and there is no CSD required. For these units, the APU engine controls monitor the alternator output frequency. If the alternator output frequency varies from 400 Hz, the APU speed control adjusts the engine rpm accordingly to keep the alternator output within limits.

Figure 9-78. *Constant-speed drive (top) and integrated drive generator (bottom).*

Figure 9-79. *A hydraulic constant speed drive for an AC alternator.*

AC Alternators Control Systems

Modern aircraft that employ AC alternators use several computerized control units, typically located in the aircraft's equipment bay for the regulation of AC power throughout the aircraft. *Figure 9-81* shows a photo of a typical equipment bay and computerized control units.

Since AC alternators are found on large transport category aircraft designed to carry hundreds of passengers, their control systems always have redundant computers that provide safety in the event of a system failure. Unlike DC systems, AC systems must ensure that the output frequency of the alternator stays within limits. If the frequency of an alternator varies from 400 Hz, or if two or more alternators connected to the same bus are out of phase, damage occurs to the system. All AC alternator control units contain circuitry that regulates both voltage and frequency. These control units also monitor a variety of factors to detect any system

Figure 9-80. *Speed control circuit.*

Figure 9-81. *Line replaceable units in an equipment rack.*

failures and take protective measures to ensure the integrity of the electrical system. The two most common units used to control AC alternators are the bus power control unit (BPCU) and the GCU. In this case, the term "generator" is used, and not alternator, although the meaning is the same.

The GCU is the main computer that controls alternator functions. The BPCU is the computer that controls the distribution of AC power to the power distribution busses located throughout the aircraft. There is typically one GCU used to monitor and control each AC alternator, and there can be one or more BPCUs on the aircraft. BPCUs are described later in this chapter; however, please note that the BPCU works in conjunction with the GCUs to control AC on modern aircraft.

A typical GCU ensures the AC alternator maintains a constant voltage, typically between 115 to 120 volts. The GCU ensures the maximum power output of the alternator is never exceeded. The GCU provides fault detection and circuit protection in the event of an alternator failure. The GCU monitors AC frequency and ensures the output if the alternator remains 400 Hz. The basic method of voltage regulation is similar to that found in all alternator systems; the output of the alternator is controlled by changing the strength of a magnetic field. As shown in *Figure 9-82*, the GCU controls the exciter field magnetism within the brushless alternator to control alternator output voltage. The frequency is controlled by the CDS hydraulic unit in conjunction with signals monitored by the GCU.

Figure 9-82. *Schematic GCU control of the exciter field magnetism.*

The GCU is also used to turn the AC alternator on or off. When the pilot selects the operation of an AC alternator, the GCU monitors the alternator's output to ensure voltage and frequency are within limits. If the GCU is satisfied with the alternator's output, the GCU sends a signal to an electrical contactor that connects the alternator to the appropriate AC distribution bus. The contactor, often call the generator breaker, is basically an electromagnetic solenoid that controls a set of large contact points. The large contact points are necessary in order to handle the large amounts of current produced by most AC alternators. This same contactor is activated in the event the GCU detects a fault in the alternator output; however, in this case the contactor would disconnect the alternator from the bus.

Aircraft Electrical Systems

Virtually all aircraft contain some form of an electrical system. The most basic aircraft must produce electricity for operation of the engine's ignition system. Modern aircraft have complex electrical systems that control almost every aspect of flight. In general, electrical systems can be divided into different categories according to the function of the system. Common systems include lighting, engine starting, and power generation.

Small Single-Engine Aircraft

Light aircraft typically have a relatively simple electrical system because simple aircraft generally require less redundancy and less complexity than larger transport category aircraft. On most light aircraft, there is only one electrical system powered by the engine-driven alternator or generator. The aircraft battery is used for emergency power and engine starting. Electrical power is typically distributed through one or more common points known as an electrical bus (or bus bar).

Almost all electrical circuits must be protected from faults that can occur in the system. Faults are commonly known as opens or shorts. An open circuit is an electrical fault that occurs when a circuit becomes disconnected. A short circuit is an electrical fault that occurs when one or more circuits create an unwanted connection. The most dangerous short circuit occurs when a positive wire creates an unwanted connection to a negative connection or ground. This is typically called a short to ground.

There are two ways to protect electrical systems from faults: mechanically and electrically. Mechanically, wires and components are protected from abrasion and excess wear through proper installation and by adding protective covers and shields. Electrically, wires can be protected using circuit breakers and fuses. The circuit breakers protect each system in the event of a short circuit. It should be noted that fuses

can be used instead of circuit breakers. Fuses are typically found on older aircraft. A circuit breaker panel from a light aircraft is shown in *Figure 9-83*.

Figure 9-83. *Light aircraft circuit breaker panel.*

Battery Circuit

The aircraft battery and battery circuit is used to supply power for engine starting and to provide a secondary power supply in the event of an alternator (or generator) failure. A schematic of a typical battery circuit is shown in *Figure 9-84*. This diagram shows the relationship of the starter and external power circuits that are discussed later in this chapter. The bold lines found on the diagram represent large wire (see the wire leaving the battery positive connection), which is used in the battery circuit due to the heavy current provided through these wires. Because batteries can supply large current flows, a battery is typically connected to the system through an electrical solenoid. At the start/end of each flight, the battery is connected/disconnected from the electrical distribution bus through the solenoid contacts. A battery master switch on the flight deck is used to control the solenoid.

Although they are very similar, there is often confusion between the terms "solenoid" and "relay." A solenoid is typically used for switching high current circuits and relays used to control lower current circuits. To help illuminate the confusion, the term "contactor" is often used when describing a magnetically operated switch. For general purposes, an aircraft technician may consider the terms relay, solenoid, and contactor synonymous. Each of these three terms may be used on diagrams and schematics to describe electrical switches controlled by an electromagnet.

Here it can be seen that the battery positive wire is connected to the electrical bus when the battery master switch is active. A battery solenoid is shown in *Figure 9-85*. The battery switch is often referred to as the master switch since it turns

Figure 9-84. *Schematic of typical battery circuit.*

Figure 9-85. *Battery solenoid.*

off or on virtually all electrical power by controlling the battery connection. Note how the electrical connections of the battery solenoid are protected from electrical shorts by rubber covers at the end of each wire.

The ammeter shown in the battery circuit is used to monitor the current flow from the battery to the distribution bus. When all systems are operating properly, battery current should flow from the main bus to the battery giving a positive indication on the ammeter. In this case, the battery is being charged. If the aircraft alternator (or generator) experiences a malfunction, the ammeter indicates a negative value. A negative indication means current is leaving the battery to power any electrical load connected to the bus. The battery is being discharged and the aircraft is in danger of losing all electrical power.

Generator Circuit

Generator circuits are used to control electrical power between the aircraft generator and the distribution bus. Typically, these circuits are found on older aircraft that have not upgraded to an alternator. Generator circuits control power to the field winding and electrical power from the generator to the electrical bus. A generator master switch is used to turn on the generator typically by controlling field current. If the generator is spinning and current is sent to the field circuit, the generator produces electrical power. The power output of the generator is controlled through the generator control unit (or voltage regulator). A simplified generator control circuit is shown in *Figure 9-86.*

As can be seen in *Figure 9-86,* the generator switch controls the power to the generator field (F terminal). The generator output current is supplied to the aircraft bus through the armature circuit (A terminal) of the generator.

Alternator Circuit

Alternator circuits, like generator circuits, must control power both to and from the alternator. The alternator is

Figure 9-86. *Simplified generator control circuit.*

controlled by the pilot through the alternator master switch. The alternator master switch in turn operates a circuit within the alternator control unit (or voltage regulator) and sends current to the alternator field. If the alternator is powered by the aircraft engine, the alternator produces electrical power for the aircraft electrical loads. The alternator control circuit contains the three major components of the alternator circuit: alternator, voltage regulator, and alternator master switch. [Figure 9-87]

The voltage regulator controls the generator field current according to aircraft electrical load. If the aircraft engine is running and the alternator master switch is on, the voltage regulator adjusts current to the alternator field as needed. If more current flows to the alternator field, the alternator

output increases and feeds the aircraft loads through the distribution bus.

All alternators must be monitored for correct output. Most light aircraft employ an ammeter to monitor alternator output. *Figure 9-88* shows a typical ammeter circuit used to monitor alternator output. An ammeter placed in the alternator circuit is a single polarity meter that shows current flow in only one direction. This flow is from the alternator to the bus. Since

Figure 9-88. *Typical ammeter circuit used to monitor alternator output.*

Figure 9-87. *Alternator control circuit.*

the alternator contains diodes in the armature circuit, current cannot reverse flow from the bus to the alternator.

When troubleshooting an alternator system, be sure to monitor the aircraft ammeter. If the alternator system is inoperative, the ammeter gives a zero indication. In this case, the battery is being discharged. A voltmeter is also a valuable tool when troubleshooting an alternator system. The voltmeter should be installed in the electrical system while the engine is running and the alternator operating. A system operating normally produces a voltage within the specified limits (approximately 14 volts or 28 volts depending on the electrical system). Consult the aircraft manual and verify the system voltage is correct. If the voltage is below specified values, the charging system should be inspected.

External Power Circuit

Many aircraft employ an external power circuit that provides a means of connecting electrical power from a ground source to the aircraft. External power is often used for starting the engine or maintenance activities on the aircraft. This type of system allows operation of various electrical systems without discharging the battery. The external power systems typically consists of an electrical plug located in a convenient area of the fuselage, an electrical solenoid used to connect external power to the bus, and the related wiring for the system. A common external power receptacle is shown in *Figure 9-89*.

Figure 9-90 shows how the external power receptacle connects to the external power solenoid through a reverse polarity diode. This diode is used to prevent any accidental connection in the event the external power supply has the incorrect polarity (i.e., a reverse of the positive and negative electrical connections). A reverse polarity connection could be catastrophic to the aircraft's electrical system. If a ground power source with a reverse polarity is connected, the diode blocks current and the external power solenoid does not close.

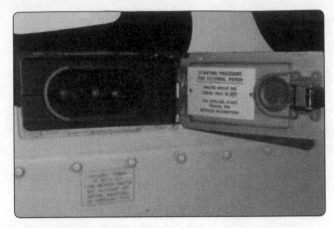

Figure 9-89. *External power receptacle.*

This diagram also shows that external power can be used to charge the aircraft battery or power the aircraft electrical loads. For external power to start the aircraft engine or power electrical loads, the battery master switch must be closed.

Starter Circuit

Virtually all modern aircraft employ an electric motor to start the aircraft engine. Since starting the engine requires several horsepower, the starter motor can often draw 100 or more amperes. For this reason, all starter motors are controlled through a solenoid. *[Figure 9-91]*

The starter circuit must be connected as close as practical to the battery since large wire is needed to power the starter motor and weight savings can be achieved when the battery and the starter are installed close to each other in the aircraft. As shown in the starter circuit diagram, the start switch can be part of a multifunction switch that is also used to control the engine magnetos. *[Figure 9-92]*

The starter can be powered by either the aircraft battery or the external power supply. Often when the aircraft battery

Figure 9-90. *A simple external power circuit diagram.*

Figure 9-91. *Starter circuit.*

Figure 9-92. *Multifunction starter switch.*

is weak or in need of charging, the external power circuit is used to power the starter. During most typical operations, the starter is powered by the aircraft battery. The battery master must be on and the master solenoid closed in order to start the engine with the battery.

Avionics Power Circuit

Many aircraft contain a separate power distribution bus specifically for electronics equipment. This bus is often referred to as an avionics bus. Since modern avionics equipment employs sensitive electronic circuits, it is often advantageous to disconnect all avionics from electrical power to protect their circuits. For example, the avionics bus is often depowered when the starter motor is activated. This helps to prevent any transient voltage spikes produced by the starter from entering the sensitive avionics. *[Figure 9-93]*

Figure 9-93. *Avionics power circuit.*

The circuit employs a normally closed (NC) solenoid that connects the avionics bus to the main power bus. The electromagnet of the solenoid is activated whenever the starter is engaged. Current is sent from the starter switch through Diode D1, causing the solenoid to open and depower the avionics bus. At that time, all electronics connected to the avionics bus will lose power. The avionics contactor is also activated whenever external power is connected to the aircraft. In this case, current travels through diodes D2 and D3 to the avionics bus contactor.

A separate avionics power switch may also be used to disconnect the entire avionics bus. A typical avionics power switch is shown wired in series with the avionics power bus. In some cases, this switch is combined with a circuit breaker and performs two functions (called a circuit breaker switch). It should also be noted that the avionics contactor is often referred to as a split bus relay, since the contactor separates (splits) the avionics bus from the main bus.

Landing Gear Circuit

Another common circuit found on light aircraft operates the retractable landing gear systems on high-performance light aircraft. These airplanes typically employ a hydraulic system to move the gear. After takeoff, the pilot moves the gear position switch to the retract position, starting an electric motor. The motor operates a hydraulic pump, and the hydraulic system moves the landing gear. To ensure correct operation of the system, the landing gear electrical system is relatively complex. The electrical system must detect the position of each gear (right, left, nose) and determine when each reaches full up or down; the motor is then controlled accordingly. There are safety systems to help prevent accidental actuation of the gear.

A series of limit switches are needed to monitor the position of each gear during the operation of the system. (A limit switch is simply a spring-loaded, momentary contact switch that is activated when a gear reaches it limit of travel.) Typically, there are six limit switches located in the landing gear wheel wells. The three up-limit switches are used to detect when the gear reaches the full retract (UP) position. Three down-limit switches are used to detect when the gear reach the full extended (DOWN) position. Each of these switches is mechanically activated by a component of the landing gear assembly when the appropriate gear reaches a given limit.

The landing gear system must also provide an indication to the pilot that the gear is in a safe position for landing. Many aircraft employ a series of three green lights when all three gears are down and locked in the landing position. These three lights are activated by the up- and down-limit switches found in the gear wheel well. A typical instrument panel showing the landing gear position switch and the three gears down indicators is shown in *Figure 9-94*.

The hydraulic motor/pump assembly located in the upper left corner of *Figure 9-95* is powered through either the UP or DOWN solenoids (top left). The solenoids are controlled by the gear selector switch (bottom left) and the six landing gear limit switches (located in the center of *Figure 9-95*). The three gear DOWN indicators are individual green lights (center of

Figure 9-94. *Instrument panel showing the landing gear position switch and the three gear down indicators.*

Figure 9-95. *Aircraft landing gear schematic while gear is in the DOWN and locked position.*

Figure 9-95) controlled by the three gear DOWN switches. As each gear reaches its DOWN position, the limit switch moves to the DOWN position, and the light is illuminated.

Figure 9-95 shows the landing gear in the full DOWN position. It is always important to know gear position

when reading landing gear electrical diagrams. Knowing gear position helps the technician to analyze the diagram and understand correct operation of the circuits. Another important concept is that more than one circuit is used to operate the landing gear. On this system, there is a low current control circuit fused at 5 amps (CB2, top right of

Figure 9-95). This circuit is used for indicator lights and the control of the gear motor contactors. There is a separate circuit to power the gear motor fused at 30 amps (CB3, top right of *Figure 9-95*). Since this circuit carries a large current flow, the wires would be as short as practical and carefully protected with rubber boots or nylon insulators.

The following paragraphs describe current flow through the landing gear circuit as the system moves the gear up and down. Be sure to refer to *Figure 9-96* often during the following discussions. *Figure 9-96* shows current flow when the gear is traveling to the extend (DOWN) position. Current flow is highlighted in red for each description.

Figure 9-96. *Landing gear moving down diagram.*

To run the gear DOWN motor, current must flow in the control circuit leaving CB2 through terminal 1 to the NOT DOWN contacts of the DOWN limit switches, through terminal 3, to the DOWN solenoid positive terminal (upper left). The negative side of the DOWN solenoid coil is connected to ground through the gear selector switch. Remember, the gear DOWN switches are wired in parallel and activated when the gear reach the full-DOWN position. All three gears must reach full-DOWN to shut off the gear DOWN motor. Also note that the gear selector switch controls the negative side of the gear solenoids. The selector switch has independent control of the gear UP and DOWN motors through control of the ground circuit to both the UP and DOWN solenoids.

When the landing gear control circuit is sending a positive voltage to the DOWN solenoid, and the gear selector switch is sending negative voltage, the solenoid magnet is energized. When the gear-DOWN solenoid is energized, the high-current gear motor circuit sends current from CB1 through the down solenoid contact points to the gear DOWN motor. When the motor runs, the hydraulic pump produces pressure and the gear begins to move. When all three gears reach the DOWN position, the gear-DOWN switches move to the DOWN position, the three green lights illuminate, and the gear motor turns off completing the gear-DOWN cycle.

Figure 9-97 shows the landing gear electrical diagram with the current flow path shown in red as the gear moves to the retract (UP) position. Starting in the top right corner of the diagram, current must flow through CB2 in the control circuit through terminal 1 to each of the three gear-UP switches. With the gear-UP switches in the not UP position, current flows to terminal 2 and eventually through the squat switch to the UP solenoid electromagnet coil. The UP solenoid coil receives negative voltage through the gear selector switch. With the UP solenoid coil activated, the UP solenoid closes and power travels through the motor circuit. To power the motor, current leaves the bus through CB1 to the terminal at the DOWN solenoid onward through the UP solenoid to the UP motor. (Remember, current cannot travel through the DOWN solenoid at this time since the DOWN solenoid is not activated.) As the UP motor runs, each gear travels to the retract position. As this occurs, the gear UP switches move from the NOT UP position to the UP position. When the last gear reaches up, the current no longer travels to terminal 2 and the gear motor turns off. It should be noted that similar to DOWN, the gear switches are wired in parallel, which means the gear motor continues to run until all three gear reach the required position.

During both the DOWN and UP cycles of the landing gear operation, current travels from the limit switches to terminal 2. From terminal 2, there is a current path through the gear selector switch to the gear unsafe light. If the gear selector disagrees with the current gear position (e.g., gear is DOWN and pilot has selected UP), the unsafe light is illuminated. The gear unsafe light is shown at the bottom of *Figure 9-96*.

The squat switch (shown mid left of *Figure 9-96*) is used to determine if the aircraft is on the GROUND or in FLIGHT. This switch is located on a landing gear strut. When the weight of the aircraft compresses the strut, the switch is activated and moved to the GROUND position. When the switch is in the GROUND position, the gear cannot be retracted and a warning horn sounds if the pilot selects gear UP. The squat switch is sometimes referred to as the weight-on-wheels switch.

A throttle switch is also used in conjunction with landing gear circuits on most aircraft. If the throttle is retarded (closed) beyond a certain point, the aircraft descends and eventually lands. Therefore, many manufacturers activate a throttle switch whenever engine power is reduced. If engine power is reduced too low, a warning horn sounds telling the pilot to lower the landing gear. Of course, this horn need not sound if the gear is already DOWN or the pilot has selected the DOWN position on the gear switch. This same horn also sounds if the aircraft is on the ground, and the gear handle is moved to the UP position. *Figure 9-96* shows the gear warning horn in the bottom left corner.

AC Supply

Many modern light aircraft employ a low-power AC electrical system. Commonly, the AC system is used to power certain instruments and some lighting that operate only using AC. The electroluminescent panel has become a popular lighting system for aircraft instrument panels and requires AC. Electroluminescent lighting is very efficient and lightweight; therefore, excellent for aircraft installations. The electroluminescent material is a paste-like substance that glows when supplied with a voltage. This material is typically molded into a plastic panel and used for lighting.

A device called an inverter is used to supply AC when needed for light aircraft. Simply put, the inverter changes DC into AC. Two types of inverters may be found on aircraft: rotary inverters and static inverters. Rotary inverters are found only on older aircraft due to its poor reliability, excess weight, and inefficiency. The rotary inverters employee a DC motor that spins an AC generator. The unit is typically one unit and contains a voltage regulator circuit to ensure voltage stability. Most aircraft have a modern static inverter instead of a rotary inverter. Static inverters, as the name implies, contain no moving parts and use electronic circuitry to convert DC to AC. *Figure 9-98* shows a static inverter. Whenever AC is used on light aircraft, a distribution circuit separated from the DC system must be employed. *[Figure 9-99]*

Figure 9-97. *Aircraft landing gear schematic while gear is moving to the UP position.*

Some aircraft use an inverter power switch to control AC power. Many aircraft simply power the inverter whenever the DC bus is powered and no inverter power switch is needed. On complex aircraft, more than one inverter may be used to provide a backup AC power source. Many inverters also offer more than one voltage output. Two common voltages found on aircraft inverters are 26VAC and 115VAC.

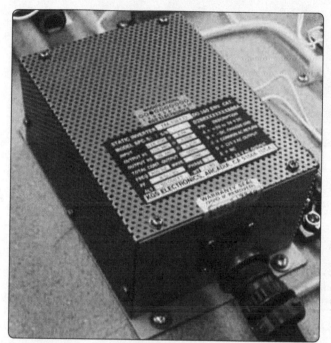

Figure 9-98. *A static inverter.*

Light Multiengine Aircraft

Multiengine aircraft typically fly faster, higher, and farther than single engine aircraft. Multiengine aircraft are designed for added safety and redundancy and, therefore, often contain a more complex power distribution system when compared to light single-engine aircraft. With two engines, these aircraft can drive two alternators (or generators) that supply current to the various loads of the aircraft. The electrical distribution bus system is also divided into two or more systems. These bus systems are typically connected through a series of circuit protectors, diodes, and relays. The bus system is designed to create a power distribution system that is extremely reliable by supplying current to most loads through more than one source.

Paralleling Alternators or Generators

Since two alternators (or generators) are used on twin engine aircraft, it becomes vital to ensure both alternators share the electrical load equally. This process of equalizing alternator outputs is often called paralleling. In general, paralleling is a simple process when dealing with DC power systems found on light aircraft. If both alternators are connected to the same load bus and both alternators produce the same output voltage, the alternators share the load equally. Therefore, the paralleling systems must ensure both power producers maintain system voltage within a few tenths of a volt. For most twin-engine aircraft, the voltage would be between 26.5-volt and 28-volt DC with the alternators operating. A simple vibrating point system used for paralleling alternators is found in *Figure 9-100*.

As can be seen in *Figure 9-100*, both left and right voltage regulators contain a paralleling coil connected to the output of each alternator. This paralleling coil works in conjunction with the voltage coil of the regulator to ensure proper alternator output. The paralleling coils are wired in series between the output terminals of both alternators. Therefore, if the two alternators provide equal voltages, the paralleling coil has no effect. If one alternator has a higher voltage output, the paralleling coils create the appropriate magnetic force to open/close the contact points, controlling field current and control alternator output.

Today's aircraft employ solid-state control circuits to ensure proper paralleling of the alternators. Older aircraft use vibrating point voltage regulators or carbon-pile regulators to monitor and control alternator output. For the most part, all carbon-pile regulators have been replaced except on historic aircraft. Many aircraft still maintain a vibrating point system, although these systems are no longer being

Figure 9-99. *Distribution circuit.*

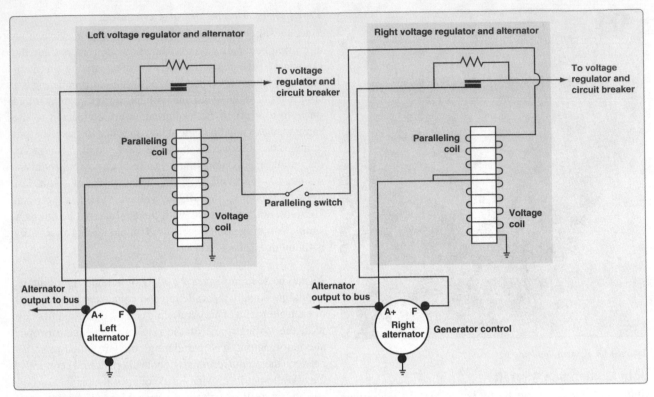

Figure 9-100. *Vibrating point system used for paralleling alternators.*

used on contemporary aircraft. The different types of voltage regulators were described earlier in this chapter.

Power Distribution on Multiengine Aircraft

The power distribution systems found on modern multiengine aircraft contain several distribution points (busses) and a variety of control and protection components to ensure the reliability of electrical power. As aircraft employ more electronics to perform various tasks, the electrical power systems becomes more complex and more reliable. One means to increase reliability is to ensure more than one power source can be used to power any given load. Another important design concept is to supply critical electrical loads from more than one bus. Twin-engine aircraft, such as a typical corporate jet or commuter aircraft, have two DC generators; they also have multiple distribution busses fed from each generator. *Figure 9-101* shows a simplified diagram of the power distribution system for a twin-engine turboprop aircraft.

This aircraft contains two starter generator units used to start the engines and generate DC electrical power. The system is typically defined as a split-bus power distribution system since there is a left and right generator bus that splits (shares) the electrical loads by connecting to each sub-bus through a diode and current limiter. The generators are operated in parallel and equally carry the loads.

The primary power supplied for this aircraft is DC, although small amounts of AC are supplied by two inverters. The aircraft diagram shows the AC power distribution at the top and mid left side of the diagram. One inverter is used for main AC power and the second operated in standby and ready as a backup. Both inverters produce 26-volt AC and 115-volt AC. There is an inverter select relay operated by a pilot controlled switch used to choose which inverter is active.

The hot battery bus (right side of *Figure 9-101*) shows a direct connection to the aircraft battery. This bus is always hot if there is a charged battery in the aircraft. Items powered by this bus may include some basics like the entry door lighting and the aircraft clock, which should always have power available. Other items on this bus would be critical to flight safety, such as fire extinguishers, fuel shut offs, and fuel pumps. During a massive system failure, the hot battery bus is the last bus on the aircraft that should fail.

If the battery switch is closed and the battery relay activated, battery power is connected to the main battery bus and the isolation bus. The main battery bus carries current for engine starts and external power. So the main battery bus must be large enough to carry the heaviest current loads of the aircraft. It is logical to place this bus as close as practical to the battery and starters and to ensure the bus is well protected from shorts to ground.

Figure 9-101. *Diagram of the power distribution system for a twin-engine turboprop aircraft.*

The isolation bus connects to the left and right busses and receives power whenever the main battery bus is energized. The isolation bus connects output of the left and right generators in parallel. The output of the two generators is then sent to the loads through additional busses. The generator busses are connected to the isolation bus through a fuse known as a current limiter. Current limiters are high amperage fuses that isolate busses if a short circuit occurs. There are several current limiters used in this system for protection between busses. As can be seen in *Figure 9-101*, a current limiter symbol looks like two triangles pointed toward each other. The current limiter between the isolation bus and the main generator busses are rated at 325 amps and can only be replaced on the ground. Most current limiters are designed for ground replacement only and only after the malfunction that caused the excess current draw is repaired.

The left and right DC generators are connected to their respective main generator busses. Each generator feeds its respective bus, and since the busses are connected under normal circumstances, the generators operate in parallel. Both generators feed all loads together. If one generator fails or a current limiter opens, the generators can operate independently. This design allows for redundancy in the event of failure and provides battery backup in the event of a dual generator failure.

In the center of *Figure 9-101* are four dual-feed electrical busses. These busses are considered dual-feed since they receive power from both the left and right generator busses. If a fault occurs, either generator bus can power any or all loads on a dual-feed bus. During the design phase of the aircraft, the electrical loads must be evenly distributed between each of the dual-feed busses. It is also important to power redundant systems from different busses. For example, the pilot's windshield heat would be powered by a different bus from the one that powers the copilot's windshield heat. If one bus fails, at least one windshield heat continues to work properly, and the aircraft can be landed safely in icing conditions.

Notice that the dual-feed busses are connected to the main generator busses through both a current limiter and a diode. Remember, a diode allows current flow in only one direction. *[Figure 9-102]*

The current can flow from the generator bus to the dual-feed bus, but the current cannot flow from the dual fed bus to the main generator bus. The diode is placed in the circuit so the main bus must be more positive than the sub bus for current flow. This circuit also contains a current limiter and a circuit breaker. The circuit breaker is located on the flight deck and can be reset by the pilot. The current limiter can only be replaced on the ground by a technician. The circuit breaker is rated at a slightly lower current value than the current limiter; therefore, the circuit breaker should open if a current overload

exists. If the circuit breaker fails to open, the current limiter provides backup protection and disconnects the circuit.

Large Multiengine Aircraft

Transport category aircraft typically carry hundreds of passengers and fly thousands of miles each trip. Therefore, large aircraft require extremely reliable power distribution systems that are computer controlled. These aircraft have multiple power sources (AC generators) and a variety of distribution busses. A typical airliner contains two or more main AC generators driven by the aircraft turbine engines, as well as more than one backup AC generator. DC systems are also employed on large aircraft and the ship's battery is used to supply emergency power in case of a multiple failures.

The AC generator (sometimes called an alternator) produces three-phase 115-volt AC at 400 Hz. AC generators were discussed previously in this chapter. Since most modern transport category aircraft are designed with two engines, there are two main AC generators. The APU also drives an AC generator. This unit is available during flight if one of the main generators fails. The main and auxiliary generators are typically similar in output capacity and supply a maximum of 110 kilovolt amps (KVA). A fourth generator, driven by an emergency ram air turbine, is also available in the event the two main generators and one auxiliary generator fail. The emergency generator is typically smaller and produces less power. With four AC generators available on modern aircraft, it is highly unlikely that a complete power failure occurs. However, if all AC generators are lost, the aircraft battery will continue to supply DC electrical power to operate vital systems.

AC Power Systems

Transport category aircraft use large amounts of electrical power for a variety of systems. Passenger comfort requires power for lighting, audio visual systems, and galley power for food warmers and beverage coolers. A variety of electrical systems are required to fly the aircraft, such as flight control systems, electronic engine controls, communication, and navigation systems. The output capacity of one engine-driven AC generator can typically power all necessary electrical

Figure 9-102. *Dual-feed bus system.*

systems. A second engine-driven generator is operated during flight to share the electrical loads and provide redundancy.

The complexity of multiple generators and a variety of distribution busses requires several control units to maintain a constant supply of safe electrical power. The AC electrical system must maintain a constant output of 115 to 120 volts at a frequency of 400 Hz (±10 percent). The system must ensure power limits are not exceeded. AC generators are connected to the appropriate distribution busses at the appropriate time, and generators are in phase when needed. There is also the need to monitor and control any external power supplied to the aircraft, as well as control of all DC electrical power.

Two electronic line replaceable units are used to control the electrical power on a typical large aircraft. The generator control unit (GCU) is used for control of AC generator functions, such as voltage regulation and frequency control. The bus power control unit (BPCU) is used to control the distribution of electrical power between the various distribution busses on the aircraft. The GCU and BPCU work together to control electrical power, detect faults, take corrective actions when needed, and report any defect to the pilots and the aircraft's central maintenance system. There is typically one GCU for each AC generator and at least one BPCU to control bus connections. These LRUs are located in the aircraft's electronics equipment bay and are designed for easy replacement.

When the pilot calls for generator power by activating the generator control switch on the flight deck, the GCU monitors the system to ensure correct operation. If all systems are operating within limits, the GCU energizes the appropriate generator circuits and provides voltage regulation for the system. The GCU also monitors AC output to ensure a constant 400-Hz frequency. If the generator output is within limits, the GCU then connects the electrical power to the main generator bus through an electrical contactor (solenoid). These contactors are often called generator breakers (GB) since they break (open) or make (close) the main generator circuit.

After generator power is available, the BPCU activates various contactors to distribute the electrical power. The BPCU monitors the complete electrical system and communicates with the GCU to ensure proper operation. The BPCU employs remote current sensors known as a current transformers (CT) to monitor the system. *[Figure 9-103]*

A CT is an inductive unit that surrounds the main power cables of the electrical distribution system. As AC power flows through the main cables, the CT receives an induced voltage. The amount of CT voltage is directly related to the

Figure 9-103. *Current transformer.*

current flowing through the cable. The CT connects to the BPCU, which allows accurate current monitoring of the system. A typical aircraft employs several CTs throughout the electrical system.

The BPCU is a dedicated computer that controls the electrical connections between the various distribution busses found on the aircraft. The BPCU uses contactors (solenoids) called bus tie breakers (BTB) for connection of various circuits. These BTBs open/close the connections between the busses as needed for system operation as called for by the pilots and the BPCU. This sounds like a simple task, yet to ensure proper operation under a variety of conditions, the bus system becomes very complex. There are three common types of distribution bus systems found on transport category aircraft: split bus, parallel bus, and split parallel.

Split-Bus Power Distribution Systems

Modern twin-engine aircraft, such as the Boeing 737, 757, 777, Airbus A-300, A-320, and A-310, employ a split-bus power distribution system. During normal conditions, each engine-driven AC generator powers only one main AC bus. The busses are kept split from each other, and two generators can never power the same bus simultaneously. This is very important since the generator output current is not phase regulated. (If two out-of-phase generators were connected to the same bus, damage to the system would occur.) The split-bus system does allow both engine-driven generators to power any given bus, but not at the same time. Generators must remain isolated from each other to avoid damage. The GCUs and BPCU ensures proper generator operation and power distribution.

On all modern split bus systems, the APU can be started and operated during flight. This allows the APU generator to provide back-up power in the event of a main generator failure. A fourth emergency generator powered by the ram air turbine is also available if the other generators fail.

The four AC generators are shown at the bottom of *Figure 9-104*. These generators are connected to their respective busses through the generator breakers. For example, generator 1 sends current through GB1 to AC bus 1. AC bus 1 feeds a variety of primary electrical loads, and also feeds sub-busses that in turn power additional loads.

With both generators operating and all systems normal, AC bus 1 and AC bus 2 are kept isolated. Typically during flight, the APB (bottom center of *Figure 9-104*) would be open and the APU generator off; the emergency generator (bottom right) would also be off and disconnected. If generator one should fail, the following happens:

1. The GB 1 is opened by the GCU to disconnect the failed generator.

2. The BPCU closes BTB 1 and BTB 2. This supplies AC power to AC bus 1 from generator 2.

3. The pilots start the APU and connect the APU generator. At that time, the BPCU and GCUs move the appropriate BTBs to correctly configure the system so the APU powers bus 1 and generator 2 powers bus 2.

Once again, two AC generators operate independently to power AC bus 1 and 2.

If all generators fail, AC is also available through the static inverter (center of *Figure 9-104*). The inverter is powered from the hot battery bus and used for essential AC loads if all AC generators fail. Of course, the GCUs and BPCU take the appropriate actions to disconnect defective units and continue to feed essential AC loads using inverter power.

To produce DC power, AC bus 1 sends current to its transformer rectifier (TR), TR 1 (center left of *Figure 9-104*). The TR unit is used to change AC to DC. The TR contains a transformer to step down the voltage from 115-volt AC to 26-volt AC and a rectifier to change the 26-volt AC to 26-volt DC. The output of the TR is therefore compatible with the aircraft battery at 26-volt DC. Since DC power is not phase sensitive, the DC busses are connected during normal operation. In the event of a bus problem, the BPCU may isolate one or more DC busses to ensure correct distribution of DC power. This aircraft contains two batteries that are used to supply emergency DC power.

Figure 9-104. *Schematic of split-bus power distribution system.*

Parallel Systems

Multiengine aircraft, such as the Boeing 727, MD-11, and the early Boeing 747, employ a parallel power distribution system. During normal flight conditions, all engine-driven generators connect together and power the AC loads. In this configuration, the generators are operated in parallel; hence the name parallel power distribution system. In a parallel system, all generator output current must be phase regulated. Before generators are connected to the same bus, their output frequency must be adjusted to ensure the AC output reaches the positive and negative peaks simultaneously. During the flight, generators must maintain this in-phase condition for proper operation.

One advantage of parallel systems is that in the event of a generator failure, the busses are already connected and the defective generator need only be isolated from the system. A paralleling bus, or synchronizing bus, is used to connect the generators during flight. The synchronizing bus is often referred to as the sync bus. Most of these systems are less automated and require that flight crew monitor systems and manually control bus contactors. BTBs are operated by the flight crew through the electrical control panel and used to connect all necessary busses. GBs are used to connect and disconnect the generators.

Figure 9-105 shows a simplified parallel power distribution system. This aircraft employs three main-engine driven generators and one APU generator. The APU (bottom right) is not operational in flight and cannot provide backup power. The APU generator is for ground operations only. The three main generators (bottom of *Figure 9-105*) are connected to their respective AC bus through GBs one, two, and three. The AC busses are connected to the sync bus through three BTBs. In this manner, all three generators share the entire AC electrical loads. Keep in mind, all generators connected to the sync bus must be in phase. If a generator fails, the flight crew would simply isolate the defective generator and the flight would continue without interruption.

The number one and two DC busses (*Figure 9-105* top left) are used to feed the DC electrical loads of the aircraft. DC bus 1 receives power form AC bus 1 though TR1. DC bus 2 is fed in a similar manner from AC bus 2. The DC busses

Figure 9-105. *Parallel power distribution system.*

also connect to the battery bus and eventually to the battery. The essential DC bus (top left) can be fed from DC bus 1 or the essential TR. A diode prevents the essential DC bus from powering DC bus 1. The essential DC bus receives power from the essential TR, which receives power from the essential AC bus. This provides an extra layer of redundancy since the essential AC bus can be isolated and fed from any main generator. *Figure 9-105* shows generator 3 powering the essential AC bus.

Split-Parallel Systems

A split-parallel bus basically employs the best of both split-bus and the parallel-bus systems. The split-parallel system is found on the Boeing 747-400 and contains four generators driven by the main engines and two APU-driven generators. The system can operate with all generators in parallel, or the generators can be operated independently as in a split-bus system. During a normal flight, all four engine-driven generators are operated in parallel. The system is operated in split-bus mode only under certain failure conditions or when using external power. The Boeing 747-400 split-parallel system is computer controlled using four GCU and two BPCU. There is one GCU controlling each generator; BPCU 1 controls the left side bus power distribution, and BPCU 2 controls the right side bus power. The GCUs and BPCUs operate similarly to those previously discussed under the split-bus system.

Figure 9-106 shows a simplified split-parallel power distribution system. The main generators (top of *Figure 9-106*) are driven by the main turbine engines. Each generator is connected to its load bus through a generator control breaker (GCB). The generator control unit closes the GCB when the pilot calls for generator power and all systems are operating normally. Each load bus is connected to various electrical systems and additional sub-busses. The BTB are controlled by the BPCU and connect each load bus to the left and right sync bus. A split systems breaker (SSB) is used to connect the left and right sync busses and is closed during a normal flight. With the SSB, GCBs, and BTBs, in the closed position the generators operate in parallel. When operating in parallel, all generators must be in phase.

If the aircraft electrical system experiences a malfunction, the control units make the appropriate adjustments to ensure all necessary loads receive electrical power. For example, if generator 1 fails, GCU 1 detects the fault and command GCB 1 to open. With GCB 1 open, load bus 1 now feeds from the sync bus and the three operating generators. In another example, if load bus 4 should short to ground, BPCU 4 opens the GCB 4 and BTB 4. This isolates the shorted bus (load bus 4). All loads on the shorted bus are no longer powered, and generator 4 is no longer available. However, with three remaining generators operational, the flight continues safely.

Figure 9-106. *Split-parallel distribution system.*

As do all large aircraft, the Boeing 747-400 contains a DC power distribution system. The DC system is used for battery and emergency operations. The DC system is similar to those previously discussed, powered by TR units. The TRs are connected to the AC busses and convert AC into 26-volt DC. The DC power systems are the final backups in the event of a catastrophic electrical failure. The systems most critical to fly the aircraft can typically receive power from the battery. This aircraft also contains two static inverters to provide emergency AC power when needed.

Wiring Installation

Wiring Diagrams

Electrical wiring diagrams are included in most aircraft service manuals and specify information, such as the size of the wire and type of terminals to be used for a particular application. Furthermore, wiring diagrams typically identify each component within a system by its part number and its serial number, including any changes that were made during the production run of an aircraft. Wiring diagrams are often used for troubleshooting electrical malfunctions.

Block Diagrams

A block diagram is used as an aid for troubleshooting complex electrical and electronic systems. A block diagram consists of individual blocks that represent several components, such as a printed circuit board or some other type of replaceable module. *Figure 9-107* is a block diagram of an aircraft electrical system.

Pictorial Diagrams

In a pictorial diagram, pictures of components are used instead of the conventional electrical symbols found in schematic diagrams. A pictorial diagram helps the maintenance technician visualize the operation of a system. *[Figure 9-108]*

Schematic Diagrams

A schematic diagram is used to illustrate a principle of operation, and therefore does not show parts as they actually appear or function. *[Figure 9-109]* However, schematic diagrams do indicate the location of components with respect to each other. Schematic diagrams are best utilized for troubleshooting.

Wire Types

The satisfactory performance of any modern aircraft depends to a very great degree on the continuing reliability of electrical systems and subsystems. Improperly or carelessly maintained wiring can be a source of both immediate and potential danger. The continued proper performance of electrical systems depends on the knowledge and techniques of the technician who installs, inspects, and maintains the electrical system wires and cables.

Procedures and practices outlined in this section are general recommendations and are not intended to replace the manufacturer's instructions and approved practices.

Figure 9-107. *Block diagram of an aircraft electrical system.*

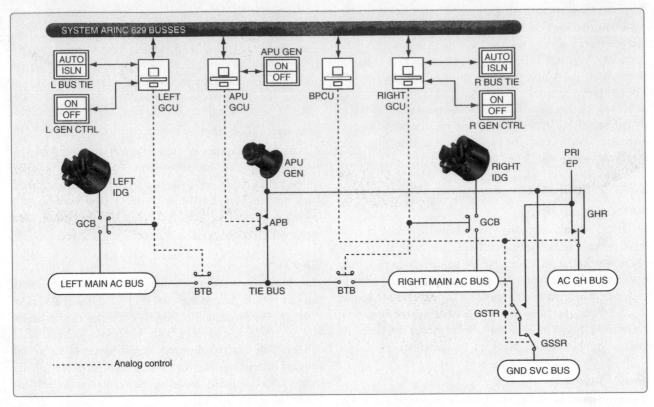

Figure 9-108. *Pictorial diagram of an aircraft electrical system.*

Figure 9-109. *Schematic diagram.*

A wire is described as a single, solid conductor, or as a stranded conductor covered with an insulating material. *Figure 9-110* illustrates these two definitions of a wire. Because of in-flight vibration and flexing, conductor round wire should be stranded to minimize fatigue breakage.

Figure 9-110. *Aircraft electrical cable.*

The term "cable," as used in aircraft electrical installations, includes:

1. Two or more separately insulated conductors in the same jacket.

2. Two or more separately insulated conductors twisted together (twisted pair).

3. One or more insulated conductors covered with a metallic braided shield (shielded cable).

4. A single insulated center conductor with a metallic braided outer conductor (radio frequency cable).

The term "wire harness" is used when an array of insulated conductors are bound together by lacing cord, metal bands, or other binding in an arrangement suitable for use only in specific equipment for which the harness was designed; it may include terminations. Wire harnesses are extensively used in aircraft to connect all the electrical components. *[Figure 9-111]*

For many years, the standard wire in light aircraft has been MIL-W-5086A, which uses a tin-coated copper conductor rated at 600 volts and temperatures of 105 °C. This basic wire is then coated with various insulating coatings. Commercial and military aircraft use wire that is manufactured under MIL-W-22759 specification, which complies with current military and FAA requirements.

Figure 9-111. *Shielded wire harness.*

The most important consideration in the selection of aircraft wire is properly matching the wire's construction to the application environment. Wire construction that is suitable for the most severe environmental condition to be encountered should be selected. Wires are typically categorized as being suitable for either open wiring or protected wiring application. The wire temperature rating is typically a measure of the insulation's ability to withstand the combination of ambient temperature and current-related conductor temperature rise.

Conductor

The two most generally used conductors are copper and aluminum. Each has characteristics that make its use advantageous under certain circumstances. Also, each has certain disadvantages. Copper has a higher conductivity; is more ductile; has relatively high tensile strength; and can be easily soldered. Copper is more expensive and heavier than aluminum. Although aluminum has only about 60 percent of the conductivity of copper, it is used extensively. Its lightness makes possible long spans, and its relatively large diameter for a given conductivity reduces corona (the discharge of electricity from the wire when it has a high potential). The discharge is greater when small diameter wire is used than when large diameter wire is used. Some bus bars are made of aluminum instead of copper where there is a greater radiating surface for the same conductance. The characteristics of copper and aluminum are compared in *Figure 9-112*.

Characteristic	Copper	Aluminum
Tensile strength (lb-in)	55,000	25,000
Tensile strength for same conductivity (lb)	55,000	40,000
Weight for same conductivity (lb)	100	48
Cross section for same conductivity (CM)	100	160
Specific resistance (ohm/mil ft)	10.6	17

Figure 9-112. *Aircraft electrical cable.*

Plating

Bare copper develops a surface oxide coating at a rate dependent on temperature. This oxide film is a poor conductor of electricity and inhibits determination of wire. Therefore, all aircraft wiring has a coating of tin, silver, or nickel that has far slower oxidation rates.

1. Tin-coated copper is a very common plating material. Its ability to be successfully soldered without highly active fluxes diminishes rapidly with time after manufacture. It can be used up to the limiting temperature of 150 °C.

2. Silver-coated wire is used where temperatures do not exceed 200 °C (392 °F).

3. Nickel-coated wire retains its properties beyond 260 °C, but most aircraft wire using such coated strands has insulation systems that cannot exceed that temperature on long-term exposure. Soldered terminations of nickel-plated conductor require the use of different solder sleeves or flux than those used with tin- or silver-plated conductor.

Insulation

Two fundamental properties of insulation materials are insulation resistance and dielectric strength. These are entirely different and distinct properties.

Insulation resistance is the resistance to current leakage through and over the surface of insulation materials. Insulation resistance can be measured with a megohmmeter/insulation tester without damaging the insulation, and data so obtained serves as a useful guide in determining the general condition of the insulation. However, the data obtained in this manner may not give a true picture of the condition of the insulation. Clean, dry insulation having cracks or other faults might show a high value of insulation resistance but would not be suitable for use.

Dielectric strength is the ability of the insulator to withstand potential difference and is usually expressed in terms of the voltage at which the insulation fails because of the electrostatic stress. Maximum dielectric strength values can be measured by raising the voltage of a test sample until the insulation breaks down.

The type of conductor insulation material varies with the type of installation. Characteristics should be chosen based on environment, such as abrasion resistance, arc resistance, corrosion resistance, cut-through strength, dielectric strength, flame resistant, mechanical strength, smoke emission, fluid resistance, and heat distortion. Such types of insulation materials (e.g., PVC/nylon, Kapton®, and Teflon®) are no longer used for new aircraft designs, but might still be installed on older aircraft. Insulation materials for new aircraft designs are made of Tefzel®, Teflon®/Kapton®/Teflon® and PTFE/Polyimide/PTFE. The development of better and safer insulation materials is ongoing.

Since electrical wire may be installed in areas where inspection is infrequent over extended periods of time, it is necessary to give special consideration to heat-aging characteristics in the selection of wire. Resistance to heat is of primary importance in the selection of wire for aircraft use, as it is the basic factor in wire rating. Where wire may be required to operate at higher temperatures due either to high ambient temperatures, high current loading, or a combination of the two, selection should be made on the basis of satisfactory performance under the most severe operating conditions.

Wire Shielding

With the increase in number of highly sensitive electronic devices found on modern aircraft, it has become very important to ensure proper shielding for many electric circuits. Shielding is the process of applying a metallic covering to wiring and equipment to eliminate electromagnetic interference (EMI). EMI is caused when electromagnetic fields (radio waves) induce high frequency (HF) voltages in a wire or component. The induced voltage can cause system inaccuracies or even failure.

Use of shielding with 85 percent coverage or greater is recommended. Coaxial, triaxial, twinaxial, or quadraxial cables should be used, wherever appropriate, with their shields connected to ground at a single point or multiple points, depending upon the purpose of the shielding. [Figure 9-113] The airframe grounded structure may also be used as an EMI shield.

Figure 9-113. *Shielded wire harness for flight control.*

Wire Substitutions

Wire Substitutions

When a replacement wire is required in the repair and modification of existing aircraft, the maintenance manual for that aircraft must first be reviewed to determine if the original aircraft manufacturer (OAM) has approved any substitution. If not, then the manufacturer must be contacted for an acceptable replacement.

Areas Designated as Severe Wind and Moisture Problem (SWAMP)

SWAMP areas differ from aircraft to aircraft but are usually wheel wells, near wing flaps, wing folds, pylons, and other exterior areas that may have a harsh environment. Wires in these areas have often an exterior jacket to protect them from the environment. Wires for these applications often have design features incorporated into their construction that may make the wire unique; therefore, an acceptable substitution may be difficult, if not impossible, to find. It is very important to use the wire type recommended in the aircraft manufacturer's maintenance handbook. Insulation or jacketing varies according to the environment. *[Figure 9-114]*

Figure 9-114. *Wire harness with protective jacket.*

Wire Size Selection

Wire is manufactured in sizes according to a standard known as the American wire gauge (AWG). As shown in *Figure 9-115*, the wire diameters become smaller as the gauge numbers become larger. Typical wire sizes range from a number 40 to number 0000.

Gauge numbers are useful in comparing the diameter of wires, but not all types of wire or cable can be measured accurately with a gauge. Larger wires are usually stranded to increase their flexibility. In such cases, the total area can be determined by multiplying the area of one strand (usually computed in circular mils when diameter or gauge number is known) by the number of strands in the wire or cable.

Several factors must be considered in selecting the size of wire for transmitting and distributing electric power.

1. Wires must have sufficient mechanical strength to allow for service conditions.

2. Allowable power loss (I2 R loss) in the line represents electrical energy converted into heat. The use of large conductors reduces the resistance and therefore the I2 R loss. However, large conductors are more expensive, heavier, and need more substantial support.

3. If the source maintains a constant voltage at the input to the lines, any variation in the load on the line causes a variation in line current and a consequent variation in the IR drop in the line. A wide variation in the IR drop in the line causes poor voltage regulation at the load. The obvious remedy is to reduce either current or resistance. A reduction in load current lowers the amount of power being transmitted, whereas a reduction in line resistance increases the size and weight of conductors required. A compromise is generally reached whereby the voltage variation at the load is within tolerable limits and the weight of line conductors is not excessive.

4. When current is drawn through the conductor, heat is generated. The temperature of the wire rises until the heat radiated, or otherwise dissipated, is equal to the heat generated by the passage of current through the line. If the conductor is insulated, the heat generated in the conductor is not so readily removed as it would be if the conductor were not insulated. Thus, to protect the insulation from too much heat, the current through the conductor must be maintained below a certain value. When electrical conductors are installed in locations where the ambient temperature is relatively high, the heat generated by external sources constitutes an appreciable part of the total conductor heating. Allowance must be made for the influence of external heating on the allowable conductor current, and each case has its own specific limitations. The maximum allowable operating temperature of insulated conductors varies with the type of conductor insulation being used.

If it is desirable to use wire sizes smaller than #20, particular attention should be given to the mechanical strength and installation handling of these wires (e.g., vibration, flexing, and termination). Wires containing less than 19 strands must not be used. Consideration should be given to the use of high-strength alloy conductors in small-gauge wires to increase mechanical strength. As a general practice, wires smaller than size #20 should be provided with additional clamps and be grouped with at least three other wires. They should also have additional support at terminations, such as connector grommets, strain relief clamps, shrinkable sleeving, or telescoping bushings. They should not be used in

Cross Section			Ohms per 1,000 ft		
Gauge Number	Diameter (mils)	Circular (mils)	Square inches	25 °C (77 °F)	65 °C (149 °F)
0000	460.0	212,000.0	0.166	0.0500	0.0577
000	410.0	168,000.0	0.132	0.0630	0.0727
00	365.0	133,000.0	0.105	0.0795	0.0917
0	325.0	106,000.0	0.0829	0.100	0.166
1	289.0	83,700.0	0.0657	0.126	0.146
2	258.0	66,400.0	0.0521	0.159	0.184
3	229.0	52,600.0	0.0413	0.201	0.232
4	204.0	41,700.0	0.0328	0.253	0.292
5	182.0	33,100.0	0.0260	0.319	0.369
6	162.0	26,300.0	0.0206	0.403	0.465
7	144.0	20,800.0	0.0164	0.508	0.586
8	128.0	16,500.0	0.0130	0.641	0.739
9	114.0	13,100.0	0.0103	0.808	0.932
10	102.0	10,400.0	0.00815	1.02	1.18
11	91.0	8,230.0	0.00647	1.28	1.48
12	81.0	6,530.0	0.00513	1.62	1.87
13	72.0	5,180.0	0.00407	2.04	2.36
14	64.0	4,110.0	0.00323	2.58	2.97
15	57.0	3,260.0	0.00256	3.25	3.75
16	51.0	2,580.0	0.00203	4.09	4.73
17	45.0	2,050.0	0.00161	5.16	5.96
18	40.0	1,620.0	0.00128	6.51	7.51
19	36.0	1,290.0	0.00101	8.21	9.48
20	32.0	1,020.0	0.000802	10.40	11.90
21	28.5	810.0	0.000636	13.10	15.10
22	25.3	642.0	0.000505	16.50	19.00
23	22.6	509.0	0.000400	20.80	24.00
24	20.1	404.0	0.000317	26.20	30.20
25	17.9	320.0	0.000252	33.00	38.10
26	15.9	254.0	0.000200	41.60	48.00
27	14.2	202.0	0.000158	52.50	60.60
28	12.6	160.0	0.000126	66.20	76.40
29	11.3	127.0	0.0000995	83.40	96.30
30	10.0	101.0	0.0000789	105.00	121.00
31	8.9	79.7	0.0000626	133.00	153.00
32	8.0	63.2	0.0000496	167.00	193.00
33	7.1	50.1	0.0000394	211.00	243.00
34	6.3	39.8	0.0000312	266.00	307.00
35	5.6	31.5	0.0000248	335.00	387.00
36	5.0	25.0	0.0000196	423.00	488.00
37	4.5	19.8	0.0000156	533.00	616.00
38	4.0	15.7	0.0000123	673.00	776.00
39	3.5	12.5	0.0000098	848.00	979.00
40	3.1	9.9	0.0000078	1,070.00	1,230.00

Figure 9-115. *American wire gauge for standard annealed solid copper wire.*

applications where they are subjected to excessive vibration, repeated bending, or frequent disconnection from screw termination. *[Figure 9-116]*

Current Carrying Capacity

In some instances, the wire may be capable of carrying more current than is recommended for the contacts of the related connector. In this instance, it is the contact rating that dictates the maximum current to be carried by a wire. Wires of larger gauge may need to be used to fit within the crimp range of connector contacts that are adequately rated for the current being carried. *Figure 9-117* gives a family of curves whereby the bundle derating factor may be obtained.

Maximum Operating Temperature

The current that causes a temperature steady state condition equal to the rated temperature of the wire should not be exceeded. Rated temperature of the wire may be based upon the ability of either the conductor or the insulation to withstand continuous operation without degradation.

1. Single Wire in Free Air

Determining a wiring system's current-carrying capacity begins with determining the maximum current that a given-sized wire can carry without exceeding the allowable temperature difference (wire rating minus ambient °C). The curves are based upon a single copper wire in free air. *[Figure 9-117]*

2. Wires in a Harness

When wires are bundled into harnesses, the current derived for a single wire must be reduced, as shown in *Figure 9-118*. The amount of current derating is a function of the number of wires in the bundle and the percentage of the total wire bundle capacity that is being used.

3. Harness at Altitude

Since heat loss from the bundle is reduced with increased altitude, the amount of current should be derated. *Figure 9-119* gives a curve whereby the altitude-derating factor may be obtained.

4. Aluminum Conductor Wire

When aluminum conductor wire is used, sizes should be selected on the basis of current ratings shown in *Figure 9-120*. The use of sizes smaller than #8 is discouraged. Aluminum wire should not be attached to engine mounted accessories or used in areas having corrosive fumes, severe vibration, mechanical stresses, or where there is a need for frequent disconnection. Use of aluminum wire is also discouraged for runs of less than 3 feet. Termination hardware should be of the type specifically designed for use with aluminum conductor wiring.

Computing Current Carrying Capacity

The following section presents some examples on how to calculate the load carrying capacity of aircraft electrical wire. The calculation is a step by step approach and several graphs are used to obtain information to compute the current carrying capacity of a particular wire.

Example 1

Assume a harness (open or braided) consisting of 10 wires, size 20, 200 °C rated copper, and 25 wires size 22, 200 °C rated copper, is installed in an area where the ambient temperature is 60 °C and the aircraft is capable of operating at a 35,000 foot altitude. Circuit analysis reveals that 7 of the 35 wires in the bundle ($^7/_{35}$ = 20 percent) are carrying power currents near or up to capacity.

Step 1—Refer to the single wire in free air curves in *Figure 9-114*. Determine the change of temperature of the wire to determine free air ratings. Since the wire is in an ambient temperature of 60 °C and rated at 200 °C, the change of the temperature is 200 °C – 60 °C = 140 °C. Follow the 140 °C temperature difference horizontally until it intersects with wire size line on *Figure 9-113*. The free air rating for size 20 is 21.5 amps, and the free air rating for size 22 is 16.2 amps.

Step 2—Refer to the bundle derating curves in *Figure 9-118*. The 20 percent curve is selected since circuit analysis indicate that 20 percent or less of the wire in the harness would be carrying power currents and less than 20 percent of the bundle capacity would be used. Find 35 (on the horizontal axis), since there are 35 wires in the bundle, and determine a derating factor of 0.52 (on the vertical axis) from the 20 percent curve.

Step 3—Derate the size 22 free air rating by multiplying 16.2 by 0.52 to get 8.4 amps in harness rating. Derate the size 20 free air rating by multiplying 21.5 by 0.52 to get 11.2 amps in-harness rating.

Step 4—Refer to the altitude derating curve of *Figure 9-119*. Look for 35,000 feet (on the horizontal axis) since that is the altitude at which the aircraft is operating. Note that the wire must be derated by a factor of 0.86 (found on the vertical axis). Derate the size 22 harness rating by multiplying 8.4 amps by 0.86 to get 7.2 amps. Derate the size 20 harness rating by multiplying 11.2 amps by 0.86 to get 9.6 amps.

Step 5—To find the total harness capacity, multiply the total number of size 22 wires by the derated capacity (25 × 7.2 = 180.0 amps) and add to that the number of size 20 wires multiplied by the derated capacity (10 × 9.6 = 96.8 amps) and multiply the sum by the 20 percent harness capacity factor. Thus, the total harness capacity is (180.0 + 96.0) × 0.20 = 55.2 amps. It has been determined that the total harness

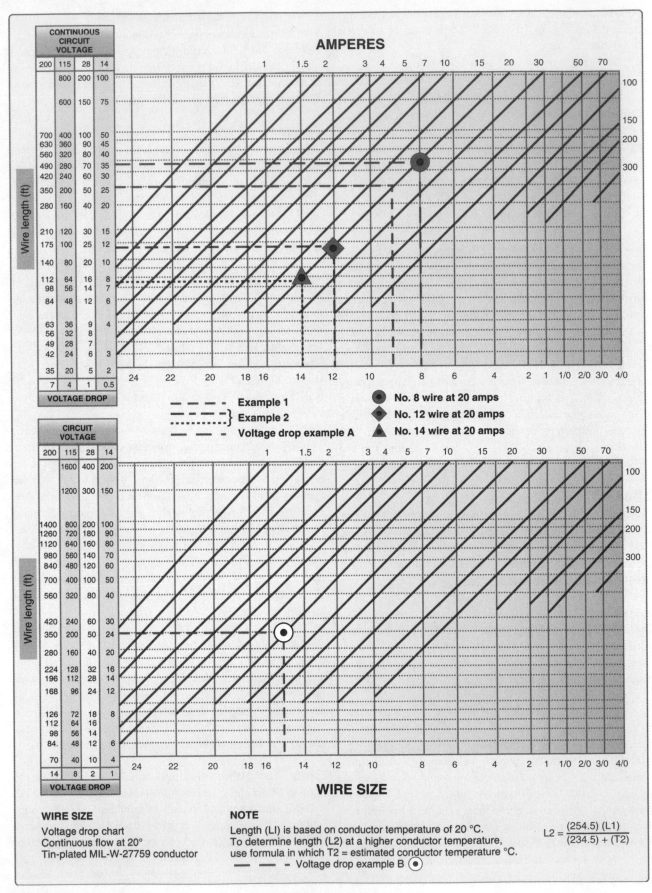

Figure 9-116. *Conductor chart, continuous (top) and intermittent flow (bottom).*

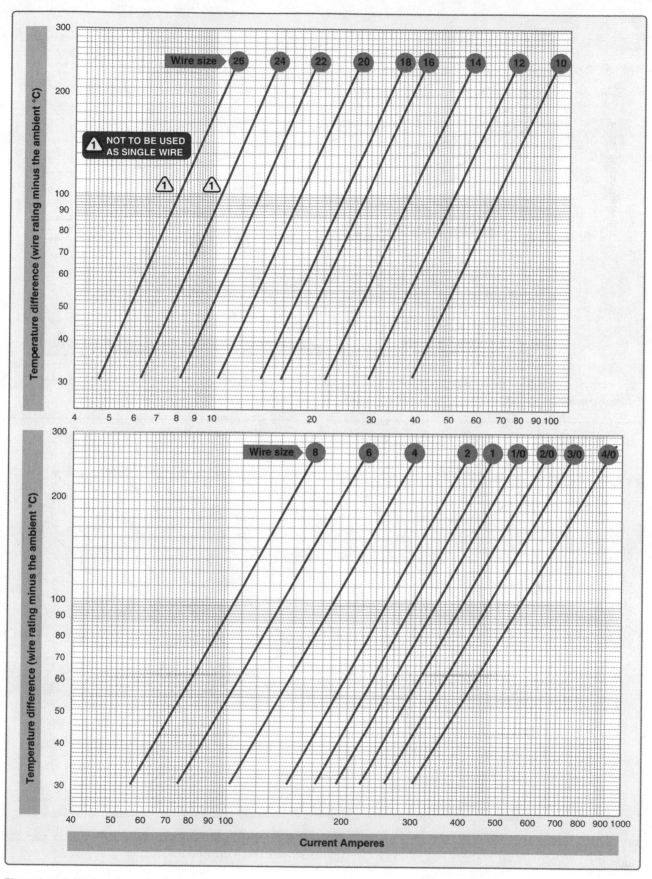

Figure 9-117. *Single copper wire in free air.*

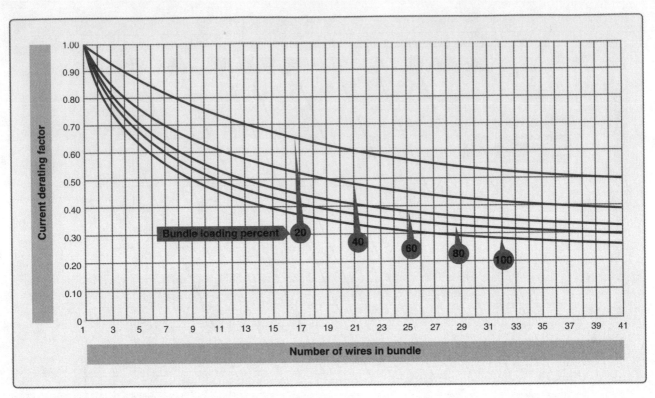

Figure 9-118. *Bundle derating curve.*

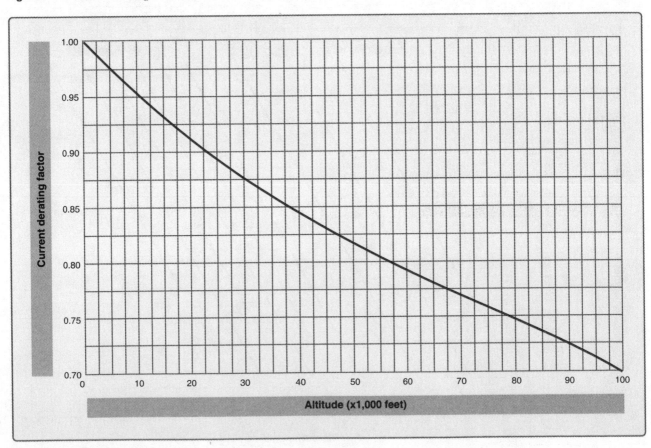

Figure 9-119. *Altitude derating curve.*

current should not exceed 55.2 A, size 22 wire should not carry more than 7.2 amps and size 20 wire should not carry more than 9.6 amps.

Step 6—Determine the actual circuit current for each wire in the bundle and for the whole bundle. If the values calculated in step 5 are exceeded, select the next larger size wire and repeat the calculations.

Example 2

Assume a harness (open or braided), consisting of 12 size 12, 200 °C rated copper wires, is operated in an ambient temperature of 25 °C at sea level and 60 °C at a 20,000-foot altitude. All 12 wires are operated at or near their maximum capacity.

Step 1—Refer to the single wire in free air curve in *Figure 9-117*, determine the temperature difference of the wire to determine free air ratings. Since the wire is in ambient temperature of 25 °C and 60 °C and is rated at 200 °C, the temperature differences are 200 °C – 25 °C = 175 °C and 200 °C – 60 °C = 140 °C, respectively. Follow the 175 °C and the 140 °C temperature difference lines on *Figure 9-116* until each intersects wire size line. The free air ratings of size 12 are 68 amps and 59 amps, respectively.

Step 2—Refer to the bundling derating curves in *Figure 9-120*. The 100 percent curve is selected because we know all 12 wires are carrying full load. Find 12 (on the horizontal axis) since there are 12 wires in the bundle and determine a derating factor of 0.43 (on the vertical axis) from the 100 percent curve.

Wire size	Continuous duty current (amp) wires in bundles, groups, or harnesses or conduits		Max. resistance ohms/1000feet
	Wire conductor temperature rating		
	@ 105 °C	@ 150 °C	@ 20 °C
#8	30	45	1.093
#6	40	61	0.641
#4	54	82	0.427
#2	76	113	0.268
#1	90	133	0.214
#0	102	153	0.169
#00	117	178	0.133
#000	138	209	0.109
#0000	163	248	0.085

Figure 9-120. *Current-carrying capacity and resistance of aluminum wire.*

Step 3—Derate the size #12 free air ratings by multiplying 68 amps and 61 amps by 0.43 to get 29.2 amps and 25.4 amps, respectively.

Step 4—Refer to the altitude derating curve of *Figure 9-119*, look for sea level and 20,000 feet (on the horizontal axis) since these are the conditions at which the load is carried. The wire must be derated by a factor of 1.0 and 0.91, respectively.

Step 5—Derate the size 12 in a bundle ratings by multiplying 29.2 amps at sea level and 25.4 amps at 20,000 feet by 1.0 and 0.91, respectively to obtain 29.2 amps and 23.1 amps. The total bundle capacity at sea level and 25 °C ambient temperature is 29.2 × 12=350.4 amps. At 20,000 feet and 60 °C ambient temperature, the bundle capacity is 23.1 × 12=277.2 amps. Each size 12 wire can carry 29.2 amps at sea level, 25 °C ambient temperature or 23.1 amps at 20,000 feet and 60 °C ambient temperature.

Step 6—Determine the actual circuit current for each wire in the bundle and for the bundle. If the values calculated in Step 5 are exceeded, select the next larger size wire and repeat the calculations.

Allowable Voltage Drop

The voltage drop in the main power wires from the generation source or the battery to the bus should not exceed 2 percent of the regulated voltage when the generator is carrying rated current or the battery is being discharged at the 5-minute rate. The tabulation shown in *Figure 9-121* defines the maximum acceptable voltage drop in the load circuits between the bus and the utilization equipment ground.

Nominal system voltage	Allowable voltage drop during continuous operation	Intermittent operation
14	0.5	1
28	1	2
115	4	8
200	7	14

Figure 9-121. *Tabulation chart (allowable voltage drop between bus and utilization equipment ground).*

The resistance of the current return path through the aircraft structure is generally considered negligible. However, this is based on the assumption that adequate bonding to the structure or a special electric current return path has been provided that is capable of carrying the required electric current with a negligible voltage drop. To determine circuit resistance, check the voltage drop across the circuit. If the voltage drop does not exceed the limit established by the aircraft or product manufacturer, the resistance value for the circuit may be considered satisfactory. When checking a circuit, the input voltage should be maintained at a constant value. *Figures 9-122* and *9-123* show formulas that may be used to determine electrical resistance in wires and some typical examples.

Voltage drop	Run lengths (feet)	Circuit current (amps)	Wire size from chart	Check calculated voltage drop (VD) = (resistance/feet) (length) (current)
1	107	20	No. 6	VD = (0.00044 ohms/feet) (107 x 20) = 0.942
0.5	90	20	No. 4	VD = (0.00028 ohms/feet) (90 x 20) = 0.504
4	88	20	No. 12	VD = (0.00202 ohms/feet) (88 x 20) = 3.60
7	100	20	No. 14	VD = (0.00306 ohms/feet) (100 x 20) = 6.12

Figure 9-122. *Determining required tin-plated copper wire size and checking voltage drop.*

Maximum Voltage drop	Wire size	Circuit current (amps)	Maximum wire run length (feet)	Check calculated voltage drop (VD) = (resistance/feet) (length) (current)
1	No. 10	20	39	VD = (0.00126 ohms/feet) (39 x 20) = 0.98
0.5	---		19.5	VD = (0.00126 ohms/feet) (19.5 x 20) = 0.366
4	---		156	VD = (0.00126 ohms/feet) (156 x 20) = 3.93
7	---		273	VD = (0.00126 ohms/feet) (273 x 20) = 6.88

Figure 9-123. *Determining maximum tin-plated copper wire length and checking voltage drop.*

The following formula can be used to check the voltage drop. The resistance/ft can be found in *Figures 9-122* and *9-123* for the wire size.

Calculated Voltage drop (VD) = resistance/ft × length × current

Electric Wire Chart Instructions

To select the correct size of electrical wire, two major requirements must be met:

1. The wire size should be sufficient to prevent an excessive voltage drop while carrying the required current over the required distance. *[Figure 9-121]*

2. The size should be sufficient to prevent overheating of the wire carrying the required current. (See Maximum Operating Temperature earlier in this chapter for computing current carrying capacity methods.)

To meet the two requirements for selecting the correct wire size using *Figure 9-116*, the following must be known:

1. The wire length in feet.

2. The number of amperes of current to be carried.

3. The allowable voltage drop permitted.

4. The required continuous or intermittent current.

5. The estimated or measured conductor temperature.

6. Is the wire to be installed in conduit and/or bundle?

7. Is the wire to be installed as a single wire in free air?

Example A.
Find the wire size in *Figure 9-116* using the following known information:

1. The wire run is 50 feet long, including the ground wire.

2. Current load is 20 amps.

3. The voltage source is 28 volts from bus to equipment.

4. The circuit has continuous operation.

5. Estimated conductor temperature is 20 °C or less. The scale on the left of the chart represents maximum wire length in feet to prevent an excessive voltage drop for a specified voltage source system (e.g., 14V, 28V, 115V, 200V). This voltage is identified at the top of scale and the corresponding voltage drop limit for continuous operation at the bottom. The scale (slant lines) on top of the chart represents amperes. The scale at the bottom of the chart represents wire gauge.

Step 1—From the left scale, find the wire length 50 feet under the 28V source column.

Step 2—Follow the corresponding horizontal line to the right until it intersects the slanted line for the 20-amp load.

Step 3—At this point, drop vertically to the bottom of the chart. The value falls between No. 8 and No. 10. Select the next larger size wire to the right, in this case No. 8. This is the smallest size wire that can be used without exceeding the voltage drop limit expressed at the bottom of the left scale. This example is plotted on the wire chart in *Figure 9-116*. Use *Figure 9-116 (top)* for continuous flow and *Figure 9-116 (bottom)* for intermittent flow.

Example B.
Find the wire size in *Figure 9-116* using the following known information:

1. The wire run is 200 feet long, including the ground wire.

2. Current load is 10 amps.

3. The voltage source is 115 volts from bus to equipment.

4. The circuit has intermittent operation.

Step 1—From the left scale, find the wire length of 200 feet under the 115V source column.

Step 2—Follow the corresponding horizontal line to the right until it intersects the slanted line for the 10 amp load.

Step 3—At this point, drop vertically to the bottom of the chart. The value falls between No. 16 and No. 14. Select the next larger size wire to the right—in this case, No. 14. This is the smallest size wire that can be used without exceeding the voltage drop limit expressed at the bottom of the left scale.

Wire Identification

The proper identification of electrical wires and cables with their circuits and voltages is necessary to provide safety of operation, safety to maintenance personnel, and ease of maintenance. All wire used on aircraft must have its type identification imprinted along its length. It is common practice to follow this part number with the five digit/letter Commercial and Government Entity (CAGE) code identifying the wire manufacturer. You can identify the performance capabilities of existing installed wire you need to replace, and avoid the inadvertent use of a lower performance and unsuitable replacement wire.

Placement of Identification Markings

Identification markings should be placed at each end of the wire and at 15-inch maximum intervals along the length of the wire. Wires less than 3 inches in length need not be identified. Wires 3 to 7 inches in length should be identified approximately at the center. Added identification marker sleeves should be located so that ties, clamps, or supporting devices need not be removed to read the identification. The wire identification code must be printed to read horizontally (from left to right) or vertically (from top to bottom). The two methods of marking wire or cable are as follows:

1. Direct marking is accomplished by printing the cable's outer covering. *[Figure 9-124B]*

2. Indirect marking is accomplished by printing a heat-shrinkable sleeve and installing the printed sleeve on the wire or cables outer covering. Indirectly-marked wire or cable should be identified with printed sleeves at each end and at intervals not longer than 6 feet. *[Figure 9-125]* The individual wires inside a cable should be identified within 3 inches of their termination. *[Figure 9-124A]*

Types of Wire Markings

The preferred method is to mark directly on the wire without causing insulation degradation. Teflon-coated wires, shielded wiring, multiconductor cable, and thermocouple wires usually require special sleeves to carry identification marks. There are some special wire marking machines available that can be used to stamp directly on the type wires mentioned above. Whatever method of marking is used, the marking should be legible and the color should contrast with the wire insulation or sleeve.

Several different methods can be used to mark directly on the wire: hot stamp marking, ink jet printers, and laser jet printers. *[Figure 9-126]* The hot stamp method can damage the insulation of a newer type of wire that utilizes thin

Figure 9-124. *Wire markings for single wire without sleeve.*

Figure 9-125. *Spacing of printed identification marks (indirect marking).*

Figure 9-126. *Laser wire printer.*

insulators. Fracture of the insulation wall and penetration to the conductor of these materials by the stamping dies have occurred. Later in service, when these openings have been wetted by various fluids or moisture, serious arcing and surface tracking have damaged wire bundles.

Identification sleeves can be used if the direct marking on the wire is not possible. *[Figure 9-127]*

Figure 9-127. *Alternate method of identifying wire bundles.*

Flexible sleeving, either clear or opaque, is satisfactory for general use. When color-coded or striped component wire is

used as part of a cable, the identification sleeve should specify which color is associated with each wire identification code. Identification sleeves are normally used for identifying the following types of wire or cable: unjacketed shielded wire, thermocouple wire, coaxial cable, multiconductor cable, and high temperature wire. In most cases, identification tape can be used in place of sleeving. For sleeving exposed to high temperatures (over 400 °F), materials, such as silicone fiberglass, should be used. Polyolefin sleeving should be used in areas where resistance to solvent and synthetic hydraulic fluids is necessary. Sleeves may be secured in place with cable ties or by heat shrinking. The identification sleeving for various sizes of wire is shown in *Figure 9-128*.

Wire size		Sleeving size	
AN #	AL #	No.	Nominal ID (inch)
24		12	0.085
22		11	0.095
20		10	0.106
18		9	0.118
16		8	0.113
14		7	0.148
12		6	0.166
10		4	0.208
8	8	2	0.263
6	6	0	0.330
4	4	3/8 inch	0.375
2	2	1/2 inch	0.500
1	1	1/2 inch	0.500
0	0	5/8 inch	0.625
00	00	5/8 inch	0.625
000	000	3/4 inch	0.750
0000	0000	3/4 inch	0.750

Figure 9-128. *Recommended size of identification sleeving.*

Wire Installation and Routing
Open Wiring

Interconnecting wire is used in point-to-point open harnesses, normally in the interior or pressurized fuselage, with each wire providing enough insulation to resist damage from handling and service exposure. Electrical wiring is often installed in aircraft without special enclosing means. This practice is known as open wiring and offers the advantages of ease of maintenance and reduced weight.

Wire Groups and Bundles and Routing

Wires are often installed in bundles to create a more organized installation. These wire bundles are often called wire harnesses. Wire harnesses are often made in the factory or electrical shop on a jig board so that the wire bundles could be preformed to fit into the aircraft. *[Figure 9-129]* As a result, each harness for a particular aircraft installation is identical in shape and length. The wiring harness could be covered by a shielding (metal braid) to avoid EMI. Grouping or bundling certain wires, such as electrically unprotected power wiring and wiring going to duplicate vital equipment, should be avoided. Wire bundles should generally be less than 75 wires, or 1½ to 2 inches in diameter where practicable. When several wires are grouped at junction boxes, terminal blocks, panels, etc., identity of the groups within a bundle can be retained.

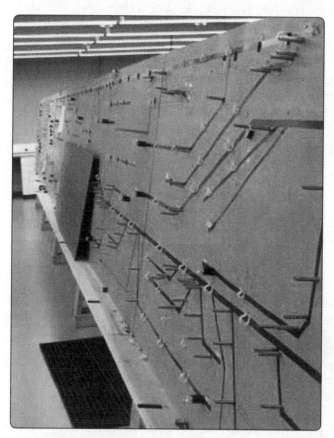

Figure 9-129. *Cable harness jig board.*

Slack in Wire Bundles

Wiring should be installed with sufficient slack so that bundles and individual wires are not under tension. Wires connected to movable or shock-mounted equipment should have sufficient length to allow full travel without tension on the bundle. Wiring at terminal lugs or connectors should have sufficient slack to allow two reterminations without replacement of wires. This slack should be in addition to the drip loop and the allowance for movable equipment. Normally, wire groups or bundles should not exceed ½ inch deflection between support points. *[Figure 9-130]* This measurement may be exceeded if there is no possibility of the wire group or bundle touching a surface that may cause abrasion. Sufficient slack should be provided at each end to permit replacement of terminals and ease of maintenance; prevent mechanical strain on the wires, cables, junctions, and supports; permit free movement of shock- and vibration-mounted equipment; and allow shifting of equipment, as necessary, to perform alignment, servicing, tuning, removal of dust covers, and changing of internal components while installed in aircraft.

Twisting Wires

When specified on the engineering drawing, or when accomplished as a local practice, parallel wires must sometimes be twisted. The following are the most common examples:

1. Wiring in the vicinity of magnetic compass or flux valve

2. Three-phase distribution wiring

3. Certain other wires (usually radio wiring) as specified on engineering drawings

Twist the wires so they lie snugly against each other, making approximately the number of twists per foot as shown in *Figure 9-131*. Always check wire insulation for damage after twisting. If the insulation is torn or frayed, replace the wire.

½" maximum with normal hand pressure

Figure 9-130. *Slack between supports of a cable harness.*

Gauge #	22	20	18	16	14	12	10	8	6	4
2 Wires	10	10	9	8	7 1/2	7	6 1/2	6	5	4
3 Wires	10	10	8 1/2	7	6 1/2	6	5 1/2	5	4	3

Figure 9-131. *Recommended number of wire twists per foot.*

Spliced Connections In Wire Bundles

Splicing is permitted on wiring as long as it does not affect the reliability and the electromechanical characteristics of the wiring. Splicing of power wires, coaxial cables, multiplex bus, and large-gauge wire must have approved data. Splicing of electrical wire should be kept to a minimum and avoided entirely in locations subject to extreme vibrations. Splicing of individual wires in a group or bundle should have engineering approval, and the splice(s) should be located to allow periodic inspection.

Many types of aircraft splice connector are available for use when splicing individual wires. Use of a self-insulated splice connector is preferred; however, a non-insulated splice connector may be used provided the splice is covered with plastic sleeving that is secured at both ends. Environmentally sealed splices that conform to MIL-T-7928 provide a reliable means of splicing in SWAMP areas. However, a non-insulated splice connector may be used, provided the splice is covered with dual-wall shrink sleeving of a suitable material.

There should be no more than one splice in any one wire segment between any two connectors or other disconnect points. Exceptions include when attaching to the spare pigtail lead of a potted connector, when splicing multiple wires to a single wire, when adjusting wire size to fit connector contact crimp barrel size, and when required to make an approved repair.

Splices in bundles must be staggered to minimize any increase in the size of the bundle, preventing the bundle from fitting into its designated space or causing congestion that adversely affects maintenance. *[Figure 9-132]*

Splices should not be used within 12 inches of a termination device, except when attaching to the pigtail spare lead of a potted termination device, to splice multiple wires to a single wire, or to adjust the wire sizes so that they are compatible with the contact crimp barrel sizes.

Bend Radii

The minimum radius of bends in wire groups or bundles must not be less than 10 times the outside diameter of the largest wire or cable, except that at the terminal strips where wires break out at terminations or reverse direction in a bundle. Where the wire is suitably supported, the radius may be three times the diameter of the wire or cable. Where it is not practical to install wiring or cables within the radius requirements, the bend should be enclosed in insulating tubing. The radius for thermocouple wire should be done in accordance with the manufacturer's recommendation and shall be sufficient to avoid excess losses or damage to the cable. Ensure that RF cables (e.g., coaxial and triaxial) are bent at a radius of no less than six times the outside diameter of the cable.

Protection Against Chafing

Wires and wire groups should be protected against chafing or abrasion in those locations where contact with sharp surfaces or other wires would damage the insulation, or chafing could occur against the airframe or other components. Damage to the insulation can cause short circuits, malfunction, or inadvertent operation of equipment.

Protection Against High Temperature

Wiring must be routed away from high-temperature equipment and lines to prevent deterioration of insulation. Wires must be rated so the conductor temperature remains within the wire specification maximum when the ambient temperature and heat rise related to current-carrying capacity are taken into account. The residual heating effects caused by exposure to sunlight when aircraft are parked for extended periods should also be taken into account. Wires, such as those used in fire detection, fire extinguishing, fuel shutoff, and fly-by-wire flight control systems that must operate during and after a fire, must be selected from types that are qualified to provide circuit integrity after exposure to fire for

Figure 9-132. *Staggered splices in wire bundle.*

a specified period. Wire insulation deteriorates rapidly when subjected to high temperatures.

Separate wires from high-temperature equipment, such as resistors, exhaust stacks, heating ducts, to prevent insulation breakdown. Insulate wires that must run through hot areas with a high-temperature insulation material, such as fiberglass or PTFE. Avoid high-temperature areas when using cables with soft plastic insulation, such as polyethylene, because these materials are subject to deterioration and deformation at elevated temperatures. Many coaxial cables have this type of insulation.

Protection Against Solvents and Fluids

An arcing fault between an electrical wire and a metallic flammable fluid line may puncture the line and result in a fire. Every effort must be made to avoid this hazard by physical separation of the wire from lines and equipment containing oxygen, oil, fuel, hydraulic fluid, or alcohol. Wiring must be routed above these lines and equipment with a minimum separation of 6 inches or more whenever possible. When such an arrangement is not practicable, wiring must be routed so that it does not run parallel to the fluid lines. A minimum of 2 inches must be maintained between wiring and such lines and equipment, except when the wiring is positively clamped to maintain at least ½-inch separation, or when it must be connected directly to the fluid-carrying equipment. Install clamps as shown in *Figure 9-133*. These clamps should not be used as a means of supporting the wire bundle. Additional clamps should be installed to support the wire bundle and the clamps fastened to the same structure used to support the fluid line(s) to prevent relative motion.

Figure 9-133. *Positive separation of wire and fluid lines and wire clamps.*

Wires, or groups of wires, should enter a junction box, or terminate at a piece of equipment in an upward direction where practicable. Ensure that a trap, or drip loop, is provided to prevent fluids or condensation from running into wire or cable ends that slope downward toward a connector, terminal block, panel, or junction block. A drip loop is an area where the wire(s) are made to travel downward and then up to the connector. *[Figure 9-134]* Fluids and moisture will flow along the wires to the bottom of the loop and be trapped there to drip or evaporate without affecting electrical conductivity in the wire, junction, or connected device.

Figure 9-134. *Drip loop.*

Where wires must be routed downwards to a junction box or electrical unit and a drip loop is not possible, the entrance should be sealed according to manufacturer's specifications to prevent moisture from entering the box/unit. Wires and cables installed in bilges and other locations where fluids collect must be routed as far from the lowest point as possible or otherwise be provided with a moisture-proof covering.

Protection of Wires in Wheel Well Areas

Wires located on landing gear and in the wheel well area can be exposed to many hazardous conditions if not suitably protected. Where wire bundles pass flex points, there must not be any strain on attachments or excessive slack when parts are fully extended or retracted. The wiring and protective tubing must be inspected frequently and replaced at the first sign of wear.

Wires should be routed so that fluids drain away from the connectors. When this is not practicable, connectors must be potted. Wiring which must be routed in wheel wells or other external areas must be given extra protection in the form of harness jacketing and connector strain relief. Conduits or flexible sleeving used to protect wiring must be equipped with drain holes to prevent entrapment of moisture.

The technician should check during inspections that wires and cables are adequately protected in wheel wells and other areas where they may be exposed to damage from impact of rocks, ice, mud, etc. (If rerouting of wires or cables is not practical, protective jacketing may be installed). This type of installation must be held to a minimum.

Clamp Installation

Wires and wire bundles must be supported by clamps or plastic cable straps. *[Figure 9-135]* Clamps and other primary support devices must be constructed of materials that are compatible with their installation and environment, in terms of temperature, fluid resistance, exposure to ultraviolet (UV) light, and wire bundle mechanical loads. They should be spaced at intervals not exceeding 24 inches. Clamps on wire bundles should be selected so that they have a snug fit without pinching wires *[Figures 9-136 through 9-138]*

Figure 9-136. *Safe angle for cable clamps.*

Figure 9-135. *Wire clamps.*

Caution: The use of metal clamps on coaxial RF cables may cause problems, if clamp fit is such that RF cable's original cross section is distorted.

Clamps on wire bundles should not allow the bundle to move through the clamp when a slight axial pull is applied. Clamps on RF cables must fit without crushing and must be snug enough to prevent the cable from moving freely through the clamp, but may allow the cable to slide through the clamp when a light axial pull is applied. The cable or wire bundle may be wrapped with one or more turns of electrical tape when required to achieve this fit. Plastic clamps or cable ties must not be used where their failure could result in interference with movable controls, wire bundle contact with movable equipment, or chafing damage to essential or unprotected wiring. They must not be used on vertical runs where inadvertent slack migration could result in chafing or other damage. Clamps must be installed with their attachment hardware positioned above them, wherever practicable, so that they are unlikely to rotate as the result of wire bundle weight or wire bundle chafing. *[Figure 9-136]*

Figure 9-137. *Typical mounting hardware for MS-21919 cable clamps.*

Figure 9-138. *Installing cable clamp to structure.*

Clamps lined with nonmetallic material should be used to support the wire bundle along the run. Tying may be used between clamps, but should not be considered as a substitute for adequate clamping. Adhesive tapes are subject to age deterioration and, therefore, are not acceptable as a clamping means. *[Figure 9-137]*

The back of the clamp, whenever practical, should be rested against a structural member. *[Figure 9-138]* Stand-offs should be used to maintain clearance between the wires and the structure. Clamps must be installed in such a manner that the electrical wires do not come in contact with other parts of the aircraft when subjected to vibration. Sufficient slack should be left between the last clamp and the electrical equipment to prevent strain at the terminal and to minimize adverse effects on shock-mounted equipment. Where wires or wire bundles pass through bulkheads or other structural members, a grommet or suitable clamp should be provided to prevent abrasion.

When a wire bundle is clamped into position, if there is less than ⅜-inch of clearance between the bulkhead cutout and the wire bundle, a suitable grommet should be installed as indicated in *Figure 9-139*. The grommet may be cut at a 45° angle to facilitate installation, provided it is cemented in place and the slot is located at the top of the cutout.

Wire and Cable Clamp Inspection
Inspect wire and cable clamps for proper tightness. Where cables pass through structure or bulkheads, inspect for proper clamping and grommets. Inspect for sufficient slack between the last clamp and the electronic equipment to prevent strain at the cable terminals and to minimize adverse effects on shock-mounted equipment. Wires and cables are supported by suitable clamps, grommets, or other devices at intervals of not more than 24 inches, except when contained in troughs,

ducts, or conduits. The supporting devices should be of a suitable size and type, with the wires and cables held securely in place without damage to the insulation.

Use metal stand-offs to maintain clearance between wires and structure. Tape or tubing is not acceptable as an alternative to stand-offs for maintaining clearance. Install phenolic blocks, plastic liners, or rubber grommets in holes, bulkheads, floors, or structural members where it is impossible to install off-angle clamps to maintain wiring separation. In such cases, additional protection in the form of plastic or insulating tape may be used.

Properly secure clamp retaining bolts so the movement of wires and cables is restricted to the span between the points of support and not on soldered or mechanical connections at terminal posts or connectors.

Movable Controls Wiring Precautions
Clamping of wires routed near movable flight controls must be attached with steel hardware and must be spaced so that failure of a single attachment point cannot result in interference with controls. The minimum separation between wiring and movable controls must be at least ½ inch when the bundle is displaced by light hand pressure in the direction of the controls.

Conduit
Conduit is manufactured in metallic and nonmetallic materials and in both rigid and flexible forms. Primarily, its purpose is for mechanical protection of cables or wires. Conduit size should be selected for a specific wire bundle application to allow for ease in maintenance, and possible future circuit expansion, by specifying the conduit inner diameter (ID) about 25 percent larger than the maximum diameter of the wire bundle. *[Figure 9-140]*

Figure 9-139. *Clamping at a bulkhead hole.*

Figure 9-140. *Flexible conduit.*

Conduit problems can be avoided by following these guidelines:

- Do not locate conduit where passengers or maintenance personnel might use it as a handhold or footstep.

- Provide drain holes at the lowest point in a conduit run. Drilling burrs should be carefully removed.

- Support conduit to prevent chafing against structure and to avoid stressing its end fittings.

Rigid Conduit

Damaged conduit sections should be repaired to preclude injury to the wires or wire bundle that may consume as much as 80 percent of the tube area. Minimum acceptable tube bend radii for rigid conduit are shown in *Figure 9-141*. Kinked or wrinkled bends in rigid conduits are not recommended and should be replaced. Tubing bends that have been flattened into an ellipse and have a minor diameter of less than 75 percent of the nominal tubing diameter should be replaced, because the tube area has been reduced by at least 10 percent. Tubing that has been formed and cut to final length should be deburred to prevent wire insulation damage. When installing replacement tube sections with fittings at both ends, care should be taken to eliminate mechanical strain.

Nominal tube OD (inches)	Minimum bend radius (inches)
1/8	3/8
3/16	7/16
1/4	9/16
3/8	15/16
1/2	1 1/4
5/8	1 1/2
3/4	1 3/4
1	3
1 1/4	3 3/4
1 1/2	5
1 3/4	7
2	8

Figure 9-141. *Minimum bend radii for rigid conduit.*

Flexible Conduit

Flexible aluminum conduit conforming to specification MIL-C-6136 is available in two types: Type I, bare flexible conduit, and Type II, rubber-covered flexible conduit. Flexible brass conduit conforming to specification MIL-C-7931 is available and normally used instead of flexible aluminum where necessary to minimize radio interference. Also available is a plastic flexible tubing. (Reference MIL-T-8191A.) Flexible conduit may be used where it is impractical to use rigid conduit, such as areas that have motion between conduit ends or where complex bends are necessary.

The use of transparent adhesive tape is recommended when cutting flexible tubing with a hacksaw to minimize fraying of the braid. The tape should be centered over the cutting reference mark with the saw cutting through the tape. After cutting the flexible conduit, the transparent tape should be removed, the frayed braid ends trimmed, burrs removed from inside the conduit, and coupling nut and ferrule installed. Minimum acceptable bending radii for flexible conduit are shown in *Figure 9-142*.

Wire Shielding

In conventional wiring systems, circuits are shielded individually, in pairs, triples, or quads depending on

Nominal ID of conduit (inches)	Minimum bending radius inside (inches)
3/16	2 1/4
1/4	2 3/4
3/8	3 3/4
1/2	3 3/4
5/8	3 3/4
3/4	4 1/4
1	5 3/4
1 1/4	8
1 1/2	8 1/4
1 3/4	9
2	9 3/4
2 1/2	10

Figure 9-142. *Minimum bending radii for flexible aluminum or brass conduit.*

each circuit's shielding requirement called out for in the engineering documentation. A wire is normally shielded when it is anticipated that the circuit can be affected by another circuit in the wire harness. When the wires come close together, they can couple enough interference to cause a detrimental upset to attached circuitry. This effect is often called crosstalk. Wires must come close enough for their fields to interact, and they must be in an operating mode that produces the crosstalk effect. However, the potential for crosstalk is real, and the only way to prevent crosstalk is to shield the wire. *[Figure 9-143]*

Figure 9-143. *Crosstalk.*

Bonding and Grounding

One of the more important factors in the design and maintenance of aircraft electrical systems is proper bonding and grounding. Inadequate bonding or grounding can lead to unreliable operation of systems, EMI, electrostatic discharge damage to sensitive electronics, personnel shock hazard, or damage from lightning strike.

Grounding

Grounding is the process of electrically connecting conductive objects to either a conductive structure or some other conductive return path for the purpose of safely completing either a normal or fault circuit. *[Figure 9-144]* If wires carrying return currents from different types of sources, such as signals of DC and AC generators, are connected to the same ground point or have a common connection in the return paths, an interaction of the currents occurs. Mixing return currents from various sources should be avoided because noise is coupled from one source to another and can be a major problem for digital systems. To minimize the interaction between various return currents, different types of ground should be identified and used. As a minimum, the design should use three ground types: (1) AC returns, (2) DC returns, and (3) all others.

Figure 9-144. *Ground wires.*

For distributed power systems, the power return point for an alternative power source would be separated. For example, in a two-AC generator (one on the right side and the other on the left side) system, if the right AC generator were supplying backup power to equipment located in the left side, (left equipment rack) the backup AC ground return should be labeled "AC Right." The return currents for the left generator should be connected to a ground point labeled "AC Left."

The design of the ground return circuit should be given as much attention as the other leads of a circuit. A requirement for proper ground connections is that they maintain an impedance that is essentially constant. Ground return circuits should have a current rating and voltage drop adequate for satisfactory operation of the connected electrical and electronic equipment. EMI problems that can be caused by a system's power wire can be reduced substantially by locating the associated ground return near the origin of the power

wiring (e.g., circuit breaker panel) and routing the power wire and its ground return in a twisted pair. Special care should be exercised to ensure replacement on ground return leads. The use of numbered insulated wire leads instead of bare grounding jumpers may aid in this respect. In general, equipment items should have an external ground connection, even when internally grounded. Direct connections to a magnesium structure must not be used for ground return because they may create a fire hazard.

Power ground connections for generators, transformer rectifiers, batteries, external power receptacles, and other heavy-current loads must be attached to individual grounding brackets that are attached to aircraft structure with a proper metal-to-metal bonding attachment. This attachment and the surrounding structure must provide adequate conductivity to accommodate normal and fault currents of the system without creating excessive voltage drop or damage to the structure. At least three fasteners, located in a triangular or rectangular pattern, must be used to secure such brackets in order to minimize susceptibility to loosening under vibration. If the structure is fabricated of a material, such as carbon fiber composite (CFC), that has a higher resistivity than aluminum or copper, it is necessary to provide an alternative ground path(s) for power return current. Special attention should be considered for composite aircraft.

Power return or fault current ground connections within flammable vapor areas must be avoided. If they must be made, make sure these connections do not arc, spark, or overheat under all possible current flow or mechanical failure conditions, including induced lightning currents. Criteria for inspection and maintenance to ensure continued airworthiness throughout the expected life of the aircraft should be established. Power return fault currents are normally the highest currents flowing in a structure. These can be the full generator current capacity. If full generator fault current flows through a localized region of the carbon fiber structure, major heating and failure can occur. CFC and other similar low-resistive materials must not be used in power return paths. Additional voltage drops in the return path can cause voltage regulation problems. Likewise, repeated localized material heating by current surges can cause material degradation. Both problems may occur without warning and cause no repeatable failures or anomalies.

The use of common ground connections for more than one circuit or function should be avoided except where it can be shown that related malfunctions that could affect more than one circuit do not result in a hazardous condition. Even when the loss of multiple systems does not, in itself, create a hazard, the effect of such failure can be quite distracting to the crew.

Bonding

Bonding is the electrical connecting of two or more conducting objects not otherwise adequately connected.

The following bonding requirements must be considered:

- Equipment bonding—low-impedance paths to aircraft structure are normally required for electronic equipment to provide radio frequency return circuits and for most electrical equipment to facilitate reduction in EMI. The cases of components that produce electromagnetic energy should be grounded to structure. To ensure proper operation of electronic equipment, it is particularly important to conform the system's installation specification when interconnections, bonding, and grounding are being accomplished.

- Metallic surface bonding—all conducting objects on the exterior of the airframe must be electrically connected to the airframe through mechanical joints, conductive hinges, or bond straps capable of conducting static charges and lightning strikes. Exceptions may be necessary for some objects, such as antenna elements, whose function requires them to be electrically isolated from the airframe. Such items should be provided with an alternative means to conduct static charges and/or lightning currents, as appropriate.

- Static bonds—all isolated conducting parts inside and outside the aircraft, having an area greater than 3 square inches and a linear dimension over 3 inches, that are subjected to appreciable electrostatic charging due to precipitation, fluid, or air in motion, should have a mechanically secure electrical connection to the aircraft structure of sufficient conductivity to dissipate possible static charges. A resistance of less than 1 ohm when clean and dry generally ensures such dissipation on larger objects. Higher resistances are permissible in connecting smaller objects to airframe structure.

Testing of Bonds and Grounds

The resistance of all bond and ground connections should be tested after connections are made before re-finishing. The resistance of each connection should normally not exceed 0.003 ohm. A high quality test instrument, an AN/USM-21A or equivalent, is required to accurately measure the very low resistance values.

Bonding Jumper Installation

Bonding jumpers should be made as short as practicable, and installed in such a manner that the resistance of each connection does not exceed .003 ohm. The jumper should not interfere with the operation of movable aircraft elements, such as surface controls, nor should normal movement of these elements result in damage to the bonding jumper. *[Figure 9-145]*

Figure 9-145. *Bonding jumpers.*

- Bonding connections—to ensure a low-resistance connection, nonconducting finishes, such as paint and anodizing films, should be removed from the attachment surface to be contacted by the bonding terminal. Electrical wiring should not be grounded directly to magnesium parts.

- Corrosion protection—one of the more frequent causes of failures in electrical system bonding and grounding is corrosion. The areas around completed connections should be post-finished quickly with a suitable finish coating.

- Corrosion prevention—electrolytic action may rapidly corrode a bonding connection if suitable precautions are not taken. Aluminum alloy jumpers are recommended for most cases; however, copper jumpers should be used to bond together parts made of stainless steel, cadmium plated steel, copper, brass, or bronze. Where contact between dissimilar metals cannot be avoided, the choice of jumper and hardware should be such that corrosion is minimized; the part likely to corrode should be the jumper or associated hardware.

- Bonding jumper attachment—the use of solder to attach bonding jumpers should be avoided. Tubular members should be bonded by means of clamps to which the jumper is attached. Proper choice of clamp material should minimize the probability of corrosion.

- Ground return connection—when bonding jumpers carry substantial ground return current, the current rating of the jumper should be determined to be adequate, and a negligible voltage drop is produced. *[Figure 9-146]*

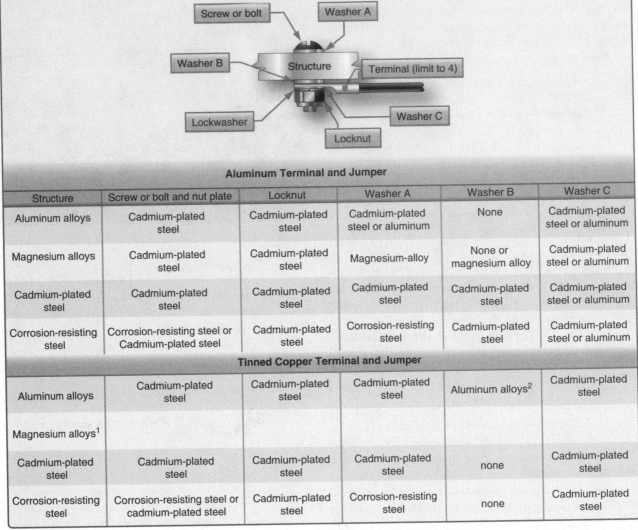

Aluminum Terminal and Jumper

Structure	Screw or bolt and nut plate	Locknut	Washer A	Washer B	Washer C
Aluminum alloys	Cadmium-plated steel	Cadmium-plated steel	Cadmium-plated steel or aluminum	None	Cadmium-plated steel or aluminum
Magnesium alloys	Cadmium-plated steel	Cadmium-plated steel	Magnesium-alloy	None or magnesium alloy	Cadmium-plated steel or aluminum
Cadmium-plated steel	Cadmium-plated steel	Cadmium-plated steel	Cadmium-plated steel	Cadmium-plated steel	Cadmium-plated steel or aluminum
Corrosion-resisting steel	Corrosion-resisting steel or Cadmium-plated steel	Cadmium-plated steel	Corrosion-resisting steel	Cadmium-plated steel	Cadmium-plated steel or aluminum

Tinned Copper Terminal and Jumper

Structure	Screw or bolt and nut plate	Locknut	Washer A	Washer B	Washer C
Aluminum alloys	Cadmium-plated steel	Cadmium-plated steel	Cadmium-plated steel	Aluminum alloys[2]	Cadmium-plated steel
Magnesium alloys[1]					
Cadmium-plated steel	Cadmium-plated steel	Cadmium-plated steel	Cadmium-plated steel	none	Cadmium-plated steel
Corrosion-resisting steel	Corrosion-resisting steel or cadmium-plated steel	Cadmium-plated steel	Corrosion-resisting steel	none	Cadmium-plated steel

[1]Avoid connecting copper to magnesium.
[2]Use washers with a conductive finish treated to prevent corrosion, such as AN960JD10L.

Figure 9-146. *Bolt and nut bonding or grounding to flat surface.*

Lacing and Tying Wire Bundles

Ties, lacing, and straps are used to secure wire groups or bundles to provide ease of maintenance, inspection, and installation. Straps may not be used in areas of SWAMP, such as wheel wells, near wing flaps, or wing folds. They may not be used in high vibration areas where failure of the strap would permit wiring to move against parts that could damage the insulation and foul mechanical linkages or other moving mechanical parts. They also may not be used where they could be exposed to UV light, unless the straps are resistant to such exposure. *[Figure 9-147]*

The single cord-lacing method and tying tape may be used for wire groups of bundles 1 inch in diameter or less. The recommended knot for starting the single cord-lacing method is a clove hitch secured by a double-looped overhand knot.

Figure 9-147. *Wire lacing.*

[Figure 9-148, step A] Use the double cordlacing method on wire bundles 1 inch in diameter or larger. When using the double cord-lacing method, employ a bowline-on-a-bight as the starting knot. *[Figure 9-149, step A]*

Tying

Use wire group or bundle ties where the supports for the wire are more than 12 inches apart. A tie consists of a clove hitch around the wire group or bundle, secured by a square knot. *[Figure 9-150]*

Figure 9-148. *Single cord lacing method.*

Figure 9-149. *Double cord lacing.*

Wrap cord twice over bundle

Clove hitch and square knot

Figure 9-150. *Tying.*

Wire Termination

Stripping Wire

Before wire can be assembled to connectors, terminals, splices, etc., the insulation must be stripped from connecting ends to expose the bare conductor. Copper wire can be stripped in a number of ways depending on the size and insulation.

Aluminum wire must be stripped using extreme care, since individual strands break very easily after being nicked. The following general precautions are recommended when stripping any type of wire:

1. When using any type of wire stripper, hold the wire so that it is perpendicular to cutting blades.

2. Adjust automatic stripping tools carefully; follow the manufacturer's instructions to avoid nicking, cutting, or otherwise damaging strands. This is especially important for aluminum wires and for copper wires smaller than No. 10. Examine stripped wires for damage. Cut off and restrip (if length is sufficient), or reject and replace any wires having more than the allowable number of nicked or broken strands listed in the manufacturer's instructions.

3. Make sure insulation is clean-cut with no frayed or ragged edges. Trim, if necessary.

4. Make sure all insulation is removed from stripped area. Some types of wire are supplied with a transparent layer of insulation between the conductor and the primary insulation. If this is present, remove it.

5. When using hand-plier strippers to remove lengths of insulation longer than ¾ inch, it is easier to accomplish in two or more operations.

6. Retwist copper strands by hand or with pliers, if necessary, to restore natural lay and tightness of strands.

A pair of handheld wire strippers is shown in *Figure 9-151*. This tool is commonly used to strip most types of wire. The

Figure 9-151. *Wire strippers.*

following general procedures describe the steps for stripping wire with a hand stripper.

1. Insert wire into exact center of correct cutting slot for wire size to be stripped. Each slot is marked with wire size.

2. Close handles together as far as they will go.

3. Release handles, allowing wire holder to return to the open position.

4. Remove stripped wire.

Terminals are attached to the ends of electrical wires to facilitate connection of the wires to terminal strips or items of equipment. *[Figure 9-152]* The tensile strength of the wire-to-terminal joint should be at least equivalent to the tensile strength of the wire itself, and its resistance negligible relative to the normal resistance of the wire.

The following should be considered in the selection of wire terminals: current rating, wire size (gauge) and insulation diameter, conductor material compatibility, stud size, insulation material compatibility, application environment, and solder versus solderless.

Figure 9-152. *Ring-tongue terminals.*

Preinsulated crimp-type ring-tongue terminals are preferred. The strength, size, and supporting means of studs and binding posts, as well as the wire size, may be considered when determining the number of terminals to be attached to any one post. In high-temperature applications, the terminal temperature rating must be greater than the ambient temperature plus current related temperature rise. Use of nickel-plated terminals and of uninsulated terminals with high-temperature insulating sleeves should be considered. Terminal blocks should be provided with adequate electrical clearance or insulation strips between mounting hardware and conductive parts.

Terminal Strips

Wires are usually joined at terminal strips. *[Figure 9-153]* A terminal strip fitted with barriers may be used to prevent the terminals on adjacent studs from contacting each other. Studs should be anchored against rotation. When more than four terminals are to be connected together, a small metal bus should be mounted across two or more adjacent studs. In all cases, the current should be carried by the terminal contact

Figure 9-153. *Terminal strip.*

surfaces and not by the stud itself. Defective studs should be replaced with studs of the same size and material since terminal strip studs of the smaller sizes may shear due to overtightening the nut. The replacement stud should be securely mounted in the terminal strip and the terminal securing nut should be tight. Terminal strips should be mounted in such a manner that loose metallic objects cannot fall across the terminals or studs. It is good practice to provide at least one spare stud for future circuit expansion or in case a stud is broken.

Terminal strips that provide connection of radio and electronic systems to the aircraft electrical system should be inspected for loose connections, metallic objects that may have fallen across the terminal strip, dirt and grease accumulation, etc. These conditions can cause arcing, which may result in a fire or system failures.

Terminal Lugs

Wire terminal lugs should be used to connect wiring to terminal block studs or equipment terminal studs. No more than four terminal lugs, or three terminal lugs and a bus bar, should be connected to any one stud. The total number of terminal lugs per stud includes a common bus bar joining adjacent studs. Four terminal lugs plus a common bus bar are not permitted on one stud. Terminal lugs should be selected with a stud hole diameter that matches the diameter of the stud. However, when the terminal lugs attached to a stud vary in diameter, the greatest diameter should be placed on the bottom and the smallest diameter on top. Tightening terminal connections should not deform the terminal lugs or the studs. Terminal lugs should be positioned so that bending of the terminal lug is not required to remove the fastening screw or nut, and movement of the terminal lugs tends to tighten the connection.

Copper Wire Terminals

Solderless crimp-style, copper wire, terminal lugs may be used which conform to MIL-T-7928. Spacers or washers should not be used between the tongues of terminal lugs. *[Figure 9-154]*

Figure 9-154. *Wire terminal.*

Aluminum Wire Terminals

The aluminum terminal lugs should be crimped to aluminum wire only. The tongue of the aluminum terminal lugs, or the total number of tongues of aluminum terminal lugs when stacked, should be sandwiched between two flat washers when terminated on terminal studs. Spacers or washers should not be used between the tongues of terminal lugs. Special attention should be given to aluminum wire and cable installations to guard against conditions that would result in excessive voltage drop and high resistance at junctions that may ultimately lead to failure of the junction. Examples of such conditions are improper installation of terminals and washers, improper torsion (torquing of nuts), and inadequate terminal contact areas.

Pre-Insulated Splices

Pre-insulated terminal lugs and splices must be installed using a high-quality crimping tool. Such tools are provided with positioners for the wire size and are adjusted for each wire size. It is essential that the crimp depth be appropriate for each wire size. If the crimp is too deep, it may break or cut individual strands. If the crimp is not deep enough, it may not be tight enough to retain the wire in the terminal or connector. Crimps that are not tight enough are also susceptible to high resistance due to corrosion buildup between the crimped terminal and the wire. [Figure 9-155]

Figure 9-155. *Terminal splices.*

Crimping Tools

Hand, portable, and stationary power tools are available for crimping terminal lugs. These tools crimp the barrel to the conductor, and simultaneously form the insulation support to the wire insulation. [Figure 9-156]

Emergency Splicing Repairs

Broken wires can be repaired by means of crimped splices, by using terminal lugs from which the tongue has been cut off, or by soldering together and potting broken strands. These repairs are applicable to copper wire. Damaged aluminum wire must not be temporarily spliced. These repairs are for temporary emergency use only and should

Figure 9-156. *Crimping pliers.*

be replaced as soon as possible with permanent repairs. Since some manufacturers prohibit splicing, the applicable manufacturer's instructions should always be consulted.

Junction Boxes

Junction boxes are used for collecting, organizing, and distributing circuits to the appropriate harnesses that are attached to the equipment. [Figure 9-157] Junction boxes are also used to conveniently house miscellaneous components, such as relays and diodes. Junction boxes that are used in high-temperature areas should be made of stainless steel.

Figure 9-157. *Junction boxes.*

Replacement junction boxes should be fabricated using the same material as the original or from a fire-resistant, nonabsorbent material, such as aluminum, or an acceptable plastic material. Where fireproofing is necessary, a stainless steel junction box is recommended. Rigid construction prevents oil-canning of the box sides that could result in internal short circuits. In all cases, drain holes should be provided in the lowest portion of the box. Cases of electrical power equipment must be insulated from metallic structure to avoid ground fault related fires.

The junction box arrangement should permit easy access to any installed items of equipment, terminals, and wires. Where marginal clearances are unavoidable, an insulating material should be inserted between current carrying parts and any grounded surface. It is not good practice to mount equipment on the covers or doors of junction boxes, since inspection for internal clearance is impossible when the door or cover is in the closed position.

Junction boxes should be securely mounted to the aircraft structure in such a manner that the contents are readily accessible for inspection. When possible, the open side should face downward or at an angle so that loose metallic objects, such as washers or nuts, tend to fall out of the junction box rather than wedge between terminals.

Junction box layouts should take into consideration the necessity for adequate wiring space and possible future additions. Electrical wire bundles should be laced or clamped inside the box so that cables do not touch other components, prevent ready access, or obscure markings or labels. Cables at entrance openings should be protected against chafing by using grommets or other suitable means.

AN/MS Connectors

Connectors (plugs and receptacles) facilitate maintenance when frequent disconnection is required. There is a multitude of types of connectors. The connector types that use crimped contacts are generally used on aircraft. Some of the more common types are the round cannon type, the rectangular, and the module blocks. Environmentally resistant connectors should be used in applications subject to fluids, vibration, heat, mechanical shock, and/or corrosive elements.

When HIRF/lightning protection is required, special attention should be given to the terminations of individual or overall shields. The number and complexity of wiring systems have resulted in an increased use of electrical connectors. [Figure 9-158] The proper choice and application of connectors is a significant part of the aircraft wiring system. Connectors must be kept to a minimum, selected, and installed to provide the maximum degree of safety and

Figure 9-158. *Electrical connectors.*

reliability to the aircraft. For the installation of any particular connector assembly, the specification of the manufacturer or the appropriate governing agency must be followed.

Types of Connector

Connectors must be identified by an original identification number derived from MIL Specification (MS) or OEM specification. *Figure 9-159* provides information about MS style connectors.

Environment-resistant connectors are used in applications where they are probably subjected to fluids, vibration, heat, mechanical shock, corrosive elements, etc. Firewall class connectors incorporating these same features should, in addition, be able to prevent the penetration of the fire through the aircraft firewall connector opening and continue to function without failure for a specified period of time when exposed to fire. Hermetic connectors provide a pressure seal for maintaining pressurized areas. When EMI/RFI protection is required, special attention should be given to the termination of individual and overall shields. Backshell adapters designed for shield termination, connectors with conductive finishes, and EMI grounding fingers are available for this purpose.

Rectangular connectors are typically used in applications where a very large number of circuits are accommodated in a single mated pair. *[Figure 9-160]* They are available with a great variety of contacts, which can include a mix of standard, coaxial, and large power types. Coupling is accomplished by various means. Smaller types are secured with screws which hold their flanges together. Larger ones have integral guide pins that ensure correct alignment, or jackscrews that both align and lock the connectors. Rack and panel connectors use integral or rack-mounted pins for alignment and box mounting hardware for couplings.

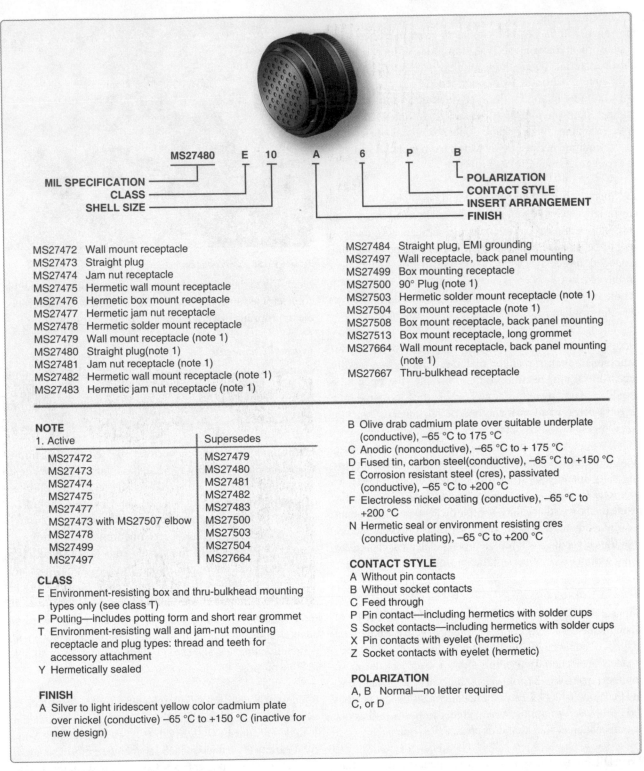

MS27480 E 10 A 6 P B

MIL SPECIFICATION
CLASS
SHELL SIZE

POLARIZATION
CONTACT STYLE
INSERT ARRANGEMENT
FINISH

MS27472 Wall mount receptacle
MS27473 Straight plug
MS27474 Jam nut receptacle
MS27475 Hermetic wall mount receptacle
MS27476 Hermetic box mount receptacle
MS27477 Hermetic jam nut receptacle
MS27478 Hermetic solder mount receptacle
MS27479 Wall mount receptacle (note 1)
MS27480 Straight plug(note 1)
MS27481 Jam nut receptacle (note 1)
MS27482 Hermetic wall mount receptacle (note 1)
MS27483 Hermetic jam nut receptacle (note 1)

MS27484 Straight plug, EMI grounding
MS27497 Wall receptacle, back panel mounting
MS27499 Box mounting receptacle
MS27500 90° Plug (note 1)
MS27503 Hermetic solder mount receptacle (note 1)
MS27504 Box mount receptacle (note 1)
MS27508 Box mount receptacle, back panel mounting
MS27513 Box mount receptacle, long grommet
MS27664 Wall mount receptacle, back panel mounting
            (note 1)
MS27667 Thru-bulkhead receptacle

NOTE

1. Active	Supersedes
MS27472	MS27479
MS27473	MS27480
MS27474	MS27481
MS27475	MS27482
MS27477	MS27483
MS27473 with MS27507 elbow	MS27500
MS27478	MS27503
MS27499	MS27504
MS27497	MS27664

CLASS

E Environment-resisting box and thru-bulkhead mounting types only (see class T)
P Potting—includes potting form and short rear grommet
T Environment-resisting wall and jam-nut mounting receptacle and plug types: thread and teeth for accessory attachment
Y Hermetically sealed

FINISH

A Silver to light iridescent yellow color cadmium plate over nickel (conductive) –65 °C to +150 °C (inactive for new design)

B Olive drab cadmium plate over suitable underplate (conductive), –65 °C to 175 °C
C Anodic (nonconductive), –65 °C to + 175 °C
D Fused tin, carbon steel(conductive), –65 °C to +150 °C
E Corrosion resistant steel (cres), passivated (conductive), –65 °C to +200 °C
F Electroless nickel coating (conductive), –65 °C to +200 °C
N Hermetic seal or environment resisting cres (conductive plating), –65 °C to +200 °C

CONTACT STYLE

A Without pin contacts
B Without socket contacts
C Feed through
P Pin contact—including hermetics with solder cups
S Socket contacts—including hermetics with solder cups
X Pin contacts with eyelet (hermetic)
Z Socket contacts with eyelet (hermetic)

POLARIZATION

A, B Normal—no letter required
C, or D

Figure 9-159. *MS connector information sheet.*

Module blocks are types of junctions that accept crimped contacts similar to those on connectors. Some use internal busing to provide a variety of circuit arrangements. They are useful where a number of wires are connected for power or signal distribution. When used as grounding modules, they save and reduce hardware installation on the aircraft.

Standardized modules are available with wire end grommet seals for environmental applications and are track mounted. Function module blocks are used to provide an easily wired package for environment-resistant mounting of small resistors, diodes, filters, and suppression networks. In-line

Figure 9-160. *Rectangular connectors.*

terminal junctions are sometimes used in lieu of a connector when only a few wires are terminated and when the ability to disconnect the wires is desired. The in-line terminal junction is environment resistant. The terminal junction splice is small and may be tied to the surface of a wire bundle when approved by the OEM.

Voltage and Current Rating

Selected connectors must be rated for continuous operation under the maximum combination of ambient temperature and circuit current load. Hermetic connectors and connectors used in circuit applications involving high-inrush currents should be derated. It is good engineering practice to conduct preliminary testing in any situation where the connector is to operate with most or all of its contacts at maximum rated current load. When wiring is operating with a high conductor temperature near its rated temperature, connector contact sizes should be suitably rated for the circuit load. This may require an increase in wire size. Voltage derating is required when connectors are used at high altitude in nonpressurized areas.

Spare Contacts for Future Wiring

To accommodate future wiring additions, spare contacts are normally provided. Locating the unwired contacts along the outer part of the connector facilitates future access. A good practice is to provide two spares on connectors with 25 or fewer contacts; 4 spares on connectors with 26 to 100 contacts; and 6 spares on connectors with more than 100 contacts. Spare contacts are not normally provided on receptacles of components that are unlikely to have added wiring. Connectors must have all available contact cavities filled with wired or unwired contacts. Unwired contacts should be provided with a plastic grommet sealing plug.

Wire Installation Into the Connector

Wires that perform the same function in redundant systems must be routed through separate connectors. On systems critical to flight safety, system operation wiring should be routed through separate connectors from the wiring used for system failure warning. It is also good practice to route a system's indication wiring in separate connectors from its failure warning circuits to the extent practicable. These steps can reduce an aircraft's susceptibility to incidents that might result from connector failures.

Adjacent Locations

Mating of adjacent connectors should not be possible. In order to ensure this, adjacent connector pairs must be different in shell size, coupling means, insert arrangement, or keying arrangement. When such means are impractical, wires should be routed and clamped so that incorrectly mated pairs cannot reach each other. Reliance on markings or color stripes is not recommended as they are likely to deteriorate with age. *[Figure 9-161]*

Figure 9-161. *Connector arrangement to avoid wrong connection.*

Sealing

Connectors must be of a type that excludes moisture entry through the use of peripheral and interfacial seal that are compressed when the connector is mated. Moisture entry through the rear of the connector must be avoided by correctly matching the wire's outside diameter with the connector's rear grommet sealing range. It is recommended that no more than one wire be terminated in any crimp style contact. The use of heat-shrinkable tubing to build up the wire diameter, or the application of potting to the wire entry area as additional means of providing a rear compatibility with the rear grommet is recommended. These extra means have inherent penalties and should be considered only where other means cannot be used. Unwired spare contacts should have a correctly sized plastic plug installed.

Drainage

Connectors must be installed in a manner that ensures moisture and fluids drain out of and not into the connector when unmated. Wiring must be routed so that moisture accumulated on the bundle drains away from connectors. When connectors must be mounted in a vertical position, as through a shelf or floor, the connectors must be potted or environmentally sealed. In this situation, it is better to have the receptacle faced downward so that it is less susceptible to collecting moisture when unmated.

Wire Support

A rear accessory back shell must be used on connectors that are not enclosed. Connectors with very small size wiring, or subject to frequent maintenance activity, or located in high-vibration areas must be provided with a strain-relief-type back shell. The wire bundle should be protected from mechanical damage with suitable cushion material where it is secured by the clamp. Connectors that are potted or have molded rear adapters do not normally use a separate strain relief accessory. Strain relief clamps should not impart tension on wires between the clamp and contact. *[Figure 9-162]*

Figure 9-162. *Backshells with strain relief.*

Sufficient wire length must be provided at connectors to ensure a proper drip loop and that there is no strain on termination after a complete replacement of the connector and its contacts.

Coaxial Cable

All wiring needs to be protected from damage. However, coaxial and triaxial cables are particularly vulnerable to certain types of damage. Personnel should exercise care while handling or working around coaxial. *[Figure 9-163]* Coaxial

Figure 9-163. *Coaxial cables.*

damage can occur when clamped too tightly, or when they are bent sharply (normally at or near connectors). Damage can also be incurred during unrelated maintenance actions around the coaxial cable. Coaxial cable can be severely damaged on the inside without any evidence of damage on the outside. Coaxial cables with solid center conductors should not be used. Stranded center coaxial cables can be used as a direct replacement for solid center coaxial. *[Figure 9-164]* Coaxial cable precautions include:

- Never kink coaxial cable.

- Never drop anything on coaxial cable.

- Never step on coaxial cable.

- Never bend coaxial cable sharply.

- Never loop coaxial cable tighter than the allowable bend radius.

- Never pull on coaxial cable except in a straight line.

- Never use coaxial cable for a handle, lean on it, or hang things on it (or any other wire).

Wire Inspection

Aircraft service imposes severe environmental condition on electrical wire. To ensure satisfactory service, inspect wire annually for abrasions, defective insulation, condition of terminations, and potential corrosion. Grounding connections for power, distribution equipment, and electromagnetic shielding must be given particular attention to ensure that electrical bonding resistance has not been significantly increased by the loosening of connections or corrosion.

Electrical System Components

Switches

Switches are devices that open and close circuits. They consist of one or more pair of contacts. The current in the circuit flows when the contacts are closed. Switches with

Figure 9-164. *Coaxial cable connectors.*

momentary contacts actuate the circuit temporarily, and they return to the normal position with an internal spring when the switch is released. Switches with continuous contacts remain in position when activated. Hazardous errors in switch operation can be avoided by logical and consistent installation. Two-position on/off switches should be mounted so that the on position is reached by an upward or forward movement of the toggle. When the switch controls movable aircraft elements, such as landing gear or flaps, the toggle should move in the same direction as the desired motion. Inadvertent operation of a switch can be prevented by mounting a suitable guard over the switch. *[Figure 9-165]*

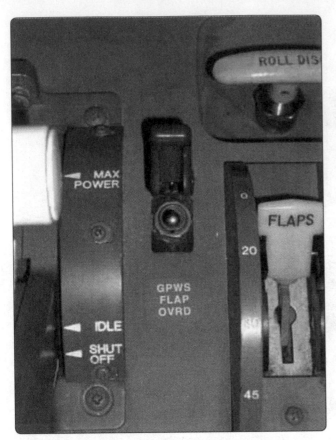

Figure 9-165. *Switch guard.*

A specifically designed switch should be used in all circuits where a switch malfunction would be hazardous. Such switches are of rugged construction and have sufficient contact capacity to break, make, and carry continuously the connected load current. Snap action design is generally preferred to obtain rapid opening and closing of contacts regardless of the speed of the operating toggle or plunger, thereby minimizing contact arcing. The nominal current rating of the conventional aircraft switch is usually stamped on the switch housing. This rating represents the continuous current rating with the contacts closed. Switches should be derated from their nominal current rating for the following types of circuits:

1. High rush-in circuits—contain incandescent lamps that can draw an initial current 15 times greater than the continuous current. Contact burning or welding may occur when the switch is closed.

2. Inductive circuits—magnetic energy stored in solenoid coils or relays is released and appears as an arc when the control switch is opened.

3. Motors—DC motors draw several times their rated current during starting, and magnetic energy stored in their armature and field coils is released when the control switch is opened.

Figure 9-166 is used for selecting the proper nominal switch rating when the continuous load current is known. This selection is essentially a derating to obtain reasonable switch efficiency and service life.

Nominal system voltage (DC)	Type of load	Derating factor
28V	Lamp	8
28V	Inductive	4
28V	Resistive	2
28V	Motor	3
12V	Lamp	5
12V	Inductive	2
12V	Resistive	1
12V	Motor	2

Figure 9-166. *Derating table for switches.*

Type of Switches

Single-pole single-throw (SPST)—opens and closes a single circuit. Pole indicates the number of separate circuits that can be activated, and throw indicates the number of current paths.

Double-pole single-throw (DPST)—turn two circuits on and off with one lever.

Single-pole double-throw (SPDT)—route circuit current to either of two paths. The switch is ON in both positions. For example, switch turns on red lamp in one position and turns on green lamp in the other position.

Double-pole double-throw (DPDT)—activates two separate circuits at the same time.

Double-throw switches—have either two or three positions.

Two position switch—pole always connected to one of the two throws. Three-position switches have a center OFF position that disconnects the pole from both throws.

Spring loaded switches—available in two types: 1) normally open (NO) and 2) normally closed (NC). The contacts of the NO switch are disconnected in the normal position and become closed when the switch is activated. The switch returns to the normal position when the applied force to the switch is released. The contacts of the NC switch are connected in the normal position and become open when the switch is activated. The switch returns to the normal position when the applied force to the switch is released.

Toggle and Rocker Switches

Toggle and rocker switches control most of aircraft's electrical components. *[Figure 9-167]* Aircraft that are

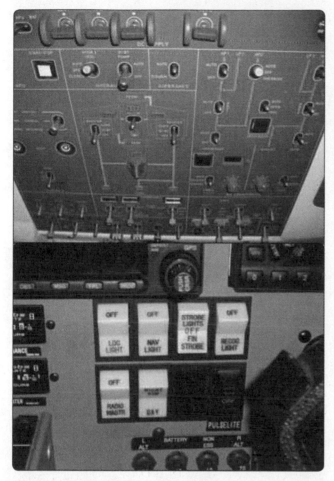

Figure 9-167. *Toggle and rocker switches.*

outfitted with a glass cockpit often use push buttons to control electrical components.

Rotary Switches

Rotary switches are activated by twisting a knob or shaft and are commonly found on radio control panels. Rotary switches are utilized for controlling more than two circuits.

Precision (Micro) Switches

Micro switches require very little pressure to activate. These types of switches are spring loaded, once the pressure is removed, the contacts return to the normal position. These types of switches are typically single pole double throw (SPDT) or double pole double throw (DPDT) and have three contacts: normally open, normally closed, and common. Micro switches are used to detect position or to limit travel of moving parts, such as landing gear, flaps, spoilers, etc. *[Figure 9-168]*

Relays and Solenoids (Electromagnetic Switches)

Relays are used to control the flow of large currents using a small current. A low-power DC circuit is used to activate the relay and control the flow of large AC currents. They are used

Figure 9-168. *A micro switch.*

to switch motors and other electrical equipment on and off and to protect them from overheating. A solenoid is a special type of relay that has a moving core. The electromagnet core in a relay is fixed. Solenoids are mostly used as mechanical actuators but can also be used for switching large currents. Relays are only used to switch currents.

Solenoids

Solenoids are used as switching devices where a weight reduction can be achieved or electrical controls can be simplified. The foregoing discussion of switch ratings is generally applicable to solenoid contact ratings. Solenoids have a movable core/armature that is usually made of steel or iron, and the coil is wrapped around the armature. The solenoid has an electromagnetic tube and the armature moves in and out of the tube. *[Figure 9-169]*

Figure 9-169. *Solenoid.*

Relays

The two main types of relays are electromechanical and solid state. Electromechanical relays have a fixed core and a moving plate with contacts on it, while solid-state relays work similar to transistors and have no moving parts. Current flowing through the coil of an electromechanical relay creates a magnetic field that attracts a lever and changes the switch contacts. The coil current can be on or off so relays have two switch positions, and they are double throw switches.

Residual magnetism is a common problem and the contacts may stay closed or are opened by a slight amount of residual magnetism. A relay is an electrically operated switch and is therefore subject to dropout under low system voltage conditions. Relays allow one circuit to switch a second circuit that can be completely separate from the first. For example, a low voltage DC battery circuit can use a relay to switch a 110-volt three-phase AC circuit. There is no electrical connection inside the relay between the two circuits; the link is magnetic and mechanical. *[Figure 9-170]*

Figure 9-170. *Relay.*

Current Limiting Devices

Conductors should be protected with circuit breakers or fuses located as close as possible to the electrical power source bus. Normally, the manufacturer of the electrical equipment specifies the fuse or circuit breaker to be used when installing equipment. The circuit breaker or fuse should open the circuit before the conductor emits smoke. To accomplish this, the time current characteristic of the protection device must fall below that of the associated conductor. Circuit protector characteristics should be matched to obtain the maximum utilization of the connected equipment. *Figure 9-171* shows a chart used in selecting the circuit breaker and fuse protection for copper conductors. This limited chart is applicable to a specific set of ambient temperatures and wire bundle sizes and is presented as typical only. It is important to consult such guides before selecting a conductor for a specific purpose. For example, a wire run individually in the open air may be protected by the circuit breaker of the next higher rating to that shown on the chart.

Fuses

A fuse is placed in series with the voltage source and all current must flow through it. *[Figure 9-172]* The fuse consists of a strip of metal that is enclosed in a glass or plastic housing. The metal strip has a low melting point and is usually made of lead, tin, or copper. When the current exceeds the capacity

Wire AN gauge copper	Circuit breaker amperage	Fuse amperage
22	5	5
20	7.5	5
18	10	10
16	15	10
14	20	15
12	30	20
10	40	30
8	50	50
6	80	70
4	100	70
2	125	100
1		150
0		150

Figure 9-171. *Wired and circuit protection chart.*

Figure 9-172. *A fuse.*

of the fuse the metal strip heats up and breaks. As a result of this, the flow of current in the circuit stops.

There are two basic types of fuses: fast acting and slow blow. The fast-acting type opens very quickly when their particular current rating is exceeded. This is important for electric devices that can quickly be destroyed when too much current flows through them for even a very small amount of time. Slow blow fuses have a coiled construction inside. They are designed to open only on a continued overload, such as a short circuit.

Circuit Breakers

A circuit breaker is an automatically operated electrical switch designed to protect an electrical circuit from damage caused by an overload or short circuit. Its basic function is to detect a fault condition and immediately discontinue electrical flow. Unlike a fuse that operates once and then has to be replaced, a circuit breaker can be reset to resume normal operation. All resettable circuit breakers should open the circuit in which they are installed regardless of the position of the operating control when an overload or circuit fault exists. Such circuit breakers are referred to as trip-free. Automatic reset circuit breakers automatically reset themselves. They should not be used as circuit protection devices in aircraft. When a circuit breaker trips, the electrical circuit should be checked and the fault removed before the circuit breaker is reset. Sometimes circuit breakers trip for no apparent reason, and the circuit breaker can be reset one time. If the circuit breaker trips again, there exists a circuit fault and the technician must troubleshoot the circuit before resetting the circuit breaker. [Figure 9-173]

Figure 9-173. *Circuit breaker panel.*

Some new aircraft designs use a digital circuit protection architecture. This system monitors the amperage through a particular circuit. When the maximum amperage for that circuit is reached, the power is rerouted away from the circuit. This system reduces the use of mechanical circuit breakers. The advantages are weight savings and the reduction of mechanical parts.

Aircraft Lighting Systems

Aircraft lighting systems provide illumination for both exterior and interior use. Lights on the exterior provide illumination for such operations as landing at night, inspection of icing conditions, and safety from midair collision. Interior lighting provides illumination for instruments, cockpits, cabins, and other sections occupied by crewmembers and passengers. Certain special lights, such as indicator and warning lights, indicate the operation status of equipment.

Exterior Lights

Position, anticollision, landing, and taxi lights are common examples of aircraft exterior lights. Some lights are required for night operations. Other types of exterior lights, such as wing inspection lights, are of great benefit for specialized flying operations.

Position Lights

Aircraft operating at night must be equipped with position lights that meet the minimum requirements specified by Title 14 of the Code of Federal Regulations. A set of position lights consist of one red, one green, and one white light. [Figures 9-174 and 9-175]

Figure 9-174. *A left wing tip position light (red) and a white strobe light.*

Figure 9-175. *A right wing tip position light, also known as a navigation light.*

On some types of installations, a switch in the cockpit provides for steady or flashing operation of the position lights. On many aircraft, each light unit contains a single lamp mounted on the surface of the aircraft. Other types of position light units contain two lamps and are often streamlined into the surface of the aircraft structure. The green light unit is always mounted at the extreme tip of the right wing. The red unit is mounted in a similar position on the left wing. The white unit is usually located on the vertical stabilizer in a position where it is clearly visible through a wide angle from the rear of the aircraft. *Figure 9-176* illustrates a schematic diagram of a position light circuit. Position lights are also known as navigation lights.

There are, of course, many variations in the position light circuits used on different aircraft. All circuits are protected by fuses or circuit breakers, and many circuits include flashing and dimming equipment. Small aircraft are usually equipped with a simplified control switch and circuitry. In some cases, one control knob or switch is used to turn on several sets of lights; for example, one type utilizes a control knob, the first movement of which turns on the position lights and the instrument panel lights. Further rotation of the control knob increases the intensity of only the panel lights. A flasher unit is seldom included in the position light circuitry of very light aircraft but is used in small twin-engine aircraft. Traditional position lights use incandescent light bulbs. LED lights have been introduced on modern aircraft because of their good visibility, high reliability, and low power consumption.

Anticollision Lights

An anticollision light system may consist of one or more lights. They are rotating beam lights that are usually installed on top of the fuselage or tail in such a location that the light does not affect the vision of the crewmember or detract from the visibility of the position lights. Large transport type aircraft use an anticollision light on top and one on the bottom

of the aircraft. *Figure 9-177* shows a typical anticollision light installation in a vertical stabilizer.

Figure 9-177. *Anticollision lights.*

Figure 9-176. *Navigation light system schematic.*

9-102

An anticollision light unit usually consists of one or two rotating lights operated by an electric motor. The light may be fixed but mounted under rotating mirrors inside a protruding red glass housing. The mirrors rotate in an arc, and the resulting flash rate is between 40 and 100 cycles per minute. Newer aircraft designs use a LED type of anticollision light. The anticollision light is a safety light to warn other aircraft, especially in congested areas.

A white strobe light is a second type of anti-collision light that is also common. Usually mounted at the wing tips and, possibly, at empennage extremities, strobe lights produce an extremely bright intermittent flash of white light that is highly visible. The light is produced by a high voltage discharge of a capacitor. A dedicated power pack houses the capacitor and supplies voltage to a sealed xenon-filled tube. The xenon ionizes with a flash when the voltage is applied. A strobe light is shown in *Figure 9-174*.

Landing and Taxi Lights

Landing lights are installed in aircraft to illuminate runways during night landings. These lights are very powerful and are directed by a parabolic reflector at an angle providing a maximum range of illumination. Landing lights of smaller aircraft are usually located midway in the leading edge of each wing or streamlined into the aircraft surface. Landing lights for larger transport category aircraft are usually located in the leading edge of the wing close to the fuselage. Each light may be controlled by a relay, or it may be connected directly into the electric circuit. On some aircraft, the landing light is mounted in the same area with a taxi light. *[Figure 9-178]* A sealed beam, halogen, or high intensity xenon discharge lamp is used.

Taxi lights are designed to provide illumination on the ground while taxiing or towing the aircraft to or from a runway, taxi strip, or in the hangar area. *[Figure 9-179]* Taxi lights are not designed to provide the degree of illumination necessary for landing lights. On aircraft with tricycle landing gear, either single or multiple taxi lights are often mounted on the non-steerable part of the nose landing gear. They are positioned at an oblique angle to the center line of the aircraft to provide illumination directly in front of the aircraft and also some illumination to the right and left of the aircraft's path. On some aircraft, the dual taxi lights are supplemented by wingtip clearance lights controlled by the same circuitry. Taxi lights are also mounted in the recessed areas of the wing leading edge, often in the same area with a fixed landing light.

Figure 9-179. *Taxi lights.*

Figure 9-178. *Landing lights.*

Many small aircraft are not equipped with any type of taxi light, but rely on the intermittent use of a landing light to illuminate taxiing operations. Still other aircraft utilize a dimming resistor in the landing light circuit to provide reduced illumination for taxiing. A typical circuit for taxi lights is shown in *Figure 9-180*.

Some large aircraft are equipped with alternate taxi lights located on the lower surface of the aircraft, aft of the nose radome. These lights, operated by a separate switch from the main taxi lights, illuminate the area immediately in front of and below the aircraft nose.

Wing Inspection Lights

Some aircraft are equipped with wing inspection lights to illuminate the leading edge of the wings to permit observation of icing and general condition of these areas in flight. These lights permit visual detection of ice formation on wing leading edges while flying at night. They are usually controlled through a relay by an on/off toggle switch in the cockpit. Some wing inspection light systems may include or be supplemented by additional lights, sometimes called nacelle lights, that illuminate adjacent areas, such a cowl flaps or the landing gear. These are normally the same type of lights and can be controlled by the same circuits.

Interior Lights

Aircraft are equipped with interior lights to illuminate the cabin. *[Figure 9-181]* Often white and red light settings are provided. Commercial aircraft have a lighting systems that illuminates the main cabin, an independent lighting system so that passengers can read when the cabin lights are off, and an emergency lighting system on the floor of the aircraft to aid passengers of the aircraft during an emergency.

Figure 9-181. *Interior cockpit and cabin light system.*

Figure 9-180. *Taxi light circuit.*

Maintenance and Inspection of Lighting Systems

Inspection of an aircraft's lighting system normally includes checking the condition and security of all visible wiring, connections, terminals, fuses, and switches. A continuity light or meter can be used in making these checks, since the cause of many troubles can often be located by systematically testing each circuit for continuity.

Glossary

Aborted takeoff. A takeoff that is terminated prematurely when it is determined that some condition exists that makes takeoff or further flight dangerous.

Absolute pressure. Pressure measured from zero pressure or a vacuum.

Absolute pressure regulator. A valve used in a pneumatic system at the pump inlet to regulate the compressor inlet air pressure to prevent excessive speed variation and/or over-speeding of the compressor.

Absolute zero. The point at which all molecular motion ceases. Absolute zero is –460 °F and –273 °C.

Accumulator. A hydraulic component that consists of two compartments separated by a movable component, such as a piston, diaphragm, or bladder. One compartment is filled with compressed air or nitrogen, and the other is filled with hydraulic fluid and is connected into the system pressure manifold. An accumulator allows an incompressible fluid to be stored under pressure by the force produced by a compressible fluid. Its primary purposes are to act as a shock absorber in the system, and to provide a source of additional hydraulic power when heavy demands are placed on the system.

Actuator. A fluid power device that changes fluid pressure into mechanical motion.

ADC. Air data computer.

ADF. Automatic direction finder

ADI. Attitude director indicator.

Advancing blade. The blade on a helicopter rotor whose tip is moving in the same direction the helicopter is moving. Adverse yaw. A condition of flight at the beginning of a turn in which the nose of an airplane momentarily yaws in the opposite direction from the direction in which the turn is to be made.

Aerodynamic drag. The total resistance to the movement of an object through the air. Aerodynamic drag is composed of both induced drag and parasite drag. See induced drag and parasite drag.

Aerodynamic lift. The force produced by air moving over a specially shaped surface called an airfoil. Aerodynamic lift acts in a direction perpendicular to the direction the air is moving.

Aeroelastic tailoring. The design of an aerodynamic surface whose strength and stiffness are matched to the aerodynamic loads that will be imposed upon it.

Aeronautical Radio Incorporated (ARINC). A corporation whose principal stockholders are the airlines. Its function is to operate certain communication links between airliners in flight and the airline ground facilities. ARINC also sets standards for communication equipment used by the airlines.

Aging. A change in the characteristics of a material with time. Certain aluminum alloys do not have their full strength when they are first removed from the quench bath after they have been heat-treated, but they gain this strength after a few days by the natural process of aging.

Agonic line. A line drawn on an aeronautical chart along which there is no angular difference between the magnetic and geographic north poles.

Air carrier. An organization or person involved in the business of transporting people or cargo by air for compensation or hire.

Air-cycle cooling system. A system for cooling the air in the cabin of a turbojet-powered aircraft. Compressor bleed air passes through two heat exchangers where it gives up some of its heat; then, it drives an expansion turbine where it loses still more of its heat energy as the turbine drives a compressor. When the air leaves the turbine, it expands and its pressure and temperature are both low.

Aircraft communication addressing and reporting system (ACARS). A two-way communication link between an airliner in flight and the airline's main ground facilities. Data is collected in the aircraft by digital sensors and is transmitted to the ground facilities. Replies from the ground may be printed out so the appropriate flight crew member can have a hard copy of the response.

Airfoil. Any surface designed to obtain a useful reaction, or lift, from air passing over it.

Airspeed indicator. A flight instrument that measures the pressure differential between the pitot, or ram, air pressure, and the static pressure of the air surrounding the aircraft. This differential pressure is shown in units of miles per hour, knots, or kilometers per hour.

Airworthiness Alert. A notice sent by the FAA to certain interested maintenance personnel identifying problems with aircraft that have been gathered from Malfunction and Defect Reports. These problems are being studied at the time the Airworthiness Alert is issued but have not been fully evaluated by the time the material went to press.

Airworthiness Directive (AD note). A notice sent out by the FAA to the registered owner of an aircraft notifying him or her of an unsafe condition that has been found on the aircraft. Compliance with AD notes is mandatory.

Alclad. A registered trade name for clad aluminum alloy.

Alodine. The registered trade name for a popular conversion coating chemical used to produce a hard, airtight, oxide film on aluminum alloy for corrosion protection.

Alphanumeric symbols. Symbols made up of all of the letters in our alphabet, numerals, punctuation marks, and certain other special symbols.

Alternator. An electrical generator that produces alternating current. The popular DC alternator used on light aircraft produces three-phase AC in its stator windings. This AC is changed into DC by a six-diode, solid-state rectifier before it leaves the alternator.

Altimeter setting. The barometric pressure at a given location corrected to mean (average) sea level.

Altitude engine. A reciprocating engine whose rated sea-level takeoff power can be produced to an established higher altitude.

Alumel. An alloy of nickel, aluminum, manganese, and silicon that is the negative element in a thermocouple used to measure exhaust gas temperature.

Ambient pressure. The pressure of the air surrounding a person or an object.

Ambient temperature. The temperature of the air surrounding a person or an object.

American wire gauge. The system of measurement of wire size used in aircraft electrical systems.

Amphibian. An airplane with landing gear that allows it to operate from both water and land surfaces.

Amplifier. An electronic circuit in which a small change in voltage or current controls a much larger change in voltage or current.

Analog electronics. Electronics in which values change in a linear fashion. Output values vary in direct relationship to changes of input values.

Analog-type indicator. An electrical meter that indicates values by the amount a pointer moves across a graduated numerical scale.

Aneroid. The sensitive component in an altimeter or barometer that measures the absolute pressure of the air. The aneroid is a sealed, flat capsule made of thin corrugated disks of metal soldered together and evacuated by pumping all of the air out of it. Evacuating the aneroid allows it to expand or collapse as the air pressure on the outside changes.

Angle of attack. The acute angle formed between the chord line of an airfoil and the direction of the air that strikes the airfoil.

Angle of attack indicator. An instrument that measures the angle between the local airflow around the direction detector and the fuselage reference plane.

Angle of incidence. The acute angle formed between the chord line of an airfoil and the longitudinal axis of the aircraft on which it is mounted.

Annual rings. The rings that appear in the end of a log cut from a tree. The number of annual rings per inch gives an indication of the strength of the wood. The more rings there are and the closer they are together, the stronger the wood. The pattern of alternating light and dark rings is caused by the seasonal variations in the growth rate of the tree. A tree grows quickly in the spring and produces the light-colored, less dense rings. The slower growth during the summer, or latter part of the growing season, produces the dark-colored, denser rings.

Annunciator panel. A panel of warning lights in plain sight of the pilot. These lights are identified by the name of the system they represent and are usually covered with colored lenses to show the meaning of the condition they announce.

Anodizing. The electrolytic process in which a hard, airtight, oxide film is deposited on aluminum alloy for corrosion protection.

Antenna. A special device used with electronic communication and navigation systems to radiate and receive electromagnetic energy.

Anti-icer system. A system that prevents the formation of ice on an aircraft structure.

Anti-icing additive. A chemical added to the turbine-engine fuel used in some aircraft. This additive mixes with water that condenses from the fuel and lowers its freezing temperature so it will not freeze and block the fuel filters. It also acts as a biocidal agent and prevents the formation of microbial contamination in the tanks.

Antidrag wire. A structural wire inside a Pratt truss airplane wing between the spars. Antidrag wires run from the rear spar inboard, to the front spar at the next bay outboard. Antidrag wires oppose the forces that try to pull the wing forward.

Antiservo tab. A tab installed on the trailing edge of a stabilator to make it less sensitive. The tab automatically moves in the same direction as the stabilator to produce an aerodynamic force that tries to bring the surface back to a streamline position. This tab is also called an antibalance tab.

Antiskid brake system. An electrohydraulic system in an airplane's power brake system that senses the deceleration rate of every main landing gear wheel. If any wheel decelerates too rapidly, indicating an impending skid, pressure to that bake is released and the wheel stops decelerating. Pressure is then reapplied at a slightly lower value.

Antitear strip. Strips of aircraft fabric laid under the reinforcing tape before the fabric is stitched to an aircraft wing.

Arbor press. A press with either a mechanically or hydraulically operated ram used in a maintenance shop for a variety of pressing functions.

Arcing. Sparking between a commutator and brush or between switch contacts that is caused by induced current when a circuit is broken.

Area. The number of square units in a surface.

Aspect ratio. The ratio of the length, or span, of an airplane wing to its width, or chord. For a nonrectangular wing, the aspect ratio is found by dividing the square of the span of the wing by its area. Aspect Ratio = span2 ÷ area.

Asymmetrical airfoil. An airfoil section that is not the same on both sides of the chord line.

Asymmetrical lift. A condition of uneven lift produced by the rotor when a helicopter is in forward flight. Asymmetrical lift is caused by the difference between the airspeed of the advancing blade and that of the retreating blade.

Attenuate. To weaken, or lessen the intensity of, an activity.

Attitude indicator. A gyroscopic flight instrument that gives the pilot an indication of the attitude of the aircraft relative to its pitch and roll axes. The attitude indicator in an autopilot is in the sensing system that detects deviation from a level-flight attitude.

Augmenter tube. A long, stainless steel tube around the discharge of the exhaust pipes of a reciprocating engine. Exhaust gases flow through the augmenter tube and produce a low pressure that pulls additional cooling air through the engine compartment. Heat may be taken from the augmenter tubes and directed through the leading edges of the wings for thermal anti-icing.

Autoclave. A pressure vessel inside of which air can be heated to a high temperature and pressure raised to a high value. Autoclaves are used in the composite manufacturing industry to apply heat and pressure for curing resins.

Autogiro. A heavier-than-air rotor-wing aircraft sustained in the air by rotors turned by aerodynamic forces rather than by engine power. When the name Autogiro is spelled with a capital A, it refers to a specific series of machines built by Juan de la Cierva or his successors.

Autoignition system. A system on a turbine engine that automatically energizes the igniters to provide a relight if the engine should flame out.

Automatic adjuster. A subsystem in an aircraft disk brake that compensates for disk or lining wear. Each time the brakes are applied, the automatic adjuster is reset for zero clearance, and when the brakes are released, the clearance between the disks or the disk and lining is returned to a preset value. A malfunctioning automatic adjuster in a multiple-disk brake can cause sluggish and jerky operation.

Automatic flight control system (AFCS). The full system of automatic flight control that includes the autopilot, flight director, horizontal situation indicator, air data sensors, and other avionics inputs.

Automatic pilot (autopilot). An automatic flight control device that controls an aircraft about one or more of its three axes. The primary purpose of an autopilot is to relieve the pilot of the control of the aircraft during long periods of flight. autorotation. Descent of a helicopter without the use of engine power. An aerodynamic force causes the rotors to rotate.

Autosyn system. A synchro system used in remote indicating instruments. The rotors in an Autosyn system are two-pole electromagnets, and the stators are delta-connected, three-phase, distributed-pole windings in the stator housings. The rotors in the transmitters and indicators are connected in parallel and are excited with 26-volt, 400-Hz AC. The rotor in the indicator follows the movement of the rotor in the transmitter.

Auxiliary power unit (APU). A small turbine or reciprocating engine that drives a generator, hydraulic pump, and air pump. The APU is installed in the aircraft and is used to supply electrical power, compressed air, and hydraulic pressure when the main engines are not running.

Aviation snips. Compound-action hand shears used for cutting sheet metal. Aviation snips come in sets of three. One pair cuts to the left, one pair cuts to the right, and the third pair of snips cuts straight.

Aviator's oxygen. Oxygen that has had almost all of the water and water vapor removed from it. Avionics. The branch of technology that deals with the design, production, installation, use, and servicing of electronic equipment mounted in aircraft. Azimuth. A horizontal angular distance, measured clockwise from a fixed reference direction to an object.

Back course. The reciprocal of the localizer course for an ILS (Instrument Landing System). When flying a back-course approach, the aircraft approaches the instrument runway from the end on which the localizer antennas are installed.

Backhand welding. Welding in which the torch is pointed away from the direction the weld is progressing.

Backplate (brake component). A floating plate on which the wheel cylinder and the brake shoes attach on an energizing-type brake.

Backup ring. A flat leather or Teflon ring installed in the groove in which an O-ring or T-seal is placed. The backup ring is on the side of the seal away from the pressure, and it prevents the pressure extruding the seal between the piston and the cylinder wall.

Balance cable. A cable in the aileron system of an airplane that connects to one side of each aileron. When the control wheel is rotated, a cable from the cockpit pulls one aileron down and relaxes the cable going to the other aileron. The balance cable pulls the other aileron up.

Balance panel. A flat panel hinged to the leading edge of some ailerons that produces a force which assists the pilot in holding the ailerons deflected. The balance panel divides a chamber ahead of the aileron in such a way that when the aileron is deflected downward, for example, air flowing over its top surface produces a low pressure that acts on the balance panel and causes it to apply an upward force to the aileron leading edge.

Balance tab. An adjustable tab mounted on the trailing edge of a control surface to produce a force that aids the pilot in moving the surface. The tab is automatically actuated in such a way it moves in the direction opposite to the direction the control surface on which it is mounted moves.

Balanced actuator. A linear hydraulic or pneumatic actuator that has the same area on each side of the piston.

Banana oil. Nitrocellulose dissolved in amyl acetate, so named because it smells like bananas.

Bank (verb). The act of rotating an aircraft about its longitudinal axis.

Barometric scale. A small window in the dial of a sensitive altimeter in which the pilot sets the barometric pressure level from which the altitude shown on the altimeter is measured. This window is sometimes called the "Kollsman" window. base. The electrode of a bipolar transistor between the emitter and the collector. Varying a small flow of electrons moving into or out of the base controls a much larger flow of electron between the emitter and the collector.

Base. The electrode of a bipolar transistor between the emitter and the collector. Varying a small flow of electrons moving into or out of the base controls a much larger flow of electrons between the emitter and the collector.

Bead (tire component). The high-strength carbon-steel wire bundles that give an aircraft tire its strength and stiffness where it mounts on the wheel.

Bead seat area. The flat surface on the inside of the rim of an aircraft wheel on which the bead of the tire seats.

Bearing strength (sheet metal characteristic). The amount of pull needed to cause a piece of sheet metal to tear at the points at which it is held together with rivets. The bearing strength of a material is affected by both its thickness and the diameter of the rivet.

Beehive spring. A hardened-steel, coil-spring retainer used to hold a rivet set in a pneumatic rivet gun. This spring gets its name from its shape. It screws onto the end of the rivet gun and allows the set to move back and forth, but prevents it being driven from the gun.

Bend allowance. The amount of material actually used to make a bend in a piece of sheet metal. Bend allowance depends upon the thickness of the metal and the radius of the bend, and is normally found in a bend allowance chart.

Bend radius. The radius of the inside of a bend.

Bend tangent line. A line made in a sheet metal layout that indicates the point at which the bend starts.

Bernoulli's principle. The basic principle that explains the relation between kinetic energy and potential energy in fluids that are in motion. When the total energy in a column of moving fluid remains constant, any increase in the kinetic energy of the fluid (its velocity) results in a corresponding decrease in its potential energy (its pressure).

Bezel. The rim that holds the glass cover in the case of an aircraft instrument.

Bias-cut surface tape. A fabric tape in which the threads run at an angle of 45° to the length of the tape. Bias-cut tape may be stretched around a compound curve such as a wing tip bow without wrinkling.

Bilge area. A low portion in an aircraft structure in which water and contaminants collect. The area under the cabin floorboards is normally called the bilge.

Bipolar transistor. A solid-state component in which the flow of current between its emitter and collector is controlled by a much smaller flow of current into or out of its base. Bipolar transistors may be of either the NPN or PNP type.

BITE. Built-in test equipment.

Blade track. The condition of a helicopter rotor in which each blade follows the exact same path as the blade ahead of it.

Black box. A term used for any portion of an electrical or electronic system that can be removed as a unit. A black box does not have to be a physical box.

Bladder-type fuel cell. A plastic-impregnated fabric bag supported in a portion of an aircraft structure so that it forms a cell in which fuel is carried.

Bleeder. A material such as glass cloth or mat that is placed over a composite lay-up to absorb the excess resin forced out of the ply fibers when pressure is applied.

Bleeding dope. Dope whose pigments are soluble in the solvents or thinners used in the finishing system. The color will bleed up through the finished coats.

Bleeding of brakes. The maintenance procedure of removing air entrapped in hydraulic fluid in the brakes. Fluid is bled from the brake system until fluid with no bubbles flows out. Blimp. A cigar-shaped, nonrigid lighter-than-air flying machine.

Blush. A defect in a lacquer or dope finish caused by moisture condensing on the surface before the finish dries. If the humidity of the air is high, the evaporation of the solvents cools the air enough to cause the moisture to condense. The water condensed from the air mixes with the lacquer or dope and forms a dull, porous, chalky-looking finish called blush. A blushed finish is neither attractive nor protective.

Bonding. The process of electrically connecting all isolated components to the aircraft structure. Bonding provides a path for return current from electrical components, and a low-impedance path to ground to minimize static electrical charges. Shock-mounted components have bonding braids connected across the shock mounts.

Boost pump. An electrically driven centrifugal pump mounted in the bottom of the fuel tanks in large aircraft. Boost pumps provide a positive flow of fuel under pressure to the engine for starting and serve as an emergency backup in the event an engine-driven pump should fail. They are also used to transfer fuel from one tank to another and to pump fuel overboard when it is being dumped. Boost pumps prevent vapor locks by holding pressure on the fuel in the line to the engine-driven pump. Centrifugal boost pumps have a small agitator propeller on top of the impeller to force vapors from the fuel before it leaves the tank.

Boundary layer. The layer of air that flows next to an aerodynamic surface. Because of the design of the surface and local surface roughness, the boundary layer often has a random flow pattern, sometimes even flowing in a direction opposite to the direction of flight. A turbulent boundary layer causes a great deal of aerodynamic drag.

Bourdon tube. A pressure-indicating mechanism used in most oil pressure and hydraulic pressure gages. It consists of a sealed, curved tube with an elliptical cross section. Pressure inside the tube tries to straighten it, and as it straightens, it moves a pointer across a calibrated dial. Bourdon-tube pressure gauges are used to measure temperature by measuring the vapor pressure in a sealed container of a volatile liquid, such as methyl chloride, whose vapor pressure varies directly with its temperature.

Brazing. A method of thermally joining metal parts by wetting the surface with a molten nonferrous alloy. When the molten material cools and solidifies, it holds the pieces together. Brazing materials melt at a temperature higher than 800 °F, but lower than the melting temperature of the metal on which they are used.

British thermal unit (BTU). The amount of heat energy needed to raise the temperature of one pound of pure water 1 °F.

Bucking bar. A heavy steel bar with smooth, hardened surfaces, or faces. The bucking bar is held against the end of the rivet shank when it is driven with a pneumatic rivet gun, and the shop head is formed against the bucking bar.

Buffeting. Turbulent movement of the air over an aerodynamic surface.

Bulb angle. An L-shaped metal extrusion having an enlarged, rounded edge that resembles a bulb on one of its legs.

Bulkhead. A structural partition that divides the fuselage of an aircraft into compartments, or bays.

Bungee shock cord. A cushioning material used with the nonshock absorbing landing gears installed on older aircraft. Bungee cord is made up of many small rubber bands encased in a loose-woven cotton braid.

Burnish (verb). To smooth the surface of metal that has been damaged by a deep scratch or gouge. The metal piled up at the edge of the damage is pushed back into the damage with a smooth, hard steel burnishing tool.

Burr. A sharp rough edge of a piece of metal left when the metal was sheared, punched, or drilled.

Bus. A point within an electrical system from which the individual circuits get their power.

Buttock line. A line used to locate a position to the right or left of the center line of an aircraft structure.

Butyl. Trade name for a synthetic rubber product made by the polymerization of isobutylene. Butyl withstands such potent chemicals as phosphate ester-base (Skydrol) hydraulic fluids.

Cage (verb). To lock the gimbals of a gyroscopic instrument so it will not be damaged by abrupt flight maneuvers or rough handling.

Calendar month. A measurement of time used by the FAA for inspection and certification purposes. One calendar month from a given day extends from that day until midnight of the last day of that month.

Calender (fabric treatment). To pass fabric through a series of heated rollers to give it a smooth shiny surface.

Calibrated airspeed (CAS). Indicated airspeed corrected for position error. See position error.

Calorie. The amount of heat energy needed to raise the temperature of one gram of pure water 1 °C.

Canted rate gyro. A rate gyro whose gimbal axis is tilted so it can sense rotation of the aircraft about its roll axis as well as its yaw axis.

Camber (wheel alignment). The amount the wheels of an aircraft are tilted, or inclined, from the vertical. If the top of the wheel tilts outward, the camber is positive. If the top of the wheel tilts inward, the camber is negative.

Canard. A horizontal control surface mounted ahead of the wing to provide longitudinal stability and control.

Cantilever wing. A wing that is supported by its internal structure and requires no external supports. The wing spars are built in such a way that they carry all the bending and torsional loads.

Cap strip. The main top and bottom members of a wing rib. The cap strips give the rib its aerodynamic shape.

Capacitance-type fuel quantity measuring system. A popular type of electronic fuel quantity indicating system that has no moving parts in the fuel tank. The tank units are cylindrical capacitors, called probes, mounted across the tank, from top to bottom. The dielectric between the plates of the probes is either fuel or the air above the fuel, and the capacitance of the probe varies with the amount of fuel in the tank. The indicator is a servo-type instrument driven by the amplified output of a capacitance bridge.

Capillary tube. A soft copper tube with a small inside diameter. The capillary tube used with vapor-pressure thermometer connects the temperature sensing bulb to the Bourdon tube. The capillary tube is protected from physical damage by enclosing it in a braided metal wire jacket.

Carbon monoxide detector. A packet of chemical crystals mounted in the aircraft cockpit or cabin where they are easily visible. The crystals change their color from yellow to green when they are exposed to carbon monoxide.

Carbon-pile voltage regulator. A type of voltage regulator used with high-output DC generators. Field current is controlled by varying the resistance of a stack of thin carbon disks. This resistance is varied by controlling the amount the stack is compressed by a spring whose force is opposed by the pull of an electromagnet. The electromagnet's strength is proportional to the generator's output voltage.

Carburizing flame. An oxyacetylene flame produced by an excess of acetylene. This flame is identified by a feather around the inner cone. A carburizing flame is also called a reducing flame.

Carcass (tire component). The layers of rubberized fabric that make up the body of an aircraft tire.

Case pressure. A low pressure that is maintained inside the case of a hydraulic pump. If a seal becomes damaged, hydraulic fluid will be forced out of the pump rather than allowing air to be drawn into the pump.

Cathode-ray tube (CRT). A display tube used for oscilloscopes and computer video displays. An electron gun emits a stream of electrons that is attracted to a positively charged inner surface of the face of the tube. Acceleration and focusing grids speed the movement of the electrons and shape the beam into a pinpoint size. Electrostatic or electromagnetic forces caused by deflection plates or coils move the beam over the face of the tube. The inside surface of the face of the tube is treated with a phosphor material that emits light when the beam of electrons strikes it.

Cavitation. A condition that exist in a hydraulic pump when there is not enough pressure in the reservoir to force fluid to the inlet of the pump. The pump picks up air instead of fluid CDI. Course deviation indicator.

CDU. Control display unit.

Center of gravity. The location on an aircraft about which the force of gravity is concentrated.

Center of lift. The location of the chord line of an airfoil at which all the lift forces produced by the airfoil are considered to be concentrated.

Center of pressure. The point on the chord line of an airfoil where all of the aerodynamic forces are considered to be concentrated.

Centering cam. A cam in the nose-gear shock strut that causes the piston to center when the strut fully extends. When the aircraft takes off and the strut extends, the wheel is straightened in its fore-and-aft position so it can be retracted into the wheel well.

Charging stand (air conditioning service equipment). A handy and compact arrangement of air conditioning servicing equipment. A charging stand contains a vacuum pump, a manifold gauge set, and a method of measuring and dispensing the refrigerant.

Chatter. A type of rapid vibration of a hydraulic pump caused by the pump taking in some air along with the hydraulic fluid.

Check (wood defect). Longitudinal cracks that extend across a log's annual rings.

Check valve. A hydraulic or pneumatic system component that allows full flow of fluid in one direction but blocks all flow in the opposite direction.

Chemical oxygen candle system. An oxygen system used for emergency or backup use. Solid blocks of material that release oxygen when they are burned are carried in special fireproof fixtures. When oxygen is needed, the candles are ignited with an integral igniter, and oxygen flows into the tubing leading to the masks.

Chevron seal. A form of one-way seal used in some fluidpower actuators. A chevron seal is made of a resilient material whose cross section is in the shape of the letter V. The pressure being sealed must be applied to the open side of the V.

Chromel. An alloy of nickel and chromium used as the positive element in a thermocouple for measuring exhaust gas temperature.

Circle. A closed plane figure with every point an equal distance from the center. A circle has the greatest area for its circumference of any enclosed shape.

Circuit breaker. An electrical component that automatically opens a circuit any time excessive current flows through it A circuit breaker may be reset to restore the circuit after the fault causing the excessive current has been corrected.

Clad aluminum. A sheet of aluminum alloy that has a coating of pure aluminum rolled on one or both of its surfaces for corrosion protection.

Clamp-on ammeter. An electrical instrument used to measure current without opening the circuit through which it is flowing. The jaws of the ammeter are opened, slipped over the current carrying wire, and then clamped shut. Current flowing through the wire produces a magnetic field which induces a voltage in the ammeter that is proportional to the amount of current.

Cleco fastener. A patented spring-type fastener used to hold metal sheets in position until they can be permanently riveted together.

Close-quarter iron. A small hand-held iron with an accurately calibrated thermostat. This iron is used for heat-shrinking polyester fabrics in areas that would be difficult to work with a large iron.

Closed angle. An angle formed in sheet metal that has been bent more than 90°.

Closed assembly time. The time elapsing between the assembly of glued joints and the application of pressure. Closed-center hydraulic system. A hydraulic system in which the selector valves are installed in parallel with each other. When no unit is actuated, fluid circulates from the pump back to the reservoir without flowing through any of the selector valves.

Closed-center selector valve. A type of flow-control valve used to direct pressurized fluid into one side of an actuator, and at the same time, direct the return fluid from the other side of the actuator to the fluid reservoir. Closed-center selector valves are connected in parallel between the pressure manifold and the return manifold.

Coaxial. Rotating about the same axis. Coaxial rotors of a helicopter are mounted on concentric shafts in such a way that they turn in opposite directions to cancel torque.

Coaxial cable. A special type of electrical cable that consists of a central conductor held rigidly in the center of a braided outer conductor. Coaxial cable, commonly called coax, is used for attaching radio receivers and transmitters to their antenna.

Coefficient of drag. A dimensionless number used in the formula for determining induced drag as it relates to the angle of attack.

Coefficient of lift. A dimensionless number relating to the angle of attack used in the formula for determining aerodynamic lift.

Coin dimpling. A process of preparing a hole in sheet metal for flush riveting. A coining die is pressed into the rivet hole to form a sharp-edged depression into which the rivet head fits.

Collective pitch control. The helicopter control that changes the pitch of all of the rotor blades at the same time. Movement of the collective pitch control increases or decreases the lift produced by the entire rotor disk.

Collodion. Cellulose nitrate used as a film base for certain aircraft dopes.

Combustion heater. A type of cabin heater used in some aircraft. Gasoline from the aircraft fuel tanks is burned in the heater.

Compass fluid. A highly refined, water-clear petroleum product similar to kerosene. Compass fluid is used to dampen the oscillations of magnetic compasses.

Compass rose. A location on an airport where an aircraft can be taken to have its compasses "swung." Lines are painted on the rose to mark the magnetic directions in 30° increments.

Compass swinging. A maintenance procedure that minimizes deviation error in a magnetic compass. The aircraft is aligned on a compass rose, and the compensating magnets in the compass case are adjusted so the compass card indicates the direction marked on the rose. After the deviation error is minimized on all headings, a compass correction card is completed and mounted on the instrument panel next to the compass.

Compensated fuel pump. A vane-type, engine-driven fuel pump that has a diaphragm connected to the pressure regulating valve. The chamber above the diaphragm is vented to the carburetor upper deck where it senses the pressure of the air as it enters the engine. The diaphragm allows the fuel pump to compensate for altitude changes and keeps the carburetor inlet fuel pressure a constant amount higher than the carburetor inlet air pressure.

Compensator port (brake system component). A small hole between a hydraulic brake master cylinder and the reservoir. When the brakes are released, this port is uncovered and the fluid in the master cylinder is vented to the reservoir. When the brake is applied, the master-cylinder piston covers the compensator port and allows pressure in the line to the brake to build up and apply the brakes. When the brake is released, the piston uncovers the compensator port. If any fluid has been lost from the brake, the reservoir will refill the master cylinder. A restricted compensator port will cause the brakes to drag or will cause them to be slow to release.

Composite. Something made up of different materials combined in such a way that the characteristics of the resulting material are different from those of any of the components.

Compound curve. A curve formed in more than one plane. The surface of a sphere is a compound curve.

Compound gauge (air conditioning servicing equipment). A pressure gauge used to measure the pressure in the low side of an air conditioning system. A compound gauge is calibrated from zero to 30 inches of mercury vacuum, and from zero to about 150-psi positive gauge pressure.

Compressibility effect. The sudden increase in the total drag of an airfoil in transonic flight caused by formation of shock waves on the surface.

Compression failure. A type of structural failure in wood caused by the application of too great a compressive load. A compression failure shows up as a faint line running at right angles to the grain of the wood.

Compression strut. A heavy structural member, often in the form of a steel tube, used to hold the spars of a Pratt truss airplane wing apart. A compression strut opposes the compressive loads between the spars arising from the tensile loads produced by the drag and antidrug wires.

Compression wood. A defect in wood that causes it to have a high specific gravity and the appearance of an excessive growth of summerwood. In most species, there is little difference between the color of the springwood and the summerwood. Any material containing compression wood is unsuited for aircraft structural use and must be rejected.

Compressor (air conditioning system component). The component in a vapor-cycle cooling system in which the low-pressure refrigerant vapors, after they leave the evaporator, are compressed to increase both their temperature and pressure before they pass into the condenser. Some compressors are driven by electric motors, others by hydraulic motors and, in the case of most light airplanes, are belt driven from the engine.

Concave surface. A surface that is curved inward. The outer edges are higher than the center.

Condenser (air conditioning system component). The component in a vapor-cycle cooling system in which the heat taken from the aircraft cabin is given up to the ambient air outside the aircraft.

Conductor (electrical). A material that allows electrons to move freely from one atom to another within the material.

Coning angle. The angle formed between the plane of rotation of a helicopter rotor blade when it is producing lift and a line perpendicular to the rotor shaft. The degree of the coning angle is determined by the relationship between the centrifugal force acting on the blades and the aerodynamic lift produced by the blades.

Constant (mathematical). A value used in a mathematical computation that is the same every time it is used. For example, the relationship between the length of the circumference of a circle and the length of its diameter is a constant, 3.1416. This constant is called by the Greek name of Pi (π).

Constant differential mode (cabin pressurization). The mode of pressurization in which the cabin pressure is maintained a constant amount higher than the outside air pressure. The maximum differential pressure is determined by the structural strength of the aircraft cabin.

Constant-displacement pump. A fluid pump that moves a specific volume of fluid each time it rotates; the faster the pump turns, the more fluid it moves. Some form of pressure regulator or relief valve must be used with a constant-displacement pump when it is driven by an aircraft engine.

Constant-speed drive (CSD). A special drive system used to connect an alternating current generator to an aircraft engine. The drive holds the generator speed (and thus its frequency) constant as the engine speed varies.

Constantan. A copper-nickel alloy used as the negative lead of a thermocouple for measuring the cylinder head temperature of a reciprocating engine.

Contactor (electrical component). A remotely actuated, heavy-duty electrical switch. Contactors are used in an aircraft electrical system to connect the battery to the main bus.

Continuity tester. A troubleshooting tool that consists of a battery, a light bulb, and test leads. The test leads are connected to each end of the conductor under test, and if the bulb lights up, there is continuity. If it does not light up, the conductor is open.

Continuous Airworthiness Inspection Program. An inspection program that is part of a continuous airworthiness maintenance program approved for certain large airplanes (to which 14 CFR Part 125 is not applicable), turbojet multi-engine airplanes, turbopropeller-powered multi-engine airplanes, and turbine-powered rotorcraft.

Continuous-duty solenoid. A solenoid-type switch designed to be kept energized by current flowing through its coil for an indefinite period of time. The battery contactor in an aircraft electrical system is a continuous-duty solenoid. Current flows through its coil all the time the battery is connected to the electrical system.

Continuous-flow oxygen system. A type of oxygen system that allows a metered amount of oxygen to continuously flow into the mask. A rebreather-type mask is used with a continuous-flow system. The simplest form of continuousflow oxygen system regulates the flow by a calibrated orifice in the outlet to the mask, but most systems use either a manual or automatic regulator to vary the pressure across the orifice proportional to the altitude being flown.

Continuous-loop fire-detection system. A fire-detection system that uses a continuous loop of two conductors separated with a thermistor-type insulation. Under normal temperature conditions, the thermistor material is an insulator; but if it is exposed to a fire, the thermistor changes into a conductor and completes the circuit between the two conductors, initiating a fire warning.

Control horn. The arm on a control surface to which the control cable or push-pull rod attaches to move the surface.

Control stick. The type of control device used in some airplanes. A vertical stick in the flight deck controls the ailerons by side-to-side movement and the elevators by foreand-aft movement.

Control yoke. The movable column on which an airplane control wheel is mounted. The yoke may be moved in or out to actuate the elevators, and the control wheel may be rotated to actuate the ailerons.

Controllability. The characteristic of an aircraft that allows it to change its flight attitude in response to the pilot's movement of the flight deck controls.

Conventional current. An imaginary flow of electricity that is said to flow from the positive terminal of a power source, through the external circuit to its negative terminal. The arrowheads in semiconductor symbols point in the direction of conventional current flow.

Converging duct. A duct, or passage, whose cross-sectional area decreases in the direction of fluid flow.

Conversion coating. A chemical solution used to form an airtight oxide or phosphate film on the surface of aluminum or magnesium parts. The conversion coating prevents air from reaching the metal and keeps it from corroding.

Convex surface. A surface that is curved outward. The outer edges are lower than the center.

Coriolis effect. The change in rotor blade velocity to compensate for a change in the distance between the center of mass of the rotor blade and the axis rotation of the blade as the blades flap in flight.

Cornice brake. A large shop tool used to make straight bends across a sheet of metal. Cornice brakes are often called leaf brakes.

Corrugated metal. Sheets of metal that have been made more rigid by forming a series of parallel ridges or waves in its surface.

Cotter pin. A split metal pin used to safety a castellated or slotted nut on a bolt. The pin is passed through the hole in the shank of the bolt and the slots in the nut, and the ends of the pin are spread to prevent it backing out of the hole.

Countersinking. Preparation of a rivet hole for a flush rivet by beveling the edges of the holes with a cutter of the correct angle.

Coverite surface thermometer. A small surface-type bimetallic thermometer that calibrates the temperature of an iron used to heat-shrink polyester fabrics.

Crabbing. Pointing the nose of an aircraft into the wind to compensate for wind drift.

Crazing. A form of stress-caused damage that occurs in a transparent thermoplastic material. Crazing appears as a series of tiny, hair-like cracks just below the surface of the plastic.

Critical Mach number. The flight Mach number at which there is the first indication of supersonic airflow over any part of the aircraft structure.

Cross coat. A double coat of aircraft finishing material in which the second coat is sprayed at right angles to the first coat, before the solvents have evaporated from the first coat.

Cross-feed valve (fuel system component). A valve in a fuel system that allows any of the engines of a multi-engine aircraft to draw fuel from any fuel tank. Cross-feed systems are used to allow a multi-engine aircraft to maintain a balanced fuel condition.

Cross-flow valve. An automatic flow-control valve installed between the gear-up and gear-down lines of the landing gear of some large airplanes. When the landing gear is released from its uplocks, its weight causes it to fall faster than the hydraulic system can supply fluid to the gear-down side of the actuation cylinder. The cross-flow valve opens and directs fluid from the gear-up side into the gear-down side. This allows the gear to move down with a smooth motion.

CRT. Cathode-ray tube.

Cryogenic liquid. A liquid which boils at temperatures of less than about 110 °F (–163 °C) at normal atmospheric pressures.

Cuno filter. The registered trade name for a particular style of edge-type fluid filter. Cuno filters are made up of a stack of thin metal disks that are separated by thin scraper blades. Contaminants collect on the edge of the disks, and they are periodically scraped out and allowed to collect in the bottom of the filter case for future removal.

Current. A general term used for electrical flow. See conventional current.

Current limiter. An electrical component used to limit the amount of current a generator can produce. Some current limiters are a type of slow-blow fuse in the generator output. Other current limiters reduce the generator output voltage if the generator tries to put out more than its rated current.

Cusp. A pointed end.

Cyclic pitch control. The helicopter control that allows the pilot to change the pitch of the rotor blades individually, at a specific point in their rotation. The cyclic pitch control allows the pilot to tilt the plane of rotation of the rotor disk to change the direction of lift produced by the rotor.

Dacron. The registered trade name for a cloth woven from polyester fibers

Damped oscillation. Oscillation whose amplitude decreases with time.

Database. A body of information that is available on any particular subject.

Data bus. A wire or group of wires that are used to move data within a computer system.

Debooster valve. A valve in a power brake system between the power brake control valve and the wheel cylinder. This valve lowers the pressure of the fluid going to the brake and increases its volume. A debooster valve increases the smoothness of brake application and aids in rapid release of the brakes.

Decay. The breakdown of the structure of wood fibers. Wood that shows any indication of decay must be rejected for use in aircraft structure.

Decomposition. The breakdown of the structure of wood fibers. Wood that shows any indication of decay must be rejected for use in aircraft structure.

Deciduous. A type of tree that sheds its foliage at the end of the growing season. Hardwoods come from deciduous trees.

Dedicated computer. A small digital computer, often built into an instrument or control device that contains a built-in program that causes it to perform a specific function.

Deep-vacuum pump. A vacuum pump capable of removing almost all of the air from a refrigeration system. A deepvacuum pump can reduce the pressure inside the system to a few microns of pressure.

Deflator cap. A cap for a tire, strut, or accumulator air valve that, when screwed onto the valve, depresses the valve stem and allows the air to escape safely through a hole in the side of the cap.

Deicer system. A system that removes ice after it has formed on an aircraft.

Delamination. The separation of the layers of a laminated material.

Delivery air duct check valve. An isolation valve at the discharge side of the air turbine that prevents the loss of pressurization through a disengaged cabin air compressor.

Delta airplane. An airplane with a triangular-shaped wing. This wing has an extreme amount of sweepback on its leading edge, and a trailing edge that is almost perpendicular to the longitudinal axis of the airplane.

Delta connection (electrical connection). A method of connecting three electrical coils into a ring or, as they are drawn on a schematic diagram as a triangle, a delta (D).

Denier. A measure of the fineness of the yarns in a fabric.

Density altitude. The altitude in standard air at which the density is the same as that of the existing air.

Density ratio (σ). The ratio of the density of the air at a given altitude to the density of the air at sea level under standard conditions.

Derated (electrical specification). Reduction in the rated voltage or current of an electrical component. Derating is done to extend the life or reliability of the device.

Desiccant (air conditioning component). A drying agent used in an air conditioning system to remove water from the refrigerant. A desiccant is made of silica-gel or some similar material.

Detent. A spring-loaded pin or tab that enters a hole or groove when the device to which it is attached is in a certain position. Detents are used on a fuel valve to provide a positive means of identifying the fully on and fully off position of the valve.

Detonation. An explosion, or uncontrolled burning of the fuel-air mixture inside the cylinder of a reciprocating engine. Detonation occurs when the pressure and the temperature inside the cylinder become higher than the critical pressure and temperature of the fuel. Detonation is often confused with preignition.

Deviation error. An error in a magnetic compass caused by localized magnetic fields in the aircraft. Deviation error, which is different on each heading, is compensated by the technician "swinging" the compass. A compass must be compensated so the deviation error on any heading is no greater than 10 degrees.

Dewar bottle. A vessel designed to hold liquefied gases. It has double walls with the space between being evacuated to prevent the transfer of heat. The surfaces in the vacuum area are made heat-reflective.

Differential aileron travel. Aileron movement in which the upward-moving aileron deflects a greater distance than the one moving downward. The up aileron produces parasite drag to counteract the induced drag caused by the down aileron. Differential aileron travel is used to counteract adverse yaw.

Differential pressure. The difference between two pressures. An airspeed indicator is a differential-pressure gauge. It measures the difference between static air pressure and pitot air pressure.

Differential-voltage reverse-current cutout. A type of reverse-current cutout switch used with heavy-duty electrical systems. This switch connects the generator to the electrical bus when the generator voltage is a specific amount higher than the battery voltage.

Digital multimeter. An electrical test instrument that can be used to measure voltage, current, and resistance. The indication is in the form of a liquid crystal display in discrete numbers.

Dihedral. The positive angle formed between the lateral axis of an airplane and a line that passes through the center of the wing or horizontal stabilizer. Dihedral increases the lateral stability of an airplane.

Diluter-demand oxygen system. A popular type of oxygen system in which the oxygen is metered to the mask, where it is diluted with cabin air by an airflow-metering aneroid assembly which regulates the amount of air allowed to dilute the oxygen on the basis of cabin altitude. The mixture of oxygen and air flows only when the wearer of the mask inhales. The percentage of oxygen in the air delivered to the mask is regulated, on the basis of altitude, by the regulator. A diluter-demand regulator has an emergency position which allows 100 percent oxygen to flow to the mask, by-passing the regulating mechanism.

Dipole antenna. A half wavelength, center-fed radio antenna. The length of each of the two arms is approximately one fourth of the wavelength of the center frequency for which the antenna is designed.

Dirigible. A large, cigar-shaped, rigid, lighter-than-air flying machine. Dirigibles are made of a rigid truss structure covered with fabric. Gas bags inside the structure contain the lifting gas, which is either helium or hydrogen.

Disc area (helicopter specification). The total area swept by the blades of a helicopter main rotor.

Divergent oscillation. Oscillation whose amplitude increases with time.

Diverging duct. A duct, or passage, whose cross-sectional area increases in the direction of fluid flow.

DME. Distance measuring equipment.

Dope proofing. The treatment of a structure to be covered with fabric to keep the solvents in the dope from softening the protective coating on the structure.

Dope roping. A condition of aircraft dope brushed onto a surface in such a way that it forms a stringy, uneven surface rather than flowing out smoothly.

Double-acting actuator (hydraulic system component). A linear actuator moved in both directions by fluid power

Double-acting hand pump (hydraulic system component). A hand-operated fluid pump that moves fluid during both strokes of the pump handle.

Doubler. A piece of sheet metal used to strengthen and stiffen a repair in a sheet metal structure.

Downtime. Any time during which an aircraft is out of commission and unable to be operated.

Downwash. Air forced down by aerodynamic action below and behind the wing of an airplane or the rotor of a helicopter. Aerodynamic lift is produced when the air is deflected downward. The upward force on the aircraft is the same as the downward force on the air.

Drag (helicopter rotor blade movement). Fore-and-aft movement of the tip of a helicopter rotor blade in its plane of rotation.

Dragging brakes. Brakes that do not fully release when the brake pedal is released. The brakes are partially applied all the time, which causes excessive lining wear and heat.

Drag wire. A structural wire inside a Pratt truss airplane wing between the spars. Drag wires run from the front spar inboard, to the rear spar at the next bay outboard. Drag wires oppose the forces that try to drag the wing backward.

Drill motor. An electric or pneumatic motor that drives a chuck that holds a twist drill. The best drill motors produce high torque, and their speed can be controlled.

Drip stick. A fuel quantity indicator used to measure the fuel level in the tank when the aircraft is on the ground. The drip stick is pulled down from the bottom of the tank until fuel drips from its opened end. This indicates that the top of the gauge inside the tank is at the level of the fuel. Note the number of inches read on the outside of the gauge at the point it contacts the bottom of the tank, and use a drip stick table to convert this measurement into gallons of fuel in the tank.

Dry air pump. An engine-driven air pump which used carbon vanes. Dry pumps do not use any lubrication, and the vanes are extremely susceptible to damage from the solid airborne particles. These pumps must be operated with filters in their inlet so they will take in only filtered air.

Dry ice. Solidified carbon dioxide. Dry ice sublimates, or changes from a solid directly into a gas, at a temperature of −110 °F (−78.5 °C).

Dry rot. Decomposition of wood fibers caused by fungi. Dry rot destroys all strength in the wood.

Ductility. The property of a material that allows it to be drawn into a thin section without breaking.

Dummy load (electrical load). A noninductive, high-power, 50-ohm resistor that can be connected to a transmission line in place of the antenna. The transmitter can be operated into the dummy load without transmitting any signal.

Duralumin. The name for the original alloy of aluminum, magnesium, manganese, and copper. Duralumin is the same as the modern 2017 aluminum alloy.

Dutch roll. An undesirable, low-amplitude coupled oscillation about both the yaw and roll axes that affects many swept wing airplanes. Dutch roll is minimized by the use of a yaw damper.

Dutchman shears. A common name for compound-action sheet metal shears.

Dynamic pressure (q). The pressure a moving fluid would have if it were stopped. Dynamic pressure is measured in pounds per square foot.

Dynamic stability. The stability that causes an aircraft to return to a condition of straight and level flight after it has been disturbed from this condition. When an aircraft is disturbed from the straight and level flight, its static stability starts it back in the correct direction; but it overshoots, and the corrective forces are applied in the opposite direction. The aircraft oscillates back and forth on both sides of the correct condition, with each oscillation smaller than the one before it. Dynamic stability is the decreasing of these restorative oscillations.

EADI. Electronic Attitude Director Indicator.

ECAM. Electronic Centralized Aircraft Monitor.

Eccentric brushing. A special bushing used between the rear spar of certain cantilever airplane wings and the wing attachment fitting on the fuselage. The portion of the bushing that fits through the hole in the spar is slightly offset from that which passes through the holes in the fitting. By rotating the bushing, the rear spar may be moved up or down to adjust the root incidence of the wing.

Eddy current damping (electrical instrument damping). Decreasing the amplitude of oscillations by the interaction of magnetic fields. In the case of a vertical-card magnetic compass, flux from the oscillating permanent magnet produces eddy currents in a damping disk or cup. The magnetic flux produced by the eddy currents opposes the flux from the permanent magnet and decreases the oscillations. Edge distance. The distance between the center of a rivet hole and the edge of the sheet of metal.

EFIS. Electronic Flight Instrument System.

EHSI. Electronic Horizontal Situation Indicator.

EICAS. Engine Indicating and Crew Alerting System.

Ejector. A form of jet pump used to pick up a liquid and move it to another location. Ejectors are used to ensure that the compartment in which the boost pumps are mounted is kept full of fuel. Part of the fuel from the boost pump flowing through the ejector produces a low pressure that pulls fuel from the main tank and forces it into the boost pump sump area.

Elastic limit. The maximum amount of tensile load, in pounds per square inch, a material is able to withstand without being permanently deformed.

Electromotive force (EMF). The force that causes electrons to move from one atom to another within an electrical circuit. Electromotive force is an electrical pressure, and it is measured in volts.

Electron current. The actual flow of electrons in a circuit. Electrons flow from the negative terminal of a power source through the external circuit to its positive terminal. The arrowheads in semiconductor symbols point in the direction opposite to the flow of electron current.

ELT (emergency locator transmitter). A self-contained radio transmitter that automatically begins transmitting on the emergency frequencies any time it is triggered by a severe impact parallel to the longitudinal axis of the aircraft.

Elevator downspring. A spring in the elevator control system that produces a mechanical force that tries to lower the elevator. In normal flight, this spring force is overcome by the aerodynamic force from the elevator trim tab. But in slow flight with an aft CG position, the trim tab loses its effectiveness and the downspring lowers the nose to prevent a stall.

Elevons. Movable control surfaces on the trailing edge of a delta wing or a flying wing airplane. These surfaces operate together to serve as elevators, and differentially to act as ailerons.

EMI. Electromagnetic interference.

Empennage. The tail section of an airplane.

Enamel. A type of finishing material that flows out to form a smooth surface. Enamel is usually made of a pigment suspended in some form of resin. When the resin cures, it leaves a smooth, glossy protective surface.

Energizing brake. A brake that uses the momentum of the aircraft to increase its effectiveness by wedging the shoe against the brake drum. Energizing brakes are also called servo brakes. A single-servo brake is energizing only when moving in the forward direction, and a duo-servo brake is energizing when the aircraft is moving either forward or backward.

Epoxy. A flexible, thermosetting resin that is made by polymerization of an epoxide. Epoxy has wide application as a matrix for composite materials and as an adhesive that bonds many different types of materials. It is noted for its durability and its chemical resistance.

Equalizing resistor. A large resistor in the ground circuit of a heavy-duty aircraft generator through which all of the generator output current flows. The voltage drop across this resistor is used to produce the current in the paralleling circuit that forces the generators to share the electrical load equally.

Ethylene dibromide. A chemical compound added to aviation gasoline to convert some of the deposits left by the tetraethyl lead into lead bromides. These bromides are volatile and will pass out of the engine with the exhaust gases.

Ethylene glycol. A form of alcohol used as a coolant for liquid-cooled engines and as an anti-icing agent.

Eutectic material. An alloy or solution that has the lowest possible melting point.

Evacuation (air conditioning servicing procedure). A procedure in servicing vapor-cycle cooling systems. A vacuum pump removes all the air from the system. Evacuation removes all traces of water vapor that could condense out, freeze, and block the system.

Evaporator (air conditioning component). The component in a vapor-cycle cooling system in which heat from the aircraft cabin is absorbed into the refrigerant. As the heat is absorbed, the refrigerant evaporates, or changes from a liquid into a vapor. The function of the evaporator is to lower the cabin air temperature.

Expander-tube brake. A brake that uses hydraulic fluid inside a synthetic rubber tube around the brake hub to force rectangular blocks of brake-lining material against the rotating brake drum. Friction between the brake drum and the lining material slows the aircraft.

Expansion wave. The change in pressure and velocity of a supersonic flow of air as it passes over a surface which drops away from the flow. As the surface drops away, the air tries to follow it. In changing its direction, the air speeds up to a higher supersonic velocity and its static pressure decreases. There is no change in the total energy as the air passes through an expansion wave, and so there is no sound as there is when air passes through a shock wave.

Extruded angle. A structural angle formed by passing metal heated to its plastic state through specially shaped dies.

FAA Form 337. The FAA form that must be filled in and submitted to the FAA when a major repair or major alteration has been completed.

Federal Aviation Administration Flight Standards District Office (FAA FSDO). An FAA field office serving an assigned geographical area staffed with Flight Standards personnel who serve the aviation industry and the general public on matters relating to certification and operation of air carrier and general aviation aircraft.

Fading of brakes. The decrease in the amount of braking action that occurs with some types of brakes that are applied for a long period of time. True fading occurs with overheated drum-type brakes. As the drum is heated, it expands in a bell-mouthed fashion. This decreases the amount of drum in contact with the brake shoes and decreases the braking action. A condition similar to brake fading occurs when there is an internal leak in the brake master cylinder. The brakes are applied, but as the pedal is held down, fluid leaks past the piston, and the brakes slowly release.

Fairing. A part of a structure whose primary purpose is to produce a smooth surface or a smooth junction where two surfaces join.

Fairlead. A plastic or wooden guide used to prevent a steel control cable rubbing against an aircraft structure.

FCC. Federal Communications Commission.

FCC. Flight Control Computer.

Feather (helicopter rotor blade movement). Rotation of a helicopter rotor blade about its pitch-change axis.

Ferrous metal. Any metal that contains iron and has magnetic characteristics.

Fiber stop nut. A form of a self-locking nut that has a fiber insert crimped into a recess above the threads. The hole in the insert is slightly smaller than the minor diameter of the threads. When the nut is screwed down over the bolt threads, the opposition caused by the fiber insert produces a force that prevents vibration loosening the nut.

File. A hand-held cutting tool used to remove a small amount of metal with each stroke.

Fill threads. Threads in a piece of fabric that run across the width of the fabric, interweaving with the warp threads. Fill threads are often called woof, or weft, threads.

Fillet. A fairing used to give shape but not strength to an object. A fillet produces a smooth junction where two surfaces meet.

Finishing tape. Another name for surface tape. See surface tape.

Fishmouth splice. A type of splice used in a welded tubular structure in which the end of the tube whose inside diameter is the same as the outside diameter of the tube being spliced is cut in the shape of a V, or a fishmouth, and is slipped over the smaller tube welded. A fishmouth splice has more weld area than a butt splice and allows the stresses from one tube to transfer into the other tube gradually. Fire pull handle. The handle in an aircraft flight deck that is pulled at the first indication of an engine fire. Pulling this handle removes the generator from the electrical system, shuts off the fuel and hydraulic fluid to the engine, and closes the compressor bleed air valve. The fire extinguisher agent discharge switch is uncovered, but it is not automatically closed.

Fire zone. A portion of an aircraft designated by the manufacturer to require fire-detection and/or fire-extinguishing equipment and a high degree of inherent fire resistance.

Fitting. An attachment device that is used to connect components to an aircraft structure.

Fixed fire-extinguishing system. A fire-extinguishing system installed in an aircraft.

Flameout. A condition in the operation of a gas turbine engine in which the fire in the engine unintentionally goes out.

Flap (aircraft control). A secondary control on an airplane wing that changes its camber to increase both its lift and its drag.

Flap (helicopter rotor blade movement). Up-and-down movement of the tip of a helicopter rotor blade.

Flap overload valve. A valve in the flap system of an airplane that prevents the flaps being lowered at an airspeed which could cause structural damage. If the pilot tries to extend the flaps when the airspeed is too high, the opposition caused by the air flow will open the overload valve and return the fluid to the reservoir.

Flash point. The temperature to which a material must be raised for it to ignite, but not continue to burn, when a flame is passed above it.

Flat pattern layout. The pattern for a sheet metal part that has the material used for each flat surface, and for all of the bends, marked out with bend-tangent lines drawn between the flats and bend allowances.

Flight controller. The component in an autopilot system that allows the pilot to maneuver the aircraft manually when the autopilot is engaged.

Fluid. A form of material whose molecules are able to flow past one another without destroying the material. Gases and liquids are both fluids.

Fluid power. The transmission of force by the movement of a fluid. The most familiar examples of fluid power systems are hydraulic and pneumatic systems.

Flutter. Rapid and uncontrolled oscillation of a flight control surface on an aircraft that is caused by a dynamically unbalanced condition.

Fly-by-wire. A method of control used by some modern aircraft in which control movement or pressures exerted by the pilot are directed into a digital computer where they are input into a program tailored to the flight characteristics of the aircraft. The computer output signal is sent to actuators at the control surfaces to move them the optimum amount for the desired maneuver.

Flying boat. An airplane whose fuselage is built in the form of a boat hull to allow it to land and takeoff from water. In the past, flying boats were a popular form of large airplane.

Flying wing. A type of heavier-than-air aircraft that has no fuselage or separate tail surfaces. The engines and useful load are carried inside the wing, and movable control surfaces on the trailing edge provide both pitch and roll control.

Foot-pound. A measure of work accomplished when a force of 1 pound moves an object a distance of 1 foot.

Force. Energy brought to bear on an object that tends to cause motion or to change motion.

Forehand welding. Welding in which the torch is pointed in the direction the weld is progressing.

Form drag. Parasite drag caused by the form of the object passing through the air.

Former. An aircraft structural member used to give a fuselage its shape.

FMC. Flight Management Computer.

Forward bias. A condition of operation of a semiconductor device such as a diode or transistor in which a positive voltage is connected to the P-type material and a negative voltage to the N-type material.

FPD. Freezing point depressant.

Fractional distillation. A method of separating the various components from a physical mixture of liquids. The material to be separated is put into a container and its temperature is increased. The components having the lowest boiling points boil off first and are condensed. Then, as the temperature is further raised, other components are removed. Kerosene, gasoline, and other petroleum products are obtained by fractional distillation of crude oil.

Frangible. Breakable, or easily broken.

Freon. The registered trade name for a refrigerant used in a vapor-cycle air conditioning system.

Frise aileron. An aileron with its hinge line set back from the leading edge so that when it is deflected upward, part of the leading edge projects below the wing and produces parasite drag to help overcome adverse yaw.

Full-bodied. Not thinned.

Fully articulated rotor. A helicopter rotor whose blades are attached to the hub in such a way that they are free to flap, drag, and feather. See each of these terms.

Frost. Ice crystal deposits formed by sublimation when the temperature and dew point are below freezing.

Fuel-flow transmitter. A device in the fuel line between the engine-driven fuel pump and the carburetor that measures the rate of flow of the fuel. It converts this flow rate into an electrical signal and sends it to an indicator in the instrument panel.

Fuel jettison system. A system installed in most large aircraft that allows the flight crew to jettison, or dump, fuel to lower the gross weight of the aircraft to its allowable landing weight. Boost pumps in the fuel tanks move the fuel from the tank into a fuel manifold. From the fuel manifold, it flows away from the aircraft through dump chutes is each wing tip. The fuel jettison system must be so designed and constructed that it is free from fire hazards.

Fuel totalizer. A fuel quantity indicator that gives the total amount of fuel remaining on board the aircraft on one instrument. The totalizer adds the quantities of fuel in all of the tanks.

Fungus (plural: fungi). Any of several types of plant life that include yeasts, molds, and mildew.

Fusible plugs. Plugs in the wheels of high-performance airplanes that use tubeless tires. The centers of the plugs are filled with a metal that melts at a relatively low temperature. If a takeoff is aborted and the pilot uses the brakes excessively, the heat transferred into the wheel will melt the center of the fusible plugs and allow the air to escape from the tire before it builds up enough pressure to cause an explosion.

Gauge (rivet). The distance between rows of rivets in a multirow seam. Gauge is also called transverse pitch.

Gauge pressure. Pressure referenced from the existing atmospheric pressure.

Galling. Fretting or pulling out chunks of a surface by sliding contact with another surface or body.

Gasket. A seal between two parts where there is no relative motion.

Gear-type pump. A constant-displacement fluid pump that contains two meshing large-tooth spur gears. Fluid is drawn into the pump as the teeth separate and is carried around the inside of the housing with teeth and is forced from the pump when the teeth come together.

General Aviation Airworthiness Alerts. Documents published by the FAA that provide an economical interchange of service experience and cooperation in the improvement of aeronautical product durability, reliability, and safety. Alerts include items that have been reported to be significant, but which have not been fully evaluated at the time the material went to press.

Generator. A mechanical device that transforms mechanical energy into electrical energy by rotating a coil inside a magnetic field. As the conductors in the coil cut across the lines of magnetic flux, a voltage is generated that causes current to flow.

Generator series field. A set of heavy field windings in a generator connected in a series with the armature. The magnetic field produced by the series windings is used to change the characteristics of the generator.

Generator shunt field. A set of field windings in a generator connected in parallel with the armature. Varying the amount of current flowing in the shunt field windings controls the voltage output of the generator.

Gerotor pump. A form of constant-displacement gear pump. A gerotor pump uses an external-tooth spur gear that rides inside of and drives an internal-tooth rotor gear. There is one more tooth space inside the rotor than there are teeth on the drive gear. As the gears rotate, the volume of the space between two of the teeth on the inlet side of the pump increases, while the volume of the space between the two teeth on the opposite side of the pump decreases.

GHz (gigahertz). 1,000,000,000 cycles per second.

Gimbal. A support that allows a gyroscope to remain in an upright condition when its base is tilted.

Glass cockpit. An aircraft instrument system that uses a few cathode-ray-tube displays to replace a large number of mechanically actuated instruments.

Glaze ice. Ice that forms when large drops of water strike a surface whose temperature is below freezing. Glaze ice is clear and heavy.

Glide slope. The portion of an ILS (Instrument Landing System) that provides the vertical path along which an aircraft descends on an instrument landing.

Goniometer. Electronic circuitry in an ADF system that uses the output of a fixed loop antenna to sense the angle between a fixed reference, usually the nose of the aircraft, and the direction from which the radio signal is being received.

Gram. The basic unit of weight or mass in the metric system. One gram equals approximately 0.035 ounce.

Graphite. A form of carbon. Structural graphite is used in composite structure because of its strength and stiffness. Greige (pronounced "gray"). The unshrunk condition of a polyester fabric as it is removed from the loom.

Ground effect. The increased aerodynamic lift produced when an airplane or helicopter is flown nearer than half wing span or rotor span to the ground. This additional lift is caused by an effective increase in angle of attack without the accompanying increase in induced drag, which is caused by the deflection of the downwashed air.

Ground. The voltage reference point in an aircraft electrical system. Ground has zero electrical potential. Voltage values, both positive and negative, are measured from ground. In the United Kingdom, ground is spoken of as "earth."

Ground-power unit (GPU). A service component used to supply electrical power to an aircraft when it is being operated on the ground.

Guncotton. A highly explosive material made by treating cotton fibers with nitric and sulfuric acids. Guncotton is used in making the film base of nitrate dope.

Gusset. A small plate attached to two or more members of a truss structure. A gusset strengthens the truss.

Gyro (gyroscope). The sensing device in an autopilot system. A gyroscope is a rapidly spinning wheel with its weight concentrated around its rim. Gyroscopes have two basic characteristics that make them useful in aircraft instruments: rigidity in space and precession. See rigidity in space and precession.

Gyroscopic precession. The characteristic of a gyroscope that causes it to react to an applied force as though the force were applied at a point 90° in the direction of rotation from the actual point of application. The rotor of a helicopter acts in much the same way as a gyroscope and is affected by gyroscopic precession.

Halon 1211. A halogenated hydrocarbon fire-extinguishing agent used in many HRD fire-extinguishing systems for powerplant protection. The technical name for Halon 1211 is bromochlorodifluoromethane.

Halon 1301. A halogenated hydrocarbon fire-extinguishing agent that is one of the best for extinguishing cabin and powerplant fires. It is highly effective and is the least toxic of the extinguishing agents available. The technical name for Halon 1301 is bromotrifluoromethane.

Hangar rash. Scrapes, bends, and dents in an aircraft structure caused by careless handling.

Hardwood. Wood from a broad-leaf tree that sheds its leaves each year.

Heading indicator. A gyroscopic flight instrument that gives the pilot an indication of the heading of the aircraft.

Heat exchanger. A device used to exchange heat from one medium to another. Radiators, condensers, and evaporators are all examples of heat exchangers. Heat always moves from the object or medium having the greatest level of heat energy to a medium or object having a lower level.

Helix. A screw-like, or spiral, curve.

Hertz. One cycle per second.

Holding relay. An electrical relay that is closed by sending a pulse of current through the coil. It remains closed until the current flowing through its contacts is interrupted.

Homebuilt aircraft. Aircraft that are built by individuals as a hobby rather than by factories as commercial products. Homebuilt, or amateur-built, aircraft are not required to meet the stringent requirements imposed on the manufacture of FAA-certified aircraft.

Horsepower. A unit of mechanical power that is equal to 33,000 foot-pounds of work done in 1 minute, or 550 foot-pounds of work done in 1 second.

Hot dimpling. A process used to dimple, or indent, the hole into which a flush rivet is to be installed. Hot dimpling is done by clamping the metal between heating elements and forcing the dies through the holes in the softened metal. Hot dimpling prevents hard metal from cracking when it is dimpled.

Hot-wire cutter. A cutter used to shape blocks of Styrofoam. The wire is stretched tight between the arms of a frame and heated by electrical current. The hot wire melts its way through the foam.

HRD. High-rate-discharge.

HSI. Horizontal situation indicator. Hydraulic actuator. The component in a hydraulic system that converts hydraulic pressure into mechanical force. The two main types of hydraulic actuators are linear actuators (cylinders and pistons) and rotary actuators (hydraulic motors).

Hydraulic fuse. A type of flow control valve that allows a normal flow of fluid in the system but, if the flow rate is excessive, or if too much fluid flows for normal operation, the fuse will shut off all further flow.

Hydraulic motor. A hydraulic actuator that converts fluid pressure into rotary motion. Hydraulic motors have an advantage in aircraft installations over electric motors, because they can operate in a stalled condition without the danger of a fire.

Hydraulic power pack. A small, self-contained hydraulic system that consists of a reservoir, pump, selector valves, and relief valves. The power pack is removable from the aircraft as a unit to facilitate maintenance and service.

Hydraulics. The system of fluid power which transmits force through an incompressible fluid

Hydrocarbon. An organic compound that contains only carbon and hydrogen. The vast majority of fossil fuels, such as gasoline and turbine-engine fuel, are hydrocarbons.

Hydroplaning. A condition that exists when a high-speed airplane is landed on a water-covered runway. When the brakes are applied, the wheels lock up and the tires skid on the surface of the water in much the same way a water ski rides on the surface. Hydroplaning develops enough heat in a tire to ruin it.

Hydrostatic test. A pressure test used to determine the serviceability of high-pressure oxygen cylinders. The cylinders are filled with water and pressurized to 5/3 of their working pressure. Standard-weight cylinders (DOT 3AA) must by hydrostatically tested every five years, and lightweight cylinders (DOT 3HT) must be tested every three years.

Hypersonic speed. Speed of greater than Mach 5 (5 times the speed of sound).

Hyperbolic navigation. Electronic navigation systems that determine aircraft location by the time difference between reception of two signals. Signals from two stations at different locations will be received in the aircraft at different times. A line plotted between two stations along which the time difference is the same forms a hyperbola.

Hypoxia. A physiological condition in which a person is deprived of the needed oxygen. The effects of hypoxia normally disappear as soon as the person is able to breathe air containing sufficient oxygen.

ICAO. The International Civil Aeronautical Organization.

Icebox rivet. A solid rivet made of 2017 or 2024 aluminum alloy. These rivets are too hard to drive in the condition they are received from the factory, and must be heat-treated to soften them. They are heated in a furnace and then quenched in cold water. Immediately after quenching they are soft, but within a few hours at room temperature they become quite hard. The hardening can be delayed for several days by storing them in a subfreezing icebox and holding them at this low temperature until they are to be used.

IFR. Instrument flight rules.

Inch-pound. A measure of work accomplished when a force of 1 pound moves an object a distance of 1 inch. Indicated airspeed (IAS). The airspeed as shown on an airspeed indicator with no corrections applied.

Induced current. Electrical current produced in a conductor when it is moved through or crossed by a magnetic field Induced drag. Aerodynamic drag produced by an airfoil when it is producing lift. Induced drag is affected by the same factors that affect induced lift.

Induction time. The time allowed an epoxy or polyurethane material between its initial mixing and its application. This time allows the materials to begin their cure.

Infrared radiation. Electromagnetic radiation whose wavelengths are longer than those of visible light.

Ingot. A large block of metal that was molded as it was poured from the furnace. Ingots are further processed into sheets, bars, tubes, or structural beams.

INS. Inertial Navigation System.

Inspection Authorization (IA). An authorization that may be issued to an experienced aviation maintenance technician who holds both an Airframe and Powerplant rating. It allows the holder to conduct annual inspections and to approve an aircraft or aircraft engine for return to service after a major repair or major alteration.

Integral fuel tank. A fuel tank which is formed by sealing off part of the aircraft structure and using it as a fuel tank. An integral wing tank is called a "wet wing." Integral tanks are used because of their large weight saving. The only way of repairing an integral fuel tank is by replacing damaged sealant and making riveted repairs, as is done with any other part of the aircraft structure.

Interference drag. Parasite drag caused by air flowing over one portion of the airframe interfering with the smooth flow of air over another portion.

Intermittent-duty solenoid. A solenoid-type switch whose coil is designed for current to flow through it for only a short period of time. The coil will overheat if current flows through it too long.

IRS. Inertial Reference System.

IRU. Inertial Reference Unit.

Iso-octane. A hydrocarbon, C8H18, which has very high critical pressure and temperature. Iso-octane is used as the high reference for measuring the antidetonation characteristics of a fuel.

Isobaric mode. The mode of pressurization in which the cabin pressure is maintained at a constant value regardless of the outside air pressure.

Isogonic line. A line drawn on an aeronautical chart along which the angular difference between the magnetic and geographic north poles is the same.

Isopropyl alcohol. A colorless liquid used in the manufacture of acetone and its derivatives and as a solvent and anti-icing agent.

Jackscrew. A hardened steel rod with strong threads cut into it. A jackscrew is rotated by hand or with a motor to apply a force or to lift an object.

Jet pump. A special venturi in a line carrying air from certain areas in an aircraft that need an augmented flow of air through them. High-velocity compressor bleed air is blown into the throat of a venturi where it produces a low pressure that pulls air from the area to which it is connected. Jet pumps are often used in the lines that pull air through galleys and toilet areas.

Joggle. A small offset near the edge of a piece of sheet metal. It allows one sheet of metal to overlap another sheet while maintaining a flush surface.

Jointer. A woodworking power tool used to smooth edges of a piece of wood.

K-factor. A factor used in sheet metal work to determine the setback for other than a 90° bend. Setback = K · (bend radius + metal thickness). For bends of less than 90°, the value of K is less than 1; for bends greater than 90°, the value of K is greater than 1.

Kevlar. A patented synthetic aramid fiber noted for its flexibility and light weight. It is to a great extent replacing fiberglass as a reinforcing fabric for composite construction.

Key (verb). To initiate an action by depressing a key or a button.

kHz (kilohertz). 1,000 cycles per second.

Kick-in pressure. The pressure at which an unloading valve causes a hydraulic pump to direct its fluid into the system manifold.

Kick-out pressure. The pressure at which an unloading valve shuts off the flow of fluid into the system pressure manifold and directs it back to the reservoir under a much reduced pressure.

Kilogram. One thousand grams.

Kinetic energy. Energy that exists because of motion.

Knot (wood defect). A hard, usually round section of a tree branch embedded in a board. The grain of the knot is perpendicular to the grain of the board. Knots decrease the strength of the board and should be avoided where strength is needed.

Knot (measure of speed). A speed measurement that is equal to one nautical mile per hour. One knot is equal to 1.15 statute mile per hour.

Kollsman window. The barometric scale window of a sensitive altimeter. See barometric scale.

Koroseal lacing. A plastic lacing material available in round or rectangular cross sections and used for holding wire bundles and tubing together. It holds tension on knots indefinitely and is impervious to petroleum products.

Kraft paper. A tough brown wrapping paper, like that used for paper bags.

Labyrinth seal. A type of seal in a Roots blower cabin supercharger that is made in the form of knife edges riding in step-shaped grooves. Air pressure is dropped in each section of the seal, and any oil in the air is trapped in the grooves.

Lacquer. A finishing material made of a film base, solvents, plasticizers, and thinners. The film base forms a tough film over the surface when it dries. The solvents dissolve the film base so it can be applied as a liquid. The plasticizers give the film base the needed resilience, and the thinners dilute the lacquer so it can be applied with a spray gun. Lacquer is sprayed on the surface as a liquid, and when the solvents and thinners evaporate, the film base remains as a tough decorative and protective coating.

Landing gear warning system. A system of lights used to indicate the condition of the landing gear. A red light illuminates when any of the gears are in an unsafe condition; a green light shows when all of the gears are down and locked, and no light is lit when the gears are all up and locked. An aural warning system is installed that sounds a horn if any of the landing gears are not down and locked when the throttles are retarded for landing.

Laminar flow. Airflow in which the air passes over the surface in smooth layers with a minimum of turbulence.

Laminated wood. A type of wood made by gluing several pieces of thin wood together. The grain of all pieces runs in the same direction.

Latent heat. Heat that is added to a material that causes a change in its state without changing its temperature. Lateral axis. An imaginary line, passing through the center of gravity of an airplane, and extending across it from wing tip to wing tip.

Lay-up. The placement of the various layers of resinimpregnated fabric in the mold for a piece of laminated composite material.

L/D ratio. A measure of efficiency of an airfoil. It is the ratio of the lift to the total drag at a specified angle of attack.

Left-right indicator. The course-deviation indicator used with a VOR navigation system.

Lightening hole. A hole cut in a piece of structural material to get rid of weight without losing any strength. A hole several inches in diameter may be cut in a piece of metal at a point where the metal is not needed for strength, and the edges of the hole are flanged to give it rigidity. A piece of metal with properly flanged lightening holes is more rigid than the metal before the holes were cut.

Linear actuator. A fluid power actuator that uses a piston moving inside a cylinder to change pressure into linear, or straight-line, motion.

Linear change. A change in which the output is directly proportional to the input.

Loadmeter. A current meter used in some aircraft electrical systems to show the amount of current the generator or alternator is producing. Load meters are calibrated in percent of the generator rated output.

Localizer. The portion of an ILS (Instrument Landing System) that directs the pilot along the center line of the instrument runway.

Lodestone. A magnetized piece of natural iron oxide.

Logic flow chart. A type of graphic chart that can be made up for a specific process or procedure to help follow the process through all of its logical steps.

Longitudinal axis. An imaginary line, passing through the center of gravity of an airplane, and extending lengthwise through it from nose to tail.

Longitudinal stability. Stability of an aircraft along its longitudinal axis and about its lateral axis. Longitudinal stability is also called pitch stability.

LORAN A. Long Range Aid to Navigation. A hyperbolic navigation system that operates with frequencies of 1,950 kHz, 1,850 kHz, and 1,900 kHz.

LORAN C. The LORAN system used in aircraft. It operates on a frequency of 100 kHz.

LRU. Line replaceable unit.

Lubber line. A reference on a magnetic compass and directional gyro that represents the nose of the aircraft. The heading of the aircraft is shown on the compass card opposite the lubber line.

Mach number. A measurement of speed based on the ratio of the speed of the aircraft to the speed of sound under the same atmospheric conditions. An airplane flying at Mach 1 is flying at the speed of sound.

Magnetic bearing. The direction to or from a radio transmitting station measured relative to magnetic north. Major alteration. An alteration not listed in the aircraft, aircraft engine, or propeller specifications. It is one that might appreciably affect weight, balance, structural strength performance, powerplant operation, flight characteristics, or other qualities affecting airworthiness, or that cannot be made with elementary operations.

Major repair. A repair to an aircraft structure or component that if improperly made might appreciably affect weight, balance, structural strength, performance, powerplant operation, flight characteristics, or other qualities affecting airworthiness, or that is not done according to accepted practices, or cannot be made with elementary operation.

Manifold cross-feed fuel system. A type of fuel system commonly used in large transport category aircraft. All fuel tanks feed into a common manifold, and the dump chutes and the single-point fueling valves are connected to the manifold. Fuel lines to each engine are taken from the manifold.

Manifold pressure. The absolute pressure of the air in the induction system of a reciprocating engine.

Manifold pressure gauge. A pressure gauge that measures the absolute pressure inside the induction system of a reciprocating engine. When the engine is not operating, this instrument shows the existing atmospheric pressure.

Master switch. A switch in an aircraft electrical system that can disconnect the battery from the bus and open the generator or alternator field circuit.

Matrix. The material used in composite construction to bond the fibers together and to transmit the forces into the fibers. Resins are the most widely used matrix materials.

Mean camber. A line that is drawn midway between the upper and lower camber of an airfoil section. The mean camber determines the aerodynamic characteristics of the airfoil.

MEK. Methyl-ethyl-ketone is an organic chemical solvent that is soluble in water and is used as a solvent for vinyl and nitrocellulose films. MEK is an efficient cleaner for preparing surfaces for priming or painting.

Mercerize. A treatment given to cotton thread to make it strong and lustrous. The thread is stretched while it is soaked in a solution of caustic soda.

MFD. Multi-function display.

MHz (megahertz). 1,000,000 cycles per second.

Microballoons. Tiny, hollow spheres of glass or phenolic material used to add body to a resin.

Microbial contaminants. The scum that forms inside the fuel tanks of turbine-engine-powered aircraft that is caused by micro-organisms. These micro-organisms live in water that condenses from fuel, and they feed on the fuel. The scum they form clogs fuel filters, lines, and fuel controls and holds water in contact with the aluminum alloy structure, causing corrosion.

Micro-Mesh. A patented graduated series of cloth-backed cushioned seats that contain abrasive crystals. Micro-Mesh is used for polishing and restoring transparency to acrylic plastic windows and windshields.

Micron ("micro meter"). A unit of linear measurement equal to one millionth of a meter, one thousandth of a millimeter, or 0.000039 inch. A micron is also called a micrometer.

Micronic filter. The registered trade name of a type of fluid filter whose filtering element is a specially treated cellulose paper formed into vertical convolutions, or wrinkles. Micronic filters prevent the passage of solids larger than about 10 microns, and are normally replaced with new filters rather than cleaned.

Micro-organism. An organism, normally bacteria or fungus, or microscopic size.

Microswitch. The registered trade name for a precision switch that uses a short throw of the control plunger to actuate the contacts. Microswitches are used primarily as limit switches to control electrical units automatically.

MIG welding. Metal inert gas welding is a form of electric arc welding in which the electrode is an expendable wire. MIG welding is now called GMA (gas metal arc) welding.

Mil. One thousandth of an inch (0.001 inch). Paint film thickness is usually measured in mils.

Mildew. A gray or white fungus growth that forms on organic materials. Mildew forms on cotton and linen aircraft fabric and destroys its strength.

Millivoltmeter. An electrical instrument that measures voltage in units of millivolts (thousandths of a volt).

Mist coat. A very light coat of zinc chromate primer. It is so thin that the metal is still visible, but the primer makes pencil marks easy to see.

Moisture separator. A component in a high-pressure pneumatic system that removes most of the water vapor from the compressed air. When the compressed air is used, its pressure drops, and this pressure drop causes a drop in temperature. If any moisture were allowed to remain in the air, it would freeze and block the system.

Mold line. A line used in the development of a flat pattern for a formed piece of sheet metal. The mold line is an extension of the flat side of a part beyond the radius. The mold line dimension of a part is the dimension made to the intersection of mold lines and is the dimension the part would have if its corners had no radius.

Mold point. The intersection of two mold lines of a part. Mold line dimensions are made between mold points.

Moment. A force that causes or tries to cause an object to rotate. The value of a moment is the product of the weight of an object (or the force), multiplied by the distance between the center of gravity of the object (or the point of application of the force) and the fulcrum about which the object rotates.

Monel. An alloy of nickel, copper, and aluminum or silicon.

Monocoque. A single-shell type of aircraft structure in which all of the flight loads are carried in the outside skin of the structure.

MSDS. Material Safety Data Sheets. MSDS are required by the Federal Government to be available in workplaces to inform workers of the dangers that may exist from contact with certain materials.

MSL. Mean sea level. When the letters MSL are used with an altitude, it means that the altitude is measured from mean, or average, sea level.

MTBF. Mean time between failures.

Multimeter. An electrical test instrument that consists of a single current-measuring meter and all of the needed components to allow the meter to be used to measure voltage, resistance, and current. Multimeters are available with either analog-or digital-type displays.

Multiple-disk brakes. Aircraft brakes in which one set of disks is keyed to the axle and remains stationary. Between each stationary disk there is a rotating disk that is keyed to the inside of the wheel. When the brakes are applied, the stationary disks are forced together, clamping the rotating disks between them. The friction between the disks slows the aircraft.

Nailing strip. A method of applying pressure to the glue in a scarf joint repair in a plywood skin. A strip of thin plywood is nailed over the glued scarf joint with the nails extending into a supporting structure beneath the skin. The strip is installed over vinyl sheeting to prevent it sticking to the skin. When the glue is thoroughly dry, the nailing strip is broken away and the nails removed.

Nap of the fabric. The ends of the fibers in a fabric. The first coat of dope on cotton or linen fabric raises the nap, and the fiber ends stick up. These ends must be carefully removed by sanding to get a smooth finish.

Naphtha. A volatile and flammable hydrocarbon liquid used chiefly as a solvent or as a cleaning fluid.

NDB. Non-directional beacons.

Negative pressure relief valve (pressurization component). A valve that opens anytime the outside air pressure is greater than the cabin pressure. It prevents the cabin altitude from ever becoming greater than the aircraft flight altitude.

Neutral axis (neutral plane). A line through a piece of material that is bent. The material in the outside of the bend is stretched and that on the inside of the bend is shrunk. The material along the neutral plane is neither shrunk nor stretched.

Neutral flame. An oxyacetylene flame produced when the ratio of oxygen and acetylene is chemically correct and there is no excess of oxygen or carbon. A neutral flame has a rounded inner cone and no feather around it.

Noise (electrical). An unwanted electrical signal within a piece of electronic equipment.

Nomex. A patented nylon material used to make the honeycomb core for certain types of sandwich materials.

Nonenergizing brake. A brake that does not use the momentum of the aircraft to increase the friction.

Nonvolatile memory. Memory in a computer that is not lost when power to the computer is lost.

Normal heptane. A hydrocarbon, C7H16, with a very low critical pressure and temperature. Normal heptane is used as the low reference in measuring the anti-detonation characteristics of a fuel.

Normal shock wave. A shock wave that forms ahead of a blunt object moving through the air at the speed of sound. The shock wave is normal (perpendicular) to the air approaching the object. Air passing through a normal shock wave is slowed to a subsonic speed and its static pressure is increased.

Normalizing. A process of strain-relieving steel that has been welded and left in a strained condition. The steel is heated to a specified temperature, usually red hot, and allowed to cool in still air to room temperature.

Nose-gear centering cam. A cam in the nose-gear shock strut that causes the piston to center when the strut fully extends. When the aircraft takes off and the strut extends, the wheel is straightened in its fore-and-aft position so it can be retracted into the wheel well.

NPN transistor. A bipolar transistor made of a thin base of P-type silicon or geranium sandwiched between a collector and an emitter, both of which are made of N-type material.

Null position. The position of an ADF loop antenna when the signal being received is canceled in the two sides of the loop and the signal strength is the weakest.

Oblique shock wave. A shock wave that forms on a sharp-pointed object moving through air at a speed greater than the speed of sound. Air passing through an oblique shock wave is slowed down, but not to a subsonic speed, and its static pressure is increased.

Oleo shock absorber. A shock absorber used on aircraft landing gear. The initial landing impact is absorbed by oil transferring from one compartment in the shock strut into another compartment through a metering orifice. The shocks of taxiing are taken up by a cushion of compressed air.

Octane rating. A rating of the anti-detonation characteristics of a reciprocating engine fuel. It is based on the performance of the fuel in a special test engine. When a fuel is given a dual rating such as 80/87, the first number is its anti-detonating rating with a lean fuel-air mixture, and the higher number is its rating with a rich mixture.

Open angle. An angle in which sheet metal is bent less than 90°.

Open assembly time. The period of time between the application of the glue and the assembly of the joint components.

Open-hydraulic system. A fluid power system in which the selector valves are arranged in series with each other. Fluid flows from the pump through the center of the selector valves, back into the reservoir when no unit is being actuated.

Open-center selector valve. A type of selector valve that functions as an unloading valve as well as a selector valve. Open-center selector valves are installed in series, and when no unit is actuated, fluid from the pump flows through the centers of all the valves and returns to the reservoir. When a unit is selected for actuation, the center of the selector valve is shut off and the fluid from the pump goes through the selector valve into one side of the actuator. Fluid from the other side of the actuator returns to the valve and goes back to the reservoir through the other selector valves. When the actuation is completed, the selector valve is placed in its neutral position. Its center opens, and fluid from the pump flows straight through the valve.

Open wiring. An electrical wiring installation in which the wires are tied together in bundles and clamped to the aircraft structure rather than being enclosed in conduit.

Orifice check valve. A component in a hydraulic or pneumatic system that allows unrestricted flow in one direction, and restricted flow in the opposite direction.

O-ring. A widely used type of seal made in the form of a rubber ring with a round cross section. An O-ring seals in both directions, and it can be used as a packing or a gasket.

Ornithopter. A heavier-than-air flying machine that produces lift by flapping its wings. No practical ornithopter has been built.

Oscilloscope. An electrical instrument that displays on the face of a cathode-ray tube the waveform of the electrical signal it is measuring.

Outflow valve (pressurization component). A valve in the cabin of a pressurized aircraft that controls the cabin pressure by opening to relieve all pressure above that for which the cabin pressure control is set.

Overvoltage protector. A component in an aircraft electrical system that opens the alternator field circuit any time the alternator output voltage is too high.

Oxidizing flame. An oxyacetylene flame in which there is an excess of oxygen. The inner cone is pointed and often a hissing sound is heard.

Ozone. An unstable form of oxygen produced when an electric spark passes through the air. Ozone is harmful to rubber products.

Packing. A seal between two parts where there is relative motion.

Paint. A covering applied to an object or structure to protect it and improve its appearance. Paint consists of a pigment suspended in a vehicle such as oil or water. When the vehicle dries by evaporation or curing, the pigment is left as a film on the surface.

Parabolic reflector. A reflector whose surface is made in the form of a parabola.

Parallel circuit. A method of connecting electrical components so that each component is in a path between the terminals of the source of electrical energy.

Paralleling circuit. A circuit in a multi-engine aircraft electrical system that controls a flow of control current which is used to keep the generators or alternators sharing the electrical load equally. The relay opens automatically to shut off the flow of paralleling current any time the output of either alternator or generator drops to zero.

Paralleling relay. A relay in multi-engine aircraft electrical system that controls a flow of control current which is used to keep the generators or alternators sharing the electrical load equally. The relay opens automatically to shut off the flow of paralleling current any time the output of either alternator or generator drops to zero.

Parasite drag. A form of aerodynamic drag caused by friction between the air and the surface over which it is flowing.

Parent metal. The metal being welded. This term is used to distinguish between the metal being welded and the welding rod.

Partial pressure. The percentage of the total pressure of a mixture of gases produced by each of the individual gases in the mixture.

Parting film. A layer of thin plastic material placed between a composite lay-up and the heating blanket. It prevents the blanket from sticking to the fabric.

Pascal's Law. A basic law of fluid power which states that the pressure in an enclosed container is transmitted equally and undiminished to all points of the container, and the force acts at right angles to the enclosing walls.

Performance number. The anti-detonation rating of a fuel that has a higher critical pressure and temperature than isooctane (a rating of 100). Iso-octane that has been treated with varying amounts of tetraethyl lead is used as the reference fuel.

Petrolatum-zinc dust compound. A special abrasive compound used inside an aluminum wire terminal being swaged onto a piece of aluminum electrical wire. When the terminal is compressed, the zinc dust abrades the oxides from the wire, and the petrolatum prevents oxygen reaching the wire so no more oxides can form.

Petroleum fractions. The various components of a hydrocarbon fuel that are separated by boiling them off at different temperatures in the process of fractional distillation.

Phased array antenna. A complex antenna which consists of a number of elements. A beam of energy is formed by the superimposition of the signals radiating from the elements. The direction of the beam can be changed by varying the relative phase of the signals applied to each of the elements.

Phenolic plastic. A plastic material made of a thermosetting phenol-formaldehyde resin, reinforced with cloth or paper. Phenolic plastic materials are used for electrical insulators and for chemical-resistant table tops.

Pilot hole. A small hole punched or drilled in a piece of sheet metal to locate a rivet hole.

Pin knot cluster. A group of knots, all having a diameter of less than approximately 1/16 inch.

Pinked-edge tape. Cloth tape whose edges have small V-shaped notches cut along their length. The pinked edges prevent the tape from raveling.

Pinking shears. Shears used to cut aircraft fabric with a series of small notches along the cut edge.

Pinion. A small gear that meshes with a larger gear, a sector of a gear, or a toothed rack.

Piston. A sliding plug in an actuating cylinder used to convert pressure into force and then into work.

Pitch (aircraft maneuver). Rotation of an aircraft about its lateral axis.

Pitch (rivet). The distance between the centers of adjacent rivets installed in the small row.

Pitch pocket (wood defect). Pockets of pitch that appear in the growth rings of a piece of wood.

Pitot pressure. Ram air pressure used to measure airspeed. The pitot tube faces directly into the air flowing around the aircraft. It stops the air and measures its pressure.

Plain-weave fabric. Fabric in which each warp thread passes over one fill thread and under the next. Plain-weave fabric typically has the same strength in both warp and fill directions.

Plan position indicator (PPI). A type of radar scope that shows both the direction and distance of the target from the radar antenna. Some radar antenna rotate and their PPI scopes are circular. Other antenna oscillate and their PPI scopes are fan shaped.

Planer. A woodworking power tool used to smooth the surfaces of a piece of wood.

Plasticizer. A constituent in dope or lacquer that gives its film flexibility and resilience.

Plastic media blasting (PMB). A method of removing paint from an aircraft surface by dry-blasting it with tiny plastic beads.

Plastics. The generic name for any of the organic materials produced by polymerization. Plastics can be shaped by molding or drawing.

Plenum. An enclosed chamber in which air can be held at a pressure higher than that of the surrounding air.

Ply rating. The rating of an aircraft tire that indicates its relative strength. The ply rating does not indicate the actual number of plies of fabric in the tire; it indicates the number of piles of cotton fabric needed to produce the same strength as the actual piles.

Plywood. A wood product made by gluing several pieces of thin wood veneer together. The grain of the wood in each layer runs at 90° or 45° to the grain of the layer next to it.

Pneumatics. The system of fluid power which transmits force by the use of a compressible fluid.

PNP transistor. A bipolar transistor made of a thin base of N-type silicon or germanium sandwiched between a collector and an emitter, both of which are made of P-type material.

Polyester fibers. A synthetic fiber made by the polymerization process in which tiny molecules are united to form a long chain of molecules. Polyester fibers are woven into fabrics that are known by their trade names of Dacron, Fortrel, and Kodel. Polyester film and sheet are known as Mylar and Celenar.

Polyester resin. A thermosetting resin used as a matrix for much of the fiberglass used in composite construction

Polyurethane enamel. A hard, chemically resistant finish used on aircraft. Polyurethane enamel is resistant to damage from all types of hydraulic fluid.

Polyvinyl chloride. A thermoplastic resin used in the manufacture of transparent tubing for electrical insulation and fluid lines which are subject to low pressures

Position error. The error in pitot-static instruments caused by the static ports not sensing true static air pressure. Position error changes with airspeed and is usually greatest at low airspeeds.

Potential energy. Energy possessed in an object because of its position, chemical composition, shape, or configuration.

Potentiometer. A variable resistor having connections to both ends of the resistance element and to the wiper that moves across the resistance.

Pot life. The length of time a resin will remain workable after the catalyst has been added. If a catalyzed material is not used within its usable pot life, it must be discarded and a new batch mixed up.

Power. The time rate of doing work. Power is force multiplied by distance (work), divided by time.

Power brakes. Aircraft brakes that use the main hydraulic system to supply fluid for the brake actuation. Aircraft that require a large amount of fluid for their brake actuation normally use power brakes, and the volume of fluid sent to the brakes is increased by the use of deboosters.

Power control valve. A hand-operated hydraulic pump unloading valve. When the valve is open, fluid flows from the pump to the reservoir with little opposition. To actuate a unit, turn the selector valve, and manually close the power control valve. Pressurized fluid flows to the unit, and when it is completely actuated, the power control valve automatically opens.

Precession. The characteristic of a gyroscope that causes a force to be felt, not at the point of application, but at a point 90° in the direction of rotation from that point.

Preflight inspection. A required inspection to determine the condition of the aircraft for the flight to be conducted. It is conducted by the pilot-in-command.

Precipitation heat treatment. A method of increasing the strength of heat-treated aluminum alloy. After the aluminum alloy has been solution-heat-treated by heating and quenching, it is returned to the oven and heated to a temperature lower than that used for the initial heat treatment. It is held at this temperature for a specified period of time, and then removed from the oven and allowed to cool slowly.

Prepreg (preimpregnated fabric). A type of composite material in which the reinforcing fibers are encapsulated in an uncured resin. Prepreg materials must be kept refrigerated to prevent them from curing before they are used.

Press-to-test light fixture. An indicator light fixture whose lens can be pressed in to complete a circuit that tests the filament of the light bulb.

Pressure. Force per unit area. Hydraulic and pneumatic pressure are normally given in units of pounds per square inch (psi).

Pressure altitude. The altitude in standard air at which the pressure is the same as that of the existing air. Pressure altitude is read on an altimeter when the barometric scale is set to the standard sea level pressure of 29.92 inches of mercury.

Pressure-demand oxygen system. A type of oxygen system used by aircraft that fly at very high altitude. This system functions as a diluter-demand system until, at about 40,000 feet, the output to the mask is pressurized enough to force the needed oxygen into the lungs, rather than depending on the low pressure produced when the wearer of the mask inhales to pull in the oxygen. (See diluter-demand oxygen system.)

Pressure fueling. The method of fueling used by almost all transport aircraft. The fuel is put into the aircraft through a single underwing fueling port. The fuel tanks are filled to the desired quantity and in the sequence selected by the person conducting the fueling operation. Pressure fueling saves servicing time by using a single point to fuel the entire aircraft, and it reduces the chances for fuel contamination.

Pressure manifold (hydraulic system component). The portion of a fluid power system from which the selector valves receive their pressurized fluid.

Pressure plate (brake component). A strong, heavy plate used in a multiple-disk brake. The pressure plate receives the force from the brake cylinders and transmits this force to the disks.

Pressure reducing valve (oxygen system component). A valve used in an oxygen system to change high cylinder pressure to low system pressure.

Pressure relief valve (oxygen system component). A valve in an oxygen system that relieves the pressure if the pressure reducing valve should fail.

Pressure vessel. The strengthened portion of an aircraft structure that is sealed and pressurized in flight.

Primer (finishing system component). A component in a finishing system that provides a good bond between the surface and the material used for the topcoats.

Profile drag. Aerodynamic drag produced by skin friction. Profile drag is a form of parasite drag.

Progressive inspection. An inspection that may be used in place of an annual or 100-hour inspection. It has the same scope as an annual inspection, but it may be performed in increments so the aircraft will not have to be out of service for a lengthy period of time.

Pump control valve. A control valve in a hydraulic system that allows the pilot to manually direct the output of the hydraulic pump back to the reservoir when no unit is being actuated.

Pureclad. A registered trade name for clad aluminum alloy.

Purge (air conditioning system operation). To remove all of the moisture and air from a cooling system by flushing the system with a dry gaseous refrigerant.

Pusher powerplant. A powerplant whose propeller is mounted at the rear of the airplane and pushes, rather than pulls, the airplane through the air.

PVC (Polyvinylchloride). A thermoplastic resin used to make transparent tubing for insulating electrical wires.

Quartersawed wood. Wood sawed from a tree in such a way that the annual rings cross the plank at an angle greater than 45°.

Quick-disconnect fitting. A hydraulic line fitting that seals the line when the fitting is disconnected. Quick-disconnect fittings are used on the lines connected to the engine-driven hydraulic pump. They allow the pump to be disconnected and an auxiliary hydraulic power system connected to perform checks requiring hydraulic power while the aircraft is in the hangar.

Rack-and-pinion actuator. A form of rotary actuator where the fluid acts on a piston on which a rack of gear teeth is cut. As the piston moves, it rotates a pinion gear which is mated with the teeth cut in the rack.

Radial. A directional line radiating outward from a radio facility, usually a VOR. When an aircraft is flying outbound on the 330° from the station.

Radius dimpling. A process of preparing a hole in sheet metal for flush riveting. A cone-shaped male die forces the edges of the rivet hole into the depression in a female die. Radius dimpling forms a round-edged depression into which the rivet head fits.

Range markings. Colored marks on an instrument dial that identify certain ranges of operation as specified in the aircraft maintenance or flight manual and listed in the appropriate aircraft Type Certificate Data Sheets or Aircraft Specifications. Color coding directs attention to approaching operating difficulties. Airspeed indicators and most pressure and temperature indicators are marked to show the various ranges of operation. These ranges and colors are the most generally used: Red radial line, do not exceed. Green arc, normal operating range. Yellow arc, caution range. Blue radial line, used on airspeed indicators to show best single-engine rate of climb speed. White arc, used on airspeed indicators to show flap operating range.

RDF. Radio direction finding

Rebreather oxygen mask. A type of oxygen mask used with a continuous flow oxygen system. Oxygen continuously flows into the bottom of the loose-fitting rebreather bag on the mask. The wearer of the mask exhales into the top of the bag. The first air exhaled contains some oxygen, and this air goes into the bag first. The last air to leave the lungs contains little oxygen, and it is forced out of the bag as the bag is filled with fresh oxygen. Each time the wearer of the mask inhales, the air first exhaled, along with fresh oxygen, is taken into the lungs.

Receiver-dryer. The component in a vapor-cycle cooling system that serves as a reservoir for the liquid refrigerant. The receiver-dryer contains a desiccant that absorbs any moisture that may be in the system.

Rectangle. A plane surface with four sides whose opposite sides are parallel and whose angles are all right angles.

Rectification (arc welding condition). A condition in AC-electric arc welding in which oxides on the surface of the metal act as a rectifier and prevent electrons flowing from the metal to the electrode during the half cycle when the electrode is positive.

Reducing flame. See carburizing flame

Reed valve. A thin, leaf-type valve mounted in the valve plate of an air conditioning compressor to control the flow of refrigerant gases into and out of the compressor cylinders.

Reinforcing tape. A narrow strip of woven fabric material placed over the fabric as it is being attached to the aircraft structure with rib lacing cord. This tape carries a large amount of the load and prevents the fabric tearing at the stitches.

Rejuvenator. A finishing material used to restore resilience to an old dope film. Rejuvenator contains strong solvents to open the dried-out film and plasticizers to restore resilience to the old dope.

Relative wind. The direction the wind strikes an airfoil.

Relay. An electrical component which uses a small amount of current flowing through a coil to produce a magnetic pull to close a set of contacts through which a large amount of current can flow. The core in a relay coil is fixed.

Relief hole. A hole drilled at the point at which two bend lines meet in a piece of sheet metal. This hole spreads the stresses caused by the bends and prevents the metal cracking.

Relief valve. A pressure-control valve that relieves any pressure over the amount for which it is set. They are damage preventing units used in both hydraulic and pneumatic systems. In an aircraft hydraulic system, pressure relief valves prevent damaging high pressures that could be caused by a malfunctioning pressure regulator, or by thermal expansion of fluid trapped in portions of the system.

Repair. A maintenance procedure in which a damaged component is restored to its original condition, or at least to a condition that allows it to fulfill its design function.

Restrictor. A fluid power system component that controls the rate of actuator movement by restricting the flow of fluid into or out of the actuator.

Retard breaker points. A set of breaker points in certain aircraft magnetos that are used to provide a late (retarded) spark for starting the engine.

Retarder (finishing system component). Dope thinner that contains certain additives that slow its rate of evaporation enough to prevent dope blushing.

Retread. The replacement of the tread rubber on an aircraft tire.

Retreating blade. The blade on a helicopter rotor whose tip is moving in the direction opposite to that in which the helicopter is moving.

Retreating blade stall. The stall of a helicopter rotor disc that occurs near the tip of the retreating blade. A retreating blade stall occurs when the flight airspeed is high and the retreating blade airspeed is low. This results in a high angle of attack, causing the stall.

Return manifold. The portion of a fluid power system through which the fluid is returned to the reservoir.

Reverse polarity welding. DC-electric arc welding in which the electrode is positive with respect to the work.

Rib thread. A series of circumferential grooves cut into the tread of a tire. This tread pattern provides superior traction and directional stability on hard-surfaced runways.

Ribbon direction. The direction in a piece of honeycomb material that is parallel to the length of the strips of material that make up the core.

Rigid conduit. Aluminum alloy tubing used to house electrical wires in areas where they are subject to mechanical damage.

Rigidity in space. The characteristic of a gyroscope that prevents its axis of rotation tilting as the earth rotates. This characteristic is used for attitude gyro instruments.

Rime ice. A rough ice that forms on aircraft flying through visible moisture, such as a cloud, when the temperature is below freezing. Rime ice disturbs the smooth airflow as well as adding weight.

Rivet cutters. Special cutting pliers that resemble diagonal cutters except that the jaws are ground in such a way that they cut the rivet shank, or stem, off square.

Rivet set. A tool used to drive aircraft solid rivets. It is a piece of hardened steel with a recess the shape of the rivet head in one end. The other end fits into the rivet gun.

RMI. Radio magnetic indicator.

Rocking shaft. A shaft used in the mechanism of a pressure measuring instrument to change the direction of movement by 90° and to amplify the amount of movement.

Roll (aircraft maneuver). Rotation of an aircraft about its longitudinal axis.

Roots-type air compressor. A positive-displacement air pump that uses two intermeshing figure-8-shaped rotors to move the air.

Rosette weld. A method of securing one metal tube inside another by welding. Small holes are drilled in the outer tube and the inner tube is welded to it around the circumference of the holes.

Rotary actuator. A fluid power actuator whose output is rotational. A hydraulic motor is a rotary actuator.

Roving. A lightly twisted roll or strand of fibers.

RPM. Revolutions per minute.

Ruddervators. The two movable surfaces on a V-tail empennage. When these two surfaces are moved together with the in-and-out movement of the control yoke, they act as elevators, and when they are moved differentially with the rudder pedals, they act as the rudder.

Saddle gusset. A piece of plywood glued to an aircraft structural member. The saddle gusset has a cutout to hold a backing block or strip tightly against the skin to allow a nailing strip to be used to apply pressure to a glued joint in the skin.

Sailplane. A high-performance glider.

Sandwich material. A type of composite structural material in which a core material is bonded between face sheets of metal or resin-impregnated fabric.

Satin-weave fabric. Fabric in which the warp threads pass under one fill thread and over several others. Satin-weave fabrics are used when the lay-up must be made over complex shapes.

Scarf joint. A joint in a wood structure in which the ends to be joined are cut in a long taper, normally about 12:1, and fastened together by gluing. A glued scarf joint makes a strong splice because the joint is made along the side of the wood fibers rather than along their ends.

Schematic diagram. A diagram of an electrical system in which the system components are represented by symbols rather than drawings or pictures of the actual devices.

Schrader valve. A type of service valve used in an air conditioning system. This is a spring-loaded valve much like the valve used to put air into a tire.

Scissors. A name commonly used for torque links. See torque links.

Scupper. A recess around the filler neck of an aircraft fuel tank. Any fuel spilled when the tank is being serviced collects in the scupper and drains to the ground through a drain line rather than flowing into the aircraft structure.

Sea level engine. A reciprocating engine whose rated takeoff power can be produced only at sea level.

Sector gear. A part of a gear wheel containing the hub and a portion of the rim with teeth.

Series circuit. A method of connecting electrical components in such a way that all the current flows through each of the components. There is only one path for current to flow.

Series-parallel circuit. An electrical circuit in which some of the components are connected in parallel and others are connected in series.

Selcal system. Selective calling system. Each aircraft operated by an airline is assigned a particular four-tone audio combination for identification purposes. A ground station keys the signal whenever contact with that particular aircraft is desired. The signal is decoded by the airborne selcal decoder and the crew alerted by the selcal warning system.

Selsyn system. A DC synchro system used in remote indicating instruments. The rotor in the indicator is a permanent magnet and the stator is a tapped toroidal coil. The transmitter is a circular potentiometer with DC power fed into its wiper which is moved by the object being monitored. The transmitter is connected to the indicator in such a way that rotation of the transmitter shaft varies the current in the sections of the indicator toroidal coil. The magnet in the indicator on which the pointer is mounted locks with the magnetic field produced by the coils and follows the rotation of the transmitter shaft.

Segmented-rotor brake. A heavy-duty, multiple-disk brake used on large, high-speed aircraft. Stators that are surfaced with a material that retains its friction characteristics at high temperatures are keyed to the axle. Rotors which are keyed into the wheels mesh with the stators. The rotors are made in segments to allow for cooling and for their large amounts of expansion.

Selector valve. A flow control valve used in hydraulic systems that directs pressurized fluid into one side of an actuator, and at the same time directs return fluid from the other side of the actuator back to the reservoir. There are two basic types of selector valves: open-center valves and closed-center valves. The four-port closed-center valve is the most frequently used type. See closed-center selector valve and open-center selector valve.

Selvage edge. The woven edge of fabric used to prevent the material unraveling during normal handling. The selvage edge, which runs the length of the fabric parallel to the warp threads, is usually removed from materials used in composite construction.

Semiconductor diode. A two-element electrical component that allows current to pass through it in one direction, but blocks its passage in the opposite direction. A diode acts in an electrical system in the same way a check valve acts in a hydraulic system.

Semimonocoque structure. A form of aircraft stressed skin structure. Most of the strength of a semimonocoque structure is in the skin, but the skin is supported on a substructure of formers and stringers that give the skin its shape and increase its rigidity.

Sensible heat. Heat that is added to a liquid causing a change in its temperature but not its physical state.

Sensitivity. A measure of the signal strength needed to produce a distortion-free output in a radio receiver.

Sequence valve. A valve in a hydraulic system that requires a certain action to be completed before another action can begin. Sequence valves are used to assure that the hydraulically actuated wheel-well doors are completely open before pressure is directed to the landing gear to lower it.

Servo. An electrical or hydraulic actuator connected into a flight control system. A small force on the flight deck control is amplified by the servo and provides a large force to move the control surface.

Servo amplifier. An electronic amplifier in an autopilot system that increases the signal from the autopilot enough that it can operate the servos that move the control surfaces. Servo tab. A small movable tab built into the trailing edge of a primary control surface of an airplane. The flight deck controls move the tab in such a direction that it produces an aerodynamic force moving the surface on which it is mounted.

Setback. The distance the jaws of a brake must be set back from the mold line to form a bend. Setback for a 90° bend is equal to the inside radius of the bend plus the thickness of the metal being bent. For a bend other than 90°, a K-factor must be used. See also K-factor.

Shake (wood defect). Longitudinal cracks in a piece of wood, usually between two annual rings.

SHF. Super-high frequency.

Shear section. A necked-down section of the drive shaft of a constant-displacement engine-driven fluid pump. If the pump should seize, the shear section will break and prevent the pump from being destroyed or the engine from being damaged. Some pumps use a shear pin rather than a shear section.

Shear strength. The strength of a riveted joint in a sheet metal structure in which the rivets shear before the metal tears at the rivet holes.

Shelf life. The length of time a product is good when it remains in its original unopened container.

Shielded wire. Electrical wire enclosed in a braided metal jacket. Electromagnetic energy radiated from the wire is trapped by the braid and is carried to ground.

Shimmy. Abnormal, and often violent, vibration of the nose wheel of an airplane. Shimmying is usually caused by looseness of the nose wheel support mechanism or an unbalanced wheel.

Shimmy damper. A small hydraulic shock absorber installed between the nose wheel fork and the nose wheel cylinder attached to the aircraft structure.

Shock mounts. Resilient mounting pads used to protect electronic equipment by absorbing low-frequency, high amplitude vibrations.

Shock wave. A pressure wave formed in the air by a flight vehicle moving at a speed greater than the speed of sound. As the vehicle passes through the air, it produces sound waves that spread out in all directions. But since the vehicle is flying faster than these waves are moving, they build up and form a pressure wave at the front and rear of the vehicle. As the air passes through a shock wave it slows down, its static pressure increases, and its total energy decreases.

Shop head. The head of a rivet which is formed when the shank is upset.

Show-type finish. The type of finish put on fabric-covered aircraft intended for show. This finish is usually made up of many coats of dope, with much sanding and rubbing of the surface between coats.

Shunt winding. Field coils in an electric motor or generator that are connected in parallel with the armature.

Shuttle valve. An automatic selector valve mounted on critical components such as landing gear actuation cylinders and brake cylinders. For normal operation, system fluid flows into the actuator through the shuttle valve, but if normal system pressure is lost, emergency system pressure forces the shuttle over and emergency fluid flows into the actuator.

Sidestick controller. A flight deck flight control used on some of the fly-by-wire equipped airplanes. The stick is mounted rigidly on the side console of the flight deck, and pressures exerted on the stick by the pilot produce electrical signals that are sent to the computer that flies the airplane.

Sight glass (air conditioning system component). A small window in the high side of a vapor-cycle cooling system. Liquid refrigerant flows past the sight glass, and if the charge of refrigerant is low, bubbles will be seen. A fully charged system has no bubbles in the refrigerant.

Sight line. A line drawn on a sheet metal layout that is one bend radius from the bend-tangent line. The sight line is lined up directly below the nose of the radius bar in a cornice brake. When the metal is clamped in this position, the bend tangent line is in the correct position for the start of the bend.

Silicon controlled rectifier (SCR). A semiconductor electron control device. An SCR blocks current flow in both directions until a pulse of positive voltage is applied to its gate. It then conducts in its forward direction, while continuing to block current in its reverse direction.

Silicone rubber. An elastomeric material made from silicone elastomers. Silicone rubber is compatible with fluids that attack other natural or synthetic rubbers.

Single-acting actuator. A linear hydraulic or pneumatic actuator that uses fluid power for movement in one direction and a spring force for its return.

Single-action hand pump. A hand-operated fluid pump that moves fluid only during one stroke of the pump handle. One stroke pulls the fluid into the pump and the other forces the fluid out.

Single-disk brakes. Aircraft brakes in which a single steel disk rotates with the wheel between two brake-lining blocks. When the brake is applied, the disk is clamped tightly between the lining blocks, and the friction slows the aircraft.

Single-servo brakes. Brakes that uses the momentum of the aircraft rolling forward to help apply the brakes by wedging the brake shoe against the brake drum.

Sintered metal. A porous material made by fusing powdered metal under heat and pressure.

Skydrol hydraulic fluid. The registered trade name for a synthetic, nonflammable, phosphate ester-base hydraulic fluid used in modern high-temperature hydraulic systems.

Slat. A secondary control on an aircraft that allows it to fly at a high angle of attack without stalling. A slat is a section of leading edge of wing mounted on curved tracks that move into and out of the wing on rollers.

Slip roll former. A shop tool used to form large radius curves on sheet metal.

Slippage mark. A paint mark extending across the edge of an aircraft wheel onto a tube-type tire. When this mark is broken, it indicates the tire has slipped on the wheel, and there is a good reason to believe the tube has been damaged.

Slipstream area. For the purpose of rib stitch spacing, the slipstream area is considered to be the diameter of the propeller plus one wing rib on each side.

Slot (aerodynamic device). A fixed, nozzle-like opening near the leading edge of an airplane wing ahead of the aileron. A slot acts as a duct to force high-energy air down on the upper surface of the wing when the airplane is flying at a high angle of attack. The slot, which is located ahead of the aileron, causes the inboard portion of the wing to stall first, allowing the aileron to remain effective throughout the stall.

Slow-blow fuse. An electrical fuse that allows a large amount of current to flow for a short length of time but melts to open the circuit if more than its rated current flows for a longer period.

Smoke detector. A device that warns the flight crew of the presence of smoke in cargo and/or baggage compartments. Some smoke detectors are of the visual type, others are photoelectric or ionization devices.

Snubber. A device in a hydraulic or pneumatic component that absorbs shock and/or vibration. A snubber is installed in the line to a hydraulic pressure gauge to prevent the pointer fluctuating.

Softwood. Wood from a tree that bears cones and has needles rather than leaves.

Soldering. A method of thermally joining metal parts with a molten nonferrous alloy that melts at a temperature below 800 °F. The molten alloy is pulled up between close-fitting parts by capillary action. When the alloy cools and hardens, it forms a strong, leak-proof connection.

Solenoid. An electrical component using a small amount of current flowing through a coil to produce a magnetic force that pulls an iron core into the center of the coil. The core may be attached to a set of heavy-duty electrical contacts, or it may be used to move a valve or other mechanical device.

Solidity (helicopter rotor characteristic). The solidity of a helicopter rotor system is the ratio of the total blade area to the disc area.

Solution heat treatment. A type of heat treatment in which the metal is heated in a furnace until it has a uniform temperature throughout. It is then removed and quenched in cold water. When the metal is hot, the alloying elements enter into a solid solution with the base metal to become part of its basic structure. When the metal is quenched, these elements are locked into place.

Sonic venture. A venture in a line between a turbine engine or turbocharger and a pressurization system. When the air flowing through the venture reaches the speed of sound, a shock wave forms across the throat of the venture and limits the flow. A sonic venture is also called a flow limited.

Specific heat. The number of BTUs of heat energy needed to change the temperature of one pound of a substance 1 °F.

Speed brakes. A secondary control of an airplane that produces drag without causing a change in the pitch attitude of the airplane. Speed brakes allow an airplane to make a steep descent without building up excessive forward airspeed.

Spike knot. A knot that runs through the depth of a beam perpendicular to the annual rings. Spike knots appear most frequently in quartersawed wood.

Spin. A flight maneuver in which an airplane descends in a corkscrew fashion. One wing is stalled and the other is producing lift.

Spirit level. A curved glass tube partially filled with a liquid, but with a bubble in it. When the device in which the tube is mounted is level, the bubble will be in the center of the tube.

Splayed patch (wood structure repair). A type of patch made in an aircraft plywood structure in which the edges of the patch are tapered for approximately five times the thickness of the plywood. A splayed patch is not recommended for use on plywood less than $\frac{1}{10}$ inch thick.

Split bus. A type of electrical bus that allows all of the voltage-sensitive avionic equipment to be isolated from the rest of the aircraft electrical system when the engine is being started or when the ground-power unit is connected.

Split-rocker switch. An electrical switch whose operating rocker is split so one half of the switch can be opened without affecting the other half. Split-rocker switches are used as aircraft master switches. The battery can be turned on without turning on the alternator, but the alternator cannot be turned on without also turning on the battery. The alternator can be turned off without turning off the battery, but the battery cannot be turned off without also turning off the alternator.

Split (wood defect). A longitudinal crack in a piece of wood caused by externally induced stress.

Spoilers. Flight controls that are raised up from the upper surface of a wing to destroy, or spoil, lift. Flight spoilers are used in conjunction with the ailerons to decrease lift and increase drag on the descending wing. Ground spoilers are used to produce a great amount of drag to slow the airplane on its landing roll.

Spongy brakes. Hydraulic brakes whose pedal has a spongy feel because of air trapped in the fluid.

Spontaneous combustion. Self-ignition of a material caused by heat produced in the material as it combines with oxygen from the air.

Springwood. The portion of an annual ring in a piece of wood formed principally during the first part of the growing season, the spring of the year. Springwood is softer, more porous, and lighter than the summerwood.

Square. A four-sided plane figure whose sides are all the same length, whose opposite sides are parallel, and whose angles are all right angles.

Squat switch. An electrical switch actuated by the landing gear scissors on the oleo strut. When no weight is on the landing gear, the oleo piston is extended and the switch is in one position, but when weight is on the gear, the oleo strut compresses and the switch changes its position. Squat switches are used in antiskid brake systems, landing gear safety circuits, and cabin pressurization systems.

Squib. An explosive device in the discharge valve of a high-rate-discharge container of fire-extinguishing agent. The squib drives a cutter into the seal in the container to discharge the agent.

SRM. Structural Repair Manual.

Stabilator. A flight control on the empennage of an airplane that acts as both a stabilizer and an elevator. The entire horizontal tail surface pivots and is moved as a unit. Stability. The characteristic of an aircraft that causes it to return to its original flight condition after it has been disturbed.

Stabilons. Small wing-like horizontal surfaces mounted on the aft fuselage to improve longitudinal stability of airplanes that have an exceptionally wide center of gravity range.

Stagnation point. The point on the leading edge of a wing at which the airflow separates, with some flowing over the top of the wing and the rest below the wing.

Stall. A flight condition in which an angle of attack is reached at which the air ceases to flow smoothly over the upper surface of an airfoil. The air becomes turbulent and lift is lost.

Stall strip. A small triangular metal strip installed along the leading edge of an airplane wing near the wing root. Stall strips cause the root section of the wing to stall before the portion of the wing ahead of the ailerons.

Standpipe. A pipe sticking up in a tank or reservoir that allows part of the tank to be used as a reserve, or standby, source of fluid.

Starter-generator. A single-component starter and generator used on many of the smaller gas-turbine engines. It is used as a starter, and when the engine is running, its circuitry is shifted so that it acts as a generator.

Static. Still, not moving.

Static air pressure. Pressure of the ambient air surrounding the aircraft. Static pressure does not take into consideration any air movement.

Static dischargers. Devices connected to the trailing edges of control surfaces to discharge static electricity harmlessly into the air. They discharge the static charges before they can build up high enough to cause radio receiver interference.

Static stability. The characteristic of an aircraft that causes it to return to straight and level flight after it has been disturbed from that condition.

Stoddard solvent. A petroleum product, similar to naphtha, used as a solvent and a cleaning fluid

STOL. Short takeoff and landing.

Stop drilling. A method of stopping the growth of a crack in a piece of metal or transparent plastic by drilling a small hole at the end of the crack. The stresses are spread out all around the circumference of the hole rather than concentrated at the end of the crack.

Straight polarity welding. DC-electric arc welding in which the electrode is negative with respect to the work.

Strain. A deformation or physical change in a material caused by a stress.

Stress. A force set up within an object that tries to prevent an outside force from changing its shape.

Stressed skin structure. A type of aircraft structure in which all or most of the stresses are carried in the outside skin. A stressed skin structure has a minimum of internal structure.

Stress riser. A location where the cross-sectional area of the part changes abruptly. Stresses concentrate at such a location and failure is likely. A scratch, gouge, or tool mark in the surface of a highly stressed part can change the area enough to concentrate the stresses and become a stress riser.

Stringer. A part of an aircraft structure used to give the fuselage its shape and, in some types of structure, to provide a small part of fuselage strength. Formers give the fuselage its cross-sectional shape and stringers fill in the shape between the formers.

Stroboscopic tachometer. A tachometer used to measure the speed of any rotating device without physical contact. A highly accurate variable-frequency oscillator triggers a high-intensity strobe light.

Sublimation. A process in which a solid material changes directly into a vapor without passing through the liquid stage.

Subsonic flight. Flight at an airspeed in which all air flowing over the aircraft is moving at a speed below the speed of sound.

Summerwood. The less porous, usually harder portion of an annual ring that forms in the latter part of the growing season, the summer of the year.

Sump. A low point in an aircraft fuel tank in which water and other contaminants can collect and be held until they can be drained out.

Supercooled water. Water in its liquid form at a temperature well below its natural freezing temperature. When supercooled water is disturbed, it immediately freezes. Superheat. Heat energy that is added to a refrigerant after it changes from a liquid to a vapor.

Super heterodyne circuit. A sensitive radio receiver circuit in which a local oscillator produces a frequency that is a specific difference from the received signal frequency. The desired signal and the output from the oscillator are mixed, and they produce a single, constant intermediate frequency. This IF is amplified, demodulated, and detected to produce the audio frequency that is used to drive the speaker. Supersonic flight. Flight at an airspeed in which all air flowing over the aircraft is moving at a speed greater than the speed of sound.

Supplemental Type Certificate (STC). An approval issued by the FAA for a modification to a type certificated airframe, engine, or component. More than one STC can be issued for the same basic alteration, but each holder must prove to the FAA that the alteration meets all the requirements of the original type certificate

Surface tape. Strips of aircraft fabric that are doped over all seams and places where the fabric is stitched to the aircraft structure. Surface tape is also doped over the wing leading edges where abrasive wear occurs. The edges of surface tape are pink, or notched, to keep them from raveling before the dope is applied.

Surfactant. A surface active agent, or partially soluble contaminant, which is a by-product of fuel processing or of fuel additives. Surfactants adhere to other contaminants and cause them to drop out of the fuel and settle to the bottom of the fuel tank as sludge.

Surveyor's transit. An instrument consisting of a telescope mounted on a flat, graduated, circular plate on a tripod. The plate can be adjusted so it is level, and its graduations oriented to magnetic north. When an object is viewed through the telescope, its azimuth and elevation may be determined.

Swashplate. The component in a helicopter control system that consists basically of two bearing races with ball bearings between them. The lower, or nonrotating, race is tilted by the cyclic control, and the upper, or rotating, race has arms which connect to the control horns on the rotor blades. Movement of the cyclic pitch control is transmitted to the rotor blades through the swashplate. Movement of the collective pitch control raises or lowers the entire swashplate assembly to change the pitch of all the blades at the same time.

Synchro system. A remote instrument indicating system. A synchro transmitter is actuated by the device whose movement is to be measured, and it is connected electrically with wires to a synchro indicator whose pointer follows the movement of the shaft of the transmitter.

Symmetrical airfoil. An airfoil that has the same shape on both sides of its chord line, or center line.

Symmetry check. A check of an airframe to determine that the wings and tail are symmetrical about the longitudinal axis.

System-pressure regulator (hydraulic system component). A type of hydraulic system-pressure control valve. When the system pressure is low, as it is when some unit is actuated, the output of the constant-delivery pump is directed into the system. When the actuation is completed and the pressure builds up to a specified kick-out pressure, the pressure regulator shifts. A check valve seals the system off and the pressure is maintained by the accumulator. The pump is unloaded and its output is directed back into the reservoir with very little opposition. The pump output pressure drops, but the volume of flow remains the same. When the system pressure drops to the specified kick-in pressure, the regulator again shifts and directs fluid into the system. Spool-type and balanced-pressure-type system pressure regulators are completely automatic in their operation and require no attention on the part of the flight crew.

TACAN (Tactical Air Navigation). A radio navigation facility used by military aircraft for both direction and distance information. Civilian aircraft receive distance information from a TACAN on their DME.

Tack coat. A coat of finishing material sprayed on the surface and allowed to dry until the solvents evaporate. As soon as the solvents evaporate, a wet full-bodied coat of material is sprayed over it.

Tack rag. A clean, lintless rag, slightly damp with thinner. A tack rag is used to wipe a surface to prepare it to receive a coat of finishing material.

Tack weld. A method of holding parts together before they are permanently welded. The parts are assembled, and small spots of weld are placed at strategic locations to hold them in position.

Tacky. Slightly sticky to the touch.

Tailets. Small vertical surfaces mounted underside of the horizontal stabilizer of some airplanes to increase the directional stability.

Takeoff warning system. An aural warning system that provides audio warning signals when the thrust levers are advanced for takeoff if the stabilizer, flaps, or speed brakes are in an unsafe condition for takeoff.

Tang. A tapered shank sticking out from the blade of a knife or a file. The handle of a knife or file is mounted on the tang.

TCAS. Traffic Alert Collision Avoidance System

Teflon. The registered trade name for a fluorocarbon resin used to make hydraulic and pneumatic seals, hoses, and backup rings.

Tempered glass. Glass that has been heat-treated to increase its strength. Tempered glass is used in bird-proof, heated windshields for high-speed aircraft.

Terminal strips. A group of threaded studs mounted in a strip of insulating plastic. Electrical wires with crimped-on terminals are placed over the studs and secured with nuts.

Terminal VOR. A low-powered VOR that is normally located on an airport.

Tetraethyl lead (TEL). A heavy, oily, poisonous liquid, $Pb(C2H5)4$, that is mixed into aviation gasoline to increase its critical pressure and temperature.

Therapeutic mask adapter. A calibrated orifice in the mask adapter for a continuous-flow oxygen system that increases the flow of oxygen to a mask being used by a passenger who is known to have a heart or respiratory problem.

Thermal dimpling. See hot dimpling.

Thermal relief valve. A relief valve in a hydraulic system that relieves pressure that builds up in an isolated part of the system because of heat. Thermal relief valves are set at a higher pressure than the system pressure relief valve.

Thermistor. A special form of electrical resistor whose resistance varies with its temperature.

Thermistor material. A material with a negative temperature coefficient that causes its resistance to decrease as its temperature increases.

Thermocouple. A loop consisting of two kinds of wire, joined at the hot, or measuring, junction and at the cold junction in the instrument. The voltage difference between the two junctions is proportional to the temperature difference between the junctions. In order for the current to be meaningful, the resistance of the thermocouple is critical, and the leads are designed for a specific installation. Their length should not be altered. Thermocouples used to measure cylinder head temperature are usually made of iron and constantan, and thermocouples that measure exhaust gas temperature for turbine engines are made of chromel and alumel.

Thermocouple fire-detection system. A fire-detection system that works on the principle of the rate-of-temperature rise. Thermocouples are installed around the area to be protected, and one thermocouple is surrounded by thermal insulation that prevents its temperature changing rapidly. In the event of a fire, the temperature of all the thermocouples except the protected one will rise immediately and a fire warning will be initiated. In the case of a general overheat condition, the temperature of all the thermocouples will rise uniformly and there will be no fire warning.

Thermoplastic resin. A type of plastic material that becomes soft when heated and hardens when cooled.

Thermosetting resin. A type of plastic material that, when once hardened by heat, cannot be softened by being heated again.

Thermostatic expansion valve (TEV). The component in a vapor-cycle cooling system that meters the refrigerant into the evaporator. The amount of refrigerant metered by the TEV is determined by the temperature and pressure of the refrigerant as it leaves the evaporator coils. The TEV changes the refrigerant from a high-pressure liquid into a low-pressure liquid.

Thixotropic agents. Materials, such as microballoons, added to a resin to give it body and increase its workability.

TIG welding. Tungsten inert welding is a form of electric arc welding in which the electrode is a nonconsumable tungsten wire. TIG welding is now called GTA (gas tungsten arc) welding.

Toe-in. A condition of landing gear alignment in which the front of the tires are closer together than the rear. When the aircraft rolls forward, the wheels try to move closer together.

Toe-out. A condition of landing gear alignment in which the front of the tires are further apart than the rear. When the aircraft rolls forward, the wheels try to move farther apart.

Torque. A force that produces or tries to produce rotation.

Torque links. The hinged link between the piston and cylinder of an oleo-type landing gear shock absorber. The torque links allow the piston to move freely in and out of the landing gear cylinder, but prevent it rotating. The torque links can be adjusted to achieve and maintain the correct wheel alignment. Torque links are also called scissors and nutcrackers.

Torque tube. A tube in an aircraft control system that transmits a torsional force from the operating control to the control surface.

Torsion rod. A device in a spring tab to which the control horn is attached. For normal operation, the torsion rod acts as a fixed attachment point, but when the control surface loads are high, the torsion rod twists and allows the control horn to deflect the spring tab.

Total air pressure. The pressure a column of moving air will have if it is stopped.

TMC. Thrust management computer.

Toroidal coil. An electrical coil wound around a ring-shaped core of highly permeable material.

Total air temperature. The temperature a column of moving air will have if it is stopped.

TR unit. A transformer-rectifie unit. A TR unit reduces the voltage of AC and changes it into DC.

Tractor powerplant. An airplane powerplant in which the propeller is mounted in the front, and its thrust pulls the airplane rather than pushes it.

Trammel (verb). To square up the Pratt truss used in an airplane wing. Trammel points are set on the trammel bar so they measure the distance between the center of the front spar, at the inboard compression strut, and at the center of the rear spar at the next compression strut outboard. The drag and antidrug wires are adjusted until the distance between the center of the rear spar at the inboard compression strut and the center of the front spar at the next outboard compression strut is exactly the same as that between the first points measured.

Trammel bar. A wood or metal bar on which trammel points are mounted to compare distances.

Trammel points. A set of sharp-pointed pins that protrude from the sides of a trammel bar.

Transducer. A device that changes energy from one form to another. Commonly used transducers change mechanical movement or pressures into electrical signals.

Transformer rectifier. A component in a large aircraft electrical system used to reduce the AC voltage and change it into DC for charging the battery and for operating DC equipment in the aircraft.

Translational lift. The additional lift produced by a helicopter rotor as the helicopter changes from hovering to forward flight

Transonic flight. Flight at an airspeed in which some air flowing over the aircraft is moving at a speed below the speed of sound, and other air is moving at a speed greater than the speed of sound.

Transverse pitch. See gauge.

Triangle. A three-sided, closed plane figure. The sum of the three angles in a triangle is always equal to 180°.

Tricresyl phosphate (TCP). A chemical compound, (CH3C6H4O)3PO, used in aviation gasoline to assist in scavenging the lead deposits left from the tetraethyl lead.

Trim tab. A small control tab mounted on the trailing edge of a movable control surface. The tab may be adjusted to provide an aerodynamic force to hold the surface on which it is mounted deflected in order to trim the airplane for handsoff flight at a specified airspeed.

Trimmed flight. A flight condition in which the aerodynamic forces acting on the control surfaces are balanced and the aircraft is able to fly straight and level with no control input.

Trip-free circuit breaker. A circuit breaker that opens a circuit any time an excessive amount of current flows, regardless of the position of the circuit breaker's operating handle.

Troubleshooting. A procedure used in aircraft maintenance in which the operation of a malfunctioning system is analyzed to find the reason for the malfunction and to find a method for returning the system to its condition of normal operation.

True airspeed (TAS). Airspeed shown on the airspeed indicator (indicated airspeed) corrected for position error and nonstandard air temperature and pressure.

Trunnion. Projections from the cylinder of a retractable landing gear strut about which the strut pivots retract.

Truss-type structure. A type of structure made up of longitudinal beams and cross braces. Compression loads between the main beams are carried by rigid cross braces. Tension loads are carried by stays, or wires, that go from one main beam to the other and cross between the cross braces.

Turbine. A rotary device actuated by impulse or reaction of a fluid flowing through vanes or blades that are arranges around a central shaft.

Turn and slip indicator. A rate gyroscopic flight instrument that gives the pilot an indication of the rate of rotation of the aircraft about its vertical axis. A ball in a curved glass tube shows the pilot the relationship between the centrifugal force and the force of gravity. This indicates whether or not the angle of bank is proper for the rate of turn. The turn and slip indicator shows the trim condition of the aircraft and serves as an emergency source of bank information in case the attitude gyro fails. Turn and slip indicators were formerly called needle and ball and turn and bank indicators.

Turnbuckle. A component in an aircraft control system used to adjust cable tension. A turnbuckle consists of a brass tubular barrel with right-hand threads in one end and left-hand in the other end. Control cable terminals screw into the two ends of the barrel, and turning the barrel pulls the terminals together, shortening the cable.

Twist drill. A metal cutting tool turned in a drill press or handheld drill motor. A twist drill has a straight shank and spiraled flutes. The cutting edge is ground on the end of the spiraled flutes.

Twist rope. A stripe of paint on flexible hose that runs the length of the hose. If this stripe spirals around the hose after it is installed, it indicates the hose was twisted when it was installed. Twist stripes are also called lay lines.

Two-terminal spot-type fire detection system. A fire detection system that uses individual thermoswitches installed around the inside of the area to be protected. These thermoswitches are wired in parallel between two separate circuits. A short or an open circuit can exist in either circuit without causing a fire warning.

Type Certificate Data Sheets (TCDS). The official specifications of an aircraft, engine, or propeller issued by the Federal Aviation Administration. The TCDS lists pertinent specifications for the device, and it is the responsibility of the mechanic and/or inspector to ensure, on each inspection, that the device meets these specifications.

UHF. Ultrahigh frequency.

Ultimate tensile strength. The tensile strength required to cause a material to break or to continue to deform under a decreasing load.

Ultraviolet-blocking dope. Dope that contains aluminum powder or some other pigment that blocks the passage of ultraviolet rays of the sun. The coat of dope protects the organic fabrics and clear dope from deterioration by these rays.

Undamped oscillation. Oscillation that continues with an unchanging amplitude once it has started.

Underslung rotor. A helicopter rotor whose center of gravity is below the point at which it is attached to the mast.

Unidirectional fabric. Fabric in which all the threads run in the same direction. These threads are often bound with a few fibers run at right angles, just enough to hold the yarns together and prevent their bunching.

Unloading valve. This is another name for system pressure regulator. See system pressure regulator.

Utility finish. The finish of an aircraft that gives the necessary tautness and fill to the fabric and the necessary protection to the metal, but does not have the glossy appearance of a show-type finish.

Vapor lock. A condition in which vapors form in the fuel lines and block the flow of fuel to the carburetor.

Vapor pressure. The pressure of the vapor above a liquid needed to prevent the liquid evaporating. Vapor pressure is always specified at a specific temperature.

Variable displacement pump. A fluid pump whose output is controlled by the demands of the system. These pumps normally have a built-in system pressure regulator. When the demands of the system are low, the pump moves very little fluid, but when the demands are high, the pump moves a lot of fluid. Most variable displacement pumps used in aircraft hydraulic systems are piston-type pumps.

Varnish (aircraft finishing material). A material used to produce an attractive and protective coating on wood or metal. Varnish is made of a resin dissolved in a solvent and thinned until it has the proper viscosity to spray or brush. The varnish is spread evenly over the surface to be coated, and when the solvents evaporate, a tough film is left.

Varsol. A petroleum product similar to naphtha used as a solvent and cleaning fluid

Veneer. Thin sheets of wood "peeled" from a log. A wideblade knife held against the surface of the log peels away the veneer as the log is rotated in the cutter. Veneer is used for making plywood. Several sheets of veneer are glued together, with the grain of each sheet placed at 45° or 90° to the grain of the sheets next to it.

Vertical axis. An imaginary line, passing vertically through the center of gravity of an airplane.

Vertical fin. The fixed vertical surface in the empennage of an airplane. The vertical fin acts as a weathervane to give the airplane directional stability.

VFR. Visual flight rules

VHF. Very high frequency.

Vibrator-type voltage regulator. A type of voltage regulator used with a generator or alternator that intermittently places a resistance in the field circuit to control the voltage. A set of vibrating contacts puts the resistor in the circuit and takes it out several times a second.

Viscosity. The resistance of a fluid to flow. Viscosity refers to the "stiffness" of the fluid, or its internal friction.

Viscosity cup. A specially shaped cup with an accurately sized hole in its bottom. The cup is submerged in the liquid to completely fill it. It is then lifted from the liquid and the time in seconds is measured from the beginning of the flow through the hole until the first break in this flow. The viscosity of the liquid relates to this time.

Vixen file. A metal-cutting hand file that has curved teeth across its faces. Vixen files are used to remove large amounts of soft metal.

V$_{NE}$. Never-exceed speed. The maximum speed the aircraft is allowed to attain in any conditions of flight.

Volatile liquid. A liquid that easily changes into a vapor.

Voltmeter multiplier. A precision resistor in series with a voltmeter mechanism used to extend the range of the basic meter or to allow a single meter to measure several ranges of voltage.

VOR. Very high frequency Omni Range navigation.

VORTAC. An electronic navigation system that contains both a VOR and a TACAN facility.

Vortex (plural vortices). A whirling motion in a fluid.

Vortex generator. Small, low-aspect-ratio airfoils installed in pairs on the upper surface of a wing, on both sides of the vertical fin just ahead of the rudder, and on the underside of the vertical stabilizers of some airplanes. Their function is to pull high-energy air down to the surface to energize the boundary layer and prevent airflow separation until the surface reaches a higher angle of attack.

Warp clock. An alignment indicator included in a structural repair manual to show the orientation of the piles of a composite material. The ply direction is shown in relation to a reference direction.

Warp threads. Threads that run the length of the roll of fabric, parallel to the selvage edge. Warp threads are often stronger than fill threads.

Warp tracers. Threads of a different color from the warp threads that are woven into a material to identify the direction of the warp threads.

Wash in. A twist in an airplane wing that increases its angle of incidence near the tip.

Wash out. A twist in an airplane wing that decreases its angle of incidence near the tip.

Watt. The basic unit of electrical power. One watt is equal to $1/_{746}$ horsepower.

Way point. A phantom location created in certain electronic navigation systems by measuring direction and distance from a VORTAC station or by latitude and longitude coordinates from Loran or GPS.

Web of a spar. The part of a spar between the caps.

Weft threads. See fill threads.

Wet-type vacuum pump. An engine-driven air pump that uses steel vanes. These pumps are lubricated by engine oil drawn in through holes in the pump base. The oil passes through the pump and is exhausted with the air. Wet-type pumps must have oil separators in their discharge line to trap the oil and return it to the engine crankcase.

Wing fences. Vertical vanes that extend chordwise across the upper surface of an airplane wing to prevent spanwise airflow.

Wing heavy. An out-of-trim flight condition in which an airplane flies hands off, with one wing low.

Wire bundle. A compact group of electrical wires held together with special wrapping devices or with waxed string. These bundles are secured to the aircraft structure with special clamps.

Woof threads. See fill threads.

Work. The product of force times distance.

Yaw. Rotation of an aircraft about its vertical axis.

Yaw damper. An automatic flight control system that counteracts the rolling and yawing produced by Dutch roll. See Dutch roll. A yaw damper senses yaw with a rate gyro and moves the rudder an amount proportional to the rate of yaw, but in the opposite direction.

Yield strength. The amount of stress needed to permanently deform a material.

Zener diode. A special type of solid-state diode designed to have a specific breakdown voltage and to operate with current flowing through it in its reverse direction.

Zeppelin. The name of large, rigid, lighter-than-air ships built by the Zeppelin Company in Germany prior to and during World War I.

Zero-center ammeter. An ammeter in a light aircraft electrical system located between the battery and the main bus. This ammeter shows the current flowing into or out of the battery.

Index

A

AC alternators 9-41
   AC alternators control systems 9-45
Acceleration 2-3
Acetone 8-2
Acetylene 5-7
Acrylic urethanes 8-5
Adhesive pot life 6-11
Adhesives 7-9
Adjusting the spray pattern 8-11
Adjustment of bend radius 4-68
Aerodynamics 2-2, 2-3
Ailerons 1-26
Air compressors 8-6
Aircraft 1-5
Aircraft batteries 9-21
   Inspection 9-26
   Ratings by specification 9-23
   Battery and charger characteristics 9-25
      Lead-acid batteries 9-25
      NiCd batteries 9-25
   Battery charging 9-24
      Constant current charging 9-24
      Constant Voltage Charging (CP) 9-24
   Battery freezing 9-23
   Battery maintenance 9-24
   Capacity 9-22
   Installation practices 9-26
      Battery hold down devices 9-27
      Battery sump jars 9-26
      Battery venting 9-26
      External surface 9-26
      Installing batteries 9-26
      Quick-disconnect type battery 9-27
      Replacing lead-acid batteries 9-26
   Lead-acid batteries 9-21
   NiCd batteries 9-22
   Storing and servicing facilities 9-23
   Temperature correction 9-23
   Ventilation systems 9-26
Aircraft electrical systems 9-47
   Large multiengine aircraft 9-60
      AC power systems 9-60
      Parallel systems 9-63
      Split-bus power distribution systems 9-61
      Split-parallel systems 9-64

   Light multiengine aircraft 9-57
      Paralleling alternators or generators 9-57
      Power distribution on multiengine aircraft ... 9-58
   Small single-engine aircraft 9-47
      AC supply 9-55
      Alternator circuit 9-48
      Avionics power circuit 9-51
      Battery circuit 9-47
      External power circuit 9-50
      Generator circuit 9-48
      Landing gear circuit 9-52
      Starter circuit 9-50
Aircraft inspection 2-60
Aircraft lighting systems 9-101
   Exterior lights 9-101
      Anticollision lights 9-102
      Landing and taxi lights 9-103
      Position lights 9-101
      Wing inspection lights 9-104
   Interior lights 9-104
   Maintenance and inspection of lighting systems 9-105
Aircraft metal structural repair 4-1
Aircraft rigging 2-41
Aircraft structures 1-1
Aircraft wood and structural repair 6-1
Airfoil 2-5
Airframe 1-42
Airplane assembly 2-41
   Aileron installation 2-41
   Empennage installation 2-41
   Flap installation 2-41
Airplane assembly and rigging 2-38
Air tools 7-20
Air Traffic Control (ATC) transponder inspection 2-63
Alcohol 8-2
Alternate pressure application 7-32
Alternating Current (AC) 9-7
   Definitions 9-8
      Cycle define 9-10
      Effective 9-9
      Frequency defined 9-11
      Instantaneous 9-8
      Peak 9-8
      Period defined 9-11
      Phase relationships 9-11
      Values of AC 9-8

Wavelength define 9-11
Alternator drive 9-42
Alternator voltage regulators 9-40
Altimeter and static system inspections 2-63
Aluminum alloys 4-30
Aluminum soldering 5-21
Amorphous thermoplastics 7-8
Amphibious aircraft 1-36
Angle adapters 4-16
Angle of attack 2-6
Angle of incidence 2-6
Annual and 100-hour inspections 2-62,2-64
Annual inspection 2-61
Anti-chafe tape 3-5
Antiservo tabs 1-34
Antitorque pedals 2-31
Antitorque system 1-45
Application of cement 7-56
Application of ohm's law 9-5
Applying the finish 8-11
Applying the glue/adhesive 6-12
Approval of repair 4-94
Aramid (Kevlar®) fiber-reinforced plastic 7-52
Arc welding procedures 5-25
Argon 5-7
Assessment of damage 4-92
Atmosphere 2-2
Audible sonic testing (coin tapping) 7-16
Autoclave 7-23
Autogyro 2-18
Automated tap test 7-16
Automatic center punch 4-6
Autorotation 2-28
Auxiliary lift devices 2-13
Aviation snips 4-13
Awl 4-7
Axes of an aircraft 2-9

B

Balance panels 1-33
Balsa wood 7-13
Band saw 4-11
Bar folding machine 4-21
Base measurement 4-59
Bead weld 5-28
Bearing 4-3
Bell stabilizer bar system 2-31
Belt drive clutch 2-37
Belt sander 4-11
Bend allowance (BA) 4-59
Bending a U-channel 4-62
Bend radius 4-60
Bend tangent line (BL) 4-60
Benzene 8-2
Bernoulli's Principle 2-4

Bias 3-3
Bidirectional (Fabric) 7-3
Biplane assembly and rigging 2-58
Bismaleimides (BMI) 7-8
Blanket method 3-12
Bleeder ply 7-21
Bleedout technique 7-29
Bleriot, Louis 1-3
Blind bolts 4-54,7-48
Blind fasteners 7-47
Blind fasteners (nonstructural) 4-57
Blind rivets 4-47
Blushing 8-13
Bolt and bushing holes 6-20
Bolted repairs 7-44
Bonded flush patch repair 7-37
Boron 7-6
Boundary layer 2-7
Box and pan brake (finger brake 4-22
Box beam 1-12,1-13
Brazing and soldering 5-20
Breather material 7-21
Brinelling 4-90
Brushing 8-5
Bucking bar 4-36
Bumping 4-59
Burnishing 4-90
Burr 4-90
Burring tool 4-14
Butt joints 5-31

C

Cable connectors 2-46
Cable drums 2-48
Cable guides 2-44
Cable inspection 2-44
Cable system installation 2-44
Cable systems 2-41
    Cable construction 2-42
    Cable designations 2-42
    Nicopress® process 2-42
    Swage-type terminals 2-42
    Woven splice 2-42
Cable tension 2-45,2-52
Cantilever design 1-11
Carbon fiber reinforced plastic 7-52
Carbon/graphite 7-6
Carburizing flam 5-13
Caul 6-11
Caul plate 7-20
Cayley, George 1-1
C-clamps 4-28,7-32
Cementing 7-56
Center of gravity 2-9
Center punch 4-6

Centrifugal clutch...2-37
Ceramic fiber...7-6
Chanute, Octave...1-2
Characteristics of a good weld.............................5-16
Chassis punch..4-7
Chattering..4-91
Checking dihedral..2-50
Checking engine alignment..................................2-52
Checking fin verticalit...2-51
Checking incidence..2-50
Check valves and flashback arrestor....................5-8
Chemical stripping...8-21
CherryBUCK® 95 KSI one-piece shear pin.........4-52
CherryMAX® bulbed blind rivet.........................4-48
Cherry Maxibolt® blind bolt system...................4-54
Cherry's E-Z Buck® (CSR90433) hollow rivet.....7-47
Chip chasers..4-20
Chrome molybdenum...5-17
Circular-cutting saws...4-8
Clamps and vises...4-28
Classification of damag.......................................4-91
Cleaning..7-57
Cleco fasteners..4-29
Close contact adhesive..6-10
Closed angle..4-60
Closed assembly time..6-11
Closed end bend (more than 90°)........................4-74
Clutch..2-37
Coaxial cable...9-96
Co-bonding..7-28
Co-curing...7-28
Collective pitch..2-29
Combinations of damages....................................7-14
Combination square...4-4
Common paint troubles..8-13
Common spray gun problems...............................8-13
Composite honeycomb sandwich repairs.............7-33
Composite patch bonded to aluminum structure....7-40
Composite repairs..7-19
Compound curve forming.....................................7-55
Compression riveting...4-39
Concave surfaces...4-79
Conduit..9-83
    Flexible conduit...9-85
    Rigid conduit..9-84
Connecting torch..5-11
Connectors
    Adjacent locations...9-95
    Drainage...9-96
    Sealing...9-95
    Spare contacts for future wiring......................9-95
    Voltage and current rating................................9-95
    Wire installation into the connector.................9-95
    Wire support...9-96

Continuous Airworthiness Maintenance
Program (CAMP)..2-68
Control...2-9
Control operating systems....................................2-41
Controls...1-46
Control surface travel..2-53
Convex surfaces..4-79
Coriolis effect..2-23
Corner joints..5-32
Cornice brake..4-22
Correct forming of a weld....................................5-16
Corrosion...4-90,7-15
    Corrosion precautions......................................7-46
    Corrosion treatment...4-94
Corrugated skin repair...4-97
Cotton covered aircraft..3-23
Count...3-3
Countersinking...4-41,7-52
    Countersinking tools...................................4-37,4-41
    Countersunk rivets...4-41
Covering processes...3-8
Cowling...1-20
Crack...4-90
Crimping..4-59
Cross coat..3-3
Curing of composite materials.............................7-32
Curing stages of resins..7-8
Current...9-2
    Conventional Current Theory and Electron Theory.....9-3
Current limiting devices.......................................9-100
    Circuit breakers...9-100
    Fuses...9-100
Curved flanged parts...4-77
Cut...4-91
Cut-off wheel...4-9
Cutting equipment...7-52
Cutting processes and precautions......................7-52
Cutting tools..4-8
Cutting torch..5-9
Cyclic pitch..2-30

D

Damage and defects..4-90
Damage necessitating replacement of parts........4-92
Damage removal..4-93
Damage repairable by insertion...........................4-92
Damage repairable by patching...........................4-91
Damage requiring core replacement and repair to one or
both faceplates..7-34
DC alternators...9-39
DC generators..9-32
    Compound wound DC generators....................9-32
    DC generator maintenance..............................9-33
    Generator ratings...9-33
    Parallel (shunt) wound DC generators.............9-32

Series wound DC generators 9-32
DC generators and controls............................9-27
   Construction features of DC generators 9-29
      Armature 9-30
      Commutators...9-31
      Field frame 9-29
   Generators 9-27
Decals..8-18
De Havilland mosquito 1-4
Delamination and debonds..............................7-14
Density 2-3
Dent..4-91
Dents at a cluster weld 5-32
Dents between clusters..................................5-32
Design of a patch for a nonpressurized area 4-96
Die grinder 4-14
Different flame 5-13
Dimpling 4-42
Dimpling dies 4-37
Dimpling inspection.....................................4-44
Dipping 8-5
Directional stability.....................................2-11
Disk sander..4-11
Display of marks 8-17
Display of nationality and registration marks.............8-17
Dissymmetry of lift 2-26
Dividers...4-4
Dollies and stakes 4-27
Dope...8-4
Double spread 6-11
Double Vacuum Debulk Principle 7-42
Downdraft tables..7-53
Drag 2-7,2-8
   Parasite drag 2-8
   Profile drag 2-8
Drill bits 4-17
   Cobalt alloy drill bits 4-17
   Step drill bits 4-17
   Twist drill bits 4-17
Drill bit sizes 4-18
Drill bushing holder types...............................4-19
Drill bushings and guides................................4-19
Drill extensions and adapters 4-16
Drilling 4-40,7-49,7-55
Drilling large holes......................................4-20
Drill lubrication...4-18
Drill press...4-15
Drill stops...4-19
Drive nut-type of blind bolt 4-55
Drive punch...4-6
Driving the rivet...4-40
Drop hammer 4-24
Dry fiber materia 7-8
Dual rotor helicopter 2-18
Dutch roll 2-11

Dynamic balance...2-38
Dynamic stability 2-11

E

Eddie-Bolt® 2 pin fastening system 4-53
Eddie-Bolt® fasteners...................................7-46
Edge distance 4-34
Edge joints 5-32
Edges of the panel 4-97
Effective Translational Lift (ETL).......................2-25
Electric resistance welding 5-6
Electromagnetic generation of power 9-5
Electromotive force (voltage) 9-3
Electronic blade tracker 2-33
Electronic method 2-34
Elevated temperature curing 7-32
Elevator 1-27
Empennage..1-22
Engine mount repairs 5-36
Engine mounts 1-20
Envelope bagging..7-31
Envelope method 3-12
Epoxy 7-7,8-4
Equal pressure torch.....................................5-9
Equipment 7-49
Equipment setup...5-10
Erosion 4-91
Evaluating the rivet.....................................4-44
Expansion and contraction of metals 5-30
Extension drill bits 4-16
External and internal inspection.........................6-3
External bonded patch repairs 7-41
External bonded repair with prepreg plies 7-41
External repair using precured laminate patches 7-43
External repair using wet layup and double vacuum
debulk method (DVD) 7-42
Extreme low frequency vibration.........................2-32
Eye protection 7-53

F

Fabric cement 3-7,3-16
Fabric heat shrinking....................................3-17
Fabric impregnation using a vacuum bag 7-30
Fabric impregnation with a brush or squeegee 7-30
Fabric patch...6-20
Fabric sealer...3-7
Fabric strength 3-9
Fabric testing devices....................................3-11
Fastener materials 7-46
Fasteners used with composite laminates 7-46
Fastener system for sandwich honeycomb structures
(SPS technologies comp tite).............................7-46
Fenestron® 1-46
Fiber breakage...7-13
Fiber forms..7-3

Fiberglass 7-4
Fiberglass coverings 3-24
Fiberglass molded mat repairs 7-41
Fiberlite 7-48
Fiber orientation 7-2
Files 4-13
Filler rod 5-10
Fillers 3-8
Fillet weld 5-28
Film adhesives 7-9
Finishing tapes 3-21
Fire protection 7-53
Fisheyes 8-15
Fixed-wing aircraft 1-5
Flag and pole 2-32
Flange 4-59
Flanged angles 4-76
Flapping 1-44
Flaps 1-28
    Fowler flaps 1-30
    Split flap 1-30
Flat 4-60
Flat position welding 5-28
Flawed fastener holes 7-14
Flight control surfaces 1-24
    Auxiliary control surfaces 1-28
    Dual purpose flight control surface ... 1-27
    Primary flight control surface 1-24
Floats 4-97
Flush patch 4-96
Flutter and vibration precautions 4-89
Fly-by-wire control 2-15
Foam 7-12
Foaming adhesives 7-10
Folding a box 4-71
Folding sheet metal 4-59
Form block or die 4-80
Formed or extruded angles 4-75
Former or bulkhead repair 4-102
Forming by bumping 4-80
Forming methods 7-55
Forming procedures and techniques 7-54
Forming process 4-57
Forming tools 4-21
Forming with an English wheel 4-26
Forms 7-55
Forward flight 2-24
Freewheeling unit 2-38
Fresh air breathing systems 8-8
Friction-locked blind rivets 4-48
Fully articulated rotor 2-18
Fully articulated rotor system 1-44
Fuselage 1-8, 1-42

G

Galling 4-91
Gap-filling adhesive 6-11
Gap seals 1-35
Gas cylinders 5-10
Gas welding and cutting equipment 5-7
Gas welding procedures 5-15
Generator controls 9-34
    Functions of generator control systems 9-35
        Differential voltage 9-35
        Overexcitation protection 9-35
        Overvoltage protection 9-35
        Parallel generator operations 9-35
        Reverse current sensing 9-35
        Voltage regulation 9-35
    Generator controls for high-output generators ... 9-35
    Generator controls for low-output generators 9-36
        Carbon pile regulators 9-36
        Current limiter 9-37
        Reverse-current relay 9-38
        Three-unit regulators 9-37
        Voltage regulator 9-37
    Theory of generator control 9-34
Glass fiber reinforced plastic 7-52
Glued joint inspection 6-4
Glue line 6-11
Glues (adhesives) 6-10
Gouge 4-91
Governor 2-30
Grain of the metal 4-59
Gravity 2-7
Gravity-feed gun 8-7
Gray enamel undercoat 8-4
Greige 3-3
Grinding wheels 4-13
Grommets 3-6, 3-21
Groove weld 5-28
Ground effect 2-23
Gussets 3-21
Gyroscopic forces 2-20

H

Hand cutting tools 4-13
Hand forming 4-74
Handling of the torch 5-14
Hand-operated shrinker and stretcher 4-27
Hand rivet set 4-36
Hand tools 4-36, 7-19
Hardwood form blocks 4-27
Heat blanket 7-24
Heat bonder 7-24
Heating 7-54
Heat lamp 7-24
Heat press forming 7-24
Heat sources 7-22

Helicopter power systems 2-35
   Powerplant 1-43,2-35
   Reciprocating engine 2-35
   Turbine engine 2-36
Helicopter structures 1-42
Helicopter vibration 2-32
Helium 5-7
Hex nut and wing nut temporary sheet fasteners 4-30
High frequency vibration 2-32
High rush-in circuits 9-98
High-speed aerodynamics 2-15
Hi-Lite® fastening system 4-51
Hi-Lok® and Huck-Spin® lockbolt fasteners 7-46
Hi-Lok® fastening system 4-51
Hi-Tigue® fastening system 4-51
Hole drilling 4-14
Hole drilling techniques 4-20
Hole duplicator 4-8
Hole preparation 4-40,4-56
Hole transfer 4-40
Honeycomb 7-11
Horizontal stabilizer stations 1-40
Hoses 5-11
Hot air system 7-24
Hot dimpling 4-43
Hovering flight 2-22
Huck Blind Bolt system 4-54
Humidity 2-3
   Absolute humidity 2-3
   Relative humidity 2-3
Hydrogen 5-7
Hydromechanical control 2-15
Hydropress forming 4-24

I

Impedance 9-15
Inclusion 4-91
Inductive circuits 9-98
Injector torch 5-9
Inside the member 4-97
Inspection 4-50
Inspection for corrosion 4-93
Inspection of damage 4-90
Inspection of riveted joints 4-92
Inspection openings 4-108
Inspection rings 3-6
Installation of high-shear fasteners 4-50
Installation of rivets 4-32
Installation procedure 4-53,7-57

J

Joggling 4-81
Junkers, Hugo 1-3

K

Keeping weight to a minimum 4-89
Kett saw 4-8
Kevlar® 7-4

L

Lacquers 8-4
Laminated structures 7-2
Landing gear 1-35,1-36,1-43
   Landing gear repairs 5-35
Lap joints 5-32
Lap joint weld 5-29
Lap or scab patch 4-95
Large coating containers 8-7
Lateral stability 2-11
Layout method 4-73
Layout or flat pattern development 4-60
Layout tools 4-4
Layup materials 7-19
Layup process (typical laminated wet layup) 7-28
Layups 7-26
Layup tapes 7-21
Layup techniques 7-28
Leading edge repair 4-105
Leg 4-59
Lift 2-7
Lightening holes 4-82
Lighting and adjusting the torch 5-13
Lightning protection fiber 7-6
Lilienthal, Otto 1-2
Linseed oil 8-3
Location and placement of marks 8-17
Lockbolt fastening systems 4-52
   Lockbolt inspection 4-53
   Lockbolt removal 4-53
Longeron repair 4-103
Longitudinal stability 2-11
Low frequency vibration 2-32

M

Machining processes and equipment 7-49
Magnesium welding 5-19
Main rotor system 1-44
   Rigid rotor system 1-44
   Semirigid rotor system 1-44
Main rotor transmission 2-36
Maintaining original contour 4-89
Maintaining original strength 4-87
Maintenance 1-38
Major components of a laminate 7-2
Making straight line bends 4-61
Male and female die forming 7-55
Manual foot-operated sheet metal shrinker 4-27
Manufacturer's inspection program 2-63
Manufacturing and in-service damage 7-13

Marking method...2-34
Marking tools 4-4
Masking and applying the trim 8-16
Masking for the trim 8-16
Masking materials..8-16
Matrix imperfections...7-13
Matrix materials 7-6
Maule punch tester..3-11
Mechanical control..2-14
Mechanical-lock blind rivets.............................4-48
Medium frequency vibration.............................2-32
Metal decals with cellophane backing 8-18
Metal decals with no adhesive 8-18
Metal decals with paper backing.......................8-18
Methylene chloride 8-2
Methyl Ethyl Ketone (MEK) 8-2
Microshavers...4-39
Mineral spirits 8-3
Minor core damage (filler and potting repairs .7-34
Mixing equipment...8-9
Mixing resins 7-30
Moisture detector 7-19
Monocoque 1-9
Monospar 1-12
Motion..2-3
Motors 9-98
Multiple pass welding..5-27
Multispar 1-12,1-13

N

Nacelles...1-19
Naphtha...8-3
National Advisory Committee for Aeronautics (NACA)
method of double flush riveting 4-46
Negligible damage 4-91
Neutral axis 4-60
Neutral flam 5-13
Neutron radiography 7-19
Newton's Laws of Motion 2-4
Nibblers 4-9
Nick..4-91
No bleedout...7-29
Nondestructive Inspection (NDI) of composites ...7-15
Nonwoven (knitted or stitched) 7-4
NOTAR...1-46
Notcher..4-12
Numbering systems...1-39
    Aileron station 1-40
    Buttock line 1-39
    Flap station 1-40
    Fuselage stations 1-39
    Nacelle station 1-40
    Water line 1-40

O

Offset flapping hinge...2-32
Ohm's Law..9-2
Open and closed bends.......................................4-74
Open and closed skin area repair 4-96
Open angle 4-60
Open assembly time...6-11
Open end bend (less than 90°) 4-74
Open wiring 9-78
Opposition to current flow of AC 9-12
    Apparent power 9-20
    Capacitive reactance.....................................9-14
    Inductive reactance.......................................9-12
    Parallel AC circuits 9-19
    Power in AC circuits 9-20
    Resistance..9-12
    True power 9-20
Optical considerations..7-54
Orange peel 8-14
Other aircraft inspection and maintenance Programs 2-66
Outside the member 4-97
Oven...7-22
Overhead position welding 5-30
Oxidizing flam 5-13
Oxy-acetylene cutting..5-14
Oxy-acetylene welding of ferrous metals 5-16
Oxy-acetylene welding of nonferrous metals 5-18
Oxygen...5-7

P

Paint 8-10
Paint booth 8-6
Paint finishes 8-19
Paint system compatibility.................................8-19
Paint touchup 8-19
Paper decals 8-18
Paste adhesives...7-9
Patches 4-95
Patch installation on the aircraft 7-42
Peel ply..7-21
Pens 4-4
Perforated release film 7-21
Periodic maintenance inspections 2-61
Phased array inspection......................................7-18
Phenolic resin...7-7
Piccolo former..4-26
Pin fastening systems (high-shear fasteners) 4-50
Pinholes..8-14
Pinked edge 3-3
Pin punch 4-7
Pitting...4-91
Plasma arc cutting..5-7
Plastic Media Blasting (PMB) 8-21
Plug patch...6-21
Ply 3-3

Ply orientation warp clock 7-29
Plywood skin repairs 6-20
Pneumatic circular cutting saw 4-8
Pneumatic drill motors 4-15
Pneumatic rivet gun 4-37
Polishing 7-57
Polybenzimidazoles (PBI) 7-8
Polyester fabric repairs 3-23
Polyester resins 7-7
Polyether Ether Ketone (PEEK) 7-8
Polyimides 7-7
Polyurethane 8-5
Poor adhesion 8-13
Pop rivets 4-57
Portable power drills 4-15
Power factor 9-20
Powerplant stations 1-40
Power systems 9-41
Power tools 4-37
Preflight 2-61
Pre-impregnated products (prepregs) 7-8
Preparation of wood for gluing 6-11
Preparing glues for use 6-12
Prepreg 7-27
Press brake 4-22
Pressing or clamping time 6-11
Pressure 2-2
    Atmospheric pressure 2-2
Pressure on the joint 6-12
Pressure regulators 5-7
Pressurization 1-10
Prick punch 4-6
Primary flight control 2-12
Primers 3-7,8-3,8-10
Processes and precautions 7-51
Progressive inspection 2-62
Protective equipment for personnel 8-22
Puddle 5-15
Pull through nutplate blind rivet 4-57
Pull-type blind bolt 4-54
Pulse echo ultrasonic inspection 7-18
Punches 4-5
Push rods (control rods) 2-47

R

Radiography 7-19
Radius dimpling 4-43
Radome repairs 7-41
Reamers 4-19
Rebalancing methods 2-40
Rebalancing procedures 2-39
Reciprocating 4-9
Red Baron's Fokker DR-1 1-4
Red iron oxide 8-3
Regulators 5-11

Reinforcing tape 3-5
Relays 9-99
Release agents 7-21
Relief hole location 4-73
Removal of decals 8-19
Removal of mechanically locked blind rivets 4-49
Removal of pin rivets 4-50
Removal of rivets 4-45
Repairability of sheet metal structure 4-92
Repair layout 4-32
Repair material selection 4-93
Repair of lightening holes 4-100
Repair of steel tubing aircraft structure by
Welding 5-32
Repair of stressed skin structure 4-95
Repair of wood aircraft components 6-13
Repair of wood aircraft structures 6-7
    Materials 6-7
    Suitable wood 6-7
Repair parts layout 4-93
Repairs 7-56
Repair safety 7-53
Repairs to a pressurized area 4-100
Replacement of a panel 4-97
Replacing rivets 4-46
Required inspections 2-61
Resin injection repairs 7-40
Respiratory protection 7-53
Reusable sheet metal fasteners 4-29
Rib and web repair 4-104
Rib bracing 3-5
Rib lacing 3-18
Rib lacing cord 3-5
Rigging 2-16
Rigging checks 2-48
Rigging fixtures 2-45
Rigging specification 2-41
    Maintenance manual 2-41
    Manufacturer's service information 2-41
    Structural Repair Manual (SRM) 2-41
    Type certificate data sheet 2-41
Right angle and 45° drill motors 4-15
Rigid rotor 2-19
Rings 3-21
Rivet cutter 4-36
Rivet head shape 4-31
Riveting procedure 4-40
Rivet installation tools 4-36
Rivet layout example 4-35
Rivet length 4-33
Rivet nut 4-56
Rivet pitch 4-35
Rivet selection 4-94
Rivet sets/headers 4-39
Rivet spacers 4-4

Rivet spacing..4-34
Rivet spacing and edge distance 4-94
Rivet strength...4-33
Room temperature curing.................................7-32
Rotary machine..4-24
Rotary punch press...4-10
Rotary-wing..2-18
Rotary-wing aircraft...1-5
Rotor blade preservation....................................2-35
Rotor blade tracking..2-32
Rotor systems...2-18
Roving..7-3
Rudder...1-27
Ruddervator..1-28

S

Safety in the paint shop.....................................8-21
Sags and runs 8-14
Sandbag bumping...4-81
Sandbags..4-28
Sanding scratches..8-15
Sandwich structures 7-10,7-34
Saturation techniques..7-30
Sawing...7-55
Scales...4-4
Scarf patch...6-24
Score...4-91
Scratch...4-91
Screws and nutplates in composite structures.....7-48
Scribes..4-5
Scroll shears...4-10
Seams...3-16
Selvage edge..3-3
Semicrystalline thermoplastics.............................7-8
Semimonocoque..1-9
Semirigid rotor..2-19
Sequence for painting a single-engine or
light twin airplane..8-13
Series wound DC generators................................9-32
Setback (SB)...4-60
Sewing thread..3-5
Seyboth..3-11
Shear strength and bearing strength....................4-88
Sheet metal forming and flat pattern layout terminology 4-59
Sheet metal hammers and mallets........................4-28
Sheet metal holding devices................................4-28
Sheet metal repair...4-86
Shop tools...4-9
Shotbags and weights...7-32
Shrinking..4-58,4-76
Shrinking and stretching tools.............................4-26
Shrinking blocks..4-28
Shrink tape...7-32
Sight line..4-60
Silver soldering...5-22

Single rotor helicopter.......................................2-18
Single side vacuum bagging.................................7-31
Single spread..6-11
Siphon feed gun...8-7
Size requirements for different aircraft................8-18
Skids..1-43
Skin protection..7-53
Skis...1-37
Slats..1-30
Sleeve bolts..4-56
Slip roll former...4-23
Snake attachment..4-16
Soft or harsh flame..5-13
Soldering..5-21
Solenoids..9-99
Solid laminates...7-37
Solid release film..7-21
Solid shank rivet...4-31
Solid-state regulators...9-40
Solutions to heat sink problems..........................7-26
Spar repair..4-103
Special fabric fasteners.......................................3-6
Specialized repairs...4-108
Special purpose fasteners...................................4-47
Speed brakes..1-30
Spin forming...4-25
Splayed patch...6-20
Spoiler...1-30
Spray dust..8-16
Spray equipment..8-6
Spray gun operation...8-11
Spray guns..8-7
Spraying...8-5
Spring-back...2-46
Squaring shear..4-9
Stabilator...1-27
Stability...2-9
Stability Augmentation Systems (SAS).................2-32
Stabilizers..1-24
Stabilizer systems...2-31
Stain..4-91
Stainless steel...5-17
Stall fence..1-34
Static balance...2-38
Static stability..2-9
Steel..5-16
Storage and handling..7-54
Storage of finishing material...............................8-22
Straight extension..4-16
Straight line bends...4-75
Straight snips..4-13
Strength characteristics.......................................7-2
Stress analysis..1-7
Stresses applied to rivets....................................4-34
Stresses in structural members.............................4-2

Stretch forming 4-24,7-55
Stretching 4-58,4-77
Stretching tools 4-27
Stretching with V-Block method 4-75
Stringer repair 4-100
Stringers 1-9
Stripping the finis 8-20
Structural alignment 2-48
Structural fasteners 4-31
Structural stresses 1-6
    Bending 1-7,4-4
    Compression 1-7,4-3
    Shear 1-7,4-3
    Tension 1-7,4-2
    Torsion 1-7,4-3
Structural support during repair 4-92
Subsonic flow 2-4
Support tooling and molds 7-20
Surface patch 6-20
Surface preparation for touchup 8-20
Surfaces 8-10
Surface tape 3-5
Swash plate assembly 2-29
Switches 9-96
    Double-pole double-throw (DPDT) 9-98
    Double-pole single-throw (DPST) 9-98
    Double-throw switches 9-98
    Precision (micro) switches 9-99
    Rotary switches 9-99
    Single-pole double-throw (SPDT) 9-98
    Single-pole single-throw (SPST) 9-98
    Spring loaded switches 9-98
    Toggle and rocker switches 9-98
    Two position switch 9-98
Symmetry check 2-52
Synthetic enamel 8-4
System air filter 8-7

T

Tabs 1-31
Tail cone 1-22
Tail rotor tracking 2-34
Tail wheel gear 1-37
Tapered shank bolt 4-56
Technical standard order 3-4
Techniques of position welding 5-28
Tee joints 5-31
Temperature variations in repair zone 7-25
Tension regulators 2-45
Terms used in the glue process 6-10
Testing glued joints 6-13
Thermal survey 7-26
    Thermal survey of repair area 7-25
Thermocouple placement 7-25
Thermocouples 7-25

Thermography 7-19
Thermoplastic resins 7-8
Thermoplastics 7-54
Thermosetting plastics 7-54
Thermosetting resins 7-6
Thixotropic agents 7-9
Throatless shear 4-10
Throttle 2-30
Through transmission ultrasonic inspection 7-17
Thrust 2-7
TIG welding 5-22
    TIG welding 4130 steel tubing 5-23
    TIG welding aluminum 5-24
    TIG welding magnesium 5-24
    TIG welding stainless steel 5-23
    TIG welding titanium 5-24
Titanium 4-85
Toluene 8-2
Topcoats 3-8
    Catalysts 3-8
    Fungicide 3-8
    Mildewicide 3-8
    Rejuvenator 3-8
    Retarder 3-8
    Thinners 3-8,8-3
Torch brazing of aluminum 5-21
Torch brazing of steel 5-20
Torches 5-9
    Torch lighters 5-10
    Torch tips 5-9
    Torque compensation 2-19
Torque tubes 2-48
Total developed width (TDW) 4-60
Trailing edge and transition area patch repairs 7-40
Trailing edge repair 4-105
Transfer punch 4-6
Translating tendency 2-22
Translational lift 2-24
Transmission 1-43,1-44
Transmission system 2-36
Transparent plastics 7-54
Transverse pitch 4-35
Tricycle gear 1-38
Trim controls 2-12
Balance tabs 2-12
Servo tabs 1-32,2-12
Spring tabs 2-12
Truss 1-8
Tube splicing with inside sleeve reinforcement 5-33
Tube splicing with outer split sleeve Reinforcement 5-34
Turbine engines 1-43
Turnbuckles 2-46
Turpentine 8-3
Two hole 4-15
Tying wire bundles 9-88

Types of damage and defects 4-90
Types of drill bits 4-17
Types of fiber 7-4
Types of welding 5-2
Typical repairs for aircraft structures 4-97

U

Ultrasonic bondtester inspection 7-18
Ultrasonic inspection 7-17
Unidirectional (tape) 7-3
Upsetting 4-91
Urethane 8-4
Urethane coating 8-5

V

Vacuum bag 7-21
Vacuum bagging techniques 7-31
Vacuum bag materials 7-21
Vacuum compaction table 7-22
Vacuum equipment 7-22
Vacuum forming with a female form 7-55
Vacuum forming without forms 7-55
Varnish 8-3
V-Blocks 4-27
Velocity 2-3
Vertical flight 2-24
Vertical position welding 5-29
Vertical stabilizer stations 1-40
Very light jet 1-5
Vinyl ester resin 7-7
Vinyl film decal 8-19
Viscosity measuring cup 8-9
Visual inspection 7-15
Vortex generators 1-34

W

Warp clock 7-3
Wash primers 8-3
Web members 1-10
Weight 2-7
Weight 2-8
Welded joints using Oxy-Acetylene torch 5-31
Welding 5-1
    Aluminum welding 5-18
    Electric arc welding 5-2
    Gas metal arc welding 5-3,5-22
    Gas tungsten arc welding 5-3
    Gas welding 5-2
    Plasma arc welding 5-6
    Seam welding 5-6
    Shielded metal arc welding 5-2
    Spot welding 5-6
Welding eyewear 5-9
Welding gases 5-7
Welding hose 5-8

Wet layups 7-26
Wet or dry grinder 4-12
Windshield installation 7-57
Winglets 1-34,2-14
Wing ribs 1-15,1-16
Wing rib repairs 6-13
Wings 1-10
Wing skin 1-17
Wing spars 1-13
Wire groups and bundles and routing 9-78
    Bend radii 9-80
    Clamp installation 9-82
    Movable controls wiring precautions 9-83
    Protection against chafing 9-80
    Protection against high temperature 9-80
    Protection against solvents and fluid 9-81
    Protection of wires in wheel well areas 9-81
    Slack in wire bundles 9-79
    Spliced connections in wire bundles 9-80
    Twisting wires 9-79
    Wire and cable clamp inspection 9-83
Wire identification 9-77
    Placement of identification marking 9-77
    Types of wire markings 9-77
Wire inspection 9-96
Wire shielding 9-85
    Bonding 9-87
    Bonding jumper installation 9-87
        Bonding connections 9-87
        Bonding jumper attachment 9-87
        Corrosion prevention 9-87
        Corrosion protection 9-87
        Ground return connection 9-87
    Grounding 9-86
    Testing of bonds and grounds 9-87
Wire size selection 9-69
    Current carrying capacity 9-71
        Allowable voltage drop 9-75
        Computing current carrying capacity 9-71
        Electric wire chart instructions 9-76
        Maximum operating temperature 9-71
Wire termination 9-90
    AN/MS connectors 9-93
    Emergency splicing repairs 9-92
    Junction boxes 9-92
    Stripping wire 9-90
    Terminal lugs 9-91
        Aluminum wire terminals 9-92
        Copper wire terminals 9-91
        Crimping tools 9-92
        Pre-insulated splices 9-92
    Terminal strips 9-91
Wire types 9-65
    Areas Designated as Severe Wind and Moisture
    Problem (SWAMP) 9-69

Conductor 9-67
Insulation 9-68
Plating 9-68
Wire shielding 9-68
Wire substitutions 9-69
Wiring diagrams 9-65
Block diagrams 9-65
Pictorial diagrams 9-65
Schematic diagrams 9-65
Wiring installation 9-65
Wood aircraft construction and repairs 6-2
Wood condition 6-5
Working Inconel® alloys 625 and 718 4-83
Working magnesium 4-84
Working stainless steel 4-83
Working titanium 4-85
Wright brothers 1-2
Wrinkling 8-15

Z
Zinc chromate 8-4